D0844356

500 CHILI RECIPES

500 CHILI RECIPES

An irresistible collection of red-hot, tongue-tingling recipes for every kind of fiery dish from around the world, shown in 500 sizzling photographs

Consultant Editor: Jenni Fleetwood

LORENZ BOOKS

This edition is published by Lorenz Books, an imprint of Anness Publishing Ltd, Hermes House, 88–89 Blackfriars Road, London SE1 8HA; tel. 020 7401 2077; fax 020 7633 9499

www.lorenzbooks.com; www.annesspublishing.com

If you like the images in this book and would like to investigate using them for publishing, promotions or advertising, please visit our website www.practicalpictures.com for more information.

UK agent: The Manning Partnership Ltd; tel. 01225 478444; fax 01225 478440; sales@manning-partnership.co.uk

UK distributor: Grantham Book Services Ltd; tel. 01476 541080; fax 01476 541061; orders@gbs.tbs-ltd.co.uk

North American agent/distributor: National Book Network; tel. 301 459 3366; fax 301 429 5746; www.nbnbooks.com

Australian agent/distributor: Pan Macmillan Australia; tel. 1300 135 113; fax 1300 135 103; customer.service@macmillan.com.au

New Zealand agent/distributor: David Bateman Ltd; tel. (09) 415 7664; fax (09) 415 8892

Publisher: Joanna Lorenz
Project Editor: Anne Hildyard
Copy-editor: Jay Thundercliffe
Production Controller: Claire Rae
Design: SMI

ETHICAL TRADING POLICY

At Anness Publishing we believe that business should be conducted in an ethical and ecologically sustainable way, with respect for the environment and a proper regard to the replacement of the natural resources we employ.

As a publisher, we use a lot of wood pulp to make high-quality paper for printing, and that wood commonly comes from spruce trees. We are therefore currently growing more than 750,000 trees in three Scottish forest plantations: Berrymoss (130 hectares/320 acres), West Touxhill (125 hectares/305 acres) and Deveron Forest (75 hectares/185 acres). The forests we manage contain more than 3.5 times the number of trees employed each year in making paper for the books we manufacture.

Because of this ongoing ecological investment programme, you, as our customer, can have the pleasure and reassurance of knowing that a tree is being cultivated on your behalf to naturally replace the materials used to make the book you are holding.

Our forestry programme is run in accordance with the UK Woodland Assurance Scheme (UKWAS) and will be certified by the internationally recognized Forest Stewardship Council (FSC). The FSC is a non-government organization dedicated to promoting responsible management of the world's forests. Certification ensures forests are managed in an environmentally sustainable and socially responsible way. For further information about this scheme, go to www.annesspublishing.com/trees

A CIP catalogue record for this book is available from the British Library.

Publisher's Note:
Although the advice and information in this book are believed to be accurate and true at the time of going to press, neither the authors nor the publisher can accept any legal responsibility or liability for any errors or omissions that may be made.

Notes

Bracketed terms are intended for American readers.

For all recipes, quantities are given in both metric and imperial measures and, where appropriate, in standard cups and spoons. Follow one set of measures, but not a mixture, because they are not interchangeable.

Standard spoon and cup measures are level. 1 tsp = 5ml, 1 tbsp = 15ml, 1 cup = 250ml/8fl oz. Australian standard tablespoons are 20ml. Australian readers should use 3 tsp in place of 1 tbsp for measuring small quantities.

American pints are 16fl oz/2 cups. American readers should use 20fl oz/2.5 cups in place of 1 pint when measuring liquids.
Electric oven temperatures in this book are for conventional ovens. When using a fan oven, the temperature will probably need to be reduced by about 10–20°C/20–40°F. Since ovens vary, you should check with your manufacturer's instruction book for guidance.
The nutritional analysis given for each recipe is calculated per portion (i.e. serving or item), unless otherwise stated. If the recipe gives a range, such as Serves 4–6, then the nutritional analysis will be for the smaller portion size, i.e. 6 servings. Measurements for sodium do not include salt added to taste.
Medium (US large) eggs are used unless otherwise stated.

Main front cover image shows Chicken with Basil and Chilli – for recipe, see page 94

Contents

Introduction

Chillies now form an important part of many of the world's major cuisines. India is the largest producer and exporter of chillies, with much of the crop used for local consumption. Japan, Thailand, Mexico, Turkey, Nigeria, Ethiopia, Uganda, Kenya and Tanzania are also prime producers.

The word *chilli* is spelt in different ways. Sometimes it is chile, sometimes chili, or chilli pepper. This last description is accurate in that it recognizes that chillies are members of the *Capsicum* family, like the sweet (bell) peppers. It also forms a link with all those spicy powders such as chilli, cayenne and paprika, which are an essential part of many national dishes.

The great explorer Columbus was responsible for confusing chillies with peppers. When he set sail in 1492, hoping to find a sea route to the spice islands, it was a source of black pepper (*Piper nigrum*) he was seeking. Not only did he fail to find his intended destination, discovering instead the Caribbean island of San Salvador (now Watling Island), but he also assumed that the hot spice flavouring the local food was black pepper. By the time it was realized that the fleshy pods of a fruit were responsible, rather than black peppercorns, it was too late. The Spanish called the flavouring *pimiento* (pepper). The name stuck, and it has led to confusion ever since.

It was the Aztecs who coined the name *chilli*. Like the Mayas and Incas, they were greatly enamoured of the brightly coloured fruit that had originated in the rainforests of South America, and used chillies both as food and for medicinal purposes. When the Spanish invaded Mexico in 1509, they found many different varieties of both fresh and dried chilli on sale at the market at Tenochtitla. Mexico remains a mecca for those who love chillies, with every region having its own special varieties. Chillies are valued for their heat and for their flavour, and accomplished Mexican cooks will often use several different types – fresh and dried – in a single dish.

In the 15th century, Vasco da Gama succeeded in finding the sea route to the spice islands. By the middle of the 16th century, a two-way trade had been established. Spices such as nutmeg, cinnamon and black pepper were brought to Europe from the East, and chillies and other plants from the New World went to Asia. The spice trade created a culinary explosion, and the chilli rapidly became an important ingredient in the food of South-east Asia, India and China. Portuguese and Arab traders introduced it to Africa. It was enthusiastically adopted, and when West African slaves were taken to the southern states of America to work the cotton plantations, they took chillies with them. Although parts of Europe adopted the chilli, universal acceptance has been relatively slow. Spain and Portugal use chillies quite extensively, which is not surprising, given the influence of those early explorers, but in France their use is limited to a few dishes, like the fiery rouille traditionally served with bouillabaisse.

Chillies are an excellent source of vitamin C and they yield beta carotene, folate, potassium and vitamin E. They stimulate the appetite and improve circulation, but can irritate the stomach. Chillies are a powerful decongestant, and can help to clear blocked sinuses.

There are more than 200 different types of chillies, but those usually available include jalapeños, cayennes, Anaheim chillies and poblanos, as well as sweet (bell) peppers. Generally, small chillies are not hotter than big ones and red chillies are not hotter than green. Most chillies start out green and ripen to red, but some start yellow and become red, and yet others start yellow and stay yellow. Chillies on the same plant can have different degrees of heat, and in one type of chilli, the top of the fruit is hotter than the bottom. What makes one chilli hotter than another is the amount of the chemical capsaicin in the seeds and fibrous white lining. Capsaicin can produce a tingle or a tidal wave of heat, and also contributes to the feel-good factor by stimulating the brain to produce hormones called endorphins. A less appealing aspect to capsaicin is that it is an irritant, and can cause severe burning to delicate parts of the face and body with which it comes into contact, so it is vital to handle chillies with care. Wear gloves or cut them up using a knife and fork. If you do handle chillies directly, wash your hands in soapy water afterwards (capsaicin does not dissolve in water alone) or use vegetable oil to remove any residue. If you bite into a chilli that burns your mouth, don't drink a glass of water; this spreads the discomfort around. Instead, take a mouthful of creamy milk, yogurt or ice cream, hold it in your mouth for a minute or so, then spit it out. Or, eat a piece of fresh bread, a cooked potato or some rice; these foods absorb the capsaicin oil.

Fiery Tomato Soup with Red Pepper Cream

This dazzling soup can be as fiery or as mild as you like. Simply increase or reduce the amount of chilli.

Serves 4

1.5kg/3¼lb plum tomatoes, halved
5 red chillies, seeded
1 red (bell) pepper, halved and seeded
2 red onions, roughly chopped
6 garlic cloves, crushed
30ml/2 tbsp sun-dried tomato paste
45ml/3 tbsp olive oil
400ml/14fl oz/1⅔ cups vegetable stock
salt and ground black pepper
wild rocket (arugula) leaves, to garnish

For the pepper cream

1 red (bell) pepper, halved and seeded
10ml/2 tsp olive oil
120ml/4fl oz/½ cup crème fraîche
few drops of Tabasco sauce

1 Preheat the oven to 200°C/400°F/Gas 6. Place the tomatoes, chillies, pepper, onions, garlic and tomato paste in a roasting pan. Toss the vegetables, drizzle with the oil and toss again. Roast for 40 minutes, until tender and the pepper skin is slightly charred.

2 Meanwhile, make the pepper cream. Lay the pepper halves skin-side up on a baking tray and brush with the oil. Roast with the mixed vegetables for about 30–40 minutes, until blistered.

3 Transfer the pepper for the pepper cream to a bowl when cooked. Cover with clear film (plastic wrap) and leave to cool. Peel the skin and purée the flesh in a food processor or blender with half the crème fraîche. Pour into a bowl and stir in the remaining crème fraîche. Season and add a dash of Tabasco.

4 Process the roasted vegetables in batches, adding enough stock to each batch to make a thick purée. Press the purée through a sieve (strainer) into a pan and add more stock if you want a thinner soup. Heat the soup gently and season well.

5 Ladle the soup into bowls and spoon red pepper cream into the centre. Pile wild rocket leaves on top to garnish.

Chilli Beansprout Broth

This gentle Korean broth is quick and easy to make and easy on the palate, with just a hint of spiciness and a refreshing nutty flavour. It is reputed to be the perfect solution for calming your stomach after a heavy drinking session.

Serves 4

200g/7oz/generous 2 cups soya beansprouts
1 red or green chilli
15 dried anchovies
1 spring onion (scallion), finely sliced
3 garlic cloves, chopped
salt

1 Wash the soya beansprouts in plenty of cold water, then trim off the tail ends.

2 Split the chilli and discard the seeds, then cut the flesh diagonally into thin slices.

3 Boil 750ml/1¼ pints/3 cups water in a pan and add the dried anchovies. After boiling for 15 minutes remove the anchovies and discard.

4 Add the soya beansprouts and boil for a further 5 minutes, ensuring the lid is kept tightly on.

5 Add the spring onion, chilli and garlic to the pan, and boil for a further 3 minutes.

6 Season to taste with salt, and then ladle the soup into warmed individual bowls and serve immediately.

Cook's Tips

- *Soya beansprouts and dried anchovies are available at supermarkets and Asian food stores. If you are unable to find any dried anchovies, then 5ml/1 tsp Thai fish sauce can be used instead.*
- *To make a spicier version of this soup simply increase the number of fresh chillies used or add 5ml/1 tsp of chilli powder to each bowl.*

Fiery Tomato Soup Energy 319kcal/1330kj; Protein 5.3g; Carbohydrate 23.5g, of which sugars 22g; Fat 23.4g, of which saturates 10g; Cholesterol 34mg; Calcium 67mg; Fibre 6.2g; Sodium 72mg.
Chilli Beansprout Broth Energy 41kcal/173kJ; Protein 4.6g; Carbohydrate 2.7g, of which sugars 1.2g; Fat 1.4g, of which saturates 0.2g; Cholesterol 7mg; Calcium 46mg; Fibre 1g; Sodium 445mg.

Corn and Red Chilli Chowder

Corn and chillies make good bedfellows, and here the cool combination of creamed corn and milk is the perfect foil for the raging heat of the chillies.

Serves 6

2 tomatoes, skinned
1 onion, roughly chopped
375g/13oz can creamed corn
2 red (bell) peppers, halved and seeded
15ml/1 tbsp olive oil, plus extra for brushing
3 red chillies, seeded and chopped
2 garlic cloves, chopped
5ml/1 tsp ground cumin
5ml/1 tsp ground coriander
600ml/1 pint/2½ cups milk
350ml/12fl oz/1½ cups chicken stock
3 corn on the cob, kernels removed
450g/1lb potatoes, finely diced
60ml/4 tbsp double (heavy) cream
60ml/4 tbsp chopped fresh parsley
salt and ground black pepper

1 Process the tomatoes and onion in a food processor or blender to a smooth purée. Add the corn and process again, then set aside. Preheat the grill to high.

2 Put the peppers, skin sides up, on a grill (broiler) rack and brush with oil. Grill (broil) for 8–10 minutes, until the skins blacken and blister. Transfer to a bowl and cover with clear film (plastic wrap), then leave to cool. Peel and dice the peppers, then set them aside.

3 Heat the oil in a large pan and add the chopped chillies and garlic. Cook, stirring, for 2–3 minutes, until softened.

4 Add the ground cumin and coriander, and cook for another minute. Stir in the corn purée and cook for about 8 minutes, stirring occasionally.

5 Pour in the milk and stock, then stir in the corn kernels, potatoes, red pepper and seasoning to taste. Cook for 15–20 minutes, until the corn and potatoes are tender.

6 Pour into deep bowls and add the cream, then sprinkle over the chopped parsley. Serve immediately.

Avocado and Lime Soup with a Green Chilli Salsa

Inspired by guacamole, this creamy soup relies on good-quality ripe avocados for its flavour and colour.

Serves 4

3 ripe avocados
juice of 1½ limes
1 garlic clove, crushed
handful of ice cubes
400ml/14fl oz/1⅔ cups vegetable stock, chilled
400ml/14fl oz/1⅔ cups milk, chilled
150ml/¼ pint/⅔ cup sour cream, chilled
few drops of Tabasco sauce
salt and ground black pepper
fresh coriander (cilantro) leaves, to garnish
extra virgin olive oil, to serve

For the salsa

4 tomatoes, peeled, seeded and finely diced
2 spring onions (scallions), finely chopped
1 green chilli, seeded and finely chopped
15ml/1 tbsp chopped fresh coriander (cilantro)
juice of ½ lime

1 Prepare the salsa first. Mix all the ingredients and season well. Chill until required.

2 Halve and stone (pit) the avocados. Scoop the flesh out of the avocado skins and place in a food processor or blender. Add the lime juice, garlic, ice cubes and 150ml/¼ pint/⅔ cup of the vegetable stock.

3 Process the soup until smooth. Pour into a large bowl and stir in the remaining stock, milk, sour cream, Tabasco and seasoning.

4 Ladle the soup into bowls or glasses and spoon a little salsa on top. Add a splash of olive oil to each portion and garnish with fresh coriander leaves. Serve immediately.

Cook's Tip
This soup may discolour if left standing for too long, but the flavour will not be spoilt. Give it a quick whisk just before serving.

Corn and Chilli Chowder Energy 294kcal/1347kj; Protein 9.4g; Carbohydrate 43.2g, of which sugars 15.7g; Fat 13.5g, of which saturates 5g; Cholesterol 18mg; Calcium 119mg; Fibre 5g; Sodium 500mg.
Avocado Soup Energy 335kcal/1390kj; Protein 7.3g; Carbohydrate 12g, of which sugars 10.6g; Fat 28.9g, of which saturates 10g; Cholesterol 28mg; Calcium 176mg; Fibre 4.7g; Sodium 76mg.

Indian Dhal Soup

This is a simple, mildly spiced lentil soup, which is a good accompaniment to heavily spiced meat dishes.

Serves 4 to 6

15ml/1 tbsp ghee
1 large onion, finely chopped
2 garlic cloves, crushed
1 green chilli, chopped
2.5ml/½ tsp ground turmeric
75g/3oz red lentils
250ml/8fl oz/1 cup water
400g/14oz can chopped tomatoes
2.5ml/½ tsp sugar
lemon juice, to taste
200g/7oz/1 cup plain boiled rice or 2 potatoes, boiled (optional)
salt
coriander (cilantro) leaves, chopped, to garnish

1 Heat the ghee in a large pan and fry the onion, garlic, chilli and turmeric together for 4–5 minutes until the onion has softened and turned translucent.

2 Add the lentils and the measured water to the pan and bring to the boil. Reduce the heat, cover and simmer until all the water has been absorbed.

3 Mash the lentils in the pan with the back of a wooden spoon until you have a smooth paste.

4 Add salt to taste and mix well. Add the chopped tomatoes, sugar and lemon juice, to taste, to the pan and stir well until thoroughly combined.

5 Chop the cooked potatoes into cubes, if using, and add to the soup, or add in the plain boiled rice, if you prefer.

6 Heat the soup until it is bubbling and all the ingredients are heated through. Serve immediately, garnished with coriander.

Cook's Tip

When using lentils, first rinse in cold water and remove any floating items. Drain them and then carefully pick through the lentils to remove any stones that may be present.

Red Hot Vegetable and Peanut Soup

This is a colourful and refreshing soup from Jakarta with more than a hint of sharpness.

Serves 4 or 8 as part of a buffet

For the spice paste
5 shallots or 1 medium red onion, sliced
3 garlic cloves, crushed
2.5cm/1in galangal, peeled and sliced
1–2 fresh red chillies, seeded and sliced
25g/1oz raw peanuts
1cm/½in cube shrimp paste, prepared
1.2 litres/2 pints/5 cups well-flavoured stock
50–75g/2–3oz salted peanuts, lightly crushed
15–30ml/1–2 tbsp soft dark brown sugar
5ml/1 tsp tamarind pulp, soaked in 75ml/5 tbsp warm water for 15 minutes
salt

For the vegetables
1 chayote, thinly peeled, seeds removed, flesh finely sliced
115g/4oz green beans, trimmed and finely sliced
50g/2oz corn kernels (optional)
handful of green leaves, such as watercress, rocket (arugula) or Chinese leaves, finely shredded
1 fresh green chilli, sliced, to garnish

1 Prepare the spice paste by grinding the shallots or onion, garlic, galangal, chillies, raw peanuts and shrimp paste until smooth in a food processor or with a mortar and pestle.

2 Pour in some of the stock to moisten and then pour this mixture into a pan or wok, adding the rest of the stock. Cook for 15 minutes with the peanuts and sugar. Strain the tamarind mixture, discarding the seeds, and reserve the juice.

3 Add the chayote slices, beans and corn, if using, to the soup and cook fairly rapidly for 5 minutes. At the last minute, add the green leaves and salt to taste.

4 Add the tamarind juice, mix well and taste for seasoning. Serve in warmed individual bowls, garnished with the slices of green chilli.

Indian Dhal Soup Energy 235kcal/991kJ; Protein 13g; Carbohydrate 28.4g, of which sugars 3.7g; Fat 8.8g, of which saturates 2.2g; Cholesterol 0mg; Calcium 66mg; Fibre 2.9g; Sodium 40mg.
Red Hot Vegetable Soup Energy 80kcal/334kJ; Protein 3.8g; Carbohydrate 6.2g, of which sugars 4.9g; Fat 4.7g, of which saturates 0.9g; Cholesterol 0mg; Calcium 46mg; Fibre 1.8g; Sodium 19mg.

South Indian Pepper Water

This is a highly soothing broth for winter evenings, also known as *mulla-ga-tani*. Serve with the whole spices or strain and reheat if you so wish. The lemon juice may be adjusted to taste, but this dish should be distinctly sour.

Serves 4 to 6

30ml/2 tbsp vegetable oil
2.5ml/½ tsp ground black pepper
5ml/1 tsp cumin seeds
2.5ml/½ tsp mustard seeds
1.5ml/¼ tsp asafoetida
2 whole dried red chillies
4–6 curry leaves
2.5ml/½ tsp ground turmeric
2 garlic cloves, crushed
300ml/½ pint/1¼ cups tomato juice
juice of 2 lemons
100ml/3½fl oz/scant ½ cup water
salt
coriander (cilantro) leaves, chopped, to garnish (optional)

1 In a large frying pan, heat the vegetable oil. Add the black pepper, cumin and mustard seeds to the pan. Fry the spices for 3–4 minutes, stirring, until the seeds start to splutter and release their fragrances.

2 Add the asafoetida, dried chillies, curry leaves, turmeric and garlic to the pan. Fry, stirring constantly, until the chillies are nearly black and the garlic has turned golden brown. Ensure that the garlic does not burn, otherwise it will impart a bitter taste to the soup.

3 Lower the heat and then add the tomato juice, lemon juice and measured water and mix well until all the ingredients are well combined. Season with a little salt.

4 Bring the soup slowly to the boil, then reduce the heat and simmer for 10 minutes, stirring occasionally. Spoon into bowls and garnish with the chopped coriander, if using, and serve.

Cook's Tip
Asafoetida is a pungent spice with a very strong odour of garlic and onion and should only be used sparingly.

Chilli and Yogurt Soup

With the addition of bhajias, this soup can be served as a substantial main dish.

Serves 4 to 6

450ml/¾ pint/1½ cups natural (plain) yogurt, beaten
60ml/4 tbsp gram flour
2.5ml/½ tsp chilli powder
2.5ml/½ tsp ground turmeric
2–3 green chillies, finely chopped
60ml/4 tbsp vegetable oil
4 whole dried red chillies
5ml/1 tsp cumin seeds
3 garlic cloves, crushed
5cm/2in piece fresh root ginger, crushed
3–4 curry leaves
salt
fresh coriander (cilantro) leaves, chopped, to garnish

1 Mix together the yogurt, gram flour, chilli powder, and turmeric. Add salt to taste. Pass the mixture through a sieve (strainer) into a pan.

2 Add the green chillies and cook gently over a low heat for about 10 minutes, stirring occasionally. Be careful not to let the soup boil over.

3 Heat the oil in a frying pan and add the dried chillies, cumin, garlic, ginger and curry leaves. Fry until the chillies turn black.

4 Pour the contents of the frying pan over the yogurt soup. Cover the pan, then remove it from the heat and leave to rest for about 5 minutes.

5 Mix the soup well and gently reheat for a further 5 minutes. Serve hot, ladled into bowls and garnished with the chopped coriander leaves.

Cook's Tip
Gram flour, also known as besan, is a pale-yellow flour made from ground chickpeas. More aromatic and with less starch content and higher protein than wheat flour, it is used widely in Indian cookery for doughs, batters and for thickening sauces. Look for it in large supermarkets or Asian food stores.

South Indian Pepper Water Energy 79kcal/328kj; Protein 1.7g; Carbohydrate 4.3g, of which sugars 2.6g; Fat 6.3g, of which saturates 0.7g; Cholesterol 0mg; Calcium 42mg; Fibre 1.1g; Sodium 178mg.
Chilli and Yogurt Soup Energy 226kcal/924kj; Protein 18.8g; Carbohydrate 9.1g, of which sugars 5.9g; Fat 14.4g, of which saturates 2.3g; Cholesterol 29mg; Calcium 177mg; Fibre 0.5g; Sodium 90mg.

Cucumber Soup with Chilli Salsa and Salmon

The refreshing flavours of cucumber and yogurt in this soup fuse with the cool chilli salsa and a hint of heat from the charred salmon to bring the taste of summer to the table.

Serves 4

3 medium cucumbers
300ml/½ pint/1¼ cups Greek (US strained plain) yogurt
250ml/8fl oz/1 cup vegetable stock, chilled
120ml/4fl oz/½ cup crème fraîche
15ml/1 tbsp chopped fresh chervil
15ml/1 tbsp chopped fresh chives
15ml/1 tbsp chopped fresh flat leaf parsley
1 small red chilli, seeded and very finely chopped
a little oil, for brushing
225g/8oz salmon fillet, skinned and cut into eight thin slices
salt and ground black pepper
fresh chervil or chives, to garnish

1 Peel two of the cucumbers and then cut them in half lengthways. Scoop out and discard the seeds, then roughly chop the flesh.

2 Purée the cucumber in a food processor or blender, then add the Greek yogurt, chilled stock, crème fraîche, chervil and chives, and process until smooth. Season the mixture with a little salt and ground black pepper. Transfer to a bowl and set aside in the refrigerator until needed.

3 Peel, halve and seed the remaining cucumber. Cut the flesh into small neat dice. Mix with the chopped parsley and chilli. Chill until required.

4 Brush a griddle or frying pan with oil and heat until very hot. Sear the salmon slices for 1–2 minutes on each side, until tender and charred.

5 Ladle the chilled soup into individual soup bowls. Top each serving with two slices of the salmon, then pile a portion of salsa into the centre of each. Garnish with the chervil and chives and serve.

Tomato, Chilli and Egg Drop Soup

Popular in southern Vietnam and Cambodia, this spicy soup with eggs is probably adapted from the traditional Chinese egg drop soup. Served on its own with chunks of crusty bread, or accompanied by jasmine or ginger rice, this is a tasty dish for a light supper.

Serves 4

30ml/2 tbsp groundnut (peanut) or vegetable oil
3 shallots, finely sliced
2 garlic cloves, finely chopped
2 Thai chillies, seeded and finely sliced
25g/1oz galangal, shredded
8 large, ripe tomatoes, skinned, seeded and finely chopped
15ml/1 tbsp sugar
30ml/2 tbsp Thai fish sauce
4 lime leaves
900ml/1½ pints/3¾ cups chicken stock
15ml/1 tbsp wine vinegar
4 eggs
sea salt and ground black pepper

For the garnish
chilli oil, for drizzling
1 small bunch fresh coriander (cilantro), finely chopped
1 small bunch fresh mint leaves, finely chopped

1 Heat the oil in a wok or heavy pan. Stir in the shallots, garlic, chillies and galangal and cook until golden and fragrant. Add the tomatoes with the sugar, Thai fish sauce and lime leaves. Stir until it resembles a sauce. Pour in the stock and bring to the boil. Reduce the heat and simmer for 30 minutes. Season.

2 Just before serving, bring a wide pan of water to the boil. Add the vinegar and half a teaspoon of salt. Break the eggs into individual cups or small bowls.

3 Stir the water rapidly to create a swirl and drop an egg into the centre of the swirl. Follow immediately with the others, or poach two at a time, and keep the water boiling to throw the whites up over the yolks. Turn off the heat, cover the pan and leave to poach until firm enough to lift. Poached eggs are traditional, but you could use lightly fried eggs instead.

4 Using a slotted spoon, lift the eggs out of the water and slip them into the hot soup. Drizzle a little chilli oil over the eggs, sprinkle with the coriander and mint, and serve.

Cucumber Soup Energy 226kcal/942kj; Protein 3.7g; Carbohydrate 64.1g; of which sugars 64.1g; Fat 16.3g; of which saturates 10.3g; Cholesterol 48mg; Calcium 125mg; Fibre 2.3g; Sodium 280mg.
Tomato and Egg Soup Energy 181kcal/756kJ; Protein 8g; Carbohydrate 12.3g, of which sugars 11.5g; Fat 11.7g, of which saturates 2.4g; Cholesterol 190mg; Calcium 52mg; Fibre 2.3g; Sodium 280mg.

Spiced Mango Soup with Yogurt

This delicious, light soup comes from Chutney Mary's, the Anglo-Indian restaurant in London. It is best when served lightly chilled.

Serves 4

2 ripe mangoes
15ml/1 tbsp gram flour
120ml/4fl oz/½ cup natural (plain) yogurt
900ml/1½ pints/3¾ cups water
2.5ml/½ tsp grated fresh root ginger
2 red chillies, seeded and finely chopped
30ml/2 tbsp olive oil
2.5ml/½ tsp mustard seeds
2.5ml/½ tsp cumin seeds
8 curry leaves
salt and ground black pepper
fresh mint leaves, shredded, to garnish
natural (plain) yogurt, to serve

1 Peel the mangoes, remove the stones (pits) and cut the flesh into even chunks. Purée the flesh in a food processor or blender until smooth.

2 Pour the puréed mango into a pan and stir in the gram flour, yogurt, water, ginger and chillies. Bring the mixture slowly to the boil, stirring occasionally. Simmer for about 4–5 minutes until the mixture has thickened slightly. Remove the pan from the heat and set aside.

3 Heat the olive oil in a frying pan. Add the mustard seeds and cook for a few seconds until they begin to pop, then add the cumin seeds.

4 Add the curry leaves to the frying pan and then cook for 5 minutes. Stir the spice mixture into the soup, return it to the heat and cook for 10 minutes.

5 Press the soup through a sieve (strainer), if you like, then season to taste.

6 Leave the soup to cool completely, then chill in the refrigerator for at least 1 hour.

7 Ladle the soup into bowls, and top each with a dollop of yogurt. Garnish with shredded mint leaves and serve.

Red-hot Red Lentil Soup with Onion and Parsley

In Istanbul and Izmir, lentil soups are light and subtly spiced, and served as an appetizer or as a snack. In Anatolia, lentil and bean soups are made with chunks of mutton and flavoured with tomato and spices, and are usually served as a meal on their own.

Serves 4 to 6

30–45ml/2–3 tbsp olive or sunflower oil
1 large onion, finely chopped
2 garlic cloves, finely chopped
1 fresh red chilli, seeded and finely chopped
5–10ml/1–2 tsp cumin seeds
5–10ml/1–2 tsp coriander seeds
1 carrot, finely chopped
scant 5ml/1 tsp ground fenugreek
5ml/1 tsp sugar
15ml/1 tbsp tomato purée (paste)
250g/9oz/generous 1 cup split red lentils
1.75 litres/3 pints/7½ cups chicken stock
salt and ground black pepper

To serve

1 small red onion, finely chopped
1 large bunch of fresh flat leaf parsley, finely chopped
4–6 lemon wedges

1 Heat the oil in a heavy pan and stir in the onion, garlic, chilli, cumin and coriander seeds. When the onion begins to colour, toss in the carrot and cook for 2–3 minutes. Add the fenugreek, sugar and tomato purée, and stir in the lentils.

2 Pour in the stock, stir well and bring to the boil. Lower the heat, partially cover the pan and simmer for 30–40 minutes, until the lentils have broken up.

3 If the soup is too thick, thin it down with a little water. Season with salt and pepper to taste.

4 Serve the soup straight from the pan or, if you prefer a smooth texture, whizz it in a blender, then reheat if necessary. Ladle the soup into bowls and sprinkle liberally with the chopped onion and parsley. Serve with a wedge of lemon to squeeze over the soup.

Spiced Mango Soup Energy 121kcal/508kJ; Protein 2.8g; Carbohydrate 14.7g, of which sugars 12.7g; Fat 6.2g, of which saturates 1g; Cholesterol 0mg; Calcium 73mg; Fibre 2.4g; Sodium 28mg.
Red-hot Red Lentil Soup Energy 203kcal/354kJ; Protein 11.1g; Carbohydrate 31.8g; of which sugars 7.3g; Fat 4.4g; of which saturates 0.6g; Cholesterol 0mg; Calcium 45mg; Fibre 3.5g; Sodium 26mg.

Chilli Coconut Soup with Pumpkin and Bamboo

This tasty soup is from Java, where it is served on its own with rice or as an accompaniment to a poached or grilled fish dish. In some parts of Java, the dish includes small prawns but, if it is packed with vegetables alone, it makes a satisfying vegetarian meal. Generally, such dishes are accompanied by a chilli sambal, which can be made by pounding chillies with shrimp paste and lime juice.

Serves 4

30ml/2 tbsp palm, groundnut (peanut) or corn oil
150g/5oz pumpkin flesh
115g/4oz yard-long beans
220g/7½oz can bamboo shoots, drained and rinsed
900ml/1½ pints coconut milk
10–15ml/2–3 tsp palm sugar (jaggery)
130g/4½oz fresh coconut, shredded
salt

For the spice paste

4 shallots, chopped
25g/1oz fresh root ginger, chopped
4 red chillies, seeded and chopped
2 garlic cloves, chopped
5ml/1 tsp coriander seeds
4 candlenuts, toasted and chopped

1 Make the spice paste. Using a mortar and pestle, grind all the ingredients together to form a smooth paste, or whizz them together in an electric blender or food processor.

2 Heat the oil in a wok or large, heavy pan, stir in the spice paste and fry until it smells fragrant. Toss the pumpkin, yard-long beans and bamboo shoots in the paste and pour in the coconut milk.

3 Add the sugar and bring to the boil. Reduce the heat and cook gently for 5–10 minutes, until the vegetables are tender. Season the soup and stir in half the fresh coconut.

4 Ladle the soup into individual warmed bowls, sprinkle with the remaining coconut and serve with bowls of cooked rice to spoon the soup over, and chilli sauce.

Spicy Pumpkin and Coconut Soup

The natural sweetness of the pumpkin is heightened by the addition of a little sugar in this attractive soup, but this is balanced by the chillies, shrimp paste and dried shrimp. Coconut cream blurs the boundaries beautifully.

Serves 4 to 6

450g/1lb pumpkin
2 garlic cloves, crushed
4 shallots, finely chopped
2.5ml/½ tsp shrimp paste
1 lemon grass stalk, chopped
2 fresh green chillies, seeded
15ml/1 tbsp dried shrimp, soaked for 10 minutes in warm water to cover
600ml/1 pint/2½ cups chicken stock
600ml/1 pint/2½ cups coconut cream
30ml/2 tbsp Thai fish sauce
5ml/1 tsp sugar
115g/4oz small cooked shelled prawns (shrimp)
salt and ground black pepper

To garnish

2 fresh red chillies, seeded and thinly sliced
10–12 fresh basil leaves

1 Peel the pumpkin and cut it into quarters with a sharp knife. Scoop out the seeds with a teaspoon and discard. Cut the flesh into chunks about 2cm/¾in thick and set aside.

2 Put the garlic, shallots, shrimp paste, lemon grass, green chillies and salt to taste in a mortar. Drain the dried shrimp, discarding the soaking liquid, and add them to the mortar. Use a pestle to grind the mixture into a paste. Alternatively, place all the ingredients in a food processor and process to a paste.

3 Bring the chicken stock to the boil in a large pan. Add the ground paste and stir well to dissolve. Add the pumpkin chunks and simmer for 10–15 minutes, or until the pumpkin is tender.

4 Stir in the coconut cream, then bring the soup back to simmering point. Do not let it boil. Add the fish sauce, sugar and ground black pepper to taste.

5 Add the prawns and cook for a further 2–3 minutes, until they are heated through. Serve in warm soup bowls, garnished with chillies and basil leaves.

Chilli Coconut Soup Energy 333kcal/1388kJ; Protein 6g; Carbohydrate 26g, of which sugars 23.8g; Fat 23.6g, of which saturates 11.7g; Cholesterol 0mg; Calcium 115mg; Fibre 4.9g; Sodium 258mg.
Spicy Pumpkin Soup Energy 77kcal/328kJ; Protein 6.8g; Carbohydrate 10.9g, of which sugars 10.2g; Fat 1g, of which saturates 0.5g; Cholesterol 56mg; Calcium 104mg; Fibre 1.3g; Sodium 877mg.

Chilli Noodle Soup with Oyster Mushrooms

Colloquially known as 'marketplace noodles' in Korea, this dish has long been enjoyed as a quick and simple lunch. The oyster mushrooms give the mild broth an appetizing richness, while the noodles have a hint of beef and a dash of chilli.

Serves 2

500ml/17fl oz/2¼ cups water
80g/3oz beef
30ml/2 tbsp light soy sauce
2 eggs, beaten
50ml/3 tbsp vegetable oil
4 oyster mushrooms
80g/3oz courgette (zucchini)
sesame oil, for drizzling
100g/4oz egg noodles
1 spring onion (scallion), finely chopped
1 dried red chilli, thinly sliced
2 garlic cloves, crushed
salt and ground white pepper
sesame seeds, to garnish

1 Pour the water into a pan and bring to the boil. Add the beef and cook for 20 minutes, then remove and slice into strips. Strain the stock into a jug (pitcher), and add the soy sauce.

2 Season the eggs with a pinch of salt. Coat a frying pan with 10ml/2 tsp vegetable oil and heat. Add the eggs and make a thin omelette, browning on each side. Cut into thin strips.

3 Cut the mushrooms and courgette into thin strips and sprinkle with salt. Pat the courgette dry with kitchen paper after 5 minutes.

4 Coat a frying pan or wok with the remaining vegetable oil and heat. Stir-fry the mushrooms and drizzle with the sesame oil then set aside. Lightly fry the courgette until it softens, then remove. Stir-fry the beef until lightly browned, and set aside.

5 Boil a pan of water and cook the plain noodles, then drain and rinse in cold water. Quickly reheat the reserved beef stock.

6 Place the noodles in a bowl. Add the mushrooms, courgette and beef. Top with the spring onion, chilli and garlic, then add the stock to cover one-third of the ingredients. Sprinkle with the sesame seeds before serving.

Green Chilli Dumpling Soup

The succulent dumplings taste fantastic in this clear soup. With ready-to-eat dumplings widely available this dish is simple and quick, and the dumpling flavours suffuse the nourishing broth.

Serves 4

750ml/1¼ pints/3 cups beef stock
16 frozen dumplings
1 spring onion (scallion), finely sliced
¼ green chilli, seeded and finely sliced
1 garlic clove, crushed
15ml/1 tbsp light soy sauce
salt and ground black pepper

1 Pour the beef stock into a heavy pan and slowly bring it to the boil.

2 Add the frozen dumplings to the stock, cover the pan, and boil for about 6–8 minutes.

3 Add the spring onion, chilli, garlic and light soy sauce to the pan, and continue to boil the soup, stirring gently, for a further 2–3 minutes.

4 Check that the dumplings are cooked through and then season the soup with salt and black pepper.

5 Spoon the soup into warmed serving bowls, adding four dumplings to each bowl, and serve piping hot. Serve with a dipping sauce, if you wish, for diners to dip their dumplings into.

Cook's Tips

- *If you would prefer to use fresh dumplings, they will only need to be cooked for 5 minutes.*
- *Soy sauce with a drop of vinegar makes a good dipping sauce for the dumplings.*
- *When cooking dumplings in this way, stir the soup as carefully as you can to avoid causing the dumplings to break apart and lose their fillings in the stock.*

Chilli Noodle Soup Energy 492kcal/2059kJ; Protein 23.1g; Carbohydrate 40.4g, of which sugars 3.3g; Fat 27.7g, of which saturates 4.9g; Cholesterol 213mg; Calcium 60mg; Fibre 2.3g; Sodium 1167mg.
Green Chilli Dumpling Soup Energy 106kcal/445kJ; Protein 2g; Carbohydrate 12.6g, of which sugars 0.6g; Fat 6.1g, of which saturates 3.4g; Cholesterol 5mg; Calcium 30mg; Fibre 0.5g; Sodium 842mg.

Hot and Sour Prawn Soup

This is a classic Thai seafood soup called *tom yam kung*, and it is one of the most popular and best-known Thai soups.

Serves 4 to 6

450g/1lb raw king prawns (jumbo shrimp), thawed if frozen
1 litre/1¾ pints/4 cups chicken stock or water
3 lemon grass stalks, roots trimmed
10 kaffir lime leaves, torn in half
225g/8oz can straw mushrooms, drained
45ml/3 tbsp Thai fish sauce
60ml/4 tbsp fresh lime juice
30ml/2 tbsp chopped spring onion (scallion)
15ml/1 tbsp fresh coriander (cilantro) leaves
4 fresh red chillies, seeded and thinly sliced
salt and ground black pepper

1 Peel the prawns, reserving the shells. Devein the prawns and set aside until needed.

2 Rinse the prawn shells under cold water, then put them into a large pan along with the chicken stock or water. Bring the pan gently to the boil.

3 Bruise the lemon grass stalks and add them to the stock with half the lime leaves. Simmer gently for 5–6 minutes, until the stock is fragrant.

4 Strain the stock through a sieve (strainer), return it to the clean pan and gently reheat.

5 Add the drained mushrooms and the prawns, then cook until the prawns turn pink.

6 Stir the Thai fish sauce, lime juice, spring onion, coriander, chillies and the remaining lime leaves into the soup.

7 Taste and adjust the seasoning if necessary. The soup should be sour, salty, spicy and hot.

8 Simmer the soup for a further 5 minutes. Divide among soup bowls and serve immediately.

Hot and Sour Pineapple Prawn Broth

This simple dish is served as an appetite enhancer because of its hot and sour flavour. It is also popular as an accompaniment to plain rice or noodles. In some restaurants, the broth is presented in a hollowed-out pineapple, halved lengthways.

Serves 4

30ml/2 tbsp vegetable oil
15–30ml/1–2 tbsp tamarind paste
15ml/1 tbsp sugar
450g/1lb fresh prawns (shrimp), peeled and deveined
4 thick fresh pineapple slices, cored and cut into bitesize chunks
salt and ground black pepper
fresh coriander (cilantro) and mint leaves, to garnish
steamed rice or plain noodles, to serve

For the spice paste

4 shallots, chopped
4 red chillies, chopped
25g/1oz fresh root ginger, peeled and chopped
1 lemon grass stalk, trimmed and chopped
5ml/1 tsp shrimp paste

1 Using a mortar and pestle or a food processor, grind the shallots, chillies, ginger and lemon grass to a paste. Add the shrimp paste and mix well.

2 Heat the oil in a wok or heavy pan. Stir in the spice paste and fry until fragrant. Stir in the tamarind paste and the sugar, then pour in 1.2 litres/2 pints/5 cups water. Mix well and bring to the boil. Reduce the heat and simmer for 10 minutes. Season the broth with salt and pepper.

3 Add the prawns and pineapple to the broth and simmer for 4–5 minutes, or until the prawns are cooked. Using a slotted spoon, lift the prawns and pineapple out of the broth and divide them among four warmed bowls. Ladle over some of the broth and garnish with coriander and mint leaves.

4 The remaining broth can be served separately as a drink, or spooned over steamed rice or plain noodles, if they are accompanying this dish.

Hot and sour Prawn Soup Energy 103kcal/434kJ; Protein 21.5g; Carbohydrate 1.1g, of which sugars 0.7g; Fat 1.4g, of which saturates 0.2g; Cholesterol 219mg; Calcium 100mg; Fibre 0.8g; Sodium 892mg.
Pineapple Prawn Broth Energy 192kcal/808kJ; Protein 20.4g; Carbohydrate 14.2g, of which sugars 13.9g; Fat 6.4g, of which saturates 0.8g; Cholesterol 219mg; Calcium 111mg; Fibre 1.3g; Sodium 216mg.

Tomato Soup with Chilli Squid and Tarragon

Oriental-style seared squid mingles with the pungent tomato and garlic flavours of the Mediterranean.

Serves 4

4 small squid (or 1–2 large squid)
60ml/4 tbsp olive oil
2 shallots, chopped
1 garlic clove, crushed
1.2kg/2½ lb ripe tomatoes, roughly chopped
15ml/1 tbsp sun-dried tomato paste
450ml/¾ pint/2 scant cups vegetable stock
about 2.5ml/½ tsp sugar
2 red chillies, seeded and chopped
30ml/2 tbsp chopped fresh tarragon
salt and ground black pepper
crusty bread, to serve

1 Wash the squid under cold water. Grasp the head and tentacles and pull the body away with the other hand. Discard the intestines that come away. Cut the tentacles away from the head in one piece and reserve; discard the head. Pull the quills out of the main body and remove any roe. Pull off the fins from the body pouch and rub off the semi-transparent, mottled skin. Wash the squid under cold water. Cut into rings and set these aside with the tentacles.

2 Heat 30ml/2 tbsp of the oil in a heavy pan. Add the shallots and garlic, and cook for 4–5 minutes, until softened. Add the tomatoes and tomato paste. Season, cover and cook for 3 minutes. Add half the stock and simmer for 5 minutes, until the tomatoes are soft. Cool the soup, then rub it through a sieve (strainer) and return it to the rinsed-out pan. Stir in the remaining stock and sugar, and reheat gently.

3 Meanwhile, heat the remaining oil in a frying pan. Add the squid rings and tentacles, and the chillies. Cook for 4–5 minutes, stirring, then remove from the heat and stir in the tarragon.

4 Adjust the seasoning if necessary. If the soup tastes slightly sharp, add a little extra sugar. Ladle the soup into bowls and spoon the chilli squid in the centre. Serve with crusty bread.

Spicy Octopus and Watercress Soup

This refreshing Korean seafood soup has a wonderfully restorative quality. Delicious octopus is cooked in a rich vegetable broth, with mooli and watercress adding an elusive flavour that is quintessentially Korean.

Serves 2 to 3

1 large octopus, cleaned and gutted
150g/5oz mooli (daikon), peeled
½ leek, sliced
20g/¾oz kelp or spinach leaves
3 garlic cloves, crushed
1 fresh red chilli, seeded and finely sliced
15ml/1 tbsp light soy sauce
75g/3oz watercress or rocket (arugula)
salt and ground black pepper

1 Rinse the octopus in salted water and cut into pieces about 2.5cm/1in long. Finely dice the mooli.

2 Pour 750ml/1¼ pints/3 cups water into a large pan and bring to the boil. Reduce the heat and add the mooli, leek, kelp or spinach, and crushed garlic.

3 Simmer over a medium heat until the radish softens and becomes clear. Discard the kelp and leek and then add the sliced chilli.

4 Add the octopus, increase the heat and boil for 5 minutes. Season with soy sauce, salt and pepper, and then add the watercress or rocket.

5 Remove from the heat, cover the pan and leave to stand for 1 minute while the leaves wilt into the liquid. Ladle into bowls and serve immediately.

Variation

If you prefer a little more heat, for a spicier version of this soup try adding a teaspoon of Korean chilli powder. This gives the dish a really tangy kick.

Tomato Soup Energy 186kcal/777kj; Protein 8.1g; Carbohydrate 10.9g, of which sugars 10.2g; Fat 12.6g, of which saturates 2g; Cholesterol 48mg; Calcium 30mg; Fibre 1.7g; Sodium 386mg.
Spicy Octopus Soup Energy 106kcal/449kJ; Protein 19.9g; Carbohydrate 2.6g, of which sugars 2.3g; Fat 1.9g, of which saturates 0.5g; Cholesterol 48mg; Calcium 108mg; Fibre 1.7g; Sodium 386mg.

Crab and Chilli Soup

Prepared fresh crab is readily available and perfect for creating an exotic soup in minutes.

Serves 4

45ml/3 tbsp olive oil
1 red onion, finely chopped
2 red chillies, seeded and finely chopped
1 garlic clove, finely chopped
450g/1lb fresh white crab meat
30ml/2 tbsp chopped fresh parsley
30ml/2 tbsp chopped fresh coriander (cilantro)
juice of 2 lemons
1 lemon grass stalk
1 litre/1¾ pints/4 cups good fish or chicken stock
15ml/1 tbsp Thai fish sauce
150g/5oz vermicelli or angel hair pasta, broken into 5–7.5cm/2–3in lengths
salt and ground black pepper

For the coriander relish

50g/2oz/1 cup fresh coriander (cilantro) leaves
1 green chilli, seeded and chopped
15ml/1 tbsp sunflower oil
25ml/1½ tbsp lemon juice
2.5ml/½ tsp ground roasted cumin seeds

1 Heat the oil in a pan and add the onion, chillies and garlic. Cook for 10 minutes until the onion is soft. Transfer to a bowl with the crab meat, parsley, coriander and lemon juice. Set aside.

2 Bruise the lemon grass and add to a pan with the stock and fish sauce. Add the lemon grass and bring to the boil, then stir in the pasta. Simmer, uncovered, for 3–4 minutes or cook for the time suggested on the packet, until the pasta is tender but al dente.

3 Meanwhile, make the coriander relish. Place the coriander, chilli, oil, lemon juice and cumin in a food processor or blender and process to form a coarse paste. Add seasoning to taste.

4 Remove and discard the lemon grass from the soup. Stir the chilli and crab mixture into the soup and season it well. Bring to the boil, then reduce the heat and simmer for 2 minutes.

5 Ladle the soup into four deep, warmed bowls and put a spoonful of the relish in the centre of each. Serve the soup immediately.

Spicy Seafood Noodle Soup

This Korean soup is a spicy, garlic-infused stew.

Serves 2

50g/2oz pork loin
50g/2oz mussels
50g/2oz prawns (shrimp)
90g/3½oz squid
15ml/1 tbsp vegetable oil
1 dried chilli, sliced
½ leek, sliced
2 garlic cloves, finely sliced
5ml/1 tsp grated fresh root ginger
30ml/2 tbsp Korean chilli powder
5ml/1 tsp mirin or rice wine
50g/2oz bamboo shoots, sliced
½ onion, roughly chopped
50g/2oz carrot, roughly chopped
2 Chinese leaves (Chinese cabbage), roughly chopped
750ml/1¼ pints/3 cups beef stock
light soy sauce, to taste
300g/11oz udon or flat wheat noodles
salt

1 Slice the pork, and set aside. Scrub the mussels' shells and rinse under cold water. Discard any that remain closed after being tapped. Scrape off any barnacles and remove the 'beards'. Rinse well. Gently pull the tail shells from the prawns. Twist off the head. Peel the body shell and the claws. Rinse well.

2 Wash the squid. Hold the body, pull away the head and tentacles. Discard the ink sac. Pull out the innards. Discard the thin purple skin, but keep the two small side fins. Slice the head across just under the eyes, severing the tentacles. Squeeze the tentacles to push out the round beak and discard. Rinse the pouch and tentacles. Score the flesh in a criss-cross pattern, and slice into 2cm/¾in pieces.

3 Heat a pan with the oil. Add the chilli, leek, garlic and ginger. Fry until the garlic has browned and add the pork. Fry quickly, add the chilli powder and mirin or rice wine. Add the bamboo shoots, onion and carrot, and fry until the vegetables are soft.

4 Add the seafood and cabbage and cook for 30 seconds. Pour in the stock and bring to the boil, then cover and simmer for 3 minutes. Season with salt. Discard any closed mussels.

5 Cook the noodles in a pan of boiling water. Place noodles in soup bowls, ladle over the soup and serve immediately.

Crab and Chilli Soup Energy 228kcal/951kJ; Protein 23.6g; Carbohydrate 5.4g, of which sugars 5g; Fat 12.6g, of which saturates 6g; Cholesterol 90mg; Calcium 199mg; Fibre 1.1g; Sodium 767mg.
Spicy Seafood Soup Energy 778kcal/3288kJ; Protein 39.5g; Carbohydrate 122.8g, of which sugars 9.4g; Fat 17.7g, of which saturates 1.4g; Cholesterol 176mg; Calcium 104mg; Fibre 6.9g; Sodium 734mg.

Hot and Sour Filipino Fish Soup

Chunky, filling and spicy, the Filipino fish soups are meals in themselves. There are many variations on the theme, depending on the region and the local fish, but most contain a lot of shellfish, and are flavoured with tamarind mixed with hot chilli, and served with coconut vinegar that is flavoured by garlic. Served on its own or with rice, this soup awakens the senses.

Serves 4 to 6

2 litres/3½ pints/8 cups fish stock
250ml/8fl oz/1 cup white wine
15–30ml/1–2 tbsp tamarind paste
30–45ml/2–3 tbsp patis (fish sauce)
30ml/2 tbsp palm sugar (jaggery)
50g/2oz fresh root ginger, grated
2–3 red or green chillies, seeded and finely sliced
2 tomatoes, skinned, seeded and cut into wedges
350g/12oz fresh fish, such as trout, sea bass, swordfish or cod, cut into bitesize chunks
12–16 fresh prawns (shrimp), in their shells
1 bunch fresh basil leaves, roughly chopped
1 bunch flat leaf parsley, roughly chopped
salt and ground black pepper

To serve
60–90ml/4–6 tbsp coconut vinegar
1–2 garlic cloves, finely chopped
1–2 limes, cut into wedges
2 red or green chillies, seeded and quartered lengthways

1 In a wok or large pan, bring the stock and wine to the boil. Stir in the tamarind paste, patis, sugar, ginger and chillies. Reduce the heat and simmer for 15–20 minutes.

2 Add the tomatoes to the broth and season with salt and pepper. Add the fish and prawns and simmer for a further 5 minutes, until the fish is cooked.

3 In a bowl, mix the coconut vinegar and garlic for serving and set aside. Stir half the basil and half the parsley into the broth

4 Ladle into bowls. Garnish with the remaining basil and parsley and serve with the spiked coconut vinegar to splash on top, the lime wedges to squeeze into the soup, and the chillies to chew on for extra heat.

Red Curry Monkfish Soup

This light and creamy coconut soup provides a base for a colourful fusion of red-curried monkfish and pad Thai, the classic stir-fried noodle dish of Thailand.

Serves 4

175g/6oz flat rice noodles
30ml/2 tbsp vegetable oil
2 garlic cloves, chopped
15ml/1 tbsp red curry paste
450g/1lb monkfish tail, cut into bitesize pieces
300ml/½ pint/1¼ cups coconut cream
750ml/1¼ pints/3 cups hot chicken stock
45ml/3 tbsp Thai fish sauce
15ml/1 tbsp palm sugar (jaggery)
60ml/4 tbsp roughly chopped roasted peanuts
4 spring onions (scallions), shredded lengthways
50g/2oz beansprouts
large handful of fresh Thai basil leaves
salt and ground black pepper
1 red chilli, seeded and cut lengthways into slivers, to garnish

1 Soak the noodles in boiling water for 10 minutes, or according to the packet instructions. Drain them and set aside until needed.

2 Heat the oil in a wok or pan over a high heat. Add the garlic and cook for 2 minutes. Stir in the curry paste and cook for 1 minute.

3 Add the monkfish and stir-fry for 4–5 minutes, until the fish is just tender. Pour the coconut cream and the hot chicken stock into the pan.

4 Stir in the Thai fish sauce and the sugar, and bring just to the boil. Add the drained noodles to the pan and cook over a medium heat for 1–2 minutes, until tender.

5 Stir in half of the peanuts, half of the spring onions, half of the beansprouts, the basil and seasoning.

6 Ladle the soup into deep bowls and sprinkle over the remaining peanuts. Garnish with the remaining spring onions, beansprouts and the red chilli.

Hot and Sour Filipino Fish Soup Energy 137kcal/576kJ; Protein 17.7g; Carbohydrate 8.1g, of which sugars 8g; Fat 1g, of which saturates 0.1g; Cholesterol 92mg; Calcium 76mg; Fibre 1.3g; Sodium 644mg.
Red Curry Monkfish Soup Energy 379kcal/1589kJ; Protein 25.5g; Carbohydrate 41.2g, of which sugars 4.7g; Fat 12g, of which saturates 2g; Cholesterol 18mg; Calcium 49mg; Fibre 0.9g; Sodium 111mg.

Hot and Spicy Fish Soup

This soup is a firm favourite to accompany a glass of rice spirit. Halibut or sea bass work as well as cod. White fish flakes have a bite of red chilli, and the watercress and spring onions add a refreshing zesty quality.

Serves 3 to 4

1 cod, filleted and skinned, head separate
225g/8oz Chinese white radish, peeled
½ onion, chopped
2 garlic cloves, crushed
22.5ml/4½ tsp Korean chilli powder
5ml/1 tsp gochujang chilli paste
2 spring onions (scallions), roughly sliced
1 block firm tofu, cubed
90g/3½oz watercress or rocket (arugula)
salt and ground black pepper

1 Slice the cod fillets into three or four large pieces and set the head aside. Cut the white radish into 2cm/¾in cubes.

2 Bring 750ml/1¼ pints/3 cups water to the boil in large pan and add the fish head. Add the radish, onion, crushed garlic and a pinch of salt. Then add the chilli powder and gochujang chilli paste, and boil for 5 minutes more.

3 Remove the fish head and add the sliced fillet to the pan. Simmer until the fish is tender, about 4 minutes, and then add the spring onions, tofu, and watercress or rocket. Simmer the soup without stirring for 2 minutes more.

4 Season with salt and pepper, and serve the soup immediately.

Cook's Tips

- *Gochujang is a savoury, pungent paste from Korea. Made from chilli powder, rice and soya beans, it is traditionally fermented for long periods in sealed jars. Look out for ready-made versions in Asian stores and food markets.*
- *For a milder version of this soup omit the chilli powder and gochujang chilli paste. The soup will still be wonderfully hearty and flavoursome.*

Chicken and Ginger Broth with Papaya

This is a traditional peasant dish that is still cooked every day in rural areas of the Philippines. In some areas, green papaya is added to the broth, which could be regarded as a version of coq au vin. Generally the chicken and broth are served with steamed rice, but the broth is also sipped during the meal to cleanse and stimulate the palate.

Serves 4 to 6

15–30ml/1–2 tbsp palm or groundnut (peanut) oil
2 garlic cloves, finely chopped
1 large onion, sliced
40g/1½oz fresh root ginger, finely grated
2 whole dried chillies
1 chicken, left whole or jointed, trimmed of fat
30ml/2 tbsp patis (fish sauce)
600ml/1 pint/2½ cups chicken stock
1.2 litres/2 pints/5 cups water
1 small green papaya, cut into fine slices or strips
1 bunch fresh young chilli or basil leaves
salt and ground black pepper
cooked rice, to serve

1 Heat the oil in a wok or a large pan that has a lid. Stir in the garlic, onion and ginger and fry until they begin to colour. Stir in the chillies, add the chicken and fry until the skin is lightly browned all over.

2 Pour in the patis, stock and water, adding more water if necessary so that the whole chicken is completely covered. Bring to the boil, reduce the heat, cover and simmer gently for about 1½ hours, until the chicken is very tender when pierced with a sharp knife.

3 Season the stock with salt and pepper and add the papaya. Continue to simmer for a further 10–15 minutes, then stir in the chilli or basil leaves.

4 Serve the chicken and broth in warmed bowls, with the same number of bowls of steamed rice. Each diner ladles some of the broth over the rice.

Hot and Spicy Fish Soup Energy 132kcal/554kJ; Protein 23.4g; Carbohydrate 2.8g, of which sugars 2.3g; Fat 3g, of which saturates 0.5g; Cholesterol 46mg; Calcium 300mg; Fibre 1.1g; Sodium 80mg.
Chicken and Ginger Broth Energy 290kcal/1219kJ; Protein 46.4g; Carbohydrate 9.8g, of which sugars 8.7g; Fat 7.5g, of which saturates 1.5g; Cholesterol 169mg; Calcium 40mg; Fibre 2.2g; Sodium 150mg.

Chicken and Rice Soup with Chilli and Lemon Grass

This tasty soup, known as *shnor chrook*, is Cambodia's answer to the chicken noodle soup that is so popular in the West. Light and refreshing, it is the perfect choice for a hot day, as well as a great pick-me-up when you are feeling low or tired.

Serves 4

2 lemon grass stalks, trimmed, cut into three, and lightly bruised
15ml/1 tbsp Thai fish sauce
90g/3½oz/½ cup short grain rice, rinsed
sea salt
ground black pepper
1 small bunch coriander (cilantro) leaves, finely chopped, and 1 green or red chilli, seeded and cut into thin strips, to garnish
1 lime, cut in wedges, to serve

For the stock

1 small chicken or 2 meaty chicken legs
1 onion, quartered
2 garlic cloves, crushed
25g/1oz fresh root ginger, sliced
2 lemon grass stalks, cut in half lengthwise and bruised
2 dried red chillies
30ml/2 tbsp Thai fish sauce

1 Put the chicken into a large pan. Add all the other stock ingredients and pour in 2 litres/3½ pints/8 cups water. Bring to the boil, then reduce the heat and simmer, covered, for 2 hours.

2 Skim any fat from the stock, strain and reserve. Remove the skin from the chicken and shred the meat. Set aside. Pour the stock back into the pan and bring to the boil, then simmer. Stir in the lemon grass, Thai fish sauce and the rice and simmer, uncovered, for 40 minutes. Add the chicken and season to taste.

3 Ladle the hot soup into bowls, garnish with the coriander and strips of chilli and serve with lime wedges to squeeze over.

Cook's Tip

• *Many Vietnamese and Cambodians often spike the soup with additional chillies as a garnish, or served on the side.*

Mackerel and Chilli Tomato Soup

All the ingredients for this unusual soup are cooked in a single pan, so it is not only quick and easy to prepare, but reduces the clearing up. Smoked mackerel gives the soup a robust flavour, but this is tempered by the citrus tones in the lemon grass and tamarind.

Serves 4

200g/7oz smoked mackerel fillets
4 tomatoes
1 litre/1¾ pints/4 cups vegetable stock
1 lemon grass stalk, finely chopped
5cm/2in piece fresh galangal, finely diced
4 shallots, finely chopped
2 garlic cloves, finely chopped
2.5ml/½ tsp dried chilli flakes
15ml/1 tbsp Thai fish sauce
5ml/1 tsp palm sugar (jaggery) or light muscovado (brown) sugar
45ml/3 tbsp thick tamarind juice, made by mixing tamarind paste with warm water
small bunch fresh chives or spring onions (scallions), to garnish

1 Prepare the smoked mackerel fillets. Remove and discard the skin, if necessary, then chop the flesh into large pieces. Remove any stray bones with your fingers or tweezers.

2 Cut the tomatoes in half, squeeze out the seeds with your fingers, then finely dice the flesh with a sharp knife. Set aside.

3 Pour the stock into a pan and add the lemon grass, galangal, shallots and garlic. Bring to the boil, then simmer for 15 minutes.

4 Add the fish, tomatoes, chilli flakes, fish sauce, sugar and tamarind juice. Simmer for 5 minutes, until the fish and tomatoes are heated through. Serve garnished with chives or spring onions.

Cook's Tips

Galangal is a rhizome used in Thai and other South-east Asian cuisine. It resembles, and is related to, ginger in appearance. In its raw form, it has a hot, ginger and pepper flavour, with a quite sour taste and pungent aroma.

Chicken and Rice Soup Energy 147kcal/615kJ; Protein 12.8g; Carbohydrate 19.8g, of which sugars 1.4g; Fat 1.7g, of which saturates 0.4g; Cholesterol 53mg; Calcium 37mg; Fibre 0.8g; Sodium 320mg.
Mackerel and Tomato Soup Energy 209kcal/868kJ; Protein 10.3g; Carbohydrate 6.6g; of which sugars 6.5g; Fat 15.9g; of which saturates 3.2g; Cholesterol 53mg; Calcium 19mg; Fibre 0.8g; Sodium 681mg.

Hot and Peppery Chicken Soup

This aromatic soup is rich with coconut milk and intensely flavoured with galangal, lemon grass and kaffir lime leaves.

Serves 4 to 6

4 lemon grass stalks, roots trimmed
2 x 400ml/14fl oz cans coconut milk
475ml/16fl oz/2 cups chicken stock
2.5cm/1in piece fresh galangal, peeled and thinly sliced
10 black peppercorns, crushed
10 kaffir lime leaves, torn
300g/11oz skinless chicken breast fillets, cut into thin strips
115g/4oz/1 cup button (white) mushrooms, halved if large
50g/2oz/½ cup baby corn cobs, quartered lengthways
60ml/4 tbsp fresh lime juice
45ml/3 tbsp Thai fish sauce
chopped fresh red chillies, spring onions (scallions) and fresh coriander (cilantro) leaves, to garnish

1 Cut off the lower 5cm/2in from each lemon grass stalk and chop it finely. Bruise the remaining pieces of stalk.

2 Bring the coconut milk and chicken stock to the boil in a large pan over a medium heat.

3 Add the chopped and bruised lemon grass, the fresh galangal, the black peppercorns and half the kaffir lime leaves to the pan.

4 Reduce the heat to low and simmer gently for 10 minutes. Strain the soup into a clean pan.

5 Return the soup to a low heat, then stir in the chicken strips, the halved mushrooms and the corn. Simmer gently over a low heat, stirring the soup occasionally, for 5–7 minutes, or until the chicken is cooked.

6 Stir the lime juice and fish sauce into the soup, then add the remaining lime leaves.

7 Ladle the soup into four to six warmed individual soup bowls and serve immediately, garnished with the chopped red chillies, the spring onions and the fresh coriander leaves.

Spicy Indonesian Chicken Broth

Colourful and crunchy, this South-east Asian soup can be served as an appetizer or as a dish on its own.

Serves 4 to 6

30ml/2 tbsp palm, groundnut (peanut) or corn oil
25g/1oz fresh root ginger, finely chopped
25g/1oz fresh turmeric, finely chopped, or 5ml/1 tsp ground turmeric
1 lemon grass stalk, finely chopped
4–5 kaffir lime leaves, crushed
4 candlenuts, coarsely ground
2 garlic cloves, crushed
5ml/1 tsp coriander seeds
5ml/1 tsp shrimp paste
2 litres/3½ pints chicken stock
corn or vegetable oil, for deep-frying
2 waxy potatoes, finely sliced
350g/12oz skinless chicken breast fillets, thinly sliced widthways
150g/5oz leafy green cabbage, finely sliced
150g/5oz mung beansprouts
3 hard-boiled eggs, thinly sliced
salt and ground black pepper

To serve

1 bunch fresh coriander (cilantro) leaves, roughly chopped
2–3 spring onions (scallions), finely sliced
2–3 hot red or green chillies, seeded and finely sliced
2 limes, cut into wedges
kecap manis

1 Arrange the ingredients for serving attractively on a platter or in serving bowls.

2 Heat the oil in a pan, stir in the ginger, turmeric, lemon grass, kaffir lime leaves, candlenuts, garlic, coriander seeds and shrimp paste. Fry until the mixture darkens and becomes fragrant. Pour in the stock, bring to the boil, then simmer for about 20 minutes.

3 Meanwhile, heat the oil for deep-frying in a wok. Fry the potato slices until crisp. Remove with a slotted spoon, drain on kitchen paper and put aside. Strain the chicken stock and reserve. Pour back into the pan and season. Return to the boil, reduce the heat and add the chicken. Simmer for 2–3 minutes.

4 Sprinkle the cabbage and beansprouts into the base of the serving bowls. Ladle in the broth and top with the eggs and potatoes, and serve. Diners help themselves to the ingredients for serving, and the kecap manis to drizzle over the top.

Hot and Peppery Soup Energy 134kcal/571kj; Protein 19.8g; Carbohydrate 10.7g, of which sugars 10.4g; Fat 1.7g, of which saturates 0.7g; Cholesterol 53mg; Calcium 66mg; Fibre 0.5g; Sodium 887mg.
Spicy Indonesian Broth Energy 296kcal/1238kJ; Protein 21.1g; Carbohydrate 14.8g, of which sugars 3g; Fat 17.5g, of which saturates 2.8g; Cholesterol 136mg; Calcium 63mg; Fibre 2.7g; Sodium 96mg.

Chilli Chicken Noodle Soup

Nowadays a signature dish of the city of Chiang Mai, this delicious noodle soup originated in Burma, now called Myanmar, which lies only a little to the north. It is also the Thai equivalent of the famous Malaysian laksa.

Serves 4 to 6

600ml/1 pint/2½ cups coconut milk
30ml/2 tbsp Thai red curry paste
5ml/1 tsp ground turmeric
450g/1lb chicken thighs, boned and cut into bitesize chunks
600ml/1 pint/2½ cups chicken stock
60ml/4 tbsp Thai fish sauce
15ml/1 tbsp dark soy sauce
juice of ½–1 lime
450g/1lb fresh egg noodles, blanched briefly in boiling water
salt and ground black pepper

To garnish
3 spring onions (scallions), chopped
4 fresh red chillies, chopped
4 shallots, chopped
60ml/4 tbsp sliced pickled mustard leaves, rinsed
30ml/2 tbsp fried sliced garlic
coriander (cilantro) leaves
4–6 fried noodle nests (optional)

1 Pour about one-third of the coconut milk into a large, heavy pan or wok. Bring to the boil over a medium heat, stirring frequently with a wooden spoon until the milk separates.

2 Add the curry paste and ground turmeric, stir to mix completely and cook until the mixture is fragrant. Add the chunks of chicken and toss over the heat for about 2 minutes, making sure that they are thoroughly coated with the paste.

3 Add the remaining coconut milk, the chicken stock, fish sauce and soy sauce. Season with salt and pepper to taste. Bring to simmering point, stirring frequently, then lower the heat and cook gently for 7–10 minutes. Remove from the heat and stir in lime juice to taste.

4 Reheat the fresh egg noodles in boiling water, drain and divide among four to six warmed bowls. Divide the chunks of chicken among the bowls and ladle in the hot soup. Top each serving with spring onions, chillies, shallots, pickled mustard leaves, fried garlic, coriander leaves and a fried noodle nest, if using. Serve immediately.

Fiery Chicken Soup with Noodles

The noodles are bathed in a chicken broth, topped with vegetables, seasoned chicken shreds and spicy sauce.

Serves 2

½ chicken, about 500g/1½lb, chopped into large pieces
2 leeks
4 garlic cloves, peeled
40g/1½oz fresh root ginger, peeled
8 dried shiitake mushrooms, soaked in warm water for 30 minutes
115g/4oz carrot
1 courgette (zucchini)
30ml/2 tbsp vegetable oil
1 onion, finely chopped
10ml/2 tsp sesame oil
light soy sauce, to taste
½ dried chilli, finely chopped
salt and ground white pepper

For the seasoning
10ml/2 tsp dark soy sauce
2 spring onions (scallions), finely chopped
2 garlic cloves, crushed
30ml/2 tbsp sesame oil
30ml/2 tbsp sesame seeds

For the noodles
225g/8oz/2 cups plain (all-purpose) flour
6 eggs, beaten

For the sauce
30ml/2 tbsp light soy sauce
2 spring onions (scallions), finely chopped
2 garlic cloves, crushed
10ml/2 tsp Korean chilli powder
10ml/2 tsp sesame seeds
15ml/1 tbsp sesame oil

1 Place the chicken in a pan. Add the leeks, garlic and ginger, and cover with water. Boil for 20 minutes. Strain the stock and reserve. Strip off the meat from the chicken. Mix the seasoning ingredients in a bowl and use to coat the chicken.

2 For the noodles, mix together the flour, a pinch of salt, the eggs and a splash of water. Knead until smooth, then roll out to about 3mm/⅛in thick. Fold the dough three times and slice into noodles.

3 Slice the mushrooms, carrot and courgette. Heat the vegetable oil in a pan and stir-fry the mushrooms, courgette, carrot and onion until just tender. Combine the sauce ingredients in a bowl.

4 Heat the stock, season with the soy sauce, salt and pepper. Add the noodles for 4 minutes, then transfer them to bowls and ladle over the broth. Top with chicken, vegetables and a sprinkling of dried chilli. Serve with the sauce.

Chilli Chicken Soup Energy 606kcal/2569kJ; Protein 39.5g; Carbohydrate 88.7g, of which sugars 10.1g; Fat 12.9g, of which saturates 3.7g; Cholesterol 135mg; Calcium 84mg; Fibre 3.3g; Sodium 1111mg.
Fiery Chicken Soup Energy 1138kcal/4767kJ; Protein 94.1g; Carbohydrate 70.4g, of which sugars 11.4g; Fat 55.6g, of which saturates 10.5g; Cholesterol 746mg; Calcium 392mg; Fibre 10.1g; Sodium 739mg.

Chicken, Chilli and Tomato Soup

This delicious, refreshing soup is perfect for a light lunch when you need a lift.

Serves 4

225g/8oz skinless chicken breast fillets
1 garlic clove, crushed
pinch of freshly nutmeg
25g/1oz/2 tbsp butter or margarine
½ onion, finely chopped
15ml/1 tbsp tomato purée (paste)
400g/14oz can tomatoes, puréed
1.2 litres/2 pints/5 cups chicken stock
1 fresh chilli, seeded and chopped
1 chayote, peeled and diced, about 350g/12oz
5ml/1 tsp dried oregano
2.5ml/½ tsp dried thyme
50g/2oz smoked haddock fillet, skinned and diced
salt and ground black pepper
fresh chopped chives, to garnish

1 Dice the chicken, place in a bowl and season with salt, pepper, garlic and nutmeg. Mix well to coat the chicken and then set aside for about 30 minutes.

2 Melt the butter or margarine in a large pan, add the chicken and cook over a moderate heat for 5–6 minutes. Stir in the onion and fry gently for a further 5 minutes until the onion is slightly softened.

3 Add the tomato purée, puréed tomatoes, stock, chilli, chayote and herbs. Bring to the boil, cover and simmer gently for 35 minutes until the chayote is tender.

4 Add the smoked fish, simmer for a further 5 minutes or until the fish is cooked through, adjust the seasoning and pour into warmed soup bowls. Garnish with a sprinkling of chopped chives and serve.

Cook's Tip
Chayote, also called christophene, is a member of the gourd family. It is the size and shape of a very large pear, with pale green skin. The flesh has a mild flavour and works well here, where it absorbs the flavours of the other ingredients.

Spicy Vegetable Broth with Minced Beef

This delicious soup is popular throughout Indonesia where it is called *sayur menir.*

Serves 6

30ml/2 tbsp groundnut (peanut) oil
115g/4oz finely minced (ground) beef
1 large onion, grated or finely chopped
1 garlic clove, crushed
1–2 chillies, seeded and chopped
1cm/½in cube shrimp paste
3 macadamia nuts or 6 almonds, finely ground
1 carrot, finely grated
5ml/1 tsp soft light brown sugar
1 litre/1¾ pints/4 cups chicken stock
50g/2oz dried shrimp, soaked in warm water for 10 minutes
225g/8oz spinach, rinsed and finely shredded
8 baby corn, sliced, or 200g/7oz canned corn kernels
1 large tomato, chopped
juice of ½ lemon
salt

1 Heat the oil in a pan. Add the beef, onion and garlic and cook, stirring, until the meat has evenly browned.

2 Add the chillies, shrimp paste, nuts, carrot and sugar to the minced beef. Add salt to taste.

3 Add the stock and bring gently to the boil. Reduce the heat to a simmer and then add the shrimp, with their soaking liquid. Simmer for about 10 minutes.

4 A few minutes before serving, add the spinach, corn, tomato and lemon juice. Simmer for a minute or two, to heat through. Do not overcook at this stage because this will spoil the appearance and the taste of the broth. Ladle into warmed individual bowls and serve immediately.

Cook's Tip
If you prefer a little more heat, to make this soup very hot and spicy simply add the seeds from inside the chillies.

Chicken and Chilli Soup Energy 133kcal/558kj; Protein 16.7g; Carbohydrate 32g, of which sugars 2.4g; Fat 6g, of which saturates 3.5g; Cholesterol 57mg; Calcium 36mg; Fibre 1.1g; Sodium 167mg.
Spicy Vegetable Broth Energy 218kcal/911kJ; Protein 12.6g; Carbohydrate 14.7g, of which sugars 8.4g; Fat 12.5g, of which saturates 2.3g; Cholesterol 54mg; Calcium 199mg; Fibre 3g; Sodium 530mg.

Green Chilli, Lamb, Bean and Pumpkin Soup

This spicy, fresh soup combines tender meaty lamb with sweet pumpkin and green bananas.

Serves 4

115g/4oz black-eyed beans (peas), soaked for 2 hours, or overnight
675g/1½lb lamb neck (US shoulder or breast), cut into medium-size chunks
5ml/1 tsp chopped fresh thyme, or 2.5ml/½ tsp dried thyme
2 bay leaves
1.2 litres/2 pints/5 cups stock or water
1 onion, sliced
225g/8oz pumpkin, diced
2 black cardamom pods
7.5ml/1½ tsp ground turmeric
15ml/1 tbsp chopped fresh coriander (cilantro)
2.5ml/½ tsp caraway seeds
1 fresh green chilli, seeded and chopped
2 green bananas
1 carrot
salt and ground black pepper

1 Drain the black-eyed beans, place them in a pan and cover with fresh cold water. Bring to the boil, then boil rapidly for 10 minutes and then reduce the heat and simmer, covered, for 40–50 minutes until tender, adding more water if necessary. Remove from the heat and set aside to cool.

2 Meanwhile, put the lamb in a large pan, add the thyme, bay leaves and stock or water and bring to the boil. Cover and simmer over a moderate heat for 1 hour, until tender.

3 Add the onion, pumpkin, cardamoms, turmeric, coriander, caraway, chilli and seasoning and stir. Bring back to a simmer and then cook, uncovered, for 15 minutes, until the pumpkin is tender, stirring occasionally.

4 When the beans are cool, spoon into a blender or food processor with their liquid and blend to a smooth purée.

5 Cut the bananas into medium slices and the carrot into thin slices. Stir into the soup with the beans and cook for 10–12 minutes, until the vegetables are tender. Adjust the seasoning and serve.

Spiced Chicken and Vegetable Soup

This creamy coconut soap, made with chicken and prawns, is substantial enough to serve on its own.

Serves 6 to 8

1 onion, ½ cut in two, ½ sliced
2 garlic cloves, crushed
1 fresh red or green chilli, seeded and sliced
1cm/½in cube shrimp paste
3 macadamia nuts or 6 almonds
1cm/½in galangal, peeled and sliced, or 5ml/1 tsp galangal powder
5ml/1 tsp sugar
vegetable oil, for frying
225g/8oz skinless chicken breast fillets, cut into 1cm/½in cubes
300ml/½ pint/1¼ cups coconut milk
1.2 litres/2 pints/5 cups chicken stock
1 aubergine (eggplant), diced
225g/8oz green beans, chopped
small wedge of crisp white cabbage, shredded
1 red (bell) pepper, seeded and finely sliced
115g/4oz cooked, peeled prawns (shrimp)
salt and ground black pepper

1 Grind the onion quarters, garlic, chilli, shrimp paste, nuts, galangal and sugar to a paste in a processor or in a mortar with a pestle.

2 Heat a wok, add the oil and then fry the paste, without browning, until it gives off a rich aroma.

3 Add the sliced onion and chicken cubes and cook for 3–4 minutes. Stir in the coconut milk and stock. Bring to the boil and simmer for a few minutes.

4 Add the diced aubergine to the soup, with the beans, and cook for a few minutes, until the beans are almost cooked.

5 A few minutes before serving, stir the cabbage, red pepper and prawns into the soup. The vegetables should be cooked so that they are still crunchy and the prawns merely need heating through.

6 Taste the soup and adjust the seasoning if necessary. Ladle the soup into warmed soup bowls and serve immediately.

Chilli and Pumpkin Soup Energy 442kcal/1855kj; Protein 40.8g; Carbohydrate 27.2g, of which sugars 13.1g; Fat 19.7g, of which saturates 9g; Cholesterol 128mg; Calcium 74mg; Fibre 6.4g; Sodium 155mg.
Spiced Chicken Soup Energy 130kcal/544kJ; Protein 11.7g; Carbohydrate 7g, of which sugars 6.3g; Fat 6.3g, of which saturates 0.8g; Cholesterol 48mg; Calcium 62mg; Fibre 2g; Sodium 89mg.

Roasted Garlic and Pork Soup with Chilli

Made with pork or chicken, this warming and sustaining rice soup combines ancient traditions of the Filipino rice culture with Spanish colonial techniques of browning and sautéeing.

Serves 4 to 6

15–30ml/1–2 tbsp palm or groundnut (peanut) oil
1 large onion, finely chopped.
2 garlic cloves, finely chopped
25g/1oz fresh root ginger, finely chopped
350g/12oz pork rump or tenderloin, cut widthways into bitesize slices
5–6 black peppercorns
115g/4oz/1 cup plus 15ml/1 tbsp short grain rice
2 litres/3½ pints/8 cups pork or chicken stock
30ml/2 tbsp patis (fish sauce)
salt

To serve

2 garlic cloves, finely chopped
2 spring onions (scallions), white parts only, finely sliced
2–3 green or red chillies, seeded and quartered lengthways

1 Heat the oil in a wok or deep, heavy pan that has a lid. Stir in the onion, garlic and ginger and fry until fragrant and beginning to colour. Add the pork and fry, stirring frequently, for 5–6 minutes, until lightly browned. Stir in the peppercorns.

2 Meanwhile, put the rice in a sieve (strainer), rinse under cold running water until the water runs clear, then drain. Toss the rice into the pan, making sure that it is coated in the mixture.

3 Pour in the stock, add the patis and bring to the boil. Reduce the heat and partially cover with a lid. Simmer for 40 minutes, stirring ocassionally to make sure that the rice doesn't stick to the bottom of the pan. Season with salt to taste.

4 Just before serving, dry-fry the garlic in a small, heavy pan until golden brown, then stir it into the soup. Ladle the soup into individual warmed bowls and sprinkle the spring onions over the top. Serve the chillies separately, to chew on.

Golden Chorizo, Chilli and Chickpea Soup

Small uncooked chorizo sausages are available from Spanish delicatessens, but ready-to-eat chorizo can be cut into chunks and used instead.

Serves 4

115g/4oz/⅔ cup dried chickpeas, soaked overnight and drained
pinch of saffron strands
45ml/3 tbsp olive oil
450g/1lb uncooked mini chorizo sausages
5ml/1 tsp dried chilli flakes
6 garlic cloves, finely chopped
450g/1lb tomatoes, roughly chopped
350g/12oz new potatoes, quartered
2 bay leaves
450ml/¾ pint/scant 2 cups water
60ml/4 tbsp chopped fresh parsley
salt and ground black pepper
30ml/2 tbsp extra virgin olive oil, to garnish
crusty bread, to serve

1 Place the chickpeas in a pan. Cover with plenty of water and bring to the boil, skimming off any scum as it forms. Cover and simmer for 2–3 hours, until tender. Add more boiling water, if necessary, to keep the chickpeas well covered. Drain, reserving the cooking liquid. Soak the saffron strands in a little warm water.

2 Heat the oil in a large frying pan. Add the chorizo and fry over for 5 minutes, until a lot of oil has seeped out of the sausages and they are pale golden brown. Drain and set aside.

3 Add the chilli flakes and garlic to the fat in the pan and cook for a few seconds. Stir in the saffron with its soaking water, tomatoes, chickpeas, potatoes, chorizo sausages and bay leaves. Pour in 450ml/¾ pint/scant 2 cups of the chickpea cooking liquid and the water, and stir in salt and pepper to taste.

4 Bring to the boil and then simmer for 45 minutes, stirring occasionally, until the soup has thickened slightly.

5 Add the parsley to the soup and adjust the seasoning. Ladle the soup into four warmed soup plates and drizzle a little extra virgin olive oil over each portion. Serve with crusty bread.

Garlic and Pork Soup Energy 195kcal/813kJ; Protein 14.8g; Carbohydrate 19.9g, of which sugars 3.4g; Fat 6.2g, of which saturates 1.3g; Cholesterol 37mg; Calcium 24mg; Fibre 0.8g; Sodium 399mg.
Chorizo and Chickpea Soup Energy 642kcal/2674kJ; Protein 21.7g; Carbohydrate 42.3g, of which sugars 8.1g; Fat 44g, of which saturates 12.5g; Cholesterol 68mg; Calcium 174mg; Fibre 6.1g; Sodium 997mg

Spicy Tripe Soup with Lemon Grass and Lime

This popular Indonesian soup is packed with spices and the refreshing flavours of lemon grass and lime.

Serves 4

250ml/8fl oz/1 cup rice wine vinegar
900g/2lb beef tripe, cleaned
2 litres/3½ pints/8 cups beef stock or water
2–3 garlic cloves, crushed whole
2 lemon grass stalks
25g/1oz fresh root ginger, finely grated
3–4 kaffir lime leaves
225g/8oz mooli (daikon) or turnip, finely sliced
15ml/1 tbsp palm, groundnut (peanut) or vegetable oil
4 shallots, finely sliced
salt and ground black pepper

For the sambal

15ml/1 tbsp palm, groundnut (peanut) or vegetable oil
2 garlic cloves, crushed
2–3 hot red chillies, seeded and finely chopped
15ml/1 tbsp chilli and shrimp paste
25ml/1½ tbsp tomato purée (paste)

1 Fill a large pan with about 2.5 litres/4½ pints/11¼ cups water and bring to the boil. Reduce the heat and add the vinegar and the tripe. Season and simmer gently for 1 hour.

2 Prepare the sambal. Heat the oil in a pan. Stir in the garlic and chillies and fry until fragrant. Stir in the chilli and shrimp paste, then add the tomato purée and mix. Set aside.

3 When the tripe is cooked, drain and cut into bitesize squares or strips. Pour the stock or water into a pan and bring to the boil. Reduce the heat and add the tripe, garlic, lemon grass, ginger, lime leaves and mooli or turnip. Cook gently for 15–20 minutes, until the mooli or turnip is tender.

4 Meanwhile, heat the oil in a frying pan. Add the shallots and fry for 5 minutes or until golden brown. Drain on kitchen paper.

5 Ladle the soup into individual warmed bowls and sprinkle the shallots over the top. Serve the soup with the spicy sambal, which can be added in a dollop and stirred in.

Hot and Spicy Beef and Fern Frond Soup

Known as *yukgejang*, this is one of the most traditional Korean soups. The smoky taste of fern fronds gives it its unique flavour, and red chilli powder provides a fierce kick and fiery colour to the combination of beef and leek. It makes a perfect lunch dish when served with a bowl of rice.

Serves 2 to 3

75g/3oz dried edible fern fronds
75g/3oz enoki mushrooms, trimmed
250g/9oz beef flank
10ml/2 tsp sesame oil
30ml/2 tbsp chilli powder
1 garlic clove, peeled and finely chopped
15ml/1 tbsp vegetable oil
75g/3oz/½ cup beansprouts, trimmed
1 leek, sliced
1 spring onion (scallion), finely sliced
salt

1 Boil the dried fern fronds for about 3 minutes. Drain and rinse with cold water. Cut the fronds into thirds and discard the tougher stem pieces, along with the enoki mushroom caps.

2 Place the beef in a medium pan and cover with water. Bring to the boil, cover and cook over high heat for 30 minutes. Then remove the beef and strain the stock into a jug (pitcher).

3 Cut the beef into thin strips and place in a bowl. Add the sesame oil, chilli powder and chopped garlic, and coat the meat.

4 Heat the vegetable oil in a pan and add the meat with the fern fronds, beansprouts, leek and spring onion. Stir-fry for 2 minutes, then reduce the heat and pour in the beef stock. Cover and cook gently for 30 minutes or so until tender. Add the mushrooms and salt and simmer for 2 minutes. Serve.

Cook's Tip

If edible fern shoots are not available the best alternative is an equivalent amount of shiitake mushrooms.

Spicy Tripe Soup Energy 160kcal/668kJ; Protein 19.2g; Carbohydrate 5.5g, of which sugars 4.8g; Fat 7g, of which saturates 1.1g; Cholesterol 163mg; Calcium 198mg; Fibre 1.9g; Sodium 299mg.
Hot and Spicy Beef Soup Energy 225kcal/935kJ; Protein 21.5g; Carbohydrate 3g, of which sugars 2g; Fat 14.1g, of which saturates 4g; Cholesterol 48mg; Calcium 28mg; Fibre 2.3g; Sodium 59mg.

Roasted Coconut Cashew Nuts with Chilli

Serve these hot and sweet cashew nuts in paper or cellophane cones at parties. Not only do they look enticing and taste terrific, but the cones help to keep clothes and hands clean and can simply be thrown away afterwards.

Serves 6 to 8

15ml/1 tbsp groundnut (peanut) oil
30ml/2 tbsp clear honey
250g/8oz/2 cups cashew nuts
115g/4oz/1⅓ cups desiccated (dry unsweetened shredded) coconut
2 small fresh red chillies, seeded and finely chopped
salt and ground black pepper

1 Heat the oil in a wok or large frying pan.

2 Stir the honey into the pan and heat for a few seconds, stirring constantly.

3 Add the nuts and the desiccated coconut and stir-fry until both are golden brown. Stir the mixture constantly to ensure that it does not stick to the base of the pan.

4 Add the chillies to the pan and season with a little salt and ground black pepper to taste. Toss until all the ingredients are well mixed.

5 Serve the nuts warm or cooled in rolled-up paper cones or on saucers.

Variations

• *Almonds would also work well in this recipe. Cashew nuts can be expensive so you could also choose peanuts for a more economical snack.*

• *Desiccated coconut is a handy ingredient to have in your pantry as it has many uses, but if you can get hold of a fresh coconut then you can also use that in this recipe. Simply grate the flesh and substitute for the desiccated version.*

Hot and Spicy Plantain Snacks

Sweet and crisp, deep-fried slices of plantain make good nibbles with drinks. Make sure the plantains are ripe – the skin should be brown and mottled – otherwise they tend to be woody rather than sweet and fruity. Be liberal with the spices as the starchy plantains can carry strong flavours.

Serves 2 to 4 as a snack

2 large ripe plantains
sunflower oil, for deep-frying
1 dried red chilli, roasted, seeded and chopped
15–30ml/1–2 tbsp zahtar
coarse salt

1 To peel the plantains, cut off their ends with a sharp knife and make two to three incisions in the skin from end to end, then peel off the skin. Cut the plantains into thick slices.

2 Heat the oil for deep-frying to 180°C/350°F, or until a cube of day-old bread browns in 30–45 seconds. Fry the plantain slices in batches until golden brown. Drain each batch on a double layer of kitchen paper.

3 While the plantain is still warm, place the pieces in a shallow bowl and sprinkle liberally with the dried roasted chilli, zahtar and salt.

4 Toss the ingredients thoroughly and serve immediately.

Cook's Tips

• *Zahtar is a spice blend popular in North Africa and the Middle East. It is usually composed of toasted sesame seeds, dried thyme, dried marjoram and sumac. It is often sprinkled over meats and vegetables as a seasoning or mixed with olive oil and used as a bread glaze. Look for it in large supermarkets or Middle Eastern food stores.*

• *To roast the chilli, place in a small frying pan and cook over a medium heat, stirring constantly, until the chilli darkens and gives off a peppery aroma.*

Roasted Nuts Energy 436kcal/1810kJ; Protein 9.7g; Carbohydrate 22.1g, of which sugars 16.6g; Fat 34.9g, of which saturates 14.8g; Cholesterol 0mg; Calcium 20mg; Fibre 4g; Sodium 128mg.
Hot and Spicy Plantain Energy 334kcal/1408kJ; Protein 1.9g; Carbohydrate 59.4g, of which sugars 14.4g; Fat 11.5g, of which saturates 1.3g; Cholesterol 0mg; Calcium 8mg; Fibre 2.9g; Sodium 4mg.

Popcorn with Lime and Chilli

If the only popcorn you've had came out of a carton at the movies, try this Mexican speciality. The lime juice and chilli powder are inspired additions, and the snack is quite a healthy choice to serve with drinks.

Makes 1 large bowl
30ml/2 tbsp vegetable oil
225g/8oz/1¼ cups corn kernels for popcorn
10ml/2 tsp chilli powder
juice of 2 limes

1 Heat the oil in a large, heavy frying pan until it is very hot. Add the popcorn and immediately cover the pan with a lid and reduce the heat.

2 After a few minutes the corn should start to pop. Resist the temptation to lift the lid to check. Shake the pan occasionally so that all corn will be cooked and browned.

3 When the sound of popping corn has stopped, quickly remove the pan from the heat and allow to cool slightly.

4 Take off the pan lid and with a spoon lift out and discard any corn kernels that have not popped. The uncooked corn will have fallen to the bottom of the pan and is completely inedible.

5 Add the chilli powder. Shake the pan again and again to make sure that all of the corn is covered with a colourful dusting of chilli.

6 Transfer the popcorn to a large bowl and keep warm. Add a squeeze of lime juice immediately before serving.

Variation
Give your popcorn an Indian flavour by replacing the chilli powder with curry powder. Omit the lime juice and add 5ml/½ tsp salt and 5ml/½ tsp sugar to the popcorn. You can also add in some flaked (sliced) almonds and sultanas (golden raisins), if you like.

Rice Cakes with Spicy Dipping Sauce

Prepare these rice cakes at least a day before you plan to serve them, as the rice needs to dry out overnight.

Serves 4 to 6
175g/6oz/1 cup Thai jasmine rice
350ml/12fl oz/1½ cups water
oil, for deep-frying and greasing

For the spicy dipping sauce
6 dried chillies, halved and seeded
2.5ml/½ tsp salt
2 shallots, chopped
2 garlic cloves, chopped
4 coriander (cilantro) roots
10 white peppercorns
250ml/8fl oz/1 cup coconut milk
5ml/1 tsp shrimp paste
115g/4oz minced (ground) pork
115g/4oz cherry tomatoes, chopped
15ml/1 tbsp Thai fish sauce
15ml/1 tbsp palm sugar (jaggery) or light muscovado (brown) sugar
30ml/2 tbsp tamarind juice (tamarind paste mixed with warm water)
30ml/2 tbsp coarsely chopped roasted peanuts
2 spring onions (scallions), chopped

1 For the sauce, soak the chillies in warm water for 20 minutes. Drain and crush in a mortar with the salt. Add the shallots, garlic, coriander and peppercorns. Pound to a coarse paste.

2 Boil the coconut milk in a pan until it separates. Add the chilli paste and cook for 2–3 minutes. Stir in the shrimp paste.

3 Add the pork and cook for 5–10 minutes. Stir in the tomatoes, fish sauce, sugar and tamarind juice. Simmer, stirring until thickened, then stir in the peanuts and spring onions. Leave to cool.

4 Preheat the oven to the lowest setting. Wash the rice in several changes of water. Put it in a pan, add the water, cover and bring to the boil. Reduce the heat and simmer for 15 minutes.

5 Fluff up the rice. Spoon on to a greased baking sheet and press down. Leave in the oven to dry out overnight.

6 Break the rice into cake-size pieces. Heat the oil in a wok or deep-fryer. Deep-fry the cakes, in batches, for about 1 minute, until they puff up. Remove and drain well. Serve with the sauce.

Popcorn with Lime and Chilli Energy 484kcal/2021kJ; Protein 8g; Carbohydrate 39g, of which sugars 5g; Fat 34g, of which saturates 4g; Cholesterol 0mg; Calcium 12mg; Fibre 3.4g; Sodium 0.4mg.
Rice Cakes Energy 316kcal/1508kJ; Protein 11.7g; Carbohydrate 42g, of which sugars 8.8g; Fat 16g, of which saturates 2.9g; Cholesterol 19mg; Calcium 38mg; Fibre 0.8g; Sodium 359mg.

Spiced Walnut and Red Chilli

Made primarily of walnuts, this spicy Turkish dip is usually served with toasted flatbread or chunks of crusty bread. It can also be served as an accompaniment to grilled, broiled or barbecued meats. Arabic in origin, this dish is traditionally made with pomegranate juice, but modern recipes often use lemon juice instead.

Serves 4 to 6

175g/6oz/1 cup broken shelled walnuts
5ml/1 tsp cumin seeds, dry-roasted and ground
5–10ml/1–2 tsp Turkish red pepper, or 1–2 fresh red chillies, seeded and finely chopped, or 5ml/1 tsp chilli powder
1–2 garlic cloves (optional)
1 slice of day-old bread, sprinkled with water and left for a few minutes, then squeezed dry
15–30ml/1–2 tbsp tomato purée (paste)
5–10ml/1–2 tsp sugar
30ml/2 tbsp pomegranate syrup or juice of 1 lemon
120ml/4fl oz/½ cup olive or sunflower oil, plus extra for serving
salt and ground black pepper
a few sprigs of fresh flat leaf parsley, to garnish
strips of pitta bread, to serve

1 Using a large mortar and pestle, pound the walnuts with the cumin seeds, red pepper or the fresh red chillies and garlic.

2 Add the soaked bread and pound to a paste, then beat in the tomato purée, sugar and pomegranate syrup or the juice of a lemon, if using.

3 Now slowly drizzle in 120ml/4fl oz/½ cup oil, beating all the time until the paste is thick and light. Season with salt and ground black pepper, and spoon into a bowl.

4 Splash a little olive oil over the top to keep it moist, and garnish with parsley leaves. Serve at room temperature.

Cook's Tip
If you have an electric blender, whizz the ingredients together.

Roast Vegetables with Fresh Herbs and Chilli Sauce

Oven roasting brings out all the flavours of these classic Mediterranean vegetables. Serve them hot with grilled or roast meat or fish.

Serves 4

2–3 courgettes (zucchini)
1 large onion
1 red (bell) pepper
16 cherry tomatoes
2 garlic cloves, chopped
pinch of cumin seeds
5ml/1 tsp fresh thyme or 4–5 torn basil leaves
60ml/4 tbsp olive oil
juice of ½ lemon
5–10ml/1–2 tsp harissa
fresh thyme sprigs, to garnish

1 Preheat the oven to 220°C/425°F/Gas 7. Cut the courgettes into long thin strips. Cut the onion into thin wedges and cut the pepper into fairly large chunks, discarding the seeds and core.

2 Place the vegetables in a roasting pan, add the tomatoes, garlic, cumin seeds and thyme or basil. Sprinkle with oil and toss to coat. Cook in the oven for 25–30 minutes until the vegetables are soft and slightly charred at the edges.

3 Blend the lemon juice and harissa and stir into the vegetables just before serving, garnished with the fresh thyme sprigs.

Variation
Try wedges of red and yellow (bell) peppers in place of one of the courgettes, or add chunks of aubergine (eggplant).

Cook's Tip
Harissa is a spicy paste made from a base of beetroot (beets) and carrots and flavoured with chillies, coriander seeds, caraway, garlic, salt and olive oil. It is a popular ingredient in northern African cooking and is sold in small pots – look out for its distinctive orangey red colour.

Spiced Walnut Energy 339kcal/1399kJ; Protein 4.8g; Carbohydrate 5.1g, of which sugars 2.8g; Fat 33.4g, of which saturates 3.5g; Cholesterol 0mg; Calcium 34mg; Fibre 1.2g; Sodium 32mg.
Roast Vegetables Energy 154kcal/635kJ; Protein 3.7g; Carbohydrate 8.2g, of which sugars 7.6g; Fat 12g, of which saturates 1.8g; Cholesterol 0mg; Calcium 48mg; Fibre 2.8g; Sodium 8mg.

Stir-fried Spinach with Chilli, Currants and Pine Nuts

There are endless versions of traditional spinach and yogurt meze dishes, ranging from plain steamed spinach served with yogurt, to this sweet and tangy Anatolian creation tamed with garlic-flavoured yogurt. Serve while still warm, with flatbread or chunks of a crusty loaf to accompany it.

Serves 3 to 4

350g/12oz fresh spinach leaves, thoroughly washed and drained
about 200g/7oz/scant 1 cup thick and natural (plain) yogurt
2 garlic cloves, crushed
30–45ml/2–3 tbsp olive oil
1 red onion, cut in half lengthways, in half again crossways, and sliced along the grain
5ml/1 tsp sugar
15–30ml/1–2 tbsp currants, soaked in warm water for 5–10 minutes and drained
30ml/2 tbsp pine nuts
5–10ml/1–2 tsp Turkish red pepper, or 1 fresh red chilli, seeded and finely chopped
juice of 1 lemon
salt and ground black pepper
a pinch of paprika, to garnish

1 Steam the spinach for 3–4 minutes, until wilted and soft. Drain off any excess water and chop the spinach.

2 In a medium bowl, beat the yogurt with the garlic. Season the mixture and set aside.

3 Heat the oil in a heavy pan and fry the onion and sugar, stirring, until the onion begins to colour. Add the currants, pine nuts and red pepper or chilli and fry until the nuts begin to darken slightly.

4 Add the spinach, tossing it around the pan until well mixed, then pour in the lemon juice and season with salt and pepper.

5 Serve the spinach straight from the pan with the yogurt spooned on top, or tip into a serving dish and make a well in the middle, then spoon the yogurt into the well, drizzling some of it over the spinach. Serve hot, garnished with a sprinkling of paprika.

Spicy Pumpkin Dip

This spicy dip is great to serve at a buffet or picnic. It can be stored in an airtight container for at least a week in the refrigerator. Serve it with chunks of bread or raw vegetables to dip into it.

Serves 6 to 8

45–60ml/3–4 tbsp olive oil
1 onion, finely chopped
5–8 garlic cloves, roughly chopped
675g/1½lb pumpkin, peeled and diced
5–10ml/1–2 tsp ground cumin
5ml/1 tsp paprika
1.5–2.5ml/¼–½ tsp ground ginger
1.5–2.5ml/¼–½ tsp curry powder
75g/3oz chopped canned tomatoes or diced fresh tomatoes and 15–30ml/1–2 tbsp tomato purée (paste)
½–1 red jalapeño or serrano chilli, chopped, or cayenne pepper, to taste
pinch of sugar, if necessary
juice of ½ lemon, or to taste
salt
30ml/2 tbsp chopped fresh coriander (cilantro) leaves, to garnish

1 Heat the oil in a frying pan, add the onion and half the garlic and fry until softened.

2 Add the pumpkin, then cover the pan and cook for about 10 minutes, or until half-tender.

3 Add the spices to the pan and cook for 1–2 minutes. Stir in the tomatoes, chilli, sugar and salt and cook over a medium-high heat until the liquid has evaporated.

4 When the pumpkin is tender, mash to a paste. Add the remaining garlic and season, then stir in the lemon juice.

5 Serve the dip at room temperature, sprinkled with the chopped fresh coriander.

Variation
Use butternut squash, or any other winter squash, in place of the pumpkin, if you prefer.

Stir-fried Spinach Energy 145kcal/603kJ; Protein 5.8g; Carbohydrate 10.2g, of which sugars 9.8g; Fat 9.3g, of which saturates 1.3g; Cholesterol 1mg; Calcium 252mg; Fibre 2.2g; Sodium 165mg.
Spicy Pumpkin Dip Energy 54kcal/224kJ; Protein 0.9g; Carbohydrate 2.9g; of which sugars 2.3g; Fat 4.4g; of which saturates 0.7g; Cholesterol 1mg; Calcium 37mg; Fibre 1.3g; Sodium 3mg.

Aubergine and Chilli Pepper Dip

This is a lovely Anatolian meze dish of smoked aubergine and peppers with a refreshing lemon and chilli tang. Arabic in origin, it is traditionally served warm with lemon wedges to squeeze over it. Increase the quantities and serve it as a main dish with yogurt and bread, or serve it as an accompaniment to a barbecue spread.

Serves 4

2 red (bell) peppers
1 large aubergine (eggplant)
30–45ml/2–3 tbsp olive oil
1 red onion, cut in half lengthways and finely sliced along the grain
1 fresh red chilli, seeded and finely sliced
2 garlic cloves, chopped
5–10ml/1–2 tsp sugar
juice of 1 lemon
dash of white wine vinegar
a big handful of fresh flat leaf parsley, roughly chopped
salt and ground black pepper
lemon wedges and toasted pitta bread, to serve

1 Place the peppers under a conventional grill (broiler), or on a rack over the hot coals of a barbecue. Turn them from time to time until the skin is charred on all sides and the flesh feels soft. Place in a plastic bag and leave for a few minutes.

2 One at a time, hold the charred vegetables under cold running water and peel off the skins of the charred vegetables. Place them on a chopping board and remove the stalks. Halve the peppers lengthways and scoop out the seeds, then chop the flesh to a pulp. Chop the aubergine flesh to a pulp too.

3 Pour the oil into a wide, heavy pan and toss in the onion, chilli, garlic and sugar. Cook over a medium heat for 2–3 minutes, until they begin to colour.

4 Add the pulped peppers and aubergine, stir in the lemon juice and vinegar and season with salt and pepper. Toss in the parsley and serve with lemon wedges and toasted pitta bread.

Herby Tomato and Chilli Dip

This Turkish meze dish is a mixture of chopped fresh vegetables. Along with cubes of honey-sweet melon and feta, or plump, juicy olives spiked with red pepper and oregano, this is meze at its simplest and best. Popular in kebab houses throughout Turkey, it makes a tasty snack or appetizer, and tastes great served with chunks of warm, crusty bread or toasted pitta to dip into the meze.

Serves 4

2 large tomatoes, skinned, seeded and finely chopped
2 Turkish green peppers or 1 green (bell) pepper, seeded and finely chopped
1 onion, finely chopped
1 green chilli, seeded and finely chopped
1 small bunch of fresh flat leaf parsley, finely chopped
a few fresh mint leaves, finely chopped
15–30ml/1–2 tbsp olive oil
salt and ground black pepper

1 Put all the finely chopped ingredients in a large bowl and mix well together until thoroughly combined.

2 Bind the mixture with the olive oil and season generously with salt and pepper.

3 Serve at room temperature, in individual bowls or a large dish.

Cook's Tip
To skin tomatoes, place in a bowl, cover with boiling water and leave for about 1 minute. The skin should peel off easily.

Variation
When you bind the chopped vegetables with the olive oil, add 15–30ml/1–2 tbsp tomato purée (paste) with a little extra chilli and 5–10ml/1–2 tsp sugar. The mixture will become a tangy paste to spread on fresh, crusty bread or toasted pitta, and it can also be used as a sauce for grilled (broiled) or barbecued meats.

Smoked Aubergine Dip Energy 102kcal/425kJ; Protein 1.8g; Carbohydrate 10.5g, of which sugars 9.8g; Fat 6.2g, of which saturates 1g; Cholesterol 0mg; Calcium 19mg; Fibre 3.1g; Sodium 6mg.
Herby Tomato and Chili Dip Energy 101kcal/420kJ; Protein 2.3g; Carbohydrate 9.3g, of which sugars 8g; Fat 6.3g, of which saturates 0.9g; Cholesterol 0mg; Calcium 66mg; Fibre 2.7g; Sodium 15mg.

Deep-fried Eggs with Red Chilli

Another name for this Chinese dish is mother-in-law eggs, which comes from a story about a prospective bridegroom who very much wanted to impress his future mother-in-law and devised a new recipe based on the only dish he knew how to make – boiled eggs.

Serves 4 to 6

30ml/2 tbsp vegetable oil
6 shallots, thinly sliced
6 garlic cloves, thinly sliced
6 fresh red chillies, sliced
oil, for deep-frying
6 hard-boiled eggs, shelled
salad leaves, to serve
sprigs of fresh coriander (cilantro), to garnish

For the sauce

75g/3oz/6 tbsp palm sugar (jaggery) or light muscovado (brown) sugar
75ml/5 tbsp Thai fish sauce
90ml/6 tbsp tamarind juice

1 Make the sauce. Put the sugar, fish sauce and tamarind juice in a pan. Bring to the boil, stirring until the sugar dissolves, lower the heat and simmer for 5 minutes. Taste and add more sugar, fish sauce or tamarind juice, if needed. Transfer to a bowl.

2 Heat the vegetable oil in a frying pan and cook the shallots, garlic and chillies for 5 minutes. Transfer to a bowl and set aside.

3 Heat the oil in a deep-fryer or wok to 190°C/375°F or until a cube of bread, added to the oil, browns in about 45 seconds. Deep-fry the eggs in the hot oil for about 3–5 minutes, or until they turn a golden brown colour. Remove from the oil and drain well on kitchen paper.

4 Cut the eggs into quarters and arrange them on a bed of salad leaves. Drizzle with the prepared sauce and sprinkle over the shallot mixture. Garnish with the coriander sprigs and serve immediately.

Cook's Tip
The level of heat varies, depending on which type of chillies are used and whether or not you include the seeds.

Hot Thai Omelette Rolls

These tasty egg rolls are made from wedges of a rolled Thai-flavoured omelette. They are very popular and are frequently served as finger food, often bought from the many street stalls in Thai cities and eaten on the way to work.

Serves 2

3 eggs, beaten
15ml/1 tbsp soy sauce
1 bunch garlic chives, thinly sliced
1–2 small fresh red or green chillies, seeded and finely chopped
small bunch fresh coriander (cilantro), chopped
pinch of sugar
salt and ground black pepper
15ml/1 tbsp groundnut (peanut) oil

For the dipping sauce

60ml/4 tbsp light soy sauce
fresh lime juice, to taste

1 Make the dipping sauce. Pour the soy sauce into a bowl. Add a generous squeeze of lime juice. Taste and add more lime juice if needed.

2 For the rolls, mix together the beaten eggs, soy sauce, chives, chillies and coriander until well combined. Add the sugar and season to taste. Heat the oil in a large frying pan, pour in the egg mixture and swirl the pan until the mixture evenly coats the base of the pan.

3 Cook for 1–2 minutes, until the omelette is just firm and the underside is golden. Slide it out on to a plate and roll up as though it were a pancake. Leave to cool completely.

4 When the omelette is cool, slice it diagonally in 1cm/½in pieces. Arrange the slices on a serving platter and serve with the bowl of dipping sauce.

Cook's Tip
Wear gloves while preparing chillies or cut them up with a knife and fork if you find that they irritate your skin. Wash your hands afterwards in warm, soapy water.

Deep-fried Eggs Energy 215kcal/894kJ; Protein 14.2g; Carbohydrate 2.4g, of which sugars 2.2g; Fat 16.9g, of which saturates 4.2g; Cholesterol 381mg; Calcium 112mg; Fibre 0.8g; Sodium 1223mg.
Thai Omelette Rolls Energy 189kcal/780kJ; Protein 11.5g; Carbohydrate 1g, of which sugars 0.9g; Fat 15.3g, of which saturates 3.9g; Cholesterol 331mg; Calcium 76mg; Fibre 0.7g; Sodium 660mg.

Italian Bread with Spicy Aromatic Tomatoes

This is a great way to keep hunger pangs at bay while you wait for the main course to come off the barbecue. As soon as the coals are hot enough, simply grill the sliced bread, heap on the sauce and drizzle over plenty of good quality extra virgin olive oil. To accompany the breads, put out little bowls of pine nuts, lightly toasted in a pan over the barbecue.

Serves 6

2 sfilatino (Italian bread sticks), sliced lengthways into 3 pieces
1 garlic clove, cut in half
leaves from 4 fresh oregano sprigs
18 kalamata olives, pitted and sliced
extra virgin olive oil, for drizzling
ground black pepper

For the aromatic tomatoes
800g/1¾lb ripe plum tomatoes
30ml/2 tbsp extra virgin olive oil
2 garlic cloves, crushed to a paste with a pinch of salt
1 small piece of dried chilli, seeds removed, finely chopped

1 Prepare the barbecue. Plunge the tomatoes into boiling water for 30 seconds, then refresh in cold water. Peel away the skins, remove the seeds and core and roughly chop the flesh. Mix the oil and crushed garlic in a large frying pan. Place on the stove over a high heat. When the garlic sizzles, add the tomatoes and the chilli. Cook for 2 minutes. The aim is to evaporate the liquid not to pulp the tomatoes, which should keep their shape.

2 Once the flames have died down, position a lightly oiled grill rack over the hot coals. When the coals are medium-hot, or with a moderate coating of ash, toast the bread on both sides. Generously rub each slice with the cut side of a piece of garlic.

3 Roughly chop all but a few of the oregano leaves and mix them into the tomato sauce. Pile the mixture on to the toasted sfilatino. Scatter over the whole oregano leaves and the olive slices. Sprinkle with plenty of pepper, drizzle with lots of extra virgin olive oil and serve immediately.

Cheese and Chilli Tortillas

These cheese-filled tortillas are the Mexican equivalent of toasted sandwiches. Serve them as soon as they are cooked, or they will become chewy. If you are making them for a crowd, fill and fold the tortillas ahead of time, but only cook them to order.

Serves 4

200g/7oz mozzarella, Monterey Jack or mild Cheddar cheese
1 fresh fresno chilli (optional)
8 wheat flour tortillas, about 15cm/6in across
Onion and Red Chilli Relish, to serve

1 If using mozzarella cheese, it must be drained thoroughly and then patted dry and sliced into thin strips. Monterey Jack and Cheddar should both be coarsely grated, as finely grated cheese will melt and ooze away when cooking. Set the cheese aside in a bowl.

2 If using the chilli, spear it on a long-handled metal skewer and roast it over the flame of a gas burner until the skin blisters and darkens. Do not let the flesh burn. Alternatively, dry fry it in a griddle pan until the skin is scorched. Place the roasted chilli in a strong plastic bag and tie the top to keep the steam in. Set aside for 20 minutes.

3 Remove the chilli from the bag and peel off the skin. Cut off the stalk, then slit the chilli and scrape out the seeds. Cut the flesh into eight thin strips.

4 Warm a large frying pan or griddle. Place one tortilla on the pan or griddle at a time, sprinkle about an eighth of the cheese on to one half and add a strip of chilli, if using. Fold the tortilla over the cheese and press the edges together gently to seal. Cook the filled tortilla for about 1 minute until the cheese is beginning to melt, then carefully turn over and cook the other side for 1 minute.

5 Remove the filled tortilla from the pan or griddle, cut it into three triangles or four strips and serve immediately, with the onion relish.

Italian Bread Energy 473kcal/2000kJ; Protein 13.7g; Carbohydrate 80.3g, of which sugars 8g; Fat 13.1g, of which saturates 2.1g; Cholesterol 0mg; Calcium 177mg; Fibre 5.1g; Sodium 1021mg.
Cheese and Chilli Tortillas Energy 418kcal/1764kJ; Protein 17g; Carbohydrate 66g, of which sugars 7g; Fat 11g, of which saturates 7g; Cholesterol 29mg; Calcium 303mg; Fibre 2.6g; Sodium 0.5mg.

Spicy Omelette

Eggs are packed with nutritional value and make wholesome and delicious dishes. This omelette, cooked with potato, onion and a touch of spices, can be put together quickly for a quick snack.

Serves 4 to 6

30ml/2 tbsp vegetable oil
1 medium onion, finely chopped
2.5ml/½ tsp cumin powder
1 clove garlic, finely crushed
1 or 2 green chillies, finely chopped
a few sprigs fresh coriander (cilantro), chopped
1 firm tomato, chopped
1 small potato, cubed and boiled
25g/1oz cooked peas
25g/1oz cooked corn
salt and pepper, to taste
2 eggs, beaten
25g/1oz grated cheese

1 Heat the oil in a pan and fry the onion for 5 minutes until softened and beginning to colour.

2 Add the cumin powder, crushed garlic and chopped chillies and cook for 1–2 minutes, stirring until well combined.

3 Add the coriander, tomato, potato cubes, peas and corn to the pan, stir until thoroughly mixed and cook until hot but the potato and tomato are still firm. Season to taste.

4 Increase the heat and pour in the beaten eggs. Shake the pan until the eggs are evenly spread around the pan and well combined with the other ingredients.

5 Reduce the heat, cover the pan and cook until the bottom of the omelette is a golden brown colour. Turn the omelette and sprinkle with the grated cheese. Place under a hot grill (broiler) and cook until the egg sets and the cheese has melted.

Variation
Other vegetables will work well here: try using a thinly sliced red (bell) pepper in place of the potato, or substitute a few chopped mushrooms instead of peas or corn.

Steamed Tofu Dumplings with Chilli and Chives

The slight spiciness and delicate texture of Korean chives make them a wonderful ingredient to add to these stuffed paper-thin steamed dumplings, called *mandu* in Korea. Here the succulent filling of tofu is combined with beef and rice wine.

Serves 4

30 dumpling skins
1 egg, beaten

For the filling
3 spring onions (scallions), finely chopped
3 garlic cloves, crushed
5ml/1 tsp finely grated fresh root ginger
5ml/1 tsp mirin or rice wine
90g/3½oz/scant ½ cup minced (ground) beef
90g/3½oz firm tofu
90g/3½oz Korean chives, finely chopped
½ onion, finely chopped
30ml/2 tbsp soy sauce
30ml/2 tbsp sesame oil
15ml/1 tbsp sugar
15ml/1 tbsp salt
10ml/2 tsp ground black pepper

For the dipping sauce
60ml/4 tbsp dark soy sauce
30ml/2 tbsp rice vinegar
5ml/1 tsp Korean chilli powder

1 To make the dipping sauce, mix the soy sauce, rice vinegar and chilli powder in a small serving bowl.

2 For the filling, put the spring onions, garlic, ginger, mirin or rice wine and beef into a bowl and mix well. Marinate for 15 minutes.

3 Meanwhile, drain off any excess liquid from the tofu, then crumble into a bowl. Add the chives to the seasoned beef, with the tofu and remaining filling ingredients. Mix together thoroughly.

4 Take a dumpling skin and brush with a little beaten egg. Place a spoonful of the stuffing in the middle and fold into a half-moon shape, crimping the edges firmly to seal. Repeat with the other dumpling skins. Place them in a steamer over a pan of boiling water and cook for 6 minutes. Or, you can just cook the dumplings in boiling water for about 3 minutes. Arrange on a serving dish and serve with the soy dipping sauce.

Spicy Omelette Energy 93kcal/388kJ; Protein 4g; Carbohydrate 3.7g, of which sugars 1.2g; Fat 7.1g, of which saturates 1.9g; Cholesterol 67mg; Calcium 46mg; Fibre 0.6g; Sodium 104mg.
Steamed Dumplings Energy 235kcal/982kJ; Protein 9.9g; Carbohydrate 26.1g, of which sugars 6.5g; Fat 10.8g, of which saturates 2.5g; Cholesterol 14mg; Calcium 208mg; Fibre 2.2g; Sodium 1054mg.

Chilli Potatoes

There are several variations on this chilli and potato dish, but the most important thing is the spicing, which is made even more piquant by adding a little vinegar. This recipe uses dried chillies, but fresh ones can be substituted.

Serves 4

675g/1½lb small new potatoes
75ml/5 tbsp olive oil
2 garlic cloves, sliced
3 dried chillies, seeded and chopped
2.5ml/½ tsp ground cumin
10ml/2 tsp paprika
30ml/2 tbsp red or white wine vinegar
1 red or green (bell) pepper, seeded and sliced
coarse sea salt, for sprinkling (optional)

1 Scrub the potatoes and put them into a pan of salted water. Bring to the boil and cook for 10 minutes, or until almost tender. Drain and leave to cool slightly. Peel, if you like, then cut into chunks.

2 Heat the olive oil in a large frying pan and fry the potatoes over a medium-high heat, turning them frequently, until they have turned a golden brown colour.

3 Meanwhile, crush together the garlic, chillies and cumin to a paste using a mortar and pestle.

4 Mix the paste with the paprika and red or white wine vinegar, then add to the potatoes with the sliced pepper and cook, stirring, for about 2 minutes. Sprinkle with sea salt, if using, and serve the potatoes hot as a tapas dish or cold as a side dish with a main course.

Cook's Tip
This potato dish is an essential part of a tapas meal in Spain, where the dish is known as patatas bravas, *literally meaning 'fierce potatoes' owing to the heat. The classic version is made as above with a spicy tomato and chilli sauce poured over before serving.*

Fresh Corn Fritters with Chilli Sauce

Sometimes it is the simplest dishes that taste the best. These fritters, packed with crunchy corn, are very easy to prepare and will prove to be very popular.

Makes 12

3 corn cobs, total weight about 250g/9oz
1 garlic clove, crushed
small bunch fresh coriander (cilantro), chopped
1 small fresh red or green chilli, seeded and finely chopped
1 spring onion (scallion), finely chopped
15ml/1 tbsp soy sauce
75g/3oz/¾ cup rice flour or plain (all-purpose) flour
2 eggs, lightly beaten
60ml/4 tbsp water
oil, for shallow frying
salt and ground black pepper
sweet chilli sauce, to serve

1 Using a sharp knife, slice the kernels from the cobs and place them in a large bowl.

2 Add the garlic, chopped coriander, red or green chilli, spring onion, soy sauce, flour, beaten eggs and water to the pan and mix until well combined.

3 Season with salt and pepper to taste and mix again. The mixture should be just firm enough to hold its shape, but not too stiff.

4 Heat the oil in a large frying pan. Add spoonfuls of the corn mixture, gently spreading each one out with the back of the spoon to make a roundish fritter. Cook for 1–2 minutes on each side.

5 Drain the fritters on kitchen paper and keep them hot while frying more fritters in the same way. Serve immediately with sweet chilli sauce for dipping.

Cook's Tip
Sweet chilli sauce is a common condiment in many South-east Asian cuisines. It is ideal as a dipping sauce for these fritters.

Chilli Potatoes Energy 255kcal/1070kJ Protein 4g; Carbohydrate 29g; of which sugars 3g; Fat 15g; of which saturates 2g; Cholesterol 0mg; Calcium 20mg; Fibre 2.4g; Sodium 0.1mg.
Fresh Corn Fritters Energy 76kcal/315kJ; Protein 2.1g; Carbohydrate 7.6g; of which sugars 0.5g; Fat 4.1g; of which saturates 0.6g; Cholesterol 32mg; Calcium 12mg; Fibre 0.5g; Sodium 102mg.

Spiced Carrot and Apricot Rolls

These sweet, herby carrot rolls are a great treat in Turkey, but rarely found elsewhere. Served with a dollop of yogurt flavoured with mint and garlic, they make a delicious light lunch or supper with a green salad and warm crusty bread.

Serves 4

8–10 carrots, cut into thick slices
2–3 slices of day-old bread, ground into crumbs
4 spring onions (scallions), finely sliced
150g/5oz/generous ½ cup ready-to-eat dried apricots, finely chopped
45ml/3 tbsp pine nuts
1 egg
5ml/1 tsp Turkish red pepper, or 1 fresh red chilli, seeded and finely chopped
1 bunch of fresh dill, chopped
1 bunch of fresh basil, finely shredded
salt and ground black pepper
plain (all-purpose) flour, for coating
sunflower oil, for shallow frying
lemon wedges, to serve

For the mint yogurt

about 225g/8oz/1 cup thick and creamy natural (plain) yogurt
juice of ½ lemon
1–2 garlic cloves, crushed
1 bunch of fresh mint, finely chopped

1 Steam the carrot slices for about 25 minutes, or until very soft. While the carrots are steaming, make the mint yogurt. Beat the yogurt in a bowl with the lemon juice and garlic, season and stir in the mint. Set aside, or chill in the refrigerator.

2 Mash the carrots to a paste. Add the breadcrumbs, spring onions, apricots and pine nuts and mix well. Beat in the egg and stir in the red pepper or chilli and herbs. Season.

3 Tip a small heap of flour on to a flat surface. Take a plum-sized portion of the carrot mixture in your fingers and mould it into an oblong roll. Coat the carrot roll in the flour and transfer it to a large plate. Repeat with rest of the mixture, to make 12 to16 rolls.

4 Heat the oil in a frying pan. Fry the carrot rolls for about 8–10 minutes, turning them occasionally, until golden brown. Drain and serve hot, with lemon wedges and the mint yogurt.

Courgette, Feta and Chilli Fritters

Ideal for lunch, supper, a savoury snack or appetizer, these tasty patties are incredibly versatile. You can even make miniature versions and serve them as tasty nibbles with drinks. If you like a little more fire on your tongue, add a little extra Turkish red pepper or chillies.

Serves 4 to 6

3 firm courgettes (zucchini)
30–45ml/2–3 tbsp olive oil
1 large onion, halved lengthways, in half again crossways, and sliced along the grain
4 garlic cloves, chopped
45ml/3 tbsp plain (all-purpose) flour
3 eggs, beaten
225g/8oz feta cheese, crumbled
1 bunch each of fresh flat leaf parsley, mint and dill, chopped
5ml/1 tsp Turkish red pepper, or 1 fresh red chilli, seeded and chopped
sunflower oil, for shallow frying
salt and ground black pepper
mint leaves, to garnish

1 Wash the courgettes and trim off the ends. Hold them at an angle and grate them, then put them in a colander or sieve (strainer) and sprinkle with a little salt. Leave them to weep for about 5 minutes.

2 Squeeze the grated courgettes in your hand to extract the juices. Heat the olive oil in a heavy frying pan, stir in the courgettes, onion and garlic and fry until they begin to take on colour. Remove from the heat and leave to cool.

3 Tip the flour into a bowl and gradually beat in the eggs to form a smooth batter. Beat in the cooled courgette mixture. Add the feta, herbs and red pepper or chilli, and season with a little pepper. Add salt if you like, but usually the feta is quite salty. Mix well.

4 Heat enough sunflower oil for shallow frying in a heavy, non-stick pan. Drop four spoonfuls of the mixture into the hot oil, leaving space between each one, then fry over a medium heat for 6–8 minutes, or until firm to the touch and golden brown on both sides. Remove from the pan with a slotted spoon and drain on kitchen paper while you fry the remainder. Serve while still warm, garnished with mint leaves.

Spiced Carrot Rolls Energy 401kcal/1673kJ; Protein 8.7g; Carbohydrate 46g, of which sugars 29.1g; Fat 21.5g, of which saturates 2.5g; Cholesterol 48mg; Calcium 144mg; Fibre 8.5g; Sodium 145mg.
Courgette Fritters Energy 327kcal/1354kJ; Protein 12.3g; Carbohydrate 12.4g, of which sugars 5.4g; Fat 25.7g, of which saturates 7.9g; Cholesterol 121mg; Calcium 214mg; Fibre 2.3g; Sodium 581mg.

Thai Green Curry Puffs

Shrimp paste and green curry sauce, used judiciously, give these puffs their distinctive, spicy, savoury flavour, and the addition of chilli steps up the heat.

Makes 24

24 small wonton wrappers, about 8cm/3¼in square, thawed if frozen
15ml/1 tbsp cornflour (cornstarch), mixed to a paste with 30ml/2 tbsp water
oil, for deep-frying

For the filling

1 small potato, about 115g/4oz, boiled and mashed
25g/1oz/3 tbsp cooked petits pois (baby peas)
25g/1oz/3 tbsp cooked corn
few sprigs fresh coriander (cilantro), chopped
1 small fresh red chilli, seeded and finely chopped
½ lemon grass stalk, finely chopped
15ml/1 tbsp soy sauce
5ml/1 tsp shrimp paste or fish sauce
5ml/1 tsp Thai green curry paste

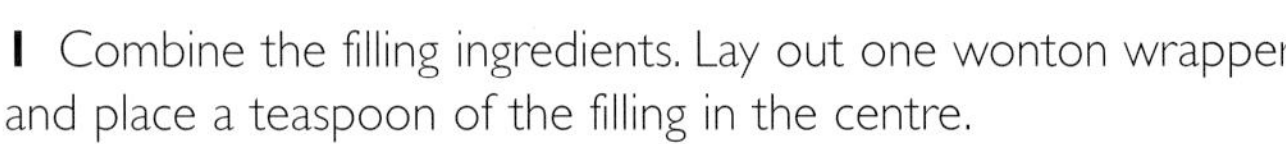

1 Combine the filling ingredients. Lay out one wonton wrapper and place a teaspoon of the filling in the centre.

2 Brush a little of the cornflour paste along two sides of the square. Fold the other two sides over to meet them, then press together to make a triangular pastry and seal in the filling. Make more pastries in the same way.

3 Heat the oil in a deep-fryer or wok to 190°C/375°F, or until a cube of bread, added to the oil, browns in about 45 seconds. Add the pastries to the oil, a few at a time, and fry them for about 5 minutes, until golden brown.

4 Remove the pastries from the fryer or wok and drain on kitchen paper. If you intend serving the puffs hot, place them in a low oven while cooking successive batches. The puffs also taste good cold.

Cook's Tip
Wonton wrappers dry out quickly, so keep them covered, using clear film (plastic wrap), until you are ready to use them.

Bean and Red Chilli Fritters

These fritters are almost always made from black-eyed beans. For a quicker version, after soaking the beans, drain them thoroughly and liquidize in a blender or processor without removing the skins.

Serves 4

250g/8oz/1¼ cups dried black-eyed beans (peas)
1 onion, chopped
1 red chilli, halved, with seeds removed (optional)
150ml/¼ pint/⅔ cup water
oil, for deep frying

1 Soak the black-eyed beans in plenty of cold water for 6–8 hours or overnight.

2 Drain the beans and then, with a brisk action, rub between the palms of your hands to remove the skins.

3 Return the beans to the bowl, top up with water so that the beans are covered and any loosened skins will float to the surface. Remove and discard the skins and soak the beans again for a further 2 hours.

4 Place the beans in a blender or food processor with the onion, chilli, if using, and a little water. Blend until the mixture forms a thick paste.

5 Pour the mixture into a large bowl and whisk for a few minutes to thoroughly combine.

6 Heat the oil for deep-frying in a large heavy pan and fry spoonfuls of the mixture for about 4 minutes until golden brown. Remove and drain on kitchen paper, then serve immediately while still hot.

Cook's Tip
Don't be tempted to use canned black-eyed beans. These are pre-soaked and cooked and will be too soft for use in this recipe as the beans here are not cooked before frying the fritters.

Thai Green Curry Puffs Energy 75kcal/314kj; Protein 1.1g; Carbohydrate 8.4g, of which sugars 0.6g; Fat 4.3g, of which saturates 0.6g; Cholesterol 0mg; Calcium 12mg; Fibre 0.4g; Sodium 70mg.
Bean Fritters Energy 238kcal/1004kj; Protein 13.7g; Carbohydrate 33.4g, of which sugars 3.7g; Fat 6.5g, of which saturates 0.9g; Cholesterol 0mg; Calcium 55mg; Fibre 5.2g; Sodium 376mg.

Hot Spring Rolls

These Thai spring rolls are filled with a tasty garlic, pork and noodle mixture.

Makes 24

24 X 15cm/6in square spring roll wrappers, thawed if frozen
30ml/2 tbsp plain (all-purpose) flour
vegetable oil, for deep-frying
sweet chilli dipping sauce, to serve

For the filling

6 Chinese dried mushrooms, soaked for 30 minutes in warm water
50g/2oz cellophane noodles
30ml/2 tbsp vegetable oil
2 garlic cloves, chopped
2 fresh red chillies, seeded and chopped
225g/8oz minced (ground) pork
50g/2oz peeled cooked prawns (shrimp), thawed if frozen
30ml/2 tbsp Thai fish sauce
5ml/1 tsp sugar
1 carrot, grated
50g/2oz piece of canned bamboo shoot, drained and chopped
50g/2oz/⅔ cup beansprouts
2 spring onions (scallions), finely chopped
15ml/1 tbsp chopped fresh coriander (cilantro)
ground black pepper

1 Drain the mushrooms. Cut off and discard the stems. Chop the caps finely. Cover the noodles with boiling water and soak for 10 minutes. Drain and snip them into 5cm/2in lengths. Heat the oil in a wok, add the garlic and chillies and stir-fry for 30 seconds. Transfer to a plate.

2 Stir-fry the pork until browned. Add the mushrooms, noodles and prawns. Stir in the fish sauce and sugar. Season with pepper. Pour into a bowl. Stir in the carrot, bamboo, beansprouts, spring onions and coriander. Mix in the reserved chilli mixture.

3 Stir a little water into the flour in a small bowl to make a paste. Place a spoonful of the filling in the centre of a wrapper. Turn the bottom edge over to cover the filling, then fold in the sides. Roll up almost to the top, then brush the top edge with the flour paste and seal. Fill the remaining wrappers.

4 Heat the oil in a deep-fryer or wok to 190°C/375°F, or until a cube of bread browns in about 45 seconds. Fry the spring rolls, in batches, until crisp and golden. Drain on kitchen paper and serve hot with sweet chilli sauce.

Spicy Split Pea or Lentil Fritters

These delicious spicy fritters, called *piaju*, come from India.

Serves 4 to 6

250g/9oz/generous 1 cup yellow split peas or red lentils, soaked overnight
3–5 garlic cloves, chopped
30ml/2 tbsp roughly chopped fresh root ginger
120ml/4fl oz/½ cup chopped fresh coriander (cilantro) leaves
2.5–5ml/½–1 tsp ground cumin
1.5–2.5ml/¼–½ tsp ground turmeric
large pinch of cayenne pepper or ½–1 fresh green chilli, chopped
120ml/4fl oz/½ cup gram flour
5ml/1 tsp baking powder
30ml/2 tbsp couscous
2 large or 3 small onions, chopped
vegetable oil, for frying
salt and ground black pepper
lemon and fresh chilli, to serve

1 Drain the split peas or lentils, reserving a little of the soaking water. Put the chopped garlic and ginger in a food processor or blender and process until finely minced (ground). Add the drained peas or lentils, 15–30ml/1–2 tbsp of the reserved soaking water and the coriander, and process to form a paste.

2 Add the cumin, turmeric, cayenne or chilli, 2.5ml/½ tsp salt, 2.5ml/½ tsp pepper, the gram flour, baking powder and couscous to the mixture and combine. The mixture should form a thick batter. If it seems too thick, add a spoonful of the soaking water. Add a little more flour or couscous if it is too watery. Mix in the onions.

3 Heat the oil in a wide, deep frying pan, to a depth of about 5cm/2in, until it is hot enough to brown a cube of bread in 30 seconds. Using two spoons, form the mixture into two-bitesize balls and slip each one gently into the hot oil. Cook until golden brown on the underside, then turn and cook the second side until golden brown.

4 Remove the fritters from the hot oil with a slotted spoon and drain well on kitchen paper. Transfer the fritters to a baking sheet and keep them warm in the oven until all the mixture is cooked. Serve the fritters hot or at room temperature with lemon wedges and chopped fresh chilli.

Hot Spring Rolls Energy 135kcal/562kj; Protein 3.1g; Carbohydrate 7.8g, of which sugars 0.5g; Fat 10.3g, of which saturates 1.4g; Cholesterol 10mg; Calcium 15mg; Fibre 0.4g; Sodium 41g.
Split Pea Fritters Energy 360kcal/1511kj; Protein 14.1g; Carbohydrate 51.3g, of which sugars 8.3g; Fat 12.3g, of which saturates 1.4g; Cholesterol 0mg; Calcium 119mg; Fibre 5.3g; Sodium 26g.

Onion Bhajias

Bhajias are a classic Indian snack. Gram flour is used to make the batter, which can also be used with a variety of other vegetables, meat or seafood to make pakoras.

Makes 20 to 25

225g/8oz/2 cups gram flour, or channa atta
2.5ml/½ tsp chilli powder
5ml/1 tsp turmeric powder
5ml/1 tsp baking powder
1.5ml/¼ tsp Asafoetida
salt, to taste
½ tsp each nigella, fennel, cumin and onion seeds, coarsely crushed
2 large onions, finely sliced
2 green chillies, finely chopped
50g/2oz coriander (cilantro) leaves, chopped
cold water, to mix
vegetable oil, for deep-frying

1 In a bowl, mix together the flour, chilli, turmeric, baking powder, Asafoetida and salt to taste. Pass the mixture through a sieve (strainer) into a large mixing bowl.

2 Add the coarsely crushed seeds, onion, green chillies and coriander leaves and toss together well. Very gradually mix in enough cold water until a thick batter forms and surrounds all the ingredients.

3 Heat enough oil in a wok for deep-frying. Drop spoonfuls of the mixture into the hot oil and fry until they are golden brown. Leave enough space to turn the fritters. Drain well and serve hot.

Cook's Tips

- *Gram flour, also known as besan, is a pale-yellow flour made from ground chickpeas. More aromatic and with less starch content and higher protein than wheat flour, it is used widely in Indian cookery for doughs, batters and for thickening sauces. Look for it in large supermarkets or Indian and Asian food stores.*
- *Asafoetida is a pungent spice obtained from the resin of a fennel-like plant. It has a very strong odour of garlic and onion and should only be used sparingly.*

Fiery Potato Cakes

Only a few communities in India make these unusual appetizers. They can also be served as a main meal accompanied with a salad.

Makes 8 to 10

15ml/1 tbsp vegetable oil
1 large onion, finely chopped
2 garlic cloves, finely crushed
5cm/2in piece fresh root ginger, finely crushed
5ml/1 tsp ground coriander
5ml/1 tsp ground cumin
2 green chillies, finely chopped
30ml/2 tbsp each chopped fresh coriander (cilantro) and mint
225g/8oz lean minced (ground) beef or lamb
50g/2oz frozen peas, thawed
juice of 1 lemon
900g/2lb potatoes, boiled and mashed
2 eggs, beaten
breadcrumbs, for coating
vegetable oil, for shallow-frying
salt
lemon wedges, to serve

1 Heat the vegetable oil in a wok or frying pan and fry the onion for 5 minutes until it begins to turn translucent. Add the garlic, ginger, coriander, cumin, chillies and fresh herbs, and cook, stirring frequently, for another 5 minutes.

2 Add the minced meat and the peas and fry until the meat is cooked, then season with salt and lemon juice to taste. The mixture should be very dry.

3 Divide the mashed potato into about eight or ten portions. Take one portion and flatten it into a pancake shape in the palm of your hand.

4 Place a spoonful of the meat mixture into the centre of the potato and gather the sides together to enclose the meat. Flatten it slightly to make a round shape. Repeat until the remaining potato portions are filled.

5 Place the beaten egg and breadcrumbs on separate small plates. Dip each potato cake first in the egg and then in the breadcrumbs, ensuring they are evenly coated. Chill for 1 hour.

6 Heat the oil in a frying pan and shallow-fry the cakes until brown and crisp all over. Serve hot, with lemon wedges.

Onion Bhajias Energy 72kcal/301kJ; Protein 1.2g; Carbohydrate 8.8g, of which sugars 1.3g; Fat 3.8g, of which saturates 0.4g; Cholesterol 0mg; Calcium 23mg; Fibre 0.7g; Sodium 2mg.
Fiery Potato Cakes Energy 207kcal/864kJ; Protein 8.1g; Carbohydrate 18g, of which sugars 3g; Fat 12g, of which saturates 2.8g; Cholesterol 52mg; Calcium 24mg; Fibre 1.6g; Sodium 43mg.

Fried Yam Balls

Yam balls are a popular snack in many African countries. They are traditionally made quite plain, but can be flavoured with chopped vegetables and herbs, as in this recipe, or with cooked meat or fish, or spices.

Makes about 24 balls

450g/1lb white yam, diced
30ml/2 tbsp finely chopped onion
45ml/3 tbsp chopped tomatoes
2.5ml/½ tsp chopped fresh thyme
1 green chilli, seeded and finely chopped
15ml/1 tbsp finely chopped spring onion (scallion)
1 garlic clove, crushed
1 egg, beaten
salt and ground black pepper
vegetable oil, for shallow frying
seasoned flour, for dusting

1 Boil the yam in salted water for about 30 minutes until tender. Drain and mash the yam. Add the onion, tomatoes, thyme, chilli, spring onion and garlic, then stir in the egg and seasoning and mix well.

2 Using a dessertspoon, scoop a little of the mixture at a time and, using your fingers, mould into small balls. Heat a little oil in a large frying pan, roll the yam balls in the seasoned flour and then fry for a few minutes until golden brown. Drain the yam balls on kitchen paper and keep them warm while cooking the rest of the mixture. Serve the balls immediately.

Cook's Tip

Yam is a tropical-vine tuber, similar in many ways to a sweet potato – although they are in fact from different plant species. You can use sweet potatoes instead if yams are hard to find.

Variation

Try adding fresh chopped herbs to the yam mixture; parsley and chives make a good combination. Mix in 30ml/2 tbsp with the egg and seasoning.

Spiced Samosas

Traditional samosa pastry requires a lot of time and hard work but spring roll pastry makes an excellent substitute and is readily available from supermarkets and Asian stores. One packet will generally make about 30 samosas. They can be frozen either before or after frying.

Makes 30

1 packet spring roll pastry, thawed and wrapped in a damp dish towel
vegetable oil, for deep-frying

For the filling

3 large potatoes, boiled and coarsely mashed
85g/3oz/¾ cup frozen peas, boiled and drained
50g/2oz/⅓ cup canned corn, drained
5ml/1 tsp ground coriander
5ml/1 tsp ground cumin
5ml/1 tsp amchur (dry mango powder)
1 small onion (red if available), finely chopped
2 green chillies, seeded and finely chopped
30ml/2 tbsp each chopped coriander (cilantro) and mint leaves
juice of 1 lemon
salt

1 Toss all the ingredients together for the samosa filling in a large mixing bowl. Mix together with a wooden spoon or your hands until thoroughly blended. Adjust the seasoning with salt and lemon juice, to taste.

2 To make the samosas, use one strip of the spring roll pastry at a time, keeping the rest under the dish towel to stop them from drying out. Place 1 tbsp of the filling mixture at one end of the strip of pastry and diagonally fold it to form a triangle.

3 Put the vegetable oil in a wide, deep frying pan or wok, so you have enough for deep-frying. Heat the oil until it is hot enough to brown a cube of bread in 30 seconds.

4 Fry the samosas in small batches of about five until they are golden brown all over. Serve hot with a fruity chutney or a sweet chilli sauce.

Fried Yam Balls Energy 179kcal/754kJ Protein 1.7g; Carbohydrate 31.8g, of which sugars 5.9g; Fat 5.9g, of which saturates 0.8g; Cholesterol 0mg; Calcium 21mg; Fibre 1.6g; Sodium 4mg.
Spiced Samosas Energy 86kcal/359kJ; Protein 1g; Carbohydrate 7g, of which sugars 1g; Fat 6g, of which saturates 1g; Cholesterol 0mg; Calcium 4mg; Fibre 0.5g; Sodium 0.1mg.

Seafood Fritters with a Fiery Pear and Chilli Dip

Succulent seafood is battered and lightly fried to create these golden fritters.

Serves 4
2 eggs, beaten
45ml/3 tbsp vegetable oil, for frying
75g/3oz/⅔ cup plain (all-purpose) flour for dusting
salt and ground black pepper

For the dipping sauce
45ml/3 tbsp light soy sauce
45ml/3 tbsp sugar
1 garlic clove, crushed
10ml/2 tsp pear juice
2.5ml/½ tsp lemon juice
1.5ml/½ tsp Korean chilli powder

For the prawn fritters
5 medium-size prawns (shrimp), peeled
juice of ½ lemon
30ml/2 tbsp white wine
2.5ml/½ tsp sesame oil
1 dried shiitake mushroom, soaked in warm water for about 30 minutes until soft
1 green chilli, finely chopped

For the crab fritters
75g/3oz crab meat
3 oyster mushrooms, finely sliced
¼ green (bell) pepper, chopped
25g/1oz Korean chives, finely sliced
1 garlic clove, thinly sliced
2 eggs, beaten
45ml/3 tbsp plain (all-purpose) flour

For the cod fritters
300g/11oz cod fillet
7.5ml/1½ tsp dark soy sauce
5ml/1 tsp white wine
2.5ml/½ tsp sesame oil

1 Combine all the ingredients for the sauce in a small bowl. For the prawn fritters, season the prawns with salt, pepper, lemon juice, white wine and sesame oil. Chop the mushroom and mix with the chilli, season with sesame oil, and dust with flour. Set aside. Dust the prawns with flour. Coat with egg and set aside.

2 To make the crab fritters, season the crab meat and place in a bowl. Add the remaining ingredients, mix well and set aside. For the cod fritters, cut into bitesize pieces and mix with the other ingredients. Dust with flour, coat with egg and set aside.

3 Heat the oil in a frying pan. Fry the fritters until browned and then add mushroom mixture to the prawn fritters. Continue frying until all are golden brown. Serve with the dipping sauce.

Hot Spicy Prawns with Coriander

This is a quick and easy way of preparing prawns for a snack or appetizer. If you increase the quantities, this dish can also be served as a main course, and is simple enough to make for a tasty midweek dinner. Select a variety of mushrooms and add them to the pan with the sauce ingredients, if you like. Serve the prawns with bread to mop up the tasty juices.

Serves 2 to 4
450g/1lb uncooked king prawns (jumbo shrimp)
60ml/4 tbsp olive oil
2–3 garlic cloves, chopped
25g/1oz fresh root ginger, peeled and shredded
1 chilli, seeded and chopped
5ml/1 tsp cumin seeds
5ml/1 tsp paprika
bunch of fresh coriander (cilantro), chopped
salt
1 lemon, cut into wedges, to serve

1 To prepare the prawns, hold each one between two fingers and gently pull off the tail shell. Twist off the head. Peel away the soft body shell and the small claws beneath and rinse thoroughly under cold water.

2 Pour the olive oil into a large, heavy frying pan, and heat the oil over a medium heat. Add the chopped garlic, stirring to ensure it does not burn, or it will taste bitter.

3 Stir in the ginger, chilli and cumin seeds. Cook the mixture briefly, stirring constantly, until the ingredients give off a lovely fragrant aroma. Add the paprika and stir in well.

4 Add the prawns to the pan. Fry them over a fairly high heat, turning them frequently, for 3–5 minutes, until just cooked.

5 Season to taste with salt and add the coriander. Serve immediately, with lemon wedges for squeezing over the prawns.

Variation
This dish is also delicious made with scallops or mussels in place of the prawns.

Seafood Fritters Energy 294kcal/1227kJ; Protein 29.3g; Carbohydrate 9.1g, of which sugars 6.1g; Fat 15.3g, of which saturates 2.8g; Cholesterol 287mg; Calcium 103mg; Fibre 1.1g; Sodium 671mg.
Hot Spicy Prawns Energy 382kcal/1591kJ; Protein 40.8g; Carbohydrate 1.1g, of which sugars 0.9g; Fat 23.9g, of which saturates 3.4g; Cholesterol 439mg; Calcium 254mg; Fibre 1.9g; Sodium 440mg.

Prawns in Chilli-chocolate Sauce

There is a long tradition in Spain, which originates in Mexico, of cooking savoury food – even shellfish – with chocolate. Known as *langostinos en chocolate* in Spanish, this is just the kind of culinary adventure that Spanish chefs love.

Serves 4

8 large raw prawns (shrimp), in the shell
15ml/1 tbsp seasoned plain (all-purpose) flour
15ml/1 tbsp pale dry sherry
juice of 1 large orange
15g/½oz dark (bittersweet) chocolate, chopped
30ml/2 tbsp olive oil
2 garlic cloves, finely chopped
2.5cm/1in piece fresh root ginger, finely chopped
1 small dried chilli, seeded and chopped
salt and ground black pepper

1 Peel the prawns, leaving just the tail sections intact. Make a shallow cut down the back of each one and carefully pull out and discard the dark intestinal tract.

2 Turn the prawns over so that the undersides are uppermost, and then carefully slit them open from tail to top, using a small sharp knife, cutting them almost, but not quite, through to the central back line.

3 Press the prawns down firmly to flatten them out. Coat with the seasoned flour and set aside.

4 Gently heat the sherry and orange juice in a small pan. When warm, remove from the heat and stir in the chopped chocolate until melted.

5 Heat the oil in a frying pan. Add the garlic, ginger and chilli and cook for 2 minutes until golden. Remove with a slotted spoon and reserve. Add the prawns, cut side down, and cook for 2–3 minutes until golden brown with pink edges. Turn the prawns and cook for a further 2 minutes.

6 Return the garlic mixture to the pan and pour the chocolate sauce over. Cook for 1 minute, turning the prawns to coat them in the glossy sauce. Season to taste and serve hot.

Seafood and Spring Onion Pancake with Mixed Chillies

This pancake combines the silky texture of squid and scallops with the crunch and piquancy of spring onions.

Serves 4

90g/3½oz squid, trimmed, cleaned, skinned and sliced
2 oysters, removed from the shell
5 clams, removed from the shell
5 small prawns (shrimp), shelled
3 scallops, removed from the shell
15ml/1 tbsp vegetable oil
5 spring onions (scallions), sliced into thin strips
½ red chilli, seeded and cut into thin strips
½ green chilli, seeded and cut into thin strips
50g/2oz enoki mushrooms
1 garlic clove, thinly sliced
salt and ground black pepper

For the batter

115g/4oz/1 cup plain (all-purpose) flour
40g/1½oz/⅓ cup cornflour (cornstarch)
2 eggs, beaten
5ml/1 tsp salt
5ml/1 tsp sugar

For the dipping sauce

90ml/6 tbsp light soy sauce
22.5ml/4½ tsp rice vinegar
1 spring onion (scallion), shredded
1 red chilli, finely shredded
1 garlic clove, crushed
5ml/1 tsp sesame oil
5ml/1 tsp sesame seeds

1 For the batter, sift the flour into a large bowl. Add the rest of the batter ingredients with 200ml/7fl oz/scant 1 cup iced water and whisk until smooth. Set aside. Put the seafood into another large bowl. Season, and leave to stand for 10 minutes.

2 Meanwhile, make the dipping sauce. Put all the ingredients in a small bowl, mixing well until combined.

3 Heat the vegetable oil in a large frying pan. Pour one-third of the batter in, spreading it evenly in the pan. Place the spring onions, chillies, mushrooms and garlic on to the pancake and then add the seafood. Pour over the remaining batter and cook, turning once, until the pancake is golden brown on both sides.

4 Slice the pancake into bitesize pieces and serve on a large plate with the dipping sauce.

Prawns Energy 133kcal/554kJ; Protein 9.5g; Carbohydrate 7.4g, of which sugars 3.6g; Fat 6.9g, of which saturates 1.5g; Cholesterol 98mg; Calcium 49mg; Fibre 0.3g; Sodium 97mg.
Seafood Pancake Energy 255kcal/1077kJ; Protein 16.5g; Carbohydrate 33.7g, of which sugars 1.9g; Fat 7.1g, of which saturates 1.4g; Cholesterol 232mg; Calcium 80mg; Fibre 1.4g; Sodium 613mg.

Steamed Mussels with Chilli and Lemon Grass

This dish, called *so hap xa*, is Vietnam's version of the French classic, *moules marinière*. Here the mussels are steamed open in a herby stock with lemon grass and chilli instead of wine and parsley. Both versions are delicious, and this one can be served with chunks of baguette to mop up the cooking liquid, just like the French do with theirs. This is also a popular Vietnamese method of steaming clams and snails. Beer is sometimes used instead of stock and it makes a rich, fragrant sauce.

Serves 4

1kg/2¼lb fresh mussels
600ml/1 pint/2½ cups chicken stock or beer, or a mixture
1 green or red Thai chilli, seeded and finely chopped
2 shallots, finely chopped
2–3 lemon grass stalks, finely chopped
1 bunch of ginger leaves
salt and ground black pepper
baguette, to serve (optional)

1 Scrub the mussels, removing any barnacles and pull away any 'beards'. Discard any mussels that do not close when tapped sharply. Place the prepared mussels in a bowl in the refrigerator until ready to use.

2 Pour the stock into a deep pan. Add the chilli, shallots, lemon grass and ginger leaves and bring it to the boil. Cover and simmer for 10–15 minutes to let the flavours mingle, then season to taste with salt and pepper.

3 Tip the mussels into the stock. Give the pan a good shake, cover tightly and cook for about 2 minutes, or until the mussels have opened.

4 Discard any mussels that remain closed. Ladle the remaining mussels into individual bowls, making sure everyone gets some of the cooking liquid.

5 Serve the mussels decorated with ginger leaves and with a chunk of baguette, if using, so each diner can mop up the juices.

Scallops in Hot Chilli Sauce

Shellfish are often cooked very simply in Mexico. Hot chilli sauce and lime are popular ingredients in many fish recipes.

Serves 4

20 scallops
2 courgettes (zucchini)
75g/3oz/6 tbsp butter
15ml/1 tbsp vegetable oil
4 garlic cloves, chopped
30ml/2 tbsp hot chilli sauce
juice of 1 lime
small bunch of fresh coriander (cilantro), finely chopped

1 If you have bought scallops in their shells, open them. Hold a scallop shell in the palm of your hand, with the flat side uppermost. Insert the blade of a knife close to the hinge that joins the shells and prise them apart. Run the blade of the knife across the inside of the flat shell to cut away the scallop. Only the white adductor muscle and the orange coral are eaten, so pull away and discard all other parts. Rinse the scallops under cold running water.

2 Cut the courgettes in half, then into four pieces. Melt the butter in the vegetable oil in a large frying pan. Add the courgettes to the pand and fry for about 5 minutes, or until soft. Remove from the pan.

3 Add the garlic to the frying pan and fry until golden. Stir in the hot chilli sauce.

4 Add the scallops to the sauce. Cook, stirring constantly, for 1–2 minutes only.

5 Stir in the lime juice, chopped coriander and the courgette pieces. Serve immediately on heated plates.

Cook's Tip

Oil is capable of withstanding higher temperatures than butter, but butter gives fried food added flavour. Using a mixture of both ingredients, as here, provides the perfect compromise because the oil prevents the butter from burning.

Steamed Mussels Energy 73kcal/311kJ; Protein 11g; Carbohydrate 3g, of which sugars 1g; Fat 2g, of which saturates 0g; Cholesterol 36mg; Calcium 37mg; Fibre 0.7g; Sodium 0.7mg.
Scallops in Chilli Sauce Energy 291kcal/1213kJ; Protein 24.2g; Carbohydrate 4.4g of which sugars 1g; Fat 19.8g of which saturates 10.6g; Cholesterol 87mg; Calcium 45mg; Fibre 0.5g; Sodium 294mg.

Rice Seaweed Roll with Spicy Squid

This Korean favourite is cooked rice, wrapped in seaweed, and then served with spicy squid and mooli. This delicious snack is perfect when accompanied by a bowl of clear soup.

Serves 2

400g/14oz/4 cups cooked rice
rice vinegar, for drizzling
sesame oil, for drizzling
150g/5oz squid, trimmed, cleaned, and skinned
90g/3½oz mooli (daikon), peeled and diced
3 large sheets dried seaweed or nori

For the squid seasoning
22.5ml/4½ tsp Korean chilli powder
7.5ml/1½ tsp sugar
1 garlic clove, crushed
5ml/1 tsp sesame oil
2.5ml/½ tsp sesame seeds

For the mooli seasoning
15ml/1 tbsp sugar
30ml/2 tbsp rice vinegar
22.5ml/4½ tsp Korean chilli powder
15ml/1 tbsp Thai fish sauce
1 garlic clove, crushed
1 spring onion (scallion), finely chopped

1 Put the cooked rice in a bowl and drizzle over some rice vinegar and sesame oil. Mix well, then set aside. Use a sharp knife to score the squid with a criss-cross pattern, and slice into pieces about 5cm/2in long and 1cm/½in wide.

2 Bring a pan of water to the boil over high heat. Blanch the squid for 3 minutes, then drain under cold running water. Combine all the squid seasoning ingredients in a bowl, and then coat the squid. Set aside to absorb the flavours.

3 Put the mooli in a bowl, then drizzle over some rice vinegar. Leave for 15 minutes and then drain the mooli and transfer to a bowl. Add the mooli seasoning ingredients, mix well and chill in the refrigerator.

4 Place the rice evenly on each of the three seaweed sheets, roll each into a cylinder and slice into bitesize pieces.

5 Arrange the rolls on a serving plate and serve with the seasoned squid and mooli.

Grilled Squid in Serrano Chilli Dressing

This is a lovely dish – sweet, charred squid served in a tangy dressing made with tamarind, lime and the intensely flavoured Thai fish sauce. It is best made with baby squid because they are tender and sweet. Traditionally, the squid are steamed for this dish, but their flavour is enhanced if they are cooked on a griddle, as here, or lightly charred on a grill over a barbecue. Serve immediately while the squid is still warm.

Serves 4

2 large tomatoes, skinned, halved and seeded
500g/1¼lb fresh baby squid
1 bunch each of fresh basil, coriander (cilantro) and mint, stalks removed, leaves chopped

For the dressing
15ml/1 tbsp tamarind paste
juice of half a lime
30ml/2 tbsp Thai fish sauce
15ml/1 tbsp raw cane sugar
1 garlic clove, crushed
2 shallots, halved and finely sliced
1–2 Serrano chillies, seeded and finely sliced

1 Put the ingredients for the dressing in a bowl and stir until thoroughly mixed. Set aside.

2 Heat a ridged griddle, wiping with oil. Cook the tomatoes until lightly charred. Chop into bitesize chunks, and put in a bowl.

3 Clean the griddle, then heat it up again and wipe with a little more oil. Cook the squid for 2–3 minutes each side until browned. Add to the tomatoes, add the herbs and the dressing and toss well. Serve immediately.

Cook's Tip

To prepare squid yourself, get a firm hold of the head and pull it from the body. Reach inside the body sac and remove the transparent back bone, as well as any stringy parts. Rinse the sac inside and out and pat dry. Cut the tentacles off and add to the pile of squid. Discard everything else.

Rice Seaweed Roll Energy 195kcal/830kJ; Protein 8.8g; Carbohydrate 36.2g, of which sugars 4.8g; Fat 2.8g, of which saturates 0.6g; Cholesterol 84mg; Calcium 32mg; Fibre 0.4g; Sodium 312mg.
Grilled Squid Energy 165kcal/701kJ; Protein 22g; Carbohydrate 15g, of which sugars 10g; Fat 3g, of which saturates 1g; Cholesterol 281mg; Calcium 105mg; Fibre 1g; Sodium 0.5mg.

Spiced Whelks

This Korean salad is a popular appetizer, often eaten as a snack with drinks. The saltiness of the whelks mingles with the heat of the chilli and the refreshing coolness of the cucumber, creating a captivating combination of tastes and textures.

Serves 2

300g/11oz cooked whelks, drained
½ medium cucumber
1 carrot
2 spring onions (scallions)
1 red chilli, finely sliced
1 green chilli, finely sliced
½ onion, finely sliced

For the dressing

45ml/3 tbsp soy sauce
45ml/3 tbsp sugar
45ml/3 tbsp rice vinegar
30ml/2 tbsp Korean chilli powder
10ml/2 tsp garlic, crushed
5ml/1 tsp sesame seeds
2.5ml/½ tsp salt
2.5ml/½ tsp ground pepper
5ml/1 tsp sesame oil

1 Wash and drain the whelks and slice them into pieces roughly 1cm/½in long.

2 Seed the cucumber and then slice it into long, thin matchstick strips. Cut the carrot into thin julienne strips and slice the spring onions into thin strips.

3 Blend all the dressing ingredients in a bowl, mixing them together thoroughly.

4 Combine the whelks with the cucumber, carrot, spring onions, chillies and onion in a large salad bowl. Pour over the dressing and toss the salad before serving.

Cook's Tips

• Korean chilli powder, called gochugaru is one of the essential ingredients in Korean cooking. Almost all spicy dishes contain it. It is one of the main ingredients of kimchi. There are many varieties, some are very hot and some are mild. Look for it in Asian markets and food stores.

Fried Anchovies with Peanuts and Chilli Paste

The Malays love these fiery fried dried anchovies, known as *ikan bilis goreng*. They are often served as a snack with bread or with coconut rice. The Malays also enjoy them with rice porridge, for breakfast.

Serves 4

4 shallots, chopped
2 garlic cloves, chopped
4 dried red chillies, soaked in warm water until soft, seeded and chopped
30ml/2 tbsp tamarind pulp, soaked in 150ml/¼ pint/⅔ cup water until soft
vegetable oil, for deep-frying
115g/4oz/1 cup peanuts
200g/7oz dried anchovies, heads removed, washed and drained
30ml/2 tbsp sugar
bread or rice, to serve

1 Using a mortar and pestle, food processor or blender, grind the shallots, garlic and chillies together until they form a coarse paste. Set the mixture aside.

2 Squeeze the tamarind pulp to help soften it in the water and press it through a sieve (strainer). Measure out 120ml/4fl oz/½ cup of the tamarind water.

3 Heat oil for deep-frying in a wok or large pan. Lower the heat and deep-fry the peanuts in a wire basket, until they colour. Drain them on kitchen paper and set aside.

4 Add the anchovies to the hot oil and deep-fry until they turn brown and become crisp. Drain the anchovies on kitchen paper and set aside.

5 Pour out most of the oil from the wok, reserving 30ml/2 tbsp. Stir in the spice paste and fry for about 1–2 minutes until the mixture releases its fragrant aroma.

6 Add the sugar, anchovies and peanuts. Gradually stir in the tamarind water, so the mixture remains dry. Serve hot or cold with bread or rice.

Spiced Whelks Energy 215kcal/907kJ; Protein 25g; Carbohydrate 17g, of which sugars 14.1g; Fat 5.7g, of which saturates 1.1g; Cholesterol 338mg; Calcium 69mg; Fibre 1.8g; Sodium 1737mg.
Fried Anchovies Energy 338kcal/1400kJ; Protein 17g; Carbohydrate 4.8g, of which sugars 2.6g; Fat 28g, of which saturates 4.4g; Cholesterol 24mg; Calcium 134mg; Fibre 2g; Sodium 1475mg.

Herring Cured with Chilli and Ginger

Generally served as an appetizer or snack in the Philippines, the herring is not cooked but cured and eaten raw. As with sushi or any other raw fish dish, the fish has to be absolutely fresh. Cured in coconut vinegar and lime juice, and flavoured with ginger and chillies, this is a delicious and refreshing snack.

Serves 4

150ml/¼ pint/⅔ cup coconut vinegar
juice of 2 limes
40g/1½oz fresh root ginger, grated
2 red chillies, seeded and finely sliced
8–10 herring fillets, cut into bitesize pieces
2 shallots, finely sliced
1 green mango, cut into julienne strips
salt and ground black pepper
fresh coriander (cilantro) sprigs, lime wedges, shredded red chillies and shredded fresh ginger, to garnish

1 Put the coconut vinegar, lime juice, ginger and chillies in a bowl and mix together. Season the mixture with salt and pepper, to taste

2 Place the herring fillets in a shallow dish, sprinkle the shallots and green mango over, and pour in the vinegar mixture.

3 Cover with clear film (plastic wrap) and leave to marinate in the refrigerator for 1–2 hours or overnight, turning the fish several times.

4 Serve the fish garnished with coriander, lime wedges to squeeze over, shredded chillies and shredded ginger.

Variation

This dish can be made with many types of seafood, including octopus, halibut and salmon, although mackerel and herring are particularly suitable.

Fried Whitebait in Spicy Dressing

Serve these tangy morsels as an appetizer with drinks or as a main course with a salad of cold mashed potatoes dressed with onions, chillies, olive oil and lemon juice.

Serves 4

800g/1¾lb whitebait or tiny white fish
juice of 2 lemons
5ml/1 tsp salt
plain (all-purpose) flour, for dusting
vegetable oil, for frying
2 onions, chopped or thinly sliced
2.5–5ml/½–1 tsp cumin seeds
2 carrots, thinly sliced
2 jalapeño chillies, chopped
8 garlic cloves, roughly chopped
120ml/4fl oz/½ cup white wine or cider vinegar
2–3 large pinches of dried oregano
15–30ml/1–2 tbsp chopped fresh coriander (cilantro) leaves
slices of corn on the cob, black olives and coriander (cilantro), to serve

1 Put the fish in a bowl, add the lemon juice and salt and leave for 30–60 minutes. Remove the fish and dust with flour.

2 Heat the oil in a deep-frying pan until hot enough to turn a cube of bread golden brown in 30 seconds. Fry the fish, in small batches, until crisp, then put in a dish and set aside.

3 In a separate pan, heat 30ml/2 tbsp of oil. Add the onions, cumin seeds, carrots, chillies and garlic and fry for 5 minutes. Stir in the vinegar, oregano and coriander and cook for 1–2 minutes.

4 Pour the onion mixture over the fried fish and leave to cool. Serve the fish at room temperature, with slices of corn on the cob, black olives and coriander leaves.

Cook's Tips

• When selecting whitebait or any other smelt, make sure the fish are very tiny as they are eaten whole.
• If you prefer, use chunks of any firm white fish such as cod or halibut instead of tiny whole fish. Simply flour the chunks of fish and fry as above.

Herring Energy 408kcal/1699kJ; Protein 36.4g; Carbohydrate 5.9g, of which sugars 5.7g; Fat 26.7g, of which saturates 6.6g; Cholesterol 100mg; Calcium 160mg; Fibre 1.9g; Sodium 260mg.
Whitebait Energy 1087kcal/4504kJ; Protein 40.3g; Carbohydrate 18.5g, of which sugars 5.9g; Fat 95.3g, of which saturates 8.9g; Cholesterol 0mg; Calcium 1734mg; Fibre 2.3g; Sodium 471mg.

Crab Cakes with a Chilli Tomato Dip

These crab cakes are quite delicious, especially when accompanied by a tangy tomato dip.

Makes about 15

225g/8oz white crab meat
115g/4oz cooked potatoes, mashed
25g/1oz/2 tbsp fresh herb seasoning
2.5ml/½ tsp mild mustard
2.5ml/½ tsp ground black pepper
½ hot chilli pepper
15ml/1 tbsp shrimp paste (optional)
2.5ml/½ tsp dried oregano, crushed
1 egg, beaten
flour, for dusting
oil, for frying
lime wedges and basil leaves, to garnish

For the tomato dip

15ml/1 tbsp butter or margarine
½ onion, finely chopped
2 canned plum tomatoes, chopped
1 garlic clove, crushed
150ml/¼ pint/⅔ cups water
5–10ml/1–2 tsp malt vinegar
15ml/1 tbsp chopped fresh coriander (cilantro)
½ hot chilli pepper, seeded and finely sliced

1 To make the crab cakes, mix together the crab meat, mashed potatoes, herb seasoning, mustard, peppers, shrimp paste, if using, oregano and egg in a large bowl. Chill for 30 minutes.

2 Meanwhile, make the tomato dip. Melt the butter or margarine in a small pan. Add the onion, tomato and garlic and sauté for about 5 minutes until the onion is soft.

3 Add the water, vinegar, coriander and hot pepper. Simmer for 10 minutes and then blend to a smooth paste in a food processor or blender and pour into a bowl. Keep warm or chill as required.

4 Using a spoon, shape the mixture into rounds and dust with flour. Heat a little oil in a frying pan and fry the crab cakes a few at a time for 2–3 minutes on each side until golden brown. Drain and keep warm while cooking the remaining cakes.

5 Serve the cakes with the warm or cold tomato dip and garnish with lime wedges and basil leaves.

Wok-fried Crab with Red Chilli

This hot and spicy crab dish is popular in Indonesia, where it is called *kepitang pedas*. Variations of this popular appetizer can be found all over Asia.

Serves 4

2 cooked crabs, about 675g/1½lb
1cm/½in cube shrimp paste
2 garlic cloves
2 fresh red chillies, seeded, or 5ml/1 tsp chopped chilli from a jar
1cm/½in piece fresh root ginger, peeled and sliced
60ml/4 tbsp sunflower oil
300ml/½ pint/1¼ cups tomato ketchup
15ml/1 tbsp soft dark brown sugar
150ml/¼ pint/⅔ cup warm water
4 spring onions (scallions), chopped, to garnish
cucumber chunks and hot toast, to serve (optional)

1 Remove the large claws of one crab and turn it on to its back, with the head facing away from you. Use your thumbs to push the body up from the main shell. Discard the stomach sac and 'dead men's fingers,' i.e. lungs and any green matter. Leave the creamy brown meat in the shell and cut the shell in half, with a cleaver or strong knife. Cut the body section in half and crack the claws with a sharp blow from a hammer or cleaver. Avoid splintering the claws. Repeat with the other crab.

2 Grind the shrimp paste, garlic, chillies and ginger to a paste in a food processor or with a pestle and mortar.

3 Heat a wok and add the oil. Fry the spice paste, stirring it all the time, without browning, for 1–2 minutes until the fragrant aromas are released.

4 Stir in the tomato ketchup, sugar and water and mix the sauce well. Continue to heat the sauce until just boiling, then add all the crab pieces and toss in the sauce until well-coated and heated through.

5 Serve in a large bowl, sprinkled with the spring onions. Place in the centre of the table for everyone to help themselves. Accompany this dish with cool cucumber chunks and hot toast for mopping up the sauce, if you like.

Crab Cakes Energy 70kcal/290kJ; Protein 3.5g; Carbohydrate 2.9g; of which sugars 0.7g; Fat 5g; of which saturates 1.1g; Cholesterol 26mg; Calcium 24mg; Fibre 0.3g; Sodium 95mg.
Wok-fried Crab Energy 286kcal/1194kJ; Protein 14g; Carbohydrate 26g; of which sugars 25g; Fat 14g; of which saturates 2g; Cholesterol 49mg; Calcium 31mg; Fibre 0.9g; Sodium 1.5mg.

Chilli Hot Salt Fish Fritters

These delicious fish fritters combine salty cod with crispy spring onion in a light batter spiked with fresh chilli.

Makes 15

115g/4oz/1 cup self-raising (self-rising) flour
115g/4oz/1 cup plain (all-purpose) flour
2.5ml/½ tsp baking powder
175g/6oz soaked salt cod, shredded
1 egg, whisked
15ml/1 tbsp chopped spring onion (scallion)
1 garlic clove, crushed
2.5ml/½ tsp ground black pepper
½ hot chilli pepper, seeded and finely chopped
1.5ml/¼ tsp turmeric
45ml/3 tbsp milk
vegetable oil, for shallow frying
sprig of dill, to garnish

1 Sift the self-raising and plain flours together into a bowl. Sift the baking powder into the flour and mix together.

2 Add the salt cod, egg, spring onion, garlic, pepper, hot pepper and turmeric. Add a little of the milk and mix well.

3 Gradually stir in the remaining milk, adding just enough to make a thick batter. Stir thoroughly so that all ingredients are completely combined.

4 Heat a little vegetable oil in a large frying pan until very hot. Add spoonfuls of the mixture then fry for a few minutes on each side until golden brown and puffy.

5 Lift out the fritters from the pan, drain on kitchen paper and keep warm while cooking the remainder of the mixture in the same way. Serve the fritters garnished with the dill sprig.

Cook's Tip
Salt cod is popular in Mediterranean countries as well as in tropical countries where it keeps well in the heat. It is called bacalhau *in Portugal and is the national dish. Salt cod needs soaking in three changes of water for about a day before use.*

Chilli-marinated Sardines

The Arabs invented marinades as a means of preserving poultry, meat and game. In Spain this method was enthusiastically adopted as a means of keeping fish fresh and they created this dish, called *escabeche*. The fish are always fried first and then stored in vinegar.

Serves 2 to 4

12–16 sardines, cleaned
seasoned plain (all-purpose) flour, for dusting
30ml/2 tbsp olive oil
roasted red onion, green (bell) pepper and tomatoes, to garnish

For the marinade
90ml/6 tbsp olive oil
1 onion, sliced
1 garlic clove, crushed
3–4 bay leaves
2 cloves
1 dried red chilli, seeded and chopped
5ml/1 tsp paprika
120ml/4fl oz/½ cup wine or sherry vinegar
120ml/4fl oz/½ cup white wine
salt and ground black pepper

1 Using a sharp knife, cut the heads off the sardines and split each of them along the belly. Turn the fish over so that the backbone is uppermost. Press down along the backbone to loosen it, then carefully lift out the backbone and as many of the remaining little bones as possible. Close the sardines up again and dust them with seasoned flour.

2 Heat the olive oil in a frying pan and fry the sardines for 2–3 minutes on each side. With a metal spatula, remove the fish from the pan to a plate and allow to cool, then pack them in a single layer in a large shallow dish.

3 To make the marinade, add the olive oil to the oil remaining in the frying pan. Fry the onion and garlic for 5–10 minutes until soft, stirring occasionally. Add the bay leaves, cloves, chilli and paprika, with pepper to taste. Fry, stirring, for 1–2 minutes.

4 Stir in the vinegar, wine and a little salt. Allow to bubble up, then pour over the sardines. The marinade should cover the fish completely. When the fish is cool, cover then chill overnight or for up to three days. Serve the sardines and their marinade, garnished with the onion, pepper and tomatoes.

Chilli Hot Saltfish Fritters Energy 109kcal/458kJ; Protein 5.8g; Carbohydrate 12.3g, of which sugars 0.8g; Fat 4.4g, of which saturates 0.6g; Cholesterol 20mg; Calcium 30mg; Fibre 0.6g; Sodium 53mg.
Chilli-marinated Sardines Energy 242kcal/1004kJ Protein 15.8g; Carbohydrate 1.7g; of which sugars 0.9g; Fat 18.1g; of which saturates 3.6g; Cholesterol 0mg; Calcium 70mg; Fibre 0.2g; Sodium 92mg.

Spicy Chicken Satay with Peanut Sauce

These miniature kebabs are popular all over South-east Asia, and they are especially delicious when cooked over a barbecue. The peanut dipping sauce is a perfect partner for the marinated, grilled chicken.

Serves 4

4 skinless chicken breast fillets

For the marinade

2 garlic cloves, crushed
2.5cm/1in piece fresh root ginger, finely grated
10ml/2 tsp Thai fish sauce
30ml/2 tbsp light soy sauce
15ml/1 tbsp clear honey

For the satay sauce

90ml/6 tbsp crunchy peanut butter
1 fresh red chilli, seeded and finely chopped
juice of 1 lime
60ml/4 tbsp coconut milk
salt

1 First, make the satay sauce. Put all the ingredients in a food processor or blender. Process the mixture until smooth, then check the seasoning and add more salt or lime juice if necessary. Spoon the sauce into a bowl, cover with clear film (plastic wrap) and set aside.

2 Using a sharp knife, slice each chicken breast fillet into four long strips. Put all the marinade ingredients in a large bowl and mix well, then add the chicken strips and toss together until thoroughly coated. Cover and leave for at least 30 minutes in the refrigerator to marinate.

3 Meanwhile, soak 16 wooden satay sticks or kebab skewers in water, to prevent them from burning during cooking.

4 Preheat the grill (broiler) to high or prepare the barbecue. Drain the satay sticks or skewers. Drain the chicken strips. Thread one strip on to each satay stick or skewer.

5 Grill (broil) the chicken skewers for 3 minutes on each side, or until it is golden brown and cooked through. Serve immediately with the satay sauce.

Fiery Chicken Wings with Blood Oranges

This is a great recipe for the barbecue – it is quick and easy, and best eaten with the fingers. The juicy oranges are there to suck after experiencing an explosion of fiery spices on the tongue. The oranges can be cooked separately or threaded alternately with the chicken wings on skewers.

Serves 4

60ml/4 tbsp fiery harissa
30ml/2 tbsp olive oil
16–20 chicken wings
4 blood oranges, quartered
icing (confectioners') sugar
small bunch of fresh coriander (cilantro), chopped
salt

1 Put the harissa in a small bowl with the olive oil and mix to form a loose paste. Add a little salt and stir to combine.

2 Brush the harissa mixture over the chicken wings so that they are well coated. Cook the wings on a hot barbecue once the coals are ready or under a hot grill (broiler) for 5 minutes on each side.

3 Once the wings begin to cook, dip the orange quarters lightly in icing sugar and grill them for a few minutes, until they are slightly burnt but not black and charred.

4 Serve the chicken wings immediately with the oranges, sprinkled with a little chopped fresh coriander.

Variations

- *Cherry tomatoes will also work well here in place of the oranges. It is the burst of juice that makes this dish so delicious.*
- *The fiery marinade on the chicken works well with the oranges but for less heat cut back on the harissa and use a little more oil – or try adding a splash of fresh orange juice to the paste before coating the chicken.*

Chicken Satay Energy 375kcal/1564kJ; Protein 42.9g; Carbohydrate 3.9g, of which sugars 2.4g; Fat 20.9g, of which saturates 5.6g; Cholesterol 196mg; Calcium 14mg; Fibre 0g; Sodium 132mg.
Fiery Chicken Wings Energy 500kcal/2077kJ; Protein 44.8g; Carbohydrate 0g, of which sugars 0g; Fat 35.6g, of which saturates 8.9g; Cholesterol 196mg; Calcium 74mg; Fibre 0g; Sodium 132mg.

Tangy Chicken Livers with Red Chilli and Roasted Hazelnuts

Sautéed offal, such as liver and kidney, is a popular appetizer in Morocco, often cooked simply in olive oil with garlic and chilli and served with lemon. This dish of chicken livers makes a delicious, tangy appetizer on its own, served with a few salad leaves, or spooned on thin slices of toasted bread. In the restaurants of Casablanca, where the French influence still lingers, the refinement of this dish is much enjoyed.

Serves 4

30–45ml/2–3 tbsp olive oil
2–3 garlic cloves, chopped
1 dried red chilli, chopped
5ml/1 tsp cumin seeds
450g/1lb chicken livers, trimmed and cut into bitesize chunks
5ml/1 tsp ground coriander
handful of roasted hazelnuts, roughly chopped
10–15ml/2–3 tsp orange flower water
½ preserved lemon, finely sliced or chopped
salt and ground black pepper
small bunch of fresh coriander (cilantro), finely chopped, to serve

1 Heat the olive oil in a heavy frying pan and stir in the garlic, chilli and cumin seeds. Add the chicken livers and toss over the heat until they are browned on all sides. Reduce the heat a little and continue to cook for 3–5 minutes.

2 When the livers are almost cooked, add the ground coriander and hazelnuts. Stir in the orange flower water and preserved lemon. Season to taste with salt and black pepper and serve immediately, sprinkled with a little fresh coriander.

Variation

Lamb's liver, trimmed and finely sliced, is also good cooked this way. The trick is to sear the outside so that the middle is almost pink and melts in the mouth. If you don't have orange flower water, try a little balsamic vinegar.

Crisp Spring Rolls with Hot Chilli Sauce

These Indonesian spring rolls are packed with vegetables and strips of chicken.

Serves 3 to 4

15–30ml/1–2 tbsp palm or corn oil
2–3 garlic cloves, finely chopped
225g/8oz chicken breast fillets, cut into fine strips
225g/8oz fresh shrimp, shelled
2 leeks, cut into matchsticks
2 carrots, cut into matchsticks
½ green cabbage, finely shredded
175g/6oz fresh beansprouts
30ml/2 tbsp patis (fish sauce)
30ml/2 tbsp kecap manis (Indonesian sweet soy sauce)
1 egg, lightly beaten
corn or vegetable oil, for deep-frying
4 red or green Thai chillies, seeded and finely sliced, to serve

For the spring roll wrappers

115g/4oz/1 cup rice flour
30ml/2 tbsp cornflour (cornstarch)
2 eggs, beaten
15ml/1 tbsp palm or coconut oil
400ml/14fl oz/scant 2 cups water
corn or vegetable oil, for frying
salt

For the dipping sauce

200ml/7fl oz kecap manis
1 red chilli, seeded and chopped

1 Sift the flours for wrappers into a bowl. Add the eggs and oil, and beat in the water until a smooth batter forms. Set aside. Mix together the ingredients for the sauce into a serving bowl.

2 Heat a little oil in a frying pan. Ladle in a little batter and cook on one side until lightly browned. Lift the wrapper on to a plate. Repeat with the remaining batter.

3 Heat 15ml/1 tbsp oil in a wok. Fry the garlic, chicken and shrimp until cooked. Set aside. Heat the remaining oil and stir-fry the leeks, carrots and cabbage for 3 minutes. Stir-fry the beansprouts for 1–2 minutes. Add the chicken, shrimp, patis and kecap manis. Tip on to a plate and leave to cool.

4 Fill the wrappers by adding a spoonful of the filling on to one side. Spread to form a log, then roll the wrapper over, tuck in the sides and continue rolling. Seal the end with beaten egg.

5 Heat the oil in a wok. Fry two rolls at a time for 4 minutes, until golden. Remove, drain and serve with sauce and chillies.

Chichen Livers Energy 242kcal/1006kJ; Protein 22.2g; Carbohydrate 1.5g, of which sugars 0.8g; Fat 16.4g, of which saturates 2.2g; Cholesterol 428mg; Calcium 54mg; Fibre 1.5g; Sodium 91mg.
Crisp Spring Rolls Energy 585kcal/2446kJ; Protein 35.4g; Carbohydrate 43.5g, of which sugars 7.2g; Fat 31.2g, of which saturates 4.5g; Cholesterol 292mg; Calcium 170mg; Fibre 5.1g; Sodium 744mg.

Mung Bean Pancakes with Chilli

These spicy mung bean pancakes are deliciously light.

Serves 3 to 4

375g/13oz/2 cups mung beans, soaked overnight in cold water
15ml/1 tbsp pine nuts
30ml/2 tbsp rice flour
75g/3oz beef flank, sliced
200g/7oz prawns (shrimp), peeled and finely chopped
15ml/1 tbsp vegetable oil, plus extra for shallow-frying
1 button (white) mushroom, sliced
½ onion, thinly sliced
½ cucumber, seeded and sliced
½ cup cabbage kimchi, thinly sliced
3 spring onions (scallions), sliced
1 red chilli, shredded
salt and ground black pepper

For the marinade

5ml/1 tsp rice wine
2.5ml/½ tsp grated fresh root ginger
5ml/1 tsp dark soy sauce
1 garlic clove, crushed
2.5l/½ tsp sesame seeds
5ml/1 tsp sesame oil
ground black pepper

For the dipping sauce

60ml/4 tbsp dark soy sauce
10ml/2 tsp rice vinegar
1 spring onion (scallion), finely chopped

1 Drain the beans and roll them between your hands to remove the skins. Rinse well, and place in a processor with the pine nuts and 120ml/4fl oz/½ cup water. Blend to a milky paste. Transfer to a bowl and add the rice flour and 5ml/1 tsp salt. Mix well.

2 Put the beef into a bowl. Pour over the rice wine for the marinade. Add the other marinade ingredients and mix well. Leave for 20 minutes. Season the prawns. Combine all the dipping sauce ingredients in a serving bowl.

3 Coat a wok with oil. Stir-fry the beef, mushroom and onion until the meat has browned. Add the cucumber, cabbage kimchi and spring onions. Mix well and then remove the mixture from the heat.

4 Heat the oil in a frying pan. Add a spoonful of the bean paste and flatten slightly to form a pancake. Spoon some beef mixture on to the pancake, with some chilli and prawns. Press flat and fry until golden on each side. Serve immediately with the soy dipping sauce.

Spiced Turkish Flatbreads

A crispy base is topped with spiced lamb, parsley, sumac and a squeeze of lemon.

Serves 2 to 4

scant 5ml/1 tsp active dried yeast
2.5ml/½ tsp sugar
150ml/¼ pint lukewarm water
350g/12oz/3 cups white bread flour
2.5ml/½ tsp salt
a few drops of sunflower oil

For the topping

15ml/1 tbsp olive oil
15ml/1 tbsp butter
1 onion, finely chopped
2 garlic cloves, finely chopped
225g/8oz/1 cup finely minced (ground) lean lamb
30ml/2 tbsp tomato purée (paste)
15ml/1 tbsp sugar
5–10ml/1–2 tsp Turkish pepper, or 1 red chilli, finely chopped
5ml/1 tsp dried mint
5–10ml/1–2 tsp ground sumac
1 bunch of fresh flat leaf parsley, roughly chopped
1 lemon, halved
salt and ground black pepper

1 Make the dough. Put the yeast and sugar into a bowl with half the water. Set aside for 15 minutes. Sift the flour and salt into a bowl, add the yeast mixture and the rest of the water. Work the mixture to a dough, adding more water if necessary.

2 Knead the dough on a floured surface until smooth and elastic. Add the sunflower oil into the bowl and roll the dough in it. Cover the bowl with a damp dish towel and leave in a warm place for about 1 hour, or until it has doubled in size.

3 Meanwhile, prepare the topping. Heat the oil and butter in a heavy pan and gently fry the onion and garlic until soft. Leave to cool in the pan. Put the lamb in a bowl, add the tomato purée, sugar, red pepper or chilli and mint, then the onion and garlic. Season, and mix well. Cover and chill until required.

4 Place two oiled baking sheets in the oven. Preheat the oven to 220°C/425°F/Gas 7. Punch down the dough, knead, then divide into two or four equal pieces. Roll into a thin flat rounds and place on the sheets. Spread with a thin layer of meat mixture. Bake for 15–20 minutes. Sprinkle with sumac and parsley. Squeeze a little lemon juice over and roll them up while the dough is pliable. Serve immediately.

Mung Bean Pancakes Energy 492kcal/2070kJ; Protein 38.2g; Carbohydrate 55.4g, of which sugars 6.9g; Fat 14.2g, of which saturates 2.2g; Cholesterol 108mg; Calcium 175mg; Fibre 11.7g; Sodium 1867mg.
Spiced Flatbreads Energy 496kcal/2092kJ; Protein 20g; Carbohydrate 75.2g, of which sugars 8.1g; Fat 14.9g, of which saturates 6.1g; Cholesterol 51mg; Calcium 167mg; Fibre 3.8g; Sodium 333mg.

Hot Lentil and Lamb Burgers

These tasty spicy patties are also known as shami kebabs. Although Indian in origin, they are also popular in Malaysia and Singapore, where they have been adapted to suit local tastes.

Serves 4

150g/5oz/generous ½ cup red, brown, yellow or green lentils, rinsed
30ml/2 tbsp vegetable oil
2 onions, finely chopped
2 garlic cloves, finely chopped
1 green chilli, seeded and finely chopped
25g/1oz fresh root ginger, finely chopped
250g/9oz lean minced (ground) lamb
10ml/2 tsp Indian curry powder
5ml/1 tsp turmeric powder
4 eggs
vegetable oil, for shallow frying
salt and ground black pepper
fresh coriander (cilantro) leaves, roughly chopped, to garnish
1 lemon, quartered, to serve

1 Put the lentils in a pan and cover with plenty of water. Bring to a gentle boil and cook until they have softened but still have a bite to them – this can take 20–40 minutes depending on the type of lentil. Drain well.

2 Heat the oil in a heavy pan and stir in the onions, garlic, chilli and ginger. Fry until they begin to colour, then add the lentils and minced lamb. Cook for a few minutes. Add the curry powder and turmeric. Season with salt and pepper and cook the mixture over a high heat until the moisture has evaporated. The mixture needs to be dry for the patties.

3 Leave the meat mixture aside until it is cool enough to handle. Beat one of the eggs in a bowl and mix it into the meat. Using your fingers, take small portions of the mixture and roll them into balls about the size of a plum or apricot. Press each ball in the palm of your hand to form thick, flat patties – if the mixture is sticky, wet your palms with a little water.

4 Beat the remaining eggs in a bowl. Heat enough oil in a pan for shallow frying. Dip each patty in the beaten egg and place them all into the oil. Fry for about 3–4 minutes each side until golden. Garnish with coriander and serve with lemon wedges.

Pork Satay with Pineapple Sauce

Satay is the Indonesian answer to kebabs. Marinated strips of meat are threaded on to skewers, grilled over charcoal and served with a piquant peanut sauce.

Serves 4

500g/1¼lb pork fillet, cut into bitesize strips, or cubes
salt and ground black pepper
bamboo or wooden skewers

For the marinade

4 shallots, chopped
4 garlic cloves, chopped
5ml/1 tsp ground coriander
5ml/1 tsp ground cumin
2.5ml/½ tsp ground turmeric
30ml/2 tbsp dark soy sauce
30ml/2 tbsp sesame oil
fresh coriander (cilantro) leaves, roughly chopped, to garnish

For the sauce

4 shallots, chopped
2 garlic cloves, chopped
4 dried red chillies, soaked in warm water until soft, seeded and chopped
1 lemon grass stalk, trimmed and chopped
25g/1oz fresh root ginger, chopped
30ml/2 tbsp sesame or groundnut (peanut) oil
200ml/7fl oz/scant 1 cup coconut milk
10ml/2 tsp tamarind paste
10ml/2 tsp palm sugar (jaggery)
1 fresh pineapple, peeled, cored and cut into slices

1 For the marinade, grind the shallots and garlic in a mortar and pestle to form a paste. Add the spices, soy sauce and oil. Rub the marinade into the meat. Cover and set aside for 2 hours.

2 Meanwhile, prepare the sauce. Using a mortar and pestle, grind the shallots, garlic, chillies, lemon grass and ginger to a paste. Heat the oil in a heavy pan and cook the paste for 2–3 minutes until fragrant, then stir in the coconut milk, tamarind paste and sugar. Bring to the boil, then simmer for 5 minutes. Season to taste and leave to cool. Using a mortar and pestle or a food processor, crush three pineapple slices and beat them into the sauce. Soak the skewers in cold water.

3 Prepare the charcoal grill. Thread the meat on to skewers and arrange over the coals. Place the remaining pineapple slices next to them until charred, then chop into chunks. Grill the meat for 3 minutes each side; serve with the pineapple and sauce.

Hot Lentil Burgers Energy 488kcal/2033kJ; Protein 28g; Carbohydrate 25.7g, of which sugars 3.7g; Fat 31.2g, of which saturates 7.4g; Cholesterol 238mg; Calcium 87mg; Fibre 3.1g; Sodium 140mg.
Pork Satay Energy 294kcal/1233kJ; Protein 27.5g; Carbohydrate 16.4g, of which sugars 16g; Fat 13.6g, of which saturates 3g; Cholesterol 79mg; Calcium 47mg; Fibre 1.4g; Sodium 145mg.

Barbecued Prawns with a Chilli and Raspberry Dip

The success of this dish stems from the quality of the prawns, so it is worth getting really good ones, such as Mediterranean prawns. A fruity, slightly spicy dip is such an easy but fabulous accompaniment.

Serves 6

30 raw Mediterranean prawns (jumbo shrimp), peeled, with heads removed but tails left on
15ml/1 tbsp sunflower oil
sea salt
30 wooden skewers

For the chilli and raspberry dip

30ml/2 tbsp raspberry vinegar
15ml/1 tbsp sugar
115g/4oz/⅔ cup raspberries
1 large fresh red chilli, seeded and finely chopped

1 Prepare the barbecue. Soak the skewers in cold water for 30 minutes. Make the dip by mixing the vinegar and sugar in a small pan. Heat gently until the sugar has dissolved, then add the raspberries.

2 When the raspberry juices start to flow, tip the mixture into a sieve (strainer) set over a bowl. Push the raspberries through the sieve using the back of a ladle. Discard the seeds. Stir the chilli into the raspberry purée. When the dip is cool, cover and place in a cool place until needed.

3 Butterfly each prawn by making an incision down the curved back, just as you would when deveining. Use a piece of kitchen paper to wipe away the dark spinal vein.

4 Mix the oil with a little sea salt in a bowl. Add the prawns and toss to coat, then thread them on to the drained skewers, spearing them head first. Once the flames have died down, position a lightly oiled grill rack over the coals to heat.

5 When the coals are hot, or with a light coating of ash, grill the prawns for about 5 minutes, depending on size, turning them over once. Serve hot, with the dip.

Spicy Shrimp and Scallop Satay

One of the tastiest satay dishes, this is succulent, spicy and extremely moreish. Serve with rice and a fruity salad or pickled vegetables and lime.

Serves 4

250g/9oz shelled shrimp or prawns, deveined and chopped
250g/9oz shelled scallops, chopped
30ml/2 tbsp potato, tapioca or rice flour
5ml/1 tsp baking powder
12–16 wooden, metal, lemon grass or sugar cane skewers
1 lime, quartered, to serve

For the spice paste

2 shallots, chopped
2 garlic cloves, chopped
2–3 red chillies, seeded and chopped
25g/1oz galangal or fresh root ginger, chopped
15g/½oz fresh turmeric, chopped or 2.5ml/½ tsp ground turmeric
2–3 lemon grass stalks, chopped
15–30ml/1–2 tbsp palm or groundnut (peanut) oil
5ml/1 tsp shrimp paste
15ml/1 tbsp tamarind paste
5ml/1 tsp palm sugar (jaggery)

1 Make the paste. In a mortar and pestle, pound the shallots, garlic, chillies, galangal, turmeric and lemon grass to form a paste.

2 Heat the oil in a wok or heavy frying pan, stir in the paste. Fry until fragrant. Add the shrimp paste, tamarind and sugar and cook, stirring, until the mixture darkens. Set aside to cool.

3 In a bowl, pound the shrimps and scallops together to form a paste, or whizz them in an electric blender or food processor. Beat in the spice paste, then the flour and baking powder, and beat until blended. Chill in the refrigerator for 1 hour. If using wooden skewers, soak them in water for about 30 minutes.

4 Meanwhile, prepare the barbecue, or, if you are using the grill (broiler), preheat 5 minutes before you start cooking. Using your fingers, scoop up lumps of the shellfish paste and wrap it around the skewers.

5 Place each skewer on the barbecue or under the grill and cook for 3 minutes on each side, until golden brown. Serve with the lime wedges to squeeze over them.

Barbecued Prawns Energy 82kcal/345kJ; Protein 12g; Carbohydrate 3.5g, of which sugars 3.5g; Fat 2.3g, of which saturates 0.3g; Cholesterol 130mg; Calcium 59mg; Fibre 0.5g; Sodium 127mg.
Spicy Shrimp Satay Energy 220kcal/922kJ; Protein 27.1g; Carbohydrate 11.5g, of which sugars 1g; Fat 7.3g, of which saturates 1g; Cholesterol 151mg; Calcium 99mg; Fibre 1.5g; Sodium 249mg.

Chilli Satay Prawns

This delicious dish, inspired by Indonesian satay, combines mild peanuts, aromatic spices, fiery chilli, coconut milk and lemon juice in the spicy dip.

Serves 4 to 6

450g/1lb king prawns (jumbo shrimp), peeled and deveined
25ml/1½ tbsp vegetable oil

For the peanut sauce

25ml/1½ tbsp vegetable oil
15ml/1 tbsp chopped garlic
1 small onion, chopped
3–4 red chillies, seeded and chopped
3 kaffir lime leaves, torn
1 lemon grass stalk, bruised and chopped
5ml/1 tsp medium curry paste
250ml/8fl oz/1 cup coconut milk
1cm/½in piece cinnamon stick
75g/3oz/⅓ cup crunchy peanut butter
45ml/3 tbsp tamarind juice, made by mixing tamarind paste with warm water
30ml/2 tbsp Thai fish sauce
30ml/2 tbsp palm sugar (jaggery) or muscovado (brown) sugar
juice of ½ lemon

For the garnish

½ bunch fresh coriander (cilantro) leaves (optional)
4 fresh red chillies, finely sliced (optional)
spring onions (scallions), sliced

1 Make the peanut sauce. Heat half the oil in a wok or heavy frying pan. Add the garlic and onion and cook, stirring, for 3–4 minutes, until the mixture has softened but not browned.

2 Add the chillies, kaffir lime leaves, lemon grass and curry paste. Cook for 2–3 minutes, then stir in the coconut milk, cinnamon stick, peanut butter, tamarind juice, fish sauce, sugar and lemon juice. Bring to the boil, then reduce the heat to low and simmer gently for 15–20 minutes, until the sauce thickens.

3 Thread the prawns on to skewers and brush with a little oil. Cook under a preheated grill (broiler) for 2 minutes on each side until they turn pink and are firm to the touch. Alternatively, pan-fry the prawns, then thread on to skewers.

4 Remove the cinnamon from the sauce and discard. Arrange the prawns on a warmed platter, garnish with spring onions and coriander and red chillies, if liked, and serve with the sauce.

Fiery Stir-fried Prawns with Noodles

One of the most appealing aspects of Thai food is its appearance. Ingredients are carefully chosen so that each dish, even a simple stir-fry like this one, is balanced in terms of colour, texture and spicy flavour.

Serves 4

130g/4½oz rice noodles
30ml/2 tbsp groundnut (peanut) oil
1 large garlic clove, crushed
150g/5oz large prawns (shrimp), peeled and deveined
15g/½oz dried shrimp
1 piece mooli (daikon), about 75g/3oz, grated
15ml/1 tbsp Thai fish sauce
30ml/2 tbsp soy sauce
30ml/2 tbsp palm sugar (jaggery) or light muscovado (brown) sugar
30ml/2 tbsp fresh lime juice
90g/3½oz/1¾ cups beansprouts
40g/1½oz/⅓ cup peanuts, chopped
15ml/1 tbsp sesame oil
chopped coriander (cilantro), 5ml/1 tsp dried chilli flakes and 2 shallots, finely chopped, to garnish

1 Soak the noodles in a bowl of boiling water for 5 minutes, or according to the packet instructions. Heat the oil in a wok or large frying pan. Add the garlic, and stir-fry over a medium heat for 2–3 minutes, until golden brown.

2 Add the prawns, dried shrimp and grated mooli and stir-fry for a further 2 minutes. Stir in the fish sauce, soy sauce, sugar and lime juice.

3 Drain the noodles thoroughly, then snip them into smaller lengths with scissors. Add to the wok or pan with the beansprouts, peanuts and sesame oil. Toss to mix, then stir-fry for 2 minutes. Serve immediately, garnished with the coriander, chilli flakes and shallots.

Cook's Tip

Some cooks like to salt the mooli before using. Leave it to drain, then rinse in cold water and dry before grating in this recipe.

Satay Prawns Energy 321kcal/1340kJ; Protein 24.6g; Carbohydrate 13.5g, of which sugars 8.2g; Fat 13.3g, of which saturates 3.6g; Cholesterol 219mg; Calcium 52mg; Fibre 1.2g; Sodium 794mg.
Fiery Prawns Energy 312kcal/1299kJ; Protein 11.8g; Carbohydrate 35.8g, of which sugars 8.2g; Fat 13.3g, of which saturates 2.4g; Cholesterol 281mg; Calcium 52mg; Fibre 1.1g; Sodium 524mg.

Prawns and Courgettes in Turmeric and Chilli Sauce

This delicious, attractively coloured dish is popular in Indonesia and combines creamy coconut milk with vegetables and chilli.

Serves 4

1–2 chayotes or 2–3 courgettes (zucchini)
2 fresh red chillies, seeded
1 onion, quartered
5mm/¼in piece galangal, sliced
1 lemon grass stalk, lower 5cm/2in sliced, top bruised
2.5cm/1in piece fresh turmeric, peeled
200ml/7fl oz/scant 1 cup water
lemon juice
400ml/14fl oz can coconut milk
450g/1lb cooked, peeled prawns (shrimp)
salt
red chilli shreds, to garnish (optional)
boiled rice, to serve

1 Peel the chayotes, remove the seeds and cut into strips. If using courgettes, cut them into 5cm/2in strips.

2 Grind the fresh red chillies, onion, galangal, sliced lemon grass and the fresh turmeric to a paste in a food processor or with a mortar and pestle. Add the water to the paste mixture, with a squeeze of lemon juice and salt to taste.

3 Pour into a pan. Add the top of the lemon grass stem. Bring to the boil and cook for 1–2 minutes. Add the chayote or courgette pieces and cook for 2 minutes. Stir in the coconut milk. Taste and adjust the seasoning.

4 Stir in the prawns and cook gently for 2–3 minutes. Remove the lemon grass stem. Garnish with shreds of chilli, if using, and serve with rice.

Cook's Tip
Galangal belongs to the same family as root ginger and is prepared in the same way. In its raw form, it has a soapy, earthy aroma and a pine-like flavour with a faint hint of citrus. Look for it in Asian stores.

Chillied Prawns in Almond Sauce

Succulent spicy prawns are served on a bed of vegetables with a nutty, creamy sauce that has a delicious hint of fresh chilli.

Serves 4

450g/1lb raw king prawns (jumbo shrimp)
600ml/1 pint/2½ cups water
3 thin slices fresh root ginger
10ml/2 tsp curry powder
2 garlic cloves, crushed
15g/½ oz/1 tbsp butter or margarine
60ml/4 tbsp ground almonds
1 green chilli, seeded and finely chopped
45ml/3 tbsp single (light) cream
salt and ground black pepper

For the vegetables
15ml/1 tbsp mustard oil
15ml/1 tbsp vegetable oil
1 onion, sliced
½ red (bell) pepper, thinly sliced
½ green (bell) pepper, thinly sliced
1 chayote, peeled, stoned (pitted) and cut into strips
salt and ground black pepper

1 Shell the prawns and place the shells in a pan with the water and ginger. Simmer, uncovered, for 15 minutes until the liquid is reduced by half. Strain into a jug (pitcher) and discard the shells.

2 Devein the prawns, place in a bowl and season with the curry powder, garlic and salt and pepper and set aside.

3 Heat the mustard and vegetable oils in a large frying pan, add all the vegetables and cook for 5 minutes, stirring constantly. Season with salt and pepper, spoon into a serving dish and keep warm.

4 Wipe out the frying pan, then melt the butter or margarine and sauté the prawns for about 5 minutes until pink. Spoon over the bed of vegetables, cover and keep warm.

5 Add the ground almonds and chilli to the pan, stir-fry for a few seconds and then add the reserved stock and bring to the boil. Reduce the heat, stir in the cream and simmer for a few minutes, without boiling.

6 Pour the creamy sauce over the vegetables and prawns before serving.

Prawns and Courgettes Energy 162kcal/658kj; Protein 28g; Carbohydrate 10g; of which sugars 9g; Fat 2g; of which saturates 1g; Cholesterol 10mg; Calcium 182mg; Fibre 1.2g; Sodium 1.9mg.
Chillied Prawns Energy 301kcal/125kj; Protein 24.3g; Carbohydrate 6.1g; of which sugars 5.1g; Fat 20.1g; of which saturates 4.8g; Cholesterol 234mg; Calcium 154mg; Fibre 2.4g; Sodium 244mg.

King Prawn with Onion and Curry Leaves

This tasty dish combines deliciously spiced prawns with curry and fenugreek leaves.

Serves 4

3 medium onions
15ml/1 tbsp corn oil
6–8 curry leaves
1.5ml/¼ tsp onion seeds
1 green chilli, seeded and finely sliced
1 red chilli, seeded and thinly sliced
12–14 frozen cooked king prawns (jumbo shrimp), thawed and peeled
5ml/1 tsp shredded fresh root ginger
5ml/1 tsp salt
15ml/1 tbsp fresh fenugreek leaves

1 Halve the three onions and cut each of the halves crossways into thin slices.

2 Heat the oil in a wok or frying pan and fry the onion slices with the curry leaves and onion seeds for about 3 minutes, stirring constantly, until the onions have softened.

3 Add the green and red chillies, and stir-fry for 2–3 minutes. Add the prawns and continue cooking for a further 4–5 minutes until the prawns are nearly cooked.

4 Add the shredded ginger to the onions, chillies and prawns and cook, stirring for 1 minute. Season with the salt to taste.

5 Finally, add the fenugreek leaves, cover the pan and cook for a further 2–3 minutes before serving.

Cook's Tip

Fenugreek is native to Asia and southern Europe. This aromatic plant has pleasantly bitter, slightly sweet seeds commonly used in Asian cuisine. The leaves are used as a vegetable and lose their bitterness on cooking. The dried leaves are often used as a flavouring in pickles and marinades.

Red-hot Prawn and Fish Curry

Bengalis are famous for their spicy seafood dishes and always use mustard oil in recipes because it imparts a uniquely delicious taste, flavour and aroma. No feast in Bengal is complete without one of these celebrated fish dishes.

Serves 4 to 6

3 cloves garlic
5cm/2in piece fresh root ginger, peeled and roughly chopped
1 large leek, roughly chopped
4 green chillies, seeded and roughly chopped, plus two whole chillies, to garnish
60ml/4 tbsp mustard oil, or vegetable oil
15ml/1 tbsp ground coriander
2.5ml/½ tsp fennel seeds
15ml/1 tbsp crushed yellow mustard seeds, or 5ml/1 tsp mustard powder
175ml/6fl oz/¾ cup thick coconut milk
225g/8oz huss, skate blobs or monkfish, chopped into bitesize pieces
225g/8oz fresh king prawns (jumbo shrimp), peeled and deveined with tails intact
salt, to taste
115g/4oz fresh coriander (cilantro) leaves, chopped

1 In a food processor, grind the garlic, ginger, leek and chillies to a coarse paste.

2 In a frying pan, heat the mustard or vegetable oil with the paste until it is well blended. Keep the window open and take care not to overheat the mixture as any smoke from the mustard oil will sting the eyes.

3 Add the ground coriander, fennel seeds, mustard and coconut milk, stirring well until thoroughly combined. Gently bring the mixture to the boil and then simmer, uncovered, for about 5 minutes.

4 Add the fish pieces and simmer for 2–3 minutes, then fold in the prawns (shrimp). Cook over a medium heat until the prawns are cooked.

5 Season with salt to taste, fold in the chopped fresh coriander leaves and serve immediately, garnished with two whole green chillies.

King Prawns Energy 97kcal/403kJ; Protein 8.03g; Carbohydrate 9.38g, of which sugars 9.38g; Fat 3.29g, of which saturates 0.45g; Cholesterol 74mg; Calcium 68mg; Fibre 1.58g; Sodium 0.94mg.
Red-hot Prawn Curry Energy 166kcal/695kJ; Protein 15.2g; Carbohydrate 6.2g, of which sugars 3.3g; Fat 9.2g, of which saturates 1.2g; Cholesterol 78mg; Calcium 108mg; Fibre 2.4g; Sodium 120mg.

Yellow Prawn Curry

Colour is an important part of Indonesian food and the word *udang*, meaning 'yellow', is used to describe this delicious and attractive prawn dish. Big, juicy prawns are particularly favoured in Bali and Java, but you can easily substitute them with scallops, squid or mussels, or a combination of all three, depending on what you have available.

Serves 4

30ml/2 tbsp coconut or palm oil
2 shallots, finely chopped
2 garlic cloves, finely chopped
2 red chillies, seeded and finely chopped
25g/1oz fresh turmeric, finely chopped, or 10ml/2 tsp ground turmeric
25g/1oz fresh root ginger, finely chopped
2 lemon grass stalks, finely sliced
10ml/2 tsp coriander seeds
10ml/2 tsp shrimp paste
1 red (bell) pepper, seeded and finely sliced
4 kaffir lime leaves
about 500g/1¼lb fresh prawns (shrimp), shelled and deveined
400g/14oz can coconut milk
salt and ground black pepper
1 green chilli, seeded and sliced, to garnish

To serve

cooked rice
4 fried shallots or fresh chillies, seeded and sliced lengthways

1 Heat the oil in a wok or heavy frying pan. Stir in the shallots, garlic, chillies, turmeric, ginger, lemon grass and coriander seeds and fry until fragrant.

2 Stir in the shrimp paste and cook the mixture for 2–3 minutes. Add the red pepper and lime leaves and stir-fry for a further 1 minute.

3 Add the prawns to the pan. Pour in the coconut milk, stirring to combine, and bring to the boil. Cook for 5–6 minutes until the prawns are cooked. Season with salt and pepper to taste.

4 Spoon the prawns on to a warmed serving dish and sprinkle with the sliced green chillies to garnish. Serve with rice and fried shallots or the fresh chillies on the side.

Spicy Scallops with Mushrooms and Chillies

Fragrant steamed scallops are here given a spicy twist with shreds of chilli pepper. Tiny enoki mushrooms and strips of sautéed egg yolk match the elegant flavours of the seafood, and lemon zest and shredded seaweed are an attractive garnish.

Serves 2

5 scallops, with shells
30ml/2 tbsp vegetable oil
10ml/2 tsp sesame oil
2 egg yolks, beaten
1 sheet dried seaweed
1 red chilli, seeded and finely sliced
½ green (bell) pepper, finely sliced
65g/2½oz enoki mushrooms
salt and ground white pepper
grated rind of 1 lemon

1 Scrub the scallop shells. Cut the hinge muscles at the scallop's base. Lift off the rounded shell. Scrape away the beard-like fringe next to the white scallop with its orange coral, and remove the intestinal thread. Ease the scallop and coral away from the shell.

2 Heat 15ml/1 tbsp vegetable oil in a wok and stir-fry the scallops until browned. Season with sesame oil, salt and pepper.

3 Place the scallop shells into a pan of boiling water and drain. Add 10ml/2 tsp oil to the wok and heat over a low flame. Pour in the beaten egg yolks and add a pinch of salt. Cook to form a thin omelette. Once the omelette is set, remove from the pan and slice into strips.

4 Cut the seaweed into julienne strips. Add the chilli and pepper to the pan, adding oil if required, and stir-fry with a pinch of salt for 3–4 minutes.

5 Place the scallop shells in a steamer, and set one scallop on each shell. Place the pepper mixture, some omelette strips and some mushrooms on each shell, and steam for 4 minutes.

6 Garnish each scallop with the seaweed strips and a sprinkling of lemon rind, and serve immediately.

Yellow Prawn Curry Energy 230kcal/965kJ; Protein 26.4g; Carbohydrate 16g, of which sugars 13.5g; Fat 7.2g, of which saturates 1g; Cholesterol 263mg; Calcium 226mg; Fibre 2.7g; Sodium 519mg.
Spicy Scallops Energy 325kcal/1356kJ; Protein 27.2g; Carbohydrate 6.8g, of which sugars 3.1g; Fat 21.3g, of which saturates 3.8g; Cholesterol 249mg; Calcium 59mg; Fibre 1.2g; Sodium 193mg.

Chilli, Honey and Lemon Grilled Scallops

Scallops are found in the Mediterranean, the Atlantic and Pacific waters, and come in different varieties. They are available in most fish markets, so you can make this delicious fiery appetizer. If you buy queen scallops on the half shell, they will be ready to go on to the grill.

Serves 4 to 6
1 mild green chilli, seeded and finely chopped
½–1 Scotch bonnet or habanero chilli, seeded and finely chopped
1 small shallot, finely chopped
15ml/1 tbsp clear honey
60ml/4 tbsp olive oil
24 queen scallops on the half shell
salt
2 lemons, cut into thin wedges

1 Prepare the barbecue. While it is heating, mix the chillies, shallot, honey and oil together in a bowl.

2 Set out the scallops on a tray. Sprinkle each one with a pinch of salt, then top with a little of the chilli mixture.

3 Once the flames have died down on the barbecue, position a grill rack over the coals to heat. When the coals are medium-hot, or with a moderate coating of ash, place the scallops, on their half shells, on the grill rack.

4 Cook the scallops for 1½–2 minutes only. Cook as many as possible at once, moving them from the edge to the centre of the grill rack as necessary. Take care not to overcook them. Place on a serving platter. Serve with the lemon wedges.

Cook's Tip
The rich variety of chillies means that there will be a particular pepper to suit everyone's taste. Scotch bonnets and habanero chillies, used here, are very hot – they can be up to 50 times hotter than jalapeño peppers, so take extra care when using. Wear gloves while you chop them to avoid their oils irritating your skin, and ensure you do not rub your eyes after handling.

Hot, Sweet and Sour Squid

The Indonesians and Malays love cooking prawns and squid in this way, expertly crunching shells and sucking tentacles to savour all the juicy chilli and tamarind flavouring. Sweetened with the ubiquitous kecap manis, the cooking aroma emanating from these scrumptious squid will make you drool.

Serves 2 to 4
500g/1¼lb fresh baby squid
30ml/2 tbsp tamarind paste
30ml/2 tbsp chilli sauce
45ml/3 tbsp kecap manis (Indonesian sweet soy sauce)
juice of 1 kalamansi or ordinary lime
25g/1oz fresh root ginger, grated
1 small bunch fresh coriander (cilantro) leaves
2–4 green chillies, seeded and quartered lengthways
ground black pepper

To serve
fresh coriander (cilantro) leaves

1 Clean the squid and remove the head and ink sac. Pull out the backbone and rinse the body sac inside and out. Trim the head above the eyes, keeping the tentacle intact. Dry the body sac and tentacles on kitchen paper and discard the rest.

2 In a bowl, mix together the tamarind paste, chilli sauce, kecap manis and lime juice. Add the ginger and a little black pepper.

3 Spoon the mixture over the squid and rub it all over the body sacs and tentacles. Cover and chill for 1 hour.

4 Meanwhile, prepare the barbecue or heat a ridged griddle. Place the squid on the rack or griddle and cook for 3 minutes on each side, brushing them with the marinade as they cook. Serve immediately, with fresh coriander leaves.

Variation
To make hot, sweet and sour prawns (shrimp), devein the prawns and remove the feelers and legs, then rinse, pat dry, and make an incision along the tail. Marinate and cook in the same way as the squid.

Chilli Scallops Energy 159kcal/666kJ; Protein 15.9g; Carbohydrate 5.1g, of which sugars 1.9g; Fat 8.6g, of which saturates 1.4g; Cholesterol 31mg; Calcium 24mg; Fibre 0g; Sodium 121mg.
Sweet and Sour Squid Energy 110kcal/468kJ; Protein 20g; Carbohydrate 2.8g, of which sugars 1.1g; Fat 2.3g, of which saturates 0.5g; Cholesterol 281mg; Calcium 43mg; Fibre 0.6g; Sodium 943mg.

Prawn and Fish Spikes with Chilli Dip

Tolee molee are Burmese bits and pieces that accompany a main course. For this dish, bowls of herbs, crispy fried onions and *balachaung*, a wonderful chilli and prawn paste that comes in a jar, make ideal choices.

Makes 12

400g/14oz Mediterranean prawns (jumbo shrimp), peeled
225g/8oz skinned cod or halibut fillet, roughly cut into pieces
pinch of ground turmeric
1.5ml/¼ tsp ground white pepper
1.5ml/¼ tsp salt
60ml/4 tbsp chopped fresh coriander (cilantro)
1 red chilli, seeded and finely chopped
30ml/2 tbsp sunflower oil
a piece of sugar cane cut into 12 spikes or 12 wooden skewers

For the tolee molee

25g/1oz coriander (cilantro) leaves
45ml/3 tbsp olive oil
300g/11oz sweet onions, halved and finely sliced
90ml/6 tbsp balachaung
15ml/1 tbsp sugar
juice of ½ lime
30ml/2 tbsp water

1 Soak the sugar cane spikes or wooden skewers in water for 30 minutes. Make a shallow cut down the centre of the curved back of each prawn. Pull out the black vein and slice the prawns roughly. Place in a food processor with the fish, turmeric, pepper and salt. Blend the mixture to a paste. Add the coriander and chilli and blend. Spoon into a bowl and chill for 30 minutes.

2 Make the tolee molee. Place the coriander in a bowl filled with cold water. Chill. Heat the olive oil in a large frying pan and fry the onion for 10 minutes, stirring occasionally and increasing the heat for the last few minutes so that the onions become golden and crisp. Pile them into a serving bowl. Place the balachaung in a serving bowl. Mix the sugar, lime juice and measured water, stir into the balachaung and set aside.

3 Prepare the barbecue. Mould the seafood mixture around the sugar cane spikes or skewers into an oval sausage shape. Once the flames have died down, position a grill rack over the coals. When the coals are medium-hot, brush the seafood with the oil and grill for 3 minutes each side until cooked through. Serve with the tolee molee.

Marinated Octopus with Fiery Sauce

The red pipian sauce is made with ancho chilli, which is sweet and hot with a fruity aroma when cooked.

Serves 8

1kg/2¼lb whole octopus, cleaned and gutted
1 onion, quartered
2 bay leaves
30ml/2 tbsp olive oil
grated rind and juice of 1 lemon
15ml/1 tbsp chopped fresh coriander (cilantro)
fresh coriander (cilantro) sprigs, to garnish

For the red pipian

1 ancho chilli (dried poblano)
4 whole garlic cloves, peeled
1 small pink onion, chopped
500g/1¼lb plum tomatoes, cored and seeded
30ml/2 tbsp olive oil
5ml/1 tsp sugar
30ml/2 tbsp pine nuts
30ml/2 tbsp pumpkin seeds
pinch of ground cinnamon
15ml/1 tbsp smoky chilli sauce
45ml/3 tbsp vegetable stock
leaves from 4 large fresh thyme sprigs, finely chopped
salt

1 Preheat the oven to 200°C/400°F/Gas 6. Make the red pipian. Cover the chilli with hot water in a bowl. Leave for 20 minutes. Place the garlic, onion and tomatoes in a roasting pan and drizzle with oil, sprinkle over sugar and a little salt. Roast for 15 minutes.

2 Add the pine nuts, pumpkin seeds and cinnamon to the pan and roast for a further 5 minutes. Meanwhile, drain the chilli, discard the seeds and chop. Transfer the roasted mixture and the chilli to a food processor. Add the chilli sauce, stock and thyme. Blend to a paste, transfer to a bowl and leave to cool.

3 Place the octopus tentacles in a large pan, cover with cold water and add the onion and bay leaves. Bring to the boil, then simmer for up to 2 hours, checking frequently, until tender.

4 Drain and rinse the tentacles, then thread on to metal skewers and place in a dish. Add the olive oil, lemon rind and juice, and coriander. Mix well and marinate for 1 hour or overnight.

5 Prepare the barbecue. When the coals are medium-hot, grill the octopus skewers for 2–4 minutes on each side, or until golden. Serve with the red pipian, garnished with the coriander.

Prawn and Fish Spikes Energy 98kcal/409kJ; Protein 9.8g; Carbohydrate 3.5g, of which sugars 2.9g; Fat 5.1g, of which saturates 0.7g; Cholesterol 74mg; Calcium 51mg; Fibre 0.7g; Sodium 78mg.
Marinated Octopus Energy 149kcal/627kJ; Protein 23.2g; Carbohydrate 3.8g, of which sugars 3.4g; Fat 4.7g, of which saturates 0.8g; Cholesterol 60mg; Calcium 62mg; Fibre 1.2g; Sodium 8mg.

Chilli-stuffed Squid Kebabs

Preparing squid may seem tricky, but it is the best way to ensure that it is fresh. The tentacles are a tasty part of the squid so do skewer them as well.

Serves 6

12 squid, total weight 675g/1½lb
45ml/3 tbsp extra virgin olive oil, plus extra for coating
2 onions, finely chopped
3 garlic cloves, crushed
25g/1oz/2 tbsp walnuts, finely chopped
7.5ml/1½ tsp ground sumac or squeeze of lemon juice
1.5ml/¼ tsp chilli flakes, finely chopped
75–90g/3–3½oz rocket (arugula), any tough stalks removed
115g/4oz/1 cup cooked rice
salt and ground black pepper
lemon and lime wedges, to serve

1 Prepare the squid. Hold the body in one hand and grasp the tentacles at their base with the other. Pull away the head and entrails. Cut the tentacles (and part of the head above the eyes) away from the entrails. Snip out the hard beak in the middle of the tentacles and discard this, along with the entrails attached to the remainder of the head. Peel the membrane away from the body, then pull out the hard quill and discard. Wash the tentacles and body well under cold water. Put the tentacles on a plate and chill. Pull the flaps or wings away from the body, chop and set aside. Reserve the body and tentacles.

2 Heat a frying pan. Add the oil, onions and garlic and fry for 5 minutes, or until the onions are soft. Add the squid wings and fry for about 1 minute, then stir in the walnuts, sumac and chilli flakes. Add the rocket and stir-fry until it has wilted. Stir in the rice, season and transfer to a bowl to cool. If using wooden skewers, soak them in water for 30 minutes.

3 Prepare the barbecue. Stuff each squid with the cold mixture and thread two on to each skewer, with two clumps of tentacles. Toss in oil and salt. When the coals are medium-hot, or with a moderate coating of ash, grill the squid for 1½ minutes on each side. When pale golden, move them to a cooler part of the grill to cook for 1½ minutes more on each side to ensure the filling is hot. Baste with any remaining oil and salt mixture as they are turned. Serve with lemon and lime wedges.

Squid in Hot Yellow Sauce

Simple fishermen's dishes such as this one are cooked the length and breadth of Malaysia's coastline. This recipe from Sabah, the northernmost state in Malaysian Borneo, includes enough chillies to set your tongue on fire. To temper the heat, the dish is often served with the local staple, sago porridge, and finely shredded green mango tossed in lime juice.

Serves 4

500g/1¼lb fresh squid
juice of 2 limes
5ml/1 tsp salt
4 shallots, chopped
4 garlic cloves, chopped
25g/1oz galangal, chopped
25g/1oz fresh turmeric, chopped
6–8 red chillies, seeded and chopped
30ml/2 tbsp vegetable or groundnut (peanut) oil
7.5ml/1½ tsp palm sugar (jaggery)
2 lemon grass stalks, crushed
4 lime leaves
400ml/14fl oz/1⅔ cups coconut milk
salt and ground black pepper
crusty bread or steamed rice, to serve

1 First prepare the squid. Hold the body sac in one hand and pull off the head with the other. Sever the tentacles just above the eyes, and discard the rest of the head and innards. Clean the body sac inside and out and remove the skin. Pat the squid dry, cut it into thick slices and put them in a bowl, along with the tentacles. Mix the lime juice with the salt and rub it into the squid. Set aside for 30 minutes.

2 Meanwhile, using a mortar and pestle or food processor, grind the shallots, garlic, galangal, turmeric and chillies to a coarse paste.

3 Heat the oil in a wok or heavy pan, and stir in the coarse paste. Cook the paste until fragrant, then add the palm sugar, lemon grass and lime leaves. Drain the squid of any juice and toss it around the wok, coating it in the flavourings. Pour in the coconut milk and bring it to the boil. Reduce the heat and simmer for 5–10 minutes, until the squid is tender. Season with salt and pepper and serve with chunks of fresh, crusty bread or steamed rice.

Chilli-stuffed Squid Energy 129kcal/546kJ; Protein 18.3g; Carbohydrate 8.3g, of which sugars 0.8g; Fat 2.8g, of which saturates 0.6g; Cholesterol 253mg; Calcium 42mg; Fibre 0.4g; Sodium 142mg.
Squid in Yellow Sauce Energy 185kcal/780kJ; Protein 19.8g; Carbohydrate 9.4g, of which sugars 7.6g; Fat 8g, of which saturates 1.4g; Cholesterol 281mg; Calcium 50mg; Fibre 0.2g; Sodium 739mg.

Chargrilled Squid with Red Chilli and White Wine

The squid in this Spanish recipe, known as *calamares a la plancha* are traditionally cooked on the hot griddle that is an essential part of every Spanish kitchen. The method is fast and simple and really brings out the flavour of the squid. This dish is an ideal first course for four people, or can be served on a bed of rice as a main dish for two.

Serves 2 to 4

2 whole cleaned squid, with tentacles, about 275g/10oz each
75ml/5 tbsp olive oil
30ml/2 tbsp sherry vinegar
2 fresh red chillies, finely chopped
60ml/4 tbsp dry white wine
salt and ground black pepper
hot cooked rice, to serve (optional)
15–30ml/1–2 tbsp chopped parsley, to garnish

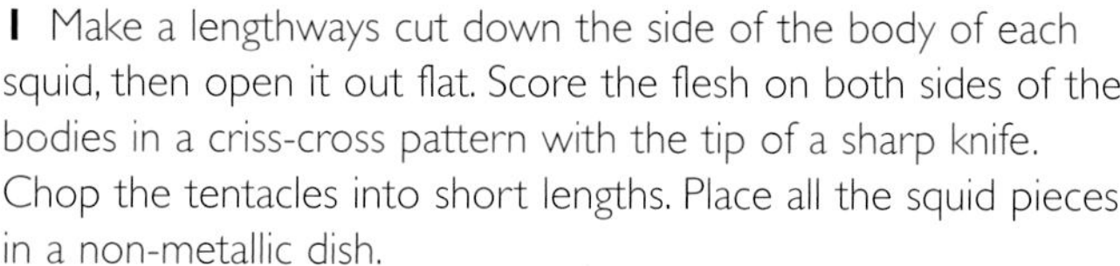

1 Make a lengthways cut down the side of the body of each squid, then open it out flat. Score the flesh on both sides of the bodies in a criss-cross pattern with the tip of a sharp knife. Chop the tentacles into short lengths. Place all the squid pieces in a non-metallic dish.

2 Whisk together the oil and vinegar in a small bowl until well combined. Season with salt and pepper to taste, pour over the squid and toss to mix. Cover the bowl and set aside to marinate for about 1 hour.

3 Heat a ridged griddle pan until hot. Add the body of one of the squid and cook over a medium heat for 2–3 minutes, pressing the squid down on to the ridges with a metal spatula to keep it flat. Repeat on the other side. Cook the other squid body in the same way.

4 Slice the bodies of the squid into diagonal strips. If serving with rice, arrange the strips over the rice and keep warm.

5 Add the chopped tentacles and chillies to the pan and toss over a medium heat for about 2–3 minutes. Stir in the white wine, then drizzle over the squid. Garnish with the parsley.

Saigon Shellfish Curry

There are many variations of this tasty curry all over the south of Vietnam. This recipe is made with prawns, squid and scallops but you could use any combination of shellfish, or even add chunks of filleted fish.

Serves 4

4cm/1½in fresh root ginger, peeled and roughly chopped
2–3 garlic cloves, roughly chopped
45ml/3 tbsp groundnut (peanut) oil
1 onion, finely sliced
2 lemon grass stalks, finely sliced
2 green or red Thai chillies, seeded and finely sliced
15ml/1 tbsp raw cane sugar
10ml/2 tsp shrimp paste
15ml/1 tbsp Thai fish sauce
30ml/2 tbsp curry powder or garam masala
550ml/18fl oz can coconut milk
juice and rind of 1 lime
4 medium squid, cleaned and cut diagonally into 3 or 4 pieces
12 king or queen scallops, shelled
20 raw prawns (shrimp), shelled and deveined
1 small bunch of fresh basil, stalks removed
1 small bunch of fresh coriander (cilantro), stalks removed, leaves finely chopped, to garnish
salt

1 Using a mortar and pestle, grind the ginger with the garlic until it almost resembles a paste. Heat the oil in a traditional clay pot, wok or heavy pan and stir in the onion. Cook until it begins to turn brown, then stir in the garlic and ginger paste.

2 Once the aromas begin to lift from the pot, add the lemon grass, chillies and sugar. Cook for 2 minutes before adding the shrimp paste, fish sauce and curry powder or garam masala. Stir the mixture well and allow the flavours to mingle and combine over the heat for 1–2 minutes.

3 Add the coconut milk, lime juice and rind. Mix well and bring the liquid to the boil. Simmer for 2–3 minutes. Season to taste with salt.

4 Gently stir in the squid, scallops and prawns. Bring the liquid to the boil once more. Reduce the heat and cook gently until the shellfish turns opaque. Add the basil leaves and sprinkle the coriander over the top. Serve immediately from the pot into individual bowls.

Squid with Chilli Energy 258kcal/1076kJ; Protein 23.5g; Carbohydrate 2g, of which sugars 0.2g; Fat 16.4g, of which saturates 2.6g; Cholesterol 338mg; Calcium 25mg; Fibre 0g; Sodium 167mg.
Saigon Shellfish Curry Energy 528kcal/2225kJ; Protein 68g; Carbohydrate 24g, of which sugars 14g; Fat 18g, of which saturates 4g; Cholesterol 699mg; Calcium 250mg; Fibre 2.5g; Sodium 1.3mg.

Chilli Crab and Tofu Stir-fry

For a light healthy meal, this speedy stir-fry is the ideal choice. The silken tofu has a fairly bland taste on its own but is excellent for absorbing all the delicious flavours of this dish – the crab meat, garlic, chillies, spring onions and soy sauce.

Serves 2

250g/9oz silken tofu
60ml/4 tbsp vegetable oil
2 garlic cloves, finely chopped
115g/4oz white crab meat
130g/4½oz/generous 1 cup baby corn, halved lengthways
2 spring onions (scallions), chopped
1 fresh red chilli, seeded and finely chopped
30ml/2 tbsp soy sauce
15ml/1 tbsp Thai fish sauce
5ml/1 tsp palm sugar (jaggery) or light muscovado (brown) sugar
juice of 1 lime
small bunch fresh coriander (cilantro), chopped, to garnish

1 Using a sharp knife, cut the silken tofu into 1cm/½in cubes.

2 Heat the oil in a wok or large, heavy frying pan. Add the tofu cubes and stir-fry until they are golden all over, taking care not to break them up while cooking. Remove from the pan with a slotted spoon and set aside.

3 Add the garlic to the wok or pan and stir-fry until just golden. Ensure that it doesn't burn otherwise it will have a slightly bitter taste.

4 Add the crab meat, tofu, corn, spring onions, chilli, soy sauce, fish sauce and sugar to the pan. Cook, stirring constantly, until the vegetables are just tender.

5 Stir in the lime juice, transfer to warmed bowls, sprinkle with the coriander and serve immediately.

Cook's Tip
This is a very economical dish to prepare as you only need a small amount of crab meat. The canned variety could also be used in this recipe, which would make it even cheaper.

Lobster and Crab Steamed in Beer and Hot Spices

Depending on the size and availability of the lobsters and crabs, you can make this delicious spicy dish for as many people as you like, because the quantities are simple to adjust.

Serves 4

4 uncooked lobsters, about 450g/1lb each
4–8 uncooked crabs, about 225g/8oz each
about 600ml/1 pint/2½ cups beer
4 spring onions (scallions), trimmed and chopped into long pieces
4cm/1½in fresh root ginger, peeled and finely sliced
2 green or red Thai chillies, seeded and finely sliced
3 lemon grass stalks, finely sliced
1 bunch of fresh dill, fronds chopped
1 bunch each of fresh basil and coriander (cilantro), stalks removed, leaves chopped
about 30ml/2 tbsp Thai fish sauce, plus extra for serving
juice of 1 lemon
salt and ground black pepper

1 Clean the lobsters and crabs well and rub them with salt and pepper. Place half of them in a large steamer and pour the beer into the base. Sprinkle half the spring onions, ginger, chillies, lemon grass and herbs over the lobsters and crabs, and steam for 10 minutes, or until the lobsters turn red. Lift them on to a serving dish. Cook the remaining half in the same way.

2 Add the lemon grass, herbs and fish sauce to the simmering beer, stir in the lemon juice, then pour into a dipping bowl. Serve the shellfish hot, dipping the lobster and crab meat into the broth and adding extra splashes of fish sauce, if you like.

Cook's Tip
Whether you cook the lobsters and crabs at the same time depends on the number of people you are cooking for and the size of your steamer. However, they don't take long to cook so it is easy to steam them in batches.

Crab Stir-fry Energy 370kcal/1532kJ; Protein 23.3g; Carbohydrate 6.2g, of which sugars 5.1g; Fat 28.1g, of which saturates 1g; Cholesterol 210mg; Calcium 185mg; Fibre 1.2g; Sodium 2487mg.
Lobster and Crab Energy 264kcal/1112kJ; Protein 48g; Carbohydrate 4g, of which sugars 1g; Fat 7g, of which saturates 1g; Cholesterol 210mg; Calcium 185mg; Fibre 0.5g; Sodium 1.3mg.

Fiery Octopus in Chilli Sauce

Here octopus is stir-fried to give it a rich meaty texture, then smothered in a fiery chilli sauce. The dish combines the deliciously charred octopus flavour with the spiciness from the gochujang – the Korean chilli paste – and the zing of jalapeño chillies. Serve with steamed rice and a bowl of soup.

Serves 2

2 small octopuses, cleaned and gutted
15ml/1 tbsp vegetable oil
½ onion, sliced 5mm/¼in thick
¼ carrot, thinly sliced
½ leek, thinly sliced
75g/3oz jalapeño chillies, trimmed
2 garlic cloves, crushed
10ml/2 tsp Korean chilli powder
5ml/1 tsp dark soy sauce
45ml/3 tbsp gochujang chilli paste
30ml/2 tbsp mirin or rice wine
15ml/1 tbsp maple syrup
sesame oil and sesame seeds, to garnish

1 First blanch the octopuses in boiling water to soften slightly. Drain well, and cut into pieces approximately 5cm/2in long.

2 Heat the oil in a large frying pan over a medium-high heat and add the onion, carrot, leek and jalapeño chillies. Stir-fry for 3 minutes.

3 Add the octopus and garlic, and sprinkle over the chilli powder. Stir-fry for 3–4 minutes, or until the octopus is tender. Add the soy sauce, gochujang paste, mirin or rice wine, and maple syrup. Mix well and stir-fry for 1 minute more.

4 Transfer to a serving platter, and garnish with a drizzle of sesame oil and a sprinkling of sesame seeds.

Cook's Tips

- *If the taste is too fiery mix some softened vermicelli noodles in with the stir-fry to dilute the chilli paste.*
- *To make the octopus more tender, knead it with a handful of plain (all-purpose) flour and rinse in salted water.*

Braised Octopus with Paprika and Chilli

This delicious spicy octopus dish is ideal to make in advance because octopus can be tough, and benefits from long cooking to tenderize it. Make as an appetizer or increase the portions for a main course.

Serves 4 to 6

1kg/2¼lb octopus, cleaned
45ml/3 tbsp olive oil
1 large red onion, chopped
3 garlic cloves, finely chopped
30ml/2 tbsp brandy
300ml/½ pint/1¼ cups dry white wine
800g/1¾lb plum tomatoes, peeled and chopped or 2 X 400g/14oz cans chopped tomatoes
1 dried red chilli, seeded and chopped
1.5ml/¼ tsp paprika
450g/1lb small new potatoes
15ml/1 tbsp chopped fresh rosemary, extra sprigs to garnish
15ml/1 tbsp fresh thyme leaves
1.2 litres/2 pints/5 cups fish stock
30ml/2 tbsp chopped fresh flat leaf parsley leaves
salt and ground black pepper
salad leaves and French bread, to serve

1 Cut the octopus into large pieces, put in a pan and pour over cold water to cover. Season with salt, bring to the boil, then simmer for 30 minutes to tenderize. Drain and cut into pieces.

2 Heat the oil in a large shallow pan. Fry the onion until lightly coloured, then add the garlic and fry for 1 minute. Add the octopus and fry for 2–3 minutes, stirring, until coloured.

3 Pour the brandy over the octopus and ignite it. When the flames have died down, add the wine, bring to the boil and then simmer for about 5 minutes. Stir in the tomatoes, with the chilli and paprika. Add the potatoes and herbs. Simmer for 5 minutes.

4 Pour in the fish stock and season. Cover and simmer for 20–30 minutes, stirring occasionally, until the octopus and potatoes are tender and the sauce has thickened slightly.

5 To serve, check the seasoning and stir in the parsley. Garnish with rosemary and accompany with salad and bread.

Fiery Octopus Energy 235kcal/988kJ; Protein 28.6g; Carbohydrate 13.2g, of which sugars 11.9g; Fat 8g, of which saturates 1.2g; Cholesterol 72mg; Calcium 76mg; Fibre 2.4g; Sodium 204mg.
Braised Octopus Energy 328kcal/1381kJ; Protein 33g; Carbohydrate 20.7g, of which sugars 8.4g; Fat 8.5g, of which saturates 1.5g; Cholesterol 80mg; Calcium 103mg; Fibre 3.2g; Sodium 27mg.

Sea Bass in Vine Leaves with Hot Chilli

This spicy dish is effortless but must be started in advance as the rice needs to be cold before it is used in the little parcels. Once the fish are wrapped, all you have to do is keep them chilled, ready to pop on to the barbecue.

Serves 8 as a first course; 4 as a main course

90g/3½oz/½ cup Chinese black rice
400ml/14fl oz/1⅔ cups boiling water
45ml/3 tbsp extra virgin olive oil
1 small onion, chopped
1 fresh mild chilli, seeded and finely chopped
8 sea bass fillets, about 75g/3oz each, with skin
16 large fresh vine leaves
salt and ground black pepper

1 Place the rice in a pan. Add the boiling water and simmer for about 5 minutes. Add salt to taste and simmer for a further 10 minutes, or until tender. Drain and transfer to a bowl.

2 Meanwhile, heat half the oil in a frying pan. Fry the onion for 5 minutes until softened. Add the chilli. Stir into the rice mixture, adjust the seasoning and cool. Cover and chill until needed.

3 Season the sea bass fillets. Wash the vine leaves in water, then pat dry with kitchen paper. Lay each leaf in the centre of a double layer of foil. Top with a sea bass fillet. Divide the rice mixture among the fillets, spooning it towards one end. Fold the fillet over the rice, trickle over the remaining oil, lay the second vine leaf on top and bring the foil up around the fish and scrunch together to seal. Chill for up to 3 hours, or until needed.

4 Prepare the barbecue. When the coals are hot, or with a light coating of ash, place the parcels on the edge of a grill rack. Cook for 5 minutes, turning them around 90 degrees halfway through. Open up the top of the foil a little and cook for 2 minutes more. Gently remove from the foil and transfer the vine parcels to individual plates and serve.

Spicy Steamed Trout Fillets

Steaming fish in banana leaves over hot charcoal is a very traditional jungle method for cooking freshwater fish. Banana leaves are large and tough, and serve as basic cooking vessels and wrappers for all sorts of fish and meat. Here, the fish is cooked in six layers of leaves, allowing for the outer ones to burn. For this simple yet extremely tasty dish, with its tangy marinade of onions, chillies and fish sauce, you could use trout, any of the catfish or carp family, or even tilapia.

Serves 4

350g/12oz freshwater fish fillets, such as trout, cut into bitesize chunks
6 banana leaves
vegetable oil, for brushing
sticky rice, noodles or salad, to serve

For the marinade

2 shallots
5cm/2in turmeric root, grated
2 spring onions (scallions), finely sliced
2 garlic cloves, crushed
1–2 green Thai chillies, seeded and finely chopped
15ml/1 tbsp Thai fish sauce
2.5ml/½ tsp raw cane sugar
salt and ground black pepper

1 To make the marinade, grate the shallots into a bowl, then combine with the other marinade ingredients, seasoning with salt and pepper. Toss the chunks of fish in the marinade, making sure they are well coated, then cover and chill for at least 6 hours, or overnight if possible.

2 Prepare a barbecue. Place one of the banana leaves on a flat surface and brush it with oil. Tip the marinated fish on to the banana leaf, spreading it out evenly, then fold over the sides to form an envelope. Place this envelope, fold side down, on top of another leaf and fold that one in the same manner. Repeat with the remaining leaves until they are all used up. Secure the last layer of banana leaves with a piece of bendy wire.

3 Place the banana leaf packet on the barbecue. Cook for about 20 minutes, turning it over from time to time to make sure it is cooked on both sides – the outer leaves will burn. Carefully untie the wire (it will be hot) and unravel the banana leaf packet, then serve the fish with sticky rice, noodles or salad.

Sea Bass Energy 160kcal/669kJ; Protein 16.8g; Carbohydrate 8.7g, of which sugars 1.1g; Fat 6.4g, of which saturates 1g; Cholesterol 65mg; Calcium 120mg; Fibre 0.4g; Sodium 57mg.
Spicy Trout Fillets Energy 155kcal/648kJ; Protein 18g; Carbohydrate 4g, of which sugars 2g; Fat 8g, of which saturates 1g; Cholesterol 59mg; Calcium 36mg; Fibre 0.7g; Sodium 200mg.

Chargrilled Fish with a Fiery Sambal

A fiery sambal is the perfect complement to succulently grilled fish.

Serves 4

30ml/2 tbsp coconut oil
60ml/4 tbsp dark soy sauce
2 garlic cloves, crushed
juice of 1 lime
1 whole sea fish, such as grouper, red snapper, or sea bass, or 4 whole smaller fish, such as sardines, gutted and cleaned
cooked rice, to serve

For the sambal

50g/2oz tamarind paste
150ml/¼ pint/⅔ cup boiling water
4 shallots, chopped
4 garlic cloves, chopped
5 red chillies, seeded and chopped
25g/1oz galangal, chopped
2 kaffir lime leaves, crumbled
10ml/2 tsp shrimp paste
10ml/2 tsp palm sugar (jaggery)
30ml/2 tbsp coconut or palm oil

1 In a small bowl, mix the coconut oil, soy sauce, garlic and lime juice together. Put the fish in a shallow dish and slash the flesh at intervals with a sharp knife. Spoon over the marinade and rub it into the skin and slashes. Leave for about 1 hour.

2 Meanwhile, make the sambal. Put the tamarind paste in a bowl, pour over the water and leave to soak for 30 minutes. Strain into a separate bowl, pressing the paste through a sieve (strainer). Discard the solids and put the tamarind juice aside.

3 Using a mortar and pestle, pound the shallots, garlic, chillies, galangal and lime leaves to a coarse paste. Add the shrimp paste and sugar and beat together until combined.

4 Heat the oil in a small wok, stir in the paste and fry for 2–3 minutes. Stir in the tamarind juice and boil until it reduces to a thick paste. Turn into a serving bowl.

5 Prepare the barbecue. Place the fish on the grill (broiler) and cook for 5 minutes each side, depending on the size of fish, basting it with any leftover marinade. Transfer the fish to a serving plate and serve with the sambal and boiled rice.

Chargrilled Swordfish with Chilli and Lime Sauce

Swordfish is excellent for the barbecue, as long as it is not overcooked. It tastes wonderful with a spicy sauce whose fire is tempered with crème fraîche.

Serves 4

2 fresh serrano chillies
4 tomatoes
45ml/3 tbsp olive oil
grated rind and juice of 1 lime
4 swordfish steaks
2.5ml/½ tsp salt
2.5ml/½ tsp ground black pepper
175ml/6fl oz/¾ cup crème fraîche
fresh flat leaf parsley, to garnish

1 Roast the serrano chillies in a dry griddle pan until the skins are blistered. Cool slightly, then put in a strong plastic bag and tie the top. Set aside for 20 minutes, then peel off the skins. Cut off the stalks, then slit the chillies, scrape out the seeds and slice the flesh.

2 Cut a cross in the base of each tomato. Place them in a heatproof bowl and pour over enough boiling water to cover. After 3 minutes, lift the tomatoes out using a slotted spoon and plunge them briefly into another bowl filled with cold water. Drain the tomatoes. Their skins will have begun to peel back from the crosses. Remove all the skin from the tomatoes, then cut them in half and squeeze out the seeds. Chop the flesh into 1cm/½in pieces.

3 Heat 15ml/1 tbsp of the olive oil in a small pan and add the strips of chilli, with the lime rind and juice. Cook the mixture for 2–3 minutes, then stir in the chopped tomatoes. Cook for 10 minutes, stirring the mixture occasionally, until the tomato has turned pulpy.

4 Brush the swordfish steaks with olive oil and season. Barbecue or grill (broil) for 3–4 minutes or until just cooked, turning once. Meanwhile, stir the crème fraîche into the sauce, heat it through gently and pour over the swordfish steaks. Serve garnished with fresh parsley.

Chargrilled Fish Energy 359kcal/1507kJ; Protein 42.3g; Carbohydrate 11.8g, of which sugars 9.3g; Fat 16.4g, of which saturates 2.3g; Cholesterol 75mg; Calcium 117mg; Fibre 1.4g; Sodium 1263mg.
Chargrilled Swordfish Energy 420kcal/1746kJ; Protein 29g; Carbohydrate 4g; of which sugars 4g; Fat 32g; of which saturates 14g; Cholesterol 111mg; Calcium 39mg; Fibre 0.9g; Sodium 500mg.

Seared Tuna with Ginger, Chilli and Watercress Salad

Tuna steaks are wonderful seared and served slightly rare with a punchy spicy sauce or salad. In this recipe the salad is served just warm as a bed for the tender tuna. Add a dab of harissa as a condiment to create a dish that will transport you to the warmth of the North African coastline.

Serves 4
30ml/2 tbsp olive oil
5ml/1 tsp harissa
5ml/1 tsp clear honey
4 X 200g/7oz tuna steaks
salt and ground black pepper
lemon wedges, to serve

For the salad
30ml/2 tbsp olive oil
a little butter
25g/1oz fresh root ginger, peeled and finely sliced
2 garlic cloves, finely sliced
2 green chillies, seeded and sliced
6 spring onions (scallions), cut into bitesize pieces
2 large handfuls of watercress
juice of ½ lemon

1 Mix the olive oil, harissa, honey and salt, and rub it over the tuna. Heat a little oil in a frying pan and sear the tuna steaks for 2 minutes on each side. They should still be pink inside.

2 Keep the tuna warm while you prepare the salad: heat the olive oil and butter in a pan. Add the ginger, garlic, chillies and spring onions, cook for a few minutes, then add the watercress. When the watercress begins to wilt, toss in the lemon juice and season well with salt and black pepper.

3 Tip the warm salad on to a serving dish or individual plates. Slice the tuna steaks and arrange on top of the salad. Serve immediately with lemon wedges for squeezing over.

Variation
Prawns (shrimp) and scallops can be cooked in the same way. The shellfish will just need to be cooked through briefly – too long and they will become rubbery.

Spicy Swordfish and Green Chilli Tacos

It is important not to overcook swordfish, or it can be tough and dry. Cooked correctly, however, it is absolutely delicious and makes a great change from beef or chicken as a spicy filling for a taco.

Serves 6
3 swordfish steaks
30ml/2 tbsp vegetable oil
2 garlic cloves, crushed
1 small onion, chopped
3 fresh green chillies, seeded and chopped
3 tomatoes
small bunch of fresh coriander (cilantro), chopped
6 fresh corn tortillas
½ iceberg lettuce, shredded
salt and ground black pepper
lemon wedges, to serve (optional)

1 Preheat the grill (broiler). Put the swordfish on an oiled rack over a grill pan and grill (broil) for 2–3 minutes on each side. When cool enough to handle, remove the skin and flake the fish into a bowl.

2 Heat the vegetable oil in a pan. Add the garlic, onion and chillies and fry for 5 minutes, or until the onion has turned soft and translucent.

3 Cut a cross in the base of each tomato, place in a heatproof bowl and pour over boiling water. After 3 minutes plunge the tomatoes into another bowl of cold water. Drain the tomatoes. Their skins will have begun to peel back from the crosses. Remove the skins, halve the tomatoes and cut out the seeds. Chop the flesh into 1cm/½in dice.

4 Add the tomatoes and swordfish to the onion mixture. Cook for 5 minutes over a low heat. Add the coriander and cook for 1–2 minutes. Season to taste.

5 Wrap the tortillas in foil and steam on a plate over a pan of boiling water until they are heated through and pliable. Place some shredded lettuce and fish mixture on to each tortilla. Fold in half, covering the filling, and serve with lemon wedges, if liked.

Seared Tuna Energy 383kcal/1604kJ; Protein 48.1g; Carbohydrate 2g, of which sugars 2g; Fat 20.4g, of which saturates 4g; Cholesterol 56mg; Calcium 59mg; Fibre 0.4g; Sodium 102mg.
Swordfish Tacos Energy 357kcal/1507kJ; Protein 32g; Carbohydrate 36g, of which sugars 3g; Fat 11g, of which saturates 2g; Cholesterol 105mg; Calcium 80mg; Fibre 2.1g; Sodium 400mg.

Fish in Spiced Tomato Herb Sauce

This is a traditional Jewish dish. The spicing is refreshing in the sultry heat of the Middle East and is very popular with Israelis. Serve this dish with flat breads such as pitta or matzos, and a refreshing salad.

Serves 8

300ml/½ pint/1¼ cups passata (bottled strained tomatoes)
150ml/¼ pint/⅔ cup fish stock
1 large onion, chopped
60ml/4 tbsp chopped fresh coriander (cilantro) leaves
60ml/4 tbsp chopped fresh parsley
5–8 garlic cloves, crushed
chopped fresh chilli or chilli paste, to taste
large pinch of ground ginger
large pinch of curry powder
1.5ml/¼ tsp ground cumin
1.5ml/¼ tsp ground turmeric
seeds from 2–3 cardamom pods
juice of 2 lemons, plus extra if needed
30ml/2 tbsp vegetable or olive oil
1.5kg/3¼lb mixed white fish fillets
salt and ground black pepper

1 Put the passata, fish stock, onion, coriander, parsley, garlic, chilli, ginger, curry powder, cumin, turmeric, cardamom, lemon juice and oil in a pan. Bring the mixture to the boil.

2 Remove the pan from the heat and add the fish fillets to the hot sauce. Return the pan to the heat and briefly bring the sauce to the boil again. Reduce the heat and simmer very gently for about 5 minutes, or until the fish fillets are all cooked. (Use a fork to test if the fish is tender. If the flesh flakes away easily, then it is cooked.)

3 Taste the sauce and adjust the seasoning, adding more lemon juice if necessary. Serve hot or warm.

Variations

- *This dish is just as delicious using only one type of fish, such as cod or flounder.*
- *Instead of poaching the fish, wrap each piece in puff pastry and bake at 190°C/375°F/Gas 5 for 20 minutes, then serve with the tomato sauce.*

Catfish with a Chilli Coconut Sauce

In this popular Indonesian dish, fish is fried and served with a fragrant and spicy sauce. Serve with rice and pickled vegetables or a green mango or papaya salad.

Serves 4

200ml/7fl oz/scant 1 cup coconut milk
30–45ml/2–3 tbsp coconut cream
30–45ml/2–3 tbsp rice flour, tapioca flour or cornflour (cornstarch)
5–10ml/1–2 tsp ground coriander
8 fresh catfish fillets
30–45ml/2–3 tbsp coconut, palm groundnut (peanut) or corn oil
salt and ground black pepper
1 lime, quartered, to serve

For the spice paste

2 shallots, chopped
2 garlic cloves, chopped
2–3 red chillies, seeded and chopped
25g/1oz galangal, chopped
15g/½ oz fresh turmeric, chopped, or 2.5ml/½ tsp ground turmeric
2–3 lemon grass stalks, chopped
15–30ml/1–2 tbsp palm or groundnut (peanut) oil
5ml/1 tsp shrimp paste
15ml/1 tbsp tamarind paste
5ml/1 tsp palm sugar (jaggery)

1 Make the paste. Using a mortar and pestle, pound the shallots, garlic, chillies, galangal, turmeric and lemon grass to a paste.

2 Heat the oil in a wok or heavy pan, stir in the paste and fry until it is fragrant and begins to colour. Add the shrimp and tamarind pastes and sugar and stir until the mixture darkens.

3 Stir the coconut milk and cream into the paste and boil for 10 minutes, until the milk and cream separate, leaving behind an oily paste. Season the sauce with salt and pepper to taste.

4 Meanwhile, mix the flour with the coriander on a plate and season. Toss the catfish fillets in the flour until lightly coated.

5 Heat the oil in a heavy frying pan and quickly fry the fillets for about 2 minutes on each side, until golden brown.

6 Transfer the catfish fillets to a warmed serving dish and serve with the spicy coconut sauce and wedges of lime to squeeze over the fish.

Fish in Spiced Sauce Energy 191kcal/803kJ; Protein 40.3g; Carbohydrate 18.5g, of which sugars 5.9g; Fat 95.3g, of which saturates 8.9g; Cholesterol 0mg; Calcium 170mg; Fibre 1.7g; Sodium 471mg.
Catfish Energy 338kcal/1412kJ; Protein 38.1g; Carbohydrate 11.9g, of which sugars 4.9g; Fat 15.3g, of which saturates 5.7g; Cholesterol 92mg; Calcium 56mg; Fibre 0.9g; Sodium 190mg.

Monkfish with Pimiento Sauce

This Spanish recipe comes from Rioja country, where a special horned red pepper grows and is used to make a spicy sauce. Here, red peppers are used with a little chilli, while cream makes a mellow pink sauce. To drink, choose a Marques de Cáceres white Rioja.

Serves 4

2 large red (bell) peppers
1kg/2¼lb monkfish tail, skinned
plain (all-purpose) flour, for dusting
30ml/2 tbsp olive oil
25g/1oz/2 tbsp butter
120ml/4fl oz/½ cup white Rioja or dry vermouth
½ dried chilli, seeded and chopped
8 raw prawns (shrimp), in the shell
150ml/¼ pint/⅔ cup double (heavy) cream
salt and ground black pepper
fresh flat leaf parsley, to garnish

1 Preheat the grill (broiler) to high and cook the peppers for 8–12 minutes, turning occasionally, until they are soft, and the skins blackened. Leave, covered, until they are cool enough to handle. Skin and discard the stalks and seeds. Transfer the flesh to a food processor or blender, strain in the juices and purée to a smooth sauce.

2 Cut the monkfish into eight steaks. (Remove bone and freeze for stock.) Season well and dust with flour.

3 Heat the oil and butter in a large frying pan and fry the fish for 3 minutes on each side. Remove to a warm dish.

4 Add the wine or vermouth and chilli to the pan and stir to deglaze the pan. Add the prawns, cook them briefly, then lift out and reserve.

5 Boil the sauce to reduce by half, then strain into a small jug (pitcher). Add the cream to the pan and boil briefly to reduce. Return the sauce to the pan, stir in the peppers and check the seasonings. Adjust to taste with salt and ground black pepper. Pour the sauce over the fish and serve garnished with the cooked prawns and parsley.

Sardines in Spicy Coconut Milk

A deliciously spiced fish dish based on coconut milk. This dish is particularly fiery but its heat is tempered by the inclusion of herbs.

Serves 4

6–8 red chillies, according to taste, seeded and chopped
4 shallots, chopped
4 garlic cloves, chopped
1 lemon grass stalk, chopped
25g/1oz galangal, chopped
30ml/2 tbsp coconut or palm oil
10ml/2 tsp coriander seeds
5ml/1 tsp cumin seeds
5ml/1 tsp fennel seeds
1 small bunch fresh mint leaves, finely chopped
1 small bunch fresh flat leaf parsley, finely chopped
15ml/1 tbsp palm sugar (jaggery)
15ml/1 tbsp tamarind paste
4 sardines or small mackerel, gutted, but kept whole
300ml/½ pint/1¼ cups coconut milk
salt and ground black pepper
steamed rice, 1 large bunch fresh flat leaf parsley and fresh basil leaves, to serve

1 Using a mortar and pestle, pound the chillies, shallots, garlic, lemon grass and galangal to a paste.

2 Heat the oil in a wok or wide, heavy pan, stir in the coriander, cumin and fennel seeds and fry until they give off a fragrant aroma. Add the spicy paste and stir until it becomes golden in colour. Add the chopped mint and parsley and stir for about 1 minute, then add the sugar and tamarind paste.

3 Carefully place the fish in the pan and toss gently to coat it thoroughly in the paste. Pour in the coconut milk and stir gently. Bring to the boil, then reduce the heat and simmer the mixture for 10–15 minutes, until the fish is tender when flaked using a fork. Season the sauce with salt and ground black pepper to taste.

4 Cover the bottom of a warmed serving dish with sprigs of flat leaf parsley and place the fish on top, then spoon the sauce over the top. Serve with a bowl of steamed rice or sago and extra stalks of fresh parsley and basil leaves to cut the spice.

Monkfish Energy 500kcal/208kJ; Protein 49.7g; Carbohydrate 7.2g, of which sugars 6.9g; Fat 27.1g, of which saturates 13.7g; Cholesterol 140mg; Calcium 70mg; Fibre 1.4g; Sodium 113mg.
Sardines with Herbs Energy 287kcal/1199kJ; Protein 22.8g; Carbohydrate 11g, of which sugars 10.2g; Fat 17.2g, of which saturates 3.7g; Cholesterol 0mg; Calcium 167mg; Fibre 2.1g; Sodium 213mg.

Grilled Fish with Spiced Mushrooms

This tasty spicy dish originates in India. The cod is grilled before it is added to the spicy mushroom sauce to prevent it from breaking up during cooking. Serve as an appetizer, or increase the portions slightly to make a delicious main course.

Serves 4

4 small cod fillets
15ml/1 tbsp lemon juice
15ml/1 tbsp olive oil
1 medium onion, chopped
1 bay leaf
4 black peppercorns, crushed
115g/4oz mushrooms
175ml/6fl oz/⅔ cup natural (plain) low-fat yogurt
5ml/1 tsp crushed ginger
5ml/1 tsp crushed garlic
2.5ml/½ tsp garam masala
2.5ml/½ tsp chilli powder
5ml/1 tsp salt
15ml/1 tbsp fresh coriander (cilantro) leaves, to garnish
lightly cooked green beans, to serve

1 Remove the skin and any bones from the cod fillets. Sprinkle with lemon juice, then grill (broil) under a preheated grill (broiler) for about 5 minutes on each side. Remove from the heat and set aside.

2 Heat the oil in a non-stick wok or frying pan and fry the onion with the bay leaf and peppercorns for 2–3 minutes. Lower the heat, then add the mushrooms and stir-fry for 4–5 minutes.

3 In a bowl mix together the yogurt, ginger and garlic, garam masala, chilli powder and salt. Pour over the onions and stir-fry for 3 minutes.

4 Add the cod to the sauce and cook for a further 2 minutes. Serve garnished with coriander leaves and accompanied by lightly cooked green beans.

Cook's Tip

Jars of ready-to-use crushed ginger and garlic, also called pulp, are very useful to the busy cook. They are widely available in supermarkets and Asian food stores.

Fried Cod with Spiced Tomato Sauce

The cod is lightly dusted with spices and cornflour before being added to the tomato sauce. Mashed potatoes are the perfect accompaniment, although roast potatoes and rice are also good.

Serves 4

30ml/2 tbsp cornflour (cornstarch)
5ml/1 tsp salt
5ml/1 tsp garlic powder
5ml/1 tsp chilli powder
5ml/1 tsp ginger powder
5ml/1 tsp ground fennel seeds
5ml/1 tsp ground coriander
2 medium cod fillets, each cut into 2 pieces
15ml/1 tbsp corn oil
mashed potatoes, to serve

For the sauce

30ml/2 tbsp tomato purée (paste)
5ml/1 tsp garam masala
5ml/1 tsp chilli powder
5ml/1 tsp crushed garlic
5ml/1 tsp crushed ginger
2.5ml/½ tsp salt
175ml/6 fl oz/⅔ cup water
15ml/1 tbsp corn oil
1 bay leaf
3–4 black peppercorns
1 cm/½ in cinnamon bark
15ml/1 tbsp chopped fresh fresh coriander (cilantro)
15ml/1 tbsp chopped fresh mint

1 Mix together the cornflour, salt, garlic powder, chilli powder, ginger powder, ground fennel seeds and ground coriander. Pour over the cod fillets and ensure that they are well coated.

2 Preheat the grill (broiler) to hot, reduce the heat to medium and place the fish under the grill. After 5 minutes, brush the cod with the oil. Turn the cod over and repeat the process. Grill (broil) for a further 5 minutes. When cooked, set aside.

3 Make the sauce by mixing together the tomato purée, garam masala, chilli powder, garlic, ginger, salt and water. Set aside.

4 Heat the oil in a non-stick wok. Add the bay leaf, peppercorns and cinnamon. Pour the sauce into the wok and reduce the heat to low. Bring to the boil and simmer for 5 minutes. Add the fish and cook for a further 2 minutes. Add the coriander and mint and serve with mashed potatoes.

Grilled Fish Energy 149kcal/626kJ; Protein 21.8g; Carbohydrate 5.9g, of which sugars 4.2g; Fat 4.6g, of which saturates 0.8g; Cholesterol 47mg; Calcium 104mg; Fibre 0.5g; Sodium 100mg.
Fried Cod Energy 294kcal/1229kJ; Protein 41.8g; Carbohydrate 2.7g, of which sugars 2.7g; Fat 12.8g, of which saturates 1.9g; Cholesterol 104mg; Calcium 26mg; Fibre 0.9g; Sodium 143mg.

Salmon in Coconut Chilli Sauce

This is an ideal dish to serve as an appetizer at dinner parties. The salmon is first marinated in a spicy coating before being cooked in a delicious coconut sauce.

Serves 4

10ml/2 tsp ground cumin
10ml/2 tsp chilli powder
2.5ml/½ tsp ground turmeric
30ml/2 tbsp white wine vinegar
1.5ml/¼ tsp salt
4 salmon steaks, about 175g/6oz each
45 ml/3 tbsp oil
1 onion, chopped
2 green chillies, seeded and chopped
2 garlic cloves, crushed
2.5cm/1in piece fresh root ginger, grated
5 ml/1 tsp ground coriander
175 ml/6 fl oz/¾ cup coconut milk
spring onion rice, to serve
fresh coriander (cilantro) sprigs, to garnish

1 In a small bowl, mix 5ml/1 tsp of the ground cumin together with the chilli powder, turmeric, vinegar and salt.

2 Rub the paste over the salmon steaks and leave to marinate for about 15 minutes.

3 Heat the oil in a large frying pan and fry the onion, chillies, garlic and ginger for 5–6 minutes. Put into a food processor or blender and process to a paste.

4 Return the paste to the pan. Add the remaining cumin, coriander and coconut milk. Bring the mixture to the boil and simmer, stirring occasionally, for 5 minutes.

5 Add the salmon steaks to the sauce. Cover the pan and cook for 15 minutes until the fish is tender. Serve with spring onion rice and garnish with coriander sprigs.

Cook's Tip
If coconut milk is unavailable, substitute coconut cream diluted with water to get the desired consistency.

Red Snapper with Tomato and Green Chilli Sauce

This dish is quick and easy to prepare, perfect for a mid-week treat.

Serves 3 to 4

1 large red snapper, cleaned
juice of 1 lemon
2.5ml/½ tsp paprika
2.5ml/½ tsp garlic granules
2.5ml/½ tsp dried thyme
2.5ml/½ tsp ground black pepper

For the sauce
30ml/2 tbsp palm or vegetable oil
1 onion
400g/14oz can chopped tomatoes
2 garlic cloves
1 thyme sprig or 2.5ml/½ tsp dried thyme
1 green chilli, seeded and chopped
½ green (bell) pepper, chopped
300ml/½ pint/1¼ cups fish stock
boiled rice, to serve

1 Preheat the oven to 200°C/400°F/Gas 6 and then prepare the sauce. Heat the oil in a pan, fry the onion for 5 minutes, then add the tomatoes, garlic, thyme and chilli.

2 Add the pepper and stock or water. Bring to the boil, stirring, then reduce the heat and simmer, covered, for about 10 minutes until the vegetables are soft.

3 Remove the pan from the heat and leave to cool. Place the mixture in a blender or food processor and blend to a purée.

4 Wash the fish well and then score the skin with a sharp knife in a criss-cross pattern. Mix together the lemon juice, paprika, garlic, thyme and black pepper, then spoon over the fish, to cover it, and rub in well.

5 Place the fish in a greased baking dish and pour over the sauce. Cover with foil and bake for about 30–40 minutes, or until the fish is cooked. Serve with boiled rice.

Cook's Tip
If you prefer less sauce, remove the foil after 20 minutes and continue baking uncovered, until cooked.

Red Snapper Energy 198kcal/837kJ; Protein 33.1g; Carbohydrate 7.4g, of which sugars 6.6g; Fat 4.3g, of which saturates 0.8g; Cholesterol 58mg; Calcium 91mg; Fibre 1.7g; Sodium 201mg.
Salmon in Coconut Sauce Energy 417kcal/1740kJ; Protein 37g; Carbohydrate 6g, of which sugars 4g; Fat 28g, of which saturates 4g; Cholesterol 88mg; Calcium 73mg; Fibre 0.6g; Sodium 200mg.

Whole Fish with Sweet and Sour Chilli Sauce

Cooking fish whole will make an impressive appetizer for dinner guests – and the spicy sauce is sure to please.

Serves 4

1 whole fish, such as red snapper or carp, about 1kg/2¼lb
30–45ml/2–3 tbsp cornflour (cornstarch)
oil for frying
salt and ground black pepper
boiled rice, to serve

For the spice paste

5 macadamia nuts or 10 almonds
2 garlic cloves
2 lemon grass stems, sliced
2.5cm/1in fresh galangal, peeled
2.5cm/1in fresh root ginger, peeled
2cm/¾in fresh turmeric, peeled, or 2.5ml/½ tsp ground turmeric

For the sauce

15ml/1 tbsp brown sugar
45ml/3 tbsp cider vinegar
350ml/12fl oz/1½ cups water
2 lime leaves, torn
4 shallots, quartered
3 tomatoes, skinned and chopped
3 spring onions (scallions), finely shredded
1 fresh red chilli, seeded and shredded

1 Ask the fishmonger to gut and scale the fish, leaving on the head and tail. Wash and dry the fish and sprinkle inside and out with salt. Set aside for 15 minutes.

2 Grind the nuts, garlic, lemon grass, galangal, ginger and turmeric to a fine paste in a food processor or with a pestle and mortar. Scrape the paste into a bowl. Stir in the sugar, cider vinegar, seasoning to taste and the water. Add the lime leaves.

3 Dust the fish with the cornflour and fry on both sides in hot oil for about 8–9 minutes, or until cooked through. Drain the fish and transfer to a serving dish. Keep warm.

4 Pour the spicy liquid into the pan and bring to the boil, then simmer for 3–4 minutes. Add the shallots and tomatoes, followed by the spring onions and chilli and simmer for 2–3 minutes.

5 Pour the sauce over the fish. Serve immediately, with plenty of boiled rice.

Indonesian Spiced Fish

If you make this tasty appetizer a day ahead, put it straight on to a serving dish after cooking and then pour over the sauce, cover and chill until required.

Serves 3 to 4

450g/1lb fish fillets, such as mackerel, cod or haddock
30ml/2 tbsp plain (all-purpose) flour
groundnut (peanut) oil for frying
1 onion, roughly chopped
1 small garlic clove, crushed
4cm/1½in fresh root ginger, peeled and grated
1–2 red chillies, seeded and sliced
1cm/½in cube shrimp paste, prepared
60ml/4 tbsp water
juice of ½ lemon
15ml/1 tbsp soft light brown sugar
30ml/2 tbsp dark soy sauce
salt
roughly torn lettuce leaves, to serve

1 Rinse the fish fillets under cold water and dry well on absorbent kitchen paper. Cut into serving portions and remove any bones.

2 Season the flour with salt and use it to dust the fish. Heat the oil in a large frying pan and fry the fish on both sides for 3–4 minutes, or until cooked. Lift on to a plate and set aside.

3 Rinse out and dry the pan. Heat a little more oil and fry the onion, garlic, ginger and chillies just to bring out the flavour. Do not brown.

4 Blend the shrimp paste with a little water. Add it to the onion mixture, with a little extra water if necessary. Cook for 2 minutes and then stir in the lemon juice, brown sugar and soy sauce.

5 Pour the sauce over the fish and serve either hot or cold, with roughly torn lettuce.

Cook's Tip
This will make an ideal dish for a buffet. Simply cut the fish into bitesize pieces or small serving portions.

Whole Fish Energy 1103kcal/4200kJ; Protein 21g; Carbohydrate 210g, of which sugars 9g; Fat 7g, of which saturates 0g; Cholesterol 0mg; Calcium 83mg; Fibre 1.9g; Sodium 0mg.
Indonesian Fish Energy 218kcal/917kJ; Protein 22.8g; Carbohydrate 11.4g, of which sugars 4.3g; Fat 9.5g, of which saturates 1.2g; Cholesterol 41mg; Calcium 36mg; Fibre 0.2g; Sodium 344mg.

Grilled Spiced Bream

This whole fish is simply grilled after being marinated in a delicious spicy paste. The fish can be cooked on an oiled rack over a barbecue if you prefer.

Serves 6

1kg/2¼lb bream, carp or pomfret (porgy), cleaned and scaled if necessary
1 fresh red chilli, seeded, or 5ml/1 tsp of chilli powder
4 garlic cloves, crushed
2.5cm/1in fresh root ginger, peeled and sliced
4 spring onions (scallions), chopped
juice of ½ lemon
30ml/2 tbsp sunflower oil
salt
boiled rice, to serve

1 Rinse the fish and dry it well inside and out with absorbent kitchen paper. Slash two or three times through the fleshy part on each side of the fish.

2 Place the chilli, garlic, ginger and spring onions in a food processor and blend to a paste, or grind the mixture together with a mortar and pestle. Add the lemon juice and salt, then stir in the oil.

3 Spoon a little of the mixture inside the fish and pour the rest over the top. Coat it completely in the spice mixture and leave to marinate for at least an hour.

4 Preheat the grill (broiler). Place a long strip of double foil under the fish to support it and to make turning it over easier.

5 Cook under the hot grill for about 5 minutes on one side. Turn the fish over and cook for a further 8 minutes on the second side, basting with the marinade during cooking. Serve with boiled rice.

Cook's Tip

There are many other fish that will work well in this dish, allowing you to use whatever is available locally. Try making it with red snapper, pompano or butterfish.

Mackerel Fillets with Chilli and Coconut

Delicious fish fillets are smothered in a spicy coconut sauce. Serve with rice for a more substantial meal. Haddock or cod fillet may be substituted in this recipe if you prefer.

Serves 6 to 8

1kg/2¼lb fresh mackerel fillets, skinned
30ml/2 tbsp tamarind pulp, soaked in 200ml/7fl oz/scant 1 cup water
1 onion
1cm/½in fresh lengkuas
2 garlic cloves
1–2 fresh red chillies, seeded, or 5ml/1 tsp chilli powder
5ml/1 tsp ground coriander
5ml/1 tsp ground turmeric
2.5ml/½ tsp ground fennel seeds
15ml/1 tbsp dark brown sugar
90–105ml/6–7 tbsp oil
200ml/7fl oz/scant 1 cup coconut cream
salt and ground black pepper
fresh chilli shreds, to garnish
cooked rice, to serve (optional)

1 Rinse the fish fillets in cold water and dry them well on kitchen paper. Put into a shallow dish and sprinkle with a little salt. Strain the tamarind and pour the juice over the fish fillets. Leave for 30 minutes.

2 Quarter the onion, peel and slice the lengkuas and peel the garlic. Grind the onion, lengkuas, garlic and chillies or chilli powder to a paste in a food processor or with a mortar and pestle. Add the ground coriander, turmeric, fennel seeds and sugar and mix well.

3 Heat half of the oil in a frying pan. Drain the fish fillets and fry them for 3–4 minutes on each side, or until cooked. Set aside.

4 Wipe out the pan and heat the remaining oil. Fry the spice paste, stirring all the time, until it gives off a spicy aroma. Do not let it turn brown. Add the coconut cream and simmer for a few minutes. Add the fish fillets and gently heat through.

5 Taste the sauce for seasoning, adjusting if necessary and serve on a bed of rice, if using, sprinkled with shredded chilli.

Grilled Spiced Bream Energy 211kcal/887kj; Protein 30g; Carbohydrate 1g, of which sugars 0g; Fat 10g, of which saturates 1g; Cholesterol 63mg; Calcium 60mg; Fibre 0.2g; Sodium 224mg.
Mackerel Fillets Energy 717kcal/297kj; Protein 34g; Carbohydrate 9g, of which sugars 8g; Fat 61g, of which saturates 27g; Cholesterol 90mg; Calcium 47mg; Fibre 0.4g; Sodium 200mg.

Salmon in Red Chilli Stock

This recipe is an Asian interpretation of gravadlax, a Scandinavian speciality. Use very fresh salmon. The raw fish is marinated for several days in a brine flavoured with Thai spices, which effectively 'cooks' it.

Serves 4 to 6

tail piece of 1 salmon, weighing about 675g/1½lb, cleaned, scaled and filleted
20ml/4 tsp coarse sea salt
20ml/4 tsp sugar
2.5cm/1in piece fresh root ginger, peeled and grated
2 lemon grass stalks, coarse outer leaves removed, thinly sliced
4 kaffir lime leaves, finely chopped or shredded
grated rind of 1 lime
1 fresh red chilli, seeded and finely chopped
5ml/1 tsp black peppercorns, coarsely crushed
30ml/2 tbsp chopped fresh coriander (cilantro)
fresh coriander (cilantro) sprigs and quartered kaffir limes, to garnish

For the dressing
150ml/¼ pint/⅔ cup mayonnaise
juice of ½ lime
10ml/2 tsp chopped fresh coriander (cilantro)

1 Remove any remaining bones from the salmon. Put the sea salt, sugar, ginger, lemon grass, lime leaves, lime rind, chilli, black peppercorns and coriander in a bowl and mix together.

2 Sprinkle one-quarter of the spice mixture in a shallow dish. Place one salmon fillet, skin down, on top. Spread two-thirds of the remaining mixture over the flesh, then place the remaining fillet on top, flesh side down. Sprinkle the rest of the spice mixture over the fish.

3 Cover with foil, then place a board on top. Add some weights, such as clean cans of food. Chill for 2–5 days, turning the fish daily in the spicy brine.

4 Make the dressing by mixing the mayonnaise, lime juice and chopped coriander in a bowl.

5 Scrape the spices off the fish. Slice it as thin as possible. Garnish with coriander and kaffir limes, and serve with the lime dressing.

Hot Smoked Salmon with Sweet Chilli Sauce

This is a fantastic way of smoking fish on a charcoal barbecue, using soaked hickory wood chips. *Mojo*, a spicy sauce popular in Cuba, cuts the richness of the hot smoked salmon.

Serves 6

6 salmon fillets, about 175g/6oz each, with skin
15ml/1 tbsp sunflower oil
salt and ground black pepper
2 handfuls hickory wood chips, soaked in cold water for at least 30 minutes

For the mojo
1 ripe mango, diced
4 drained canned pineapple slices, diced
1 small red onion, finely chopped
1 fresh long mild red chilli, seeded and finely chopped
15ml/1 tbsp good quality sweet chilli sauce
grated rind and juice of 1 lime
leaves from 1 small basil plant or 45ml/3 tbsp fresh coriander (cilantro) leaves, chopped

1 Place the salmon fillets, skin side down, on a platter. Sprinkle the flesh lightly with salt. Cover and leave for about 30 minutes.

2 Make the mojo by putting the mango, pineapple slices, onion and chilli in a bowl. Add the chilli sauce, lime rind and juice, and the herb leaves. Mix well. Cover and set aside until needed.

3 Prepare the barbecue. Pat the salmon fillets with kitchen paper, then brush with a little oil. When the coals are medium-hot, and with a moderate coating of ash, add the salmon fillets, placing them on an oiled rack skin side down. Cover with a lid or tented heavy-duty foil and cook the fish for about 3 minutes.

4 Drain the hickory chips into a colander and sprinkle a third of them over the coals. Carefully drop them through the grill racks, taking care not to sprinkle the ash as you do so.

5 Replace the barbecue cover and continue cooking for a further 8 minutes, adding a small handful of hickory chips twice more during this time. Serve the salmon hot or cold, with the mojo.

Salmon in Red Chilli Stock Energy 509kcal/2108kJ; Protein 26g; Carbohydrate 7g, of which sugars 6g; Fat 42g, of which saturates 7g; Cholesterol 91mg; Calcium 44mg; Fibre 0g; Sodium 1700mg.
Hot Smoked Salmon Energy 365kcal/1522kJ; Protein 36g; Carbohydrate 7.8g, of which sugars 7.5g; Fat 21.3g, of which saturates 3.6g; Cholesterol 88mg; Calcium 61mg; Fibre 1.3g; Sodium 83mg.

Steamed Fish with Spices and Chilli Sauce

Steaming is one of the best methods of cooking fish. By leaving the fish whole and on the bone, more flavour is retained and the flesh remains moist.

Serves 4

1 large or 2 medium firm fish such as sea bass or grouper, scaled and cleaned
30ml/2 tbsp rice wine
3 fresh red chillies, seeded and thinly sliced
2 garlic cloves, finely chopped
2cm/¾in piece fresh root ginger, peeled and finely shredded
2 lemon grass stalks, chopped
2 spring onions (scallions), chopped
30ml/2 tbsp Thai fish sauce
juice of 1 lime
1 fresh banana leaf

For the chilli sauce
10 fresh red chillies, seeded and chopped
4 garlic cloves, chopped
60ml/4 tbsp Thai fish sauce
15ml/1 tbsp sugar
75ml/5 tbsp fresh lime juice

1 Thoroughly rinse the fish under cold running water. Pat it dry with kitchen paper. With a sharp knife, slash the skin of the fish a few times on both sides.

2 Mix together the rice wine, chillies, garlic, shredded ginger, lemon grass and spring onions in a non-metallic bowl. Add the fish sauce and lime juice and mix to a paste. Place the fish on the banana leaf and spread the spice paste evenly over it, rubbing it in well where the skin has been slashed.

3 Put a rack or a small upturned plate in the base of a wok. Pour in boiling water to a depth of 5cm/2in. Lift the banana leaf, together with the fish, and place it on the rack or plate. Cover with a lid and steam for 10–15 minutes, or until the fish is cooked.

4 Meanwhile, make the sauce. Place all the ingredients in a food processor and blend until smooth. If the mixture seems to be too thick, add a little cold water. Scrape into a serving bowl.

5 Serve the fish hot, on the banana leaf if you like, with the sweet chilli sauce to spoon over the top.

Fiery Fish in a Banana Leaf Parcel

This delicious Indian dish will make an excellent appetizer for a dinner party and your guests will enjoy opening up their own individual parcels and finding the spicy aromatic fish.

Serves 6

50g/2oz fresh coconut, skinned and grated, or 65g/2½oz/ scant 1 cup desiccated (dry unsweetened shredded) coconut, soaked in 30ml/2 tbsp water
1 large lemon, skin, pith and seeds removed, roughly chopped
4 large garlic cloves, crushed
3 large fresh mild green chillies, seeded and chopped
50g/2oz fresh coriander (cilantro), roughly chopped
25g/1oz fresh mint leaves, roughly chopped
5ml/1 tsp ground cumin
5ml/1 tsp sugar
2.5ml/½ tsp fenugreek seeds, finely ground
5ml/1 tsp salt
2 large, whole banana leaves
6 salmon fillets, total weight about 1.2kg/2½lb, skinned

1 Place all the ingredients except the banana leaves and salmon in a food processor. Pulse to a fine paste. Scrape the mixture into a bowl, cover and chill for 30 minutes.

2 Prepare the barbecue. While it is heating, make the parcels. Cut each banana leaf widthways into three and cut off the hard outside edge. Put the pieces of leaf and the edge strips in a bowl of hot water and soak for 10 minutes. Drain, wipe off any white residue, and rinse. Pour over boiling water to soften. Drain, then place the leaves, smooth side up, on a clean board.

3 Smear the top and bottom with coconut paste. Place a fillet on each leaf. Bring the trimmed edge over, then fold in the sides. Bring up the remaining edge to make a parcel. Tie with a leaf strip.

4 Lay each parcel on a sheet of foil, bring up the edges and scrunch the tops together to seal. When the coals are medium-hot, or with a moderate coating of ash, place the salmon parcels on the grill rack and cook for 10 minutes, turning once.

5 Place on individual plates and leave for 2–3 minutes. Remove the foil, then unwrap and eat the fish straight out of the parcel.

Fish with Spices Energy 123kcal/519kJ; Protein 23.3g; Carbohydrate 0.8g, of which sugars 0.7g; Fat 3g, of which saturates 0.5g; Cholesterol 95mg; Calcium 158mg; Fibre 0.1g; Sodium 616mg.
Fiery Fish in a Parcel Energy 225kcal/943kJ; Protein 27.6g; Carbohydrate 14.1g, of which sugars 10.4g; Fat 6.9g, of which saturates 1.2g; Cholesterol 58mg; Calcium 51mg; Fibre 2.5g; Sodium 79mg.

Trout with Tamarind Chilli Sauce

Sometimes trout can taste rather bland, but this spicy sauce really gives it a zing. If you like your food very spicy, add an extra chilli.

Serves 4

4 trout, cleaned
6 spring onions (scallions), sliced
60ml/4 tbsp soy sauce
15ml/1 tbsp vegetable oil
30ml/2 tbsp chopped fresh coriander (cilantro) and strips of fresh red chilli, to garnish

For the sauce

50g/2oz tamarind pulp
105ml/7 tbsp boiling water
2 shallots, coarsely chopped
1 fresh red chilli, seeded and finely chopped
1cm/½in piece fresh root ginger, peeled and chopped
5ml/1 tsp soft light brown sugar
45ml/3 tbsp Thai fish sauce

1 Slash each trout diagonally four or five times on each side. Place them in a shallow dish that is large enough to hold them all in a single layer.

2 Fill the cavities with spring onions and douse each fish with soy sauce. Carefully turn the fish over to coat both sides with the sauce. Sprinkle any remaining spring onions over the top.

3 Make the sauce. Put the tamarind pulp in a small bowl and pour on the boiling water. Mash well with a fork until the pulp is thoroughly softened. Transfer the tamarind mixture to a food processor or blender. Add the shallots, fresh chilli, fresh root ginger, sugar and fish sauce. Process to a coarse pulp. Scrape into a bowl.

4 Heat the oil in a large heavy frying pan or wok and cook the trout, one at a time if necessary, for about 5 minutes on each side, until the skin is crisp and browned and the flesh cooked.

5 Put the fish on warmed plates and spoon over some of the chilli sauce. Sprinkle with the coriander and chilli and serve with the remaining sauce.

Fragrant Trout with Hot Spices

Cooking doesn't get much simpler than this. The beauty of this paste is that it is easy to make in a food processor. The deliciously-spiced paste is then smeared over the fish, which are briefly cooked on the grill.

Serves 4

2 large fresh green chillies, seeded and coarsely chopped
5 shallots, peeled
5 garlic cloves, peeled
30ml/2 tbsp fresh lime juice
30ml/2 tbsp Thai fish sauce
15ml/1 tbsp palm sugar (jaggery) or light muscovado (brown) sugar
4 kaffir lime leaves, rolled into cylinders and thinly sliced
2 trout or similar firm-fleshed fish, about 350g/12oz each, cleaned
fresh garlic chives, to garnish
boiled rice, to serve

1 Wrap the chillies, shallots and garlic in a foil package. Place the package under a hot grill (broiler) for about 10 minutes, until the contents have softened.

2 When the package is cool enough to handle, pour the contents into a mortar or food processor and pound with a pestle or process to a paste.

3 Add the lime juice, fish sauce, sugar and lime leaves to the spice paste and mix well.

4 With a teaspoon, stuff the paste inside each fish. Smear a little over the skin as well.

5 Grill (broil) the fish for about 5 minutes on each side, until just cooked. The flesh should flake easily when tested with a knife.

6 Lift each fish on to a platter, garnish with garlic chives and serve with rice.

Cook's Tip

This hot paste can be used as a marinade for any fish or meat. It also makes a wonderful spicy dip for grilled (broiled) meat.

Trout with Tamarind Energy 247kcal/1038kJ; Protein 36.6g; Carbohydrate 3.5g, of which sugars 3.3g; Fat 9.7g, of which saturates 2g; Cholesterol 147mg; Calcium 65mg; Fibre 0.2g; Sodium 1736mg.
Fragrant Trout Energy 117kcal/490kJ; Protein 14.8g; Carbohydrate 7.9g, of which sugars 6.7g; Fat 3.1g, of which saturates 0.7g; Cholesterol 59mg; Calcium 36mg; Fibre 0.7g; Sodium 57mg.

Lime and Pasilla Chilli Baked Trout

Lime juice, chillies and leeks are perfect partners for the oily trout.

Serves 4

2 fresh chillies
4 rainbow trout, cleaned
4 garlic cloves
10ml/2 tsp dried oregano
juice of 2 limes
50g/2oz/½ cup slivered almonds
salt and ground black pepper

1 Roast the chillies in a dry frying pan until the skins blister. Put them in a strong plastic bag and tie the top to keep the steam in. Set aside for 20 minutes.

2 Meanwhile, rub a little salt into the cavities in the trout, to ensure they are completely clean, then rinse them under cold running water. Drain and pat dry with kitchen paper.

3 Remove the chillies from the bag and peel off the skins. Cut off the stalks, then slit the chillies and scrape out the seeds. Chop the flesh roughly and put it in a mortar. Crush with a pestle until the mixture forms a paste.

4 Place the paste in a shallow dish that will hold all the trout in a single layer. Slice the garlic lengthways and add to the dish. Add the oregano and 10ml/2 tsp salt, then stir in the lime juice and pepper to taste. Add the trout, turning to coat them in the mixture. Cover the dish and set aside for at least 30 minutes, turning the trout again halfway through.

5 Preheat the oven to 200°C/400°F/Gas 6. Have ready four pieces of foil, large enough to wrap a fish. Top each with a sheet of baking parchment of the same size.

6 Place a trout on each piece of parchment, moisten with the marinade. Sprinkle a quarter of the almonds over. Bring up the sides of the paper and fold to seal, then fold the foil to make a parcel. Repeat with the other fish, then place in a single layer in a roasting pan. Bake the parcels in the oven for 25 minutes.

7 Serve each parcel on an individual plate, or unwrap before serving. This dish goes well with new potatoes and vegetables.

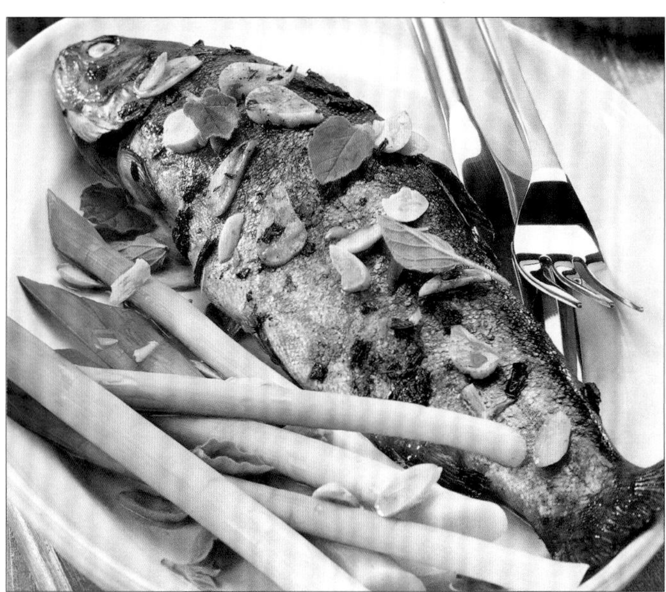

Sea Trout with Chilli and Lime

Sea trout is best served with strong flavours such as chillies and lime that cut the richness of the flesh.

Serves 6

6 sea trout cutlets, about 115g/4oz each, or wild or farmed salmon
2 garlic cloves, chopped
1 fresh long red chilli, seeded and chopped
45ml/3 tbsp chopped Thai basil
15ml/1 tbsp palm sugar (jaggery) or granulated (white) sugar
3 limes
400ml/14fl oz/1⅔ cups coconut milk
15ml/1 tbsp Thai fish sauce

1 Place the fish in a dish. Using a pestle, pound the garlic and chilli in a large mortar to break it up. Add 30ml/2 tbsp of the Thai basil with the sugar and continue to pound to a paste. Grate the rind from one lime and squeeze it. Mix the rind and juice into the paste, with the coconut milk. Pour over the fish, cover and chill for 1 hour. Cut the remaining limes into wedges.

2 Prepare the barbecue. Remove the fish from the refrigerator. Once the flames have died down, position a lightly oiled grill rack over the coals to heat. When the coals are cool to medium-hot, or with a thick to moderate coating of ash, remove the cutlets from the marinade. Place them in an oiled hinged wire fish basket or directly on the grill rack. Cook the fish for 4 minutes on each side, trying not to move them. They may stick to the grill rack if not seared first.

3 Strain the remaining marinade into a pan, and reserve the contents of the sieve (strainer). Bring the marinade to the boil, then simmer for 5 minutes. Stir in the contents of the sieve and cook for 1 minute more. Add the Thai fish sauce and the remaining Thai basil. Lift each fish cutlet on to a plate, pour over the sauce and serve with the lime wedges.

Variation

If sea trout is not in season, use good quality environmentally sound farmed salmon or, if your budget can stretch to it, buy wild salmon.

Lime Baked Trout Energy 257kcal/1077kJ; Protein 31.1g; Carbohydrate 1.5g, of which sugars 1.1g; Fat 14.1g, of which saturates 2g; Cholesterol 92mg; Calcium 59mg; Fibre 1.3g; Sodium 75mg.
Sea Trout with Chilli Energy 139kcal/587kJ; Protein 21.3g; Carbohydrate 4.1g, of which sugars 4.1g; Fat 4.3g, of which saturates 0.1g; Cholesterol 0mg; Calcium 30mg; Fibre 0g; Sodium 253g.

Baked Spicy Cod Steaks

Serve this delicious dish with a large fresh salad, or some little boiled potatoes and garlicky green beans, for a main course if you wish.

Serves 4

4 cod or hake steaks
2 or 3 sprigs of fresh flat leaf parsley
4 slices white bread, toasted, then crumbed in a food processor
salt and ground black pepper

For the sauce

75–90ml/5–6 tbsp extra virgin olive oil
175ml/6fl oz/¾ cup white wine
2 garlic cloves, crushed
60ml/4 tbsp finely chopped flat leaf parsley
1 fresh red or green chilli, seeded and finely chopped
400g/14oz ripe tomatoes, peeled and finely diced
salt and ground black pepper

1 Mix all the sauce ingredients in a bowl, and add some salt and pepper. Set the mixture aside.

2 Preheat the oven to 190°C/375°F/Gas 5. Rinse the fish steaks then pat them dry with kitchen paper. Arrange them in a single layer in an oiled baking dish and sprinkle over the parsley. Season with salt and pepper.

3 Spoon the sauce over the fish, distributing it evenly over each steak. Then sprinkle over half of the breadcrumbs, again evenly covering each steak. Bake for 10 minutes, then baste with the juices in the dish, trying not to disturb the breadcrumbs.

4 Sprinkle the remaining breadcrumbs over the top of the dish. Return to the oven and bake for a further 10–15 minutes, until the fish are cooked and the breadcrumbs are crisp and have turned golden brown.

Variation

If you like, use two whole fish, such as sea bass or grey mullet, total weight about 1kg/2¼lb. Rinse thoroughly inside and out, pat dry, then tuck the parsley sprigs inside. Add the sauce and breadcumbs as above. Bake the fish for about 15 minutes, then turn them over carefully, and bake for 20–25 minutes more.

Chilli-coated Fish in Banana Leaves

Cooking fish in banana leaves is a delightful method that can be found throughout South-east Asia. The banana leaves impart their own flavour and the fish remains beautifully succulent, with a wonderful fragrance from the spices inside the leaf.

Serves 4

500g/1¼lb fresh fish fillets, cut into chunks
juice of 2 limes
4–6 shallots, chopped
2 red chillies, seeded and chopped
25g/1oz fresh root ginger, chopped
15g/½oz fresh turmeric, chopped
2 lemon grass stalks, chopped
3–4 candlenuts, ground
10ml/2 tsp palm sugar (jaggery)
1–2 banana leaves, cut into 4 big squares
salt

To serve

cooked rice
chilli sambal

1 In a large bowl, toss the fish fillets in the lime juice then leave to marinate at room temperature for 10–15 minutes.

2 Meanwhile, using a mortar and pestle, pound the shallots, chillies, ginger, turmeric and lemon grass to a coarse paste. Add the ground candlenuts with the sugar and season with salt. Transfer the paste to the bowl with the fish and toss to coat the fish in it.

3 Place the banana leaves on a flat surface and divide the fish mixture equally among them. Tuck in the sides and fold over the ends to form a neat parcel. Secure with string.

4 Place the banana leaf parcels in a steamer and steam for 25–30 minutes until tender. Serve hot with rice and a sambal.

Cook's Tip

Banana leaves are available in South-east Asian, Chinese and African food shops but, if you cannot find them, you can use foil instead and bake the fish in the oven at 180°C/350°F/Gas 4 rather than steaming them.

Baked Spicy Cod Energy 362kcal/1,510kJ; Protein 31g; Carbohydrate 13.1g, of which sugars 3.7g; Fat 17.9g, of which saturates 2.7g; Cholesterol 36mg; Calcium 49mg; Fibre 1.3g; Sodium 274mg.
Chilli-coated Fish Energy 225kcal/943kJ; Protein 27.6g; Carbohydrate 14.1g, of which sugars 10.4g; Fat 6.9g, of which saturates 1.2g; Cholesterol 58mg; Calcium 51mg; Fibre 2.5g; Sodium 79mg.

Filipino Fish with Ginger and Chilli

Coconut vinegar is used in this tasty dish. Served with rice and topped with plenty of chillies, it makes a good lunchor supper dish. Trout, mackerel, herring or sea bass are all suitable fish to use in this recipe.

Serves 4

1 small bitter melon, cut into thick bitesize slices
1 small aubergine (eggplant), thickly sliced
4 spring onions (scallions), cut into 2.5cm/1in lengths
2 fresh green chillies, seeded and sliced
25g/1oz fresh root ginger, grated
4–6 black peppercorns
1 whole fish, gutted and cleaned, or fish fillets, total weight 500g/1¼ lb
250ml/8fl oz/1 cup coconut, rice or white wine vinegar
200ml/7fl oz/scant 1 cup water
30ml/2 tbsp light soy sauce
salt and ground black pepper

To serve

cooked rice
soy sauce
fresh chillies, seeded and sliced lengthways

1 Arrange the bitter melon and aubergine in the bottom of a wide, heavy pan. Sprinkle the spring onions, chillies, ginger and peppercorns over the top.

2 Carefully place the whole fish, or arrange the fillets, over the top of the vegetables in the pan.

3 In a bowl, mix the vinegar, water and soy sauce together, then pour the mixture over the fish and vegetables. Season the dish with a little salt and lots of black pepper.

4 Bring the mixture to the boil, reduce the heat, cover and simmer gently for about 1 hour.

5 Carefully transfer the fish to a serving dish and spoon the vegetables and cooking liquid over and around the fish. Leave to cool. Serve the fish with rice, soy sauce and plenty of sliced red chillies.

Mackerel with Red and Green Chilli

Oily fish such as mackerel is a perfect match for the clean, dry taste of sake. Garlic and chilli mute the strong flavour of the fish, while the diced mooli absorbs all the flavours of the cooking liquid for a unique and delicious taste.

Serves 2–3

1 large mackerel, filleted
300g/11oz mooli (daikon), peeled
120ml/4fl oz/½ cup light soy sauce
30ml/2 tbsp sake or rice wine
30ml/2 tbsp maple syrup
3 garlic cloves, crushed
10ml/2 tsp Korean chilli powder
½ onion, chopped
1 fresh red chilli, seeded and finely sliced
1 fresh green chilli, seeded and finely sliced

1 Slice the mackerel into medium pieces. Cut the mooli into 2.5cm/1in cubes, and then arrange evenly across the base of a large pan. Cover with a layer of mackerel.

2 Pour the soy sauce over the fish and add 200ml/7fl oz/scant 1 cup water, the sake or rice wine, and the maple syrup. Sprinkle the crushed garlic and chilli powder into the pan, and gently stir the liquid, trying not to disturb the fish and mooli. Add the onion and sliced fresh red and green chillies, and cover the pan.

3 Place the pan over a high heat and bring the liquid to the boil. Reduce the heat and simmer for 8–10 minutes, or until the fish is tender, spooning the soy liquid over the fish as it cooks. Ladle the mixture into two or three warmed serving bowls and serve immediately.

Variation

If mooli is not available then potatoes make a good alternative. They will give a sweeter, more delicate flavour to the fish, while a handful of coriander (cilantro) leaves will add more of a Thai flavour to the recipe.

Filipino Fish Energy 151kcal/636kJ; Protein 20.7g; Carbohydrate 8.5g, of which sugars 8.3g; Fat 4g, of which saturates 0.9g; Cholesterol 80mg; Calcium 54mg; Fibre 1.2g; Sodium 647mg.
Mackerel Fillets Energy 207kcal/861kJ; Protein 13.4g; Carbohydrate 11.4g, of which sugars 10.9g; Fat 11g, of which saturates 2.3g; Cholesterol 36mg; Calcium 33mg; Fibre 1.2g; Sodium 81mg.

Fried Fish in Chilli Coconut Sauce

This tasty dish is easy to make and diners will enjoy the partnership of succulent fish with a creamy ginger and coconut sauce that has a nice kick from the chillies.

Serves 4

4 medium pomfret, porgy or butterfish
juice of 1 lemon
5ml/1 tsp garlic granules
salt and ground black pepper
vegetable oil, for shallow frying

For the coconut sauce

450ml/¾ pint/scant 2 cups water
2 thin slices fresh root ginger
150ml/¼ pint/⅔ cup coconut cream
30ml/2 tbsp vegetable oil
1 red onion, sliced
2 garlic cloves, crushed
1 green chilli, seeded and thinly sliced
15ml/1 tbsp chopped fresh coriander (cilantro)

1 Cut the fish in half and sprinkle inside and out with the lemon juice. Season with the garlic granules and salt and pepper and set aside to marinate for a few hours.

2 Heat a little oil in a frying pan. Pat away the excess lemon juice from the fish. Fry for 10 minutes, turning once. Set aside.

3 To make the sauce, place the water in a pan with the slices of ginger, bring to the boil and simmer until the liquid is reduced to just over 300ml/½ pint/1¼ cups.

4 Take out the slices of ginger from the pan and reserve. Add the coconut cream to the pan and stir well.

5 Heat the oil in a wok or large frying pan and fry the onion and garlic for 4–5 minutes until the onions are beginning to soften and turn translucent.

6 Add the reserved ginger and coconut stock, the chilli and coriander, stir well and then gently add the fish. Simmer for 10 minutes, until the fish is cooked through.

7 Transfer the fish to a serving plate, adjust the seasoning for the sauce and pour over the fish. Serve immediately.

Fish in a Spicy Turmeric, Mango and Tomato Sauce

Tilapia is widely used in African cooking, but can be found in most fishmongers.

Serves 4

4 tilapia
½ lemon
2 garlic cloves, crushed
2.5ml/½ tsp dried thyme
30ml/2 tbsp chopped spring onions (scallions)
vegetable oil, for shallow frying
flour, for dusting
30ml/2 tbsp groundnut (peanut) oil
15g/½oz/1 tbsp butter
1 onion, finely chopped
3 tomatoes, peeled and chopped
5ml/1 tsp ground turmeric
60ml/4 tbsp white wine
1 green chilli, seeded and chopped
600ml/1 pint/2½ cups fish stock
5ml/1 tsp sugar
1 medium underripe mango, peeled and diced
15ml/1 tbsp chopped fresh parsley
salt and ground black pepper

1 Place the fish in a shallow bowl, squeeze the lemon juice all over the fish and gently rub in the garlic, thyme and salt and pepper. Place the spring onions in the cavity of each fish, cover loosely with clear film (plastic wrap) and leave to marinate for a few hours or overnight in the refrigerator.

2 Heat a little vegetable oil in a large frying pan, coat the fish with a little flour, then fry on both sides for a few minutes until golden brown. Transfer to a plate and set aside.

3 Heat the groundnut oil and butter in a pan and fry the onion for 5 minutes, until soft. Add the tomatoes and cook for a few minutes. Add the turmeric, white wine, chilli, stock and sugar, stir well and bring to the boil, then simmer, covered, for 10 minutes.

4 Add the fish and cook gently for about 15–20 minutes, until cooked through. Add the mango, arranging it around the fish, and cook briefly for 1–2 minutes to heat through.

5 Arrange the fish on a serving plate with the mango and tomato sauce poured over. Garnish with parsley and serve.

Fried Fish in Coconut Sauce Energy 325kcal/1356kJ; Protein 33g; Carbohydrate 4g, of which sugars 3g; Fat 20g, of which saturates 6g; Cholesterol 0mg; Calcium 142mg; Fibre 0.6g; Sodium 400mg.
Fish in a Spicy Sauce Energy 238kcal/998kJ; Protein 23.4g; Carbohydrate 10.1g, of which sugars 9.6g; Fat 10.8g, of which saturates 3.1g; Cholesterol 8mg; Calcium 168mg; Fibre 2g; Sodium 97mg.

Halibut Steaks with Lemon, Red Chilli and Coriander

Succulent fish steaks are first marinated in herbs and spices then cooked in a tasty stock with chillies and coriander, and served with a red onion topping.

Serves 4

4 halibut or cod steaks, about 175g/6oz each
juice of 1 lemon
5ml/1 tsp garlic granules
5ml/1 tsp paprika
5ml/1 tsp ground cumin
5ml/1 tsp dried tarragon
about 60ml/4 tbsp olive oil
flour, for dusting
300ml/½ pint/1¼ cups fish stock
2 red chillies, seeded and finely chopped
30ml/2 tbsp chopped fresh coriander (cilantro)
1 red onion, cut into rings
salt and ground black pepper

1 Place the fish in a shallow bowl. Mix together the lemon juice, garlic, paprika, cumin, tarragon and a little salt and pepper.

2 Spoon the lemon mixture over the fish, cover loosely with clear film (plastic wrap) and set aside to marinate for a few hours or overnight in the fridge.

3 Gently heat all of the oil in a large non-stick frying pan, dust the fish with flour and then fry the fish for a few minutes each side, until golden brown all over.

4 Pour the fish stock around the fish, and then simmer gently, covered, for about 5 minutes, stirring occasionally until the fish is thoroughly cooked through.

5 Add the chopped red chillies and 15ml/1 tbsp of the coriander to the pan. Simmer for 5 minutes.

6 Carefully transfer the fish steaks to a serving plate. Spoon the sauce over the fish and keep warm.

7 Wipe the pan, heat some olive oil and stir fry the onion rings until speckled brown. Sprinkle over the fish with the remaining chopped coriander and serve immediately.

Monkfish Stir-fry with Spices

Monkfish is a rather expensive fish these days, but it is ideal to use in a stir-fry recipe as it is a robust fish and will not break up easily.

Serves 4

30ml/2 tbsp corn oil
2 medium onions, sliced
5ml/1 tsp crushed garlic
5ml/1 tsp ground cumin
5ml/1 tsp ground coriander
5ml/1 tsp chilli powder
175g/6oz monkfish, cut into bitesize cubes
30ml/2 tbsp fresh fenugreek leaves
2 tomatoes, seeded and sliced into wedges
1 courgette (zucchini), sliced
15ml/1 tbsp lime juice
salt

1 Heat the oil in a non-stick wok or heavy frying pan and fry the onions over a low heat until they are soft and have turned slightly translucent.

2 Meanwhile, in a small bowl mix together the garlic, cumin, coriander and chilli powder, stirring until thoroughly combined.

3 Add this spice mixture to the onions in the pan and stir for about 1–2 minutes, until the mixture starts to release a fragrant spicy aroma.

4 Add the fish to the wok or pan and continue to stir-fry the mixture for 3–5 minutes, until the fish pieces are well cooked through and tender.

5 Add the fenugreek leaves, tomatoes and courgette to the pan. Season with salt to taste, and stir-fry for a further 2–3 minutes until all the ingredients are well heated. Sprinkle with lime juice before serving.

Variation

Try to use monkfish for this recipe, but if it is not available, or your budget won't stretch that far, then either cod or prawns (shrimp) will make a suitable substitute. You can even use a mixture of seafood if that is what you have to hand.

Halibut Steaks Energy 265kcal/1106kJ; Protein 33g; Carbohydrate 5.4g, of which sugars 1.2g; Fat 12.5g, of which saturates 1.8g; Cholesterol 81mg; Calcium 47mg; Fibre 0.9g; Sodium 109mg.
Monkfish Stir-fry Energy 86kcals/360kJ; Protein 9.18g; Carbohydrate 8.30g, of which sugars 2.3g; Fat 2.38g, of which saturates 0.35g; Cholesterol 16mg; Calcium 98mg; Fibre 1.87g; Sodium 270mg.

Coriander and Chilli-spiced Red Mullet

Chermoula is a herby spiced marinade used in north African cooking and gives this dish its distinct flavour.

Serves 4

30–45ml/2–3 tbsp olive oil, plus extra for brushing
1 onion, chopped
1 carrot, chopped
½ preserved lemon, finely chopped
4 plum tomatoes, peeled and chopped
600ml/1 pint/2½ cups fish stock or water
4 new potatoes, peeled and cubed
4 small red mullet or snapper, gutted and filleted
handful of black olives, pitted and halved
small bunch of fresh coriander (cilantro), chopped
small bunch of mint, chopped
salt and ground black pepper
couscous, to serve

For the chermoula

small bunch of fresh coriander (cilantro), finely chopped
2–3 garlic cloves, chopped
5–10ml/1–2 tsp ground cumin
pinch of saffron threads
60ml/4 tbsp olive oil
juice of 1 lemon
1 hot red chilli, seeded and chopped
5ml/1 tsp salt

1 Make the chermoula. Pound the ingredients in a mortar with a pestle, or process them in a food processor, and set aside.

2 Heat the olive oil in a pan. Add the onion and carrot and cook until softened. Stir in half the preserved lemon, along with 30ml/2 tbsp of the chermoula. Add the tomatoes and the stock or water. Bring to the boil, simmer, covered, for 30 minutes and add the potatoes. Simmer for a further 10 minutes, until tender.

3 Preheat the grill (broiler) on the hottest setting. Brush a baking sheet or grill pan with oil. Brush oil and a little chermoula onto the fillets. Season, then put the fillets, skin side up, on the sheet or pan and grill for 5–6 minutes.

4 Meanwhile, stir the olives, the remaining chermoula and preserved lemon into the sauce and check the seasoning. Serve the fish fillets with couscous in wide bowls, spoon the sauce over and sprinkle with chopped coriander and mint.

Barbecued Red Snapper

The grilled fish is perfect for dipping into the chilli sauce.

Serves 4

2 red snapper, each 900g/2lb, cleaned and scaled
15ml/1 tbsp olive oil
5cm/2in piece of fresh root ginger, thinly sliced
4 banana shallots, total weight about 150g/5oz, thinly sliced
3 garlic cloves, thinly sliced
30ml/2 tbsp sugar
3 lemon grass stalks, 1 thinly sliced
grated rind and juice of 1 lime
5ml/1 tsp salt
4 small fresh green or red chillies, thinly sliced
2 whole banana leaves
30ml/2 tbsp chopped fresh coriander (cilantro)

For the dipping sauce

1 large fresh red chilli, seeded and finely chopped
juice of 2 limes
30ml/2 tbsp fish sauce
5ml/1 tsp sugar
60ml/4 tbsp water

1 Make the dipping sauce. Mix together the ingredients in a bowl. Cover and chill until needed. Make four slashes in either side of each fish and rub the skin with oil.

2 Place half the ginger, shallots and the garlic in a mortar. Add half the sugar, the sliced lemon grass, a little lime juice, the salt and chillies and pound. Mix in the remaining sugar and lime juice, with the rind. Rub into the slashes and cavity of each fish.

3 Trim the hard edge from each banana leaf and discard. Soak in hot water for 10 minutes, then drain. Rinse, then pour over boiling water to soften. Drain again. Lay a fish on each leaf and sprinkle over the remaining ginger and shallots. Split the lemon grass stalks lengthways and lay over each fish. Bring the sides of the leaves up over the fish and secure each with three wooden skewers. Wrap in clear film (plastic wrap), and chill for 30 minutes.

4 Prepare the barbecue. Remove the film from each leaf. Enclose each leaf in a sheet of foil. When the coals are medium-hot, or have a coating of ash, lay the parcels on the grill rack and cook for 15 minutes. Turn over and cook for 10 minutes until cooked through. Place on a serving dish, open and sprinkle with the coriander. Serve with the sauce.

Red Mullet Energy 374kcal/1558kj; Protein 24.7g; Carbohydrate 13.8g, of which sugars 7.2g; Fat 24.9g, of which saturates 2.9g; Cholesterol 0mg; Calcium 193mg; Fibre 0.3g; Sodium 704mg.
Red Snapper Energy 382kcal/1591kJ; Protein 30.7g; Carbohydrate 8.6g, of which sugars 8.3g; Fat 25.2g, of which saturates 3.9g; Cholesterol 56mg; Calcium 97mg; Fibre 2.4g; Sodium 970mg.

Red-hot Red Snapper Burritos

Fish makes a great filling for a tortilla, especially when it is succulent red snapper mixed with rice, chilli and tomatoes.

Serves 6

3 red snapper fillets
90g/3½oz/½ cup long grain white rice
30ml/2 tbsp vegetable oil
1 small onion, finely chopped
5ml/1 tsp ground achiote seed (annatto powder)
1 pasilla or similar dried chilli, seeded and ground
75g/3oz/¾ cup slivered almonds
200g/7oz can chopped tomatoes in tomato juice
150g/5oz/1¼ cups grated Monterey Jack or mild Cheddar cheese
8 X 20cm/8in wheat flour tortillas
fresh flat-leaved parsley to garnish
lime wedges (optional)

1 Preheat the grill (broiler). Cook the fish fillets on an oiled rack for about 5 minutes, turning once. When cool, remove the skin and flake the fish into a bowl. Set it aside.

2 Meanwhile, put the rice in a pan, cover with cold water, cover and bring to the boil. Drain, rinse and drain again.

3 Heat the oil in a pan and fry the onion until soft and translucent. Stir in the ground achiote and the chilli and cook for 5 minutes.

4 Add the rice, stir well, then stir in the fish and almonds. Add the tomatoes, with their juice. Cook over a moderate heat until all the juice is absorbed and the rice is tender. Stir in the cheese and remove from the heat. Warm the tortillas.

5 Divide the filling among the tortillas and fold them as shown, to make neat parcels. Garnish with fresh parsley and serve with lime wedges, if liked. A green salad makes a good accompaniment.

Cook's Tip

If red snapper is not available this dish will also be delicious with other fish such as grey mullet, pompano or butterfish.

Sea Bass Steamed in Coconut Milk with Ginger and Red Chilli

This is a delicious spicy recipe for any whole white fish, such as sea bass or cod, or for large chunks of trout or salmon.

Serves 4

200ml/7fl oz coconut milk
10ml/2 tsp raw cane or muscovado (molasses) sugar
about 15ml/1 tbsp sesame or vegetable oil
2 garlic cloves, finely chopped
1 red Thai chilli, seeded and finely chopped
4cm/1½in fresh root ginger, peeled and grated
750g/1⅔lb sea bass, gutted and skinned on one side
1 star anise, ground
1 bunch of fresh basil, stalks removed
30ml/2 tbsp cashew nuts
sea salt and ground black pepper

1 Heat the coconut milk with the sugar in a small pan, stirring until the sugar dissolves, then remove from the heat. Add the oil to a small frying pan and stir in the garlic, chilli and ginger. Cook until they begin to brown, then add the mixture to the coconut milk and mix well to combine.

2 Place the fish, skin side down, on a wide piece of foil and tuck up the sides to form a boat-shaped container. Using a sharp knife, cut several diagonal slashes into the flesh on the top and rub with the ground star anise. Season with salt and pepper and spoon the coconut milk over the top.

3 Sprinkle about half the basil leaves over the top of the fish and pull the sides of the foil over the top, so that it is almost enclosed. Gently lay the foil packet in a steamer. Cover the steamer, bring the water to the boil, then reduce the heat and simmer for 20–25 minutes, or until just cooked.

4 Meanwhile, roast the cashew nuts in the small frying pan, adding a little extra oil if necessary. Drain the nuts on kitchen paper, then grind them to crumbs. When cooked, lift the fish out of the foil and transfer it to a serving dish. Spoon the cooking juices over, sprinkle with the cashew nut crumbs and garnish with the remaining basil leaves. Serve immediately.

Snapper Burritos Energy 519kcal/2177kj; Protein 30g; Carbohydrate 54.4g, of which sugars 2.9g; Fat 20.7g, of which saturates 6.7g; Cholesterol 52mg; Calcium 326mg; Fibre 3g; Sodium 430mg.
Sea Bass Energy 235kcal/983kJ; Protein 26g; Carbohydrate 8g, of which sugars 6g; Fat 11g, of which saturates 2g; Cholesterol 100mg; Calcium 217mg; Fibre 0.3g; Sodium 300mg

Thai Green Fish Curry

This dish combines many of the delicious spicy flavours of South-east Asian cuisine – coconut, coriander, garlic and, of course, chilli.

Serves 4

1.5ml/¼ tsp ground turmeric
30ml/2 tbsp lime juice
pinch of salt
4 cod fillets, skinned and cut into 5cm/2in chunks
1 onion, chopped
1 green chilli, roughly chopped
1 garlic clove, crushed
25g/1oz/¼ cup cashew nuts
2.5ml/½ tsp fennel seeds
30ml/2 tbsp desiccated (dry unsweetened shredded) coconut
30 ml/2 tbsp vegetable oil
1.5ml/¼ tsp cumin seeds
1.5ml/¼ tsp ground coriander
1.5ml/¼ tsp ground cumin
1.5ml/¼ tsp salt
150ml/¼ pint/⅔ cup water
175ml/6fl oz/¾ cup single (light) cream
45ml/3 tbsp finely chopped fresh coriander (cilantro)
fresh coriander (cilantro) sprig, to garnish
boiled rice, to serve

1 Mix together the turmeric, lime juice and salt and rub over the fish fillets until thoroughly coated. Cover and leave to marinate for 15 minutes.

2 Meanwhile, in a food processor or mortar and pestle, grind the onion, chilli, garlic, cashew nuts, fennel seeds and desiccated coconut to a coarse paste. Spoon the paste into a small bowl and set aside.

3 Heat the oil in a wok or large frying pan and fry the cumin seeds for 2 minutes until they begin to release their aroma and splutter slightly.

4 Add the spice paste to the pan and fry for 5 minutes, then stir in the ground coriander, cumin, salt and water and fry for a further 2–3 minutes.

5 Add the single cream and the fresh coriander. Simmer for 5 minutes. Add the fish and carefully stir in. Cover and cook gently for 10 minutes until the fish is tender. Serve with rice, garnished with a coriander sprig.

Indian-spiced Fish Casserole

A spicy fish stew made with potatoes, peppers and traditional Indian spices.

Serves 4

30 ml/2 tbsp oil
5 ml/1 tsp cumin seeds
1 onion, chopped
1 red pepper, thinly sliced
1 garlic clove, crushed
2 red chillies, finely chopped
2 bay leaves
2.5 ml/½ tsp salt
5 ml/1 tsp ground cumin
5 ml/1 tsp ground coriander
5 ml/1 tsp chilli powder
400 g/14 oz can chopped tomatoes
2 large potatoes, cut into 2.5 cm/1 in chunks
300 ml/½ pint/1¼ cups fish stock
4 cod fillets
chapatis, to serve

1 Heat the oil in a large, deep-sided frying pan and fry the cumin seeds for 2 minutes until they begin to splutter. Add the onion, pepper, garlic, chillies and bay leaves and fry for 5–7 minutes until the onions have browned.

2 Add the salt, ground cumin, ground coriander and chilli powder and cook for 3–4 minutes.

3 Stir in the tomatoes, potatoes and fish stock. Bring to the boil and simmer for a further 10 minutes.

4 Add the fish, then cover and simmer for 10 minutes, or until the fish is tender. Serve with chapatis.

Variations

- *In place of chappatis, serve this fish curry with pilau or plain rice with a few chopped herbs (coriander and parsley) added.*
- *If you prefer another fish, try haddock or another firm fish such as monkfish or hake.*
- *To ring the changes, use 450ml/¾pint/scant 2 cups coconut milk in place of the chopped tomatoes.*
- *For a change of flavour, replace the red chillies with green chillies. Deseed and finely chop them.*
- *Add another vegetable or replace the potatoes with two bulbs of fennel, sliced.*

Fish Curry Energy 575kcal/2390kJ; Protein 40g; Carbohydrate 6.2g, of which sugars 4.9g; Fat 43.5g, of which saturates 5.9g; Cholesterol 6mg; Calcium 132mg; Fibre 0g; Sodium 362mg.
Spiced Casserole Energy 332kcal/1396kJ; Protein 36.9g; Carbohydrate 27.6g, of which sugars 7.9g; Fat 9.2g, of which saturates 1.3g; Cholesterol 81mg; Calcium 59mg; Fibre 2.9g; Sodium 132mg.

Red-hot Fish Curry

The island of Bali has wonderful fish, surrounded as it is by sparkling blue sea. This simple fish curry is packed with many of the characteristic flavours associated with Indonesia.

Serves 4 to 6

675g/1½lb cod or haddock fillet
1cm/½in cube shrimp paste
2 red or white onions
2.5cm/1in fresh root ginger, peeled and sliced
1cm/½in fresh galangal, peeled and sliced
2 garlic cloves
1–2 fresh red chillies, seeded, or 10ml/2 tsp chilli sambal, or 5–10ml/1–2 tsp chilli powder
90ml/6 tbsp sunflower oil
15ml/1 tbsp dark soy sauce
5ml/1 tsp tamarind pulp, soaked in 30ml/2 tbsp warm water
250ml/8fl oz/1 cup water
celery leaves or chopped fresh chilli, to garnish
boiled rice, to serve

1 Skin the fish fillets, remove any bones and then cut the flesh into bitesize pieces. Pat the fish dry with kitchen paper and set aside until needed.

2 Grind the shrimp paste, onions, ginger, fresh galangal, garlic and fresh chillies, if using, to a paste in a food processor or with a mortar and pestle. Stir in the chilli sambal or chilli powder, if using.

3 Heat 30ml/2 tbsp of the oil and fry the spice mixture, stirring, until it gives off a rich aroma.

4 Add the soy sauce to the pan. Strain the soaked tamarind pulp and add the juice and water, mixing well. Cook gently for 2–3 minutes.

5 In a separate pan, fry the fish fillets in the remaining oil for 2–3 minutes. Turn the fish once only so that the pieces stay whole and don't break apart. Lift out with a slotted spoon and place them in the pan with the sauce.

6 Simmer the fish in the sauce for a further 3 minutes and serve with boiled rice. Garnish with feathery celery leaves or a little chopped fresh chilli, if you like.

Monkfish and Okra Curry

An interesting combination of flavours and textures is used to make this delicious fish dish.

Serves 4

450g/1lb monkfish
5ml/1 tsp ground turmeric
2.5ml/½ tsp chilli powder
2.5ml/½ tsp salt
5ml/1 tsp cumin seeds
2.5ml/½ tsp fennel seeds
2 dried red chillies
45ml/3 tbsp vegetable oil
1 onion, finely chopped
2 garlic cloves, crushed
4 tomatoes, skinned and finely chopped
150ml/¼ pint/⅔ cup water
225g/8oz okra, trimmed and cut into 2.5cm/1in lengths
5ml/1 tsp garam masala
tomato rice, to serve

1 Remove the membrane and bones from the monkfish, cut into 2.5cm/1in cubes and place in a dish. Mix together the turmeric, chilli powder and 1.5ml/¼ tsp of the salt and rub the mixture all over the fish. Marinate for 15 minutes.

2 Put the cumin seeds, fennel seeds and chillies in a wok or a large frying pan and dry-roast for about 3–4 minutes until a fragrant aroma is released. Put the spices into a blender, or use a mortar and pestle, and grind to a coarse powder.

3 Heat 30ml/2 tbsp of the oil in the frying pan and and fry the fish for about 4–5 minutes, turning occasionally. Remove with a slotted spoon and drain on kitchen paper.

4 Add the remaining oil to the pan and gently fry the onion and garlic for about 5 minutes, until soft and translucent. Add the spice powder and the remaining salt to the pan and fry for a further 2–3 minutes.

5 Stir the chopped tomatoes and the water into the pan. Simmer the mixture gently for 5 minutes, stirring occasionally.

6 Add the prepared okra and cook for about 5–7 minutes. Return the fish to the pan with the garam masala. Cover and simmer for 5–6 minutes or until the fish is tender. Serve with tomato rice.

Red-hot Curry Energy 322kcal/1342kJ; Protein 33g; Carbohydrate 8g, of which sugars 5g; Fat 18g,of which saturates 2g; Cholesterol 84mg; Calcium 53mg; Fibre 1.1g; Sodium 200mg.
Monkfish Curry Energy 203kcal/851kJ; Protein 20.9g; Carbohydrate 7.7g, of which sugars 5.4g; Fat 10.2g, of which saturates 1.5g; Cholesterol 16mg; Calcium 119mg; Fibre 3.5g; Sodium 36mg.

Northern Fish Curry with Chillies, Shallots and Lemon Grass

This is a thin, soupy curry with wonderfully strong Thai flavourings of lemon grass, garlic,chillies and the classic fish sauce.

Serves 4

450g/1lb salmon fillet
500ml/17fl oz/2¼ cups vegetable stock
4 shallots, finely chopped
2 garlic cloves, finely chopped
2.5cm/1in piece fresh galangal, finely chopped
1 lemon grass stalk, finely chopped
2.5ml/½ tsp dried chilli flakes
15ml/1 tbsp Thai fish sauce
5ml/1 tsp palm sugar (jaggery) or light muscovado (brown) sugar

1 Place the salmon fillet in the freezer for 30–40 minutes to firm up the flesh slightly, ready for slicing.

2 Remove and discard the skin on the salmon, then use a sharp knife to cut the fish into bitesize pieces, about 2.5cm/1in cubes, removing any stray bones with your fingers or with tweezers as you do so.

3 Pour the vegetable stock into a large, heavy pan and bring it to the boil over a medium heat.

4 Add the shallots, garlic, galangal, lemon grass, chilli flakes, fish sauce and sugar. Bring back to the boil, stir well, then reduce the heat and simmer gently for 15 minutes.

5 Add the fish to the pan, bring the mixture back to the boil, then turn off the heat.

6 Leave the curry to stand for 10–15 minutes until the fish is cooked through, then serve in warmed bowls.

Cook's Tip

A bowl of this curry will make a perfect appetizer, or serve with lots of sticky rice for a more substantial lunch or main course.

Spicy Fish Curry with Tamarind

The addition of tamarind to this Goan curry gives a slightly sour note to the spicy coconut sauce.

Serves 4

7.5ml/1½ tsp ground turmeric
5ml/1 tsp salt
450g/1lb monkfish fillet, cut into eight pieces
15ml/1 tbsp lemon juice
5ml/1 tsp cumin seeds
5ml/1 tsp coriander seeds
5ml/1 tsp black peppercorns
1 garlic clove, chopped
5cm/2in piece fresh root ginger, finely chopped
25g/1oz tamarind paste
150ml/¼ pint/⅔ cup hot water
30ml/2 tbsp vegetable oil
2 onions, halved and sliced lengthways
400ml/14fl oz/1⅔ cups coconut milk
4 mild green chillies, seeded and cut into thin strips
16 large prawns (shrimp), peeled
30ml/2 tbsp chopped fresh coriander (cilantro) leaves, to garnish

1 Mix together the ground turmeric and salt in a bowl. Place the fish in a shallow dish and sprinkle over the lemon juice, then rub the turmeric mixture over the fish. Cover and chill.

2 Put the cumin and coriander seeds and peppercorns in a blender or food processor and blend to a powder. Add the garlic and ginger and process for a few seconds more.

3 Preheat the oven to 200°C/400°F/Gas 6. Mix the tamarind paste and hot water and set aside. Heat the oil in a frying pan, add the onions and cook for 5–6 minutes, until softened and golden. Transfer the onions to a shallow earthenware dish. Add the fish to pan, and fry over a high heat, turning to seal on all sides. Remove from the pan and place on top of the onions.

4 Fry the ground spice mixture in the pan, stirring constantly, for 1–2 minutes. Stir in the tamarind liquid, coconut milk and chilli strips then bring to the boil. Pour over the fish.

5 Cover the dish and cook in the oven for 10 minutes. Add the prawns, and cook for a further 5 minutes, or until the prawns are pink. Do not overcook them or they will toughen. Check the seasoning, sprinkle with coriander leaves and serve.

Northern Fish Curry Energy 212kcal/882kJ; Protein 23.1g; Carbohydrate 1.7g, of which sugars 1.6g; Fat 12.5g, of which saturates 2.2g; Cholesterol 56mg; Calcium 28mg; Fibre 0.2g; Sodium 267mg.
Spicy Fish Curry Energy 220kcal/926kJ; Protein 28g; Carbohydrate 12.8g, of which sugars 10.5g; Fat 6.8g, of which saturates 1g; Cholesterol 113mg; Calcium 103mg; Fibre 1.4g; Sodium 720mg.

Sour Fish, Star Fruit and Chilli Stew

Somewhere between a stew and a soup, this refreshing dish is just one of many variations on the theme of sour fish stew found throughout South-east Asia. The star fruit are added towards the end of cooking so that they retain a bite.

Serves 4 to 6

30ml/2 tbsp coconut or palm oil
900ml/1½ pints/3¾ cups water
2 lemon grass stalks, bruised
25g/1oz fresh root ginger, finely sliced
about 675g/1½lb freshwater or saltwater fish, such as trout or sea bream, cut into thin steaks
2 firm star fruit (carambola), sliced
juice of 1–2 limes

For the spice paste

4 shallots, chopped
4 red chillies, seeded and chopped
2 garlic cloves, chopped
25g/1oz galangal, chopped
25g/1oz fresh turmeric, chopped
3–4 candlenuts, chopped

To serve

1 bunch fresh basil leaves
1 lime, cut into wedges
steamed rice

1 Using a mortar and pestle or food processor, grind all the spice paste ingredients together to form a coarse paste.

2 Heat the oil in a wok or wide, heavy pan, stir in the spice paste and fry until fragrant. Pour in the water and add the lemon grass and ginger. Bring to the boil, stirring all the time, then reduce the heat and simmer for 10 minutes.

3 Slip the fish steaks into the pan, making sure there is enough cooking liquid to cover the fish and adding more water if necessary. Simmer gently for 3–4 minutes, then add the star fruit and lime juice. Simmer for a further 2–3 minutes, until the fish is cooked.

4 Divide the fish and star fruit between four to six warmed serving bowls and add a little of the cooking liquid. Garnish with basil leaves and a wedge of lime to squeeze over it. Serve the stew with bowls of steamed rice, which is moistened by spoonfuls of the remaining cooking liquid.

Malaysian Fish Curry with Dried Red Chillies

The fish curries of Malaysia differ slightly from region to region, but most of them include Indian spices and coconut milk. The Malay food stalls often feature a fish, chicken or beef curry, which is usually served with bread or rice, pickles and extra chillies.

Serves 4

30ml/2 tbsp vegetable oil
7.5ml/1½ tsp tamarind paste
8 thick fish cutlets, each about 90g/3½oz, such as grouper, red snapper, trout or mackerel
900ml/1½ pints coconut milk
salt
fresh coriander (cilantro) leaves, roughly chopped, to garnish
rice or crusty bread, to serve

For the curry paste

4 shallots, chopped
4 garlic cloves, chopped
50g/2oz fresh root ginger, peeled and chopped
25g/1oz fresh turmeric, chopped
4–6 dried red chillies, softened in warm water, seeded and chopped
15ml/1 tbsp coriander seeds, roasted
15ml/1 tbsp cumin seeds, roasted
10ml/2 tsp fish curry powder
5ml/1 tsp fennel seeds
2.5ml/½ tsp black peppercorns

1 First make the paste. Using a mortar and pestle or food processor, grind the shallots, garlic, ginger, turmeric and chillies to a paste and transfer to a bowl.

2 Again, using the mortar and pestle or food processor, grind the roasted coriander and cumin seeds, fish curry powder, fennel seeds and peppercorns to a powder and add to the paste. Bind with 15ml/1 tbsp water and mix together.

3 Heat the oil in a wok or heavy pan. Stir in the paste and fry until fragrant. Add the tamarind paste and mix well. Add the fish cutlets and cook for 1 minute on each side. Pour in the coconut milk. Bring to the boil, then simmer for 10–15 minutes.

4 Season to taste with salt. Sprinkle the coriander over the top and serve with rice for a substantial meal, or with chunks of crusty bread for an appetizer.

Sour Fish Stew Energy 240kcal/1001kJ; Protein 25.9g; Carbohydrate 7.3g, of which sugars 4.7g; Fat 12.1g, of which saturates 1.2g; Cholesterol 0mg; Calcium 27mg; Fibre 1.7g; Sodium 67mg.
Malaysian Fish Curry Energy 264kcal/1109kJ; Protein 36.6g; Carbohydrate 12.7g, of which sugars 12.1g; Fat 7.7g, of which saturates 1.3g; Cholesterol 89mg; Calcium 110mg; Fibre 1g; Sodium 354mg.

Chicken Fillets with a Chilli Marmalade

The aji amarillo is a hot yellowy-orange Peruvian chilli. It is best to make the marmalade a day ahead so the flavours can mellow.

Serves 4

500g/1¼lb skinless chicken breast fillets each cut into 4 long strips
2 garlic cloves, crushed to a paste with 2.5ml/½ tsp salt
30ml/2 tbsp olive oil
ground black pepper
flat bread, to serve

For the chilli marmalade

50g/2oz dried aji amarillo chillies
120ml/4fl oz/½ cup water
20ml/4 tsp olive oil
2 onions, finely chopped
3 garlic cloves, crushed
5ml/1 tsp ground cumin
10ml/2 tsp Mexican oregano
130g/4½oz/scant ¾ cup sugar
200ml/7fl oz/scant 1 cup cider or white wine vinegar
2 small orange (bell) peppers, quartered and seeded

1 Make the marmalade. Heat a frying pan, add the dried chillies and roast, stirring, for 1½ minutes. Put them in a bowl with enough hot water to cover. Rehydrate for about 2 hours.

2 Discard the chilli seeds and dice the flesh. Place in a food processor, add the water and process to a purée. Heat the oil in a heavy pan. Cook the onions and garlic for 5 minutes. Add the cumin, oregano and chilli purée. Add the sugar and stir until turning syrupy. Add the vinegar. Boil, then simmer for 30 minutes.

3 Heat a griddle. Roast the peppers, skin side down to char the skins. Place in a bowl and cover. When cool, rub off the skins and dice the flesh. Add to the chilli mixture. Simmer for 25 minutes, or until the marmalade thickens. Transfer to a bowl. When cool, cover and chill until needed.

4 Spread the chicken pieces in a shallow dish and coat with the garlic, oil and pepper. Cover and set aside for 30–45 minutes.

5 Prepare the barbecue. When the coals are medium-hot, and with a covering of ash, grill the chicken pieces for 2½–3 minutes on each side. Serve with the marmalade and toasted flat bread.

Spicy Chicken Satay with Chilli Relish

This spicy marinade quickly gives an exotic flavour to tender chicken. The satays can be cooked on a barbecue or under the grill.

Serves 4

4 skinless chicken breast fillets, about 175g/6oz each
60ml/4 tbsp sambal kecap

1 Cut the chicken breast fillets into 2.5cm/1in cubes and place in a bowl with the sambal kecap. Mix thoroughly so the chicken is well coated. Cover and leave in a cool place to marinate for at least 1 hour.

2 Soak eight bamboo skewers in cold water for 30 minutes so they don't burn while cooking the chicken.

3 Pour the chicken and the marinade into a sieve (strainer) placed over a pan and leave to drain for a few minutes. Set the sieve aside.

4 Add 30ml/2 tbsp hot water to the marinade and bring to the boil. Lower the heat and simmer for 2 minutes, then pour into a bowl and leave to cool.

5 Drain the skewers, thread them with the chicken and cook under a grill (broiler) or on a barbecue for about 10 minutes, turning regularly until the chicken is golden brown and cooked through. Serve with the sambal kecap as a dip.

Cook's Tip

Sambal kecap is a popular Indonesian sauce. Look for it in Asian food stores or, if unavailable, try making your own version. In a bowl, mix together 30ml/2 tbsp dark soy sauce; juice of ½ a lemon or 1 lime; 2 hot chilli peppers, crushed, or 5ml/1 tsp chilli powder; 2 shallots, sliced very thin; 1 clove of garlic, crushed (optional); 15ml/1 tbsp hot water. Leave to stand for 30 minutes before serving to let the flavours mingle.

Chicken with Marmalade Energy 348kcal/1467kJ; Protein 31.4g; Carbohydrate 41.6g, of which sugars 40.9g; Fat 7.3g, of which saturates 1.3g; Cholesterol 88mg; Calcium 35mg; Fibre 1.8g; Sodium 82mg.
Spicy Chicken Satay Energy 265kcal/1120kJ; Protein 55.2g; Carbohydrate 3.5g, of which sugars 2g; Fat 3.4g, of which saturates 1g; Cholesterol 158mg; Calcium 19mg; Fibre 0.6g; Sodium 1204mg.

Chicken Satay with Hot Cashew Nut Sambal

Delicious satay skewers are grilled then served with a spicy sambal sauce.

Serves 6

about 1kg/2¼lb skinless chicken breast fillets
30ml/2 tbsp olive oil
5ml/1 tsp ground coriander
2.5ml/½ tsp ground cumin
2.5cm/1in piece of fresh root ginger, finely grated
2 garlic cloves, crushed
5ml/1 tsp caster (superfine) sugar
2.5ml/½ tsp salt
18 long pandanus leaves, each halved to give 21cm/8½in lengths
36 bamboo or wooden skewers

For the hot cashew nut sambal

2 garlic cloves, roughly chopped
4 small fresh hot green chillies (not tiny birdseye chillies), seeded and sliced
50g/2oz/⅓ cup cashew nuts
10ml/2 tsp sugar, preferably palm sugar (jaggery)
75ml/5 tbsp light soy sauce
juice of ½ lime
30ml/2 tbsp coconut cream

1 To make the sambal, grind the garlic and chillies quite finely in a mortar with a pestle. Add the nuts and grind until the mixture is almost smooth, with a bit of texture. Pound in the remaining ingredients, cover and put in a cool place.

2 Soak the bamboo or wooden skewers in water for 30 minutes. Slice the chicken horizontally into thin pieces and then into strips about 2.5cm/1in wide. Toss in the oil. Mix the spices, ginger, garlic, sugar and salt together. Rub this mixture into the chicken. Leave to marinate while you prepare the barbecue.

3 Thread a strip of pandanus leaf and a piece of chicken on to each skewer. Once the flames have died down, rake the coals to one side. Position an oiled grill rack over the coals to heat.

4 When the coals are medium-hot, or with a moderate coating of ash, place the satays meat side down on the rack and cover with a lid or tented heavy-duty foil and cook for 5–7 minutes. Once the meat has seared, move the satays around so that the leaves don't scorch. Serve hot, with the sambal.

Tandoori Drumsticks with Chilli Salad

A delicious tandoori chicken with a chilli onion salad.

Serves 6

12 chicken drumsticks, skinned
3 garlic cloves, crushed to a paste with a pinch of salt
150ml/¼ pint/⅔ cup Greek (US strained plain) yogurt
10ml/2 tsp ground coriander
5ml/1 tsp ground cumin
5ml/1 tsp ground turmeric
1.5ml/¼ tsp cayenne pepper
2.5ml/½ tsp garam masala
15ml/1 tbsp curry paste
juice of ½ lemon
salt
warmed naan breads, to serve

For the chilli onion salad

2 pink onions, halved and sliced
10ml/2 tsp salt
4cm/1½in piece of fresh root ginger, finely shredded
2 fresh long green chillies, seeded and finely chopped
20ml/4 tsp palm sugar (jaggery)
juice of ½ lemon
60ml/4 tbsp chopped fresh coriander (cilantro)

1 Score each drumstick around the flesh that attaches itself to the tip of the bone so it is easier to remove the end of the chunky knuckle later. Put the garlic, yogurt, spices, curry paste and lemon juice in a food processor and whizz until smooth. Pour over the drumsticks, cover and chill overnight.

2 Two hours before serving make the salad. Put the onion in a bowl, sprinkle with the salt, cover and set aside for 1 hour. Rinse, then drain and pat dry. Chop the slices and put them in a serving bowl. Add the remaining ingredients and mix well. An hour before cooking, drain the drumsticks over a bowl. Remove the knuckle bone at the end of each drumstick and scrape the flesh so the bone is clean. Return to the marinade.

3 Prepare the barbecue. Salt the drumsticks. When the coals are medium-hot, wrap the drumstick tips with strips of foil to prevent them from burning, then place on the grill rack so that they are not directly over the coals. Cover with a lid or tented heavy-duty foil and cook for 5 minutes, turning frequently. Brush with a little of the marinade and cook for 5–7 minutes more, or until cooked. Serve hot with the salad and naan breads.

Chicken Satay Energy 197kcal/835kJ; Protein 42.5g; Carbohydrate 2.4g, of which sugars 2g; Fat 2g, of which saturates 0.5g; Cholesterol 123mg; Calcium 15mg; Fibre 0.4g; Sodium 640mg.
Tandoori Drumsticks Energy 155kcal/654kJ; Protein 23g; Carbohydrate 6.4g, of which sugars 6.1g; Fat 4.5g, of which saturates 1.3g; Cholesterol 108mg; Calcium 81mg; Fibre 0.6g; Sodium 160mg.

East African-spiced Roast Chicken

A delicious, and impressive whole roast chicken stuffed with a tasty African paste.

Serves 6

1.8kg/4lb chicken
30ml/2 tbsp softened butter, plus extra for basting
3 garlic cloves, crushed
5ml/1 tsp ground black pepper
5ml/1 tsp ground turmeric
2.5ml/½ tsp ground cumin
5ml/1 tsp dried thyme
15ml/1 tbsp finely chopped fresh coriander (cilantro)
60ml/4 tbsp thick coconut milk
60ml/4 tbsp medium-dry sherry
5ml/1 tsp tomato purée (paste)
salt and chilli powder
coriander (cilantro) leaves, to garnish

1 Remove the giblets from the chicken, if necessary, rinse out the cavity and pat the skin dry.

2 Put the softened butter together with all the remaining ingredients in a large bowl and mix together well to form a thick paste.

3 Gently ease the skin of the chicken away from the flesh and rub generously with the herb and butter mixture. Rub more of the mixture over the skin, legs and wings of the chicken and into the neck cavity.

4 Place the chicken in a roasting pan, cover loosely with foil and leave to marinate for about 4 hours or overnight in the refrigerator, if possible.

5 Preheat the oven to 190°C/375°F/Gas 5. Cover the chicken with clean foil and roast for 1 hour.

6 Take the chicken out of the oven, turn the chicken over and baste thoroughly with the pan juices. Cover again with foil, and cook for a further 30 minutes.

7 Remove the foil and place the chicken breast side up. Rub all over with a little extra butter and roast for a further 10–15 minutes until the skin is golden brown and the juices run clear when the thickest part of the chicken is pierced with a skewer. Serve with a rice dish or a salad, garnished with coriander.

Spiced Chicken Wings

Fresh crushed ginger is used in the marinade and this spicy dish is also garnished with shredded ginger. Try to buy chicken wings that are already skinned, as it is very hard to skin them yourself.

Serves 4

10–12 chicken wings, skinned
175ml/6fl oz/⅔ cup natural (plain) low-fat yogurt
7.5ml/1½ tsp crushed ginger
5ml/1 tsp salt
5ml/1 tsp Tabasco sauce
15ml/1 tbsp tomato ketchup
5ml/1 tsp crushed garlic
15ml/1 tbsp lemon juice
15ml/1 tbsp fresh coriander (cilantro) leaves
15ml/1 tbsp corn oil
2 medium onions, sliced
15ml/1 tbsp grated fresh root ginger
salt and ground black pepper

1 Place the chicken wings in a large mixing bowl, season and set aside while making the marinade.

2 Pour the yogurt into another bowl along with the crushed ginger, salt, Tabasco, tomato ketchup, crushed garlic, lemon juice and half the coriander.

3 Whisk all the ingredients together, pour over the chicken wings and mix well until the chicken is thoroughly coated.

4 Heat the oil in a non-stick wok or frying pan and fry the onions until they begin to soften and turn translucent.

5 Add the chicken wings to the pan. Cook over a medium heat, stirring occasionally, for 10–15 minutes. Add the remaining coriander and the shredded ginger and cook for 1–2 minutes. Serve immediately, garnished with the rest of the coriander.

Variation
This dish will work just as well with other cuts of chicken. You can substitute drumsticks or chicken breast portions for the wings in this recipe. Remember to increase the cooking time depending on what part of the chicken you are using.

African-spiced Chicken Energy 439kcal/1824kJ; Protein 43.3g; Carbohydrate 1.2g, of which sugars 1.2g; Fat 27.9g, of which saturates 10.7g; Cholesterol 2.6mg; Calcium 23mg; Fibre 0g; Sodium 211mg.
Chicken Wings Energy 224kcals/936kJ; Protein 24.33g; Carbohydrate 12.07g, of which sugars; 10g; Fat 9.00g, of which saturates 2.2g; Cholesterol 124mg; Calcium 50g; Fibre 1.24g; Sodium 0.66mg.

Tangy Barbecued Jerk Chicken

Jerk refers to the blend of herb and spice seasoning rubbed into meat, before it is roasted over charcoal. In Jamaica, jerk seasoning was originally used only for pork, but jerked chicken is equally delicious.

Serves 4

8 chicken pieces

For the marinade

5ml/1 tsp ground allspice
5ml/1 tsp ground cinnamon
5ml/1 tsp dried thyme
1.5ml/¼ tsp freshly grated nutmeg
10ml/2 tsp demerara sugar
2 garlic cloves, crushed
15ml/1 tbsp finely chopped onion
15ml/1 tbsp chopped spring onion (scallion)
15ml/1 tbsp vinegar
30ml/2 tbsp vegetable oil
15ml/1 tbsp lime juice
1 hot chilli pepper, chopped
salt and ground black pepper
salad leaves, to serve

1 Combine all the marinade ingredients in a small bowl. Using a fork, mash them together well to form a thick paste.

2 Lay the chicken pieces on a plate or board and make several lengthways slits in the flesh. Rub the seasoning all over the chicken and into the slits.

3 Place the chicken pieces in a dish, cover with clear film (plastic wrap) and marinate overnight in the fridge.

4 Shake off any excess seasoning from the chicken. Brush with oil and either place on a baking sheet or on a barbecue grill if barbecuing. Cook under a preheated grill (broiler) for 45 minutes, turning often. Or, if cooking on a barbecue, light the coals and when ready, cook over the coals for 30 minutes, turning often. Serve hot with salad leaves.

Cook's Tip

The flavour is best if you marinate the chicken overnight. Sprinkle the charcoal with aromatic herbs such as bay leaves for even more flavour.

Hot Chilli Chicken

Not for the faint-hearted, this delicious fiery, hot curry is made with a spicy chilli masala paste.

Serves 4

30ml/2 tbsp tomato purée (paste)
2 garlic cloves, roughly chopped
2 green chillies, roughly chopped
5 dried red chillies
2.5ml/½ tsp salt
1.5ml/¼ tsp sugar
5ml/1 tsp chilli powder
2.5ml/½ tsp paprika
15ml/1 tbsp curry paste
30ml/2 tbsp vegetable oil
2.5ml/½ tsp cumin seeds
1 onion, finely chopped
2 bay leaves
5ml/1 tsp ground coriander
5ml/1 tsp ground cumin
1.5ml/¼ tsp ground turmeric
400g/14oz can chopped tomatoes
150ml/¼ pint/⅔ cup water
8 chicken thighs, skinned
5ml/1 tsp garam masala
sliced green chillies, to garnish
chappatis and natural (plain) yogurt, to serve

1 Put the tomato purée, garlic, green and dried red chillies, salt, sugar, chilli powder, paprika and curry paste into a food processor or blender and process to a smooth paste. Alternatively, grind all the ingredients together using a mortar and pestle.

2 Heat the oil in a large heavy pan and fry the cumin seeds for 2 minutes. Add the onion and bay leaves and fry for a further 5 minutes.

3 Add the spice paste and fry for 2–3 minutes until it releases a fragrant aroma. Add the remaining ground spices and cook for 2 minutes.

4 Add the chopped tomatoes and the measured water to the pan. Bring the mixture to the boil and simmer for 5 minutes until the sauce thickens.

5 Add the chicken and garam masala to the sauce. Cover the pan and simmer for 25–30 minutes until the chicken is tender. Serve with chapatis and natural yogurt, garnished with sliced green chillies.

Tangy Barbecued Jerk Chicken Energy 210l/kJ; Protein 31 Carbohydrate 6g, of which sugars 5g; Fat 7g, of which saturates 1g; Cholesterol 88mg; Calcium 38mg; Fibre 1.5g; Sodium 200mg.
Hot Chilli Chicken Energy 269kcal/1128kJ; Protein 27g; Carbohydrate 9g, of which sugars 7g; Fat 15g,0 of which saturates 3g; Cholesterol 120mg; Calcium 68mg; Fibre 1.5g; Sodium 400g.

Fragrant Grilled Chicken with Fresh Red Chillies

If you have time, prepare the chicken in advance and leave it to marinate in the refrigerator for several hours – or even overnight – until ready to cook.

Serves 4

450g/1lb chicken breast fillets, with the skin on
30ml/2 tbsp sesame oil
2 garlic cloves, crushed
2 coriander (cilantro) roots, finely chopped
2 small fresh red chillies, seeded and finely chopped
30ml/2 tbsp Thai fish sauce
5ml/1 tsp sugar
cooked rice, to serve
lime wedges, to garnish

For the sauce

90ml/6 tbsp rice vinegar
60ml/4 tbsp sugar
2.5ml/½ tsp salt
2 garlic cloves, crushed
1 small fresh red chilli, seeded and finely chopped
115g/4oz/2 cups fresh coriander (cilantro), finely chopped

1 Lay the chicken breast fillets between two sheets of clear film (plastic wrap), baking parchment or foil and beat with the side of a rolling pin or the flat side of a meat tenderizer until the meat is about half its original thickness. Place in a large, shallow dish or bowl.

2 Mix together the sesame oil, garlic, coriander roots, red chillies, fish sauce and sugar in a bowl. Stir until the sugar has dissolved. Pour over the chicken. Cover with clear film and set aside to marinate in a cool place for at least 20 minutes.

3 Meanwhile, make the sauce. Heat the vinegar in a pan, add the sugar and salt and stir until the mixture begins to thicken. Add the remaining sauce ingredients, stir well, then spoon the sauce into a serving bowl.

4 Preheat the grill (broiler) and cook the chicken for 5 minutes. Turn and baste with the marinade, then cook for a further 5 minutes, or until cooked through and golden brown. Serve with rice and the sauce, garnished with lime wedges.

Chargrilled Chicken with Garlic and Chilli Peppers

An imaginative marinade can make all the difference to chicken. This garlicky marinade, with mustard and chilli, gives tender chicken a real punch.

Serves 4 to 6

1½ chickens, total weight about 2.25kg/5lb, jointed, or 12 chicken pieces
2 or 3 red or green (bell) peppers, quartered and seeded
4 or 5 ripe tomatoes, halved horizontally
lemon wedges, to serve

For the marinade

90ml/6 tbsp extra virgin olive oil
juice of 1 large lemon
5ml/1 tsp French mustard
4 garlic cloves, crushed
2 fresh red or green chillies, seeded and chopped
5ml/1 tsp dried oregano
salt and ground black pepper

1 If you are jointing the chicken yourself, divide the legs into two. Make a couple of slits in the deepest part of the flesh of each piece of chicken, using a small sharp knife. This helps the marinade to be absorbed more efficiently and will also let the chicken cook thoroughly.

2 Mix together all the marinade ingredients in a large bowl. Add the chicken and turn over to coat them thoroughly. Cover with clear film (plastic wrap) and place in the refrigerator for 4–8 hours, turning the pieces over in the marinade occasionally.

3 Prepare the barbecue. When the coals are ready, lift the chicken pieces out of the marinade and place them on the grill rack. Add the pepper quarters and the tomatoes to the marinade and set it aside for 15 minutes. Grill the chicken pieces for 20–25 minutes. Watch them closely and move them away from the area where the heat is most fierce if they start to burn.

4 Turn the chicken pieces over and cook them for 20–25 minutes more. Meanwhile, thread the peppers on two long metal skewers. Add them to the barbecue grill, with the tomatoes, for the last 15 minutes of cooking. Remember to keep an eye on them and turn them over at least once. Serve with the lemon wedges.

Fragrant Chicken Energy 243kcal/1022kJ; Protein 28g; Carbohydrate 17.7g, of which sugars 17.6g; Fat 7.1g, of which saturates 1.2g; Cholesterol 79mg; Calcium 73mg; Fibre 1.5g; Sodium 502mg.
Chargrilled Chicken Energy 760kcal/3,156kJ; Protein 61.7g; Carbohydrate 11.1g, of which sugars 10.8g; Fat 52.2g, of which saturates 13.3g; Cholesterol 313mg; Calcium 40mg; Fibre 3.1g; Sodium 235mg.

Spicy Roast Chicken with Chilli and Lemon Grass

This tasty roasted chicken is stuffed with a spicy paste and infused with lemon grass.

Serves 4 to 6

1 chicken, total weight about 1.2kg/2½lb
6 lemon grass stalks, bruised
2–3 large sweet potatoes, peeled or unpeeled, cut into wedges
40g/1½oz fresh root ginger, cut into matchsticks
30–45ml/2–3 tbsp coconut or groundnut (peanut) oil
salt and ground black pepper
green papaya salad, to serve

For the paste
90g/3½oz fresh root ginger, chopped
2–3 lemon grass stalks, chopped
3 garlic cloves, chopped
90ml/6 tbsp light soy sauce
juice of 1 kalamansi lime or 1 ordinary lime or lemon
30ml/2 tbsp palm sugar (jaggery)
ground black pepper

For the sweet chilli vinegar
90ml/6 tbsp coconut vinegar
15–30ml/1–2 tbsp granulated (white) or soft light brown sugar
2 red chillies, seeded and chopped

1 Preheat the oven to 180°C/350°F/Gas 4. First make the paste. Using a mortar and pestle, grind the ginger, lemon grass and garlic to a coarse paste. Beat in the soy sauce and lime juice. Add the sugar and mix until it dissolves. Season with pepper.

2 Put the chicken on a flat surface and gently massage the skin to loosen it. Make a few incisions in the skin and flesh and rub the paste into the slits and under the skin. Put the chicken in a roasting pan and stuff with four of the lemon grass stalks. Place the sweet potatoes in the pan with the remaining lemon grass stalks and the ginger. Drizzle with oil and season.

3 Roast in the oven for 1–1¼ hours, until the chicken juices run clear. Baste the chicken and potatoes after 50 minutes. Meanwhile, make the chilli vinegar. Mix the vinegar and sugar in a bowl until the sugar dissolves. Stir in the chillies and set aside.

4 When the chicken and potatoes are cooked, serve immediately with the sweet chilli vinegar to splash over it and a green papaya salad.

Chargrilled Quails in a Chilli and Pomegranate Marinade

This is a simple and tasty way of serving small birds, such as quails, poussins or grouse. The sharp marinade tenderizes the meat, as well as enhancing its flavour. Served straight off the charcoal grill with warm flat bread and a crunchy salad, they are delicious for lunch or supper, or you may like to include them in a barbecue spread.

Serves 4

4 quails, cleaned and boned
juice of 4 pomegranates
juice of 1 lemon
30ml/2 tbsp olive oil
5–10ml/1–2 tsp Turkish red pepper, or 5ml/1 tsp chilli powder
30–45ml/2–3 tbsp thick and creamy natural (plain) yogurt
salt
1 bunch of fresh flat leaf parsley
seeds of ½ pomegranate, to garnish

1 Soak eight wooden skewers in hot water for about 15 minutes, then drain. Thread one skewer through the wings of each bird and a second skewer through the legs to keep them together.

2 Place the skewered birds in a wide, shallow dish. Beat the pomegranate and lemon juice with the oil and red pepper or chilli powder, pour over the quails and rub it into the skin. Cover with foil and leave to marinate in a cold place or the refrigerator for 2–3 hours, turning the birds over occasionally.

3 Get the barbecue ready for cooking. Lift the birds out of the marinade and pour what is left of it into a bowl. Beat the yogurt into the leftover marinade and add a little salt.

4 Brush some of the yogurt mixture over the birds and place them on the prepared barbecue.

5 Cook for 4–5 minutes on each side, brushing with the yogurt as they cook to form a crust.

6 Chop some of the parsley and lay the rest on a serving dish. Place the cooked quails on the parsley and garnish with the pomegranate seeds and the chopped parsley. Serve hot.

Spicy Roast Chicken Energy 434kcal/1812kJ; Protein 26.2g; Carbohydrate 28.6g, of which sugars 12.6g; Fat 24.6g, of which saturates 6.5g; Cholesterol 128mg; Calcium 42mg; Fibre 2.5g; Sodium 1209mg.
Chargrilled Quails Energy 288kcal/1207kJ; Protein 37.4g; Carbohydrate 5.8g, of which sugars 5.8g; Fat 13g, of which saturates 2.7g; Cholesterol 0mg; Calcium 84mg; Fibre 0.5g; Sodium 111mg.

Stir-fried Chicken with Chillies

This is good, home cooking – simple spicy food that you can enjoy as an everyday meal. There are variations of this dish, using pork or seafood, throughout South-east Asia so this is a good place to start. The essential elements of this dish, as with many dishes from the area, are the fragrant lemon grass and the fire of the chillies, so add as much as you like. Serve with a table salad, rice wrappers and a dipping sauce.

Serves 4

15ml/1 tbsp sugar
30ml/2 tbsp sesame or groundnut (peanut) oil
2 garlic cloves, finely chopped
2–3 green or red Thai chillies, seeded and finely chopped
2 lemon grass stalks, finely sliced
1 onion, finely sliced
350g/12oz skinless chicken breast fillets, cut into bitesize strips
30ml/2 tbsp soy sauce
15ml/1 tbsp Thai fish sauce
1 bunch fresh coriander (cilantro), stalks removed, leaves chopped
salt and ground black pepper
nuoc cham, to serve

1 To make a caramel sauce, put the sugar into a small pan with a few splashes of water, but not enough to soak it. Heat it gently until the sugar has dissolved and turned golden. Set aside.

2 Heat a wok or heavy pan and add the oil. Stir in the garlic, chillies and lemon grass, and cook until they become fragrant. Add the onion and stir-fry for 1 minute, then add the chicken.

3 When the chicken begins to brown a little, add the soy sauce, fish sauce and caramel sauce. Keep the chicken moving around the wok for a minute or two, then season with a little salt and pepper. Toss the fresh coriander into the chicken and serve immediately with nuoc cham to drizzle over it.

Cook's Tip
Nuoc cham is a chilli sauce popular in Vietnam and can be found in Asian food stores. It is used as a condiment and dipping sauce and is usually made from dried red chillies, garlic and sugar, processed with water, fish sauce and lime juice.

Chicken with Basil and Chilli

This easy chicken dish is an excellent introduction to Thai cuisine. Thai basil, which is sometimes known as holy basil, has a unique, pungent flavour that is both spicy and sharp. Deep-frying the leaves adds another dimension to this dish.

Serves 4 to 6

45ml/3 tbsp vegetable oil
4 garlic cloves, thinly sliced
2–4 fresh red chillies, seeded and finely chopped
450g/1lb skinless boneless chicken breast portions, cut into bitesize pieces
45ml/3 tbsp Thai fish sauce
10ml/2 tsp dark soy sauce
5ml/1 tsp sugar
10–12 fresh Thai basil leaves
2 fresh red chillies, seeded and finely chopped, and about 20 deep-fried Thai basil leaves, to garnish

1 Heat the oil in a wok or large frying pan. Add the garlic and chillies and stir-fry for 1–2 minutes until the garlic is golden. Take care not to let the garlic burn, otherwise it will taste bitter.

2 Add the pieces of chicken to the wok or pan, in batches if necessary, and stir-fry until the chicken changes colour.

3 Stir in the fish sauce, soy sauce and sugar. Stir-fry the mixture for 3–4 minutes, or until the chicken is cooked and golden brown.

4 Stir in the fresh Thai basil leaves. Spoon the mixture on to a warm platter. Garnish with the chopped chillies and deep-fried Thai basil and serve immediately.

Cook's Tip
To deep-fry Thai basil leaves, first make sure that the leaves are completely dry or they will splutter when added to the oil. Heat vegetable or groundnut (peanut) oil in a wok or deep-fryer to 190°C/375°F or until a cube of bread, added to the oil, browns in about 45 seconds. Add the leaves and deep-fry them briefly until they are crisp and translucent – this will take only about 30–40 seconds. Lift out the leaves using a slotted spoon or wire basket and leave them to drain on kitchen paper before using.

Stir-fried Chicken Energy 202kcal/847kJ; Protein 22g; Carbohydrate 9g, of which sugars 7g; Fat 9g, of which saturates 1g; Cholesterol 61mg; Calcium 32mg; Fibre 0.6g; Sodium 800mg.
Chicken with Basil Energy 214kcal/899kJ; Protein 28g; Carbohydrate 4g, of which sugars 10g; Fat 10g, of which saturates 1g; Cholesterol 79mg; Calcium 14mg; Fibre 0.1g; Sodium 700mg.

Stir-fried Chicken and Cashews

Although it is not native to South-east Asia, the cashew tree is highly prized in Thailand and the classic partnership of these slightly sweet nuts with chicken is immensely popular both in Thailand and abroad.

Serves 4 to 6

450g/1lb boneless chicken breast portions
1 red (bell) pepper
2 garlic cloves
4 dried red chillies
30ml/2 tbsp vegetable oil
30ml/2 tbsp oyster sauce
15ml/1 tbsp soy sauce
pinch of sugar
1 bunch spring onions (scallions), cut into 5cm/2in lengths
175g/6oz/1½ cups cashews, roasted
coriander (cilantro) leaves, to garnish

1 Remove and discard the skin from the chicken breasts and trim off any excess fat. With a sharp knife, cut the chicken into bitesize pieces and set aside.

2 Cut the red pepper in half, scrape out the seeds and the paler membranes and discard, then cut the flesh into 2cm/¾in dice. Peel and thinly slice the garlic and finely chop the dried red chillies.

3 Preheat a wok and then heat the oil. The best way to do this is to drizzle the oil around the inner rim, so that it runs down and coats the entire wok.

4 Add the garlic and dried chillies to the wok and stir-fry over a medium heat until golden. Do not let the garlic burn, otherwise it will taste bitter.

5 Add the chicken to the wok and stir-fry until it is cooked through, then add the red pepper. If the mixture is very dry, add a little water.

6 Stir in the oyster sauce, soy sauce and sugar. Add the spring onions and cashew nuts. Stir-fry for 1–2 minutes more, until heated through. Spoon into a warm dish and serve immediately, garnished with the coriander leaves.

Chicken Marinated in Chilli Paste

Hot, spicy, garlicky and a little sweet, this is a truly tasty dish.

Serves 4

900g/2lb chicken breast fillet or boneless thighs
2 round (butterhead) lettuces
vegetable oil
4 spring onions (scallions), shredded

For the marinade
60ml/4 tbsp gochujang chilli paste
45ml/3 tbsp mirin or rice wine
15ml/1 tbsp dark soy sauce
4 garlic cloves, crushed
25ml/5 tsp sesame oil
15ml/1 tbsp grated fresh root ginger
2 spring onions (scallions), finely chopped
10ml/2 tsp ground black pepper
15ml/1 tbsp lemonade

1 Combine all the marinade ingredients in a large mixing bowl and stir thoroughly so they are well combined.

2 Cut the chicken into bitesize pieces, add to the bowl and stir to coat it with the marinade. Transfer to an airtight container and marinate in the refrigerator for about 3 hours.

3 Remove the outer leaves from the heads of lettuce, keeping them whole. Rinse well and place in a serving dish.

4 Lightly coat a heavy griddle pan or frying pan with vegetable oil and place it over a medium heat (the griddle can be used over charcoal). Griddle the chicken for 15 minutes, or until the meat is cooked and has turned a deep brown. Increase the heat briefly to scorch the chicken and give it a smoky flavour.

5 Serve by wrapping the chicken pieces in lettuce leaves with a few shredded spring onions.

Cook's Tip
Gochujang is a popular savoury condiment throughout Korea. Made from red chilli powder, glutinous rice powder, fermented soya beans, and salt, it was traditionally fermented over years in large earthen pots outdoors. Look for the ready-made paste in jars and bottles available in Asian stores.

Stir-fried Chicken Energy 458kcal/1909kJ; Protein 37.1g; Carbohydrate 17.7g, of which sugars 17.6g; Fat 7.1g, of which saturates 1.2g; Cholesterol 79mg; Calcium 26mg; Fibre 0g; Sodium 447mg.
Chicken Marinated in Chilli Energy 279kcal/1178kJ; Protein 55g; Carbohydrate 2g, of which sugars 2g; Fat 5.7g, of which saturates 1.1g; Cholesterol 158mg; Calcium 39mg; Fibre 0.9g; Sodium 405mg.

Cajun Chicken Piquante

The spicy tomato sauce used here, known as *sauce piquante*, goes with everything that runs, flies or swims in Louisiana. It is based on the brown Cajun roux and has chilli peppers to give it heat: vary the heat by the amount you use.

Serves 4

4 chicken legs or 2 legs and 2 breast fillets
75ml/5 tbsp cooking oil
50g/2oz/½ cup plain (all-purpose) flour
1 medium onion, chopped
2 celery sticks, sliced
1 sweet green (bell) pepper, seeded and diced
2 garlic cloves, crushed
1 bay leaf
2.5ml/½ tsp dried thyme
2.5ml/½ tsp dried oregano
1–2 red chilli peppers, seeded and finely chopped
400g/14oz can chopped tomatoes
300ml/¼ pint/1¼ cups chicken stock
salt and ground black pepper
watercress, to garnish
boiled potatoes, to serve

1 Halve the chicken legs through the joint, or the breast fillets across the middle, to give eight pieces. In a heavy frying pan, fry the chicken pieces in half the oil until brown on all sides.

2 Pour the oil from the frying pan into a large heavy pan. Over a low heat, add the flour, and stir until the roux is the colour of peanut butter. Add the onion, celery and pepper and cook for 3 minutes. Mix in the garlic, bay leaf, thyme, oregano and chillies. Stir for 1 minute, then lower the heat and stir in the tomatoes.

3 Gradually stir in the stock. Add the chicken pieces, cover and leave to simmer for 45 minutes, until the chicken is tender. If there is too much sauce, remove the lid for the last 15 minutes.

4 Serve garnished with watercress and accompanied by boiled potatoes, or perhaps a salad of your choice.

Cook's Tip
If you prefer to err on the side of caution, use just 1 chilli and hot up the sauce at the end with a dash or two of Tabasco sauce.

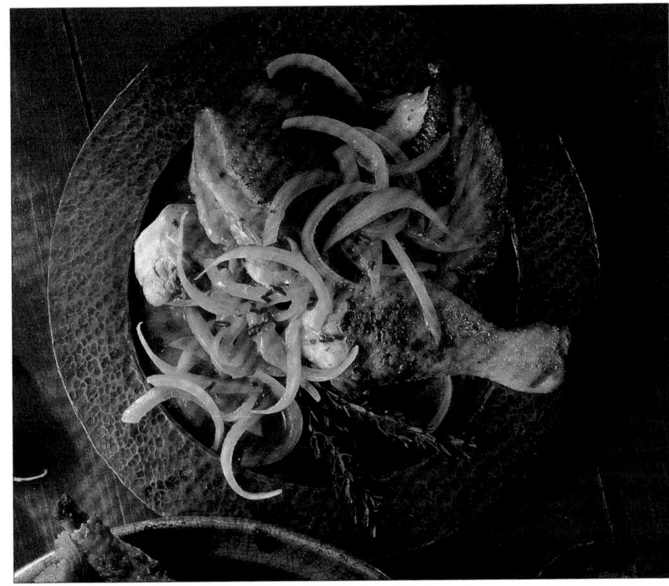

Chilli Lemon Chicken

This is a popular spicy and tangy dish in West Africa, where it is known as *yassa*. Instead of frying the chicken, African cooks often grill it before adding it to the sauce. For a less citrus taste, add less lemon juice, although the flavour does mellow.

Serves 4

150ml/¼ pint/⅔ cup lemon juice
60ml/4 tbsp malt vinegar
3 onions, sliced
60ml/4 tbsp groundnut (peanut) oil or vegetable oil
1kg/2¼lb chicken pieces
1 sprig thyme
1 green chilli, seeded and finely chopped
2 bay leaves
450ml/¾ pint/scant 2 cups chicken stock

1 In a bowl, mix together the lemon juice, vinegar, sliced onions and 30ml/2 tbsp of the oil until well combined,

2 Place the chicken pieces in a shallow dish and pour over the lemon mixture. Cover the dish with clear film (plastic wrap) and leave in a cool place to marinate for 3 hours, or overnight in the refrigerator.

3 Heat the remaining oil in a large frying pan. Cook the chicken pieces for 4–5 minutes, until browned on all sides.

4 Add the onions from the lemon marinade to the chicken. Fry for 3 minutes, then add the rest of the marinade, thyme, chilli, bay leaves and half the stock.

5 Cover the pan and simmer gently over a moderate heat for about 35 minutes, until the chicken is cooked through, adding more stock as the sauce evaporates. Serve hot.

Cook's Tip
This dish is originally from Senegal and Gambia, although it is popular throughout West Africa. For a more traditional taste, brown the chicken on a barbecue before adding it to the pan.

Cajun Chicken Piquante Energy 317kcal/1327kJ; Protein 24g; Carbohydrate 18g, of which sugars 6g; Fat 17g, of which saturates 2g; Cholesterol 105mg; Calcium 62mg; Fibre 2.5g; Sodium 400mg.
Chilli Lemon Chicken Energy 462kcal/1918kJ; Protein 37g; Carbohydrate 8.9g, of which sugars 6.3g; Fat 31g, of which saturates 8g; Cholesterol 163mg; Calcium 43mg; Fibre 1.6g; Sodium 141mg.

Peanut Chicken with Chilli

This is a variation of the popular sauce from Ghana, which was originally made from fish. In Sierra Leone, peanut butter is often added, as in this version.

Serves 4

675g/1½lb skinless chicken breast fillets
2 garlic cloves, crushed
30ml/2 tbsp butter
30ml/2 tbsp palm or vegetable oil
1 onion, finely chopped
4 tomatoes, peeled and chopped
30ml/2 tbsp peanut butter
600ml/1 pint/2½ cups chicken stock or water
1 thyme sprig or 5ml/1 tsp dried thyme
225g/8oz frozen leaf spinach, defrosted and chopped
1 fresh chilli, seeded and chopped
salt and ground black pepper
boiled yams, rice or ground rice, to serve

1 Cut the chicken fillets into thin slices, place in a bowl and stir in the garlic and season.

2 Melt the butter in a large frying pan and fry the chicken over a moderate heat, turning once or twice to brown evenly. Transfer to a plate and set aside.

3 Heat the oil in a large pan and fry the onion and tomatoes over a high heat for 5 minutes until soft. Reduce the heat, add the peanut butter and half the stock or water and stir well.

4 Cook for 4–5 minutes, stirring all the time to prevent the peanut butter burning, then add the remaining stock or water, thyme, spinach, chilli and seasoning. Stir in the chicken slices and cook over a moderate heat for about 10–15 minutes until the chicken is cooked through.

5 Pour into a warmed serving dish and serve with boiled yams, rice or ground rice.

Cook's Tip

If you're short of time, frozen spinach is more convenient, but chopped fresh spinach adds a fresher flavour to this recipe.

Spicy Spanish Chicken

This chicken dish has a spicy red pepper sauce. In the past, the dried choricero pepper – the one that gives chorizos their colour and spice – was used alone, but nowadays the dish is often made with fresh red peppers, spiced with chilli.

Serves 4

675g/1½lb red (bell) peppers
4 free-range chicken portions
10ml/2 tsp paprika
30ml/2 tbsp olive oil
1 large onion, chopped
2 garlic cloves, finely chopped
200g/7oz Serrano or other ham, in one piece, or a gammon chop
200g/7oz can chopped tomatoes
1 dried guindilla or other hot dried chilli, chopped, or 2.5ml/½ tsp chilli powder, to taste
salt and ground black pepper
chopped fresh parsley, to garnish
small new potatoes, to serve

1 Preheat the grill (broiler) to high. Put the peppers on a baking sheet and grill (broil) for 8–12 minutes, turning occasionally, until the skins have blistered and blackened. Place the peppers in a bowl, cover with clear film (plastic wrap) and leave to cool.

2 Rub salt and paprika into the chicken portions. Heat the oil in a frying pan and add the chicken, skin side down. Fry over a medium-low heat, turning until golden on all sides.

3 Meanwhile, select a casserole into which the chicken will fit comfortably. Spoon in 45ml/3 tbsp fat from the other pan. Fry the onion and garlic until soft. Dice the ham or gammon and add, stirring occasionally, for a few minutes.

4 Add the chopped tomatoes to the casserole, with the chopped dried chilli or chilli powder. Cook for 4–5 minutes.

5 Peel the skins off the peppers and discard with the seeds. Put the peppers into a blender and strain in the juices. Process, then add the paste to the casserole. Heat through.

6 Add the chicken pieces to the casserole, ensuring they are covered in sauce. Cook, covered, for 15 minutes and check the seasonings, adding more if necessary. Garnish with a little parsley and serve with small new potatoes.

Peanut Chicken Energy 387kcal/1615kJ; Protein 41.1g; Carbohydrate 7.2g, of which sugars 5.8g; Fat 21.7g, of which saturates 7.3g; Cholesterol 89mg; Calcium 131mg; Fibre 2.9g; Sodium 280mg.
Spicy Chicken Energy 332kcal/1396kJ; Protein 47.6g; Carbohydrate 13.8g, of which sugars 12.4g; Fat 10g, of which saturates 2.1g; Cholesterol 134mg; Calcium 33mg; Fibre 3.2g; Sodium 702mg.

Chicken Chilli Parcels

These fried burritos are a common sight on street stalls and in cafés along the Mexican border with Texas, but are not so well known farther south.

Serves 4

2 skinless chicken breast fillets
1 chipotle chilli, seeded
15ml/1 tbsp vegetable oil
oil, for frying
2 onions, finely chopped
4 garlic cloves, crushed
2.5ml/½ tsp ground cumin
2.5ml/½ tsp ground coriander
2.5ml/½ tsp ground cinnamon
2.5ml/½ tsp ground cloves
300g/11oz/scant 2 cups drained canned tomatillos
400g/14oz/2¾ cups cooked pinto beans
8 X 20–25cm/8–10in fresh wheat flour tortillas
salt and ground black pepper

1 Put the chicken in a large pan, pour over water to cover and add the chilli. Bring to the boil, and then simmer for 10 minutes or until the chicken is cooked and the chilli has softened. Remove the chilli and chop finely. Transfer the chicken on to a plate. Leave to cool slightly, then shred with two forks.

2 Heat the oil in a frying pan. Fry the onions until translucent, then add the garlic and ground spices and cook for 3 minutes. Add the tomatillos and pinto beans. Cook over a moderate heat for 5 minutes, stirring to break up the tomatillos and some of the beans. Simmer for 5 minutes. Add the chicken and season.

3 Wrap the tortillas in foil and place them on a plate. Stand the plate over boiling water for about 5 minutes until they become pliable. Alternatively, wrap them in microwave-safe film and heat them in a microwave on full power for 1 minute.

4 Spoon one-eighth of the bean filling into the centre of a tortilla, fold in both sides, then fold the bottom of the tortilla up and the top down to form a neat parcel. Secure with a cocktail stick (toothpick).

5 Heat the oil in a large frying pan and fry the tortilla parcels in batches until crisp, turning once. Remove them from the oil with a slotted spoon and drain on kitchen paper. Serve hot.

Hot Caribbean Peanut Chicken

Peanut butter is used in many Caribbean dishes. It adds a richness to this spicy dish, and a delicious flavour all of its own.

Serves 4

4 skinless chicken breast fillets, cut into thin strips
225g/8oz/generous 1 cup white long grain rice
30ml/2 tbsp groundnut oil
15g/½oz/1 tbsp butter, plus extra for greasing
1 onion, finely chopped
2 tomatoes, peeled, seeded and chopped
1 green chilli, seeded and sliced
60ml/4 tbsp smooth peanut butter
450ml/¾ pint/scant 2 cups chicken stock
lemon juice, to taste
salt and ground black pepper
lime wedges and sprigs of fresh flat leaf parsley, to garnish

For the marinade

15ml/1 tbsp sunflower oil
1–2 garlic cloves, crushed
5ml/1 tsp chopped fresh thyme
25ml/1½ tbsp medium curry powder
juice of half a lemon

1 Mix all the marinade ingredients in a large bowl and stir in the chicken. Cover loosely with clear film (plastic wrap) and set aside in a cool place for 2–3 hours.

2 Meanwhile, cook the rice in boiling water until tender. Drain well and turn into a generously buttered casserole.

3 Preheat the oven to 180°C/350°F/Gas 4. Heat 15ml/1 tbsp of the oil and butter in a flameproof casserole and fry the chicken for 4–5 minutes until evenly brown. Transfer to a plate. Add the onion to the casserole and fry for 5–6 minutes until lightly browned. Stir in the tomatoes and chilli. Cook for 3–4 minutes, stirring occasionally.

4 Mix the peanut butter with the stock. Mix into the tomato and onion mixture, then add the chicken. Stir in the lemon juice, season, then spoon the mixture into the casserole over the rice.

5 Cover the casserole. Cook in the oven for 15–20 minutes or until hot. Toss the rice with the chicken. Serve immediately, garnished with the lime wedges and parsley sprigs.

Chicken Parcels Energy 468kcal/1968kJ; Protein 27.5g; Carbohydrate 51.1g, of which sugars 6g; Fat 18.5g, of which saturates 2.3g; Cholesterol 61mg; Calcium 105mg; Fibre 3.3g; Sodium 271mg.
Hot Caribbean Peanut Chicken Energy 574kcal/2412kJ; Protein 39g; Carbohydrate 56g, of which sugars 5g; Fat 23g, of which saturates 6g; Cholesterol 95mg; Calcium 73mg; Fibre 2.6g; Sodium 600mg.

Fiery Chicken Casserole

This warming stew is filled with vegetables and spices. Chillies and gochujang chilli paste supply a vivid red colour and give the chicken a fiery quality.

Serves 4

3 potatoes
1 carrot
2 onions
1 chicken, about 800g/1¾lb
30ml/2 tbsp vegetable oil
2 garlic cloves, crushed
3 green chillies, seeded and sliced
1 red chilli, seeded and sliced
15ml/1 tbsp sesame oil
salt and ground black pepper
2 spring onions (scallions), finely chopped, to garnish

For the marinade

30ml/2 tbsp mirin or rice wine
salt and ground black pepper

For the seasoning

15ml/1 tbsp sesame seeds
10ml/2 tsp light soy sauce
30ml/2 tbsp gochujang chilli paste
45ml/3 tbsp Korean chilli powder

1 Peel the potatoes and cut into bitesize pieces. Soak in cold water for 15–20 minutes and drain. Peel the carrot and onions and cut into medium pieces. Cut the chicken, with skin and bone, into bitesize pieces and mix with the marinade ingredients. Stir to coat and leave for 10 minutes.

2 Heat 15ml/1 tbsp vegetable oil in a frying pan or wok, and quickly stir-fry the crushed garlic. Add the chicken and stir-fry, draining off any fat. When lightly browned, place the chicken on kitchen paper to remove any excess oil.

3 For the seasoning, grind the sesame seeds in a mortar and pestle. Combine the soy sauce, gochujang paste, chilli powder and ground sesame seeds in a bowl.

4 Heat the remaining oil and add the potatoes, carrot and onions. Cook gently, stirring well. Add the chicken. Pour in water to cover two-thirds of the meat and vegetables. Bring to the boil. Add the chilli seasoning. Simmer until the sauce has reduced by a third.

5 Add the sliced chillies and simmer for a little longer until the liquid has thickened slightly. Add the sesame oil, transfer to deep serving bowls and garnish with the chopped spring onion.

Spicy Chicken Casserole with Okra

This Turkish dish is found throughout the Middle East. A generous dose of hot red pepper is added to give a fiery kick. It is often served on its own with chunks of bread to mop up the sauce.

Serves 4

30ml/2 tbsp olive oil
30ml/2 tbsp butter
1 small free-range chicken, trimmed of excess fat and quartered
2 onions, finely sliced
2–3 garlic cloves, finely chopped
5–10ml/1–2 tsp Turkish red pepper, or 1 fresh red chilli, seeded and finely chopped
10ml/2 tsp coriander seeds
10ml/2 tsp dried oregano
5–10ml/1–2 tsp sugar
15ml/1 tbsp tomato purée (paste)
400g/14oz can chopped tomatoes
450g/1lb fresh okra, prepared as in Cook's Tip
juice of 1 lemon
salt and ground black pepper
thick and creamy natural (plain) yogurt, to serve

1 Heat the oil and butter in a wide, heavy pan or flameproof casserole. Add the chicken and brown on all sides. Set aside.

2 Add the onions, garlic, red pepper or chilli, coriander seeds and oregano to the pan. Stir in the sugar and cook until the onions begin to colour, then stir in the tomato purée and tomatoes and add 150ml/¼ pint/⅔ cup water. Bubble up the liquid for 2–3 minutes. Add the chicken pieces and baste them with the sauce. Cover the pan and cook gently for 30 minutes.

3 Sprinkle the okra over the chicken and pour in the lemon juice. Cover again and cook gently for a further 20 minutes. Transfer the chicken to a serving dish. Toss the okra into the tomato sauce, season and spoon over and around the chicken. Serve immediately, with a bowl of yogurt on the side.

Cook's Tip

To retain colour and reduce sliminess, prepare okra as follows. Cut off the stalks, then place in a bowl. Sprinkle with 15ml/1 tbsp salt and 30–45ml/2–3 tbsp white wine vinegar or cider vinegar. Mix and leave for 1–2 hours. Rinse thoroughly and pat dry.

Fiery Chicken Casserole Energy 470kcal/1955kJ; Protein 27.4g; Carbohydrate 20.4g, of which sugars 4.7g; Fat 31.5g, of which saturates 7.5g; Cholesterol 128mg; Calcium 56mg; Fibre 2.3g; Sodium 296mg.
Spicy Chicken Casserole Energy 386kcal/1617kJ; Protein 47.3g; Carbohydrate 16g, of which sugars 13.1g; Fat 15.2g, of which saturates 5.7g; Cholesterol 139mg; Calcium 224mg; Fibre 7g; Sodium 181mg.

Sweet and Spicy Chicken

This deep-fried chicken dish has a spicy kick, mellowed by the sweetness of pineapple and maple syrup.

Serves 3

675g/1½lb chicken breast fillets or boneless thighs
175g/6oz/1½ cups cornflour (cornstarch)
vegetable oil, for deep-frying
2 green chillies, sliced
2 dried red chillies, seeded and sliced
3 walnuts, finely chopped
salt and ground black pepper

For the marinade
15ml/1 tbsp white wine
15ml/1 tbsp dark soy sauce
3 garlic cloves, crushed
¼ onion, finely chopped

For the sauce
15ml/1 tbsp chilli oil
2.5ml/½ tsp gochujang chilli paste
30ml/2 tbsp dark soy sauce
7.5ml/1½ tsp pineapple juice
15 garlic cloves, peeled
30ml/2 tbsp maple syrup
15ml/1 tbsp sugar

1 Slice the chicken into bitesize strips and season with the salt and pepper. Combine all the marinade ingredients in a large bowl. Mix well and add the chicken, rubbing the mixture thoroughly into the meat. Leave to marinate for 20 minutes.

2 Sprinkle the marinated chicken with cornflour, making sure you cover the meat evenly. Fill a wok or medium heavy pan one-third full of oil and heat over high heat to 170°C/340°F, or when a piece of bread dropped in the oil browns in 15 seconds.

3 Add the chicken and deep-fry for 3–5 minutes, or until golden brown. Remove the chicken and drain on kitchen paper to remove any excess oil.

4 Blend all the sauce ingredients together in a large pan, adding the garlic cloves whole, and heat over medium heat.

5 Once the sauce is bubbling, add the fried chicken and stir to coat the meat with the sauce. Leave to simmer until the sauce has formed a sticky glaze over the chicken, and then add the chillies. Stir well and transfer to a shallow serving dish. Garnish with the walnuts before serving.

Coconut Chicken Curry with Chillies, Coriander and Cumin

A mild coconut curry from Thailand flavoured with turmeric, coriander and cumin seeds.

Serves 4

60ml/4 tbsp vegetable oil
1 large garlic clove, crushed
1 chicken, weighing about 1.6kg/3½lb, chopped into 12
400ml/14fl oz/1⅔ cups coconut cream
250ml/8fl oz/1 cup chicken stock
30ml/2 tbsp Thai fish sauce
30ml/2 tbsp sugar
juice of 2 limes
rice noodles, to serve

For the garnish
2 small fresh red chillies, seeded and finely chopped
1 bunch spring onions (scallions), thinly sliced

For the curry paste
5ml/1 tsp dried chilli flakes
2.5ml/½ tsp salt
5cm/2in piece fresh turmeric or 5ml/1 tsp ground turmeric
2.5ml/½ tsp coriander seeds
2.5ml/½ tsp cumin seeds
5ml/1 tsp dried shrimp paste

1 First make the curry paste. Put all the ingredients in a mortar, food processor or spice grinder and pound, process or grind to a smooth paste.

2 Heat the oil in a wok or frying pan and cook the garlic until golden. Add the chicken and cook until golden. Remove the chicken and set aside.

3 Reheat the oil and add the curry paste and then half the coconut cream. Cook for a few minutes until fragrant.

4 Return the chicken to the wok or pan, add the stock, mixing well, then add the remaining coconut cream, the fish sauce, sugar and lime juice. Stir well and bring to the boil, then lower the heat and simmer for 15 minutes.

5 Turn the curry into four warm serving bowls and sprinkle with the chopped fresh chillies and spring onions to garnish. Serve immediately with rice noodles.

Sweet and Spicy Chicken Energy 655kcal/2749kJ; Protein 56.4g; Carbohydrate 45.3g, of which sugars 14.4g; Fat 28.8g, of which saturates 3.5g; Cholesterol 158mg; Calcium 34mg; Fibre 0.4g; Sodium 1249mg.
Chicken Curry Energy 612kcal/254kJ; Protein 38.5g; Carbohydrate 9g, of which sugars 2.7g; Fat 47.1g, of which saturates 26.4g; Cholesterol 139mg; Calcium 22mg; Fibre 0g; Sodium 447mg.

Hot Chicken and Lemon Grass Curry with Peanuts and Coriander

This fragrant curry takes less than 20 minutes to prepare and cook – a perfect mid-week meal.

Serves 4
45ml/3 tbsp vegetable oil
2 garlic cloves, crushed
500g/1 ¼lb skinless, boneless chicken thighs, chopped into small pieces
45ml/3 tbsp Thai fish sauce
120ml/4fl oz/½ cup chicken stock
5ml/1 tsp sugar
1 lemon grass stalk, chopped into 4 sticks and lightly crushed
5 kaffir lime leaves, rolled into cylinders and thinly sliced across, plus extra to garnish
chopped roasted peanuts and chopped fresh coriander (cilantro), to garnish

For the curry paste
1 lemon grass stalk, coarsely chopped
2.5cm/1in piece fresh galangal, peeled and coarsely chopped
2 kaffir lime leaves, chopped
3 shallots, coarsely chopped
6 coriander (cilantro) roots, coarsely chopped
2 garlic cloves
2 fresh green chillies, seeded and coarsely chopped
5ml/1 tsp shrimp paste
5ml/1 tsp ground turmeric

1 Make the paste. Place all the ingredients in a mortar, or food processor, and pound with a pestle or process to a smooth paste.

2 Heat the oil in a wok or large, heavy frying pan, add the garlic and cook over a low heat, stirring frequently, until golden brown. Add the curry paste and stir-fry with the garlic for about 30 seconds more.

3 Add the chicken pieces to the pan and stir until thoroughly coated with the curry paste. Stir in the fish sauce, chicken stock and sugar. Cook, stirring constantly, for 2 minutes.

4 Add the lemon grass and lime leaves, reduce the heat and simmer for 10 minutes. If it looks dry, add a little more stock.

5 Remove the lemon grass, if you like. Serve garnished with the lime leaves, peanuts and coriander.

Chicken with Red-hot Chipotle Sauce

It is important to seek out dried chipotle chillies for this recipe, as they impart a wonderfully rich and smoky flavour to the chicken. The spicy paste can be made ahead of time, making this an ideal recipe to make when entertaining.

Serves 6
6 chipotle chillies
200ml/7fl oz/scant 1 cup chicken stock
3 onions
6 boneless chicken breast fillets
45ml/3 tbsp vegetable oil
salt and ground black pepper
fresh oregano, to garnish
boiled rice, to serve

1 Put the dried chillies in a bowl and pour over hot water to cover. Leave for about 30 minutes until soft. Drain, reserving the soaking water in a bowl. Cut off the stalk from each chilli, then slit lengthways and discard the seeds.

2 Preheat the oven to 180°C/350°F/Gas 4. Chop the flesh of the chillies roughly and put in a food processor or blender. Add enough chicken stock to the soaking water to make it up to 400ml/14fl oz/1⅔ cups. Pour into the processor or blender and process at maximum power until smooth.

3 Halve the onions and thinly slice. Remove the skin from the chicken breast fillets, then trim off any stray pieces of fat or membrane. Heat the oil in a large frying pan, add the onions and cook over a medium heat for 5 minutes, or until they have softened but not coloured.

4 Using a slotted spoon, transfer the onion to a casserole that is large enough to hold all the chicken in a single layer. Sprinkle the onion slices with salt and ground black pepper. Arrange the chicken on the onion. Season with salt and black pepper.

5 Pour the chipotle paste over the chicken in the casserole, making sure that each piece is evenly coated.

6 Bake in the preheated oven and bake for 45–60 minutes or until the chicken is cooked through, but is still moist and tender. Garnish with oregano. Serve with boiled white rice.

Hot Chicken Curry Energy 212kcal/891kJ; Protein 30.1g; Carbohydrate 1.4g, of which sugars 1.3g; Fat 9.6g, of which saturates 1.4g; Cholesterol 88mg; Calcium 8mg; Fibre 0g; Sodium 342mg.
Chicken with Chipotle Energy 229kcal/963kJ; Protein 36.7g; Carbohydrate 4.5g, of which sugars 3.3g; Fat 7.3g, of which saturates 1.1g; Cholesterol 105mg; Calcium 21mg; Fibre 0.8g; Sodium 92mg.

Ginger Chicken with Spiced Lemon and Lentils

This delicious tangy chicken stew comes from Kenya. The amount of lemon juice can be reduced, if you would prefer a less sharp sauce.

Serves 4 to 6

6 chicken thighs or pieces
2.5–4ml/½–¾ tsp ground ginger
50g/2oz mung beans
60ml/4 tbsp corn oil
2 onions, finely chopped
2 garlic cloves, crushed
5 tomatoes, peeled and chopped
1 green chilli, seeded and finely chopped
30ml/2 tbsp lemon juice
300ml/½ pint/1¼ cups coconut milk
300ml/½ pint/1¼ cups water
15ml/1 tbsp chopped fresh coriander (cilantro)
salt and ground black pepper
green vegetable, to serve

1 Place the chicken pieces in a large bowl, season with the ginger and a little salt and pepper and set aside in a cool place to marinate.

2 Meanwhile, boil the mung beans in a pan with plenty of water for 35 minutes until soft, then mash well.

3 Heat the oil in a large pan over a moderate heat and fry the chicken pieces, in batches if necessary, until evenly browned. Transfer to a plate and set aside, reserving the oil and chicken juices in the pan.

4 Add the onions to the same pan and cook them with the garlic for 5 minutes. Add the tomatoes and chilli and cook for a further 1–2 minutes, stirring well.

5 Add the mashed mung beans, lemon juice and coconut milk to the pan. Simmer for 5 minutes, then add the chicken pieces and a little water if the sauce is too thick.

6 Stir in the chopped coriander to the pan and simmer for about 35 minutes until the chicken is cooked through. Season with salt and pepper, if necessary. Serve with a green vegetable and rice or chapatis, if you like.

Chicken in Spicy Onions

This is one of the few dishes of India in which onions appear prominently. Chunky onion slices infused with toasted cumin seeds, shredded ginger and green chillies add a delicious contrast to the flavour of the chicken.

Serves 4 to 6

1.3kg/3lb chicken, jointed and skinned
2.5ml/½ tsp ground turmeric
2.5ml/½ tsp chilli powder
salt, to taste
60ml/4 tbsp vegetable oil
4 small onions, finely chopped
175g/6oz coriander (cilantro) leaves, coarsely chopped
5cm/2in piece fresh root ginger, finely shredded
2 green chillies, finely chopped
10ml/2 tsp cumin seeds, dry-roasted
75ml/5 tbsp/⅓ cup natural (plain) yogurt
75ml/5 tbsp/⅓ cup double (heavy) cream
2.5ml/½ tsp cornflour (cornstarch)

1 Rub the chicken joints with the turmeric, chilli powder and salt and leave to marinate for 1 hour.

2 Heat the oil in a frying pan and fry the chicken pieces without overlapping until both sides are sealed. Remove and keep warm.

3 Reheat the oil and fry three of the chopped onions, 150g/5oz of the coriander leaves, half the ginger, the green chillies and the cumin seeds until the onions are beginning to soften and turn translucent.

4 Return the chicken to the pan with any juices and mix well. Cover and cook gently for 15 minutes.

5 Remove the pan from the heat and allow to cool a little. In a bowl, mix together the natural yogurt, cream and cornflour until well combined. Gradually fold the mixture into the chicken pieces, mixing well.

6 Return the pan to the heat and gently cook until the chicken is tender and cooked through. Just before serving, stir in the reserved onion, coriander and ginger. Serve hot.

Ginger Chicken Energy 221kcal/928kJ; Protein 20g; Carbohydrate 16.5g, of which sugars 10.1g; Fat 8.9g, of which saturates 1.3g; Cholesterol 47mg; Calcium 66mg; Fibre 2.8g; Sodium 111mg.
Chicken in Spicy Onions Energy 439kcal/1840kJ; Protein 62.8g; Carbohydrate 7.8g, of which sugars 5.6g; Fat 17.7g, of which saturates 5.9g; Cholesterol 192mg; Calcium 120mg; Fibre 2.4g; Sodium 175mg.

West African Chilli Chicken and Rice

Serve this colourful and mildly spiced West African dish at a dinner party or other special occasion.

Serves 4

1kg/2¼lb chicken, cut into 4 to 6 pieces
2 garlic cloves, crushed
5ml/1 tsp dried thyme
30ml/2 tbsp palm or vegetable oil
400g/14oz can chopped tomatoes
15ml/1 tbsp tomato purée (paste)
1 onion, chopped
450ml/¾ pint/scant 2 cups chicken stock or water
30ml/2 tbsp dried shrimps or crayfish, ground
1 green chilli, seeded and finely chopped
350g/12oz/1½ cups long grain rice, washed

1 Rub the chicken pieces all over with the garlic and dried thyme and set aside.

2 Heat the oil in a pan until hot but not smoking and cook the chicken pieces until evenly browned. Stir in the chopped tomatoes, tomato purée and onion.

3 Cook over a moderately high heat for about 5 minutes, stirring occasionally at first and then more frequently as the tomatoes thicken.

4 Add the stock to the tomatoes and chicken and stir well. Bring to the boil, then reduce the heat, cover the pan and simmer for about 40 minutes. Add the shrimps or crayfish and the chilli. Simmer for a further 5 minutes, stirring occasionally.

5 Put the rice in a pan. Scoop 300ml/½ pint/1¼ cups of sauce into a jug (pitcher), top up with water to 450ml/¾ pint/scant 2 cups and add to the rice. Cook for 10 minutes to partly absorb the liquid.

6 Place a piece of foil on top of the rice, cover and cook over a low heat for 10 minutes, adding a little more water if necessary. Transfer the chicken pieces to a serving plate. Simmer the sauce until reduced by half. Pour over the chicken and serve immediately with the rice.

Baby Chicken in a Chilli Tamarind Sauce

The tamarind in this recipe gives the dish a tasty sweet-and-sour flavour. This is also quite a hot balti.

Serves 4 to 6

60ml/4 tbsp tomato ketchup
15ml/1 tbsp tamarind paste
60ml/4 tbsp water
7.5ml/1½ tsp chilli powder
7.5ml/1½ tsp salt
15ml/1 tbsp sugar
7.5ml/1½ tsp crushed ginger
7.5ml/1½ tsp crushed garlic
30ml/2 tbsp desiccated (dry unsweetened shredded) coconut
30ml/2 tbsp sesame seeds
5ml/1 tsp poppy seeds
5ml/1 tsp ground cumin
7.5ml/1½ tsp ground coriander
2 X 450g/1lb baby chickens, skinned and cut into 6–8 pieces each
75ml/5 tbsp corn oil
about 20 curry leaves
2.5ml/½ tsp onion seeds
3 large dried red chillies
2.5ml/½ tsp fenugreek seeds
10–12 cherry tomatoes
45ml/3 tbsp chopped fresh coriander (cilantro)
2 fresh green chillies, chopped

1 Put the tomato ketchup, tamarind paste and water into a large mixing bowl and use a fork to blend everything together.

2 Add the chilli powder, salt, sugar, ginger, garlic, coconut, sesame and poppy seeds, ground cumin and ground coriander to the mixture.

3 Add the chicken pieces and stir until they are well coated with the spice mixture. Set to one side.

4 Heat the oil in a deep frying pan or a large karahi. Add the curry leaves, onion seeds, dried red chillies and fenugreek seeds and fry for about 1 minute.

5 Add the chicken pieces to the pan, along with their spice paste, mixing as you go. Simmer gently for about 12–15 minutes, or until the chicken is thoroughly cooked.

6 Add the tomatoes, fresh coriander and green chillies, and serve immediately.

Chilli Chicken Energy 719kcal/2998kJ; Protein 44.1g; Carbohydrate 76.3g, of which sugars 5.4g; Fat 25.9g, of which saturates 7.4g; Cholesterol 163mg; Calcium 54mg; Fibre 1.3g; Sodium 187mg.
Baby Chicken Energy 268kcal/1120kJ; Protein 26g; Carbohydrate 4.1g, of which sugars 4g; Fat 16.6g, of which saturates 4.5g; Cholesterol 70mg; Calcium 60mg; Fibre 2.2g; Sodium 152mg.

Balti Chicken with Chillied Lentils and Tomatoes

This is rather an unusual combination of flavours, but highly recommended. The mango powder gives a delicious tangy flavour to this spicy dish.

Serves 4 to 6

75g/3oz/½ cup chana dhal (split yellow lentils)
60ml/4 tbsp corn oil
2 medium leeks, chopped
6 large dried red chillies
4 curry leaves
5ml/1 tsp mustard seeds
10ml/2 tsp mango powder
2 medium tomatoes, chopped
2.5ml/½ tsp chilli powder
5ml/1 tsp ground coriander
5ml/1 tsp salt
450g/1lb chicken, skinned, boned and cubed
15ml/1 tbsp chopped fresh coriander (cilantro)

1 Wash the split yellow lentils and remove any stones.

2 Put the lentils into a pan with enough water to cover, and boil for about 10 minutes until they are soft but not mushy. Drain and set aside in a bowl.

3 Heat the oil in a medium karahi or large frying pan. Lower the heat slightly and add the leeks, dried red chillies, curry leaves and mustard seeds to the pan. Stir-fry gently for a few minutes until the leeks soften and the spices are fragrant.

4 Add the mango powder, tomatoes, chilli powder, ground coriander, salt and chicken, and stir-fry for 8–10 minutes.

5 Mix in the cooked lentils and fry for a further 2 minutes, or until you are sure that the chicken is cooked right through.

6 Garnish with fresh coriander and serve with naan or paratha.

Cook's Tip
Chana dhal, a split yellow lentil, is available from Asian stores. However, split yellow peas are a good substitute.

Chicken Pasanda with Fresh Green Chillies and Coriander

Spicy, creamy and delicious – little wonder that pasanda dishes are firm favourites in Pakistan.

Serves 4

60ml/4 tbsp Greek (US strained plain) yogurt
2.5ml/½ tsp black cumin seeds
4 cardamom pods
6 whole black peppercorns
10ml/2 tsp garam masala
2.5cm/1in cinnamon stick
15ml/1 tbsp ground almonds
5ml/1 tsp crushed garlic
5ml/1 tsp crushed ginger
5ml/1 tsp chilli powder
5ml/1 tsp salt
675g/1½lb chicken, skinned, boned and cubed
75ml/5 tbsp corn oil
2 medium onions, diced
3 fresh green chillies, chopped
30ml/2 tbsp chopped fresh coriander (cilantro)
120ml/4fl oz/½ cup single (light) cream

1 Mix the yogurt, cumin seeds, cardamoms, peppercorns, garam masala, cinnamon stick, ground almonds, garlic, ginger, chilli powder and salt in a medium mixing bowl.

2 Add the chicken pieces to the bowl, ensuring they are thoroughly coated in the marinade. Set aside to marinate for about 2 hours.

3 Heat the oil in a large karahi or large frying pan. Add the onions and fry for 2–3 minutes.

4 Pour in the chicken mixture and stir until it is well blended with the onions.

5 Cook over a medium heat for about 12–15 minutes, or until the sauce has thickened and the chicken pieces are tender and cooked through.

6 Add the green chillies and fresh coriander to the pan and mix well. Stir in the cream. Bring to the boil and heat through for a minute or two. Transfer to a serving dish and garnish with more coriander, if you like.

Balti Chicken Energy 196kcal/822kJ; Protein 20.3g; Carbohydrate 9.8g, of which sugars 2.6g; Fat 8.7g, of which saturates 1.2g; Cholesterol 47mg; Calcium 41mg; Fibre 2.5g; Sodium 51mg.
Chicken Pasanda Energy 434kcal/1812kJ; Protein 44.9g; Carbohydrate 13.2g, of which sugars 7.4g; Fat 23g, of which saturates 6g; Cholesterol 135mg; Calcium 107mg; Fibre 1.4g; Sodium 129mg.

Ground Chicken with Green and Red Chillies

Minced chicken is seldom cooked in Indian or Pakistani homes. However it works very well in this delicious spicy dish.

Serves 4

275g/10oz skinless chicken breast fillets
2 thick red chillies
3 thick green chillies
45ml/3 tbsp corn oil
6 curry leaves
3 medium onions, sliced
7.5ml/1½ tsp crushed garlic
7.5ml/1½ tsp ground coriander
7.5ml/1½ tsp crushed ginger
5ml/1 tsp chilli powder
5ml/1 tsp salt
15ml/1 tbsp lemon juice
30ml/2 tbsp chopped fresh coriander leaves
chapatis and lemon wedges, to serve

1 Cut the chicken breast fillets into medium pieces. Add to a pan of boiling water for about 10 minutes until soft and cooked through. Drain.

2 Place the chicken in a food processor to mince (grind), or use a meat mincer if available.

3 Cut the chillies in half lengthways and remove the seeds, if desired. If you want a fiery dish, retain the seeds and add to the pan with the rest of the chillies. Cut the chilli flesh into strips.

4 Heat the oil in a non-stick wok or frying pan and fry the curry leaves and onions until the onions are a soft golden brown. Lower the heat and add the crushed garlic, ground coriander, crushed ginger, chilli powder and salt.

5 Add the minced chicken to the pan and stir-fry for about 3–5 minutes until it is beginning to brown.

6 Add the lemon juice, the chilli strips and most of the fresh coriander leaves. Stir for a further 3–5 minutes, then serve, garnished with the remaining coriander leaves and accompanied by chapatis and lemon wedges.

Balti Chicken in a Hot Orange and Black Pepper Sauce

Use virtually fat-free fromage frais to give this spicy sauce a rich, creamy flavour. Low-fat cream cheese can be used as a substitute if fromage frais is not available.

Serves 4

225g/8oz fromage frais or low-fat cream cheese
50ml/2fl oz/¼ cup natural (plain) low-fat yogurt
120ml/4fl oz/½ cup orange juice
7.5ml/1½ tsp crushed ginger
5ml/1 tsp crushed garlic
5ml/1 tsp ground black pepper
5ml/1 tsp salt
5ml/1 tsp ground coriander
1 baby chicken, about 675g/1½lb, skinned and cut into 8 pieces
15ml/1 tbsp corn oil
1 bay leaf
1 large onion, chopped
15ml/1 tbsp fresh mint leaves
1 green chilli, seeded and chopped

1 In a large mixing bowl, whisk together the fromage frais or cream cheese, natural yogurt, orange juice, ginger, garlic, pepper, salt and coriander.

2 Add the chicken pieces to the bowl, ensuring it is well coated, and set aside for 3–4 hours to marinate.

3 Heat the oil with the bay leaf in a wok or large frying pan and fry the onion until soft and translucent.

4 Pour the chicken mixture into the pan and cook for about 3–5 minutes over a medium heat. Lower the heat, cover with a lid and cook for 10–12 minutes, adding a little water if the sauce is too thick. When the chicken is cooked through, add the fresh mint and chilli and cook for 1–2 minutes. Serve immediately.

Cook's Tip

If you prefer the taste of curry leaves, you can use them instead of the bay leaf, but you need to double the quantity. Try to find fresh leaves in Asian food stores and markets – dried leaves lose much of their spicy aroma.

Ground Chicken Energy 196kcal/819kJ; Protein 18.4g; Carbohydrate 10.2g, of which sugars 7.3g; Fat 9.4g, of which saturates 1.2g; Cholesterol 48mg; Calcium 60mg; Fibre 2.4g; Sodium 49mg.
Balti Chicken Energy 268kcal/1129kJ; Protein 34.9g; Carbohydrate 14.8g, of which sugars 11.9g; Fat 8.3g, of which saturates 2.8g; Cholesterol 99mg; Calcium 96mg; Fibre 0.3g; Sodium 111mg.

Yellow Chicken and Papaya with a Chilli Curry Paste

The pairing of slightly sweet coconut milk and fruit with savoury chicken and spices is a comforting, refreshing and exotic combination.

Serves 4

300ml/½ pint/1¼ cups chicken stock
30ml/2 tbsp thick tamarind juice, made by mixing tamarind paste with warm water
15ml/1 tbsp sugar
200ml/7fl oz/scant 1 cup coconut milk
1 green papaya, peeled, seeded and thinly sliced
250g/9oz skinless chicken breast fillets, diced
juice of 1 lime
lime slices, to garnish

For the curry paste

1 fresh red chilli, seeded and coarsely chopped
4 garlic cloves, coarsely chopped
3 shallots, coarsely chopped
2 lemon grass stalks, sliced
5cm/2in piece fresh turmeric, coarsely chopped, or 5ml/1 tsp ground turmeric
5ml/1 tsp shrimp paste
5ml/1 tsp salt

1 Make the paste. Put the red chilli, garlic, shallots, lemon grass and turmeric in a mortar or food processor. Add the shrimp paste and salt. Pound or process to a paste.

2 Pour the stock into a wok or medium pan and bring it to the boil. Stir in the curry paste. Bring back to the boil and add the tamarind juice, sugar and coconut milk. Add the papaya and chicken and cook over a medium to high heat for about 15 minutes, stirring frequently, until the chicken is cooked.

3 Stir in the lime juice, transfer to a warm dish and serve immediately, garnished with lime slices.

Cook's Tip

Fresh turmeric resembles root ginger in appearance and is a member of the same family. When preparing it, wear gloves to protect your hands from staining.

Mild Green Curry of Chicken and Vegetables

Coconut milk creates a rich sauce that is sweet with fruit and fragrant with herbs and spices.

Serves 4

4 garlic cloves, chopped
15ml/1 tbsp chopped fresh root ginger
2–3 chillies, chopped
½ bunch fresh coriander (cilantro) leaves, roughly chopped
1 onion, chopped
juice of 1 lemon
pinch of cayenne pepper
2.5ml/½ tsp curry powder
2.5ml/½ tsp ground cumin
2–3 pinches of ground cloves
large pinch of ground coriander
3 skinless chicken breast fillets or thighs, cut into bitesize pieces
30ml/2 tbsp vegetable oil
2 cinnamon sticks
250ml/8fl oz/1 cup chicken stock
250ml/8fl oz/1 cup coconut milk
15–30ml/1–2 tbsp sugar
1–2 bananas
¼ pineapple, peeled and chopped
handful of sultanas (golden raisins)
handful of raisins or currants
2–3 sprigs of mint, thinly sliced
juice of ¼–½ lemon
salt
flat bread, to serve

1 Purée the garlic, ginger, chillies, fresh coriander, onion, lemon juice, cayenne pepper, curry powder, cumin, cloves, ground coriander and salt in a food processor or blender. Toss together the chicken pieces with about 15–30ml/1–2 tbsp of the spice mixture and set aside.

2 Heat the oil in a wok or frying pan, then add the remaining spice mixture and cook over a medium heat, stirring, for 10 minutes, or until the paste is lightly browned.

3 Stir the cinnamon sticks, stock, coconut milk and sugar into the pan, bring to the boil, then simmer for 10 minutes.

4 Stir the chicken into the sauce and cook for 2 minutes, or until the chicken becomes opaque.

5 Meanwhile, thickly slice the bananas. Stir all the fruit into the pan and cook for 1–2 minutes. Add the mint and lemon juice. Serve immediately, with flat bread.

Chicken and Papaya Energy 125kcal/533kJ; Protein 15.7g; Carbohydrate 52.8g, of which sugars 51.5g; Fat 7.5g, of which saturates 1.2g; Cholesterol 79mg; Calcium 92mg; Fibre 2.6g; Sodium 150mg.
Mild Green Curry Energy 383kcal/1622kJ; Protein 29.5g; Carbohydrate 11.9g, of which sugars 11.7g; Fat 10.4g, of which saturates 2g; Cholesterol 140mg; Calcium 78mg; Fibre 1.1g; Sodium 462mg.

Green Chicken Curry with Fresh Chillies and Coriander

Use one or two fresh green chillies in this dish, depending on how hot you like your curry. The mild aromatic flavour of the rice is a good foil for the spicy chicken.

Serves 3 to 4

4 spring onions (scallions), trimmed and coarsely chopped
1–2 fresh green chillies, seeded and coarsely chopped
2cm/¾in piece fresh root ginger
2 garlic cloves
5ml/1 tsp Thai fish sauce
bunch fresh coriander (cilantro)
small handful of fresh parsley
30–45ml/2–3 tbsp water
30ml/2 tbsp sunflower oil
4 skinless, boneless chicken breast portions, diced
1 green (bell) pepper, thinly sliced
600ml/1 pint/2½ cups coconut milk or 75g/3oz piece creamed coconut dissolved in 400ml/14fl oz/1⅔ cups boiling water
salt and ground black pepper
hot coconut rice, to serve

1 Put the spring onions, green chillies, ginger, garlic, fish sauce, coriander and parsley in a food processor or blender. Pour in 30ml/2 tbsp of the water and process to a smooth paste.

2 Heat half the oil in a large frying pan. Cook the diced chicken until evenly browned. Transfer to a plate until needed.

3 Heat the remaining oil in the pan. Add the green pepper and stir-fry for 3–4 minutes, then add the spice paste. Stir-fry for 3–4 minutes, until the mixture becomes fairly thick.

4 Return the chicken to the pan and add the coconut liquid. Season with salt and pepper and bring to the boil, then reduce the heat, half cover the pan and simmer for 8–10 minutes.

5 When the chicken is cooked, transfer it, with the green pepper, to a plate. Boil the cooking liquid remaining in the pan for 10–12 minutes, until it is well reduced and fairly thick.

6 Return the chicken and pepper to the green curry sauce, stir well and cook gently for 2–3 minutes to heat through. Spoon the curry over the coconut rice, and serve immediately.

Red-hot Chicken Curry with Fresh Red Chillies

Bamboo shoots give this fiery curry a crunchy texture.

Serves 4 to 6

1 litre/1¾ pints/4 cups coconut milk
450g/1lb skinless chicken breast fillets, diced
30ml/2 tbsp Thai fish sauce
15ml/1 tbsp sugar
1–2 drained canned bamboo shoots, total weight about 225g/8oz, rinsed and sliced
5 kaffir lime leaves, torn
salt and ground black pepper
chopped fresh red chillies and kaffir lime leaves, to garnish

For the red curry paste
5ml/1 tsp coriander seeds
2.5ml/½ tsp cumin seeds
12–15 fresh red chillies, seeded and coarsely chopped
4 shallots, thinly sliced
2 garlic cloves, chopped
15ml/1 tbsp chopped fresh galangal
2 lemon grass stalks, chopped
3 kaffir lime leaves, chopped
4 fresh coriander (cilantro) roots
10 black peppercorns
good pinch ground cinnamon
5ml/1 tsp ground turmeric
2.5ml/½ tsp shrimp paste
30ml/2 tbsp vegetable oil

1 Make the paste. Dry-fry the coriander and cumin seeds for 1–2 minutes, then put in a mortar or food processor with the remaining ingredients except the oil. Pound or process to a paste. Gradually stir in the oil. Cover and chill until ready to use.

2 Pour half of the coconut milk into a large pan. Bring to the boil, stirring constantly until the milk has separated. Stir in 30ml/2 tbsp of the red curry paste and cook the mixture, stirring, for 2–3 minutes.

3 Add the diced chicken, fish sauce and sugar to the pan. Stir well, then lower the heat and cook gently for 5–6 minutes, stirring until the chicken changes colour and is cooked through. Take care that the curry does not stick to the base of the pan.

4 Add the remaining coconut milk to the pan. Add the bamboo shoots and lime leaves. Bring back to the boil, stirring.

5 To serve, spoon the curry into a warmed serving dish and garnish with the chopped chillies and lime leaves.

Green Chicken Curry Energy 334kcal/1413kJ; Protein 49.4g; Carbohydrate 11.9g, of which sugars 11.7g; Fat 10.4g; of which saturates 2g, Cholesterol 140mg; Calcium 78mg; Fibre 1.1g; Sodium 462mg.
Red-hot Chicken Curry Energy 255kcal/1077kJ; Protein 29.5g; Carbohydrate 18g, of which sugars 16.9g; Fat 7.8g; of which saturates 1.5g, Cholesterol 79mg; Calcium 92mg; Fibre 0.9g; Sodium 1104mg.

Chicken Tikka Masala with Ginger and Chillies

Tender chicken pieces cooked in a creamy, spicy tomato sauce and served on naan bread.

Serves 4

675g/1 ½lb skinless chicken breast fillets
90ml/6 tbsp tikka paste
60ml/4 tbsp natural (plain) yogurt
30ml/2 tbsp vegetable oil
1 onion, chopped
1 garlic clove, crushed
1 green chilli, seeded and chopped
2.5cm/1in piece fresh root ginger, grated
15ml/1 tbsp tomato purée (paste)
15ml/1 tbsp ground almonds
250ml/8fl oz/1 cup water
45ml/3 tbsp butter, melted
50ml/2fl oz/¼ cup double (heavy) cream
15ml/1 tbsp lemon juice
fresh coriander (cilantro) sprigs, natural (plain) yogurt and toasted cumin seeds, to garnish
naan bread, to serve

1 Cut the chicken into 2.5cm/1in pieces. Put 45ml/3 tbsp of the tikka paste and all of the yogurt into a bowl. Add the chicken, coat thoroughly and leave to marinate for 20 minutes.

2 For the tikka sauce, heat the oil and fry the onion, garlic, chilli and ginger for 5 minutes. Add the remaining tikka paste and fry for 2 minutes. Stir in the tomato purée, almonds and water. Simmer for 15 minutes.

3 Meanwhile, thread the chicken on to wooden skewers. Preheat the grill (broiler).

4 Brush the chicken with the butter and grill (broil) under a medium heat for 15 minutes, turning occasionally.

5 Pour the tikka sauce into a food processor or blender and process until smooth. Return the sauce to the pan.

6 Add the cream and lemon juice, remove the chicken pieces from the skewers and add to the pan, then simmer for 5 minutes. Serve on naan bread and garnish with fresh coriander, yogurt and toasted cumin seeds.

Spicy Chicken Jalfrezi

A Jalfrezi curry is a stir-fried dish cooked with onions, ginger and garlic in a rich pepper sauce.

Serves 4

675g/1 ½lb skinless chicken breast fillets
30ml/2 tbsp vegetable oil
5ml/1 tsp cumin seeds
1 onion, finely chopped
1 green (bell) pepper, finely chopped
1 red (bell) pepper, finely chopped
1 garlic clove, crushed
2cm/¾in piece fresh root ginger, finely chopped
15ml/1 tbsp curry paste
1.5ml/¼ tsp chilli powder
5ml/1 tsp ground coriander
5ml/1 tsp ground cumin
2.5ml/½ tsp salt
400g/14oz can chopped tomatoes
30ml/2 tbsp chopped fresh coriander (cilantro), plus leaves, to garnish
plain rice, to serve

1 Remove any visible fat from the chicken and cut it into 2.5cm/1in pieces.

2 Heat the oil in a wok or large frying pan and fry the cumin seeds for 2–3 minutes until they begin to splutter.

3 Add the onion, green and red peppers, garlic and ginger to the pan and fry for 6–8 minutes.

4 Add the curry paste to the pan and fry for about 2 minutes, stirring constantly, until it releases its fragrant aromas.

5 Stir in the chilli powder, ground coriander, cumin and salt and add 15ml/1 tbsp cold water. Cook, stirring constantly, for a further 2 minutes.

6 Add the chicken to the pan and cook for about 5 minutes, stirring occasionally. Add the chopped tomatoes and the fresh coriander to the pan and stir well.

7 Cover the pan and simmer for about 15 minutes, or until the chicken is cooked through and tender. Garnish with the coriander and serve immediately with rice, if you like.

Chicken Tikka Energy 416kcal/1730kJ; Protein 46g; Carbohydrate 2.1g, of which sugars 0.2g; Fat 24.8g, of which saturates 8.5g; Cholesterol 203mg; Calcium 21mg; Fibre 0.5g; Sodium 172mg.
Spicy Chicken Jalfrezi Energy 338kcal/1422kJ; Protein 44.8g; Carbohydrate 20.1g, of which sugars 14g; Fat 9.5g, of which saturates 1.5g; Cholesterol 118mg; Calcium 66mg; Fibre 3.8g; Sodium 120mg.

Chicken Dhansak with Chillies

Dhansak curries originate from the Parsee community and are traditionally made with lentils and meat.

Serves 4

75g/3oz/½ cup green lentils
475ml/16fl oz/2 cups chicken stock
45ml/3 tbsp vegetable oil
5ml/1 tsp cumin seeds
2 curry leaves
1 onion, finely chopped
2.5cm/1in piece fresh root ginger, chopped
1 green chilli, seeded and finely chopped
5ml/1 tsp ground cumin
5ml/1 tsp ground coriander
1.5ml/¼ tsp salt
1.5ml/¼ tsp chilli powder
400g/14oz can chopped tomatoes
8 chicken pieces, skinned
60ml/4 tbsp chopped fresh coriander (cilantro)
5ml/1 tsp garam masala
fresh coriander (cilantro) sprigs, to garnish
plain and yellow rice, to serve

1 Rinse the lentils under cold running water, and carefully pick through to remove any stones. Put the lentils into a large heavy pan with the chicken stock. Bring to the boil, cover the pan and simmer for about 15–20 minutes. Drain, discard the liquid and set aside.

2 Heat the oil in a karahi or large heavy pan. Fry the cumin seeds and curry leaves for 2 minutes until the fragrant aromas are released and the cumin seeds begin to splutter.

3 Add the onion, ginger and chilli to the pan. Cook for about 5 minutes, until the onions begin to soften and turn translucent. Stir in the ground cumin, ground coriander, salt and chilli powder with 30ml/2 tbsp water.

4 Add the chopped tomatoes and the chicken pieces. Cover the pan and simmer for 10–15 minutes.

5 Add the lentils with the chicken stock, fresh coriander and garam masala and cook for 10 minutes, or until the chicken is cooked through and tender when pierced with a knife. Transfer the chicken to a bowl. Garnish with coriander sprigs and serve with plain and yellow rice.

Hot Chicken with Spices and Soy Sauce

This spicy dish is an Indonesian favourite, known as *ayam kecap*. Any leftovers taste equally good when reheated the following day.

Serves 4

1.6kg/3½lb chicken, jointed and cut into 16 pieces
3 onions, sliced
1 litre/1¾ pints/4 cups water
3 garlic cloves, crushed
3–4 red chillies, seeded and sliced, or 15ml/1 tbsp chilli powder
45–60ml/3–4 tbsp vegetable oil
2.5ml/½ tsp ground nutmeg
6 whole cloves
5ml/1 tsp tamarind pulp, soaked in 45ml/3 tbsp warm water
30–45ml/2–3 tbsp dark or light soy sauce
salt
fresh red chilli shreds, to garnish
boiled rice, to serve

1 Prepare the chicken and place the pieces in a large pan with one of the onions. Pour over enough water to just cover. Bring to the boil and then simmer gently for 20 minutes.

2 Meanwhile, grind the remaining onions, with the garlic and chillies, to a fine paste in a food processor or with a mortar and pestle. Heat a little of the oil in a wok or frying pan and cook the paste to bring out the flavour, but do not allow to brown.

3 Lift the chicken out of the stock in the pan using a slotted spoon and put it straight into the spicy mixture. Toss everything together over a fairly high heat so that the spices permeate the chicken pieces. Reserve 300ml/½ pint/1¼ cups of the chicken stock to add to the pan later.

4 Stir in the nutmeg and cloves. Strain the tamarind and add the tamarind juice and the soy sauce to the chicken. Cook for a further 2–3 minutes, then add the reserved stock.

5 Taste and adjust the seasoning and cook, uncovered, for a further 25–35 minutes, until the chicken pieces are tender.

6 Serve the chicken in a bowl, garnished with shredded chilli, and eat with boiled rice.

Chicken Dhansak Energy 392kcal/1653kJ; Protein 54.9g; Carbohydrate 16.7g, of which sugars 4g; Fat 12.4g, of which saturates 1.9g; Cholesterol 140mg; Calcium 52mg; Fibre 2.9g; Sodium 135mg.
Hot Chicken with Spices Energy 630kcal/2615kJ; Protein 48.8g; Carbohydrate 13.8g, of which sugars 10.7g; Fat 42.5g, of which saturates 10.6g; Cholesterol 248mg; Calcium 52mg; Fibre 2.6g; Sodium 798mg.

Spicy Duck and Sesame Stir-fry

This recipe comes from northern Thailand and is intended for game birds, as farmed duck would have too much fat. Use wild duck if you can get it. If you do use farmed duck, you should remove the skin and fat layer.

Serves 4

250g/9oz boneless wild duck meat or farmed duck, skinned and fat removed
15ml/1 tbsp sesame oil
15ml/1 tbsp vegetable oil
4 garlic cloves, finely sliced
2.5ml/½ tsp dried chilli flakes
15ml/1 tbsp Thai fish sauce
15ml/1 tbsp light soy sauce
120ml/4fl oz/½ cup water
1 head broccoli, cut into small florets
coriander (cilantro) and 15ml/1 tbsp toasted sesame seeds, to garnish

1 Cut the duck meat into bitesize pieces. Heat the sesame and vegetable oils in a wok or large, heavy frying pan and stir-fry the garlic over a medium heat until it is golden brown – do not let it burn or it will taste bitter.

2 Add the duck pieces to the pan and stir-fry for a further 2 minutes, until the meat begins to brown.

3 Stir in the chilli flakes, fish sauce, soy sauce and the measured water. Continue to cook for 1–2 minutes.

4 Add the broccoli to the pan and continue to stir-fry for about 2 minutes, until the duck is just cooked through.

5 Serve immediately on warmed plates, garnished with the coriander and sesame seeds.

Variations
- *Pak choi (bok choy), also known as Chinese flowering cabbage and celery cabbage, can be used in this recipe instead of broccoli.*
- *Other game birds will also work in this dish. Try making it with partridge, pheasant or pigeon in place of the wild duck.*

Hot Sweet and Sour Duck Casserole

This tasty casserole can be made with any game bird. It is a distinctively sweet, sour and hot dish. It is best eaten with boiled rice as an accompaniment.

Serves 4 to 6

1.3kg/3lb duck, jointed and skinned
4 bay leaves
3 tbsp salt
75ml/2½fl oz/⅓ cup vegetable oil
juice of 5 lemons
8 medium-sized onions, finely chopped
50g/2oz garlic, crushed
50g/2oz chilli powder
300ml/½ pint/1¼ cups pickling vinegar
115g/4oz fresh ginger, finely sliced or shredded
115g/4oz/½ cup sugar
50g/2oz garam masala

1 Place the duck pieces, bay leaves and salt in a large pan and cover with cold water. Bring to the boil, then simmer until the duck is fully cooked.

2 Remove the pieces of duck and keep warm. Reserve the liquid as a base for stock or soups.

3 In a large pan, heat the oil and lemon juice until it reaches smoking point. Add the onions, garlic and chilli powder and fry the onions until they are golden brown.

4 Add the vinegar, ginger and sugar and simmer until the sugar dissolves and the oil has separated from the masala.

5 Return the duck to the pan and add the garam masala. Mix well, then reheat until the masala clings to the pieces of duck and the gravy is thick.

6 Adjust the seasoning if necessary. If you prefer a thinner gravy, add a little of the reserved stock. Serve immediately.

Variation
Use pieces of rabbit in place of the duck, if you like.

Spicy Duck Stir-fry Energy 152kcal/634kJ; Protein 14.4g; Carbohydrate 1.3g, of which sugars 1.1g; Fat 10g, of which saturates 2.1g; Cholesterol 69mg; Calcium 33mg; Fibre 1.1g; Sodium 517mg.
Hot Casserole Energy 383kcal/1607kJ; Protein 26.9g; Carbohydrate 33.2g, of which sugars 25g; Fat 19g, of which saturates 2.8g; Cholesterol 128mg; Calcium 123mg; Fibre 3.6g; Sodium 184mg.

Balinese Spiced Duck

This delicious recipe is popular in Bali. Slow-cooked pieces of duck are enlivened by fragrant herbs and spices.

Serves 4

8 duck portions, fat trimmed and reserved
50g/2oz desiccated (dry unsweetened shredded) coconut
175ml/6fl oz/¾ cup coconut milk
salt and ground black pepper
fried onions, salad leaves or fresh herb sprigs, to garnish

For the spice paste

1 small onion or 4–6 shallots, sliced
2 garlic cloves, sliced
2.5cm/½in fresh root ginger, peeled and sliced
1cm/½in fresh galangal, peeled and sliced
2.5cm/1in fresh turmeric or 2.5ml/½ tsp ground turmeric
1–2 red chillies, seeded and sliced
4 macadamia nuts or 8 almonds
5ml/1 tsp coriander seeds, dry-fried

1 Place the duck fat trimmings in a heated frying pan, without oil, to render. Reserve the fat. Dry-fry the desiccated coconut in a preheated pan until it turns crisp and brown in colour.

2 To make the paste, blend the onion or shallots, garlic, ginger, galangal, fresh or ground turmeric, chillies, nuts and coriander seeds to a paste in a food processor or with a mortar and pestle.

3 Spread the spice paste over the duck portions and leave to marinate in a cool place for 3–4 hours. Preheat the oven to 160°C/325°F/Gas 3. Shake off the spice paste and transfer the duck pieces to an oiled roasting pan. Cover with a double layer of foil and cook the duck in the oven for 2 hours.

4 Turn the oven temperature up to 190°C/375°F/Gas 5. Heat the reserved duck fat in a pan, add the spice paste and fry for 1–2 minutes. Stir in the coconut milk and simmer for 2 minutes. Discard the duck juices then cover the duck with the spice mixture and sprinkle with the toasted coconut. Cook in the oven for 20–30 minutes.

5 Arrange the duck on a warm serving platter and sprinkle with the fried onions. Season to taste and serve with the salad leaves or fresh herb sprigs of your choice.

Duck Sausages with Chilli Sauce

Rich duck sausages are best baked in their own juices for 30 minutes. Creamy mashed sweet potatoes and spicy plum sauce complement and contrast with the richness of the sausages.

Serves 4

8–12 duck sausages

For the sweet potato mash

1.5kg/3¼lb sweet potatoes, cut into chunks
25g/1oz/2 tbsp butter
60ml/4 tbsp milk
salt and ground black pepper

For the plum sauce

30ml/2 tbsp olive oil
1 small onion, chopped
1 small red chilli, seeded and finely chopped
450g/1lb plums, stoned and chopped
30ml/2 tbsp red wine vinegar
45ml/3 tbsp clear honey

1 Preheat the oven to 190°C/375°F/Gas 5. Arrange the duck sausages in a single layer in a large, shallow ovenproof dish and bake, uncovered, for 25–30 minutes, turning the sausages two or three times during cooking, to ensure that they brown and cook evenly.

2 Meanwhile, put the sweet potatoes in a pan and pour in enough water to cover them. Bring to the boil, reduce the heat and simmer for 20 minutes, or until tender.

3 Drain and mash the sweet potatoes, then place the pan over a low heat. Stir frequently for about 5 minutes to dry out the mashed potatoes. Beat in the butter and milk, and season with salt and pepper.

4 Heat the oil in a frying pan and fry the onion and chilli gently for about 5 minutes until the onion is soft and translucent. Stir in the plums, vinegar and honey, then simmer gently for about 10 minutes.

5 Divide the freshly cooked sausages among four plates and serve immediately with the sweet potato mash and piquant plum sauce.

Balinese Spiced Duck Energy 305kcal/1270kJ; Protein 18.7g; Carbohydrate 9.2g, of which sugars 4.2g; Fat 22g, of which saturates 9.3g; Cholesterol 63mg; Calcium 79mg; Fibre 2.8g; Sodium 108mg.
Duck Sausages Energy 894kcal/3755kJ; Protein 17.8g; Carbohydrate 110.8g, of which sugars 42.9g; Fat 45.5g, of which saturates 17.9g; Cholesterol 67mg; Calcium 170mg; Fibre 11.6g; Sodium 1052mg.

Smoked Duck in a Chilli Spice Paste

In the villages of Indonesia, this dish of slow-cooked, tender duck is prepared for celebratory feasts. Smeared with spices and herbs and tightly wrapped in banana or pandanus leaves, the duck is smoked in the embers of a fire made from coconut husks until the aromatic meat is so tender it falls off the bone.

Serves 4

1.8kg/4lb oven-ready duck
1 large banana leaf or foil
salt and ground black pepper

For the spice paste

6–8 shallots, chopped
4 garlic cloves, chopped
4 chillies, seeded and chopped
25g/1oz fresh root ginger, chopped
50g/2oz fresh turmeric, chopped, or 25ml/1½ tbsp ground turmeric
2 lemon grass stalks, chopped
4 lime leaves, crumbled
4 candlenuts, chopped
10ml/2 tsp coriander seeds
15ml/1 tbsp shrimp paste
15–30ml/1–2 tbsp water

1 First make the paste. Using a mortar and pestle or a food processor, grind all the ingredients, except the shrimp paste and water, together to form a smooth mixture, then add the shrimp paste and water and mix together.

2 Preheat the oven to 160°C/325°F/Gas 3. Rub the spice paste all over the duck, inside and out, and sprinkle with salt and pepper. Place the duck in the centre of the banana leaf or a sheet of foil. If using a banana leaf, secure it with string to hold the filling in place. If using foil, tuck in the short sides and fold the long sides over the top to form a parcel. Place the parcel in a roasting pan.

3 Roast the duck for 4–5 hours, then open the parcel to reveal the top of the duck and roast for a further 30–45 minutes to brown the skin. Serve immediately.

Cook's Tip

This method will also work with a whole chicken, or try it with other game birds such as pheasant or partridge.

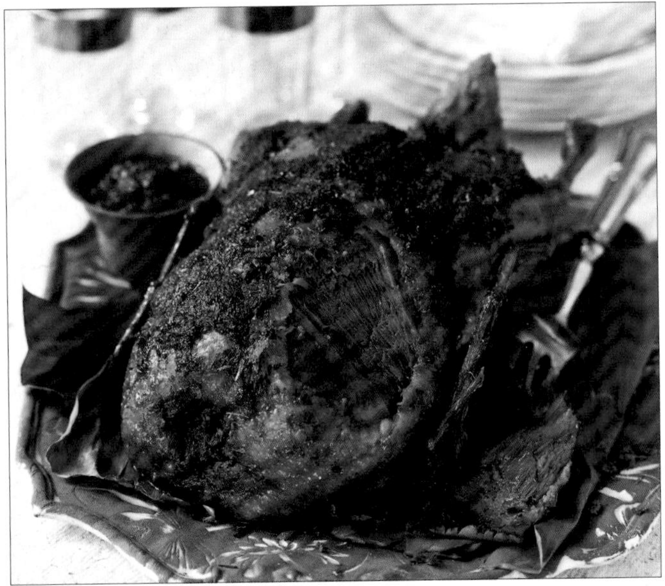

Chinese Duck Curry

A richly spiced curry in which the duck is best marinated for as long as possible, although it tastes good even if you only have time to marinate it briefly.

Serves 4

4 skinless duck breast fillets
30ml/2 tbsp five-spice powder
30ml/2 tbsp sesame oil
grated rind and juice of 1 orange
1 medium butternut squash, peeled and cubed
10ml/2 tsp Thai red curry paste
30ml/2 tbsp Thai fish sauce
15ml/1 tbsp palm sugar (jaggery) or muscovado (brown) sugar
300ml/½ pint/1¼ cups coconut milk
2 fresh red chillies, seeded
4 kaffir lime leaves, torn
small bunch coriander (cilantro), chopped, to garnish
noodles, to serve

1 Cut the duck meat into bitesize pieces and place in a bowl with the five-spice powder, sesame oil and orange rind and juice. Stir well to mix all the ingredients and coat the duck in the marinade. Cover the bowl with clear film (plastic wrap) and set aside in a cool place to marinate for at least 15 minutes.

2 Meanwhile, bring a pan of water to the boil. Add the squash and cook for 10–15 minutes, until tender. Drain and set aside.

3 Pour the marinade from the duck into a wok and heat until boiling. Stir in the curry paste and cook for 2–3 minutes. Add the duck and cook for 3–4 minutes until browned on all sides.

4 Add the fish sauce and palm sugar and cook for 2 minutes more. Stir in the coconut milk until the mixture is smooth, then add the cooked squash, with the chillies and lime leaves.

5 Simmer gently, stirring frequently, for 5 minutes, then spoon into a dish, sprinkle with the coriander and serve with noodles.

Variation

This dish works just as well with skinless chicken breast fillets in place of the duck.

Smoked Duck Energy 234kcal/982kJ; Protein 26.9g; Carbohydrate 12.8g, of which sugars 8.4g; Fat 8.8g, of which saturates 2.7g; Cholesterol 135mg; Calcium 75mg; Fibre 3g; Sodium 161mg.
Chinese Duck Curry Energy 297kcal/634kJ Protein 14.4g; Carbohydrate 1.3g, of which sugars 1.1g; Fat 10g, of which saturates 2.1g; Cholesterol 69mg; Calcium 33mg; Fibre 1.1g; Sodium 517mg.

Jungle Spiced Curry of Guinea Fowl

A traditional spicy curry from Thailand.

Serves 4

1 guinea fowl or similar game bird
15ml/1 tbsp vegetable oil
10ml/2 tsp green curry paste
15ml/1 tbsp Thai fish sauce
2.5cm/1in piece fresh galangal, peeled and finely chopped
15ml/1 tbsp fresh green peppercorns
3 kaffir lime leaves, torn
15ml/1 tbsp whisky, preferably Mekhong
300ml/½ pint/1¼ cups chicken stock
50g/2oz yard-long beans, cut into 2.5cm/1in lengths (about ½ cup)
225g/8oz/3¼ cups chestnut mushrooms, sliced
1 piece drained canned bamboo shoot, about 50g/2oz, shredded
5ml/1 tsp dried chilli flakes, to garnish (optional)

1 Cut up the guinea fowl, remove the skin, then strip the meat off the bones. Chop into bitesize pieces and set aside.

2 Heat the oil in a wok or frying pan and add the paste. Stir-fry over a medium heat for 30 seconds, until it gives off its aroma.

3 Add the fish sauce and the guinea fowl meat and stir-fry until the meat is browned all over. Add the galangal, peppercorns, lime leaves and whisky, then pour in the stock.

4 Bring to the boil. Add the vegetables, return to a simmer and cook gently for 2–3 minutes, until they are just cooked. Spoon into a dish, sprinkle with chilli flakes, if you like, and serve.

Cook's Tips

• Guinea fowl originated in West Africa and was regarded as a game bird, but has been domesticated in Europe for over 500 years. Their average size is about 1.2kg/2½lb. American readers could substitute two or three Cornish hens, depending on size.

• Fresh green peppercorns are simply unripe berries. They are sold on the stem. Look for them at Thai and Asian supermarkets. If unavailable, substitute bottled green peppercorns, but rinse well and drain them first.

Turkey Stew with Chilli and Sesame

This rich Mexican stew is traditionally served on a festive occasion.

Serves 4

115g/4oz/¾ cup sesame seeds
50g/2oz/½ cup whole blanched almonds
50g/2oz/½ cup shelled unsalted peanuts, skinned
50g/2oz/¼ cup white cooking fat, or 60ml/4 tbsp oil
1 small onion, finely chopped
2 garlic cloves, crushed
50g/2oz/⅓ cup canned tomatoes
1 ancho chilli and 1 guajillo chilli, seeded, soaked in hot water for 30 minutes and chopped
1 ripe plantain, sliced diagonally
50g/2oz/⅓ cup raisins
75g/3oz/½ cup ready-to-eat prunes, pitted
5ml/1 tsp dried oregano
2.5ml/½ tsp ground cloves
2.5ml/½ tsp crushed allspice berries
5ml/1 tsp ground cinnamon
25g/1oz/¼ cup unsweetened cocoa powder
4 turkey breast steaks
tortillas, to serve

1 Toast the sesame seeds in a frying pan until golden all over. Set aside 45ml/3 tbsp of the toasted seeds for the garnish and tip the rest into a bowl. Toast the almonds and peanuts in the same way and add them to the bowl.

2 Heat half the cooking fat or oil in a frying pan. Cook the onion and garlic for 2–3 minutes. Add the tomatoes and chilli. Cook gently for 10 minutes.

3 Add the plantain, raisins, prunes, dried oregano, spices and cocoa to the pan. Stir in 250ml/8fl oz/1 cup of the chilli water. Add the toasted sesame seeds, almonds and peanuts. Simmer for 10 minutes, stirring frequently, then allow to cool slightly. Blend the sauce in a food processor or blender until smooth.

4 Heat the remaining fat or oil in a flameproof casserole. Add the turkey and brown over a moderate heat. Pour the sauce over the steaks and cover the casserole. Simmer for 25 minutes or until the turkey is cooked, and the sauce has thickened. Sprinkle with sesame seeds and serve with warm tortillas.

Jungle Spiced Curry Energy 368kcal/1540kJ; Protein 56.8g; Carbohydrate 1.4g, of which sugars 0.9g; Fat 14g, of which saturates 3.2g; Cholesterol 0mg; Calcium 82mg; Fibre 1.1g; Sodium 454mg.
Turkey Stew Energy 700kcal/2920kJ; Protein 50.6g; Carbohydrate 27.7g, of which sugars 19.1g; Fat 43.8g, of which saturates 6.9g; Cholesterol 86mg; Calcium 267mg; Fibre 7g; Sodium 178mg.

Moghul-style Spicy Roast Lamb

This superb dish is just one of many fine examples of fabulous rich food once enjoyed by Moghul Emperors. Try it as a spicy variation to roast beef.

Serves 4 to 6

4 large onions, chopped
4 garlic cloves
5cm/2in piece fresh root ginger, chopped
45ml/3 tbsp ground almonds
10ml/2 tsp ground cumin
10ml/2 tsp ground coriander
10ml/2 tsp ground turmeric
10ml/2 tsp garam masala
4–6 green chillies
juice of 1 lemon
salt, to taste
300ml/½ pint/1¼ cups natural (plain) yogurt, beaten
1.8kg/4lb leg of lamb
8–10 cloves
4 firm tomatoes, halved and grilled, to serve
15ml/1 tbsp flaked (sliced) almonds, to garnish

1 Place the first 11 ingredients in a food processor and blend to a smooth paste, or grind in a mortar and pestle. Gradually add the yogurt and blend. Grease a large roasting pan and preheat the oven to 190°C/375°F/Gas Mark 5.

2 Remove most of the fat and skin from the lamb. Using a sharp knife, make deep pockets above the bone at each side of the thick end. Make deep diagonal gashes on both sides.

3 Push the cloves into the leg of lamb at random intervals, ensuring they are well embedded.

4 Push some of the spice mixture into the pockets and gashes and spread the remainder evenly all over the meat, working it in with your hands.

5 Place the lamb on the roasting pan and loosely cover the whole pan with foil. Roast for about 2–2½ hours, or until the lamb is cooked, removing the foil for the last 10 minutes of cooking time.

6 Remove the pan from the oven and allow the meat to rest for 10 minutes before carving. Serve with grilled tomatoes and garnish the joint with flaked almonds.

Chilli Lamb Chops

It is best to marinate the chops overnight as this makes them very tender and also helps them to absorb the maximum amount of spicy flavour. Serve with a crisp salad.

Serves 4

8 small lean spring lamb chops
1 large red chilli, seeded
30ml/2 tbsp chopped fresh coriander (cilantro)
15ml/1 tbsp chopped fresh mint
5ml/1 tsp salt
5ml/1 tsp soft light brown sugar
5ml/1 tsp garam masala
5ml/1 tsp crushed garlic
5ml/1 tsp crushed ginger
175ml/6fl oz/⅔ cup natural (plain) low-fat yogurt
10ml/2 tsp corn oil

1 Trim the lamb chops to remove any excess fat. Place them in a large bowl.

2 Finely chop the chilli, then mix with the coriander, mint, salt, brown sugar, garam masala, crushed garlic and crushed ginger.

3 Pour the yogurt into the herb mixture and, using a small whisk or a fork, mix thoroughly.

4 Pour this mixture over the top of the chops and turn them with your fingers to make sure that they are completely covered. Leave to marinate overnight in the refrigerator.

5 Heat the oil in a wok or large frying pan and add the chops. Lower the heat and allow to cook over a medium heat. Turn the chops over then continue frying until they are cooked right through, about 20 minutes, turning again if needed.

6 When the lamb is cooked, place on to warmed plates and serve with a crisp salad.

Cook's Tip
These chops can also be cooked under a grill (broiler), and they are great for cooking on a barbecue. Remember to baste the meat with oil before grilling (broiling).

Spicy Roast Lamb Energy 517kcal/2154kJ; Protein 43.5g; Carbohydrate 20.4g, of which sugars 13.1g; Fat 29.9g, of which saturates 9.7g; Cholesterol 146mg; Calcium 162mg; Fibre 2.3g; Sodium 160mg.
Chilli Lamb Energy 183kcal/764kJ; Protein 15.5g; Carbohydrate 14.1g, of which sugars 9.1g; Fat 7.8g, of which saturates 3.2g; Cholesterol 43mg; Calcium 102mg; Fibre 1.8g; Sodium 77mg.

Lamb Satay with a Chilli Sauce

These tasty spicy skewers are poplar throughout South-east Asia.

Makes 25 to 30 skewers

1kg/2¼lb leg of lamb, boned
3 garlic cloves, crushed
15–30ml/1–2 tbsp chilli sauce or 3–4 fresh chillies, seeded and ground, or 5–10ml/1–2 tsp chilli powder
60–90ml/4–6 tbsp dark soy sauce
juice of 1 lemon
salt and ground black pepper
vegetable oil for brushing
small onion pieces and cucumber wedges, to serve

For the sauce

6 garlic cloves, crushed
15ml/1 tbsp chilli sauce or 2–3 fresh chillies, seeded and ground
90ml/6 tbsp dark soy sauce
25ml/1½ tbsp lemon juice
30ml/2 tbsp boiling water

1 Cut the lamb into thick slices and then into 1cm/½in cubes. Remove any gristle but do not trim off any of the fat because this keeps the satays moist and enhances the flavour.

2 Blend the garlic, the chilli sauce, the ground fresh chillies or chilli powder, soy sauce, lemon juice and seasoning to a paste in a food processor or with a mortar and pestle. Pour over the lamb. Cover and leave for at least an hour. Soak wooden or bamboo skewers in water so they won't burn during cooking.

3 Prepare the sauce. In a bowl, mix the garlic, chilli sauce or chillies, soy sauce, lemon juice and boiling water.

4 Thread the cubed meat on to the skewers. Brush them with oil and cook under the grill (broiler), turning often. Coat each satay with a little sauce and serve hot, with small pieces of onion, cucumber and the remaining sauce.

Variation
Lamb neck fillet is now widely available in supermarkets and can be used instead of boned leg. Brush the lamb fillet with oil before grilling.

Fiery Meat Kebabs

Serve this tasty Indian snack in a bun, as you would a hamburger. Extra chilli sauce will go down a treat for chilli-lovers. Serve with a crisp salad as a main course or unaccompanied as an appetizer.

Serves 4 to 6

2 onions, finely chopped
250g/9oz lean lamb, cut into small cubes
50g/2oz Bengal gram
5ml/1 tsp cumin seeds
5ml/1 tsp garam masala
4–6 green chillies
5cm/2in piece fresh root ginger, crushed
salt, to taste
175ml/6fl oz/¾ cup water
a few coriander (cilantro) and mint leaves, chopped
juice of 1 lemon
15ml/1 tbsp gram flour
2 eggs, beaten
vegetable oil, for shallow-frying
limes, to serve

1 Put the first eight ingredients and the water into a pan and bring to the boil. Reduce the heat and simmer, covered, until the meat and gram are cooked. Cook uncovered to reduce the excess liquid. Cool, and grind to a paste.

2 Place the mixture in a mixing bowl and add the coriander and mint leaves, lemon juice and gram flour. Knead well.

3 Divide the mixture into 10–12 portions and roll each into a ball, then flatten slightly. Chill for about 1 hour. Dip the kebabs in the beaten egg and shallow-fry each side until golden brown. Serve immediately, with lime halves.

Cook's Tips
- *Gram flour, also known as besan, is a pale-yellow flour made from ground chickpeas. More aromatic and with less starch content and higher protein than wheat flour, it is used widely in Indian cookery for doughs, batters and for thickening sauces. Look for it in supermarkets or Indian and Asian food stores.*
- *Bengal gram is a smaller, rusty-coloured variety of chickpea, also known as the black chickpea. It is the most widely grown pulse in India. Use gram flour if unavailable.*

Lamb Satay Energy 72kcal/300kJ; Protein 4.2g; Carbohydrate 0.4g, of which sugars 0.3g; Fat 6g, of which saturates 1.2g; Cholesterol 15mg; Calcium 3mg; Fibre 0g; Sodium 342mg.
Fiery Meat Kebabs Energy 219kcal/909kJ; Protein 11.6g; Carbohydrate 8.1g, of which sugars 3.8g; Fat 15.9g, of which saturates 3.6g; Cholesterol 92mg; Calcium 39mg; Fibre 1.3g; Sodium 59mg.

Italian Lamb Meatballs with Chilli Tomato Sauce

Serve these piquant Italian-style meatballs with pasta and a leafy salad. Sprinkle with a little grated Parmesan cheese for that extra Italian touch.

Serves 4

450g/1lb lean minced (ground) lamb
1 large onion, grated
1 garlic clove, crushed
50g/2oz/1 cup fresh white breadcrumbs
15ml/1 tbsp chopped fresh parsley
1 small egg, lightly beaten
30ml/2 tbsp olive oil
salt and ground black pepper
60ml/4 tbsp finely grated Parmesan cheese, pasta and rocket (arugula) leaves, to serve

For the sauce

1 onion, finely chopped
400g/14oz can chopped tomatoes
200ml/7fl oz/scant 1 cup passata (bottled strained tomatoes)
5ml/1 tsp sugar
2 green chillies, seeded and finely chopped
30ml/2 tbsp chopped fresh oregano
salt and ground black pepper

1 Soak a small clay pot in cold water for 15 minutes, then drain. Place the minced lamb, onion, garlic, breadcrumbs, parsley and seasoning in a bowl and mix well. Add the beaten egg and mix to bind the meatball mixture together.

2 Roll the mixture in your hands and shape into about 20 even balls, about the size of walnuts. Wetting your hands slightly will prevent the mixture sticking to them.

3 Heat the olive oil in a frying pan, add the meatballs and cook over a high heat, stirring occasionally, until browned all over.

4 Meanwhile, to make the sauce, mix together the chopped onion, tomatoes, passata, sugar, seeded and chopped chillies and oregano. Season well and pour the sauce into the clay pot.

5 Place the meatballs in the sauce, then cover and place in an unheated oven. Set the oven to 200°C/400°F/Gas 6 and cook for 1 hour, stirring after 30 minutes. Serve over pasta with Parmesan cheese and rocket.

Lamb Tagine with Lemon and Spices

Meatballs are poached gently with lemon and spices to make a dish that is quite light and ideal for lunch. Serve it with a salad or plain couscous. A popular dish in Morocco, it has no discernible boundaries. It can be found in the tiniest rural villages, in street stalls in the towns and cities, or in the finest restaurants of Casablanca, Fez and Marakesh.

Serves 4

450g/1lb finely minced (ground) lamb
3 large onions, grated
small bunch of flat leaf parsley, chopped
5–10ml/1–2 tsp ground cinnamon
5ml/1 tsp ground cumin
pinch of cayenne pepper
40g/1½oz/3 tbsp butter
25g/1oz fresh root ginger, peeled and finely chopped
1 hot chilli, seeded and finely chopped
pinch of saffron threads
small bunch of fresh coriander (cilantro), finely chopped
juice of 1 lemon
300ml/½ pint/1¼ cups water
1 lemon, quartered
salt and ground black pepper
crusty bread, to serve

1 To make the meatballs, pound the minced lamb in a bowl by using your hand to lift it up and slap it back down into the bowl. Knead in half the grated onions, the parsley, cinnamon, cumin and cayenne pepper. Season with salt and pepper, and continue pounding the mixture by hand for a few minutes. Break off pieces and shape them into walnut-size balls.

2 In a heavy lidded frying pan, melt the butter and add the remaining onion with the ginger, chilli and saffron. Stirring frequently, cook just until the onion begins to colour, then stir in the coriander and lemon juice.

3 Pour in the water, season with salt and bring to the boil. Drop in the meatballs, reduce the heat and cover the pan. Poach the meatballs gently, turning them occasionally, for about 20 minutes.

4 Remove the lid, tuck the lemon quarters around the meatballs and cook, uncovered, for a further 10 minutes to reduce the liquid slightly. Serve hot, straight from the pan with lots of crusty fresh bread to mop up the delicious juices.

Italian Lamb Meatballs Energy 443kcal/1853kJ; Protein 33.1g; Carbohydrate 22.5g, of which sugars 11.1g; Fat 25.3g, of which saturates 10.3g; Cholesterol 148mg; Calcium 246mg; Fibre 3g; Sodium 389mg.
Lamb Tagine Energy 362kcal/1503kJ; Protein 424.5g; Carbohydrate 12.9g, of which sugars 9.3g; Fat 24g, of which saturates 12.2g; Cholesterol 108mg; Calcium 134mg; Fibre 4g; Sodium 155mg.

Lamb Cutlets with Piquant Tomato Sauce

Lamb cutlets are more readily available in Turkey, but veal can also be used for this recipe. Very fine cutlets are prepared by bashing them flat with a heavy meat cleaver. The cutlets are then quickly cooked on a griddle in their own fat, or a little butter, and served with a sprinkling of dried oregano, as in this recipe, or with wedges of lemon. For a tasty supper, serve this dish with a pilaff, or with sautéed potatoes.

Serves 4

30ml/2 tbsp olive oil
10ml/2 tsp butter
12 lamb cutlets (US rib chops), trimmed and flattened with a cleaver
1 onion, finely chopped
1 fresh green chilli, seeded and finely chopped
2 garlic cloves, finely chopped
5ml/1 tsp sugar
5–10ml/1–2 tsp white wine vinegar
2–3 large tomatoes, skinned and chopped, or 400g/14oz can chopped tomatoes
1 green (bell) pepper, seeded and finely chopped
a sprinkling of dried oregano
salt and ground black pepper

1 Heat the oil and butter in a large, heavy pan and quickly fry the cutlets on both sides until evenly browned.

2 Remove the cutlets from the pan, add the onion, chilli and garlic, and fry until the onion begins to brown.

3 Stir in the sugar and vinegar, then add the tomatoes and green pepper. Lower the heat, cover and simmer for about 30 minutes, until the mixture is thick and saucy. Season with salt and pepper.

4 Return the cutlets to the pan, covering them in the sauce. Cook for about 15 minutes, until the meat is tender.

5 Transfer the cutlets to a serving dish, arranging them around the edge with the bones sticking outwards. Sprinkle with the dried oregano, spoon the sauce into the middle of the cutlets and serve immediately.

Chargrilled Chilli Kebabs

This is the ultimate kebab: spicy chargrilled meat served on a *pide*, a Turkish flat bread, with yogurt and tomatoes.

Serves 4

12 plum tomatoes
30ml/2 tbsp butter
1 large pide, or 4 pitta or small naan, cut into bitesize chunks
5ml/1 tsp ground sumac
5ml/1 tsp dried oregano
225g/8oz/1 cup thick and creamy natural (plain) yogurt
salt and ground black pepper
1 bunch fresh flat leaf parsley, chopped, to garnish

For the kebabs

500g/1¼lb minced (ground) lamb
2 onions, finely chopped
1 green chilli, seeded and chopped
4 garlic cloves, crushed
5ml/1 tsp Turkish red pepper or paprika
5ml/1 tsp ground sumac
1 bunch flat leaf parsley, chopped

For the sauce

30ml/2 tbsp olive oil
15ml/1 tbsp butter
1 onion, finely chopped
2 garlic cloves, finely chopped
1 green chilli, seeded and chopped
5–10ml/1–2 tsp sugar
400g/14oz can chopped tomato

1 Make the kebabs. Put the lamb in a bowl with all the other ingredients and knead to a paste. Cover and chill for 15 minutes.

2 Make the sauce. Heat the oil and butter in a pan, stir in the onion, garlic and chilli and cook until they colour. Add the sugar and tomatoes and cook for 30 minutes. Season and set aside.

3 Light the barbecue and shape the kebabs. Cook on the barbecue for 6–8 minutes, turning once. Meanwhile, thread the tomatoes on to skewers and cook on the barbecue until charred.

4 While the kebabs are cooking, melt the butter in a heavy pan and fry the pide or other bread until golden. Sprinkle with sumac and oregano, then arrange on a serving dish. Splash a little sauce over the pide and spoon half the yogurt on top.

5 Cut the kebab meat into bitesize pieces. Arrange on the bread with the tomatoes, sprinkle with salt and the rest of the sumac and oregano, and garnish with the chopped parsley. Serve hot, topped with dollops of the remaining sauce and yogurt.

Lamb Cutlets Energy 683kcal/2822kJ; Protein 23.2g; Carbohydrate 7.4g, of which sugars 6.9g; Fat 62.4g, of which saturates 29.2g; Cholesterol 122mg; Calcium 24mg; Fibre 1.7g; Sodium 114mg.
Chargrilled Kebabs Energy 642kcal/2688kJ; Protein 35.2g; Carbohydrate 52.8g, of which sugars 24.1g; Fat 33.9g, of which saturates 15.1g; Cholesterol 121mg; Calcium 253mg; Fibre 6.3g; Sodium 456mg.

Lamb Stew with Chilli Sauce

The chillies in this stew add depth and richness to the sauce; the potato slices ensure that it is a fairly substantial meal.

Serves 6

6 guajillo chillies, seeded
2 pasilla chillies, seeded
250ml/8fl oz/1 cup hot water
3 garlic cloves, peeled
5ml/1 tsp ground cinnamon
2.5ml/½ tsp ground cloves
2.5ml/½ tsp ground black pepper
15ml/1 tbsp vegetable oil
1kg/2¼lb lean boneless lamb shoulder, cut into 2cm/¾in cubes
400g/14oz potatoes, scrubbed and cut into 1cm/½ in thick slices
salt
strips of red pepper and fresh oregano to garnish
cooked rice, to serve

1 Snap or tear the dried chillies into large pieces, put them in a bowl and pour over the hot water. Leave them to soak for 30 minutes, then transfer into a food processor or blender. Add the garlic, cinnamon, cloves and black pepper. Process the mixture to a smooth paste.

2 Heat the oil in a large pan. Add the lamb cubes, in batches, and stir-fry over a high heat until the cubes are evenly browned on all sides.

3 Return all the lamb cubes to the pan, spread them out, then cover them with a layer of potato slices. Add salt to taste. Put a lid on the pan and cook over a medium heat for about 10 minutes.

4 Pour over the chilli mixture and mix well. Replace the lid then simmer over a low heat for about 1 hour, or until the meat and the potatoes are tender. Serve with a rice dish, and garnish with strips of red pepper and fresh oregano.

Cook's Tip
When frying the lamb, don't be tempted to cook too many cubes at one time, as the meat will steam rather than fry. Cook them in batches, a large handful at a time.

Spanish-style Lamb Stew with Green Olives and Chillies

This spicy dish draws on Spanish culinary tradition, with the lamb first marinated in alcohol to tenderize it and then browned before being braised.

Serves 4

900g/2lb boneless leg or shoulder of lamb, cut into bitesize cubes
45ml/3 tbsp groundnut (peanut) oil
15g/½oz/1 tbsp butter
2 red onions, thickly sliced
8 garlic cloves, crushed whole
2–3 red or green chillies, seeded and sliced
2 red or green (bell) peppers, seeded and sliced
5–10ml/1–2 tsp paprika
15–30ml/1–2 tbsp palm sugar (jaggery) or cane sugar
400g/14oz can plum tomatoes, drained
15–30ml/1–2 tbsp tomato purée (paste)
2–3 bay leaves
225g/8oz green olives
300ml/½ pint/1¼ cups water
salt and ground black pepper
1 bunch fresh flat leaf parsley, roughly chopped, to garnish
cooked rice, to serve

For the marinade

250ml/8fl oz/1 cup red wine
250ml/8fl oz/1 cup port
120ml/4fl oz/½ cup coconut or rice vinegar
1 onion, roughly sliced
2 garlic cloves, crushed whole
8 black peppercorns
2–3 bay leaves

1 Mix all the marinade ingredients in a bowl. Add the lamb, mix well, then cover and chill for 6 hours. When ready, transfer the lamb to another bowl. Reserve the marinade.

2 Heat the oil and butter in a large pan. Fry the meat until browned on all sides. Remove and set aside. Add the onions, garlic, chillies and peppers to the pan and fry for 5 minutes. Stir in the paprika and sugar and return the meat to the pan.

3 Add the tomatoes, purée, bay leaves and olives. Pour in the reserved marinade and the water and bring to the boil then simmer, covered, for 2 hours.

4 Season the stew with salt and pepper to taste. Sprinkle with chopped parsley to garnish and serve with rice.

Lamb with Chilli Sauce Energy 367kcal/1536kJ; Protein 34g; Carbohydrate 11.8g, of which sugars 1.9g; Fat 20.8g, of which saturates 9g; Cholesterol 127mg; Calcium 19mg; Fibre 0.9g; Sodium 151mg.
Spanish-style Stew Energy 654kcal/2722kJ; Protein 47.4g; Carbohydrate 19.2g, of which sugars 16.7g; Fat 43.6g, of which saturates 15.8g; Cholesterol 179mg; Calcium 93mg; Fibre 5.4g; Sodium 1498mg.

Lamb, New Potato and Red Chilli Curry

This dish makes the most of an economical cut of meat by cooking it slowly until the meat is falling from the bone. Chillies and coconut cream give it lots of flavour.

Serves 4

25g/1oz/2 tbsp butter
4 garlic cloves, crushed
2 onions, sliced into rings
2.5ml/½ tsp each ground cumin, ground coriander, turmeric and cayenne pepper
2–3 red chillies, seeded and finely chopped
300ml/½ pint/1¼ cups hot chicken stock
200ml/7fl oz/scant 1 cup coconut cream
4 lamb shanks, all excess fat removed
450g/1lb new potatoes, halved
6 ripe tomatoes, quartered
salt and ground black pepper
coriander (cilantro) leaves, to garnish
spicy rice, to serve

1 Preheat the oven to 160°C/325°F/Gas 3. Melt the butter in a large flameproof casserole, add the garlic and onions and cook over a low heat for 15 minutes, until golden. Stir in the spices and chillies, then cook for a further 2 minutes.

2 Add the hot stock and coconut cream. Place the lamb shanks in the liquid and cover the casserole with foil. Cook in the oven for 2 hours, turning the shanks twice, first after about an hour or so and again about half an hour later.

3 Par-boil the potatoes for 10 minutes, drain and add to the casserole with the tomatoes, then cook uncovered in the oven for a further 35 minutes. Season to taste, garnish with coriander leaves and serve with the spicy rice.

Cook's Tip

Make this dish a day in advance if possible. Cool and chill overnight, then skim off the excess fat that has risen to the surface. Reheat thoroughly before you serve it.

Spicy Javanese Curry

This popular spicy goat dish is from Java but there are many variations all over the Indonesian archipelago.

Serves 4

30–60ml/2–4 tbsp palm, coconut or groundnut (peanut) oil
10ml/2 tsp shrimp paste
15ml/1 tbsp palm sugar (jaggery)
5ml/1 tsp coriander seeds
5ml/1 tsp cumin seeds
2.5ml/½ tsp grated nutmeg
2.5ml/½ tsp ground black pepper
2–3 lemon grass stalks, halved and bruised
700g/1lb 9oz boneless shoulder or leg of goat, or lamb, cut into bitesize pieces
400g/14oz can coconut milk
200ml/7fl oz/scant 1 cup water (if necessary)
12 yard-long beans
1 bunch fresh coriander (cilantro) leaves, roughly chopped
cooked rice and 2–3 chillies, seeded and finely chopped, to serve

For the spice paste

2–3 shallots, chopped
2–3 garlic cloves, chopped
3–4 chillies, seeded and chopped
25g/1oz galangal, chopped
40g/1½oz fresh turmeric, chopped, or 10ml/2 tsp ground turmeric
1 lemon grass stalk, chopped
2–3 candlenuts, finely ground

1 Using a mortar and pestle or food processor, grind all the spice paste ingredients together. Heat 15–30ml/1–2 tbsp of the oil in a heavy pan. Fry the paste until fragrant. Add the shrimp paste and sugar and stir-fry for 2 minutes.

2 Heat the remaining oil in a large pan. Stir in the coriander seeds, cumin seeds, nutmeg and black pepper, then add the paste and lemon grass. Stir-fry for 2–3 minutes, until dark and fragrant.

3 Stir the meat into the pan, making sure that it is well coated in the paste. Pour in the coconut milk and water, bring to the boil, then cover and simmer for about 3 hours, until the meat is tender.

4 Add the beans and cook for 10–15 minutes. Check the meat occasionally and add the water if the curry is too dry.

5 Toss a few coriander leaves into the curry and season to taste. Transfer the curry into a warmed serving dish and garnish with the remaining coriander. Serve with rice and chillies.

Lamb and Chilli Curry Energy 364kcal/1528kJ; Protein 23.5g; Carbohydrate 30.5g, of which sugars 12.1g; Fat 17.4g, of which saturates 8.8g; Cholesterol 89mg; Calcium 58mg; Fibre 3.5g; Sodium 205mg.
Spicy Javanese Curry Energy 450kcal/1877kJ; Protein 37.9g; Carbohydrate 10.8g, of which sugars 9.1g; Fat 28.7g, of which saturates 10.3g; Cholesterol 146mg; Calcium 129mg; Fibre 2.4g; Sodium 375mg.

Balti Spiced Lamb with Peas and Potatoes

Fresh mint leaves are used in this dish, but if they are obtainable, use ready-minted frozen peas to bring an added freshness to the spicy sauce.

Serves 4

225g/8oz lean spring lamb
120ml/4 fl oz/½ cup natural (plain) low-fat yogurt
1 cinnamon stick
2 green cardamom pods
3 black peppercorns
5ml/1 tsp crushed garlic
5ml/1 tsp crushed ginger
5ml/1 tsp chilli powder
5ml/1 tsp garam masala
5ml/1 tsp salt
30ml/2 tbsp chopped fresh mint
15ml/3 tbsp corn oil
2 medium onions, sliced
300ml/½ pint/1¼ cups water
1 large potato, diced
115g/4oz frozen peas
1 firm tomato, skinned, seeded and diced
cooked rice, to serve

1 Using a sharp knife, cut the lamb into even strips, then place the pieces in a bowl.

2 Add the yogurt, cinnamon, cardamoms, peppercorns, garlic, ginger, chilli powder, garam masala, salt and half the mint. Leave to marinate for about 2 hours.

3 Heat the oil in a non-stick wok or frying pan and fry the onions until golden brown. Stir in the lamb and the marinade and stir-fry for about 3 minutes.

4 Pour in the water, lower the heat and simmer gently until the meat is cooked right through, about 15 minutes, depending on the age of the lamb.

5 Meanwhile, cook the potato in boiling water until it is just soft, but not mushy.

6 Add the peas and potato to the lamb and stir to mix gently.

7 Finally, add the remaining mint and the tomato and cook for a further 5 minutes. Serve immediately with cooked rice.

Stir-fried Lamb with Chilli, Ginger and Coriander

This dish benefits from being cooked a day in advance and kept in the refrigerator, which helps the flavours to deepen.

Serves 4

225–275g/8–10oz boned lean spring lamb
3 medium onions
15ml/1 tbsp olive oil
15ml/1 tbsp tomato purée (paste)
5ml/1 tsp crushed garlic
7.5ml/1½ tsp crushed ginger
5ml/1 tsp salt
1.5ml/¼ tsp ground turmeric
600ml/1 pint/2½ cups water
15ml/1 tbsp lemon juice
15ml/1 tbsp grated fresh root ginger
15ml/1 tbsp chopped fresh coriander (cilantro)
15ml/1 tbsp chopped fresh mint
1 red chilli, seeded and chopped
chapatis, to serve

1 Cut the lamb into small cubes. Dice the onions. Heat the oil in a non-stick wok or frying pan and fry the onions until soft.

2 Meanwhile, mix the tomato purée, garlic, ginger, salt and turmeric. Add to the wok and briefly stir-fry until fragrant.

3 Add the lamb and stir-fry for about 2–3 minutes. Add the water, lower the heat, cover and cook for 15–20 minutes, stirring occasionally.

4 When the water has almost evaporated, start bhooning over a medium heat (see the Cook's Tip below), making sure that the sauce does not catch on the bottom of the wok. Continue for 5–7 minutes.

5 Pour in the lemon juice, followed by the ginger, coriander, mint and red chilli, then serve immediately with chapatis.

Cook's Tip
Bhooning is a traditional way of stir-frying which involves scraping the bottom of the wok each time in the centre.

Balti Lamb Energy 317kcal/1322kJ; Protein 18.1g; Carbohydrate 25.6g, of which sugars 10.7g; Fat 16.8g, of which saturates 4.4g; Cholesterol 43mg; Calcium 113mg; Fibre 3.8g; Sodium 89mg.
Stir-fried Lamb Energy 184kcal/767kJ; Protein 13.3g; Carbohydrate 11.7g, of which sugars 7.5g; Fat 9.8g, of which saturates 3.4g; Cholesterol 43mg; Calcium 44mg; Fibre 1.9g; Sodium 554mg.

Keema Lamb with Curry Leaves and Green Chillies

This delicious dry curry is made by cooking minced lamb in its own juices with a few spices and herbs, but no other liquid.

Serves 4

10ml/2 tsp corn oil
2 medium onions, chopped
10 curry leaves
6 green chillies
350g/12oz lean minced (ground) lamb
5ml/1 tsp crushed garlic
5ml/1 tsp crushed ginger
5ml/1 tsp chilli powder
1.5ml/¼ tsp ground turmeric
5ml/1 tsp salt
2 tomatoes, skinned and quartered
15ml/1 tbsp chopped fresh coriander (cilantro)

1 Heat the oil in a non-stick wok or frying pan. Stir-fry the onions together with the curry leaves and three of the whole green chillies for 3–4 minutes, until the onions begin to soften and turn translucent.

2 Put the lamb into a mixing bowl and add the garlic and crushed ginger, chilli powder, turmeric and salt. Blend everything together thoroughly.

3 Add the lamb mixture to the pan with the onions and stir-fry for about 7–10 minutes, lowering the heat to medium if necessary.

4 Add the tomatoes and coriander to the pan. Stir in the remaining whole green chillies. Continue to stir-fry for a further 2 minutes before serving.

Cook's Tip

- *This curry also makes a terrific brunch. Serve with fried eggs and light Indian breads such as pooris or chapatis.*
- *This curry would make an ideal filling for samosas, the spicy Indian snacks. Cook as above but ensure that all the ingredients are finely chopped before using.*

Spiced Lamb in a Yogurt and Garam Masala Sauce

The lamb is first marinated and then cooked slowly in a hot yogurt sauce. It is served with dried apricots that have been lightly sautéed with cinnamon and cardamom.

Serves 4

15ml/1 tbsp tomato purée (paste)
175ml/6fl oz/⅔ cup natural (plain) low-fat yogurt
5ml/1 tsp garam masala
1.5ml/¼ tsp cumin seeds
5ml/1 tsp salt
5ml/1 tsp crushed garlic
5ml/1 tsp crushed ginger
5ml/1 tsp chilli powder
225g/8oz lean spring lamb, cut into strips
15ml/3 tsp corn oil
2 medium onions, finely sliced
25g/1oz low-fat spread
2.5cm/1in cinnamon stick
2 green cardamom pods
5 ready-to-eat dried apricots, quartered
15ml/1 tbsp fresh coriander (cilantro) leaves

1 In a bowl, blend together the tomato purée, yogurt, garam masala, cumin seeds, salt, garlic, ginger and chilli powder. Place the lamb in the sauce and leave to marinate for about 1 hour.

2 Heat 10ml/2 tsp of the oil in a non-stick wok or frying pan and fry the onions until crisp and golden brown.

3 Remove the onions using a slotted spoon, allow to cool and then grind down by processing briefly in a food processor or with a pestle in a mortar. Reheat the remaining oil and return the onions to the wok.

4 Add the lamb and stir-fry for about 2 minutes. Cover, lower the heat and cook for 15 minutes, or until the meat is cooked through. If required, add about 150ml/¼ pint/⅔ cup water during the cooking. Remove from the heat and set aside.

5 Heat the low-fat spread with the remaining oil and drop in the cinnamon stick and cardamoms. Add the dried apricots and stir over a low heat for about 2 minutes. Pour this over the lamb. Serve garnished with the coriander.

Keema Lamb Energy 239kcal/998kJ; Protein 19.7g; Carbohydrate 13.5g, of which sugars 9.3g; Fat 12.3g, of which saturates 4.9g; Cholesterol 67mg; Calcium 50mg; Fibre 2.5g; Sodium 578mg.
Spiced Lamb Energy 302kcal/1259kJ; Protein 16.4g; Carbohydrate 19.6g, of which sugars 15.4g; Fat 18.3g, of which saturates 4.9g; Cholesterol 44mg; Calcium 139mg; Fibre 2.7g; Sodium 141mg.

Spiced Lamb with Chillies

This is a fairly hot stir-fry dish, although you can, of course, make it less so by reducing the amount of chilli you use.

Serves 4

225g/8oz lean lamb fillet
120ml/4fl oz/½ cup natural (plain) low-fat yogurt
1.5ml/¼ tsp ground cardamom
5ml/1 tsp crushed ginger
5ml/1 tsp crushed garlic
5ml/1 tsp chilli powder
5ml/1 tsp garam masala
5ml/1 tsp salt
15ml/1 tbsp corn oil
2 medium onions, chopped
1 bay leaf
300ml/½ pint/1¼ cups water
2 red chillies, seeded and sliced lengthways
2 green chillies, seeded and sliced lengthways
30ml/2 tbsp fresh coriander (cilantro) leaves

1 Using a sharp knife, cut the lamb into even strips. Mix together the yogurt, cardamom, ginger, garlic, chilli powder, garam masala and salt. Add the lamb, mix well, and leave for 1 hour to marinate.

2 Heat the oil in a non-stick wok or frying pan and fry the onions for 3–5 minutes, or until golden brown.

3 Add the bay leaf, then add the lamb with the yogurt and spices and stir-fry for 2–3 minutes over a medium heat.

4 Pour over the water, cover and cook for 15–20 minutes over a low heat, checking occasionally. Once the water has evaporated, stir-fry the mixture for 1 minute more.

5 Add the red and green chillies and the fresh coriander, and stir well. Serve immediately.

Cook's Tip
Garam masala, meaning 'warm spice', is a blend of ground spices commonly used in Indian cuisine. Typically it will contain black pepper, black cumin, cinnamon, cloves, mace, cardamom, coriander seed, nutmeg, fennel and bay leaf, all dry-fried or roasted then dried and ground.

Caribbean Lamb Curry

This popular national dish of Jamaica is known as curry goat although goat meat, lamb or mutton can be used to make it.

Serves 4 to 6

900g/2lb boned leg of mutton or lamb
50g/2oz/4 tbsp curry powder
3 garlic cloves, crushed
1 large onion, chopped
4 thyme sprigs or 5ml/1 tsp dried thyme
3 bay leaves
5ml/1 tsp ground allspice
30ml/2 tbsp vegetable oil
50g/2oz/4 tbsp butter or margarine
900ml/1½ pints/3¾ cups stock or water
1 fresh hot chilli pepper, seeded and chopped
coriander (cilantro) sprigs, to garnish
cooked rice, to serve

1 Cut the meat into 5cm/2in cubes, removing and discarding any excess fat and gristle.

2 Place the curry powder, garlic, onion, thyme, bay leaves, allspice and oil in a large bowl and mix well. Add the mutton or lamb and mix thoroughly until all the meat is well coated. Marinate in a cool place for at least 3 hours or overnight in the refrigerator.

3 Melt the butter or margarine in a large heavy pan, add the mutton or lamb and fry over a moderate heat for about 10 minutes, turning the meat frequently, until it is evenly browned all over.

4 Stir in the stock and chilli and bring to the boil. Reduce the heat, cover the pan and simmer for 1½ hours, or until the meat is tender. Serve with rice, garnished with coriander.

Cook's Tip
The cheaper cuts of mutton and lamb are usually more bony, but they are well suited for use in spicy dishes that involve lengthy simmering, making curries that are full of flavour.

Spiced Lamb Energy 183kcal/764kJ; Protein 15.5g; Carbohydrate 14.1g, of which sugars 9.1g; Fat 7.8g, of which saturates 3.2g; Cholesterol 43mg; Calcium 102mg; Fibre 1.8g; Sodium 77mg.
Caribbean Lamb Curry Energy 609kcal/2535kJ; Protein 46g; Carbohydrate 7g, of which sugars 14g; Fat 44g, of which saturates 20g; Cholesterol 203mg; Calcium 89mg; Fibre 2.5g; Sodium 600mg.

Balti Lamb with Cauliflower

Cauliflower and lamb go beautifully together. This curry is given a final *tarka* – an Indian garnish – of cumin seeds and curry leaves, which enhances the flavour.

Serves 4

10ml/2 tsp corn oil
2 medium onions, sliced
7.5ml/1½ tsp crushed ginger
5ml/1 tsp chilli powder
5ml/1 tsp crushed garlic
1.5ml/¼ tsp ground turmeric
2.5ml/½ tsp ground coriander
30ml/2 tbsp fresh fenugreek leaves
275g/10oz boned lean spring lamb, cut into strips
1 small cauliflower, cut into small florets
300ml/½ pint/1¼ cups water
30ml/2 tbsp fresh coriander (cilantro) leaves
½ red (bell) pepper, sliced
15ml/1 tbsp lemon juice

For the tarka

10ml/2 tsp corn oil
2.5ml/½ tsp white cumin seeds
4–6 curry leaves

1 Heat the oil in a non-stick wok or frying pan and fry the onions until golden brown. Lower the heat and add the crushed ginger, chilli powder, crushed garlic, turmeric and ground coriander, followed by the fenugreek.

2 Add the lamb strips to the wok and stir-fry until the lamb is completely coated with the spices. Add half the cauliflower florets and stir the mixture well.

3 Pour in the water, cover the wok, and simmer for 5–7 minutes until the cauliflower and lamb are almost cooked through.

4 Add the remaining cauliflower, half the fresh coriander, the red pepper and lemon juice and stir-fry for about 5 minutes, making sure that the sauce does not catch on the bottom of the wok.

5 Check that the lamb is completely cooked, then remove from the heat and set aside.

6 To make the tarka, heat the oil and fry the seeds and curry leaves for about 30 seconds. While it is still hot, pour the seasoned oil over the cauliflower and lamb and serve garnished with the remaining fresh coriander leaves.

Spicy Lamb Korma

This is a delicious creamy and aromatic dish with no 'hot' taste. So it is perfect for guests who like the spiciness of Asian cuisine without the extra fiery kick.

Serves 4 to 6

15ml/1 tbsp white sesame seeds
15ml/1 tbsp white poppy seeds
50g/2oz almonds, blanched
2 green chillies, seeded
5cm/2in piece fresh root ginger, sliced
6 garlic cloves, sliced
1 onion, finely chopped
45ml/3 tbsp ghee or vegetable oil
6 green cardamoms
5cm/2in piece cinnamon stick
4 cloves
900g/2lb lean lamb, cubed
5ml/1 tsp ground cumin
5ml/1 tsp ground coriander
salt, to taste
300ml/½ pint/1¼ cups double (heavy) cream mixed with ½ tsp cornflour (cornstarch)
roasted sesame seeds, to garnish

1 Heat a frying pan without any liquid and dry-roast the sesame and poppy seeds, almonds, chillies, ginger, garlic and onion for about 3–5 minutes until the fragrances of the spices are released.

2 Cool the mixture and grind to a fine paste using a mortar and pestle or a food processor. Heat the ghee or oil in a wok or frying pan.

3 Add the cardamoms, cinnamon and cloves to the pan. Stir-fry the spices until the cloves begin to swell.

4 Add the lamb, ground cumin and coriander, and the prepared paste to the pan. Season with salt, to taste.

5 Cover the pan and cook over a low heat until the lamb is almost done, about 30–40 minutes.

6 Remove the pan from the heat, leave it to cool a little and then gradually fold in the double cream, reserving 15ml/1 tsp to use as a garnish.

7 To serve, gently reheat the lamb uncovered and serve hot, garnished with the sesame seeds and the remaining cream.

Balti Lamb Energy 277kcals/1154kJ; Protein 18.7g; Carbohydrate 14.4g, of which sugars 9g; Fat 16.7g, of which saturates 4.7g; Cholesterol 52mg; Calcium 62mg; Fibre 3.2g; Sodium 73mg
Spicy Lamb Korma Energy 220kcal/916kJ; Protein 14.2g; Carbohydrate 14.5g, of which sugars 11.1g; Fat 12.2g, of which saturates 3.8g; Cholesterol 42mg; Calcium 101mg; Fibre 2.1g; Sodium 90mg.

Kashmiri-style Lamb with Chilli

This deliciously creamy curry originated in Kashmir in north-west India.

Serves 4 to 6

60ml/4 tbsp vegetable oil
1.5ml/¼ tsp asafoetida
900g/2lb lean lamb, cubed
5cm/2in piece fresh root ginger, crushed
2 garlic cloves, crushed
60ml/4 tbsp rogan josh masala paste
5ml/1 tsp chilli powder or 10ml/2 tsp paprika
8–10 strands saffron (optional)
salt, to taste
150ml/¼ pint/⅔ cup natural (plain) low-fat yogurt, beaten
flaked (sliced) almonds, to garnish

1 Heat the oil in a frying pan and fry the asafoetida and lamb, stirring well to seal the meat. Reduce the heat, cover, then cook for about 10 minutes.

2 Add the remaining ingredients except the yogurt and almonds and mix well. If the meat is too dry, add a very small quantity of boiling water. Cover and cook on a low heat for a further 10 minutes.

3 Remove the pan from the heat and leave to cool a little. Add the yogurt, 15ml/1 tbsp at a time, stirring constantly to avoid curdling. Cook uncovered over a low heat until the gravy becomes thick. Spoon the curry on to a large serving dish. Garnish with the flaked almonds and serve immediately while still hot with a spoonful of yogurt.

Cook's Tips

- *Ready-made spice pastes are the perfect way to speed up the time you spend in the kitchen. There are many varieties and they are widely available in large supermarkets and Asian stores so you are sure to find one that suits your dish without too much trouble.*
- *Saffron strands are the dried stigmas of a crocus flower, which impart a fabulous yellow-orange colour to this dish. Harvesting and processing saffron is very labour-intensive, therefore it is by far the most expensive spice in the world.*

Lamb Dhansak with Green Chillies

This is a Parsee dish with a hot, sweet and sour flavour, often eaten for Sunday lunch.

Serves 4 to 6

90ml/6 tbsp vegetable oil
5 green chillies, chopped
2.5cm/1in piece fresh root ginger, crushed
3 garlic cloves, crushed
1 clove garlic, sliced
2 bay leaves
5cm/2in cinnamon stick
900g/2lb lean lamb, cubed
600ml/1 pint/2½ cups water
175g/6oz red gram
50g/2oz each bengal gram, husked moong and red lentils
2 potatoes, chopped
1 aubergine (eggplant), chopped
4 onions, finely sliced, deep-fried and drained
50g/2oz fresh spinach, trimmed, washed and chopped
25g/1oz fresh fenugreek leaves
115g/4oz carrots, or pumpkin
115g/4oz fresh coriander (cilantro) leaves, chopped
50g/2oz mint leaves, chopped
30ml/2 tbsp dhansak masala
30ml/2 tbsp sambhar masala
salt, to taste
10ml/2 tsp soft light brown sugar
60ml/4 tbsp tamarind juice

1 Heat 45ml/3 tbsp of oil in a frying pan. Cook the chillies, ginger and crushed garlic for 2 minutes. Add the bay leaves, cinnamon, lamb and water. Boil, then simmer until the lamb is half cooked.

2 Drain the water into another pan and put the lamb aside. Add the gram and lentils to the water and cook until they are tender. Mash with the back of a spoon.

3 Add the aubergine and potatoes to the lentils with three of the deep-fried onions, the spinach, fenugreek and carrot or pumpkin. When the vegetables are tender, mash coarsely.

4 Heat 15ml/1 tbsp of the oil and fry the coriander and mint leaves, saving a little to garnish, with the dhansak and sambhar masala, salt and sugar. Add the lamb and fry for 5 minutes. Stir into the vegetable mixture. Heat gently until the lamb is cooked.

5 Add the tamarind juice. Heat the remaining oil. Fry the sliced garlic until golden. Pour over the dhansak. Garnish with the remaining deep-fried onion and reserved coriander and mint.

Kashmiri-style Lamb Energy 410kcal/1709kJ; Protein 32.2g; Carbohydrate 5.4g, of which sugars 1.9g; Fat 29.3g, of which saturates 9.4g; Cholesterol 114mg; Calcium 78mg; Fibre 0g; Sodium 153mg.
Lamb Dhansak Energy 627kcal/2626kJ; Protein 43.6g; Carbohydrate 48.6g, of which sugars 12g; Fat 30.3g, of which saturates 9.4g; Cholesterol 114mg; Calcium 141mg; Fibre 6.5g; Sodium 177mg.

Fiery Dry Lamb Curry

This dish is nearly as hot as a *phaal*, the dish renowned as India's hottest curry. Although fiery, the spices can still be distinguished above the chilli.

Serves 4 to 6

30ml/2 tbsp vegetable oil
1 large onion, finely sliced
5cm/2in piece fresh root ginger, crushed
4 garlic cloves, crushed
6–8 curry leaves
45ml/3 tbsp extra hot curry paste, or 60ml/4 tbsp hot curry powder
15ml/1 tbsp chilli powder
5ml/1 tsp five-spice powder
5ml/1 tsp ground turmeric
900g/2lb lean lamb, beef or pork, cubed
175ml/6fl oz/¾ cup thick coconut milk
salt, to taste
2 large tomatoes, finely chopped, to garnish

1 Heat the oil in a large frying pan and fry the onion, ginger, garlic and curry leaves until the onion is soft and turning translucent. Add the curry paste, chilli and five-spice powder, turmeric and salt. Stir-fry for 1–2 minutes until the spices release their fragrances.

2 Add the meat and stir well over a medium heat to seal and evenly brown the meat pieces. Keep stirring until the oil separates. Cover and cook for about 20 minutes.

3 Add the coconut milk, mix well and simmer until the meat is cooked. Towards the end of cooking, uncover the pan to reduce the excess liquid. Garnish and serve immediately.

Cook's Tip

Hotter even than a vindaloo, the phaal has achieved notoriety as the hottest curry dish, often with up to 12 chillies per serving. If the above dish is still not quite hot enough for you seek out a phaal in an Indian restaurant. However, such is the reputed heat in a phaal that many curry houses will not actually have it listed on their menu so you may need to specifically ask for it.

Rogan Josh with Spices and Tomato

The most popular dish of all Indian lamb dishes. The meat is traditionally marinated in yogurt, then cooked with spices and tomatoes, which give the dish a rich, red colour.

Serves 4

900g/2lb lamb fillet
45ml/3 tbsp lemon juice
250ml/8fl oz/1 cup natural (plain) yogurt
5ml/1 tsp salt
2 garlic cloves, crushed
2.5cm/1in piece fresh root ginger, grated
60ml/4 tbsp oil
2.5ml/½ tsp cumin seeds
2 bay leaves
4 green cardamom pods
1 onion, finely chopped
10ml/2 tsp ground coriander
10ml/2 tsp ground cumin
5ml/1 tsp chilli powder
400g/14oz can chopped tomatoes
30ml/2 tbsp tomato purée (paste)
toasted cumin seeds and bay leaves, to garnish
plain rice, to serve

1 Trim away any excess fat from the lamb and discard. Cut the meat into 2.5cm/1in cubes.

2 In a large bowl, mix together the lemon juice, yogurt, salt, 1 garlic clove and the ginger. Add the lamb, coat thoroughly, and leave in the marinade overnight in the refrigerator.

3 Heat the oil in a large frying pan and fry the cumin seeds for 2 minutes or until they begin to splutter. Add the bay leaves and cardamom pods and fry for a further 2 minutes.

4 Add the onion and remaining garlic and fry for 5 minutes. Stir in the ground coriander, cumin and chilli powder and fry for a further 2 minutes.

5 Remove the lamb from its marinade and add to the pan. Cook for 5 minutes, stirring occasionally.

6 Add the tomatoes, tomato purée and 150ml/¼ pint/⅔ cup water. Bring to the boil, then reduce the heat. Cover and simmer for about 1–1½ hours, or until the meat is tender. Serve with plain boiled rice and garnish with toasted cumin seeds and bay leaves.

Rogan Josh Energy 559kcal/2343kJ; Protein 54.4g; Carbohydrate 20.5g, of which sugars 18.8g; Fat 29.6g, of which saturates 13.5g; Cholesterol 191mg; Calcium 139mg; Fibre 4.6g; Sodium 278mg.
Lamb Curry Energy 559kcal/2343kJ; Protein 54.4g; Carbohydrate 20.5g, of which sugars 18.8g; Fat 29.6g, of which saturates 13.5g; Cholesterol 191mg; Calcium 139mg; Fibre 4.6g; Sodium 278mg.

Stir-fried Pork with Peanuts, Chillies and Lime

Pork or chicken stir-fried with nuts and herbs, with a splash of citrus flavour or fish sauce, is everyday home cooking in Vietnam. The combination of chilli, lime, basil and mint in this recipe makes it particularly refreshing and tasty. Serve with steamed or sticky rice, or with rice wrappers, salad and a dipping sauce.

Serves 4

45ml/3 tbsp vegetable or groundnut (peanut) oil
450g/1lb pork tenderloin, cut into fine strips
4 spring onions (scallions), chopped
4 garlic cloves, finely chopped
4cm/1½in fresh root ginger, finely chopped
2 green or red Thai chillies, seeded and finely chopped
100g/3½oz/generous ½ cup shelled, unsalted peanuts
grated rind and juice of 2 limes
30ml/2 tbsp nuoc mam
30ml/2 tbsp grated fresh coconut
25g/1oz/½ cup chopped fresh mint leaves
25g/1oz/½ cup chopped fresh basil leaves
25g/1oz/½ cup chopped fresh coriander (cilantro) leaves

1 Heat a wok or heavy pan and pour in 30ml/2 tbsp of the oil. Add the pork and sear over a high heat, until browned. Transfer the meat and juices on to a plate and set aside.

2 Heat the remaining oil and add the spring onions, garlic, ginger and chillies. When the aromas begin to rise from the pan, add the peanuts and stir-fry for 1–2 minutes.

3 Add the meat back into the wok. Stir in the lime rind and juice, and the nuoc mam. Add the coconut and herbs, and serve.

Cook's Tip
Nuoc mam is a Vietnamese fish sauce, which is used in moderation because it is so intensely flavoured. It is traditionally made by fermenting anchovies with salt in wooden boxes. The fish are then slowly pressed, yielding the salty, fishy liquid.

Pork with Dried Shrimp

You might expect the dried shrimp to give this dish a fishy flavour, but instead it simply imparts a delicious savoury taste.

Serves 4

250g/9oz pork fillet (tenderloin), sliced
30ml/2 tbsp vegetable oil
2 garlic cloves, finely chopped
45ml/3 tbsp dried shrimp
10ml/2 tsp dried shrimp paste or 5mm/¼in piece from block of shrimp paste
30ml/2 tbsp soy sauce
juice of 1 lime
15ml/1 tbsp palm sugar (jaggery) or muscovado (brown) sugar
1 small fresh red or green chilli, seeded and finely chopped
4 pak choi (bok choy) or 450g/1lb spring greens (collards), shredded

1 Place the pork in the freezer for about 30 minutes, until firm, to make slicing the meat easier. Using a sharp knife, cut it into thin slices.

2 Heat the oil in a wok or frying pan and cook the garlic until golden brown. Add the pork and stir-fry for about 4 minutes, until just cooked through.

3 Add the dried shrimp, then stir in the shrimp paste, with the soy sauce, lime juice and sugar. Add the chilli and pak choi or spring greens and toss over the heat until the vegetables are just wilted.

4 Transfer the stir-fry to warm individual bowls and serve immediately.

Cook's Tip
Shrimp paste has a strong fishy and salty flavour. It is used in a wide range of Asian dishes such as soups, sauces and rice dishes. The condiment is made from fermented ground shrimp, sun-dried and then cut into blocks. To many Westerners unfamiliar with this condiment, the pungent smell can be repellent; however, it does diminish a little after cooking and it is an essential ingredient in many curries and sauces.

Stir-fried Pork Energy 401kcal/1668kJ; Protein 32g; Carbohydrate 7g, of which sugars 3g; Fat 27g, of which saturates 5g; Cholesterol 71mg; Calcium 42mg; Fibre 1.8g; Sodium 400mg.
Pork with Dried Shrimp Energy 202kcal/843kJ; Protein 32.1g; Carbohydrate 6.6g, of which sugars 6.2g; Fat 9.4g, of which saturates 1.7g; Cholesterol 96mg; Calcium 377mg; Fibre 3.8g; Sodium 554mg.

Spicy Pork Stir-fry

This simple dish is quick to prepare and makes thinly sliced pork fabulously spicy. The potent flavour of gochujang chilli paste predominates in the seasoning for the pork and will set the tastebuds aflame. Serve with rice to help counterbalance the fiery character of the dish.

Serves 2

400g/14oz pork shoulder
1 onion
½ carrot
2 spring onions (scallions)
15ml/1 tbsp vegetable oil
½ red chilli, finely sliced
½ green chilli, finely sliced
steamed rice and miso soup, to serve

For the seasoning

30ml/2 tbsp dark soy sauce
30ml/2 tbsp gochujang chilli paste
30ml/2 tbsp mirin or rice wine
15ml/1 tbsp Korean chilli powder
1 garlic clove, finely chopped
1 spring onion (scallion), finely chopped
15ml/1 tbsp grated fresh root ginger
15ml/1 tbsp sesame oil
30ml/2 tbsp sugar
ground black pepper

1 Freeze the pork shoulder for 30 minutes, to make slicing easier, and then slice it thinly, to about 5mm/¼in thick. Cut the onion and carrot into thin strips, and slice the spring onions into lengthways strips.

2 To make the seasoning, combine the seasoning ingredients in a large bowl, mixing together thoroughly to form a paste. If the mixture is too dry, add a splash of water.

3 Heat a wok or large frying pan, and add the vegetable oil. Once the oil is smoking, add the pork, onion, carrot, spring onions and chillies. Stir-fry the ingredients, ensuring that they are kept moving all the time in the pan.

4 Once the pork has lightly browned, add the seasoning, and thoroughly coat the meat and vegetables. Stir-fry for 2 minutes more, or until the pork is cooked through.

5 Serve immediately with rice and a bowl of miso soup to help balance the spicy flavours of the dish.

Lemon Grass Pork with Chillies and Garlic

Chillies and lemon grass flavour this simple stir-fry, while peanuts add an interesting contrast in texture and the chillies add a satisfying kick. Look for jars of chopped lemon grass, which are handy when the fresh vegetable isn't available.

Serves 4

675g/1½lb boneless pork loin
2 lemon grass stalks, finely chopped
4 spring onions (scallions), thinly sliced
5ml/1 tsp salt
12 black peppercorns, coarsely crushed
30ml/2 tbsp groundnut (peanut) oil
2 garlic cloves, chopped
2 fresh red chillies, seeded and chopped
5ml/1 tsp soft light brown sugar
30ml/2 tbsp Thai fish sauce
25g/1oz/¼ cup roasted unsalted peanuts, chopped
ground black pepper
cooked rice noodles, to serve
coarsely torn coriander (cilantro) leaves, to garnish

1 Trim any excess fat from the pork. Cut the meat across into 5mm/¼in thick slices, then cut each slice into 5mm/¼in strips.

2 Put the pork into a large bowl with the lemon grass, spring onions, salt and crushed peppercorns; mix well. Cover the bowl with clear film (plastic wrap) and leave to marinate in a cool place for 30 minutes.

3 Preheat a wok, add the oil and swirl it around. Add the pork mixture and stir-fry over a medium heat for about 3 minutes, until browned all over.

4 Add the garlic and red chillies and stir-fry for a further 5–8 minutes over a medium heat, until the pork is cooked through and tender.

5 Add the sugar, fish sauce and chopped peanuts and toss to mix, then season to taste with black pepper. Serve immediately on a bed of rice noodles, garnished with the coarsely torn coriander leaves.

Spicy Pork Stir-fry Energy 430kcal/1799kJ; Protein 44.1g; Carbohydrate 21.3g, of which sugars 20.4g; Fat 19.2g, of which saturates 4.3g; Cholesterol 126mg; Calcium 44mg; Fibre 1.2g; Sodium 1216mg.
Lemon Grass Pork Energy 12kcal/49kJ; Protein 1.5g; Carbohydrate 0.1g, of which sugars 0.1g; Fat 0.6g, of which saturates 0.2g; Cholesterol 4mg; Calcium 1mg; Fibre 0g; Sodium 34mg.

Pork Chops with Field Mushrooms and Chilli Sauce

In Thailand, meat is frequently cooked over a brazier or open fire, so it isn't surprising that many tasty barbecue-style dishes come from there. These fabulous pork chops in a spicy sauce are great favourites with everyone.

Serves 4

4 pork chops
4 large mushrooms
45ml/3 tbsp vegetable oil
4 fresh red chillies, seeded and thinly sliced
45ml/3 tbsp Thai fish sauce
90ml/6 tbsp fresh lime juice
4 shallots, chopped
5ml/1 tsp roasted ground rice
30ml/2 tbsp spring onions (scallions), chopped, plus shredded spring onions to garnish
tagliatelle, to serve

For the marinade

2 garlic cloves, chopped
15ml/1 tbsp granulated (white) sugar
15ml/1 tbsp Thai fish sauce
30ml/2 tbsp soy sauce
15ml/1 tbsp sesame oil
15ml/1 tbsp whisky or dry sherry
2 lemon grass stalks, finely chopped
2 spring onions (scallions), chopped

1 Make the marinade. Combine the garlic, sugar, sauces, oil and whisky or sherry in a large, shallow dish. Stir in the lemon grass and spring onions.

2 Add the pork chops, turning to coat them in the marinade. Cover and leave to marinate for 1–2 hours.

3 Lift the chops out of the marinade and place them on a barbecue grill over hot coals or on a grill (broiler) rack. Add the mushrooms and brush them with 15ml/1 tbsp of the oil. Cook the pork chops for 5–7 minutes on each side and the mushrooms for about 2 minutes. Brush both with the marinade while cooking.

4 Heat the remaining oil in a wok or small frying pan, then remove the pan from the heat and stir in the chillies, fish sauce, lime juice, shallots, ground rice and spring onions. Serve the pork chops and mushrooms and spoon over the sauce. Garnish with the shredded spring onion and serve with the tagliatelle.

Enchiladas with Pork and Spicy Green Sauce

The tomatillo sauce goes perfectly with the pork and dried cascabel chilli.

Serves 3 to 4

500g/1¼lb pork shoulder, diced
1 cascabel chilli
30ml/2 tbsp oil
2 garlic cloves, crushed
1 onion, finely chopped
300g/11oz/scant 2 cups drained canned tomatillos
6 fresh corn tortillas
75g/3oz/¾ cup grated Monterey Jack or mild Cheddar cheese
tomato salad, to serve

1 Put the diced pork in a pan and pour over water to cover. Bring to the boil, lower the heat and simmer for 40 minutes.

2 Meanwhile, soak the chilli in hot water for 30 minutes until soft. Drain, then slit open and discard the stalk and seeds.

3 Drain the pork and let it cool slightly, then shred it, using two forks. Put the pork in a bowl and set it aside.

4 Heat the oil in a frying pan and fry the garlic and onion for 3–4 minutes until translucent. Chop and add the chilli with the tomatillos. Cook, stirring constantly, until the tomatillos start to break up. Lower the heat and simmer the sauce for 10 minutes more. Cool slightly, then purée in a blender.

5 Preheat the oven to 180°C/350°F/Gas 4. Soften the tortillas by wrapping them in foil and steaming on a plate over boiling water for a few minutes until pliable.

6 Spoon one-sixth of the shredded pork on to the centre of a tortilla and roll it up to make an enchilada. Place it in a shallow baking dish which is large enough to hold the enchiladas in one layer. Fill and roll the remaining tortillas.

7 Pour the sauce over the enchiladas to cover completely. Sprinkle evenly with cheese. Bake for 25–30 minutes, or until the cheese bubbles. Serve immediately. A tomato salad makes a good accompaniment for this dish.

Pork Chops Energy 339kcal/1418kJ; Protein 39.7g; Carbohydrate 2.3g, of which sugars 1g; Fat 19.1g, of which saturates 4.1g; Cholesterol 90mg; Calcium 26mg; Fibre 1g; Sodium 678mg.
Enchiladas with Pork Energy 613kcal/2574kJ; Protein 48.9g; Carbohydrate 53.5g, of which sugars 6.2g; Fat 23.4g, of which saturates 8.9g; Cholesterol 129mg; Calcium 299mg; Fibre 3.5g; Sodium 534mg.

Tostadas with Shredded Pork and Spices

Crisp fried tortillas topped with refried beans and spiced shredded pork make a delectable treat.

Serves 6

6 corn tortillas, freshly made or a few days old
oil, for frying

For the topping

500g/1¼ lb pork shoulder, cut into 2.5cm/1in cubes
2.5ml/½ tsp salt
15ml/1 tbsp oil
1 small onion, halved and sliced
1 garlic clove, crushed
1 pasilla chilli, seeded and ground
5ml/1 tsp ground cinnamon
2.5ml/½ tsp ground cloves
175g/6oz/1 cup refried beans
90ml/6 tbsp sour cream
2 tomatoes, seeded and diced
115g/4oz feta cheese, crumbled
fresh oregano sprigs, to garnish

1 Make the topping. Place the pork cubes in a pan, pour over water to cover and bring to the boil. Lower the heat, cover and simmer for 40 minutes. Drain, discarding the cooking liquid. Shred the pork, using two forks. Put it in a bowl and season with the salt.

2 Heat the oil in a large frying pan. Add the onion, garlic, chilli and spices. Stir over the heat for 2–3 minutes, then add the shredded meat and cook until the meat is thoroughly heated and has absorbed the flavourings. Heat the refried beans in a separate, small pan.

3 Meanwhile, cook the tortillas. Pour oil into a large frying pan to a depth of 2cm/¾in. Heat the oil and fry one tortilla at a time, pressing down with a metal spatula or a pair of tongs to keep it flat. As soon as a tortilla is crisp, lift it out and drain it on kitchen paper.

4 Place each tortilla on a plate. Top with refried beans. Add a little of the meat mixture, then spoon 15ml/1 tbsp of the sour cream over each. Divide the chopped tomato among the tostadas and top with crumbled feta. Serve immediately, garnished with fresh oregano.

Wild Boar Chops with Fiery Chilli Romesco Sauce

Romesco is a fiery Spanish sauce that takes its name from the small dried red chillies used for making it. Often served cold as a dip for vegetables, it is also good served hot with meat.

Serves 4

4 wild boar loin chops, about 175g/6oz each
olive oil, for shallow frying
braised Savoy cabbage, to serve

For the romesco sauce

3 dried red chillies
150ml/¼ pint/⅔ cup olive oil
1 slice white bread, crusts removed
3 garlic cloves, chopped
3 tomatoes, peeled, seeded and roughly chopped
25g/1oz/¼ cup ground almonds
60ml/4 tbsp balsamic vinegar
60ml/4 tbsp red wine vinegar
salt and ground black pepper

1 To make the romesco sauce, deseed the chillies, then soak in warm water for 30 minutes. Drain and dry, then chop finely.

2 Heat 45ml/3 tbsp of the oil in a frying pan and fry the bread until golden on both sides. Lift out with a slotted spoon and drain on kitchen paper, then crumble into a blender or food processor.

3 Add the garlic to the oil in the frying pan and cook gently for 2–3 minutes, then cool for a few minutes. Add the chillies, tomatoes and almonds to the bread in the food processor. Add the garlic, with the oil in which it was cooked. Blend to a paste.

4 With the motor running, gradually add the remaining oil and the balsamic and red wine vinegars. When the sauce is smooth, scrape it into a bowl and season. Cover and chill for 2 hours.

5 Season the boar with pepper. Heat the oil in a frying pan. Fry the chops for 15 minutes each side, until golden brown.

6 When the chops are almost cooked, place the sauce in a pan and heat gently. If it is too thick, stir in a little boiling water. Serve with the wild boar, accompanied by braised cabbage.

Tostadas with Pork Energy 334kcal/1397kJ; Protein 25.5g; Carbohydrate 22.9g, of which sugars 3.8g; Fat 16.1g, of which saturates 6.7g; Cholesterol 75mg; Calcium 152mg; Fibre 3.8g; Sodium 836mg.
Wild Boar with Romesco Sauce Energy 559kcal/2322kJ; Protein 40g; Carbohydrate 6.9g, of which sugars 3.6g; Fat 41.4g, of which saturates 7.1g; Cholesterol 110mg; Calcium 42mg; Fibre 1.6g; Sodium 168mg.

Curried Meat with Spicy Peas

This spicy dish can be served as a main course, or try mixing it with fried or scrambled eggs for a delicious brunch. It also makes a good pizza topping, and can be used as a filling for samosas.

Serves 4 to 6

5ml/1 tsp vegetable oil
1 large onion, finely chopped
2 garlic cloves, crushed
5cm/2in piece fresh root ginger, crushed
4 green chillies, chopped
30ml/2 tbsp curry powder
450g/1lb lean minced (ground) pork, beef, or lamb
225g/8oz frozen peas, thawed
salt, to taste
juice of 1 lemon
a few coriander (cilantro) leaves, chopped

1 Heat the vegetable oil in a wok or large frying pan. Add the chopped onion and cook for 2–3 minutes until it is just beginning to soften.

2 Add the garlic, ginger and chillies to the pan and cook, stirring constantly, for 4–5 minutes until the onion has turned translucent.

3 Turn the heat down to low, add the curry powder to the pan and mix well. Cook for a minute until the curry powder releases its fragrances.

4 Add the meat to the pan and stir well, pressing the meat down with the back of a spoon. Cook, stirring frequently, for 8–10 minutes until the meat is just cooked through and evenly browned all over.

5 Add the peas, salt and lemon juice to the pan, mix well, cover and simmer for 4–5 minutes until the peas are tender. Mix in the fresh coriander. Serve immediately.

Variation
This dish is equally delicious if made with minced lean lamb or pork. Simply substitute the same amount of lamb or pork for the minced beef. Or try using half pork and half beef.

Pork Satays with Peanut and Chilli

These satays are made by marinating pork, then cooking it on skewers on the barbecue, and serving with a spicy nutty sauce. Beef or lamb could be used for these satays instead.

Makes 12 to 16 skewers

500g/1¼lb pork fillet (tenderloin)
lime wedges and fried onions, to serve

For the marinade
150ml/¼ pint/⅔ cup dark soy sauce
3–4 garlic cloves, crushed
45ml/3 tbsp groundnut (peanut) oil
50g/2oz peanuts, finely crushed
salt and ground pepper

For the sauce
1 onion, finely chopped
2–3 fresh red chillies, seeded and ground, or 15ml/1 tbsp chilli sauce
75ml/3fl oz/⅓ cup dark soy sauce
60–90ml/4–6 tbsp water
juice of 1–2 limes or 1 large lemon
50g/2oz peanuts, coarsely ground

1 Wipe and trim the meat. Cut the pork into 2.5cm/1in cubes or into thin strips about 1cm/½in wide by 5cm/2in long.

2 Blend the dark soy sauce, garlic and oil together with the seasoning and the crushed peanuts. Pour over the meat and allow to marinate for at least 1 hour.

3 If using wooden or bamboo skewers, soak them in water for at least 1 hour so that they don't burn when the satays are being cooked. Then thread three or four pieces of meat on to one end of each of the skewers.

4 Make the sauce. Put the onion, chillies or chilli sauce, soy sauce and water in a pan. Bring to the boil, and simmer for 4–5 minutes. Cool, then add the lime or lemon juice. Add the crushed peanuts just before serving. Preheat the grill (broiler) or barbecue.

5 Cook the satays for about 5–8 minutes, turning frequently, until they are tender. Place on a large platter. Garnish with lime or lemon wedges and fried onions and serve with the sauce.

Curried Meat with Peas Energy 199kcal/827kJ; Protein 17.5g; Carbohydrate 7.3g, of which sugars 2.7g; Fat 11.3g, of which saturates 4.8g; Cholesterol 58mg; Calcium 40mg; Fibre 2.6g; Sodium 61mg.
Pork Satays Energy 189kcal/784kJ; Protein 14.5g; Carbohydrate 2.9g, of which sugars 2.2g; Fat 13.3g, of which saturates 5.8g; Cholesterol 35mg; Calcium 25mg; Fibre 0.9g; Sodium 70mg.

Hot Portuguese Pork

This deliciously fiery dish displays the influence of Portuguese cooking on Indian cuisine.

Serves 4 to 6

30ml/2 tbsp vegetable oil
1 onion
4 fresh red chillies, seeded and finely chopped or 5ml/1 tsp chilli powder
60ml/4 tbsp vindaloo masala paste
90ml/6 tbsp white wine vinegar
90ml/6 tbsp tomato purée (paste)
2.5ml/½ tsp fenugreek seeds
5ml/1 tsp ground turmeric
5ml/1 tsp crushed mustard seeds, or 2.5ml/½ tsp mustard powder
7.5ml/1½ tsp sugar
900g/2lb boneless pork spareribs
250ml/8fl oz/1 cup water
salt, to taste
plain boiled rice, to serve

1 Heat the oil in a wok or large frying pan. Finely chop the onion and add to the pan. Cook for 2–3 minutes until beginning to soften.

2 Add the fresh chilli or chilli powder and stir-fry for 2 minutes. Add the vindaloo paste and fry for a minute, stirring constantly until it releases its fragrances.

3 Pour in the white wine vinegar, mixing well. Add the tomato purée, fenugreek seeds, turmeric and mustard seeds or mustard powder. Season with salt, to taste, and add the sugar. Mix well until all the ingredients are throughly combined. Remove from the heat and leave to cool slightly.

4 Cut the pork spareribs into bitesize cubes and add to the pan, ensuring that it is thoroughly coated in the sauce. Set aside to marinate for 2 hours.

5 Add the water to the pan and mix with the other ingredients. Bring to the boil and then simmer gently for about 2 hours. Taste the sauce and adjust the seasoning if necessary.

6 Transfer the meat and the sauce to a large serving dish. Serve immediately with the plain boiled rice.

Spicy Barbecued Pork Spare Ribs

Sticky and spicy, these pork spare ribs are a delectable messy treat.

Serves 4

1kg/2¼lb pork spare ribs
1 onion
2 garlic cloves
2.5cm/1in fresh root ginger
75ml/2½fl oz/⅓ cup dark soy sauce
1–2 fresh red chillies, seeded and chopped
5ml/1 tsp tamarind pulp, soaked in 75ml/2½fl oz/⅓ cup water
15–30ml/1–2 tbsp soft dark brown sugar
30ml/2 tbsp groundnut (peanut) oil
salt and ground black pepper

1 Wipe the pork ribs and place them in a wok, wide frying pan or large flameproof casserole.

2 Finely chop the onion, crush the garlic and peel and slice the ginger. Blend the soy sauce, onion, garlic, ginger and chopped chillies together to a paste in a food processor or with a pestle and mortar.

3 Strain the tamarind and reserve the juice. Add the tamarind juice, brown sugar, oil and seasoning to taste to the onion mixture and mix well together.

4 Pour the sauce over the ribs and toss well to coat. Bring to the boil and then simmer, uncovered and stirring frequently, for 30 minutes. Add extra water if necessary.

5 Put the ribs on a rack in a roasting pan, place under a preheated grill (broiler), on a barbecue or in the oven at 200°C/400°F/Gas 6 and cook until the ribs are tender, about 20 minutes, depending on thickness. Baste the ribs with the sauce and turn occasionally. Serve immediately.

Cook's Tip
Children will love these messy ribs, but ensure they can handle the chillies. You can always reduce the heat if necessary.

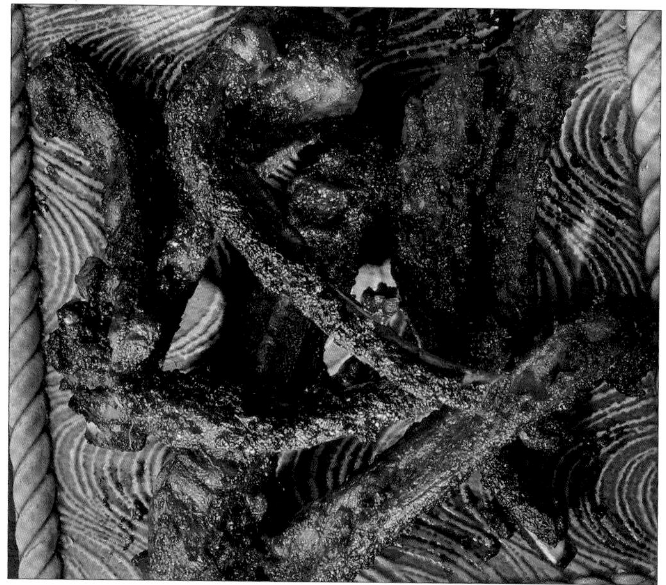

Hot Portuguese Pork Energy 267kcal/1119kJ; Protein 34.6g; Carbohydrate 11.3g, of which sugars 7.3g; Fat 9.6g, of which saturates 2.5g; Cholesterol 95mg; Calcium 68mg; Fibre 2.2g; Sodium 166mg.
Spicy Barbecued Pork Spareribs Energy 160kcal/668kJ; Protein 7g; Carbohydrate 14g, of which sugars 11g; Fat 9g, of which saturates 2g; Cholesterol 17mg; Calcium 19mg; Fibre 0.6g; Sodium 120mg.

Sticky Pork Ribs with Ginger and Chilli

Ginger, garlic and chilli are used to flavour the sweet-and-sour sauce that coats these ribs. Cook the pork ribs in a covered clay pot first to tenderize the meat, then uncover the dish so the ribs become deliciously sticky and brown.

Serves 4

16–20 small meaty pork ribs, about 900g/2lb total weight
1 onion, finely chopped
5cm/2in piece fresh root ginger, peeled and grated
2 garlic cloves, crushed
2.5–5ml/½–1 tsp chilli powder
60ml/4 tbsp soy sauce
45ml/3 tbsp tomato purée (paste)
45ml/3 tbsp clear honey
30ml/2 tbsp red wine vinegar
45ml/3 tbsp dry sherry
60ml/4 tbsp water
salt and ground black pepper

1 Soak the clay pot in cold water for 20 minutes, then drain. Place the ribs in the clay pot, arranging them evenly.

2 Mix together the onion, ginger, garlic, chilli powder, soy sauce, tomato purée, honey, wine vinegar, sherry and water.

3 Pour the sauce over the ribs and toss to coat them. Cover the clay pot and place in an unheated oven. Set the oven to 220°C/425°F/Gas 7. Cook for 1 hour.

4 Remove the lid, baste the ribs and season to taste with salt and pepper. Cook uncovered for 15–20 minutes, basting the ribs two to three times during the cooking until they are sticky and dark brown.

Cook's Tips

- *For a stronger flavour, coat the ribs evenly with the sauce and leave to marinate for 2 hours before cooking in the clay pot.*
- *If you cannot find fresh root ginger, crushed ginger, also known as ginger pulp, is available from supermarkets. Use 10ml/2 tsp of the paste instead of 5cm/2in of fresh root ginger.*

Sichuan Pork Ribs with Ginger, Garlic and Chilli Relish

This spicy dish works best when the pork ribs are grilled in whole, large slabs, then sliced to serve.

Serves 4

4 pork rib slabs, each with 6 ribs, total weight about 2kg/4½lb
40g/1½oz/3 tbsp light muscovado sugar
3 garlic cloves, crushed
5cm/2in piece fresh root ginger, finely grated
10ml/2 tsp Sichuan peppercorns, finely crushed
2.5ml/½ tsp ground black pepper
5ml/1 tsp finely ground star anise
5ml/1 tsp Chinese five-spice powder
90ml/6 tbsp dark soy sauce
45ml/3 tbsp sunflower oil
15ml/1 tbsp sesame oil

For the relish

60ml/4 tbsp sunflower oil
300g/11oz banana shallots, finely chopped
9 garlic cloves, crushed
7.5cm/3in piece fresh root ginger, finely grated
60ml/4 tbsp rice wine vinegar
45ml/3 tbsp sweet chilli sauce
105ml/7 tbsp tomato ketchup
90ml/6 tbsp water
60ml/4 tbsp chopped fresh coriander (cilantro) leaves
salt

1 Lay the slabs of pork ribs in a large dish. Mix the remaining ingredients and pour over the ribs. Cover and chill overnight.

2 Make the relish. Heat the oil in a heavy pan, add the shallots and cook for 5 minutes. Add the garlic and ginger and cook for 4 minutes. Add the remaining ingredients except the fresh coriander. Cover and simmer for 10 minutes. Stir in the coriander.

3 Prepare the barbecue. Remove the ribs from the marinade. Pour the marinade into a pan. Boil, then simmer for 3 minutes.

4 When the coals are hot, lay the ribs on a rack and cook for 3 minutes on each side. Move them to a cooler part of the barbecue, cover with a lid or tented foil and cook for 30 minutes, turning and basting occasionally with the marinade, until tender.

5 Stop basting with the marinade 5 minutes before the end of the cooking time. Cut into single ribs to serve, with the relish.

Sticky Pork Ribs Energy 633kcal/2637kJ; Protein 42.9g; Carbohydrate 11.5g, of which sugars 11.2g; Fat 45.2g, of which saturates 14.1g; Cholesterol 149mg; Calcium 43mg; Fibre 0.5g; Sodium 250mg.
Sichuan Pork Ribs Energy 633kcal/2637kJ; Protein 42.9g; Carbohydrate 11.5g, of which sugars 11.2g; Fat 45.2g, of which saturates 14.1g; Cholesterol 149mg; Calcium 43mg; Fibre 0.5g; Sodium 250mg.

Pork Belly with Sesame Dip and Chilli Sauce

Thinly sliced pork belly is griddled until the outside is crisp, leaving a smooth texture at the centre. The meat is then immersed in a salty sesame dip, before being wrapped in lettuce leaves with a spoonful of red chilli paste.

Serves 3

675g/1½lb pork belly
2 round (butterhead) lettuces

For the dip

45ml/3 tbsp sesame oil
10ml/2 tsp salt
ground black pepper

For the sauce

45ml/3 tbsp gochujang chilli paste
75ml/5 tbsp doenjang soya bean paste
2 garlic cloves, crushed
1 spring onion (scallion), finely chopped
5ml/1 tsp sesame oil

1 Freeze the pork belly for 30 minutes and then slice it very thinly, to about 3mm/⅛in thick. (You could ask the butcher to do this, or buy the meat pre-sliced at an Asian store.)

2 To make the dip, combine the sesame oil, salt and pepper in a small serving bowl.

3 To make the sauce, blend the chilli paste, doenjang soya bean paste, garlic, spring onion and sesame oil in a bowl, mixing the oil thoroughly into the paste. Transfer to a serving bowl.

4 Remove the outer leaves from the heads of lettuce, keeping them whole. Rinse well and place in a serving dish.

5 Heat a griddle pan or heavy frying pan over high heat (the griddle can be used over charcoal). Add the pork to the pan and cook until the surface is crisp and golden brown.

6 Serve the pork with the accompanying dishes of lettuce, sesame dip and chilli sauce. To eat, take a strip of pork and dip it into the sesame dip. Then place the meat in the middle of a lettuce leaf and add a small spoonful of the chilli sauce. Fold the sides of the leaf inwards and roll up into a parcel.

Jamaican Jerk Pork with Red Chillies

This is a Jamaican way of spicing meat or poultry before roasting in the oven or over a fire.

Serves 4

15ml/1 tbsp oil
2 onions, finely chopped
2 fresh red chillies, seeded and finely chopped
1 garlic clove, crushed
2.5cm/1in piece fresh root ginger, grated
5ml/1 tsp dried thyme
5ml/1 tsp ground allspice
5ml/1 tsp hot pepper sauce
30ml/2 tbsp rum
grated rind and juice of 1 lime
4 pork chops
salt and ground black pepper
fresh thyme, small red chillies and lime wedges, to garnish

1 Heat the oil in a frying pan. Add the onions and cook for 10 minutes until soft and translucent.

2 Add the chillies, garlic, ginger, thyme and allspice and fry for 2 minutes. Stir in the hot pepper sauce, rum, lime rind and juice.

3 Lower the heat and simmer gently until the mixture has formed a dark paste. Season with salt and pepper to taste, and set aside to cool.

4 Rub the paste all over the chops, ensuring they are well covered. Place them in a shallow dish, cover and marinate overnight in the refrigerator.

5 Preheat the oven to 190°C/375°F/Gas 5. Place the chops on a rack in a roasting pan and roast in the oven for 30 minutes until fully cooked.

6 Serve garnished with thyme, chillies and lime wedges.

Variation
Chicken joints or even a whole chicken can also be coated with this delicious spicy paste before roasting.

Pork Belly Energy 991kcal/4093kJ; Protein 37g; Carbohydrate 1.1g, of which sugars 0.6g; Fat 93.1g, of which saturates 31.4g; Cholesterol 162mg; Calcium 37mg; Fibre 1.2g; Sodium 1475mg.
Jerk Pork Energy 271kcal/1134kJ; Protein 33.9g; Carbohydrate 9.2g, of which sugars 5.6g; Fat 9.4g, of which saturates 2.5g; Cholesterol 95mg; Calcium 42mg; Fibre 1.4g; Sodium 109mg.

Chilli Pork with Chickpeas and Orange

This winter speciality is a familiar dish in the Aegean islands, particularly in Crete. It is traditionally offered to family and close friends on the night before a wedding. This version comes from the island of Chios. All you need to serve with this spicy dish is fresh bread to mop up the juices and a bowl of black olives.

Serves 4

350g/12oz/1¾ cups dried chickpeas, soaked overnight in water to cover
75–90ml/5–6 tbsp olive oil
675g/1½lb boneless leg of pork, cut into large cubes
1 large onion, sliced
2 garlic cloves, chopped
400g/14oz can chopped tomatoes
grated rind of 1 orange
1 small dried red chilli
salt and ground black pepper

1 Drain the chickpeas, rinse them under cold water and drain again. Place them in a large pan. Pour in enough cold water to cover generously, put a lid on the pan and bring to the boil.

2 Skim the surface, cover and cook gently for 1–1½ hours. Alternatively, cook them in a pressure cooker for 20 minutes under full pressure. When the chickpeas are soft, drain them, reserving the cooking liquid, and set them aside.

3 Heat the olive oil in a pan and brown the meat in batches. Transfer the cubes to a plate as they brown. When the meat is done, add the onion to the oil remaining in the pan and fry until golden. Add the garlic, then add the tomatoes and orange rind.

4 Crumble in the chilli. Return the chickpeas and meat to the pan, and pour in enough of the reserved cooking liquid to cover. Add the black pepper, but not salt at this stage.

5 Mix well, cover the pan and simmer for 1 hour, or until the meat is tender. Stir occasionally and add more of the reserved liquid if needed. The result should be a moist casserole; not soupy, but not dry either. Season to taste with salt and serve immediately.

Pork and Pineapple Coconut Curry

The heat of this curry balances out its sweetness to make a smooth and fragrant dish. It takes very little time to cook, so is ideal for a quick supper before going out, or for a mid-week family meal on a busy evening.

Serves 4

400ml/14fl oz can or carton coconut milk
10ml/2 tsp Thai red curry paste
400g/14oz pork loin steaks, trimmed and thinly sliced
15ml/1 tbsp Thai fish sauce
5ml/1 tsp palm sugar (jaggery) or light muscovado (brown) sugar
15ml/1 tbsp tamarind juice, made by mixing tamarind paste with warm water
2 kaffir lime leaves, torn
½ medium pineapple, peeled and chopped
1 fresh red chilli, seeded and finely chopped

1 Pour the coconut milk into a bowl and let it settle, so that the cream rises to the surface. Scoop the cream into a measuring jug (cup). You should have about 250ml/8fl oz/1 cup of cream. If necessary, mix a little of the coconut milk into the jug to achieve that quantity.

2 Pour the coconut cream into a large heavy pan and bring it slowly to the boil.

3 Cook the coconut cream for about 10 minutes, until the cream separates, stirring frequently to prevent it from sticking to the base of the pan and scorching.

4 Add the red curry paste and stir well until thoroughly combined with the cream. Cook, stirring occasionally, for about 4 minutes, until the paste is fragrant.

5 Add the sliced pork and stir in the fish sauce, sugar and tamarind juice. Cook, stirring constantly, for 1–2 minutes, until the sugar has dissolved and the pork is no longer pink.

6 Add the remaining coconut milk and the lime leaves. Bring to the boil, then stir in the pineapple. Reduce the heat and simmer gently for 3 minutes, or until the pork is fully cooked. Sprinkle over the chilli and serve.

Chilli Pork Energy 663kcal/2,781kJ; Protein 56.7g; Carbohydrate 54.4g, of which sugars 11g; Fat 25.7g, of which saturates 4.9g; Cholesterol 106mg; Calcium 184mg; Fibre 11.8g; Sodium 164mg.
Pork Curry Energy 191kcal/807kJ; Protein 22.2g; Carbohydrate 16.4g, of which sugars 16.3g; Fat 4.5g, of which saturates 1.6g; Cholesterol 63mg; Calcium 55mg; Fibre 1.2g; Sodium 449mg.

Asian Black Pudding with Chilli

Prepared entirely with pig offal, this Philippine dish is similar to black pudding, although it is traditionally cooked to a smooth mixture in a pan rather than rolled into a neat sausage. Flavoured with garlic and ginger, it is served hot with noodles or rice and chillies as a popular street snack at any time of day. In this recipe though, rather than boiling the offal until it is soft, the meat is fried and served straight from the pan with toasted bread.

Serves 4

30ml/2 tbsp groundnut (peanut) or vegetable oil
1 onion, finely chopped
2 garlic cloves, finely chopped
25g/1oz fresh root ginger, finely chopped or grated
50g/2oz pig's fat, finely chopped
225g/8oz pig's liver, chopped
115g/4oz pig's kidney, finely chopped
115g/4oz pig's heart, chopped
15–30ml/1–2 tbsp Thai fish sauce
a handful of fresh chilli leaves or flat leaf parsley, finely chopped, plus extra to garnish
about 8 slices French bread or any crusty rustic loaf
salt and ground black pepper
2 red or green chillies, seeded and quartered lengthways, to serve

1 Heat the groundnut or vegetable oil in a wok or large, heavy frying pan, stir in the onion, garlic and ginger and fry until fragrant and lightly browned.

2 Add the chopped fat and the liver, kidney and heart and fry gently until lightly browned.

3 Stir in the fish sauce and the chopped chilli leaves or parsley and fry, stirring constantly, for 1–2 minutes. Season with salt and lots of black pepper.

4 Lightly toast the slices of bread under a preheated grill (broiler) until golden brown on both sides.

5 Spoon the fried offal on top of each slice of bread and garnish with chilli leaves or parsley. Serve as a snack or a light lunch, and serve the chillies to chew on.

Braised Spicy Pork with Tofu and Mushrooms

This hearty pork and kimchi dish is a rich, spicy stew bubbling with flavour and piquancy, traditionally cooked in a heavy clay bowl called a tukbaege. The slow cooking allows the flavours to mingle and create complex, enticing taste combinations.

Serves 4

4 dried shiitake mushrooms, soaked in warm water for about 30 minutes
150g/5oz firm tofu
200g/7oz boneless pork chop
300g/11oz cabbage kimchi
45ml/3 tbsp vegetable oil
1 garlic clove, crushed
15ml/1 tbsp Korean chilli powder
750ml/1¼ pints/3 cups vegetable stock or water
2 spring onions (scallions), finely sliced
salt

1 When the soaked shiitake mushrooms have reconstituted and become soft, drain and slice them, discarding the stems. Dice the tofu into cubes approximately 2cm/¾in square. Dice the pork into bitesize cubes, and slice the kimchi into similar size pieces. Squeeze any excess liquid out of the kimchi.

2 Pour the vegetable oil into a pan or wok and place over medium heat. Add the pork and garlic, and fry until crisp. Once the pork has turned dark brown add the kimchi and chilli powder, and stir-fry for 60 seconds more.

3 Pour the stock or water into the pan and bring to the boil. Add the tofu, mushrooms and spring onions, cover then simmer gently for 10–15 minutes. Season with salt to taste and serve bubbling from the pan.

Cook's Tip

Kimchi is a pungent condiment served at almost every Korean meal. Various vegetables – such as cabbage or turnips – are pickled, then stored in tightly sealed pots or jars to ferment.

Asian Black Pudding Energy 518kcal/2175kJ; Protein 26g; Carbohydrate 56.7g, of which sugars 7g; Fat 22.6g, of which saturates 6.9g; Cholesterol 181mg; Calcium 133mg; Fibre 3.2g; Sodium 893mg.
Braised Spicy Pork Energy 185kcal/770kJ; Protein 15.1g; Carbohydrate 4.2g, of which sugars 4g; Fat 12.1g, of which saturates 1.9g; Cholesterol 32mg; Calcium 234mg; Fibre 1.8g; Sodium 534mg.

Cabbage Leaves with Spicy Pork

In South-east Asia, spicy pork or shellfish mixtures are often wrapped in leaves and steamed, or stuffed into bamboo stems and smoked over open fires.

Serves 4 to 6

1 leafy green cabbage
15–30ml/1–2 tbsp palm or groundnut (peanut) oil
10ml/2 tsp coriander seeds
2 shallots, finely chopped
2 garlic cloves, finely chopped
2–3 red chillies, seeded and finely chopped
25g/1oz galangal, finely chopped
2–3 spring onions (scallions), finely chopped
10ml/2 tsp palm sugar (jaggery)
2–3 tomatoes, skinned, seeded and finely chopped
30ml/2 tbsp coconut cream
1 small bunch fresh coriander (cilantro) leaves, finely chopped
225g/8oz minced (ground) pork
50g/2oz pig's liver, finely chopped
50g/2oz pig's heart, finely chopped
salt and ground black pepper
kecap manis, for dipping

1 Prepare the cabbage. Pull the cabbage apart so that you have about 20 leaves. Steam or blanch the leaves to soften, drain and refresh under cold water. Cut off any thick stems and set aside.

2 Heat the oil in a wok or heavy pan, stir in the coriander seeds and fry for 1 minute. Add the chopped shallots, garlic, the finely chopped chillies, galangal, spring onions and sugar and stir-fry until they begin to colour. Stir in the tomatoes, coconut cream and coriander leaves and cook for 5 minutes until the mixture resembles a thick sauce. Season with salt and pepper and transfer to a bowl to cool.

3 Add the minced pork and liver and, using your hand or a fork, mix well together. Place a cabbage leaf on a flat surface in front of you and place a spoonful of the mixture in the centre. Fold in the sides of the leaf and roll it up into a log, making sure that all of the meat is enclosed. Repeat the process with the remaining leaves.

4 Place the stuffed leaves in a steamer, seam side down, and steam for 25–30 minutes, until the meat is cooked. Serve hot with kecap manis for dipping.

Spicy Stuffed Pork Tenderloin

This is a very easy dish to make and looks extremely impressive. It is good for a bulk cookout as you can get several tenderloins on a barbecue grill, and each one yields about eight chunky slices. Serve the pork with a chickpea salad topped with finely chopped onions and parsley, and flavoured with a mustardy dressing.

Serves 6 to 8

2 pork fillets (tenderloins), each about 350g/12oz
45ml/3 tbsp olive oil
40g/1½oz/1½ cups fresh basil leaves, chopped
50g/2oz Pecorino cheese, grated
2.5ml/½ tsp chilli flakes
salt and ground black pepper

1 Make a 1cm/½in slit down the length of one of the tenderloins. Continue to slice, cutting along the fold of the meat, until you can open it out flat. Lay between two sheets of baking parchment and pound with a rolling pin to an even thickness of about 1cm/½in. Lift off the top sheet of parchment and brush the meat with a little oil. Press half the basil leaves on to the surface, then sprinkle over half the Pecorino cheese and chilli flakes. Add a little pepper.

2 Roll up lengthways to form a sausage and tie with kitchen string. Repeat with the second tenderloin. Place in a shallow bowl with the remaining oil, cover and put in a cool place until needed.

3 Prepare the barbecue. Twenty minutes before you are ready to cook, season the meat with salt. Wipe any excess oil off the meat. Once the flames have died down, rake the hot coals to one side and insert a drip tray flat beside them. Position a lightly oiled grill rack over the coals to heat.

4 When the coals are hot, or with a light coating of ash, put the tenderloins on to the grill rack over the coals. Grill for 5 minutes over the coals, turning to sear on all sides, then move them over the drip tray and grill for 15 minutes more. Cover with a lid or tented heavy-duty foil, and turn them over from time to time. When done, remove then wrap in foil. Leave to rest for 10 minutes before slicing into rounds and serving.

Cabbage Leaves Energy 183kcal/764kJ; Protein 12.6g; Carbohydrate 7.3g, of which sugars 7g; Fat 11.8g, of which saturates 5g; Cholesterol 56mg; Calcium 55mg; Fibre 2.2g; Sodium 53mg.
Spicy Stuffed Pork Energy 169kcal/703kJ; Protein 20.9g; Carbohydrate 0.2g, of which sugars 0.1g; Fat 9.3g, of which saturates 2.8g; Cholesterol 60mg; Calcium 79mg; Fibre 0.3g; Sodium 118mg.

Chilli Pork in Chinese Leaves

Meltingly tender pork, imbued with the flavours of Korean doenjang soya bean paste and garlic, is combined with a refreshingly zesty mooli stuffing and wrapped in parcels of Chinese leaves.

Serves 3 to 4

1 head Chinese leaves (Chinese cabbage)
5 garlic cloves, roughly chopped
½ onion, roughly chopped
1 leek, roughly chopped
15ml/1 tbsp doenjang soya bean paste
100ml/3½fl oz/scant ½ cup sake or rice wine
675g/1½lb pork neck
salt
sugar

For the stuffing

500g/1¼lb mooli (daikon), peeled and thinly sliced
3 chestnuts, sliced
½ Asian pear, sliced
65g/2½oz watercress, or rocket (arugula), chopped
45ml/3 tbsp Korean chilli powder
5ml/1 tsp Thai fish sauce
2 garlic cloves, crushed
2.5ml/½ tsp grated fresh root ginger
5ml/1 tsp honey
5ml/1 tsp sesame seeds

1 Soak the whole head of Chinese leaves in salty water (using 50g/2oz/¼ cup of salt) for about 1 hour, or until softened.

2 Make the stuffing. Put the mooli into a colander and sprinkle with salt. Leave to stand for 10 minutes, then rinse well and transfer to a large bowl. Add the chestnuts, pear and chopped watercress or rocket to the bowl and mix well. Add all the other stuffing ingredients, with salt to taste, and mix well.

3 Prepare the poaching liquid. Put the garlic, onion and leek in a large pan. Mix in the doenjang paste and sake or rice wine, and add the pork. Add water to cover then bring to the boil. Cook the pork for 30–40 minutes, until tender.

4 Drain the Chinese leaves and tear off whole leaves and place on a serving plate. Transfer the stuffing mixture to a serving dish. Slice the pork into bitesize pieces.

5 Place a slice of pork on a Chinese leaf. Spoon stuffing on to the meat, and wrap it into a parcel before eating it.

Chipotle Chilli Meatballs

The chipotle chilli gives the sauce a distinctive, slightly smoky flavour.

Serves 4

225g/8oz minced (ground) pork
225g/8oz lean minced (ground) beef
1 onion, finely chopped
50g/2oz/1 cup fresh white breadcrumbs
5ml/1 tsp dried oregano
2.5ml/½ tsp ground cumin
2.5ml/½ tsp salt
2.5ml/½ tsp ground black pepper
1 egg, beaten
vegetable oil, for frying
fresh oregano sprigs, to garnish
boiled rice, to serve

For the sauce

1 chipotle chilli, seeded
15ml/1 tbsp vegetable oil
1 onion, finely chopped
2 garlic cloves, crushed
175ml/6fl oz/¾ cup beef stock
400g/14oz can chopped tomatoes
105ml/7 tbsp passata (strained tomatoes)

1 Mix the minced pork and beef in a bowl. Add the onion, breadcrumbs, oregano, cumin, salt and pepper. Mix with clean hands until all the ingredients are well combined.

2 Stir in the egg, mix well, then roll into 4cm/1½in balls. Put these on a baking sheet and chill while you make the sauce.

3 Soak the dried chilli in hot water for 15 minutes. Heat the oil in a pan and fry the onion and garlic for 3–4 minutes until soft.

4 Drain the chilli, reserving the soaking water, then chop it and add it to the onion mixture. Fry for 1 minute, then stir in the beef stock, tomatoes, passata and soaking water, with salt and pepper to taste. Bring to the boil, lower the heat and simmer, stirring occasionally, while you cook the meatballs.

5 Heat the oil for frying in a frying pan and fry the meatballs in batches for about 5 minutes, turning occasionally, until browned.

6 Drain off the oil and transfer the meatballs to a shallow casserole. Pour over the sauce and simmer for 10 minutes, stirring occasionally so that the meatballs are coated. Garnish with the oregano and serve with boiled rice, if you like.

Chilli Pork Energy 332kcal/1391kJ; Protein 40.2g; Carbohydrate 18.7g, of which sugars 14.9g; Fat 7.9g, of which saturates 2.6g; Cholesterol 106mg; Calcium 136mg; Fibre 5.9g; Sodium 507mg.
Chilli Meatballs Energy 412kcal/1717kJ; Protein 26.2g; Carbohydrate 16g, of which sugars 5.9g; Fat 27.6g, of which saturates 7.7g; Cholesterol 118mg; Calcium 50mg; Fibre 1.9g; Sodium 265mg.

Stir-fried Chilli Beef with Ginger, Chilli and Oyster Sauce

In Thailand this spicy dish is often made with just straw mushrooms, which are readily available fresh, but oyster mushrooms make a good substitute and if you use a mixture, the dish will be more interesting.

Serves 4 to 6

450g/1lb rump (round) steak
30ml/2 tbsp soy sauce
15ml/1 tbsp cornflour (cornstarch)
45ml/3 tbsp vegetable oil
15ml/1 tbsp chopped garlic
15ml/1 tbsp chopped fresh root ginger
225g/8oz/3¼ cups mixed mushrooms such as shiitake, oyster and straw
30ml/2 tbsp oyster sauce
5ml/1 tsp sugar
4 spring onions (scallions), cut into short lengths
ground black pepper
2 fresh red chillies, seeded and cut into strips, to garnish

1 Place the steak in the freezer for 30 minutes, until firm, then slice diagonally into long thin strips. Mix the soy sauce and cornflour in a bowl. Add the steak, turning to coat well, cover with clear film (plastic wrap) and leave to marinate for 1–2 hours.

2 Heat half the oil in a wok or large, heavy frying pan. Add the garlic and ginger and cook for 1–2 minutes, until fragrant. Drain the steak, add it to the wok or pan and stir well. Cook, stirring frequently, for 1–2 minutes, until the steak is browned all over and tender. Remove from the wok or pan and set aside.

3 Heat the remaining oil in the wok or pan. Add the shiitake, oyster and straw mushrooms. Stir-fry over a medium heat until golden brown.

4 Return the steak to the wok and mix it with the mushrooms. Spoon in the oyster sauce and sugar, stir well, then add ground black pepper to taste. Toss over the heat until all the ingredients are thoroughly combined.

5 Stir in the spring onions. Tip the mixture on to a serving platter, garnish with the strips of red chilli and serve.

Chilli Beef with Sesame Sauce

Variations of this dish can be found all over Vietnam and Cambodia. This version has a deliciously rich, spicy and nutty flavour.

Serves 4

450g/1lb beef sirloin or fillet, cut into thin strips
15ml/1 tbsp groundnut (peanut) or sesame oil
2 garlic cloves, finely chopped
2 red Thai chillies, seeded and finely chopped
7.5ml/1½ tsp sugar
30ml/2 tbsp sesame paste
30–45ml/2–3 tbsp beef stock or water
coarse sea salt and ground black pepper
red chilli strips, to garnish
1 lemon, cut into quarters, to serve

For the marinade
15ml/1 tbsp groundnut (peanut) oil
30ml/2 tbsp tuk trey
30ml/2 tbsp soy sauce

1 In a bowl, mix together the ingredients for the marinade. Toss in the beef, making sure it is well coated. Leave to marinate for about 30 minutes.

2 Heat the groundnut or sesame oil in a wok or heavy pan. Add the garlic and chillies and cook until golden and fragrant. Stir in the sugar. Add the beef, tossing it in the wok to sear it.

3 Stir in the sesame paste and enough stock or water to thin it down. Cook for 1–2 minutes, making sure the beef is coated with the sauce. Season with salt and pepper, garnish with chilli strips and and serve with lemon wedges.

Variation
Chicken breast fillet or pork fillet (tenderloin) can be used in this recipe instead of beef.

Cook's Tip
Jars of sesame paste, also known as tahini, are available in South-east Asian and Middle Eastern stores.

Chilli Beef Energy 282kcal/1177kJ; Protein 25.4g; Carbohydrate 10.7g, of which sugars 3.4g; Fat 15.5g, of which saturates 4.2g; Cholesterol 69mg; Calcium 16mg; Fibre 0.8g; Sodium 697mg.
Sesame Chilli Beef Energy 269kcal/1119kJ; Protein 26.2g; Carbohydrate 20g, of which sugars 2.0g; Fat 18g, of which saturates 5g; Cholesterol 65mg; Calcium 31mg; Fibre 0.3g; Sodium 73mg.

Fiery Beef with Spiced Cabbage

Marinated beef is served in this Korean dish with bowls of *sigumchi namul* – a mix of spinach, sesame oil and seeds.

Serves 4

500g/1¼lb beef fillet
15ml/1 tbsp sugar
30ml/2 tbsp light soy sauce
30ml/2 tbsp sesame oil
2 garlic cloves, mashed to a paste with a further 5ml/1 tsp sugar
2.5ml/½ tsp ground black pepper

For the kimchi

500g/1¼lb Chinese leaves (Chinese cabbage), sliced across into 2.5cm/1in pieces
60ml/4 tbsp sunflower oil
15ml/1 tbsp sesame oil
50g/2oz/¼ cup sugar
105ml/7 tbsp white rice vinegar
2.5cm/1in piece of fresh root ginger, finely chopped
3 garlic cloves, finely chopped
1 fresh fat medium hot red chilli
2 spring onions (scallions), thinly sliced

For the sigumchi namul

350g/12oz baby spinach leaves
10ml/2 tsp sesame oil
30ml/2 tbsp light soy sauce
15ml/1 tbsp mirin
10ml/2 tsp sesame seeds, toasted

1 Freeze the beef for 1 hour, then use a sharp knife to slice it as thinly as possible. Layer in a shallow dish, sprinkling each layer with sugar. Cover and chill for 30 minutes. Mix the soy sauce, sesame oil, garlic paste and pepper in a bowl and pour over the beef, ensuring it is thoroughly coated in the mixture. Cover and chill overnight.

2 Make the kimchi. Blanch the Chinese leaves in boiling water for about 5 seconds, drain and refresh under cold water. Put the leaves in a bowl with the remaining kimchi ingredients. Mix, cover and chill.

3 Make the sigumchi namul. Blanch the spinach in boiling water for 1 minute, drain and refresh under cold water. Put into a bowl with the oil, soy sauce and mirin. Mix well and add the sesame seeds. Cover and keep in a cool place.

4 Heat a griddle on the stove over a high heat until very hot. Flash-fry the meat in batches for 15–20 seconds on each side. Serve immediately with the sigumchi namul and the kimchi.

Braised Beef Strips with Jalapeño Chillies, Soy and Ginger

Fine strips of braised beef are enhanced by a rich, dark soy and garlic sauce, with a piquant kick of root ginger. Muscovado sugar adds an almost imperceptible sweetness, complemented by hot jalapeño chillies. This dish makes an excellent side serving to accompany a larger stew or noodle dish.

Serves 2 to 3

450g/1lb beef frying (flank) steak
25g/1oz fresh root ginger, peeled
100ml/3½fl oz/scant ½ cup dark soy sauce
75g/3oz light muscovado (brown) sugar
12 garlic cloves, peeled
6 jalapeño chillies

1 Bring a large pan of water to the boil and add the beef. Cook for around 40 minutes until tender. Drain the meat and rinse it in warm water. Leave the beef to cool, then roughly slice it into strips about 5cm/2in long.

2 Place the peeled root ginger in a large pan with the beef and add 300ml/½ pint/1¼ cups water. Bring to the boil, cover, then reduce the heat and simmer for 30 minutes. Skim the fat from the surface of the liquid as the meat cooks. The liquid should have reduced to half its initial volume.

3 Add the soy sauce, muscovado sugar and garlic, and simmer for a further 20 minutes. Then add the jalapeño chillies, and cook for a further 5 minutes.

4 Discard the root ginger from the pan, and serve the beef strips in warmed bowls with generous quantities of the garlic cloves and chillies.

Cook's Tip
If you're using any beef cut other than frying steak, the meat should be cut into thin strips or torn by hand to ensure that it is tender when cooked.

Fiery Beef Energy 657kcal/2730kJ; Protein 41.4g; Carbohydrate 25.1g, of which sugars 24.9g; Fat 43.5g, of which saturates 10g; Cholesterol 94mg; Calcium 231mg; Fibre 4.5g; Sodium 504mg.
Braised Beef Strips Energy 408kcal/1713kJ; Protein 37.8g; Carbohydrate 34.3g, of which sugars 29.1g; Fat 14.2g, of which saturates 5.7g; Cholesterol 87mg; Calcium 33mg; Fibre 1.4g; Sodium 2472mg.

Kneaded Sirloin Steak in a Spring Onion and Chilli Marinade

The marinade does not contain any complex ingredients, rather the recipe relies on the taste of high quality sirloin steak. Kneading the meat with salt makes it deliciously tender, and the simple seasoning provides a delicate garlic flavour. Accompanied by a bowl of doenjang soup, this dish is without equal.

Serves 4

450g/1lb beef sirloin
2 round (butterhead) lettuces

For the marinade

8 garlic cloves, chopped
75g/3oz oyster mushrooms, sliced
3 spring onions (scallions), finely chopped
20ml/4 tsp mirin or rice wine
10ml/2 tsp salt
ground black pepper

For the spring onion mixture

8 shredded spring onions (scallions)
20ml/4 tsp rice vinegar
20ml/4 tsp Korean chilli powder
10ml/2 tsp sugar
10ml/2 tsp sesame oil

1 Slice the beef into thin bitesize strips and place in a bowl. Add the garlic, mushrooms and spring onions and mix well.

2 Pour the mirin or rice wine into the bowl with the beef mixture and add the salt and several twists of black pepper.

3 Mix the marinade together, making sure that the beef strips are evenly coated. Knead the meat well to tenderize. Chill, and leave for at least 2 hours.

4 Make the spring onion mixture. In a bowl, mix all the ingredients together until well combined.

5 Remove the outer leaves from the lettuce and rinse well.

6 Place a griddle pan over medium heat, and add the marinated beef. Cook gently until the meat has darkened, and then remove.

7 Serve by wrapping the meat in a lettuce leaf with a chopstick pinch of the seasoned shredded spring onion mixture.

Spicy Mexican Pie

Spiced beef is mixed with rice and layered between tortillas, with a hot salsa sauce.

Serves 4

1 onion, chopped
2 garlic cloves, crushed
1 fresh red chilli, seeded and sliced
350g/12oz rump (round) steak, cut into small cubes
15ml/1 tbsp oil
225g/8oz/2 cups cooked rice
beef stock, to moisten
3 large wheat tortillas

For the salsa picante

2 X 400g/14oz cans chopped tomatoes
2 garlic cloves, halved
1 onion, quartered
1–2 fresh red chillies, seeded and roughly chopped
5ml/1 tsp ground cumin
2.5–5ml/½–1 tsp cayenne pepper
5ml/1 tsp fresh oregano or 2.5ml/½ tsp dried oregano
tomato juice or water, if required

For the cheese sauce

50g/2oz/4 tbsp butter
50g/2oz/½ cup plain (all-purpose) flour
600ml/1 pint/2½ cups milk
115g/4oz/1 cup grated Cheddar cheese
salt and ground black pepper

1 Preheat the oven to 180°C/350°F/Gas 4. Make the salsa picante. Place the tomatoes, garlic, onion and chillies in a blender or food processor and process until smooth. Pour into a small pan, add the spices and oregano and season with salt. Bring to the boil, stirring occasionally. Boil for 1–2 minutes, then cover and simmer for 15 minutes.

2 Make the cheese sauce. Melt the butter and stir in the flour. Cook for 1 minute. Add the milk and cook until the sauce thickens. Stir in all but 30ml/2 tbsp of the cheese and season. Set aside.

3 Mix the onion, garlic and chilli in a bowl. Add the beef and mix well. Heat the oil in a frying pan and stir-fry the mixture for 10 minutes. Stir in the rice and beef stock to moisten. Season to taste. Pour a quarter of the cheese sauce into an ovenproof dish. Add a tortilla. Spread over half the salsa, then half the meat.

4 Repeat these layers, then add half the remaining cheese sauce and the last tortilla. Pour over the last of the sauce and sprinkle the reserved cheese on top. Bake for 15–20 minutes until golden.

Kneaded Sirloin Steak Energy 188kcal/786kJ; Protein 27.6g; Carbohydrate 4g, of which sugars 3.9g; Fat 6.9g, of which saturates 2.6g; Cholesterol 57mg; Calcium 26mg; Fibre 0.9g; Sodium 83mg.
Mexican Pie Energy 595kcal/2516kJ; Protein 30.3g; Carbohydrate 91.2g, of which sugars 11.3g; Fat 14.7g, of which saturates 4.7g; Cholesterol 53mg; Calcium 153mg; Fibre 4.0g; Sodium 379mg.

Beef with Coconut Milk and Red Chillies

A delicious dish, cooked slowly to achieve sumptuous tenderness and create a rich, thick sauce.

Serves 6

1kg/2¼lb beef, such as topside (pot roast) or rump (round) steak, or buffalo, cut into cubes
15ml/1 tbsp tamarind paste
90ml/6 tbsp water
115g/4oz fresh coconut, grated
45ml/3 tbsp coconut, corn or groundnut (peanut) oil
2 onions, sliced
3 lemon grass stalks, halved and bruised
2 cinnamon sticks
3–4 lime leaves
1.2 litres/2 pints/5 cups coconut milk
15ml/1 tbsp sugar
salt and ground black pepper

For the spice paste

8–10 dried red chillies
8 shallots, chopped
4–6 garlic cloves, chopped
50g/2oz galangal, chopped
25g/1oz fresh turmeric, chopped
15ml/1 tbsp coriander seeds
10ml/2 tsp cumin seeds
5ml/1 tsp black peppercorns

To serve

15ml/1 tbsp groundnut (peanut) oil
6–8 shallots, sliced
cooked rice and a salad

1 Make the paste. Soak the chillies in warm water for 30 minutes, until soft. Drain, remove the seeds, then squeeze the chillies until dry. Using a mortar and pestle or a food processor, grind the chillies, shallots, garlic, galangal and turmeric to a smooth paste.

2 In a frying pan, dry-fry the coriander, cumin seeds and peppercorns. Grind the spices to a powder. Add to the paste.

3 Put the beef or buffalo in a large bowl, add the paste and mix. Marinate for at least 1 hour if using beef or 2 hours if using buffalo.

4 Meanwhile, soak the tamarind paste in the water for 30 minutes until soft. In a frying pan, dry-fry the coconut until it is brown. Using a mortar and pestle, or a food processor, grind the coconut. Set aside. Squeeze the tamarind to help soften it and then strain to extract the juice. Discard the pulp.

5 Heat the oil in a wok with a lid or large, flameproof casserole. Add the onions, lemon grass, cinnamon stick and lime leaves, and fry for 5–10 minutes until the onions begin to colour.

6 Add the beef with all the paste and stir-fry until browned. Pour in the coconut milk and tamarind juice and bring to the boil, stirring all the time, then simmer for 2–4 hours for beef (4 hours for buffalo) until the sauce begins to thicken.

7 Stir in the sugar and the ground coconut, cover and continue to simmer very gently between 2–4 hours if using beef, and for 4 hours if using buffalo meat, stirring occasionally, until the meat is tender and the reduced sauce is very thick.

8 Meanwhile, heat the oil in a frying pan, stir in the shallots and fry for 10 minutes until almost caramelized. Drain and set aside.

9 Season the meat and serve. Sprinkle with fried shallots and serve immediately with rice and a salad.

Beef Enchiladas with Chilli Sauce

Enchiladas are usually made with corn tortillas, although in parts of northern Mexico flour tortillas may be used. The chilli sauce gives this dish a satisfying kick.

Serves 3 to 4

500g/1¼lb rump (round) steak, cut into 5cm/2in cubes
2 ancho chillies, seeded
2 pasilla chillies, seeded
2 garlic cloves, crushed
10ml/2 tsp dried oregano
2.5ml/½ tsp ground cumin
30ml/2 tbsp vegetable oil
7 fresh corn tortillas
shredded onion and flat-leaved parsley, to garnish
salsa, to serve

1 Put the steak in a deep frying pan and cover with water. Bring to the boil, then lower the heat and simmer for 1–1½ hours, or until very tender.

2 Meanwhile, put the dried chillies in a small bowl and just cover with hot water. Leave to soak for 30 minutes, then transfer the chillies to a blender and blend, gradually adding some of the soaking water to make a smooth paste.

3 Drain the steak and leave to cool, reserving 250ml/8fl oz/1 cup of the cooking liquid. Meanwhile, fry the garlic, oregano and cumin in the oil for 2 minutes.

4 Stir in the chilli paste and the reserved cooking liquid from the beef. Tear one of the tortillas into small pieces and add it to the mixture. Bring to the boil, then lower the heat. Simmer for 10 minutes, stirring occasionally, until the sauce has thickened. Shred the steak, using two forks, and stir it into the sauce. Heat through for a few minutes.

5 Wrap the tortillas in foil and steam them on a plate over boiling water until pliable.

6 Spoon some of the meat mixture on to each tortilla and roll it up to make an enchilada. Keep the enchiladas in a warmed dish until you have rolled them all. Garnish with shreds of onion and fresh flat-leaved parsley and then serve immediately with the salsa.

Beef with Milk Energy 494kcal/2064kJ; Protein 40.6g; Carbohydrate 20.9g, of which sugars 18.8g; Fat 28.2g, of which saturates 17g; Cholesterol 97mg; Calcium 95mg; Fibre 3.9g; Sodium 335mg.
Beef Enchiladas Energy 503kcal/2121kJ; Protein 43g; Carbohydrate 51.9g, of which sugars 2.9g; Fat 15.1g, of which saturates 3.7g; Cholesterol 98mg; Calcium 101mg; Fibre 2.5g; Sodium 335mg.

Red-hot Meatballs with Roasted Coconut

These Indonesian meatballs are versatile, spicy and delicious. Moulded into small balls, they can be served as an appetizer with a drink; as a snack dipped in kecap manis; or as a main dish with rice and a salad.

Serves 4

5ml/1 tsp coriander seeds
5ml/1 tsp cumin seeds
175g/6oz freshly grated coconut or desiccated (dry unsweetened shredded) coconut
15ml/1 tbsp coconut oil
4 shallots, finely chopped
2 garlic cloves, finely chopped
1–2 red chillies, seeded and finely chopped
350g/12oz minced (ground) beef
beaten egg (if necessary)
rice flour, to coat
corn oil, for shallow frying
salt and ground black pepper

To serve

30–45ml/2–3 tbsp freshly grated coconut or desiccated (dry unsweetened shredded) coconut, dry-fried
1 lime, quartered
kecap manis (Indonesian sweet soy sauce)

1 In a small, heavy pan, dry-fry the coriander and cumin seeds until they give off a nutty aroma. Using a mortar and pestle or electric spice grinder, grind the roasted seeds to a powder. In the same pan, dry-fry the coconut until it begins to colour. Transfer the coconut on to a plate and leave to cool.

2 Heat the coconut oil, stir in the shallots, garlic and chillies and fry until beginning to colour. Transfer to a plate and leave to cool.

3 Put the beef into a bowl and add the ground spices, dry-fried coconut and shallot mixture. Season with salt and pepper. Bind all the ingredients together, adding a little egg if necessary. Knead the mixture with your hands and mould it into little balls, no bigger than a fresh apricot. Coat the balls in rice flour.

4 Heat a thin layer of corn oil in a large frying pan and fry the meatballs for about 5 minutes until they are golden brown. Drain then arrange on a serving dish. Sprinkle with the coconut and serve with the lime wedges, and kecap manis for drizzling.

Black Bean Chilli con Carne

Dried and fresh chillies add plenty of fire to this spicy Tex-Mex classic.

Serves 6

225g/8oz/1 ¼ cups dried black beans
500g/1 ¼lb braising steak
30ml/2 tbsp oil
2 onions, chopped
1 garlic clove, crushed
1 fresh green chilli, seeded and finely chopped
15ml/1 tbsp paprika
10ml/2 tsp ground cumin
10ml/2 tsp ground coriander
400g/14oz can chopped tomatoes
300ml/½ pint/1 ¼ cups beef stock
1 dried red chilli, crumbled
5ml/1 tsp hot pepper sauce
1 fresh red (bell) pepper, seeded and chopped
30ml/2 tbsp fresh coriander (cilantro) leaves
salt
plain boiled rice, to serve

1 Put the beans in a pan. Add water to cover, bring to the boil and boil vigorously for 10–15 minutes. Drain, transfer to a clean bowl, cover with cold water and leave to soak for about 8 hours or overnight.

2 Preheat the oven to 150°C/300°F/Gas 2. Cut the beef into very small dice. Heat the oil in a large flameproof casserole. Add the onion, garlic and green chilli and cook them gently for 5 minutes until soft. Using a slotted spoon, transfer the mixture to a plate.

3 Increase the heat. Add the meat to the pan and fry until browned all over. Stir in the paprika, cumin and ground coriander, and mix well.

4 Add the tomatoes, stock, dried chilli and hot pepper sauce. Drain the beans and add them to the casserole, with enough water to cover. Bring to simmering point, cover and cook in the oven for 2 hours. Stir the casserole occasionally and add extra water, if necessary, to prevent it from drying out.

5 Season with salt and add the red pepper. Return to the oven and cook for 30 minutes more, until the meat and beans are tender. Sprinkle over the coriander and serve with rice.

Red-hot Meatballs Energy 559kcal/2312kJ; Protein 20.2g; Carbohydrate 8g, of which sugars 3.7g; Fat 49.6g, of which saturates 30.4g; Cholesterol 53mg; Calcium 23mg; Fibre 6.3g; Sodium 83mg.
Chilli Con Carne Energy 374kcal/1575kJ; Protein 39g; Carbohydrate 27.9g, of which sugars 7.4g; Fat 12.6g, of which saturates 4.1g; Cholesterol 83mg; Calcium 60mg; Fibre 4.7g; Sodium 111mg.

Minced Meat with Chilli and Charred Aubergine

Variations of this deliciously spiced dish crop up in different parts of South-east Asia. To attain its smoky flavour, the aubergines are charred over a flame, or charcoal grill, then skinned, chopped to a pulp and added to the dish – a method more associated with the cooking of India, the Middle East, and North Africa than Asia.

Serves 4
2 aubergines (eggplants)
15ml/1 tbsp vegetable or groundnut (peanut) oil
2 shallots, finely chopped
4 garlic cloves, peeled and finely chopped
1 red Thai chilli, finely chopped
350g/12oz minced (ground) beef
30ml/2 tbsp Thai fish sauce
sea salt and ground black pepper
crusty bread or rice and salad, to serve

1 Place the aubergines directly over an open flame. Turn them over from time to time, until the skin is charred all over. Put the aubergines into a plastic bag to sweat for a few minutes.

2 Hold each aubergine by its stalk under cold running water, while you peel off the skin. Squeeze out the excess water and chop them roughly on a board.

3 Heat the oil in a large, heavy pan. Stir in the shallots, garlic and chilli and fry until golden. Add the minced beef and stir-fry for about 5 minutes.

4 Stir in the fish sauce and the aubergine and cook gently for about 20 minutes, until the meat is tender. Season with salt and pepper and serve with crusty bread or boiled rice and a tossed green salad.

Variation
This dish can also be made with beef or pork – either way it is delicious served with chunks of fresh, crusty bread.

Oxtail in Hot Tangy Sauce

Considered a delicacy in some parts of South-east Asia, oxtail and the tails of water buffalo are generally cooked for special feasts and celebrations. In Malaysia and Singapore, oxtail is occasionally cooked in European-style stews but the many Malays and Indonesians prefer to cook it slowly in a hot, tangy sauce. Served with steamed rice, or chunks of fresh, crusty bread, it makes a very tasty supper dish.

Serves 4 to 6
8 shallots, chopped
8 garlic cloves, chopped
6 red chillies, seeded and chopped
25g/1oz fresh galangal, chopped
30ml/2 tbsp rice flour or plain (all-purpose) flour
15ml/1 tbsp ground turmeric
8–12 oxtail joints, cut to roughly the same size and trimmed of fat
45ml/3 tbsp vegetable oil
400g/14oz can plum tomatoes, drained
2 lemon grass stalks, halved and bruised
a handful of fresh kaffir lime leaves
225g/8oz tamarind pulp, soaked in 600ml/1 pint/2½ cups water, squeezed and strained
30–45ml/2–3 tbsp sugar
salt and ground black pepper
fresh coriander (cilantro) leaves, roughly chopped

1 Using a mortar and pestle or food processor, grind the shallots, garlic, chillies and galangal to a coarse paste. Mix the flour with the ground turmeric and spread it on a flat surface. Roll the oxtail in the flour and set aside.

2 Heat the oil in a heavy pan or earthenware pot. Stir in the spice paste and cook until fragrant and golden. Add the oxtail joints and brown on all sides. Add the tomatoes, lemon grass stalks, lime leaves and tamarind juice. Add enough water to cover the oxtail, and bring it to the boil. Skim off any fat from the surface. Reduce the heat, put the lid on the pan and simmer the oxtail for 2 hours.

3 Stir in the sugar, season with salt and pepper and continue to cook, uncovered, for a further 30–40 minutes, until the meat is very tender. Garnish with the chopped coriander and serve straight from the pan.

Minced Meat with Chilli Energy 245kcal/1019kJ; Protein 19g; Carbohydrate 4g, of which sugars 3.4g; Fat 17g, of which saturates 6g; Cholesterol 53mg; Calcium 23mg; Fibre 2.2g; Sodium 607mg.
Oxtail in Tangy Sauce Energy 386kcal/1611kJ; Protein 34.5g; Carbohydrate 11.3g, of which sugars 6.6g; Fat 22.6g, of which saturates 7.7g; Cholesterol 125mg; Calcium 31mg; Fibre 1.2g; Sodium 191mg.

Spicy Meat Loaf

This mouthwatering meat loaf has a deliciously fiery kick from the fresh green chillies. It is simply baked in the oven and will provide a hearty lunch on cold days, or a tasty mid-week meal.

Serves 4 to 6

5 eggs
450g/1lb lean minced (ground) beef
30ml/2 tbsp ground ginger
30ml/2 tbsp ground garlic
6 green chillies, seeded and chopped
2 small onions, finely chopped
2.5ml/½ tsp ground turmeric
50g/2oz coriander (cilantro) leaves, chopped
175g/6oz potato, grated
salt, to taste

1 Preheat the oven to 180°C/350°F/Gas Mark 4. Grease a small baking tray. Beat two eggs in a bowl until fluffy and pour into the greased baking tray.

2 In a large mixing bowl, knead the meat, ginger and garlic, four of the green chillies, half the chopped onion, one beaten egg, the turmeric, coriander leaves, potato and salt.

3 Pack the meat mixture into the baking tray and smooth the surface with a metal spatula. Put the tray in the preheated oven and cook for 45 minutes.

4 Beat the remaining eggs in a bowl and fold in the remaining green chillies and onion. Remove the baking tray from the oven and pour the mixture all over the meat. Return to the oven and cook until the eggs have set.

5 Carefully transfer the meat loaf on to a serving plate and serve immediately, cut up into slices.

Cook's Tip
Meat loaf is great for all the family, but reduce the amount of chillies in this version if serving to children.

Beef Satay with a Chilli and Peanut Sauce

The spicy peanut paste, satay, is a great favourite in South-east Asia. Although it is more associated with Thai cooking, it is thought to have originated in India. In southern Vietnam, it is used for grilling and stir-frying meats, as well as for dressing noodles and spiking marinades. This is a great barbecue dish that works with pork, chicken, prawns or shrimp. Jars of satay are available to buy but they taste nothing like the home-made paste, which you can pep up with as much garlic and chilli as you like.

Serves 4 to 6

500g/1¼lb beef sirloin, sliced against the grain in bitesize pieces
15ml/1 tbsp groundnut (peanut) oil
1 bunch each of fresh coriander (cilantro) and mint, stalks removed

For the satay

60ml/4 tbsp groundnut (peanut) or vegetable oil
4–5 garlic cloves, crushed
4–5 dried Serrano chillies, seeded and ground
5–10ml/1–2 tsp curry powder
50g/2oz/⅓ cup roasted peanuts, finely ground

1 To make the satay, heat the oil in a heavy pan and stir in the garlic until it begins to colour. Add the chillies, curry powder and peanuts and stir over a gentle heat until the mixture forms a paste. Remove from the heat and leave to cool.

2 Put the beef into a bowl. Beat the groundnut oil into the satay and tip the mixture on to the beef. Mix well, so that the beef is evenly coated. Soak four to six wooden skewers in water for 30 minutes. Prepare a barbecue. Thread the meat on to the skewers and cook for 2–3 minutes on each side. Serve the meat with the herb leaves for wrapping.

Cook's Tip
The beef is also delicious served with a salad, rice wrappers and a light dipping sauce.

Spicy Meat Loaf Energy 272kcal/1133kJ; Protein 22.1g; Carbohydrate 7.3g, of which sugars 2g; Fat 17.6g, of which saturates 6.6g; Cholesterol 204mg; Calcium 73mg; Fibre 1.5g; Sodium 129mg.
Beef Satay Energy 433kcal/1798kJ; Protein 34g; Carbohydrate 4g, of which sugars 1g; Fat 31g, of which saturates 7g; Cholesterol 64mg; Calcium 68mg; Fibre 1.5g; Sodium 100mg.

Beef and Aubergine Curry with Fresh Red Chillies

Serves 6

120ml/4fl oz/½ cup sunflower oil
2 onions, thinly sliced
2.5cm/1in fresh root ginger, sliced and cut in matchsticks
1 garlic clove, crushed
2 fresh red chillies, seeded and very finely sliced
2.5cm/1in fresh turmeric, peeled and crushed, or 5ml/1 tsp ground turmeric
1 lemon grass stem, lower part sliced finely, top bruised
675g/1½ lb braising steak, cut in even-size strips
400ml/14fl oz can coconut milk
300ml/½ pint/1¼ cups water
1 aubergine, sliced and patted dry
5ml/1 tsp tamarind pulp, soaked in 60ml/4 tbsp warm water
salt and ground black pepper
finely sliced chilli, (optional) and fried onions, to garnish
boiled rice, to serve

1 Heat half the oil and fry the onions, ginger and garlic until they give off a rich aroma. Add the chillies, turmeric and the lower part of the lemon grass. Push to one side and then turn up the heat and add the steak, stirring until the meat changes colour.

2 Add the coconut milk, water, lemon grass top and seasoning to taste. Cover and simmer gently for 1½ hours, or until the meat is tender.

3 Towards the end of the cooking time heat the remaining oil in a frying pan. Fry the aubergine slices until brown on both sides.

4 Add the browned aubergine slices to the beef curry and cook for a further 15 minutes. Stir gently from time to time. Strain the tamarind and stir the juice into the curry. Taste and adjust the seasoning. Put into a warm serving dish. Garnish with the sliced chilli, if using, and Deep-fried Onions, and serve with boiled rice.

Cook's Tip

If you want to make this curry ahead, follow the above method to the end of step 2 and finish later.

Chilli Beef and Tomato Curry

When served with boiled yam or rice, this delicious curry makes a hearty dish, certain to be popular with anybody who likes their food spicy.

Serves 4

450g/1lb stewing beef
5ml/1 tsp dried thyme
45ml/3 tbsp palm or vegetable oil
1 large onion, finely chopped
2 garlic cloves, crushed
4 canned plum tomatoes, chopped, plus 60ml/4 tbsp of the juice
15ml/1 tbsp tomato purée (paste)
2.5ml/½ tsp mixed spice
1 fresh red chilli, seeded and chopped
900ml/1½ pints/3¾ cups chicken stock or water
1 large aubergine (eggplant), about 350g/12oz
salt and ground black pepper

1 Cut the beef into cubes and season with 2.5ml/½ tsp of the thyme and salt and pepper.

2 Heat 15ml/1 tbsp of the oil in a large pan and fry the meat, in batches if necessary, for 8–10 minutes, stirring constantly, until evenly browned all over. Transfer to a bowl using a slotted spoon and set aside.

3 Heat the remaining oil in the pan and fry the onion and garlic for a few minutes until the onion begins to soften.

4 Add the tomatoes and tomato juice to the pan and simmer for a further 8–10 minutes, stirring occasionally.

5 Add the tomato purée, mixed spice, chilli and remaining thyme to the pan and stir well.

6 Add the cubed beef and the chicken stock or water to the pan. Bring to the boil, reduce the heat, cover the pan and simmer gently for 30 minutes.

7 Cut the aubergine into 1cm/½in dice. Stir into the beef mixture and cook, covered, for a further 30 minutes until the beef is completely tender. Taste the sauce, adjust the seasoning if necessary and serve immediately.

Beef and Aubergine Curry Energy 394kcal/1638kJ; Protein 26g; Carbohydrate 12g, of which sugars 10g; Fat 27g, of which saturates 5g; Cholesterol 71mg; Calcium 54mg; Fibre 203g; Sodium 700mg.
Chilli Beef Curry Energy 251kcal/1050kJ; Protein 27.2g; Carbohydrate 7.2g, of which sugars 6.2g; Fat 12.8g, of which saturates 2.9g; Cholesterol 75mg; Calcium 29mg; Fibre 3g; Sodium 87mg.

Spicy Beef and Mushroom Casserole

In this perfect example of a spicy Korean casserole dish, wild mushrooms are slow-cooked together in a sauce seasoned with garlic and sesame. Ideal as a warming winter dish, its earthy mushroom flavour is enlivened with spring onions and chillies.

Serves 2

150g/5oz beef
2 dried shiitake mushrooms, soaked in warm water for about 30 minutes until softened
25g/1oz enoki mushrooms
1 onion, sliced
400ml/14fl oz/1⅔ cups water or beef stock
25g/1oz oyster mushrooms, thinly sliced
6 pine mushrooms, cut into thin strips
10 spring onions (scallions), sliced
2 chrysanthemum leaves, and ½ red and ½ green chilli, seeded and shredded, to garnish
steamed rice, to serve

For the seasoning

30ml/2 tbsp dark soy sauce
3 spring onions (scallions), sliced
2 garlic cloves, crushed
10ml/2 tsp sesame seeds
10ml/2 tsp sesame oil

1 Slice the beef into thin strips and place in a bowl. Add the seasoning ingredients and mix well, coating the beef evenly. Set aside for 20 minutes so the beef strips can absorb the flavours of the seasonings.

2 When the soaked shiitake mushrooms have reconstituted and become soft, drain and thinly slice them, discarding the stems. Discard the caps from the enoki mushrooms.

3 Place the seasoned beef and the onion in a heavy pan or flameproof casserole and add the water or beef stock. Add all the mushrooms and the spring onions, and bring to the boil.

4 Once the mixture is bubbling in the pan, reduce the heat and simmer gently for 20 minutes.

5 Transfer to a serving dish or serve from the casserole. Garnish with the chrysanthemum leaves and shredded chilli, and then serve with steamed rice.

Beef Stew with Star Anise and Chilli Spices

The Vietnamese eat this dish for breakfast, and on chilly mornings people queue up for a steaming bowl of this spicy stew on their way to work. In southern Vietnam, it is often served with chunks of baguette, but in the other regions it is served with noodles. For the midday or evening meal, it is served with steamed or sticky rice. Traditionally, it has an orange hue from the oil in which annatto seeds have been fried, but in this recipe the colour comes from the turmeric.

Serves 4 to 6

500g/1¼lb lean beef, cut into bitesize cubes
10–15ml/2–3 tsp ground turmeric
30ml/2 tbsp sesame or vegetable oil
3 shallots, chopped
3 garlic cloves, chopped
2 red chillies, seeded and chopped
2 lemon grass stalks, cut into several pieces and bruised
15ml/1 tbsp curry powder
4 star anise, roasted and ground to a powder
700ml/scant 1¼ pints hot beef or chicken stock, or boiling water
45ml/3 tbsp Thai fish sauce
30ml/2 tbsp soy sauce
15ml/1 tbsp raw cane sugar
1 bunch of fresh basil, stalks removed
salt and ground black pepper
1 onion, halved and finely sliced, and chopped fresh coriander (cilantro) or leaves, to garnish

1 Toss the beef in the ground turmeric and set aside. Heat a wok or heavy pan and add the oil. Stir in the shallots, garlic, chillies and lemon grass, and cook until they become fragrant.

2 Add the curry powder and all but 10ml/2 tsp of the roasted star anise, followed by the beef. Brown the beef a little, then pour in the stock or water, the fish sauce, soy sauce and sugar. Stir well and bring to the boil. Reduce the heat and simmer for 40 minutes, or until the meat is tender and the liquid has reduced.

3 Season to taste with salt and pepper, stir in the reserved roasted star anise, and add the basil. Transfer the stew to a serving dish and garnish with the onion and coriander leaves.

Spicy Beef Casserole Energy 227kcal/945kJ; Protein 21.1g; Carbohydrate 5.5g, of which sugars 4.4g; Fat 13.6g, of which saturates 3.9g; Cholesterol 44mg; Calcium 72mg; Fibre 2.4g; Sodium 1125mg.
Beef Stew Energy 314kcal/1312kJ; Protein 33g; Carbohydrate 17g, of which sugars 11g; Fat 14g, of which saturates 4g; Cholesterol 64mg; Calcium 64mg; Fibre 1.7g; Sodium 1500mg

Thick Beef Curry in Sweet Peanut and Chilli Sauce

This curry is deliciously rich and thicker than most other Thai curries.

Serves 4 to 6

600ml/1 pint/2½ cups coconut milk
45ml/3 tbsp Thai red curry paste
45ml/3 tbsp Thai fish sauce
30ml/2 tbsp palm sugar (jaggery) or light muscovado (brown) sugar
2 lemon grass stalks, bruised
450g/1lb rump (round) steak, cut into thin strips
75g/3oz/¾ cup roasted peanuts, ground
2 fresh red chillies, sliced
5 kaffir lime leaves, torn
salt and ground black pepper
2 salted eggs, cut in wedges, and 15 Thai basil leaves, to garnish

1 Pour half the coconut milk into a large, heavy pan. Place over a medium heat and bring to the boil, stirring constantly until the milk separates.

2 Stir the red curry paste into the pan and cook for about 2–3 minutes until the mixture is fragrant and thoroughly blended. Add the fish sauce, sugar and bruised lemon grass stalks. Mix well.

3 Continue to cook until the colour deepens. Gradually add the remaining coconut milk, stirring constantly. Bring the mixture back to the boil.

4 Add the beef and peanuts to the pan. Cook, stirring constantly, for 8–10 minutes, or until most of the liquid has evaporated. Add the chillies and lime leaves. Season to taste with salt and black pepper. Serve immediately, garnished with wedges of salted eggs and Thai basil leaves.

Cook's Tip

If you don't have the time to make your own red curry paste, you can buy ready-made jars of Thai curry paste, which are great time-savers. There is a wide range available in most Asian food stores and large supermarkets.

Dry Beef Curry with Peanut and Lime

This spicy dry curry can be served with a moist dish such as a vegetable curry.

Serves 4 to 6

400g/14oz can coconut milk
900g/2lb stewing steak, cubed
300ml/½ pint/1¼ cups beef stock
30ml/2 tbsp crunchy peanut butter
juice of 2 limes, plus lime slices, chopped coriander (cilantro) and chilli slices, to garnish
boiled rice, to serve

For the red curry paste

30ml/2 tbsp coriander seeds
5ml/1 tsp cumin seeds
seeds from 6 cardamom pods
2.5ml/½ tsp grated nutmeg
1.5ml/¼ tsp ground cloves
2.5ml/½ tsp ground cinnamon
20ml/4 tsp paprika
pared rind of 1 mandarin orange, finely chopped
4–5 small fresh red chillies, seeded and finely chopped
25ml/5 tsp sugar
2.5ml/½ tsp salt
1 piece lemon grass, shredded
3 garlic cloves, crushed
2cm/¾in piece fresh galangal, peeled and finely chopped
4 red shallots, finely chopped
2cm/¾in piece shrimp paste
50g/2oz coriander (cilantro) root or stem, chopped
juice of ½ lime
30ml/2 tbsp vegetable oil

1 Strain the coconut milk into a bowl, retaining the thicker coconut milk in the sieve (strainer). Pour the thin milk into a large pan, then scrape in half the residue from the sieve. Reserve the remaining thick milk. Add the steak and the stock and bring to the boil, then simmer, covered, for 50 minutes.

2 Make the paste. Dry-fry all the seeds for 1–2 minutes. Transfer into a bowl and add the nutmeg, cloves, cinnamon, paprika and orange rind. Pound the chillies with the sugar and salt. Add the spice mixture, lemon grass, garlic, galangal, shallots and shrimp paste and pound. Mix in the coriander, lime juice and oil.

3 Strain the beef, and place a cupful of the cooking liquid in a wok. Stir in 30–45ml/2–3 tbsp of the paste. Boil until the liquid has evaporated. Stir in the reserved thick coconut milk, the peanut butter and beef. Simmer, uncovered, for 15–20 minutes.

4 Before serving, stir in the lime juice. Serve in bowls over rice, garnished with the lime slices, coriander and sliced red chillies.

Thick Beef Curry Energy kcal310/1296kJ; Protein 29.1g; Carbohydrate 9.7g, of which sugars 8.5g; Fat 17.4g, of which saturates 5.3g; Cholesterol 69mg; Calcium 59mg; Fibre 1.2g; Sodium 215mg.
Dry Beef Curry Energy 406kcal/1703kJ; Protein 55.4g; Carbohydrate 6.4g, of which sugars 5.9g; Fat 18g, of which saturates 5.1g; Cholesterol 170mg; Calcium 92mg; Fibre 0.6g; Sodium 812mg.

Aubergines with Chillies, Lemon Grass and Coconut Milk

One of the treasures of Malaysia is the round, orange aubergine, which has a delicate flavour. It is particularly tasty cooked in coconut milk with lots of chillies, ginger and lemon grass. Use the purple variety if you can't find orange ones.

Serves 4

15ml/1 tbsp ground turmeric
5ml/1 tsp chilli powder
3 slender orange aubergines (eggplants) or 8 baby aubergines, cut in wedges
45ml/3 tbsp vegetable or groundnut (peanut) oil
2 lemon grass stalks, trimmed, halved and bruised
600ml/1 pint/2½ cups coconut milk
salt and ground black pepper
a small bunch fresh coriander (cilantro), roughly chopped, to garnish
jasmine or coconut rice and 2 green chillies, seeded and quartered lengthways (optional), to serve

For the spice paste

4–6 dried red chillies, soaked in warm water until soft, squeezed dry and seeded
4 garlic cloves, chopped
4 shallots, chopped
25g/1oz fresh root ginger, peeled and chopped
2 lemon grass stalks, trimmed and chopped

1 First make the spice paste. Using a mortar and pestle or food processor, grind the chillies, garlic, shallots, ginger and lemon grass to a coarse paste. Grind in the dried shrimp and beat in the shrimp paste.

2 Mix the turmeric and chilli powder together. Rub the mixture all over the aubergine.

3 Heat the oil in a wok or heavy pan. Stir in the paste and lemon grass. Add the aubergine, and cook until lightly browned. Pour in the coconut milk, stir well, and boil it to thicken. Reduce the heat and cook gently for 15–20 minutes until the aubergine is tender. Season with salt and pepper.

4 Sprinkle the coriander over and serve straight from the wok with extra chillies, if you like. Serve with jasmine or coconut rice.

Spicy Aubergine Curry

Aubergine curries are popular throughout South-east Asia, the Thai version being the most famous. All are hot and aromatic, enriched with coconut milk. This Khmer recipe uses the trademark herbal paste, kroeung.

Serves 4 to 6

15ml/1 tbsp vegetable oil
4 garlic cloves, crushed
2 shallots, sliced
2 dried chillies
45ml/3 tbsp kroeung
15ml/1 tbsp palm sugar (jaggery)
600ml/1 pint/2½ cups coconut milk
250ml/8fl oz/1 cup vegetable stock
4 aubergines (eggplants), trimmed and cut into bitesize pieces
6 kaffir lime leaves
1 bunch fresh basil, stalks removed
jasmine rice and 2 limes, cut into quarters, to serve
salt and ground black pepper

1 Heat the oil in a wok or heavy pan. Stir in the garlic, shallots and whole chillies and stir-fry until they begin to colour.

2 Stir in the kroeung and palm sugar and fry, stirring constantly, until the spice mixture begins to darken.

3 Pour the coconut milk and the chicken stock into the pan, stirring until thoroughly combined. Add the aubergine pieces and lime leaves.

4 Partially cover the pan and simmer over a gentle heat for about 25 minutes until the aubergines are tender.

5 Stir in the basil and check the seasoning. Serve with jasmine rice and lime quarters.

Cook's Tip

Kroeung is a popular condiment in Cambodian cuisine. A wide variety of ingredients can be used in the spicy paste, but the most common are lemon grass, kaffir lime, galangal, turmeric, garlic, shallots, and dried red chillies. The ingredients are ground into a paste using either a pestle and mortar or a food processor or electric grinder.

Aubergines with Chillies Energy 154kcal/644kJ; Protein 6.2g; Carbohydrate 11.9g, of which sugars 11g; Fat 9.5g, of which saturates 1.4g; Cholesterol 38mg; Calcium 175mg; Fibre 3g; Sodium 497mg.
Spicy Aubergine Curry Energy 72kcal/305kJ; Protein 1.6g; Carbohydrate 11.2g, of which sugars 10.7g; Fat 3g, of which saturates 1g; Cholesterol 0mg; Calcium 46mg; Fibre 2.8g; Sodium 113mg.

Stuffed Aubergine with a Sizzling Ginger Sauce

The succulent egg filling complements the creamy texture of the braised aubergine, and the dish is infused by the flavours of rice wine and ginger, with a fiery kick from the chillies.

Serves 2

2 aubergines (eggplants)
1 egg
25ml/1½ tbsp vegetable oil
90g/3½oz/scant ½ cup minced (ground) textured vegetable protein (TVP)
15ml/1 tbsp mirin or rice wine
15ml/1 tbsp dark soy sauce
1 garlic clove, crushed
5ml/1 tsp sesame oil
1 red chilli, seeded and shredded
1 green chilli, seeded and shredded
salt and ground black pepper
steamed rice, to serve

For the sauce

30ml/2 tbsp mirin or rice wine
30ml/2 tbsp dark soy sauce
5ml/1 tsp fresh root ginger, peeled and grated
1 sheet dried seaweed

1 Clean the aubergines, and cut into slices about 2.5cm/1in thick. Make two cross slits down the length of each slice, making sure not to cut all the way through. Sprinkle with salt and set aside.

2 Beat the egg and season with salt. Heat 10ml/2 tsp oil in a frying pan. Add the egg and make an omelette, browning gently on each side. Cut into thin strips. Cool, then chill.

3 Heat the remaining oil in a frying pan. Cut the seaweed into strips. Stir-fry with the TVP, mirin or rice wine, soy sauce and garlic. Cook for 5 minutes then drizzle with sesame oil and set aside.

4 Place the chillies in a bowl. Add the egg strips and TVP, and mix well. Rinse the aubergine slices and stuff with TVP mixture.

5 Place all the sauce ingredients in a frying pan, add 200ml/7fl oz/scant 1 cup of water and salt to taste, and bring to the boil. Add the aubergine, spoon the sauce over and simmer for 15 minutes, or until the aubergines are soft.

6 Transfer to a shallow dish and serve with steamed rice.

Aubergine and Sweet Potato Stew

Scented with fragrant lemon grass, ginger, chilli and lots of garlic, this is a particularly tasty combination of flavours.

Serves 6

400g/14oz baby aubergines (eggplants) or 2 large aubergines
60ml/4 tbsp groundnut (peanut) oil
225g/8oz Thai red shallots or other shallots or pickling onions
5ml/1 tsp fennel seeds, crushed
4–5 garlic cloves, thinly sliced
25ml/1½ tbsp finely chopped fresh root ginger
475ml/16fl oz/2 cups stock
2 lemon grass stalks, outer layers discarded, finely chopped
15g/½oz coriander (cilantro), stalks and leaves chopped separately
3 kaffir lime leaves, lightly bruised
2–3 small fresh red chillies
60ml/4 tbsp Thai green curry paste
675g/1½lb sweet potatoes, peeled and cut into chunks
400ml/14fl oz coconut milk
5ml/1 tsp palm sugar (jaggery)
250g/9oz mushrooms, thickly sliced
juice of 1 lime, to taste
salt and ground black pepper
boiled rice and 18 fresh Thai basil or ordinary basil leaves, to serve

1 Slice baby aubergines in half. Cut large aubergines into chunks. Heat half the oil in a frying pan. Add the aubergines and cook, stirring occasionally, until lightly browned on all sides. Set aside.

2 Slice 4–5 of the shallots. Cook the whole shallots in the oil left in the pan until lightly browned. Set aside. Add the remaining oil and cook the sliced shallots, fennel seeds, garlic and ginger over a low heat for 5 minutes.

3 Pour in the stock, then add the lemon grass, coriander stalks, lime leaves and whole chillies. Cover and simmer for 5 minutes.

4 Stir in 30ml/2 tbsp of the curry paste and the sweet potatoes. Simmer for about 10 minutes, then return the aubergines and shallots to the pan and cook for a further 5 minutes.

5 Stir in the coconut milk and the sugar. Season to taste, then stir in the mushrooms and simmer for 5 minutes, or until all the vegetables are cooked and tender.

6 Stir in lime juice to taste, followed by the coriander leaves. Sprinkle basil leaves over and serve immediately with rice.

Stuffed Aubergine Energy 273kcal/1134kJ; Protein 14.3g; Carbohydrate 5.9g, of which sugars 5.3g; Fat 19.9g, of which saturates 5.2g; Cholesterol 122mg; Calcium 42mg; Fibre 4g; Sodium 1145mg.
Aubergine Stew Energy 236kcal/992kJ; Protein 3.5g; Carbohydrate 30.2g, of which sugars 12.4g; Fat 12.2g, of which saturates 2.2g; Cholesterol 0mg; Calcium 65mg; Fibre 1.3g; Sodium 210mg.

Herby Potatoes baked with Tomatoes, Olives and Feta

This tasty potato dish comes from western Anatolia. Traditionally baked in an earthenware dish, it makes a fabulous accompaniment to meat, poultry or fish. Or serve it on its own as a main course with a squeeze of lemon or a dollop of yogurt, and a green salad.

Serves 4 to 6

675g/1½lb organic new potatoes
15ml/1 tbsp butter
2 red onions, halved lengthways, halved again crossways, and sliced along the grain
45ml/3 tbsp olive oil
3–4 garlic cloves, chopped
5–10ml/1–2 tsp cumin seeds, crushed
5–10ml/1–2 tsp Turkish red pepper, or 1 fresh red chilli, seeded and chopped
10ml/2 tsp dried oregano
10ml/2 tsp sugar
15ml/1 tbsp white wine vinegar
400g/14oz can chopped tomatoes, drained of juice
12–16 black olives
115g/4oz feta cheese, crumbled
salt and ground black pepper
extra olive oil, for drizzling
1 lemon, cut into wedges

1 Preheat the oven to 200°C/400°F/ Gas 6. Cook the potatoes for 15–20 minutes, until tender. Drain and refresh in cold water. Peel and cut the potatoes into thick slices or bitesize wedges.

2 Heat the butter and 30ml/2 tbsp of the oil in a heavy pan, stir in the onions and garlic and cook until soft. Add the cumin seeds, red pepper or chilli and most of the oregano, then add the sugar, vinegar and tomatoes. Season with salt and pepper.

3 Put the potatoes and olives into a baking dish and top with the tomato mixture. Crumble the feta on top and sprinkle with the reserved oregano. Drizzle with the remaining oil, then bake for 25–30 minutes. Pour the eggs over the mixture, drawing in the sides to let the eggs spread. Cover and leave to cook until they have set.

4 Serve the omelette hot, straight from the pan, or leave it to cool and serve it at room temperature.

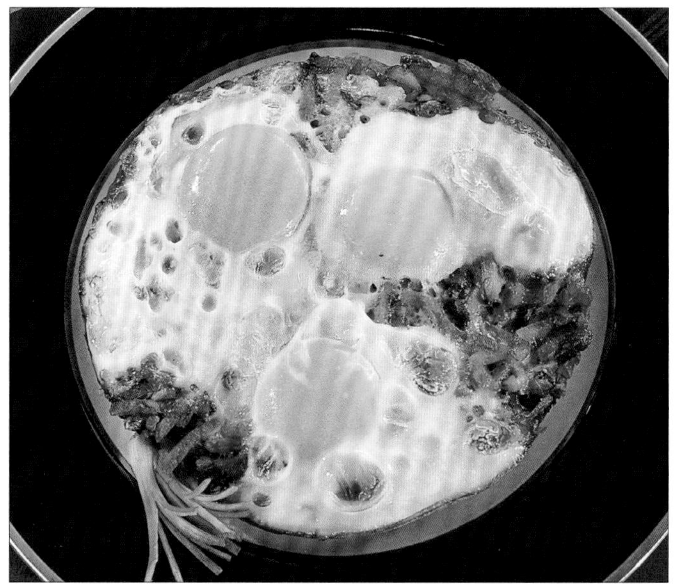

Eggs with Chilli Chipsticks

This egg-based dish, which includes chillies and chipsticks, is very quick and simple to make.

Serves 4 to 6

225g/8oz ready-salted chipsticks
2 green chillies, finely chopped
a few coriander (cilantro) leaves, finely chopped
1.5ml/¼ tsp ground turmeric
60ml/4 tbsp vegetable oil
75ml/5 tbsp/⅓ cup water
6 eggs
salt and ground black pepper
3 sprigs spring onions (scallions), finely chopped

1 In a bowl, gently mix together the chipsticks, chillies, coriander and turmeric until well combined.

2 Heat 30ml/2 tbsp of the oil in a large frying pan. Add the chipstick mixture and the measured water.

3 Cook the mixture, stirring frequently, until the chipsticks have softened, then continue to fry until crisp.

4 Place a plate over the frying pan, turn the pan over and remove the chipstick pancake on to it.

5 Reheat the remaining oil in the pan and slide the pancake back to the frying pan to brown the other side.

6 Gently break the eggs over the pancake, tilting the pan slightly so the eggs spread evenly. Cover the frying pan and allow the eggs to set over a low heat.

7 Season and sprinkle with the spring onions. Cook until the base is crisp. Serve immediately.

Cook's Tips

The inclusion of chipsticks in this recipe will have children rushing to try it. Ensure that the chilli heat won't be too hot for them by reducing the amount or removing the seeds first.

Herby Potatoes Energy 243kcal/1016kJ; Protein 6.3g; Carbohydrate 27.5g, of which sugars 9.3g; Fat 12.8g, of which saturates 5g; Cholesterol 19mg; Calcium 102mg; Fibre 2.9g; Sodium 447mg.
Eggs with Chilli Energy 276kcal/1153kJ; Protein 8.7g; Carbohydrate 20.4g, of which sugars 0.6g; Fat 18.5g, of which saturates 6.8g; Cholesterol 190mg; Calcium 58mg; Fibre 2.5g; Sodium 373mg.

Boiled Egg Curry

This spicy Indian dish is usually served with a biryani or pilau rice but it is equally good served with some Indian bread such as naan or chapati.

Serves 4 to 6

10ml/2 tsp white poppy seeds
10ml/2 tsp white sesame seeds
10ml/2 tsp whole coriander seeds
10ml/2 tbsp desiccated (dry unsweetened shredded) coconut
350ml/12fl oz/1½ cups tomato juice
10ml/2 tsp gram flour
5ml/1 tsp grated fresh root ginger
5ml/1 tsp chilli powder
1.5ml/¼ tsp asafoetida
5ml/1 tsp sugar
6 hard-boiled eggs, halved
10ml/2 tbsp sesame oil
5ml/1 tsp cumin seeds
4 whole dried red chillies
6–8 curry leaves
4 garlic cloves, finely sliced
salt

1 Heat a frying pan and dry-fry the poppy, sesame and coriander seeds for 3–4 minutes until they release their fragrances and begin to splutter.

2 Add the coconut and dry-fry until it browns. Cool and grind the ingredients together using a mortar and pestle or a food processor.

3 Pour a little of the tomato juice into a small bowl and mix with the gram flour to form a smooth paste.

4 Add the ginger, chilli powder, asafoetida, salt and sugar and the ground spices to the paste. Mix well until combined.

5 Add the remaining tomato juice to the bowl, mix well. Transfer the contents of the bowl into a pan and simmer gently for 10 minutes.

6 Add the hard-boiled eggs to the pan and cover with the sauce. Heat the oil in a frying pan and fry the remaining ingredients until the chillies turn dark brown.

7 Pour the spices and oil over the egg curry, mix gently together and reheat for a minute. Serve immediately.

Vietnamese Vegetable Curry with Thai Chillies

Variations of this fiery, flavoursome vegetable curry are found all over southern Vietnam. A favourite with the Buddhist monks and often sold from countryside stalls, it can be served with plain rice or noodles, or chunks of crusty bread.

Serves 4

30ml/2 tbsp vegetable oil
2 onions, roughly chopped
2 lemon grass stalks, roughly chopped and bruised
4 green Thai chillies, seeded and finely sliced
4cm/1½in galangal or fresh root ginger, peeled and chopped
3 carrots, peeled, halved lengthways and sliced
115g/4oz yard-long beans
grated rind of 1 lime
10ml/2 tsp soy sauce
15ml/1 tbsp rice vinegar
10ml/2 tsp Thai fish sauce
5ml/1 tsp black peppercorns, crushed
15ml/1 tbsp sugar
10ml/2 tsp ground turmeric
115g/4oz canned bamboo shoots
75g/3oz spinach, steamed and roughly chopped
150ml/¼ pint/⅔ cup coconut milk
salt
chopped fresh coriander (cilantro) and mint leaves, to garnish

1 Heat a wok or heavy pan and add the oil. Once hot, stir in the onions, lemon grass, chillies and galangal or ginger. Add the carrots and beans with the lime rind and stir-fry for 1–2 minutes.

2 Stir in the soy sauce, rice vinegar and fish sauce. Add the crushed peppercorns, sugar and turmeric, then stir in the bamboo shoots and the chopped spinach.

3 Stir in the coconut milk and simmer for 10 minutes, until the vegetables are tender. Season with salt and serve immediately, garnished with fresh coriander and mint.

Cook's Tip
This curry should be fiery, almost dominated by the chilli. In Vietnam it is eaten for breakfast as a great pick-me-up.

Boiled Egg Curry Energy 229kcal/953kJ; Protein 10.7g; Carbohydrate 4.6g, of which sugars 3.7g; Fat 19g, of which saturates 6.7g; Cholesterol 254mg; Calcium 81mg; Fibre 1.7g; Sodium 276mg.
Vietnamese Vegetable Curry Energy 159kcal/660kJ; Protein 3g; Carbohydrate 19g, of which sugars 16g; Fat 8g, of which saturates 1g; Cholesterol 0mg; Calcium 68mg; Fibre 3.7g; Sodium 200mg.

Chilli Lentils and Spiced Vegetables

This deliciously spicy curry is often served for breakfast with Indian pancakes or rice dumplings and can also be eaten as a main course.

Serves 4 to 6

60ml/4 tbsp vegetable oil
2.5ml/½ tsp mustard seeds
2.5ml/½ tsp cumin seeds
2 whole dried red chillies
1.5ml/¼ tsp asafoetida
6–8 curry leaves
2 garlic cloves, crushed
30ml/2 tbsp desiccated (dry unsweetened shredded) coconut
225g/8oz red lentils picked, washed and drained
10ml/2 tsp sambhar masala
2.5ml/½ tsp ground turmeric
450ml/¾ pint/scant 2 cups water
450g/1lb mixed vegetables (okra, courgettes/zucchini, cauliflower, shallots and sweet peppers)
60ml/4 tbsp tamarind juice
4 firm tomatoes, quartered
60ml/4 tbsp vegetable oil
2 garlic cloves, finely sliced
a handful coriander (cilantro) leaves, chopped

1 Heat the vegetable oil in a large frying pan. Add the mustard seeds and cumin seeds and fry for 1–2 minutes until fragrant and beginning to splutter.

2 Add the chillies, asafoetida, curry leaves, garlic and desiccated coconut to the pan. Cook the mixture over a medium heat, stirring constantly, for 4–5 minutes until the coconut begins to brown.

3 Stir the lentils into the pan, mixing well until combined. Add the sambhar masala and ground turmeric and mix. Pour in the measured water and bring the mixture to the boil.

4 Reduce the heat and simmer until the lentils are tender and mushy. Add all the vegetables, tamarind juice and tomatoes to the pan. Simmer gently for about 10–15 minutes, until the vegetables are just tender. They should still have a little crunch.

5 Transfer the mixture to a large bowl. Fry the garlic slices and coriander. Scatter over the lentils and vegetables and serve.

Spicy Chickpeas with Potato Cakes and Green Chillies

The potato cakes in this recipe are given a slightly sour-sweet flavour by the addition of amchur, a powder that is made from unripe or green mangos.

Makes 10 to 12

30ml/2 tbsp vegetable oil
30ml/2 tbsp ground coriander
30ml/2 tbsp ground cumin
2.5ml/½ tsp ground turmeric
2.5ml/½ tsp salt
2.5ml/½ tsp sugar
30ml/2 tbsp flour paste
450g/1lb boiled chickpeas, drained
2 fresh green chillies, chopped
1 piece fresh ginger, 5cm/2in long, finely crushed
85g/3oz fresh coriander (cilantro) leaves, chopped
2 firm tomatoes, chopped

For the potato cakes

450g/1lb potatoes, boiled and coarsely mashed
4 green chillies, finely chopped
50g/2oz coriander (cilantro) leaves, finely chopped
7.5ml/1½ tsp ground cumin
5ml/1 tsp amchur (dry mango powder)
salt, to taste
vegetable oil, for shallow-frying

1 Make the spicy chickpeas. Heat the oil in a pan and fry the coriander, cumin, turmeric, salt, sugar and flour paste until the water has evaporated and the oil separated.

2 Add the chickpeas, chillies, ginger, fresh coriander and tomatoes. Mix well and simmer for 5 minutes. Transfer to a serving dish and keep warm.

3 To make the potato cakes, mix the mashed potato in a large bowl with the green chillies, coriander, ground cumin, amchur and salt, to taste. Mix well until all the ingredients are thoroughly blended.

4 Using your hands, shape the potato mixture into little cakes. Heat the oil in a shallow frying pan or griddle and fry them on both sides until golden brown. Transfer to a serving dish and serve with the spicy chickpeas.

Chilli Lentils Energy 229kcal/963kJ; Protein 11.5g; Carbohydrate 27.5g, of which sugars 5.4g; Fat 9g, of which saturates 1.2g; Cholesterol 0mg; Calcium 54mg; Fibre 3.2g; Sodium 23mg.
Spicy Chickpeas Energy 163kcal/684kJ; Protein 5.2g; Carbohydrate 17.3g, of which sugars 1.6g; Fat 8.8g, of which saturates 1.1g; Cholesterol 0mg; Calcium 68mg; Fibre 3g; Sodium 96mg.

Chilli Dhal Curry

This is an Anglo-Indian version of dhal, a spicy dish made from lentils or other beans and peas. It is characteristically hot and spicy and can be served as a meal in itself with some Indian breads or plain rice or as part of a main course with a dry meat curry.

Serves 4 to 6

175g/6oz Bengal gram, washed
450ml/¾ pint/scant 2 cups water
60ml/4 tbsp vegetable oil
2 fresh green chillies, chopped
1 onion, chopped
2 garlic cloves, crushed
5cm/2in piece fresh root ginger, crushed
6–8 curry leaves
5ml/1 tsp chilli powder
5ml/1 tsp ground turmeric
450g/1lb bottle gourd or marrow (large zucchini), courgettes (zucchini), squash or pumpkin, peeled, pithed and sliced
60ml/4 tbsp tamarind juice
2 tomatoes, chopped
a handful fresh coriander (cilantro) leaves, chopped
salt

1 In a large pan, cook the Bengal gram in the measured water until the grains are tender but not mushy. Set aside without draining away any excess water.

2 Heat the vegetable oil in a large pan. Add the chillies, onion, garlic, ginger, curry leaves, chilli powder, turmeric and salt to the pan. Fry the mixture for 4–5 minutes, stirring constantly, until the onions begin to soften and turn translucent.

3 Add the gourd pieces, or other vegetables if using, to the spice mixture and stir until well combined. Cover the pan and cook gently, stirring frequently, until the vegetables are just beginning to soften.

4 Add the Bengal gram and the cooking water to the vegetable pan. Stir well and bring the mixture to the boil.

5 Stir in the tamarind juice, tomatoes and coriander to the pan. Reduce the heat and simmer until the vegeatables are tender.

6 Serve immediately with rice or Indian breads.

Spicy Black-eyed Bean and Potato Curry

This spicy curry can be served for a light lunch or supper, or use as a side dish as part of a larger meal.

Serves 4 to 6

225g/8oz/2¼ cups black-eyed beans (peas), soaked overnight and drained
1.5ml/¼ tsp bicarbonate of soda (baking soda)
5ml/1 tsp five-spice powder
1.5ml/¼ tsp asafoetida
2 onions, finely chopped
2.5cm/1in piece fresh root ginger, crushed
a few mint leaves
450ml/¾ pint/scant 2 cups water
60ml/4 tbsp vegetable oil
2.5ml/½ tsp each ground turmeric, coriander, cumin and chilli powder
4 fresh green chillies, chopped
75ml/2½fl oz/⅓ cup tamarind juice
2 potatoes, peeled, cubed and boiled
115g/4oz coriander (cilantro) leaves, chopped
2 firm tomatoes, chopped
salt

1 Place the black-eyed beans with the bicarbonate of soda, five-spice powder, asafoetida, onion, ginger and mint in a large, heavy pan. Pour in the measured water.

2 Bring the mixture to the boil, reduce the heat and simmer gently until the beans are soft, about 1–2 hours depending on the age of the dried beans. Remove any excess water from the pan and reserve.

3 Heat the vegetable oil in a large pan. Add the ground spices, chillies and tamarind juice, and fry gently for 3–4 minutes until the spices release their fragrances.

4 Pour the black-eyed bean mixture into the pan with the spice paste and stir until thoroughly combined.

5 Add the potatoes, coriander leaves, tomatoes and salt to the pan. Mix well, and if the curry is a little dry, add a little of the reserved water. Reheat the curry for a few minutes until just bubbling. Serve immediately.

Chilli Dhal Curry Energy 196kcal/828kJ; Protein 10.7g; Carbohydrate 29.2g, of which sugars 5.7g; Fat 5g, of which saturates 0.7g; Cholesterol 0mg; Calcium 47mg; Fibre 3.1g; Sodium 20mg.
Spicy Beans Energy 266kcal/1118kJ; Protein 11.8g; Carbohydrate 36.8g, of which sugars 8.5g; Fat 9g, of which saturates 1.1g; Cholesterol 0mg; Calcium 110mg; Fibre 8.8g; Sodium 28mg.

Indian-spiced Vegetable Curry

This is a very delicately spiced vegetable dish that makes a light meal when served with plain yogurt. It is also a good partner to a heavily spiced meat curry.

Serves 4

350g/12oz mixed vegetables: beans, peas, potatoes, cauliflower, carrots, cabbage, mangetouts (snow peas) and button (white) mushrooms
30ml/2 tbsp vegetable oil
5ml/1 tsp cumin seeds, roasted
2.5ml/½ tsp mustard seeds
2.5ml/½ tsp onion seeds
5ml/1 tsp ground turmeric
2 garlic cloves, crushed
6–8 curry leaves
1 whole dried red chilli
5ml/1 tsp sugar
150ml/¼ pint/⅔ cup natural (plain) yogurt mixed with 5ml/1 tsp cornflour (cornstarch)
salt
boiled rice and Indian breads, to serve

1 Prepare all the vegetables you have chosen: string the beans; thaw the peas, if frozen; cube the potatoes; cut the cauliflower into florets; dice the carrots; shred the cabbage; top and tail the mange-touts; wash the mushrooms and leave whole.

2 Heat a large pan with enough water to cook all the vegetables and bring to the boil. First add the potatoes and carrots and cook until nearly tender, then add all the other vegetables and cook until still firm. All the vegetables should be crunchy except the potatoes. Drain well.

3 Heat the oil in a frying pan and add the cumin, mustard and onion seeds. Fry gently for 1–2 minutes, stirring constantly until the seeds begin to splutter.

4 Add the turmeric, garlic, curry leaves and dried red chilli to the pan. Fry gently until the garlic is golden brown and the chilli nearly burnt. Reduce the heat.

5 Fold in the drained vegetables, add the sugar and season with salt. Gradually add the yogurt mixed with the cornflour (cornstarch) and stir well. Heat the curry until bubbling and serve immediately with rice and Indian breads.

Curried Spinach and Potato with Mixed Chillies

This delicious curry, suitable for vegetarians, is mildly spiced with a warming flavour from the fresh and dried chillies.

Serves 4 to 6

60ml/4 tbsp vegetable oil
225g/8oz potato
2.5cm/1in piece fresh root ginger, crushed
4 garlic cloves, crushed
1 onion, coarsely chopped
2 green chillies, chopped
2 whole dried red chillies, coarsely broken
5ml/1 tsp cumin seeds
225g/8oz fresh spinach, trimmed, washed and chopped or 225g/8oz frozen spinach, thawed and drained
salt
2 firm tomatoes, coarsely chopped, to garnish

1 Wash the potatoes and cut into quarters. If using small new potatoes, leave them whole. Heat the oil in a frying pan and fry the potatoes until brown on all sides. Remove and set aside.

2 Remove the excess oil leaving 15ml/1 tbsp in the pan. Fry the ginger, garlic, onion, green chillies, dried chillies and cumin seeds until the onion is golden brown.

3 Add the potatoes and salt to the pan and stir well. Cover the pan and cook gently until the potatoes are tender and can be easily pierced with a sharp knife.

4 Add the spinach and stir well. Cook with the pan uncovered until the spinach is tender and all the excess fluids in the pan have evaporated. Transfer the curry to a serving plate, garnish with the chopped tomatoes and serve immediately.

Cook's Tip

India is blessed with over 18 varieties of spinach. If you have access to an Indian or Chinese grocer, look out for some of the more unusual varieties.

Indian-spiced Curry Energy 92kcal/384kJ; Protein 3.1g; Carbohydrate 10.2g, of which sugars 3.4g; Fat 4.7g, of which saturates 0.7g; Cholesterol 0mg; Calcium 99mg; Fibre 0.9g; Sodium 61mg.
Curried Spinach Energy 135kcal/560kJ; Protein 3g; Carbohydrate 13.5g, of which sugars 5.9g; Fat 8g, of which saturates 1g; Cholesterol 0mg; Calcium 86mg; Fibre 2.6g; Sodium 62mg.

Curried Mushrooms, Peas and Paneer with Green Chillies

Paneer is a traditional cheese made from rich milk and is most popular with northern Indians. This makes a great dish for lunch when eaten with thick parathas.

Serves 4 to 6

90ml/6 tbsp ghee or vegetable oil
225g/8oz paneer, cubed
1 onion, finely chopped
a few mint leaves, chopped
50g/2oz coriander (cilantro) leaves, chopped
3 green chillies, chopped
3 garlic cloves
2.5cm/1in piece fresh root ginger, sliced
5ml/1 tsp ground turmeric
5ml/1 tsp chilli powder (optional)
5ml/1 tsp garam masala
225g/8oz tiny button (white) mushrooms, washed
225g/8oz frozen peas, thawed and drained
175ml/6fl oz/¾ cup natural (plain) yogurt, mixed with 5ml/1 tsp cornflour (cornstarch)
salt
tomatoes and coriander (cilantro) leaves, to garnish

1 Heat the ghee or oil in a frying pan and fry the paneer cubes until they are golden brown on all sides. Remove and drain on kitchen paper.

2 Grind the onion, mint, coriander, chillies, garlic and ginger in a mortar and pestle or food processor to a fairly smooth paste.

3 Transfer the paste to a bowl and mix in the turmeric, chilli powder, if using, garam masala and salt.

4 Remove any excess ghee or oil from the pan, leaving about 15ml/1 tbsp. Heat the oil and fry the paste until the raw onion smell disappears and the oil separates.

5 Add the mushrooms, peas and paneer to the pan. Mix well. Cool the mixture slightly and gradually fold in the yogurt. Simmer for about 10 minutes.

6 Garnish with tomatoes and coriander and serve immediately.

Corn and Pea Chilli Curry

Tender corn is cooked in a spicy tomato sauce. Use fresh corn on the cob when it is in season.

Serves 4

6 pieces of frozen corn on the cob
45ml/3 tbsp vegetable oil
2.5ml/½ tsp cumin seeds
1 onion, finely chopped
2 garlic cloves, crushed
1 green chilli, finely chopped
15ml/1 tbsp curry paste
5ml/1 tsp ground coriander
5ml/1 tsp ground cumin
1.5ml/¼ tsp ground turmeric
2.5ml/½ tsp salt
2.5ml/½ tsp sugar
400g/14oz can chopped tomatoes
15ml/1 tbsp tomato purée (paste)
150ml/¼ pint/⅔ cup water
115g/4oz frozen peas, thawed
30ml/2 tbsp chopped fresh coriander (cilantro)
chapatis, to serve (optional)

1 Use a sharp knife and cut each piece of corn in half crossways to make 12 equal pieces in total.

2 Bring a large pan of water to the boil and cook the corn cob pieces for 10–12 minutes. Drain well.

3 Heat the oil in pan and fry the cumin seeds for 2 minutes, or until they begin to splutter. Add the chopped onion, garlic and chilli and fry for 5–6 minutes until the onions are golden.

4 Add the curry paste and fry for 2 minutes. Stir in the remaining spices, salt and sugar and fry for 2–3 minutes.

5 Add the tomatoes and tomato purée with the water and simmer for 5 minutes. Add the peas and cook for 5 minutes.

6 Add the pieces of corn and fresh coriander and cook for a further 6–8 minutes, or until the corn and peas are tender. Serve with chapatis, for mopping up the rich sauce, if you like.

Variation
If you don't like peas then you can replace them with the same quantity of frozen corn.

Curried Mushrooms Energy 154kcal/643kJ; Protein 10.4g; Carbohydrate 13g, of which sugars 4.9g; Fat 7.2g, of which saturates 1.7g; Cholesterol 6mg; Calcium 139mg; Fibre 2.6g; Sodium 133mg.
Corn and Pea Curry Energy 260kcal/1089kJ; Protein 8.6g; Carbohydrate 29.7g, of which sugars 7.1g; Fat 12.9g, of which saturates 1.7g; Cholesterol 0mg; Calcium 68mg; Fibre 5.6g; Sodium 46mg.

Yard-long Bean Stew with Chillies

The southern Luzon peninsula in the Philippines is renowned for its fiery food, laced with hot chillies and coconut milk. In typical style, this rich, pungent dish is hot and, believe it or not, it is served with extra chillies to chew on.

Serves 3 to 4

30–45ml/2–3 tbsp coconut or groundnut (peanut) oil
1 onion, finely chopped
2–3 garlic cloves, finely chopped
40g/1 ½oz fresh root ginger, finely chopped
1 lemon grass stalk, bruised and finely chopped
4–5 red chillies, seeded and finely chopped
15ml/1 tbsp shrimp paste
15–30ml/1–2 tbsp tamarind paste
15–30ml/1–2 tbsp palm sugar (jaggery)
2 X 400g/14oz cans unsweetened coconut milk
4 kaffir lime leaves
500g/1 ¼lb yard-long beans
salt and ground black pepper
1 bunch of fresh coriander (cilantro) leaves, roughly chopped, to garnish

To serve
cooked rice
raw chillies

1 Heat the oil in a wok or large, heavy frying pan that has a lid. Stir in the onion, garlic, ginger, lemon grass and chillies and fry until fragrant and beginning to colour. Add the shrimp paste, tamarind paste and sugar and mix well. Stir in the coconut milk and the lime leaves.

2 Bring the mixture to the boil, reduce the heat and toss in the whole yard-long beans. Partially cover the pan and cook the beans gently for 6–8 minutes until tender.

3 Season the stew with salt and pepper and garnish with chopped coriander. Serve with rice and extra chillies, if you like.

Cook's Tip
If you prefer, you can reduce the quantity of chillies used in the recipe to suit your taste buds, and omit the extra chillies served with the stew, if you like.

Spicy Soya Bean Stew

Although this rich Korean stew has the same fermented soya bean paste foundation as many soups, it is an altogether thicker and heartier casserole. The slow-cooking process imparts a deep, complex flavour full of piquancy. It is a satisfyingly spicy and warming dish, ideal for cold winter evenings, and particularly suits the flavour of flame-grilled meat as an accompaniment.

Serves 2

½ courgette (zucchini)
25g/1oz enoki mushrooms
15ml/1 tbsp sesame oil, plus extra for drizzling
30ml/2 tbsp doenjang soya bean paste
¼ onion, finely chopped
10ml/2 tsp finely chopped garlic
550ml/18fl oz/2½ cups vegetable stock
1 red chilli, sliced diagonally
¼ block firm tofu, diced
1 spring onion (scallion), sliced, to garnish

1 Chop the courgette into thick slices, and then cut each slice into quarters. Discard the caps from the enoki mushrooms.

2 In a casserole dish or heavy pan, heat the sesame oil over high heat. Add the soya bean paste to the pan and cook for a few minutes. Then add the onion and garlic to the pan and fry gently. Add the vegetable stock, stir well, and bring to the boil.

3 Add the chillies and courgette and boil for 5 minutes. Add the tofu and mushrooms and boil for a further 2 minutes. Reduce the heat and simmer the stew gently for 15 minutes.

4 Ladle the stew into warmed individual bowls. Garnish each serving with the sliced spring onion and a drizzle of sesame oil, and serve immediately.

Cook's Tip
Enoki mushrooms, or Enokitake, are small, white, delicately flavoured mushrooms with very thin stalks. They are available from most Asian stores and can also be found in good supermarkets.

Snake Bean Stew Energy 200kcal/840kJ; Protein 5.5g; Carbohydrate 24.4g, of which sugars 22.9g; Fat 9.7g, of which saturates 1.5g; Cholesterol 19mg; Calcium 158mg; Fibre 3.4g; Sodium 384mg.
Spicy Soya Stew Energy 166kcal/690kJ; Protein 13g; Carbohydrate 4.8g, of which sugars 3.2g; Fat 10.7g, of which saturates 2.2g; Cholesterol 15mg; Calcium 169mg; Fibre 3.1g; Sodium 25mg.

Hot Pineapple and Coconut Curry

This sweet and spicy curry from the Maluku spice islands in Indonesia benefits from being made the day before eating, enabling the flavours to mingle longer. It is often eaten at room temperature, but it is also delicious hot.

Serves 4

1 small, firm pineapple
15–30ml/1–2 tbsp palm or coconut oil
4–6 shallots, finely chopped
2 garlic cloves, finely chopped
1 red chilli, seeded and finely chopped
15ml/1 tbsp palm sugar (jaggery)
400ml/14fl oz/1⅔ cups coconut milk
salt and ground black pepper
1 small bunch fresh coriander (cilantro) leaves, finely chopped, to garnish

For the spice paste

4 cloves
4 cardamom pods
1 small cinnamon stick
5ml/1 tsp coriander seeds
2.5ml/½ tsp cumin seeds
5–10ml/1–2 tsp water

1 First make the spice paste. Using a mortar and pestle or electric spice grinder, grind all the spices together to a powder. In a small bowl, mix the spice powder with the water to make a paste. Put aside.

2 Remove the skin from the pineapple, then cut the flesh lengthways into quarters and remove the core. Cut each quarter widthways into chunky slices and put aside.

3 Heat the oil in a wok or large, heavy frying pan, stir in the shallots, garlic and chilli and stir-fry until fragrant and beginning to colour. Stir in the spice paste and fry for 1 minute. Toss in the pineapple, making sure the slices are coated in the spicy mixture.

4 Stir the sugar into the coconut milk and pour into the wok. Stir and bring to the boil. Reduce the heat and simmer for 3–4 minutes to thicken the sauce, but do not allow the pineapple to become too soft. Season with salt and pepper to taste.

5 Transfer the curry to a serving dish and sprinkle with the coriander to garnish. Serve hot or at room temperature.

Tofu and Green Bean Red Chilli Curry

This is one of those versatile recipes that should be in every chilli-loving cook's repertoire. This version uses green beans, but other types of vegetable work equally well. The tofu takes on the flavour of the spice paste and also boosts the nutritional value.

Serves 4 to 6

600ml/1 pint/2½ cups canned coconut milk
15ml/1 tbsp Thai red curry paste
45ml/3 tbsp Thai fish sauce
10ml/2 tsp palm sugar (jaggery) or light muscovado (brown) sugar
225g/8oz/3¼ cups button (white) mushrooms
115g/4oz/scant 1 cup green beans, trimmed
175g/6oz firm tofu, rinsed, drained and cut into 2cm/¾in cubes
4 kaffir lime leaves, torn
2 fresh red chillies, seeded and sliced
fresh coriander (cilantro) leaves, to garnish

1 Pour about one-third of the coconut milk into a wok or pan. Cook until it starts to separate and an oily sheen appears on the surface.

2 Add the red curry paste, fish sauce and sugar to the coconut milk. Mix thoroughly. Add the button mushrooms. Stir the mixture and cook for 1–2 minutes.

3 Stir in the remaining coconut milk. Bring the mixture slowly back to the boil. Add the green beans and tofu cubes. Reduce the heat and simmer gently for 4–5 minutes more.

4 Stir in the kaffir lime leaves and sliced red chillies. Heat the curry for a couple of minutes until bubbling. Spoon the curry into warmed individual bowls. Sprinkle the coriander leaves over the top of each serving as a garnish and serve at once.

Cook's Tip

Tofu or bean curd is quite bland in flavour but it readily picks up strong tastes, such as chillies and spices.

Hot Pineapple Curry Energy 135kcal/573kJ; Protein 1.6g; Carbohydrate 25.4g, of which sugars 23.6g; Fat 3.8g, of which saturates 0.5g; Cholesterol 0mg; Calcium 87mg; Fibre 2.9g; Sodium 131mg.
Tofu and Bean Curry Energy 110kcal/460kJ; Protein 5.7g; Carbohydrate 10.2g, of which sugars 9.6g; Fat 5.5g, of which saturates 0.9g; Cholesterol 0mg; Calcium 282mg; Fibre 1.3g; Sodium 437mg.

Root Vegetable Gratin with Indian Spices

Subtly spiced with curry powder, turmeric, coriander and mild chilli powder, this rich gratin is substantial enough to serve on its own for lunch or supper. It is also a good accompaniment to a vegetable or bean curry.

Serves 4

2 large potatoes, about 450g/1lb total weight
2 sweet potatoes, about 275g/10oz total weight
175g/6oz celeriac
15ml/1 tbsp unsalted (sweet) butter
5ml/1 tsp curry powder
5ml/1 tsp ground turmeric
2.5ml/½ tsp ground coriander
5ml/1 tsp mild chilli powder
3 shallots, chopped
150ml/¼ pint/⅔ cup single (light) cream
150ml/¼ pint/⅔ cup milk
salt and ground black pepper
chopped fresh flat leaf parsley, to garnish

1 Cut the potatoes, sweet potatoes and celeriac into thin, even slices using a sharp knife or the slicing attachment on a food processor. Immediately place the vegetables in a bowl of cold water to prevent them from discolouring.

2 Preheat the oven to 180°C/350°F/Gas 4. Heat half the butter in a heavy pan, add the curry powder, ground turmeric and coriander and half the chilli powder. Cook for 2 minutes, then leave to cool slightly. Drain the vegetables, then pat them dry with kitchen paper. Place in a bowl, add the spice mixture and the shallots and mix well.

3 Arrange the vegetables in a shallow baking dish, seasoning well with salt and pepper between the layers. Mix together the cream and milk, pour the mixture over the vegetables, then sprinkle the remaining chilli powder on top.

4 Cover the dish with baking parchment and bake for 45 minutes. Remove the baking parchment, dot the vegetables with the remaining butter and bake for a further 50 minutes, or until the top is golden brown. Serve the gratin garnished with chopped parsley.

Courgette and Jalapeño Chilli Torte

This spicy dish looks like a Spanish omelette, which is traditionally served at room temperature. Serve warm or prepare it in advance and leave to cool, but do not refrigerate.

Serves 4 to 6

500g/1¼lb courgettes (zucchini)
60ml/4 tbsp vegetable oil
1 small onion
3 fresh jalapeño chillies, seeded and cut in strips
3 large eggs
50g/2oz/½ cup self-raising (self-rising) flour
115g/4oz/1 cup grated Monterey Jack or mild Cheddar cheese
2.5ml/½ tsp cayenne pepper
15g/½oz/1 tbsp butter
salt

1 Preheat the oven to 180°C/350°F/Gas 4. Top and tail the courgettes, then slice them thinly.

2 Heat the oil in a large frying pan. Add the courgettes and cook for a few minutes, turning them over at least once, until they are soft and beginning to brown. Using a slotted spoon, transfer them to a bowl.

3 Slice the onion and add it to the oil left in the pan, with most of the jalapeño strips, reserving some for the garnish. Fry until the onions have softened and are golden.

4 Using a slotted spoon, transfer the onions and jalapeños to the bowl with the courgettes.

5 Beat the eggs in a large bowl. Add the self-raising flour, cheese and cayenne. Mix well, then stir in the courgette mixture, with salt to taste.

6 Grease a 23cm/9in round shallow ovenproof dish with the butter. Pour in the courgette mixture and bake in the oven for 30 minutes until it has risen, is firm to the touch and golden brown all over. Allow to cool.

7 Serve the courgette torte in thick wedges and garnish with the remaining jalapeño strips. A tomato salad, sprinkled with chives, makes a colourful accompaniment.

Root Vegetable Gratin Energy 268kcal/1129kJ; Protein 5.8g; Carbohydrate 37.7g, of which sugars 9.8g; Fat 11.6g, of which saturates 7.1g; Cholesterol 31mg; Calcium 127mg; Fibre 3.6g; Sodium 117mg.
Courgette Torte Energy 421kcal/1747kJ; Protein 18.8g; Carbohydrate 13.2g, of which sugars 3.2g; Fat 32g, of which saturates 12.9g; Cholesterol 216mg; Calcium 356mg; Fibre 1.7g; Sodium 359mg.

Stuffed Green Chillies

Stuffed chillies are popular all over Mexico. The type of chilli used differs from region to region. Poblanos and anaheims are quite mild, but you can use hotter chillies if you prefer.

Makes 6

6 fresh poblano or Anaheim chillies
2 potatoes, total weight about 400g/14oz
200g/7oz/scant 1 cup cream cheese
200g/7oz/1¾ cups grated mature (sharp) Cheddar cheese
5ml/1 tsp salt
2.5ml/½ tsp ground black pepper
2 eggs, separated
115g/4oz/1 cup plain (all-purpose) flour
2.5ml/½ tsp white pepper
oil, for frying
chilli flakes to garnish, (optional)

1 Cut a slit down one side of each chilli. Dry-fry the chillies in a pan, turning frequently, until they blister. Place in a plastic bag and tie the top to keep the steam in. Set aside for 20 minutes, then peel off the skins and remove the seeds through the slits, keeping the chillies whole. Dry with kitchen paper and set aside.

2 Scrub or peel the potatoes and cut them into 1cm/½in dice. Bring a large pan of water to the boil, add the potatoes and return to the boil. Lower the heat and simmer for 5 minutes, or until the potatoes are just tender. Drain them thoroughly.

3 Put the cream cheese in a bowl with the mature cheese. Add 2.5ml/½ tsp of the salt and the black pepper. Mix in the potato. Spoon potato filling into each chilli. Put them on a plate, cover with clear film (plastic wrap) and chill for 1 hour to firm up.

4 Put the egg whites in a clean, grease-free bowl and whisk to firm peaks. In another bowl, beat the yolks until pale, then fold in the whites. Scrape the mixture into a large, shallow dish. Spread out the flour in another shallow dish and season it with the remaining salt and the white pepper.

5 Heat the oil for deep-frying to 190°C/375°F. Coat a few chillies first in flour and then in egg before frying the chillies in batches until golden and crisp. Drain on kitchen paper and serve hot, garnished with a sprinkle of chilli flakes for extra heat, if desired.

Roasted Vegetable and Cheese Chilli Tortillas

This spicy recipe shows how the griddle and grill rack can cope with many ingredients. Have a griddle on one side of the grill rack for the onions and peppers; the aubergines can cook over the coals on the other side.

Serves 6 to 8

1 yellow and 1 orange (bell) pepper, quartered
2 red (bell) peppers, quartered
2 red onions, cut into wedges with root intact
8 long baby aubergines (eggplant), total weight about 175g/6oz, halved lengthways
30ml/2 tbsp olive oil
400g/14oz mozzarella cheese
2 fresh green chillies, seeded and sliced into rounds
15ml/1 tbsp Mexican tomato sauce
8 corn or wheat flour tortillas
handful of fresh basil leaves
salt and ground black pepper

1 Prepare a barbecue. Once the flames have died down, heat a lightly oiled grill rack. When the coals are ready, heat a griddle.

2 Toss the peppers, onions and aubergines in the oil on a large baking tray. Place the peppers, skin side down, on the griddle and cook until seared. Transfer to a bowl, cover and set aside.

3 Grill the onions and aubergines until they have softened and are branded with grill marks, then set aside. Rub the skins off the peppers, cut each piece in half and add to the other vegetables.

4 Cut the mozzarella into 20 slices. Place them, along with the roasted vegetables, into a large bowl and add the chillies and tomato sauce. Stir well and season. Place the griddle over a medium heat and cook all the tortillas on one side only.

5 Lay a tortilla on the griddle, cooked side up, and pile about a quarter of the vegetable mixture into the centre. Sprinkle over some basil leaves. When the tortilla browns underneath, put another tortilla on top, cooked side down. Carefully turn the tortilla over and continue to cook until the underside has browned and the cheese just starts to melt. Remove from the pan and serve immediately.

Stuffed Chillies Energy 498kcal/2072kJ; Protein 14.9g; Carbohydrate 27.8g, of which sugars 3.2g; Fat 36.5g, of which saturates 18.6g; Cholesterol 127mg; Calcium 322mg; Fibre 1.8g; Sodium 374mg.
Vegetable Tortillas Energy 375kcal/1562kJ; Protein 19.3g; Carbohydrate 13.5g, of which sugars 5.7g; Fat 27.1g, of which saturates 10g; Cholesterol 315mg; Calcium 305mg; Fibre 2.6g; Sodium 589mg.

Chilli and Herb Grilled Polenta with Tangy Pebre

Here polenta is flavoured with pasilla chillies. Serve with a tangy salsa from Chile called pebre.

Serves 6

10ml/2 tsp crushed dried pasilla chilli flakes
1.3 litres/2¼ pints/5⅔ cups water
250g/9oz quick-cook polenta
50g/2oz/¼ cup butter
75g/3oz Parmesan cheese, grated
30ml/2 tbsp chopped fresh dill
30ml/2 tbsp chopped fresh coriander (cilantro)
30ml/2 tbsp olive oil
salt

For the pebre

½ pink onion, finely chopped
4 drained bottled sweet cherry peppers, finely chopped
1 fresh medium hot red chilli, seeded and finely chopped
1 small red (bell) pepper, quartered and seeded
10ml/2 tsp raspberry vinegar
30ml/2 tbsp olive oil
4 tomatoes, halved, cored, seeded and roughly chopped
45ml/3 tbsp chopped fresh coriander (cilantro)

1 Chop the dried chilli flakes. Put them in a pan with the water. Bring to the boil and add salt to taste. Add the polenta, whisking all the time. Reduce the heat and whisk for a few minutes. When the polenta is thick, whisk in the butter, Parmesan and herbs and season. Pour into a greased 33 × 23cm/13 × 9in baking tray. Leave uncovered to firm the surface and chill overnight.

2 About an hour before you plan to serve the meal, make the pebre. Place the onion, sweet cherry peppers and chilli in a mortar. Slice the skin from the red pepper. Dice the flesh and add it to the mortar with the vinegar and oil. Pound with a pestle for about 1 minute, then transfer to a serving dish. Stir in the tomatoes and coriander. Cover and leave in a cool place.

3 Remove the polenta from the refrigerator and leave for 30 minutes. Cut into 12 triangles and brush the top with oil. Heat a griddle and grill the polenta triangles in batches oiled side down for 2 minutes, then turn through 180 degrees and cook for a minute, to get a criss-cross effect. Serve with the chilled pebre.

Chilli Chickpea Dumplings

Falling between a Chinese dumpling and Italian pasta, this dish is a popular snack in eastern Anatolia. The chickpea filling is good for vegetarians. Serve as a hot snack, or as a meal on its own with a green salad.

Serves 4 to 6

450g/1lb/4 cups plain (all-purpose) flour
2.5ml/½ tsp salt
1 whole egg, beaten with 1 yolk
salt and ground black pepper

For the filling

400g/14oz can chickpeas, drained and thoroughly rinsed
5ml/1 tsp cumin seeds, crushed
5ml/1 tsp Turkish red pepper or paprika

For the yogurt

about 90ml/6 tbsp thick and creamy natural (plain) yogurt
2–3 garlic cloves, crushed

For the sauce

15ml/1 tbsp olive oil
15ml/1 tbsp butter
1 onion, finely chopped
2 garlic cloves, finely chopped
5ml/1 tsp Turkish red pepper, or 1 fresh red chilli, seeded and finely chopped
5–10ml/1–2 tsp granulated (white) sugar
5–10ml/1–2 tsp dried mint
400g/14oz can chopped tomatoes, drained of juice
600ml/1 pint/2½ cups vegetable or chicken stock
1 bunch each of parsley and coriander (cilantro), chopped

1 Make the dough. Sift the flour and salt into a wide bowl and make a well in the middle. Pour in the egg and 50ml/2fl oz/¼ cup water. Draw the flour into the liquid and mix to a dough. Knead the dough for 10 minutes, cover the bowl with a damp dish towel and leave the dough to rest for 1 hour.

2 Meanwhile, prepare the filling and yogurt. In a bowl, mash the chickpeas with a fork. Beat in the cumin, pepper or paprika and seasoning to taste. In another bowl, beat the yogurt with the garlic and season with salt and pepper.

3 Make the sauce. Heat the oil and butter in a heavy pan and fry the onion and garlic until soft. Add the pepper or chilli, sugar and mint, then stir in the tomatoes and cook for 15 minutes, until the sauce is thick. Season and remove from the heat.

4 Preheat the oven to 200°C/400°F/ Gas 6. Roll out the dough as thinly as possible on a lightly floured surface. Using a sharp knife, cut the dough into small squares (roughly 2.5cm/1in).

5 Spoon a little chickpea mixture into the centre of each square and bunch the corners together to form a pouch. Place the parcels in a greased ovenproof dish, stacking them next to each other. Bake, uncovered, for 15–20 minutes, until golden brown.

6 Pour the stock into a pan and bring to the boil. Take the pasta parcels out of the oven and pour the stock over them.

7 Return the dish to the oven and bake for 15–20 minutes, until almost all the stock has been absorbed. Meanwhile, reheat the tomato sauce.

8 Transfer the dumplings to a serving dish and spoon the yogurt over them. Top the cool yogurt with the tomato sauce and sprinkle with the chopped herbs.

Chilli and Herb Polenta Energy 176kcal/732kJ; Protein 4.8g; Carbohydrate 16.4g, of which sugars 1.2g; Fat 10g, of which saturates 4g; Cholesterol 15mg; Calcium 87mg; Fibre 1g; Sodium 98mg.
Chickpea Dumplings Energy 416kcal/1760kJ; Protein 14.8g; Carbohydrate 73.7g, of which sugars 5.9g; Fat 9g, of which saturates 2.6g; Cholesterol 71mg; Calcium 179mg; Fibre 5.9g; Sodium 360mg.

Tortillas with Salsa and Guacamole

This is just the right spicy dish to keep hungry guests from feeling the effects of too many preprandial drinks. The fieriness of the salsa will depend on the chilli sauce used, so choose one to suit your tastes.

Serves 6

30ml/2 tbsp chipotle or other chilli oil
15ml/1 tbsp sunflower oil
8 yellow corn tortillas

For the salsa

4 tomatoes
30ml/2 tbsp chopped fresh basil
juice of ½ lime
20ml/4 tsp good quality sweet chilli sauce
1 small red onion, finely chopped
salt and ground black pepper

For the guacamole

4 avocados
juice of ½ lime
1 fat mild chilli, seeded and chopped

1 Make the salsa one or two hours ahead to allow the flavours to blend. Cut the tomatoes in half, remove the cores and scoop out the seeds. Dice the flesh. Add the chopped basil, lime juice and sweet chilli sauce. Stir in the onion, then season to taste.

2 Make the guacamole. Cut the avocados in half, prize out the stones (pits), then scoop the flesh into a bowl. Add the lime juice, chilli and season. Mash with a fork to a fairly rough texture.

3 Prepare the barbecue. Mix together the chilli and sunflower oils. Stack the tortillas on a board. Lift the first tortilla off the stack and brush it lightly with the oil mixture. Turn it over and place it on the board, then brush the exposed side with oil. Repeat with the remaining tortillas, to make a new, second stack. Slice the whole stack diagonally into six pointed triangles.

4 Once the flames have died down, position a lightly oiled rack over the coals to heat. When the coals are hot, or with a light coating of ash, heat a griddle on the rack. Grill the tortilla wedges for 30 seconds on each side.

5 Transfer them to a bowl, so that they are supported by its sides. As they cool, they will shape themselves to the curve of the bowl. Serve with the salsa and guacamole.

Crispy Fried Tempeh with Chilli Spices

Often cooked at street stalls, this crispy fried tempeh can be served as a snack or as part of a selection of Indonesian dishes. For a substantial meal, try serving it with stir-fried noodles or rice and pickled vegetables.

Serves 3 to 4

45–60ml/3–4 tbsp coconut or groundnut (peanut) oil
500g/1¼lb tempeh, cut into bitesize strips
4 shallots, finely chopped
4 garlic cloves, finely chopped
25g/1oz fresh galangal or fresh root ginger, finely chopped
3–4 red chillies, seeded and finely chopped
150ml/¼ pint/⅔ cup kecap manis (Indonesian sweet soy sauce)
30–45ml/2–3 tbsp unsalted peanuts, crushed
1 small bunch fresh coriander (cilantro) leaves, roughly chopped
noodles or rice, to serve

1 Heat 30–45ml/2–3 tbsp of the oil in a wok or large, heavy frying pan. Add the tempeh and stir-fry until golden brown all over. Using a slotted spoon, transfer the tempeh to kitchen paper to drain, then set aside.

2 Wipe the wok or frying pan clean with kitchen paper. Heat the remaining 15ml/1 tbsp oil in the wok or pan, stir in the shallots, garlic, galangal and chillies and fry until fragrant and beginning to colour. Stir in the kecap manis and add the fried tempeh. Stir-fry until the sauce has reduced and is clinging to the tempeh.

3 Transfer the tempeh to a serving dish and sprinkle with the peanuts and coriander leaves. Serve immediately with stir-fried noodles or cooked rice.

Variation

Tempeh, which is fermented tofu, can be bought from Chinese and South-east Asian supermarkets. If you are unable to purchase it, then tofu can be used as an alternative.

Tortillas with Salsa Energy 340kcal/1421kJ; Protein 5.6g; Carbohydrate 34.8g, of which sugars 4.4g; Fat 20.7g, of which saturates 3.8g; Cholesterol 0mg; Calcium 69mg; Fibre 4.5g; Sodium 232mg.
Crispy Fried Tempeh Energy 258kcal/1071kJ; Protein 14.8g; Carbohydrate 7.7g, of which sugars 5.5g; Fat 18.9g, of which saturates 2.6g; Cholesterol 0mg; Calcium 682mg; Fibre 1.7g; Sodium 2680mg.

Potato Cakes with Pickled Chillies

Quick and easy to make, these potato cakes are very moreish. They are also versatile. Try serving them with salsa as a light meal, or they will be great as a spicy accompaniment to roast or pan-fried meats.

Makes 10

600g/1lb 6oz potatoes
115g/4oz/1 cup grated Cheddar cheese
2.5ml/½ tsp salt
50g/2oz/⅓ cup drained pickled jalapeño chilli slices, finely chopped (optional)
1 egg, beaten
small bunch of fresh coriander (cilantro), finely chopped
plain (all-purpose) flour, for shaping
oil, for shallow frying
fresh citrus salsa, to serve

1 Peel the potatoes and halve them if large. Add them to a pan of cold water. Bring the water to the boil.

2 Reduce the heat slightly and cook the potatoes for about 30 minutes, until tender. Drain, return to the pan and mash. The mash should not be smooth.

3 Scrape the potato into a bowl and stir in the grated cheese, with the salt and the chopped jalapeños, if using. Mix well.

4 Stir the beaten egg and most of the chopped coriander into the potato bowl. Mix well to form a dough.

5 When the dough is cool enough to handle, put it on a board. With floured hands, divide it into ten pieces of roughly equal size. Shape each piece into a ball, then press down with your hand to form a cake.

6 Heat the oil in a large frying pan. Fry the potato cakes, in batches if necessary, for 2–3 minutes over a moderate heat. Turn them over and cook until both sides are golden.

7 Pile the cooked cakes on to a serving platter, sprinkle with salt and the remaining chopped coriander and serve immediately with the fruity salsa.

Spicy Corn Patties

Serve these spicy treats with fresh lime wedges and a dollop of chilli sambal to give that extra fiery kick.

Serves 4

2 fresh corn on the cob
3 shallots, chopped
2 garlic cloves, chopped
25g/1oz galangal or fresh root ginger, chopped
1–2 chillies, seeded and chopped
2–3 candlenuts or macadamia nuts, ground
5ml/1 tsp ground coriander
5ml/1 tsp ground cumin
15ml/1 tbsp coconut oil
3 eggs
45–60ml/3–4 tbsp grated fresh coconut or desiccated (dry unsweetened shredded) coconut
2–3 spring onions (scallions), white parts only, finely sliced
corn or groundnut (peanut) oil, for shallow frying
1 small bunch fresh coriander (cilantro) leaves, chopped
salt and ground black pepper
1 lime, quartered, for serving
chilli sambal, for dipping

1 Put the corn on the cob into a large pan of water, bring to the boil and boil for about 8 minutes, until cooked but still firm. Drain the cobs and refresh under running cold water. Using a sharp knife, scrape all the corn off the cob and set aside.

2 Using a mortar and pestle, grind the shallots, garlic, galangal and chillies until they form a paste. Add the candlenuts, ground coriander and cumin and beat well together.

3 Heat the coconut oil in a small wok or heavy pan, stir in the spice paste and stir-fry until the paste becomes fragrant and begins to colour. Transfer on to a plate and leave to cool.

4 Beat the eggs in a large bowl. Add the coconut and spring onions and beat in the corn and the paste. Season the mixture.

5 Heat a thin layer of corn oil in a heavy frying pan. Working in batches, drop spoonfuls of the corn mixture into the oil and fry the patties for 2–3 minutes, until golden brown on both sides.

6 Drain the patties on kitchen paper and arrange on a serving dish on top of the coriander. Serve hot or at room temperature with wedges of lime to squeeze over and a chilli sambal.

Potato Cakes Energy 149kcal/621kJ; Protein 4.8g; Carbohydrate 9.8g, of which sugars 0.9g; Fat 10.1g, of which saturates 3.4g; Cholesterol 30mg; Calcium 101mg; Fibre 0.8g; Sodium 197mg.
Spicy Corn Patties Energy 368kcal/1531kJ; Protein 10.8g; Carbohydrate 18.1g, of which sugars 8.2g; Fat 28.7g, of which saturates 9.7g; Cholesterol 143mg; Calcium 68mg; Fibre 4.1g; Sodium 196mg.

Gado Gado with Chilli Peanut Sauce

Served at room temperature with a bowl of rice, this spicy Indonesian dish makes a tasty vegetarian meal.

Serves 4 to 6

500g/1¼lb tofu block
corn oil, for deep frying
4 shallots, finely sliced
3 carrots, sliced diagonally
about 12 yard-long beans, cut into bitesize pieces
225g/8oz kangkung (water spinach), washed and thinly sliced
1 firm mango, cut into bitesize chunks
½ pineapple, cut into bitesize chunks
225g/8oz mung bean sprouts
2–3 hard-boiled eggs, quartered
salt
1 small bunch fresh coriander (cilantro) leaves, roughly chopped, to garnish

For the peanut sauce

30ml/2 tbsp coconut or groundnut (peanut) oil
3 shallots, finely chopped
3 garlic cloves, finely chopped
3–4 red chillies, seeded and finely chopped
175g/6oz/1 cup unsalted roasted peanuts, finely ground
15g/½oz galangal or fresh root ginger, finely chopped
5–10ml/1–2 tsp shrimp paste
15ml/1 tbsp palm sugar (jaggery)
600ml/1 pint/2½ cups coconut milk
juice of 1 lime
30ml/2 tbsp kecap manis (Indonesian sweet soy sauce)

1 First make the peanut sauce. Heat the oil in a wok or heavy pan, stir in the shallots, garlic and chillies and fry until beginning to colour. Add the peanuts, galangal, shrimp paste and palm sugar and fry for about 4 minutes, until the peanuts begin to darken and ooze a little oil.

2 Pour the coconut milk, lime juice and kecap manis into the pan and bring to the boil. Reduce the heat and simmer gently for 15–20 minutes, until the sauce has reduced a little and thickened. Leave to cool.

3 Cut the tofu into four rectangular pieces. Heat enough oil in a wok for deep-frying, add the tofu pieces and fry until golden brown. Using a slotted spoon, remove from the pan and drain on kitchen paper. Cut the tofu into slices and put aside.

4 Heat 15–30ml/1–2 tbsp of the oil in a small, heavy pan, add the shallots and fry until deep golden in colour. Drain on kitchen paper and put aside.

5 Fill a large pan a third of the way up with water and place a steaming basket over it. Bring the water to the boil and put the carrots and yard-long beans in the steaming basket. Put the lid on, reduce the heat, and steam for 3–4 minutes. Add the kangkung for a minute, then drain the vegetables and refresh under cold running water.

6 Put the vegetables in a large bowl. Add the mango, pineapple and bean sprouts and pour in half the peanut sauce. Toss well then transfer to a serving dish.

7 Arrange the egg quarters and tofu slices around the edge of the dish and drizzle the remaining peanut sauce over the top. Sprinkle with the reserved fried shallots and chopped coriander to garnish, and serve immediately.

Aubergines in a Chilli Sauce

This dish is a great Indonesian favourite, both in the home and at the street stall. You can make it with large aubergines, cut in half and baked, or with small ones, butterflied. The dip is served in aubergine skins.

Serves 4

2 large aubergines (eggplants), cut in half lengthways, or 4 small auberines, butterflied
45–60ml/3–4 tbsp coconut oil
4 shallots, finely chopped
4 garlic cloves, finely chopped
25g/1oz fresh root ginger, finely chopped
3–4 red chillies, seeded and finely chopped
400g/14oz can tomatoes, drained
5–10ml/1–2 tsp palm sugar (jaggery)
juice of 2 limes
salt
1 small bunch fresh coriander (cilantro), finely chopped, to garnish

1 Preheat the oven to 180°C/350°F/Gas 4. Put the prepared aubergines on a baking tray and brush with 30ml/2 tbsp of the coconut oil. Bake in the oven for 40 minutes, until they are soft and tender.

2 Using a mortar and pestle, or a food processor, grind the shallots, garlic, ginger and chillies to a paste.

3 Heat the remaining 15ml/1 tbsp of oil in a wok or frying pan, stir in the spice paste and cook for 1–2 minutes, until it becomes fragrant and its colour begins to darken.

4 Add the tomatoes and sugar to the pan and cook for a further 3–4 minutes, until heated, then stir in the lime juice and a little salt to taste.

5 Put the baked aubergines in a serving dish and gently press down the flesh using the back of a wooden spoon to create a small hollow. Fill this with the sauce and spoon more of the sauce over the aubergines.

6 Garnish the aubergines with the chopped coriander and serve immediately if you want them warm, or leave to cool before serving at room temperature.

Gado Gado Energy 449kcal/1873kJ; Protein 22.2g; Carbohydrate 24.5g, of which sugars 20.7g; Fat 30g, of which saturates 5.1g; Cholesterol 108mg; Calcium 611mg; Fibre 5.1g; Sodium 675mg.
Aubergines Energy 100kcal/419kJ; Protein 2.1g; Carbohydrate 9.4g, of which sugars 8.8g; Fat 6.4g, of which saturates 0.9g; Cholesterol 0mg; Calcium 42mg; Fibre 3.7g; Sodium 15mg.

Chilli-stuffed Pan-fried Tofu

An easy accompaniment for a main course, or a great lunch. Squares of fried tofu stuffed with a blend of chilli and chestnut give a piquant jolt to the delicate flavour.

Serves 2

2 blocks firm tofu
30ml/2 tbsp Thai fish sauce
5ml/1 tsp sesame oil
2 eggs
7.5ml/1½ tsp cornflour (cornstarch)
vegetable oil, for shallow-frying

For the filling

2 green chillies, finely chopped
2 chestnuts, finely chopped
6 garlic cloves, crushed
10ml/2 tsp sesame seeds

1 Cut the block of tofu into 2cm/¾in slices, and then cut each slice in half. Place the tofu slices on a piece of kitchen paper to absorb any excess water.

2 Mix together the Thai fish sauce and sesame oil. Transfer the tofu slices to a plate and coat them evenly with the fish sauce mixture. Leave to marinate for 20 minutes. Meanwhile, put all the filling ingredients into a bowl and combine them thoroughly. Set aside until needed.

3 Beat the egg in a shallow dish. Add the cornflour and whisk until the mixture is well combined. Take the slices of tofu and dip them into the beaten egg mixture, ensuring an even coating on all sides.

4 Place a frying pan over medium heat and add the vegetable oil. Add the tofu slices to the pan and fry, turning over once, until golden brown.

5 Once cooked, make a slit down the middle of each slice with a sharp knife, without cutting all the way through. Gently push a large pinch of the filling into each slice, and serve.

Variation
Alternatively, you could serve the tofu with a light soy dip instead of the spicy filling.

Green Beans with Tofu and Chilli Flakes

Yard-long beans are so-called because they grow to 35cm/14in in length, and more. Look for them in Asian stores and markets, but if you have trouble finding them, you can substitute other green beans in their place.

Serves 4

500g/1¼lb yard-long beans, thinly sliced
200g/7oz silken tofu, cut into cubes
2 shallots, thinly sliced
200ml/7fl oz/scant 1 cup coconut milk
115g/4oz/1 cup roasted peanuts, chopped
juice of 1 lime
10ml/2 tsp palm sugar (jaggery) or light muscovado (brown) sugar
60ml/4 tbsp soy sauce
5ml/1 tsp dried chilli flakes

1 Bring a pan of lightly salted water to the boil. Add the beans and blanch them for 30 seconds.

2 Drain the beans immediately, then refresh under cold running water and drain again, shaking them well to remove as much water as possible. Place in a serving bowl and set aside until needed.

3 Put the tofu and shallots in a pan, then add the coconut milk. Heat gently, stirring constantly, until the tofu begins to crumble.

4 Add the peanuts, lime juice, sugar, soy sauce and chilli flakes to the pan. Heat, stirring frequently, until the sugar has dissolved. Pour the sauce over the prepared beans, toss to combine and serve immediately.

Variation
The sauce also works very well with other vegetables, for example, mangetouts (snow peas). Alternatively, stir in sliced yellow or red (bell) pepper.

Chilli-stuffed Tofu Energy 291kcal/1213kJ; Protein 23g; Carbohydrate 7.8g, of which sugars 1.3g; Fat 19.1g, of which saturates 3.4g; Cholesterol 209mg; Calcium 1014mg; Fibre 0.8g; Sodium 88mg.
Beans with Tofu Energy 263kcal/1091kJ; Protein 14.5g; Carbohydrate 13.3g, of which sugars 10g; Fat 17.2g, of which saturates 3g; Cholesterol 0mg; Calcium 335mg; Fibre 4.7g; Sodium 1353mg.

Tofu and Vegetable Thai Chilli Curry

Traditional Thai ingredients – chillies, galangal, lemon grass and kaffir lime leaves – give this curry a wonderfully fragrant aroma.

Serves 4
175g/6oz firm tofu
45ml/3 tbsp dark soy sauce
15ml/1 tbsp sesame oil
5ml/1 tsp chilli sauce
2.5cm/1in piece fresh root ginger, peeled and finely grated
1 head broccoli, about 225g/8oz
½ head cauliflower, about 225g/8oz
30ml/2 tbsp vegetable oil
1 onion, sliced
400ml/14fl oz/1⅔ cups coconut milk
150ml/¼ pint/⅔ cup water
1 red (bell) pepper, seeded and chopped
175g/6oz/generous 1 cup green beans, halved
115g/4oz shiitake or button (white) mushrooms, halved
shredded spring onions (scallions), to garnish
jasmine rice or noodles, to serve

For the curry paste
2 fresh red or green chillies, seeded and chopped
1 lemon grass stalk, chopped
2.5cm/1in piece fresh galangal, chopped
2 kaffir lime leaves
10ml/2 tsp ground coriander
a few fresh coriander (cilantro) sprigs, including the stalks
45ml/3 tbsp water

1 Rinse and drain the tofu. Using a sharp knife, cut it into 2.5cm/1in cubes. Place the cubes in an ovenproof dish that is large enough to hold them all in a single layer.

2 Mix together the soy sauce, sesame oil, chilli sauce and grated ginger in a jug (pitcher) and pour over the tofu. Toss gently to coat all the cubes evenly, cover with clear film (plastic wrap) and leave to marinate for at least 2 hours or overnight if possible, turning and basting the tofu occasionally.

3 Make the curry paste. Place the chillies, lemon grass, galangal, lime leaves, ground coriander and fresh coriander in a food processor or blender and whizz until well blended. Add the water and process to a thick paste.

4 Preheat the oven to 190°C/375°F/Gas 5. Cut the broccoli and cauliflower into small florets. Cut any stalks into thin slices.

5 Heat the vegetable oil in a frying pan and add the sliced onion. Cook over a low heat for about 8 minutes, until soft and lightly browned. Stir in the curry paste and the coconut milk. Add the water and bring to the boil.

6 Stir in the red pepper, green beans, broccoli and cauliflower. Transfer to a terracotta pot or earthenware casserole. Cover and place towards the bottom of the oven.

7 Stir the tofu and marinade, then place the dish on a shelf near the top of the oven. Cook for 30 minutes. Remove both the dish and the terracotta pot or casserole from the oven. Add the tofu, with any remaining marinade, to the curry, with the mushrooms, and stir well.

8 Return the pot or casserole to the oven, reduce the temperature to 180°C/350°F/Gas 4 and cook for 15 minutes. Garnish with spring onions and serve with the rice or noodles.

Blanched Tofu with Chilli and Soy Dressing

The silky consistency of the tofu absorbs the dark smoky taste of the soy dressing in this rich and flavourful dish. Tofu has a nutty quality that blends agreeably with the salty sweetness of the soy sauce and the hints of garlic, chilli and spring onion. Several flavoured tofus are available, such as smoked tofu, which could also be used in this recipe.

Serves 2
2 blocks firm tofu
salt

For the dressing
10ml/2 tsp finely sliced spring onion (scallion)
5ml/1 tsp finely chopped garlic
60ml/4 tbsp dark soy sauce
10ml/2 tsp chilli powder
5ml/1 tsp sugar
10ml/2 tsp sesame seeds

1 To make the dressing, mix the spring onion and garlic in a bowl with the soy sauce, chilli powder, sugar and sesame seeds. Leave the dressing to stand for a few minutes, allowing the flavours to mingle.

2 Meanwhile, bring a large pan of water to the boil and season with a pinch of salt. Place the whole blocks of tofu in the water, being careful not to let them break apart.

3 Blanch the tofu for 3 minutes. Remove and place on kitchen paper to remove any excess water.

4 Transfer the tofu to a warmed serving plate. Pour the dressing evenly over the plate of tofu. Serve immediately, slicing the tofu as desired.

Cook's Tip
Koreans traditionally eat this dish without slicing the tofu, preferring instead to either eat it directly with a spoon or pick it apart with chopsticks. It may be easier, however, to slice it in advance if you are serving it as an accompanying dish.

Tofu and Vegetable Curry Energy 210kcal/873kJ; Protein 11g; Carbohydrate 13.1g, of which sugars 13.1g; Fat 12g, of which saturates 1.8g; Cholesterol 0mg; Calcium 328mg; Fibre 5g; Sodium 927g.
Blanched Tofu with Dressing Energy 160kcal/669kJ; Protein 16.1g; Carbohydrate 6.7g, of which sugars 5.6g; Fat 7.8g, of which saturates 0.9g; Cholesterol 0mg; Calcium 954mg; Fibre 0.1g; Sodium 2144mg.

Chilli Tofu with Lemon Grass, Basil and Peanuts

This very tasty dish is a wonderful way to cook tofu. In Vietnam, you might find that aromatic pepper leaves are used as the herb element but, because these are quite difficult to find outside South-east Asia, you can use basil leaves. Equally, lime, coriander or curry leaves would work well in this simple stir-fry that can be served on its own with rice or with other vegetable dishes and salads. For the tastiest results, the tofu should be left to marinate for the full hour.

Serves 3 to 4

3 lemon grass stalks, finely chopped
45ml/3 tbsp soy sauce
1–2 red Serrano chillies, seeded and finely chopped
2 garlic cloves, crushed
5ml/1 tsp ground turmeric
10ml/2 tsp sugar
300g/11oz tofu, rinsed, drained, patted dry and cut into bitesize cubes
30ml/2 tbsp groundnut (peanut) oil
45ml/3 tbsp roasted peanuts, roughly chopped
1 bunch fresh basil, stalks removed
salt

1 In a bowl, mix together the lemon grass, soy sauce, chillies, garlic, turmeric and sugar until the sugar has dissolved. Add a little salt to taste then add the tofu, making sure it is well coated. Leave to marinate for 1 hour.

2 Heat a wok or heavy pan. Pour in the oil, and stir in the marinated tofu, turning it frequently to make sure it is evenly cooked. Add the peanuts and most of the basil leaves.

3 Transfer the tofu to a dish, sprinkle with the remaining basil leaves and serve either hot or at room temperature.

Cook's Tip
Serrano chillies are roughly halfway between jalapeño and Thai chillies in terms of heat, measured on the Scoville scale.

Spicy Soft Tofu Stew with Chilli and Mushrooms

A medley of tasty vegetables and a few clams and prawns enhance this piquant stew, in which creamy tofu is fired up by red and green chillies.

Serves 2 to 3

1 block soft tofu
15ml/1 tbsp light soy sauce
6 prawns (shrimp)
6 clams
25g/1oz enoki mushrooms
15ml/1 tbsp vegetable oil
7.5ml/1½ tsp chilli powder
5ml/1 tsp crushed garlic
500ml/17fl oz/generous 2 cups water or beef stock
⅓ leek, sliced
½ red chilli, sliced
½ green chilli, sliced
2.5ml/½ tsp dark soy sauce
1.5ml/¼ tsp Thai fish sauce
salt

1 Break the tofu into small pieces, place in a bowl then marinate with the light soy sauce and a pinch of salt for 1 hour.

2 Hold each prawn between two fingers and gently pull off the tail shell. Twist off the head. Peel away the soft body shell and the small claws beneath. Rinse well. Scrub the clams in cold running water. Discard the caps from the enoki mushrooms.

3 In a flameproof casserole dish or heavy pan, heat the vegetable oil over high heat. Add the chilli powder, garlic and a splash of water. Cook for a few minutes, then add the water or stock and bring to the boil. Add the clams, prawns and tofu, and boil for a further 4 minutes.

4 Reduce the heat slightly and add the sliced leek, red and green chillies and mushrooms. Continue to cook until the leek has softened, then stir in the soy sauce and fish sauce. Season with salt, and serve.

Cook's Tip
To give the dish an extra spicy tang, stir in 50g/2oz chopped kimchi so that the flavours can mingle.

Chilli Tofu Energy 120kcal/500kJ; Protein 3g; Carbohydrate 5g, of which sugars 3g; Fat 10g, of which saturates 2g; Cholesterol 0mg; Calcium 36mg; Fibre 3.3g; Sodium 200mg.
Spicy Soft Tofu Stew Energy 170kcal/709kJ; Protein 21.4g; Carbohydrate 2.1g, of which sugars 1.5g; Fat 8.4g, of which saturates 1.5g; Cholesterol 140mg; Calcium 378mg; Fibre 0.8g; Sodium 734mg.

Crispy Rolls with Pumpkin, Tofu, Peanuts and Chillies

This is one of the best Vietnamese 'do-it-yourself' dishes. You place all the ingredients on the table with the rice wrappers for everyone to assemble their own rolls.

Serves 4 to 5

about 30ml/2 tbsp groundnut (peanut) or sesame oil
175g/6oz tofu, rinsed and patted dry
4 shallots, halved and sliced
2 garlic cloves, finely chopped
350g/12oz pumpkin flesh, cut into strips
1 carrot, cut into strips
15ml/1 tbsp soy sauce
3–4 green Thai chillies, seeded and finely sliced
1 crispy lettuce, torn into strips
1 bunch fresh basil, stalks removed
115g/4oz/⅔ cup roasted peanuts, chopped
100ml/3½fl oz/scant ½ cup hoisin sauce
20 dried rice wrappers
salt
chilli sauce (optional), to serve

1 Heat a heavy pan and smear with oil. Place the tofu in the pan and sear on both sides. Transfer to a plate and cut into thin strips.

2 Heat 30ml/2 tbsp oil in the pan and stir in the shallots and garlic. Add the pumpkin and carrot, then pour in the soy sauce and 120ml/4fl oz/½ cup water. Add a little salt and cook gently until the vegetables have softened but still have a bite to them.

3 Meanwhile, arrange the tofu, chillies, lettuce, basil, peanuts and hoisin sauce in separate dishes and put them on the table. Fill a bowl with hot water and place it on the table or fill a bowl for each person, and place the wrappers beside it. Transfer the vegetable mixture to a dish and place on the table.

4 To eat, dip a wrapper in the water for a few seconds to soften. Lay it flat on the table or on a plate and, just off-centre, spread a few strips of lettuce, then the pumpkin mixture, some tofu, a sprinkling of chillies, some hoisin sauce, some basil leaves and peanuts, to layer the ingredients. Pull the shorter edge (the side with filling on it) over the stack, tuck in the sides and roll into a cylinder. Dip the roll into chilli sauce, if you like.

Sweet and Sour Vegetables with Spicy Tofu

Big, bold and beautiful, this is a hearty stir-fry that will satisfy the hungriest guests. Stir-fries are always a good choice when entertaining as you can prepare the ingredients ahead of time and then they take such a short time to cook.

Serves 4

4 shallots
3 garlic cloves
30ml/2 tbsp groundnut (peanut) oil
250g/9oz Chinese leaves (Chinese cabbage), shredded
8 baby corn cobs, sliced on the diagonal
2 red (bell) peppers, seeded and thinly sliced
200g/7oz/1¾ cups mangetouts (snow peas), trimmed and sliced
250g/9oz tofu, rinsed, drained and cut in 1cm/½in cubes
60ml/4 tbsp vegetable stock
30ml/2 tbsp light soy sauce
15ml/1 tbsp sugar
30ml/2 tbsp rice vinegar
2.5ml/½ tsp dried chilli flakes
small bunch coriander (cilantro), chopped

1 Slice the shallots thinly using a sharp knife and then finely chop the garlic.

2 Heat the oil in a wok or large frying pan and cook the shallots and garlic for 2–3 minutes over a medium heat, until golden. Do not let the garlic burn or it will taste bitter.

3 Add the shredded cabbage to the pan, toss over the heat for 30 seconds, then add the corn cobs and repeat the process.

4 Add the red peppers, mangetouts and tofu in the same way, each time adding a single ingredient then tossing it over the heat for about 30 seconds before adding the next ingredient.

5 Pour the stock and soy sauce into the pan. Mix together the sugar and vinegar in a small bowl, stirring until the sugar has completely dissolved, then add the mixture to the wok or pan. Sprinkle over the chilli flakes and chopped coriander, toss to mix well and serve immediately.

Crispy Rolls Energy 402kcal/1669kJ; Protein 14g; Carbohydrate 29g, of which sugars 13g; Fat 26g, of which saturates 5g; Cholesterol 0mg; Calcium 321mg; Fibre 4.1g; Sodium 0.4g.
Sweet Sour Vegetables Energy 177kcal/736kJ; Protein 10.5g; Carbohydrate 13.7g, of which sugars 12.5g; Fat 9.2g, of which saturates 1.5g; Cholesterol 0mg; Calcium 461mg; Fibre 4.3g; Sodium 844mg.

Aubergines and Peppers Stuffed with Lamb and Chillies

Aubergines and sweet peppers are stuffed with an aromatic lamb filling.

Serves 6

3 small aubergines (eggplants)
1 each red, green and yellow (bell) peppers
boiled rice, to serve

For the stuffing

45ml/3 tbsp corn oil
3 medium onions, sliced
5ml/1 tsp chilli powder
1.5ml/¼ tsp ground turmeric
5ml/1 tsp ground coriander
5ml/1 tsp ground cumin
5ml/1 tsp crushed ginger
5ml/1 tsp crushed garlic
5ml/1 tsp salt
450g/1lb minced (ground) lamb
3 fresh green chillies, chopped
30ml/2 tbsp chopped fresh coriander (cilantro)

For the fried onions

45ml/3 tbsp corn oil
5ml/1 tsp mixed onion, mustard, fenugreek and white cumin seeds
4 dried red chillies
3 medium onions, roughly chopped
5ml/1 tsp salt
5ml/1 tsp chilli powder
2 medium tomatoes, sliced
2 fresh green chillies, chopped
30ml/2 tbsp chopped fresh coriander (cilantro)

1 Prepare the vegetables. Slit the aubergines lengthways; keep the stalks intact. Cut the tops off the peppers and remove the seeds. Retain the pepper tops for lids once stuffed, if you like.

2 For the stuffing, heat the oil and fry the onions for a few minutes. Add the chilli powder, turmeric, coriander, cumin, ginger, garlic and salt, and stir-fry for 1 minute. Add the lamb and stir-fry for 10 minutes. Add the chillies and coriander towards the end.

3 Make the onions. Heat the oil in a large frying pan. Add the mixed seeds and the dried chillies, and fry for a minute. Stir in the onions and fry for 2 minutes. Add the salt, chilli powder, tomatoes, chillies and coriander. Cook for 1 minute, then set aside.

4 Fill the vegetables with the meat mixture. Place on top of the onions in the pan. Cover with foil and cook over a low heat for about 15 minutes until tender. Serve with plain boiled rice.

Aubergine and Chilli Curry

A simple and deliciously spicy way of cooking aubergines, which retains their full flavour.

Serves 4

2 large aubergines, about 450g/1lb each
45ml/3 tbsp vegetable oil
2.5ml/½ tsp black mustard seeds
1 bunch spring onions (scallions), finely chopped
115g/4oz button (white) mushrooms, halved
2 garlic cloves, crushed
1 red chilli, seeded and finely chopped
2.5ml/½ tsp chilli powder
5ml/1 tsp ground cumin
5ml/1 tsp ground coriander
1.5ml/¼ tsp ground turmeric
5ml/1 tsp salt
400g/14oz can chopped tomatoes
15ml/1 tbsp chopped fresh coriander (cilantro), plus fresh coriander (cilantro) sprig, to garnish

1 Preheat the oven to 200°C/400°F/Gas 6. Brush both of the aubergines with 15ml/1 tbsp of the oil and prick all over with a fork. Bake in the oven for about 30–35 minutes, until the aubergines are tender.

2 Meanwhile, heat the remaining oil in a pan and fry the mustard seeds for 2 minutes until they begin to splutter. Add the onions, mushrooms, garlic and chilli and fry for 5 minutes. Stir in the chilli powder, cumin, coriander, turmeric and salt and fry for 3–4 minutes. Add the tomatoes and simmer for about 5 minutes.

3 Cut each of the aubergines in half lengthways and scoop out the soft flesh into a bowl. Mash the flesh briefly.

4 Add the mashed aubergines and fresh coriander to the pan. Bring to the boil and simmer for 5 minutes, or until the sauce thickens. Serve, garnished with a fresh coriander sprig.

Cook's Tip

If you want to reduce the amount of oil in this recipe, you can wrap the aubergines in foil and bake in the oven for 1 hour.

Stuffed vegetables Energy 346kcal/1441kJ; Protein 19.6g; Carbohydrate 20.2g, of which sugars 15.1g; Fat 21.5g, of which saturates 5.6g; Cholesterol 57mg; Calcium 69mg; Fibre 5.4g; Sodium 81mg.
Aubergine and Chilli Curry Energy 84kcal/359kJ; Protein 5.5g; Carbohydrate 11.8g, of which sugars 11g; Fat 2.2g, of which saturates 0.5g; Cholesterol 0mg; Calcium 62mg; Fibre 9.1g; Sodium 21mg.

Courgette Spicy Curry

This is an excellent to spice up an everyday vegetable. The courgettes are thickly sliced and then combined with authentic Indian spices for a delicious, colourful vegetable curry.

Serves 4

675g/1½lb courgettes (zucchini)
45ml/3 tbsp vegetable oil
2.5ml/½ tsp cumin seeds
2.5ml/½ tsp mustard seeds
1 onion, thinly sliced
2 garlic cloves, crushed
1.5ml/¼ tsp ground turmeric
1.5ml/¼ tsp chilli powder
5ml/1 tsp ground coriander
5ml/1 tsp ground cumin
2.5ml/½ tsp salt
15ml/1 tbsp tomato purée (paste)
400g/14oz can chopped tomatoes
150ml/¼ pint/⅔ cup water
15ml/1 tbsp chopped fresh coriander (cilantro)
5ml/1 tsp garam masala

1 Trim the ends from the courgettes, then cut them into 1cm/½in thick slices.

2 Heat the oil in a wok or large pan and fry the cumin with the mustard seeds for 2 minutes until they begin to splutter and release their fragrances.

3 Add the onion and garlic to the pan and fry for about 5–6 minutes until the onion begins to soften.

4 Add the ground turmeric, chilli powder, coriander, cumin and salt and fry for about 2–3 minutes, stirring constantly.

5 Add the sliced courgettes to the pan all at once, and cook for about 5 minutes.

6 Mix together the tomato purée and chopped tomatoes in a bowl and add to the pan with the water. Mix well until all the ingredients are well combined. Cover the pan and simmer for 10 minutes until the sauce thickens.

7 Stir in the fresh coriander and the garam masala, then cook for 5 minutes or until the courgettes are tender. Transfer to a serving dish and serve immediately.

Shredded Cabbage with Chilli and Cumin

This cabbage dish is only lightly spiced and is a good accompaniment to many other dishes, or it will make a great main dish for a lunch or a mid-week dinner.

Serves 4

15ml/1 tbsp corn oil
50g/2oz/4 tbsp butter
2.5ml/½ tsp coriander seeds, crushed
2.5ml/½ tsp white cumin seeds
6 dried red chillies
1 small Savoy cabbage, shredded
12 mangetouts (snow peas)
3 fresh red chillies, seeded and sliced
12 baby corn cobs
salt, to taste
25g/1oz/¼ cup flaked (sliced) almonds, toasted
5ml/1 tbsp chopped fresh coriander (cilantro)

1 Heat the oil and butter in a wok or a large, heavy frying pan and add the crushed coriander seeds, white cumin seeds and dried red chillies. Stir-fry for 1–2 minutes until the spices release their fragrances.

2 Add the shredded cabbage and the mangetouts to the pan and fry, stirring constantly, for about 5 minutes, until the vegetables are just tender.

3 Finally add the fresh red chillies, baby corn cobs and salt, and fry for a further 3 minutes.

4 Garnish with the toasted almonds and fresh coriander, and serve immediately.

Variations

• *Lots of other vegetables will work equally as well in this dish. If mangetouts are out of season, you could replace them with any other green beans. Or try adding some bell peppers in place of the baby corn cobs.*

• *If you prefer a little more heat, you can keep the seeds in the chillies or increase the amount of chillies used.*

Courgette Curry Energy 161kcal/666kJ; Protein 5.8g; Carbohydrate 11g, of which sugars 6.5g; Fat 10.9g, of which saturates 1.5g; Cholesterol 0mg; Calcium 73mg; Fibre 2.6g; Sodium 24mg.
Shredded Cabbage Energy 230kcal/952kJ; Protein 6.2g; Carbohydrate 11.3g, of which sugars 7.1g; Fat 18.2g, of which saturates 7.3g; Cholesterol 27mg; Calcium 104mg; Fibre 3.8g; Sodium 416mg.

Vegetable Curry with Ginger and Chilli

This is a delicious vegetable curry, in which fresh mixed vegetables are cooked in a spicy, aromatic yogurt sauce.

Serves 4

10ml/2 tsp cumin seeds
8 black peppercorns
2 green cardamom pods, seeds only
5cm/2in cinnamon stick
2.5ml/½ tsp grated nutmeg
45ml/3 tbsp vegetable oil
1 green chilli, chopped
2.5cm/1in piece fresh root ginger, grated
5ml/1 tsp chilli powder
2.5ml/½ tsp salt
2 large potatoes, cut into 2.5cm/1in chunks
225g/8oz cauliflower, broken into florets
225g/8oz okra, thickly sliced
150ml/¼ pint/⅔ cup natural (plain) yogurt
150ml/¼ pint/⅔ cup vegetable stock
toasted flaked (sliced) almonds and fresh coriander (cilantro) sprigs, to garnish

1 Grind the cumin seeds, peppercorns, cardamom seeds, cinnamon stick and nutmeg to a fine powder using a blender or a mortar and pestle.

2 Heat the oil in a large pan and fry the chilli and ginger for about 2 minutes, stirring all the time.

3 Add the chilli powder, salt and ground spice mixture and fry for about 2–3 minutes, stirring all the time to prevent the spices from sticking.

4 Stir in the potatoes, cover, and cook for 10 minutes over a low heat, stirring occasionally.

5 Add the cauliflower and okra to the pan and mix well. Cook for about 5 minutes.

6 Add the yogurt and stock. Bring to the boil, then reduce the heat. Cover and simmer for 20 minutes, or until all the vegetables are tender. Garnish with toasted almonds and coriander sprigs, and serve immediately.

Spicy Spinach Dhal

There are many different types of dhals eaten in India, with each region having its own speciality. This is a delicious, lightly spiced dish with a mild nutty flavour from the lentils, which combine beautifully with the spinach. Serve as a main meal with rice and breads or with a meat dish.

Serves 4

175g/6oz/1 cup chana dhal or yellow split peas
175ml/6fl oz/¾ cup water
30ml/2 tbsp vegetable oil
1.5ml/¼ tsp black mustard seeds
1 onion, thinly sliced
2 garlic cloves, crushed
2.5cm/1in piece fresh root ginger, grated
1 red chilli, seeded and finely chopped
275g/10oz frozen spinach, thawed
1.5ml/¼ tsp chilli powder
2.5ml/½ tsp ground coriander
2.5ml/½ tsp garam masala
2.5ml/½ tsp salt

1 Wash the chana dhal or split peas in several changes of cold water, carefully picking through it to remove any stones. Place in a bowl and cover with plenty of cold water. Leave to soak for 30 minutes.

2 Drain the chana dhal or split peas and place in a large pan with the measured water. Bring to the boil, cover the pan, and simmer for about 20–25 minutes, or until the dhal or peas are soft and tender.

3 Meanwhile, heat the oil in a wok or large frying pan and fry the mustard seeds for 2 minutes until they begin to splutter.

4 Add the onion, garlic, ginger and chilli to the pan and fry for 5–6 minutes, stirring constantly. Add the spinach and cook for about 10 minutes, or until the spinach is dry and the liquid has been absorbed.

5 Stir in the chilli powder, coriander, garam masala and salt and cook for a further 2–3 minutes.

6 Drain the chana dhal or split peas, add to the spinach mixture and cook for about 5 minutes. Serve immediately.

Vegetable Curry Energy 238kcal/996kJ; Protein 9.1g; Carbohydrate 26.7g, of which sugars 6.9g; Fat 11.6g, of which saturates 1.8g; Cholesterol 1mg; Calcium 202mg; Fibre 4.3g; Sodium 56mg.
Spicy Spinach Dhal Energy 226kcal/949kJ; Protein 13.3g; Carbohydrate 28.7g, of which sugars 2.9g; Fat 7.3g, of which saturates 0.9g; Cholesterol 0mg; Calcium 152mg; Fibre 3.8g; Sodium 114mg.

Curried Kidney Beans with Chilli

This a very popular Punjabi-style dish using red kidney beans, but you can substitute the same quantity of other beans, if you prefer, such as butter beans or black-eyed beans.

Serves 4

225g/8oz dried red kidney beans
30ml/2 tbsp vegetable oil
2.5ml/½ tsp cumin seeds
1 onion, thinly sliced
1 green chilli, finely chopped
2 garlic cloves, crushed
2.5cm/1in piece fresh root ginger, grated
30ml/2 tbsp curry paste
5ml/1 tsp ground cumin
5ml/1 tsp ground coriander
2.5ml/½ tsp chilli powder
2.5ml/½ tsp salt
400g/14oz can chopped tomatoes
30ml/2 tbsp chopped fresh coriander (cilantro)

1 Place the kidney beans in a large bowl of cold water, then leave them to soak overnight.

2 Drain the beans and place in a large pan with double the volume of water. Boil vigorously for 10 minutes. Skim off any scum from the surface of the water. Cover the pan and cook for about 1–1½ hours, or until the beans are soft.

3 Meanwhile, heat the oil in a large frying pan and fry the cumin seeds for 2 minutes until they begin to splutter. Add the onion, chilli, garlic and ginger and fry for 5 minutes. Stir in the curry paste, cumin, coriander, chilli powder and salt and cook for 5 minutes.

4 Add the tomatoes and simmer for about 5 minutes. Add the beans and fresh coriander to the pan, reserving a little coriander for the garnish. Cover and cook for 15 minutes, adding a little water if necessary. Serve immediately, garnished with the reserved coriander.

Cook's Tip
If you want to reduce the cooking time, cook the beans in a pressure cooker for 20–25 minutes.

Yellow Lentils with Courgettes and Green Chillies

Spicy dhal dishes are often runny but this one provides texture with the addition of the courgettes.

Serves 4 to 6

175g/6oz moong dhal
2.5ml/½ tsp ground turmeric
300ml/½ pint/1¼ cups water
60ml/4 tbsp vegetable oil
1 large onion, finely sliced
2 garlic cloves, crushed
2 green chillies, chopped
2.5ml/½ tsp mustard seeds
2.5ml/½ tsp cumin seeds
1.5ml/¼ tsp asafoetida
a few coriander (cilantro) and mint leaves, chopped
6–8 curry leaves
2.5ml/½ tsp sugar
200g/7oz can chopped tomatoes
225g/8oz courgettes (zucchini), cut into small pieces
60ml/4 tbsp lemon juice
salt, to taste

1 In a pan, boil the moong dhal and turmeric in the water and then simmer until the dhal is cooked but not mushy. Drain and reserve both the liquid and the dhal.

2 Heat the oil in a wok or frying pan and fry the onion for about 3–4 minutes, until it has softened. Add the garlic, chillies, spice seeds and asafoetida, and fry for a few minutes.

3 Add the coriander, mint and curry leaves, sugar, tomatoes and courgettes. Cover and cook until the courgettes are tender but still crunchy.

4 Stir in the dhal and the lemon juice. If the dish is dry, add a little of the reserved water. Reheat and serve immediately.

Cook's Tip
Asafoetida is a pungent spice obtained from the resin of a fennel-like plant. It has a very strong odour of garlic and onion and should only be used sparingly. Its pungency may seem too much at first, but it will reduce somewhat while cooking, and does add a deep onion flavour to the dish.

Curried Beans Energy 274kcal/1155kJ; Protein 15.9g; Carbohydrate 34.5g, of which sugars 4.7g; Fat 9.2g, of which saturates 1.1g; Cholesterol 0mg; Calcium 168mg; Fibre 12.8g; Sodium 76mg.
Yellow Lentils with Courgettes Energy 210kcal/878kJ; Protein 9.4g; Carbohydrate 25.1g, of which sugars 6.1g; Fat 8.7g, of which saturates 1.1g; Cholesterol 0mg; Calcium 52mg; Fibre 3g; Sodium 18mg.

Madras Sambal with Chilli and Spices

There are many variations of this dish but it is regularly cooked in one form or another in many Indian homes and served as part of a meal. You can use any combination of vegetables that are in season.

Serves 4

225g/8 oz/1 cup toovar dhal or red split lentils
600ml/1 pint/2½ cups water
2.5ml/½ tsp ground turmeric
2 large potatoes, cut into 2.5cm/1in chunks
30ml/2 tbsp vegetable oil
2.5ml/½ tsp black mustard seeds
1.5ml/¼ tsp fenugreek seeds
4 curry leaves
1 onion, thinly sliced
115g/4oz green beans, cut into 2.5cm/1in lengths
5ml/1 tsp salt
2.5ml/½ tsp chilli powder
15ml/1 tbsp lemon juice
60ml/4 tbsp desiccated (dry unsweetened shredded) coconut
toasted coconut, to garnish

1 Wash the toovar dhal or lentils in several changes of water, picking through to remove any stones. Place in a heavy pan with the water and the turmeric. Cover and simmer for about 30–35 minutes, until the lentils are soft.

2 Par-boil the potatoes in a large pan of boiling water for about 10 minutes until they are just tender. Drain well and set aside.

3 Heat the oil in a large frying pan and fry the mustard seeds, fenugreek seeds and curry leaves for 2–3 minutes, stirring constantly, until the seeds begin to splutter.

4 Add the onion and the green beans to the pan and fry for 7–8 minutes. Add the potatoes and cook, stirring, for a further 2 minutes.

5 Stir in the lentils with the salt, chilli powder and lemon juice and simmer for 2 minutes. Stir in the coconut and simmer for about 5 minutes, until the vegetables are tender. Garnish with toasted coconut and serve immediately.

Spicy Mung Beans with Potatoes

Mung beans are one of the quicker-cooking pulses which do not require soaking and are therefore very easy to use. In this recipe they are cooked with potatoes and traditional Indian spices to give a tasty, nutritious dish.

Serves 4

175g/6oz/1 cup mung beans
750ml/1¼ pints/3 cups water
225g/8oz potatoes, cut into 2cm/¾in chunks
30ml/2 tbsp vegetable oil
2.5ml/½ tsp cumin seeds
1 green chilli, finely chopped
1 garlic clove, crushed
2.5cm/1in piece fresh root ginger, finely chopped
1.5ml/¼ tsp ground turmeric
2.5ml/½ tsp chilli powder
5ml/1 tsp salt
5ml/1 tsp sugar
4 curry leaves
5 tomatoes, skinned and finely chopped
15ml/1 tbsp tomato purée (paste)
curry leaves, to garnish
plain rice, to serve

1 Wash the beans. Bring to the boil in a large pan with the measured water. Cover the pan, reduce the heat and simmer until the beans are soft, about 30 minutes.

2 In a separate pan, par-boil the potatoes for about 10 minutes until just tender, then drain well.

3 Heat the oil in a wok or frying pan and fry the cumin seeds until they start to splutter.

4 Add the chilli, garlic and ginger to the pan and fry, stirring constantly, for 3–4 minutes until fragrant. Be careful not to let the garlic burn or it will taste bitter.

5 Add the turmeric, chilli powder, salt and sugar and cook for about 2 minutes, stirring constantly to prevent the mixture from sticking to the pan.

6 Add the curry leaves, tomatoes and tomato purée to the pan, mix well and simmer for 5 minutes until the sauce thickens. Add the tomato sauce and potatoes to the mung beans and mix together. Serve immediately with plain boiled rice, and garnish with the curry leaves.

Madras Sambal Energy 401kcal/1687kJ; Protein 16.7g; Carbohydrate 50.8g, of which sugars 5.1g; Fat 16g, of which saturates 8.9g; Cholesterol 0mg; Calcium 52mg; Fibre 6.7g; Sodium 36mg.
Spicy Mung Beans Energy 265kcal/1118kJ; Protein 13.8g; Carbohydrate 37.4g, of which sugars 5.7g; Fat 7.9g, of which saturates 1.1g; Cholesterol 0mg; Calcium 58mg; Fibre 5.8g; Sodium 34mg.

Chickpea Masala with Chillies

Chickpeas are used and cooked in a variety of ways all over India. Tamarind gives this dish a deliciously sharp, tangy flavour, and the chillies add a satisfying kick.

Serves 4

225g/8oz/1¼ cups dried chickpeas
50g/2oz tamarind pulp
120ml/4fl oz/½ cup boiling water
45ml/3 tbsp vegetable oil
2.5ml/½ tsp cumin seeds
1 onion, finely chopped
2 garlic cloves, crushed
2.5cm/1in piece fresh root ginger, grated
1 green chilli, seeded and finely chopped
5ml/1 tsp ground cumin
5ml/1 tsp ground coriander
1.5ml/¼ tsp ground turmeric
2.5ml/½ tsp salt
225g/8oz tomatoes, skinned and finely chopped
2.5ml/½ tsp garam masala
chopped chillies and chopped onion, to garnish

1 Put the chickpeas in a large bowl and cover with plenty of cold water. Leave to soak overnight.

2 Drain the chickpeas and place in a large pan with double the volume of cold water. Bring to the boil and boil vigorously for 10 minutes. Skim off any scum from the surface. Cover the pan, reduce the heat and simmer for about 1½–2 hours, or until the chickpeas are soft.

3 Meanwhile, break up the tamarind and soak in the boiling water for about 15 minutes. Rub the tamarind through a sieve (strainer) into a bowl, discarding any stones and fibre.

4 Heat the oil in a large pan and fry the cumin seeds for about 2 minutes until they start to splutter. Add the onion, garlic, ginger and chilli and fry for 5 minutes.

5 Add the cumin, coriander, turmeric and salt and fry for about 3–4 minutes. Add the tomatoes and tamarind pulp. Bring to the boil and simmer for 5 minutes.

6 Add the chickpeas and garam masala. Cover and simmer for about 15 minutes. Garnish with chopped chillies and onion.

Mixed Bean Curry with Green Chillies

You can use any combination of beans that you have available for this spicy recipe.

Serves 4

50g/2oz/⅓ cup red kidney beans
50g/2oz/⅓ cup black-eyed beans (peas)
50g/2oz/⅓ cup haricot (navy) beans
50g/2oz/⅓ cup flageolet or cannellini beans
30ml/2 tbsp vegetable oil
5ml/1 tsp cumin seeds
5ml/1 tsp black mustard seeds
1 onion, finely chopped
2 garlic cloves, crushed
2.5cm/1in piece fresh root ginger, grated
2 green chillies, finely chopped
30ml/2 tbsp curry paste
2.5ml/½ tsp salt
400g/14oz can chopped tomatoes
30ml/2 tbsp tomato purée (paste)
250ml/8fl oz/1 cup water
30ml/2 tbsp chopped fresh coriander (cilantro), plus extra, to garnish

1 Put the beans in a large bowl and cover with plenty of cold water. Leave to soak overnight, mixing occasionally.

2 Drain the beans and put into a large heavy pan with double the volume of cold water. Boil vigorously for 10 minutes. Skim off any scum. Cover and simmer for 1¼ hours, or until the beans are soft.

3 Heat the oil in a large pan and fry the cumin seeds and mustard seeds for 2 minutes until the seeds begin to splutter. Add the onion, garlic, ginger and chilli and fry for 5 minutes.

4 Add the curry paste and fry for a further 2–3 minutes, stirring, then add the salt.

5 Add the tomatoes, tomato purée and the water, mix well and simmer for 5 minutes.

6 Add the drained beans and the coriander. Cover and simmer for 30–40 minutes until the sauce thickens and the beans are cooked. Garnish with fresh coriander and serve immediately.

Chickpea Masala Energy 298kcal/1252kJ; Protein 14g; Carbohydrate 34.3g, of which sugars 4.1g; Fat 12.8g, of which saturates 1.5g; Cholesterol 0mg; Calcium 116mg; Fibre 6.8g; Sodium 286mg.
Mixed Bean Curry Energy 239kcal/1007kJ; Protein 13.7g; Carbohydrate 30.2g, of which sugars 5.4g; Fat 8g, of which saturates 1g; Cholesterol 0mg; Calcium 105mg; Fibre 10.2g; Sodium 61mg.

Balti Corn with Cauliflower and Chilli

This quick, tasty and nutritious vegetable dish is a great side dish to serve with a more substantial curry. It will also make a delicious main course if served with plain boiled rice, a dhal-based dish or simply with some Indian bread such as naan, chapati or paratha.

Serves 4

30ml/2 tbsp corn oil
4 curry leaves
1.5ml/¼ tsp onion seeds
2 medium onions, diced
1 red chilli, seeded and chopped
175g/6oz frozen corn
½ small cauliflower, cut into small florets
3–7 mint leaves

1 Heat the oil in a wok or large frying pan. Add the curry leaves and the onion seeds and cook, stirring constantly, for about 30 seconds.

2 Add the onions to the pan and fry them for 5–8 minutes until golden brown.

3 Add the chilli, corn and cauliflower to the pan and cook, stirring frequently, for 5–8 minutes.

4 Finally, add the mint leaves and heat for 2–3 minutes until the vegetables are tender. Serve immediately.

Variation
Using frozen corn means this dish is very quick and simple to prepare, but, if you prefer, use fresh corn that has been sliced from a couple of cooked cobs.

Cook's Tip
It is best to cook this dish immediately before you are ready to serve and eat, as the flavours tend to diminish if it is kept warm for too long.

Balti Stir-fried Vegetables with Chilli and Cashew Nuts

This versatile stir-fry will accommodate most other combinations of vegetables – you do not have to use the selection suggested here.

Serves 4

2 medium carrots
1 medium red (bell) pepper, seeded
1 medium green (bell) pepper, seeded
2 courgettes (zucchini)
115g/4oz green beans, halved
1 medium bunch spring onions (scallions)
15ml/1 tbsp extra virgin olive oil
4–6 curry leaves
2.5ml/½ tsp white cumin seeds
4 dried red chillies
10–12 cashew nuts
5ml/1 tsp salt
30ml/2 tbsp lemon juice
fresh mint leaves, to garnish

1 Prepare the vegetables. Cut the carrots, peppers and courgettes into matchsticks, keeping all the slices an even size so they cook in the same time. Cut the green beans in halves and finely chop the spring onions. Set aside.

2 Heat the oil in a wok or frying pan. Fry the curry leaves, cumin seeds and dried chillies for about 1 minute, stirring constantly, until the seeds start to splutter and the fragrances are released from the spices.

3 Add the vegetables and nuts to the pan and stir them around gently for 3–5 minutes until just beginning to soften. Add the salt and lemon juice. Continue to stir and cook for about 3–5 minutes.

4 Transfer to a serving dish and serve immediately, garnished with the mint leaves.

Cook's Tip
If you are very short of time, use frozen mixed vegetables, which also work well in this dish. Use vegetables that freeze well such as corn, peas and green beans.

Balti Corn with Cauliflower and Chilli Energy 124kcals/519kJ; Protein 4.g; Carbohydrate 19g, of which sugars 4g; Fat 4g, of which saturates 1 g; Cholesterol 0mg; Fibre 3g; Sodium 120mg.
Balti Vegetables Energy 89kcals/371kJ; Protein 3g; Carbohydrate 9g, of which sugars 8g; Fat 5g, of which saturates 1g; Cholesterol 0mg; Calcium 46mg; Fibre 3.1g; Sodium 500mg.

Yellow Lentils with Chilli and Tomato

Toor dhal has a wonderfully rich texture, which is best appreciated if served with plain boiled rice. Fresh fenugreek leaves, which are available from Asian grocers, impart a stunning aroma.

Serves 4

115g/4oz toor dhal
45ml/3 tbsp corn oil
1.5ml/¼ tsp onion seeds
1 medium bunch spring onions (scallions), roughly chopped
5ml/1 tsp crushed garlic
1.5ml/¼ tsp ground turmeric
7.5ml/1½ tsp crushed ginger
5ml/1 tsp chilli powder
30ml/2 tbsp fresh fenugreek leaves
5ml/1 tsp salt
150ml/¼ pint/⅔ cup water
6–8 cherry tomatoes
30ml/2 tbsp fresh coriander (cilantro) leaves
½ green (bell) pepper, seeded and sliced
15ml/1 tbsp lemon juice
shredded spring onion (scallion) tops and fresh coriander (cilantro) leaves, to garnish

1 Cook the dhal in boiling water until it is soft and mushy. Set aside.

2 Heat the oil with the onion seeds in a non-stick wok or frying pan for a few seconds until hot. Add the dhal to the wok or frying pan and stir-fry for about 3 minutes.

3 Add the spring onions followed by the garlic, turmeric, ginger, chilli powder, fenugreek leaves and salt and continue to stir-fry for 5–7 minutes.

4 Pour in enough water to loosen the mixture. Add the cherry tomatoes, coriander, green pepper and lemon juice. Serve garnished with shredded onion tops and coriander leaves.

Cook's Tip

Any remaining fresh fenugreek leaves can be frozen in a plastic bag. Use spinach if you cannot get fenugreek.

Chickpea, Sweet Potato and Aubergine Chilli Dhal

Spicy and delicious – this is a great dish to serve when you want a meal that is nutritious and aromatic.

Serves 3 to 4

45ml/3 tbsp olive oil
1 red onion, chopped
3 garlic cloves, crushed
115g/4oz sweet potatoes, peeled and diced
3 garden eggs or 1 large aubergine (eggplant), diced
425g/15oz can chickpeas, drained
5ml/1 tsp dried tarragon
2.5ml/½ tsp dried thyme
5ml/1 tsp ground cumin
5ml/1 tsp ground turmeric
2.5ml/½ tsp ground allspice
5 canned plum tomatoes, chopped with 60ml/4 tbsp reserved juice
6 ready-to-eat dried apricots
600ml/1 pint/2½ cups well-flavoured vegetable stock
1 green chilli, seeded and finely chopped
30ml/2 tbsp chopped fresh coriander (cilantro)
salt and ground black pepper

1 Heat the olive oil in a large pan. Add the onion, garlic and potatoes and cook until the onion has softened.

2 Stir in the garden eggs or aubergine, then add the chickpeas and the herbs and spices. Stir well to mix and cook over a gentle heat for a few minutes.

3 Add the tomatoes and their juice, the apricots, stock, chilli and seasoning. Stir well, bring to the boil and cook for 15 minutes.

4 When the sweet potatoes are tender, add the coriander, stir, taste, and adjust the seasoning if necessary. Serve immediately.

Cook's Tip

Garden egg is a small variety of aubergine used in West Africa. It is round and white, which may explain its other name – eggplant. You can peel the aubergine for this dish, if you prefer, but it is not necessary. Either white or orange sweet potatoes can be used and you can add less chickpeas, if you wish.

Yellow Lentils Energy 192kcal/806kJ; Protein 8.2g; Carbohydrate 20.2g, of which sugars 3.3g; Fat 9.4g, of which saturates 1.4g; Cholesterol 0mg; Calcium 34mg; Fibre 2.3g; Sodium 16mg.
Chickpea Dhal Energy 322kcal/1356kJ; Protein 12g; Carbohydrate 41.6g, of which sugars 16.6g; Fat 13.5g, of which saturates 1.7g; Cholesterol 0mg; Calcium 107mg; Fibre 9.3g; Sodium 260mg.

Spiced Potatoes and Tomatoes

Diced potatoes are cooked gently in a fresh and spicy tomato sauce, which is flavoured with curry leaves and green chillies.

Serves 4

2 medium potatoes
15ml/1 tbsp olive oil
2 medium onions, finely chopped
4 curry leaves
1.5ml/¼ tsp onion seeds
1 green chilli, seeded and chopped
4 tomatoes, sliced
5ml/1 tsp crushed ginger
5ml/1 tsp crushed garlic
5ml/1 tsp chilli powder
5ml/1 tsp ground coriander
5ml/1 tsp lemon juice
15ml/1 tbsp chopped fresh coriander (cilantro)
salt
3 hard-boiled eggs, to garnish

1 Peel the potatoes and cut into bitesize cubes. Try to keep them to a uniform size so they cook at the same time.

2 Heat the oil in a non-stick wok or frying pan over a medium heat. Fry the onions, curry leaves, onion seeds and green chilli for about 2–3 minutes, until the seeds start to splutter and the onions are softened slightly.

3 Add the tomato slices to the pan and continue to cook for about 3 minutes over a low heat, stirring occasionally, until the tomatoes are just heated through.

4 Add the ginger, garlic, chilli powder and ground coriander to the pan, mixing well. Add salt to the mixture and taste the sauce, adding more salt if necessary. Continue to cook, stirring constantly, for about 1–2 minutes.

5 Add the potatoes to the pan. Cover the pan and continue to cook over a low heat, stirring occasionally, for 8–10 minutes until the potatoes are tender.

6 Add the lemon juice and the fresh coriander and stir well to mix together.

7 Shell the hard-boiled eggs, cut into quarters and add as a garnish to the finished dish. Serve immediately.

Red Bean Chilli

This vegetarian chilli can be adapted to accommodate meat eaters by adding either minced beef or lamb in place of the lentils. Add the meat once the onions are soft and fry until nicely browned before adding the tomatoes.

Serves 4

30ml/2 tbsp vegetable oil
1 onion, chopped
400g/14oz can chopped tomatoes
2 garlic cloves, crushed
300ml/½ pint/1¼ cups white wine
about 300ml/½ pint/1¼ cups vegetable stock
115g/4oz red lentils
2 thyme sprigs or 5ml/1 tsp dried thyme
10ml/2 tsp ground cumin
45ml/3 tbsp dark soy sauce
½ hot chilli pepper, finely chopped
5ml/1 tsp mixed spice
15ml/1 tbsp oyster sauce (optional)
225g/8oz can red kidney beans, drained
10ml/2 tsp sugar
salt
boiled rice and corn, to serve

1 Heat the oil in a large pan and fry the onion over a moderate heat for a few minutes until slightly softened.

2 Add the tomatoes and garlic, cook for 10 minutes, then stir in the wine and stock.

3 Add the lentils, thyme, cumin, soy sauce, hot pepper, mixed spice and oyster sauce, if using.

4 Cover and simmer for 40 minutes, or until the lentils are soft, stirring occasionally and adding water if the lentils dry out.

5 Stir in the kidney beans and sugar and continue cooking for 10 minutes, adding a little extra stock or water if necessary. Season to taste with salt and serve hot with boiled rice and corn.

Cook's Tip

Fiery chillies can irritate the skin, so always wash your hands well after handling them and take care not to touch your eyes. If you like really hot, spicy food, then include the seeds from the chilli in this dish.

Spiced Potatoes and Tomatoes Energy 188kcals/790kJ; Protein 8.54g; Fat 7.62g; Saturated Fat 1.66g; Carbohydrate 23.40g; Fibre 3.10g; Added Sugar 0.01g; Salt 570mg.
Red Bean Chilli Energy 240kcal/1011kJ Protein 13g; Carbohydrate 35g; of which sugars 10g; Fat 7g; of which saturates 1g; Cholesterol 0mg; Calcium 79mg; Fibre 5.4g; Sodium 1200mg.

Chilli Bean Loaf

This recipe is a vegetarian dish using delicious flavours, such as pickled ginger, which is available at Asian stores.

Serves 4

225g/8oz/1¼ cups red kidney beans, soaked overnight
15g/½oz/1 tbsp butter or margarine
1 onion, finely chopped
2 garlic cloves, crushed
½ red (bell) pepper, seeded and chopped
½ green (bell) pepper, seeded and chopped
1 green chilli, seeded and finely chopped
5ml/1 tsp mixed herbs
2 eggs
15ml/1 tbsp lemon juice
75ml/5 tbsp gari (pickled ginger)
salt and ground black pepper

1 Drain the kidney beans, then place in a pan, cover with water and boil rapidly for 15 minutes. Reduce the heat and continue boiling for about 1 hour, until the beans are tender, adding more water if needed. Drain, reserving the cooking liquid. Preheat the oven to 190°C/375°F/Gas 5 and grease a 900g/2lb loaf tin (pan).

2 Melt the butter or margarine in a large frying pan and fry the onion, garlic and peppers for 5 minutes, then add the chilli, mixed herbs and a little salt and pepper.

3 Place the cooked kidney beans in a large bowl or in a food processor and mash or process to a pulp. Add the onion and pepper mixture and stir well. Cool slightly, then stir in the eggs and lemon juice.

4 Place the gari in a separate bowl and sprinkle generously with warm water. The gari should become soft and fluffy after about 5 minutes.

5 Pour the gari into the bean and onion mixture and stir together thoroughly. If the consistency is too stiff, add a little of the bean liquid. Spoon the mixture into the prepared loaf tin and bake in the oven for 35–45 minutes, until firm to the touch.

6 Cool the loaf in the tin and then turn out on to a plate. Cut into thick slices and serve immediately.

Vegetables in Spicy Peanut Sauce

This nutritious and aromatic dish is quick and easy to prepare, ideal for when you want a little spice for a mid-week dinner.

Serves 4

15ml/1 tbsp palm or vegetable oil
1 onion, chopped
2 garlic cloves, crushed
400g/14oz can chopped tomatoes, puréed
45ml/3 tbsp smooth peanut butter, preferably unsalted
750ml/1¼ pint/3 cups water
5ml/1 tsp dried thyme
1 green chilli, seeded and finely chopped
1 vegetable stock (bouillon) cube
2.5ml/½ tsp ground allspice
2 carrots
115g/4oz white cabbage
175g/6oz okra
½ red (bell) pepper
150ml/¼ pint/⅔ cup good quality vegetable stock
salt

1 Heat the oil in a wok or large frying pan. Cook the onion and garlic over a moderate heat for 5 minutes, stirring frequently until the onion has softened. Be careful not to burn the garlic or it will taste bitter.

2 Add the puréed tomatoes and the peanut butter to the pan and stir well until combined. Cook for a further 1–2 minutes until the tomatoes begin to bubble.

3 Stir in the measured water, thyme, chopped chilli, stock cube, allspice and a little salt, to taste. Bring the mixture to the boil, reduce the heat and then simmer gently, uncovered, for about 35 minutes.

4 Prepare the vegetables. Cut the carrots into even sticks, finely shred the white cabbage, top and tail the okra, and seed and slice the red pepper.

5 Place the vegetables in a separate pan with the vegetable stock. Bring to the boil, then simmer until tender but still with a little crunch, about 7–10 minutes.

6 Drain the vegetables and place in a warmed serving dish. Pour the sauce over the top and serve immediately.

Chilli Bean Loaf Energy 304kcal/1280kJ; Protein 17.7g; Carbohydrate 44.2g, of which sugars 5.3g; Fat 7g, of which saturates 2.9g; Cholesterol 103mg; Calcium 83mg; Fibre 9.9g; Sodium 70mg.
Vegetables in Peanut Sauce Energy 172kcal/719kJ; Protein 7g; Carbohydrate 15g, of which sugars 12g; Fat 10g, of which saturates 2g; Cholesterol 0mg; Calcium 130mg; Fibre 3.5g; Sodium 600mg.

Chilli, Tomato and Olive Pasta

The delicious sauce for this pasta dish packs a satisfying punch, thanks to the robust flavours of red chillies, anchovies and capers.

Serves 4

45ml/3 tbsp olive oil
2 garlic cloves, crushed
2 fresh red chillies, seeded and chopped
6 drained canned anchovy fillets
675g/1½lb ripe tomatoes, peeled, seeded and chopped
30ml/2 tbsp sun-dried tomato purée (paste)
30ml/2 tbsp drained capers
115g/4oz/1 cup pitted black olives, roughly chopped
350g/12oz/3 cups penne
salt and ground black pepper
chopped fresh basil, to garnish

1 Heat the olive oil in a pan and gently fry the garlic and chilli for about 2–3 minutes, or until the garlic is just beginning to turn brown.

2 Add the anchovy fillets to the pan, mashing them with a fork, then stir in the chopped tomatoes, sun-dried tomato purée, capers and olives.

3 Season with salt and pepper to taste. Simmer uncovered, for about 20 minutes, stirring occasionally.

4 Meanwhile, bring a large pan of lightly salted water to the boil and cook the penne according to the instructions on the packet, or until *al dente*.

5 Drain the pasta and immediately transfer to the pan with the sauce. Stir well until the pasta is evenly coated.

6 Transfer the pasta to a warmed serving dish, garnish with basil and serve immediately.

Cook's Tip

This dish is best made with ripe, well-flavoured tomatoes, but if they are not available, use two 400g/14oz cans of good quality chopped tomatoes.

Spaghetti with Garlic, Chilli and Oil

This classic Italian dish always includes a chilli to give the dish some bite.

Serves 4

400g/14oz fresh or dried spaghetti
90ml/6 tbsp extra virgin olive oil
2–4 garlic cloves, crushed
1 dried red chilli
1 small handful fresh flat leaf parsley, roughly chopped
salt

1 Cook the pasta according to the packet instructions, adding plenty of salt to the water.

2 Meanwhile, heat the oil very gently in a small frying pan. Add the crushed garlic and whole dried chilli and stir over a low heat until the garlic is just beginning to brown. Discard the chilli.

3 Drain the pasta and transfer it to a warmed large bowl. Pour on the oil and garlic mixture, add the parsley and toss vigorously until the pasta glistens. Serve immediately.

Penne with Tomato and Chilli Sauce

This is one of Rome's most famous pasta dishes – penne tossed in tomato sauce flavoured with chilli, known to Italians as *arrabbiata*, meaning 'enraged' or 'furious'. But the presence of chillies means it should be translated as 'fiery'.

Serves 4

25g/1oz dried porcini mushrooms
90g/3½oz/7 tbsp butter
150g/5oz pancetta or smoked streaky (fatty) bacon
1–2 dried red chillies, to taste
2 garlic cloves, crushed
8 ripe Italian plum tomatoes, peeled and chopped
a few fresh basil leaves, torn, plus extra to garnish
350g/12oz/3 cups fresh or dried penne
50g/2oz/½ cup freshly grated Parmesan cheese
25g/1oz/¼ cup freshly grated Pecorino cheese
salt

1 Soak the mushrooms in warm water for 15–20 minutes. Drain, then squeeze dry with your hands and finely chop them.

2 Melt half the butter in a frying pan. Dice the pancetta or bacon and stir-fry over a medium heat until golden and slightly crispy. Remove with a slotted spoon and set aside.

3 Add the mushrooms to the pan and cook in the same way. Remove and set aside. Crumble a chilli into the pan, add the garlic and cook, stirring, for a few minutes until golden.

4 Add the tomatoes and basil and season. Simmer for 15 minutes. Cook the penne according to the packet instructions. Add the pancetta or bacon and the mushrooms to the sauce.

5 Drain the pasta and transfer to a warmed serving bowl. Toss the remaining butter and cheeses with the pasta. Pour the tomato sauce over the pasta, toss well and serve immediately, with a few basil leaves sprinkled on top.

Chilli and Olive Pasta Energy 449kcal/1897kJ; Protein 13.9g; Carbohydrate 71.3g, of which sugars 9.3g; Fat 14.1g, of which saturates 1.9g; Cholesterol 3mg; Calcium 72mg; Fibre 5.3g; Sodium 861mg.
Spaghetti with Garlic Energy 549kcal/2308kJ; Protein 12g; Carbohydrate 75g, of which sugars 4g; Fat 24g, of which saturates 3g; Cholesterol 0mg; Calcium 33mg; Fibre 3.2g; Sodium 100mg.
Penne with Chilli Sauce Energy 681kcal/2856kJ; Protein 25.1g; Carbohydrate 69.7g, of which sugars 7.7g; Fat 35.5g, of which saturates 19g; Cholesterol 91mg; Calcium 264mg; Fibre 4.1g; Sodium 830mg.

Bucatini with Chilli Sauce

The chilli sauce in this recipe is called Amatriciana, named after the town of Amatrice in Lazio. If you visit Rome, you will see it in many restaurants served with bucatini or spaghetti.

Serves 4

15ml/1 tbsp olive oil
1 small onion, finely sliced
115g/4oz smoked pancetta or rindless smoked streaky (fatty) bacon, diced
1 fresh red chilli, seeded and cut into thin strips
400g/14oz can chopped Italian plum tomatoes
30–45ml/2–3 tbsp dry white wine or water
350g/12oz dried bucatini
30–45ml/2–3 tbsp freshly grated Pecorino cheese, plus extra to serve (optional)
salt and ground black pepper

1 Heat the oil in a medium pan and cook the onion, pancetta or bacon and chilli over a low heat for 5–7 minutes, stirring, until the onion is soft and the pancetta is slightly crisp.

2 Add the tomatoes and wine or water, with salt and pepper to taste. Bring to the boil, stirring, then cover and simmer for 15–20 minutes, stirring occasionally. If the sauce is too dry, stir in a little of the pasta water.

3 Meanwhile, cook the pasta in a pan of salted boiling water according to the packet instructions.

4 Drain the pasta and transfer it into a warmed bowl. Taste the sauce for seasoning, pour it over the pasta and add the grated Pecorino. Toss well. Serve immediately, with more grated cheese handed separately, if you like.

Cook's Tip

Bucatini is a long, hollow pasta, which is similar to spaghetti, but much thicker. If you prefer something in between bucatini and spaghetti, you could try linguine, which is long but slightly fatter in width than spaghetti.

Spicy Octopus and Pasta Bake

A mouthwatering dish, this slow-cooked combination of octopus and pasta in a spicy tomato sauce is quite an everyday affair in Greece.

Serves 4

2 octopuses, total weight about 675–800g/1½–1¾lb, cleaned
150ml/¼ pint/⅔ cup extra virgin olive oil
2 large onions, sliced
3 garlic cloves, chopped
1 fresh red or green chilli, seeded and thinly sliced
1 or 2 bay leaves
5ml/1 tsp dried oregano
1 piece of cinnamon stick
pinch ground allspice (optional)
175ml/6fl oz/¾ cup red wine
30ml/2 tbsp tomato purée (paste) diluted in 300ml/½ pint/1¼ cups warm water
300ml/½ pint/1¼ cups boiling water
225g/8oz/2 cups dried penne or small macaroni-type pasta
ground black pepper
45ml/3 tbsp finely chopped fresh flat leaf parsley, to garnish (optional)

1 Rinse the octopuses well, cut into large cubes and place the pieces in a heavy pan over a low heat. Cook gently; they will produce some liquid, the colour of the flesh will change and they will become bright scarlet. Keep turning the pieces of octupus until all the liquid has evaporated.

2 Add the oil to the pan and fry the octopus for about 5 minutes, then add the sliced onions. Cook the onions for 4–5 minutes, stirring them constantly until they start to turn golden.

3 Stir in the garlic, chilli, bay leaf or leaves, oregano, cinnamon stick and allspice, if using. When the garlic becomes aromatic, pour in the wine and let it bubble and evaporate for 2 minutes. Add the diluted tomato purée, add some black pepper, cover then cook gently for 1½ hours, until the octopus is soft.

4 Preheat the oven to 160°C/325°F/Gas 3. Bring the octopus mixture to the boil, and then add the boiling water, stirring.

5 Stir in the dried pasta. Transfer to a large roasting dish and level the surface. Bake for 30–35 minutes, stirring occasionally. Sprinkle the parsley on top, if using, and serve immediately.

Bucatini with Chilli Energy 681kcal/2856kJ; Protein 25.1g; Carbohydrate 69.7g, of which sugars 7.7g; Fat 35.5g, of which saturates 19g; Cholesterol 91mg; Calcium 264mg; Fibre 4.1g; Sodium 830mg.
Spicy Octopus Bake Energy 637kcal/2,669kJ; Protein 38.9g; Carbohydrate 52.9g, of which sugars 10.2g; Fat 28.5g, of which saturates 4.2g; Cholesterol 81mg; Calcium 108mg; Fibre 3.6g; Sodium 25mg.

Fiery Prawn Noodles

In Malaysia and Singapore, there are endless stir-fried noodle dishes. Some of these are classic Chinese recipes; others have been influenced by the Chinese but adapted to suit the tastes of the different communities. The rice vermicelli in this popular snack are stir-fried with prawns and lots of chilli.

Serves 4

30ml/2 tbsp vegetable oil
1 carrot, cut into matchsticks
225g/8oz fresh prawns (shrimp), peeled
120ml/4fl oz/½ cup chicken stock or water
30ml/2 tbsp light soy sauce
15ml/1 tbsp dark soy sauce
175g/6oz beansprouts
115g/4oz mustard greens or pak choi (bok choy), shredded
225g/8oz dried rice vermicelli, soaked in lukewarm water until pliable, and drained
1–2 fresh red chillies, seeded and finely sliced, and fresh coriander (cilantro) leaves, roughly chopped, to garnish

For the spice paste
4 dried red chillies, soaked until soft and seeded
4 garlic cloves, chopped
4 shallots, chopped
25g/1oz fresh root ginger, peeled and chopped
5ml/1 tsp ground turmeric

1 Place all the ingredients for the spice paste in a mortar and pestle or food processor and grind to a smooth paste.

2 Heat the oil in a wok or heavy pan and stir in the spice paste until it begins to colour and become fragrant.

3 Add the carrots to the pan and cook, stirring constantly, for a minute. Then add the prawns to the pan and mix well.

4 Pour in the stock or water and soy sauces and mix well until combined. Cook for about 1–2 minutes. Add the beansprouts and mustard greens to the pan, followed by the noodles. Toss well to make sure the vegetables noodles are well coated and heated through.

5 Transfer the noodles to a warmed serving plate. Garnish with the sliced chillies and coriander.

Chinese Stir-fried Noodles with Red Chillies

This Chinese dish of stir-fried rice noodles and seafood is one of the most popular at the hawker stalls. Breakfast, lunch, supper, mid-morning, mid-afternoon or late evening, you will find this dish anywhere at any time of day. Variations include red snapper, clams and pork. Use the broad, fresh rice noodles available in Chinese markets.

Serves 3 to 4

45ml/3 tbsp vegetable oil
2 garlic cloves, finely chopped
2 red chillies, seeded and finely sliced
1 Chinese sausage, finely sliced
12 fresh prawns (shrimp), peeled
2 small squid, trimmed, cleaned, skinned and sliced
500g/1¼lb fresh rice noodles
30ml/2 tbsp light soy sauce
45ml/3 tbsp kecap manis (Indonesian sweet soy sauce)
2–3 mustard green leaves, chopped
a handful of beansprouts
2 eggs, lightly beaten
ground black pepper
fresh coriander (cilantro) leaves, finely chopped, to serve

1 Heat a wok or large frying pan and add the oil. Stir in the garlic and chillies and fry until fragrant.

2 Add the Chinese sausage, followed by the prawns and squid, tossing them to mix thoroughly.

3 Toss in the noodles and mix well. Add the soy sauce and kecap manis, and toss in the mustard leaves and beansprouts.

4 Stir in the eggs for a few seconds until set. Season with black pepper, garnish with coriander and serve immediately.

Cook's Tip

Kecap manis is an Indonesian soya bean condiment similar to soy sauce but sweeter and with a more complex flavour. If it is not available you can replace it with the same quantity of dark soy sauce mixed with a little sugar.

Fiery Prawn Noodles Energy 330kcal/1377kJ; Protein 17.5g; Carbohydrate 49.9g, of which sugars 4.5g; Fat 6.6g, of which saturates 0.8g; Cholesterol 110mg; Calcium 125mg; Fibre 1.9g; Sodium 960mg.
Chinese Noodles Energy 618kcal/2582kJ; Protein 24.8g; Carbohydrate 100g, of which sugars 1.1g; Fat 12.9g, of which saturates 2.1g; Cholesterol 217mg; Calcium 96mg; Fibre 0.5g; Sodium 717mg.

Red-hot Noodles with Chillies and Sesame

The Vietnamese have put their own particularly delicious stamp on spicy Singapore noodles, which are a popular dish throughout South-east Asia. At home, you can make this dish with any kind of noodles – egg or rice, fresh or dried.

Serves 4

30ml/2 tbsp sesame oil
1 onion, finely chopped
3 garlic cloves, finely chopped
3–4 green or red chillies, seeded and finely chopped
4cm/1½in fresh root ginger, peeled and finely chopped
6 spring onions (scallions), finely chopped
1 skinless chicken breast fillet, cut into bitesize strips
90g/3½oz pork, cut into bitesize strips
90g/3½oz prawns (shrimp), shelled
2 tomatoes, skinned, seeded and chopped
30ml/2 tbsp tamarind paste
15ml/1 tbsp Thai fish sauce
juice and rind of 1 lime
10ml/2 tsp sugar
150ml/¼ pint/⅔ cup water or fish stock
225g/8oz fresh rice sticks (vermicelli)
salt and ground black pepper
1 bunch each of fresh basil and mint, stalks removed, leaves shredded, and chilli dipping sauce, to serve

1 Heat a wok or heavy pan and add the oil. Stir in the onion, garlic, chillies and ginger, and cook until they begin to colour.

2 Add the spring onions and cook for 1 minute, add the chicken and pork, and cook for 2 minutes, then add the prawns.

3 Add the tomatoes, followed by the tamarind paste, fish sauce, lime juice and rind, and sugar. Pour in the water or fish stock, and cook gently for 2–3 minutes.

4 Toss the noodles in a pan of boiling water and cook for a few minutes until tender. Drain and add to the chicken mixture.

5 Season with salt and ground black pepper and serve immediately, with plenty of basil and mint sprinkled over the top, and drizzled with spoonfuls of chilli dipping sauce.

Spicy Thai Seafood Noodles

This delicious dish is made with rice noodles and is considered one of the national dishes of Thailand.

Serves 4 to 6

16 tiger prawns (jumbo shrimp)
350g/12oz rice noodles
45ml/3 tbsp vegetable oil
15ml/1 tbsp chopped garlic
2 eggs, lightly beaten
15ml/1 tbsp dried shrimp, rinsed
30ml/2 tbsp pickled mooli (daikon)
50g/2oz fried tofu, cut into slivers
2.5ml/½ tsp dried chilli flakes
1 large bunch garlic chives, about 115g/4oz, cut into 5cm/2in lengths
225g/8oz/2½ cups beansprouts
50g/2oz/½ cup roasted peanuts, coarsely ground
5ml/1 tsp sugar
15ml/1 tbsp dark soy sauce
30ml/2 tbsp Thai fish sauce
30ml/2 tbsp tamarind juice, made by mixing tamarind paste with warm water
fresh coriander (cilantro) leaves and lime wedges. to garnish

1 Peel the prawns, leaving the tails intact. Carefully cut along the back of each prawn and remove the dark vein. Place the rice noodles in a bowl, add warm water to cover and leave to soak for 20–30 minutes, then drain thoroughly and set aside.

2 Heat 15ml/1 tbsp of the oil in a wok. Fry the garlic until golden. Add the prawns and cook for 1–2 minutes, then set aside.

3 Heat 15ml/1 tbsp of the remaining oil in the wok. Add the eggs and tilt the wok to make a thin layer. Stir to scramble and break up. Remove from the wok and set aside with the prawns.

4 Heat the remaining oil in the same wok. Add the dried shrimp, pickled mooli, tofu slivers and dried chilli flakes. Stir briefly. Add the noodles and stir-fry for about 5 minutes.

5 Add the garlic chives, half the beansprouts and half the peanuts. Add the sugar, then season with soy sauce, fish sauce and tamarind juice. Cook until the noodles are heated through.

6 Return the prawn and egg mixture to the wok and mix with the noodles. Serve topped with the remaining beansprouts and peanuts. Garnish with the coriander leaves and lime wedges.

Red-hot Noodles Energy 420kcal/1756kJ; Protein 23g; Carbohydrate 59g, of which sugars 9g; Fat 10g, of which saturates 2g; Cholesterol 86mg; Calcium 119mg; Fibre 1.3g; Sodium 500mg.
Spicy Fried Noodles Energy 580kcal/2416kJ; Protein 21.2g; Carbohydrate 76g, of which sugars 2.7g; Fat 20g, of which saturates 3.1g; Cholesterol 169mg; Calcium 256mg; Fibre 1.6g; Sodium 647mg.

Fresh Rice Noodles with Chilli and Ginger

A variety of dried noodles is available in Asian stores and supermarkets, but fresh ones are quite different and not that difficult to make. The freshly-made noodle sheets can be served as a snack, drenched in sugar or honey, or dipped into a savoury sauce of your choice. Otherwise, cut them into wide strips and gently stir-fry them with garlic, ginger, chillies and fish sauce or soy sauce.

Serves 4

225g/8oz/2 cups rice flour
600ml/1 pint/2½ cups water
a pinch of salt
15ml/1 tbsp vegetable oil, plus extra for brushing
slivers of red chilli and fresh root ginger, and fresh coriander (cilantro) leaves, to garnish (optional)

1 Place the flour in a bowl and stir in some water to form a paste. Pour in the rest of the water, beating it to make a smooth batter. Add the salt and oil and leave to stand for 15 minutes.

2 Meanwhile, fill a wide pan with water. Cut a piece of smooth cotton cloth a little larger than the diameter of the pan. Stretch it over the top of the pan, pulling the edges tautly down over the sides, then wind a piece of string around the edge, to secure. Using a sharp knife, make three small slits, about 2.5cm/1in from the edge of the cloth, at regular intervals.

3 Boil the water. Stir the batter and ladle 30–45ml/2–3 tbsp on to the cloth, swirling it to form a 13–15cm/5–6in wide circle. Cover with a domed lid, such as a wok lid, and steam for about 1 minute, or until the noodle sheet is translucent.

4 Iinsert a metal spatula or knife under the noodle sheet and prise it off the cloth. (If it doesn't peel off easily, steam it a little longer.) Transfer the noodle sheet to a lightly oiled baking tray, brush with oil, and cook the remaining batter in the same way. From time to time, you may need to top up the water through one of the slits and tighten the cloth again. Toss noodles with chosen garnish and serve.

Plain Noodles with Four Spicy Flavours

A wonderfully simple way of serving noodles, this dish allows each individual diner to season their own, sprinkling over the four flavours as they like. Little bowls with flavourings are always put out whenever noodles are served.

Serves 4

4 small fresh red or green chillies
60ml/4 tbsp Thai fish sauce
60ml/4 tbsp rice vinegar
sugar
mild or hot chilli powder
350g/12oz fresh or dried noodles

1 Prepare the four flavours. For the first, finely chop 2 small red or green chillies, discarding the seeds or leaving them in, depending on how hot you like your flavouring. Place them in a small bowl and add the Thai fish sauce.

2 For the second flavour, chop the remaining chillies finely and mix them with the rice vinegar in a small bowl. Put the sugar and chilli powder in separate small bowls.

3 Cook the noodles until tender, following the instructions on the packet. Drain well, transfer to a large bowl and serve immediately with the four flavours handed separately.

Buckwheat Noodles with Chilli

This chilled Korean noodle salad is perfect for a summer lunch dish. The coolness of the buckwheat noodles contrasts with the spiciness of the dressing, and Asian pear adds a delicious sweetness.

Serves 2

90g/3½oz naengmyun buckwheat noodles
1 hard-boiled egg
½ cucumber
½ Asian pear
ice cubes, to serve

For the sauce

30ml/2 tbsp gochujang chilli paste
5ml/1 tsp Korean chilli powder
30ml/2 tbsp sugar
10ml/2 tsp sesame oil
1 garlic clove, finely chopped
2.5ml/½ tsp soy sauce
5ml/1 tsp sesame seeds

1 Cook the noodles in a large pan of boiling water for 5 minutes. Drain them, and then rinse two or three times in cold water until the water runs clear. Chill for 30 minutes.

2 Slice the hard-boiled egg in half. Seed the cucumber and peel and core the Asian pear. Slice the pear and the cucumber into long, thin matchstick strips.

3 In a large bowl, combine all the ingredients for the sauce and blend well together. Arrange the noodles in the centre of a large serving platter.

4 Pour the sauce over the noodles and then sprinkle with the Asian pear and cucumber. Place the egg on the top and add ice cubes to the plate before serving.

Fresh Rice Noodles Energy 251kcal/1046kJ; Protein 4g; Carbohydrate 45g, of which sugars 0g; Fat 5g, of which saturates 1g; Cholesterol 0mg; Calcium 24mg; Fibre 1.1g; Sodium 200g.
Noodles with Four Flavours Energy 55kcal/236kJ; Protein 2g; Carbohydrate 11.6g, of which sugars 0.4g; Fat 0.5g, of which saturates 0.1g; Cholesterol 5mg; Calcium 5mg; Fibre 0.5g; Sodium 191mg.
Buckwheat Noodles Energy 337kcal/1421kJ; Protein 9.4g; Carbohydrate 58.3g, of which sugars 25.1g; Fat 9g, of which saturates 1.3g; Cholesterol 105mg; Calcium 52mg; Fibre 3.3g; Sodium 133mg.

Spiced Stir-fried Noodles

Originally from China, spicy stir-fried noodles are very popular at street stalls throughout Indonesia, and are just as varied and equally delicious.

Serves 4

450g/1lb fresh egg noodles
15–30ml/1–2 tbsp palm, groundnut (peanut) or corn oil, plus extra for shallow frying
2 shallots, finely chopped
2–3 spring onions (scallions), finely chopped
2–3 garlic cloves, crushed
3–4 Thai chillies, seeded and finely chopped
15ml/1 tbsp shrimp paste
15ml/1 tbsp tomato purée (paste)
15–30ml/1–2 tbsp kecap manis (Indonesian sweet soy sauce)
4 eggs
salt

For the garnish
15ml/1 tbsp palm or corn oil
3–4 shallots, finely sliced

1 First prepare the garnish. Heat the oil in a heavy pan, stir in the shallots and fry until deep golden brown. Drain on kitchen paper and put aside.

2 Fill a deep pan with water and bring it to the boil. Drop in the egg noodles, untangling them with chopsticks, and cook for about 3 minutes until tender but still firm to the bite. Drain and refresh under running cold water.

3 Heat the oil in a wok or large, heavy frying pan and fry the shallots, spring onions, garlic and chillies until fragrant. Add the shrimp paste and cook until the mixture darkens.

4 Toss the noodles into the pan, making sure that they are thoroughly coated in the mixture. Add the tomato purée and kecap manis, toss thoroughly, and cook for 2–3 minutes. Season the noodles with salt to taste. Divide the noodles between four warmed bowls and keep warm.

5 Heat a thin layer of oil in a large, heavy frying pan, and crack the eggs into it. Fry for 1–2 minutes until the whites are cooked but the yolks remain runny. Place on the noodles and serve immediately with the fried shallots sprinkled over the top.

Mee Krob Crispy Chilli Noodles

This Thai dish is a stunning combination of sweet and hot, salty and sour, while the texture contrives to be both crisp and chewy.

Serves 1

vegetable oil, for deep-frying
130g/4½oz rice vermicelli noodles

For the sauce
30ml/2 tbsp vegetable oil
130g/4½oz fried tofu, cut into thin strips
2 garlic cloves, finely chopped
2 small shallots, finely chopped
15ml/1 tbsp light soy sauce
30ml/2 tbsp palm sugar (jaggery) or light muscovado (brown) sugar
60ml/4 tbsp vegetable stock
juice of 1 lime
2.5ml/½ tsp dried chilli flakes

For the garnish
15ml/1 tbsp vegetable oil
1 egg, lightly beaten with 15ml/1 tbsp cold water
25g/1oz/⅓ cup beansprouts
1 spring onion (scallion), thinly shredded
1 fresh red chilli, seeded and finely chopped
1 whole head pickled garlic, sliced across to resemble a flower

1 Heat the oil for deep-frying in a wok or large pan to 190°C/375°F, or until a cube of bread, added to the oil, browns in about 45 seconds. Add the noodles and deep-fry until golden and crisp. Drain on kitchen paper and set aside.

2 Make the sauce. Heat the oil in a wok, add the fried tofu and cook over a medium heat until crisp. Using a slotted spoon, transfer it to a plate.

3 Add the garlic and shallots to the pan and cook until golden brown. Stir in the soy sauce, sugar, stock, lime juice and chilli flakes. Cook, stirring, until the mixture caramelizes. Add the reserved tofu and stir. Remove the wok from the heat and set aside.

4 Prepare the egg garnish. Heat the oil in a wok or frying pan. Pour in the egg in a thin stream to form trails. As soon as it sets, lift it out with a metal spatula and place on a plate.

5 Crumble the noodles into the tofu sauce, mix well, then spoon into serving bowls. Sprinkle with the beansprouts, spring onion, fried egg strips, chilli and pickled garlic and serve.

Spiced Noodles Energy 549kcal/2317kJ; Protein 20.5g; Carbohydrate 82.9g, of which sugars 3.9g; Fat 17.6g, of which saturates 4.5g; Cholesterol 224mg; Calcium 68mg; Fibre 3.7g; Sodium 549mg.
Chilli Noodles Energy 1293kcal/5362kJ; Protein 28.8g; Carbohydrate 109.1g, of which sugars 5.2g; Fat 80.5g, of which saturates 10.6g; Cholesterol 509mg; Calcium 733mg; Fibre 0.4g; Sodium 1180mg.

Noodles with Spicy Beansprout Broth

The components for this dish are served separately so diners can help themselves.

Serves 4 to 6
250g/9oz tofu block
corn or vegetable oil, for deep-frying
200g/7oz/1 cup long grain jasmine rice
4–6 spring onions (scallions), sliced
chilli sambal

For the broth
15ml/1 tbsp palm or corn oil
2 garlic cloves, finely chopped
1–2 red or green chillies, seeded and finely chopped
1 lemon grass stalk, finely chopped
45ml/3 tbsp soy sauce
2 litres/3½ pints chicken stock
450g/1lb fresh mung beansprouts

For the noodles
500g/1¼lb fresh egg noodles or 225g/8oz dried egg noodles, softened in warm water
30ml/2 tbsp palm or corn oil
4 shallots, finely sliced
2 garlic cloves, finely chopped
450g/1lb fresh shelled prawns (shrimp)
30ml/2 tbsp kecap manis (Indonesian sweet soy sauce)
ground black pepper

1 Prepare the tofu. Cut it into four rectangles. Heat enough oil in a wok or heavy pan for deep-frying. Add the tofu and fry for 2–3 minutes, until golden brown. Drain on kitchen paper. Cut the tofu into thin slices and pile on a serving plate. Set aside.

2 Rinse the rice under cold water, then drain. Place in a pan with 600ml/1 pint/2½ cups water. Bring to the boil, then simmer for 15 minutes. Turn off the heat, cover and steam for 10–15 minutes.

3 Make the broth. Heat the oil in a heavy pan, fry the garlic, chillies and lemon grass until fragrant. Add 15ml/1 tbsp soy sauce and the stock. Bring to the boil, then simmer for 10–15 minutes. Season with soy sauce and pepper and stir in the beansprouts.

4 Prepare the noodles. Heat the oil in a wok, fry the shallots and garlic for 2 minutes. Cook the prawns for 2 minutes. Stir in the kecap manis with 30ml/2 tbsp water. Add the noodles and season.

5 Transfer the rice and noodles on to warmed serving dishes. Serve with the tofu, a bowl of spring onions, chilli sambal and a bowl of the broth, so that everyone can help themselves.

Thai Noodles with Chinese Chives and Chilli

This is a filling and tasty vegetarian dish, ideal for a weekend lunch.

Serves 4
350g/12oz dried rice noodles
1cm/½in piece fresh root ginger, peeled and grated
30ml/2 tbsp light soy sauce
45ml/3 tbsp vegetable oil
225g/8oz Quorn (mycoprotein), cut into small cubes
2 garlic cloves, crushed
1 large onion, cut into thin wedges
115g/4oz fried tofu, thinly sliced
1 fresh green chilli, seeded and thinly sliced
175g/6oz/2 cups beansprouts
2 large bunches garlic chives, total weight about 115g/4oz, cut into 5cm/2in lengths
50g/2oz/½ cup roasted peanuts, ground
30ml/2 tbsp dark soy sauce
30ml/2 tbsp chopped fresh coriander (cilantro), and 1 lemon, cut into wedges, to garnish

1 Place the noodles in a bowl, cover with warm water and leave to soak for 30 minutes. Drain and set aside.

2 Mix the ginger, light soy sauce and 15ml/1 tbsp of the oil in a bowl. Add the Quorn, then set aside for 10 minutes. Drain, reserving the marinade.

3 Heat 15ml/1 tbsp of the remaining oil in a frying pan and cook the garlic for a few seconds. Add the Quorn and stir-fry for 3–4 minutes. Transfer to a plate and set aside.

4 Heat the remaining oil in the pan and stir-fry the onion for 3–4 minutes, until softened and tinged brown. Add the tofu and chilli, stir-fry briefly and then add the noodles. Stir-fry over a medium heat for 4–5 minutes.

5 Stir in the beansprouts, garlic chives and most of the peanuts, reserving a little for the garnish. Stir well, then add the Quorn, the dark soy sauce and the reserved marinade.

6 When hot, spoon on to serving plates and garnish with the remaining ground peanuts, the coriander and lemon.

Noodles with Broth Energy 690kcal/2900kJ; Protein 32.6g; Carbohydrate 97g, of which sugars 5.9g; Fat 20.7g, of which saturates 3.6g; Cholesterol 171mg; Calcium 328mg; Fibre 4.2g; Sodium 833mg.
Thai Noodles Energy 444kcal/1857kJ; Protein 16g; Carbohydrate 77.6g, of which sugars 4.3g; Fat 6.5g, of which saturates 0.9g; Cholesterol 0mg; Calcium 230mg; Fibre 5g; Sodium 1227mg.

Fragrant Thai Noodles with Crab

This is a Vietnamese dish of contrasting flavours, textures and colours.

Serves 4

25g/1oz dried cloud ear (wood ear) mushrooms, soaked in warm water for 20 minutes
115g/4oz dried bean thread (cellophane) noodles, soaked in warm water for 20 minutes
30ml/2 tbsp vegetable or sesame oil
3 shallots, halved and thinly sliced
2 garlic cloves, crushed
2 green or red Thai chillies, seeded and sliced
1 carrot, peeled and cut into thin diagonal rounds
5ml/1 tsp sugar
45ml/3 tbsp oyster sauce
15ml/1 tbsp soy sauce
400ml/14fl oz/1⅔ cups water or chicken stock
225g/8oz fresh, raw crab meat, cut into bitesize chunks
ground black pepper
fresh coriander (cilantro) leaves, to garnish

1 Discard the centres from the soaked cloud ears and cut in half. Drain the noodles and cut them into 30cm/12in pieces.

2 Heat a wok or heavy pan and add 15ml/1 tbsp of the oil. Stir in the shallots, garlic and chillies, and cook until fragrant. Add the carrot and cook for 1 minute, then add the cloud ears. Stir in the sugar with the oyster and soy sauces, then the noodles. Add the water or stock, and cook, covered, for 5 minutes.

3 Heat the remaining oil in a pan. Add the crab meat and cook until it is tender. Season with black pepper. Arrange the noodles and crab meat on a serving dish and garnish with coriander.

Spicy Fried Noodles

A tasty dish with pork, chicken and plenty of spice.

Serves 4

225g/8oz egg thread noodles
60ml/4 tbsp vegetable oil
2 garlic cloves, finely chopped
175g/6oz pork fillet (tenderloin), sliced into thin strips
1 skinless chicken breast fillet, sliced into thin strips
115g/4oz cooked peeled prawns (shrimp), rinsed if canned
45ml/3 tbsp fresh lemon juice
45ml/3 tbsp Thai fish sauce
30ml/2 tbsp soft light brown sugar
2 eggs, beaten
½ fresh red chilli, seeded and finely chopped
50g/2oz/⅔ cup beansprouts
60ml/4 tbsp roasted peanuts, chopped
3 spring onions (scallions), cut into 5cm/2in lengths and shredded
45ml/3 tbsp chopped fresh coriander (cilantro)

1 Cover the noodles with just-boiled water and leave for 5 minutes. Heat 45ml/3 tbsp of oil in a wok. Cook the garlic for 30 seconds. Fry the pork and chicken until brown. Fry the prawns for 2 minutes. Add the lemon juice, fish sauce and sugar and cook for 1 minute.

2 Drain the noodles and add to the wok with the remaining oil. Pour the eggs over. Stir-fry until almost set, then add the chilli and beansprouts. Divide the peanuts, spring onions and coriander into two portions, add one to the pan and stir-fry for 2 minutes.

3 Transfer the noodles to a serving dish. Sprinkle the remaining peanuts, spring onions and coriander over and serve immediately.

Noodles and Vegetables in Coconut Sauce with Fresh Red Chillies

When everyday vegetables are given the Thai treatment, the result is a delectable dish which everyone is certain to enjoy.

Serves 4 to 6

30ml/2 tbsp sunflower oil
1 lemon grass stalk, finely chopped
15ml/1 tbsp Thai red curry paste
1 onion, thickly sliced
3 courgettes (zucchini), thickly sliced
115g/4oz Savoy cabbage, thickly sliced
2 carrots, thickly sliced
150g/5oz broccoli, stem sliced and head separated into florets
2 X 400ml/14fl oz cans coconut milk
475ml/16fl oz vegetable stock
150g/5oz dried egg noodles
15ml/1 tbsp Thai fish sauce
30ml/2 tbsp soy sauce
60ml/4 tbsp chopped fresh coriander (cilantro)

For the garnish

2 lemon grass stalks
1 bunch fresh coriander (cilantro)
8–10 small fresh red chillies

1 Heat the oil in a large pan or wok. Add the lemon grass and red curry paste and stir-fry for 2–3 seconds. Add the onion and cook over a medium heat, stirring occasionally, for about 5–10 minutes, until the onion has softened but not browned.

2 Add the courgettes, cabbage, carrots and slices of broccoli stem. Toss the vegetables with the onion mixture. Reduce the heat and cook gently, stirring occasionally, for 5 minutes.

3 Increase the heat to medium, stir in the coconut milk and vegetable stock and bring to the boil. Add the broccoli florets and the noodles, then simmer gently for 20 minutes.

4 Meanwhile, make the garnish. Split the lemon grass stalks lengthways. Gather the coriander into a small bouquet and lay it on a platter, following the curve of the rim. Tuck the lemon grass halves into the bouquet and add chillies to resemble flowers.

5 Stir the fish sauce, soy sauce and chopped coriander into the noodle mixture. Spoon on to the platter, taking care not to disturb the herb bouquet, and serve immediately.

Fragrant Noodles Energy 292kcal/1224kJ; Protein 16g; Carbohydrate 30g, of which sugars 5g; Fat 13g, of which saturates 2g; Cholesterol 36mg; Calcium 29mg; Fibre 2.5g; Sodium 1000mg.
Spicy Noodles Energy 597kcal/2504kJ; Protein 39.3g; Carbohydrate 50.8g, of which sugars 10.3g; Fat 27.8g, of which saturates 5.5g; Cholesterol 226mg; Calcium 76mg; Fibre 2.9g; Sodium 250mg.
Noodles with Chillies Energy 293kcal/1235kJ; Protein 8.9g; Carbohydrate 44.7g, of which sugars 17.3g; Fat 10g, of which saturates 2.1g; Cholesterol 11mg; Calcium 131mg; Fibre 4.2g; Sodium 1007mg.

Special Chow Mein with Chinese Sausage and Chilli

Lap cheong is a spicy Chinese sausage, available from most Chinese markets.

Serves 4 to 6

450g/1lb egg noodles
45ml/3 tbsp vegetable oil
2 garlic cloves, sliced
5ml/1 tsp chopped fresh root ginger
2 fresh red chillies, seeded and chopped
2 lap cheong, about 75g/3oz in total, rinsed and sliced (optional)
1 skinless chicken breast fillet, thinly sliced
16 uncooked tiger prawns (jumbo shrimp), peeled, tails left intact, and deveined
115g/4oz/2 cups green beans
225g/8oz/2½ cups beansprouts
small bunch garlic chives, about 50g/2oz
30ml/2 tbsp soy sauce
15ml/1 tbsp oyster sauce
15ml/1 tbsp sesame oil
salt and ground black pepper
2 shredded spring onions (scallions) and fresh coriander (cilantro) leaves, to garnish

1 Cook the noodles in a large pan of boiling water, according to the instructions on the packet. Drain well.

2 Heat 15ml/1 tbsp of the oil in a wok or large frying pan. Add the garlic, ginger and chillies and stir-fry for about 2 minutes. Add the lap cheong, if using, chicken, prawns and beans. Stir-fry over a high heat for a further 2 minutes, or until the chicken and prawns are cooked through. Transfer the mixture to a bowl then set aside.

3 Heat the rest of the oil in the wok. Toss in the beansprouts and garlic chives and stir-fry for 1–2 minutes. Add the drained noodles and toss over the heat to mix. Season with the soy sauce, oyster sauce and salt and pepper to taste.

4 Return the prawn mixture to the wok. Mix well with the noodles and toss until heated through.

5 Stir the sesame oil into the noodles. Spoon into a warmed bowl and serve immediately, garnished with the spring onions and coriander leaves.

Cellophane Noodles with Spicy Pork

The magic paste in this dish is a mix of garlic, coriander root and white pepper.

Serves 2

200g/7oz cellophane noodles
30ml/2 tbsp vegetable oil
15ml/1 tbsp magic paste
200g/7oz minced (ground) pork
1 fresh green or red chilli, seeded and finely chopped
300g/11oz/3½ cups beansprouts
5 spring onions (scallions), sliced
30ml/2 tbsp soy sauce
30ml/2 tbsp Thai fish sauce
30ml/2 tbsp sweet chilli sauce
15ml/1 tbsp palm sugar (jaggery) or light muscovado (brown) sugar
30ml/2 tbsp rice vinegar
30ml/2 tbsp roasted peanuts, chopped, and chopped fresh coriander (cilantro), to garnish

1 Place the noodles in a large bowl, cover with boiling water and soak for 10 minutes. Drain the noodles and set aside.

2 Heat the oil in a wok or large, heavy frying pan. Add the magic paste and stir-fry for 2–3 seconds, then add the pork. Stir-fry the meat for 2–3 minutes, until browned all over.

3 Add the chilli to the meat and stir-fry for 3–4 seconds. Add the beansprouts and spring onions, stir-frying for a few seconds after each addition.

4 Cut the noodles into 5cm/2in lengths and add to the wok, with the soy sauce, fish sauce, chilli sauce, sugar and rice vinegar.

5 Toss the ingredients together until well combined and the noodles have warmed through. Pile into a large bowl. Sprinkle over the peanuts and coriander and serve immediately.

Chilli Ribs in Noodle Soup

This slow-cooked dish of ribs in a rich soup includes a piquant chilli seasoning.

Serves 4

900g/2lb beef short ribs, cut into 5cm/2in squares
350g/12oz mooli (daikon), peeled
5ml/1 tsp salt
90g/3½oz dangmyun noodles

For the seasoning
45ml/3 tbsp soy sauce
15ml/1 tbsp chilli powder
50g/2oz spring onions (scallions), roughly chopped
5ml/1 tsp sesame oil
1 chilli, finely sliced
ground black pepper

1 Soak the ribs in cold water for 10 hours, changing the water halfway through. Drain and place in a large pan, cover with fresh water. Bring to the boil, then rinse in cold water and set aside.

2 Cut the mooli into 2cm/¾in cubes. Place the seasoning ingredients in a bowl and mix thoroughly.

3 Place the ribs in a pan and cover with 1 litre/1¾ pints/4 cups water. Simmer for 20 minutes. Add the mooli and salt and cook for 7 minutes. Add the noodles and cook for 3 minutes more.

4 Ladle the soup into bowls and add a generous spoonful of the seasoning just before serving.

Chow Mein Energy 624kcal/2631kJ; Protein 29.3g; Carbohydrate 84.5g, of which sugars 4.6g; Fat 21.2g, of which saturates 4.2g; Cholesterol 107mg; Calcium 76mg; Fibre 4.8g; Sodium 808mg.
Noodles with Pork Energy 720kcal/3009kJ; Protein 29.4g; Carbohydrate 99.9g, of which sugars 15.4g; Fat 21.6g, of which saturates 5.1g; Cholesterol 66mg; Calcium 58mg; Fibre 2.4g; Sodium 1933mg.
Chilli Ribs Energy 437kcal/1830kJ; Protein 52.1g; Carbohydrate 19.8g, of which sugars 3.1g; Fat 17g, of which saturates 6.7g; Cholesterol 126mg; Calcium 40mg; Fibre 1.6g; Sodium 1174mg.

Chilli Meatballs, Chinese Leaves and Noodles

This fragrant combination of spiced meatballs, noodles and vegetables cooked slowly in a richly flavoured broth makes for a very hearty, warming soup.

Serves 4

10 dried shiitake mushrooms, soaked in hot water for 30 minutes, soaking liquid reserved
90g/3½oz bean thread noodles
675g/1½lb minced (ground) beef
10ml/2 tsp finely grated garlic
10ml/2 tsp finely grated fresh root ginger
1 red chilli, seeded and chopped
6 spring onions (scallions), sliced
1 egg white
15ml/1 tbsp cornflour (cornstarch)
15ml/1 tbsp Chinese rice wine
30ml/2 tbsp sunflower oil
1.5 litres/2½ pints/6¼ cups chicken or beef stock
50ml/2fl oz/¼ cup light soy sauce
5ml/1 tsp sugar
150g/5oz enoki mushrooms, trimmed
200g/7oz Chinese leaves (Chinese cabbage), very thinly sliced
salt and ground black pepper
sesame oil and chilli oil (optional)

1 Discard the stems from the reconstituted mushrooms and then thickly slice the caps and set aside. Put the noodles in a large bowl and pour over boiling water to cover. Leave to soak for 3–4 minutes, then drain, rinse and set aside.

2 Place the beef, garlic, ginger, chilli, spring onions, egg white, cornflour, rice wine and seasoning in a food processor. Process to combine well. Divide into 30 portions, then shape into balls.

3 Heat the oil in a wok. Fry the meatballs for 2–3 minutes on each side until browned. Remove and drain on kitchen paper. Wipe out the wok and add the stock, soy sauce, sugar and shiitake mushrooms with the soaking liquid and bring to the boil.

4 Add the meatballs to the boiling stock, reduce the heat and cook gently for 20–25 minutes. Add the noodles, enoki mushrooms and cabbage to the wok and cook gently for 4–5 minutes. Serve ladled into wide shallow bowls. Drizzle with sesame oil and chilli oil, if you like.

Thai Crispy Noodles with Chilli Beef

Rice vermicelli is deep-fried before being added to this dish, and in the process the vermicelli expands to at least four times its original size.

Serves 4

450g/1lb rump (round) steak
teriyaki sauce, for brushing
175g/6oz rice vermicelli
groundnut (peanut) oil, for deep-frying and stir-frying
8 spring onions (scallions), diagonally sliced
2 garlic cloves, crushed
4–5 carrots, cut into julienne strips
1–2 fresh red chillies, seeded and finely sliced
2 small courgettes (zucchini), diagonally sliced
5ml/1 tsp grated fresh root ginger
60ml/4 tbsp rice vinegar
90ml/6 tbsp light soy sauce
475ml/16fl oz/2 cups spicy stock

1 Beat the steak to about 2.5cm/1in thick. Place in a shallow dish, brush with the teriyaki sauce and set aside for 2–4 hours. Separate the rice vermicelli into manageable loops. Pour oil into a large wok to a depth of about 5cm/2in, and heat until a strand of vermicelli cooks as soon as it is lowered into the oil.

2 Add a loop of vermicelli to the oil. Almost immediately, turn to cook on the other side, then remove and drain on kitchen paper. Repeat with the remaining loops. Transfer the cooked noodles to a separate wok or serving bowl and keep warm.

3 Strain the oil from the wok into a heatproof bowl and set it aside. Heat 15ml/1 tbsp groundnut oil in the clean wok. When it sizzles, fry the steak for about 30 seconds on each side, until browned. Transfer to a board and cut into thick slices. The meat should be well browned on the outside but pink inside. Set aside.

4 Add a little extra oil to the wok, add the spring onions, garlic and carrots and fry for 5–6 minutes, until the carrots are just soft. Add the chillies, courgettes and ginger and fry for 1–2 minutes. Stir in the rice vinegar, soy sauce and stock. Cook for about 4 minutes, or until the sauce has thickened slightly. Return the slices of steak to the wok and cook for a further 1–2 minutes.

5 Spoon the steak, vegetables and sauce over the noodles and toss lightly and carefully to mix. Serve immediately.

Meatballs and Noodles Energy 548kcal/2279kJ; Protein 36.8g; Carbohydrate 24.9g, of which sugars 3g; Fat 33.3g, of which saturates 12.4g; Cholesterol 101mg; Calcium 52mg; Fibre 1.7g; Sodium 161mg.
Thai Crispy Noodles Energy 493kcal/2052kJ; Protein 29.5g; Carbohydrate 43.4g, of which sugars 7.2g; Fat 21.9g, of which saturates 5.7g; Cholesterol 65mg; Calcium 43mg; Fibre 2g; Sodium 1697mg.

Curried Spicy Rice with Fenugreek

This dish is prominently flavoured with fenugreek and soured with dried mangosteen. Lemon juice will provide the same effect.

Serves 4 to 6

175g/6oz Bengal gram
600ml/1 pint/2½ cups water
2.5ml/½ tsp ground turmeric
50g/2oz fried onions, crushed
45ml/3 tbsp green masala paste
a few mint and coriander (cilantro) leaves, chopped
350g/12oz basmati rice, cooked
30ml/2 tbsp ghee
a little water
60ml/4 tbsp vegetable oil
2.5ml/¼ tsp fenugreek seeds
15g/½oz dried fenugreek leaves
2 garlic cloves, crushed
5ml/1 tsp ground coriander
5ml/1 tsp cumin seeds
5ml/1 tsp chilli powder
60ml/4 tbsp gram flour mixed with 60ml/4 tbsp water
450g/1lb bottle gourd peeled, pith and seeds removed, cut into bitesize pieces or marrow (large zucchini) or courgettes (zucchini)
175ml/6fl oz/¾ cup tomato juice
juice of 3 lemons
salt, to taste
coriander (cilantro) leaves, to garnish

1 For the rice, boil the bengal gram in the water with the turmeric until the grains are just soft. Drain, reserving the water.

2 Toss the bengal gram gently with the deep-fried onions, green masala paste, chopped mint and coriander leaves, and salt

3 Grease a heavy pan and place a layer of rice in the bottom. Add the bengal gram mixture and another layer of the remaining rice. Place small knobs of ghee on top, sprinkle with a little water and gently heat until steam gathers in the pan.

4 To make the curry, heat the oil in a pan and fry the fenugreek seeds and leaves and garlic until the garlic turns golden brown.

5 Mix the ground spices to a paste with a little water. Add to the pan and simmer until all the water evaporates.

6 Add the remaining ingredients, and cook until the gourd is soft and transparent. Garnish with the coriander leaves and serve immediately.

Chillies with Green Gram and Rice

The whole spices in this tasty dish are edible, although it is advisable to warn the diners about them to avoid any unexpected surprises.

Serves 4 to 6

60ml/4 tbsp ghee
1 onion, finely chopped
2 garlic cloves, crushed
2.5cm/1in piece fresh root ginger, shredded
4 green chillies, chopped
4 whole cloves
2.5cm/1in cinnamon stick
4 whole green cardamoms
60ml/1 tsp turmeric
salt, to taste
350g/12oz patna rice, washed and soaked for 20 minutes
175g/6oz split green gram, washed and soaked for 20 minutes
600ml/1pint/2½ cups water

1 Gently heat the ghee in a large heavy pan with a tight-fitting lid. Fry the onion, garlic, ginger, chillies, cloves, cinnamon, cardamoms, turmeric and salt until the onion is beginning to turn soft and translucent.

2 Drain the rice and the green gram, and then add to the spices in the pan and fry for 2–3 minutes.

3 Add the water to the pan and bring to the boil. Reduce the heat, cover and simmer for about 20–25 minutes, or until all the water has been absorbed.

4 Take the pan off the heat and leave to rest for 5 minutes. Gently toss the mixture together until well combined and serve immediately.

Cook's Tip

Ghee is a clarified unsalted butter widely used in Indian cooking. It has a nutty, caramel flavor and aroma and is made by simmering the butter until all water has boiled off and the milk solids have settled to the bottom. The lack of water and solids mean that it has a longer life and a higher smoking point than normal butter.

Spicy Rice Energy 481kcal/2015kJ; Protein 14.8g; Carbohydrate 72.6g, of which sugars 4.1g; Fat 15.2g, of which saturates 3.5g; Cholesterol 0mg; Calcium 65mg; Fibre 2.8g; Sodium 82mg.
Chillies with Gram Energy 397kcal/1662kJ; Protein 11.6g; Carbohydrate 63.8g, of which sugars 1.3g; Fat 10.7g, of which saturates 4.8g; Cholesterol 0mg; Calcium 31mg; Fibre 1.6g; Sodium 12mg.

Fried Rice with Okra and Chillies

Okra features in many tasty Indian and Asian dishes and is here cooked with rice.

Serves 3 to 4

30ml/2 tbsp vegetable oil
15ml/1 tbsp butter or margarine
1 garlic clove, crushed
½ red onion, finely chopped
115g/4oz okra, topped and tailed
30ml/2 tbsp diced green and red (bell) peppers
2.5ml/½ tsp dried thyme
2 green chillies, finely chopped
2.5ml/½ tsp five-spice powder
1 vegetable stock (bouillon) cube
30ml/2 tbsp soy sauce
15ml/1 tbsp chopped fresh coriander (cilantro)
225g/8oz/2½ cups cooked rice
salt and ground black pepper
coriander (cilantro) sprigs, to garnish

1 Heat the oil and butter or margarine in a frying pan or wok, add the garlic and onion and cook over a moderate heat for 5 minutes until soft.

2 Thinly slice the okra, add to the pan or wok and fry gently for a further 6–7 minutes.

3 Add the green and red peppers, the dried thyme, the green chillies and five-spice powder and cook, stirring constantly, for 3 minutes, then crumble in the stock cube. Stir well to dissolve the stock cube.

4 Add the soy sauce, the chopped fresh coriander and the cooked rice to the pan and heat through, stirring well.

5 Season with salt and ground black pepper to taste. Serve the dish immediately, garnished with the sprigs of fresh coriander.

Cook's Tip
Okra, also known as lady's fingers, has a ridged skin and a tapered, oblong shape. Buy okra that is firm and brightly coloured. When cooked, okra gives off a viscous substance that helps to thicken any liquid in which it is cooked.

Chilli Coconut Rice

This is a delicious, mildly spiced and creamy rice dish. Use thin coconut milk, which is rich enough and won't dominate the other ingredients in the dish.

Serves 4

30ml/2 tbsp vegetable oil
1 onion, chopped
30ml/2 tbsp tomato purée (paste)
600ml/1 pint/2½ cups coconut milk
2 carrots
1 yellow (bell) pepper
5ml/1 tsp dried thyme
2.5ml/½ tsp mixed spice
1 fresh green chilli, seeded and chopped
350g/12oz/1½ cups long grain rice
salt

1 Heat the oil in a large pan and fry the onion for about 2–3 minutes, until it is beginning to soften and turn translucent.

2 Add the tomato purée to the pan and cook over a moderate heat for 5–6 minutes, stirring all the time.

3 Pour the coconut milk into the pan and stir until well combined. Bring the mixture to the boil.

4 Roughly chop the carrots. Remove the seeds from the yellow pepper and roughly chop the flesh.

5 Stir the carrots, pepper, thyme, mixed spice, chilli and rice into the onion mixture, season with salt and bring to the boil.

6 Cover the pan and simmer over a low heat until the rice has absorbed most of the liquid.

7 Cover the rice with foil, secure with the lid and steam very gently until the rice is fully cooked. Serve immediately.

Cook's Tip
If you prefer a little more heat, then use the seeds from the chilli pepper or increase the amount of chillies you use.

Fried Rice with Okra Energy 247kcal/1034kJ; Protein 5g; Carbohydrate 29g, of which sugars 3g; Fat 13g, of which saturates 4g; Cholesterol 11mg; Calcium 99mg; Fibre 2.2g; Sodium 1100mg.
Coconut Rice Energy 448kcal/1876kJ; Protein 8.6g; Carbohydrate 87.8g, of which sugars 17g; Fat 6.9g, of which saturates 1.1g; Cholesterol 0mg; Calcium 82mg; Fibre 2.6g; Sodium 194mg.

Yellow Rice with Pickled Chillies

This rice dish owes its striking colour and distinctive flavour to ground achiote seed, which is derived from annatto.

Serves 6

200g/7oz/1 cup long grain white rice
30ml/2 tbsp vegetable oil
5ml/1 tsp ground achiote seed (annatto powder)
1 small onion, finely chopped
2 garlic cloves, crushed
475ml/16fl oz/2 cups chicken stock
50g/2oz/⅓ cup drained pickled jalapeño chilli slices, chopped
salt
fresh coriander (cilantro) leaves, to garnish

1 Put the rice in a heatproof bowl, pour over boiling water to cover and leave to stand for 20 minutes. Drain, rinse under cold water and drain again.

2 Heat the oil in a pan, add the ground achiote seed and cook for 2–3 minutes. Add the onion and garlic and cook for a further 3–4 minutes, or until the onion is translucent.

3 Add the drained rice to the pan and stir well. Continue to cook for 5 minutes.

4 Pour in the stock, mix well and bring to the boil. Lower the heat, cover the pan with a tight-fitting lid and simmer for about 25–30 minutes, until all the liquid has been absorbed.

5 Add the chopped jalapeños to the pan and stir well to distribute them evenly in the rice mixture.

6 Add salt to taste, then spoon the rice into a warmed serving dish and garnish with the coriander leaves. Serve immediately.

Cook's Tip

Achiote, the seed of the annatto tree, is used as a food colouring and flavouring throughout Latin America. You can buy it in specialist spice shops and ethnic food stores.

Indonesian Spicy Fried Rice

This dish of fried rice is one of Indonesia's national dishes. Generally made with leftover cooked grains, the fried rice is served with crispy shallots and chillies or it is tossed with shrimp or crabmeat, and chopped vegetables.

Serves 4

½ cucumber
30–45ml/2–3 tbsp vegetable or groundnut (peanut) oil, plus extra for shallow frying
4 shallots, finely chopped
4 garlic cloves, finely chopped
3–4 fresh red chillies, seeded and chopped
45ml/3 tbsp kecap manis (Indonesian sweet soy sauce)
15ml/1 tbsp tomato purée (paste)
350g/12oz/1¾ cups cooked long grain rice
4 eggs

1 Peel the cucumber, cut it in half lengthways and scoop out the seeds. Cut the flesh into thin sticks. Put aside until it is required.

2 Heat the oil in a wok or large frying pan. Add the shallots, garlic and chillies to the pan and fry, stirring constantly, until they begin to colour.

3 Add the kecap manis and tomato purée and stir for about 2 minutes until thick, to form a sauce.

4 Add the cooked rice to the pan and continue to cook, stirring occasionally, for about 5 minutes until the rice is well coated with the sauce and heated through.

5 Meanwhile, in a large frying pan, heat a thin layer of oil for frying and crack the eggs into it. Fry for 1–2 minutes until the whites are cooked but the yolks remain runny.

6 Spoon the rice into four deep bowls. Alternatively, use one bowl as a mould to invert each portion of rice on to each individual plate, then lift off the bowl to reveal the mound of rice beneath. Place a fried egg on top of each serving and garnish with the cucumber sticks.

Rice with Chillies Energy 159kcal/662kJ; Protein 2.7g; Carbohydrate 27.9g, of which sugars 1.1g; Fat 3.9g, of which saturates 0.4g; Cholesterol 0mg; Calcium 10mg; Fibre 0.3g; Sodium 1000mg.
Indonesian Spicy Rice Energy 273kcal/1146kJ; Protein 9.9g; Carbohydrate 33g, of which sugars 4.7g; Fat 12.3g, of which saturates 2.5g; Cholesterol 190mg; Calcium 67mg; Fibre 1.1g; Sodium 884mg.

Spiced Vietnamese Chilli Rice

Although plain steamed rice is served at almost every meal in Vietnam, many families like to sneak in a little spice too. Chilli for fire, turmeric for colour, and coriander for its cooling flavour, are all that's needed.

Serves 4

15ml/1 tbsp vegetable oil
2–3 green or red Thai chillies, seeded and finely chopped
2 garlic cloves, finely chopped
2.5cm/1in piece fresh root ginger, chopped
5ml/1 tsp sugar
10–15ml/2–3 tsp ground turmeric
225g/8oz/generous 1 cup long grain rice
30ml/2 tbsp Thai fish sauce
600ml/1 pint/2½ cups water or stock
1 bunch of fresh coriander (cilantro), stalks removed, leaves finely chopped
salt and ground black pepper

1 Heat the oil in a large, heavy pan. Stir in the chillies, garlic and ginger with the sugar. As the spices begin to colour, stir in the ground turmeric.

2 Add the rice, coating it well, then pour in the fish sauce and the water or stock – the liquid should sit about 2.5cm/1in above the rice.

3 Season with salt and ground black pepper and bring the liquid to the boil. Reduce the heat, cover the pan and simmer for about 25 minutes, or until the water has been absorbed. Remove from the heat and leave the rice to steam for a further 10 minutes.

4 Transfer the rice on to a serving dish. Add some of the coriander and lightly toss together using a fork. Garnish with the remaining coriander.

Cook's Tip
This rice goes well with grilled (broiled) and stir-fried fish and shellfish dishes, but you can serve it as an alternative to plain rice. Add extra chillies, if you like.

Red-hot Mexican Rice

Versions of this dish, a relative of Spanish rice, are popular all over Latin America. It is a delicious medley of rice, tomatoes and aromatic flavourings.

Serves 6

200g/7oz/1 cup long grain rice
200g/7oz can chopped tomatoes in tomato juice
½ onion, roughly chopped
2 garlic cloves, roughly chopped
30ml/2 tbsp vegetable oil
450ml/¾ pint/scant 2 cups chicken stock
2.5ml/½ tsp salt
3 fresh fresno chillies or other fresh green chillies, trimmed
150g/5oz/1 cup frozen peas (optional)
ground black pepper

1 Put the rice in a large heatproof bowl and pour over boiling water to cover. Stir once, then leave to stand for 10 minutes. Transfer into a strainer over the sink, rinse under cold water, then drain again. Set aside to dry slightly.

2 Pour the tomatoes and juice into a food processor or blender, add the onion and garlic and process until smooth.

3 Heat the oil in a large, heavy pan, add the rice and cook over a moderate heat until it turns a delicate golden brown. Stir occasionally to ensure that the rice does not stick to the pan.

4 Add the tomato mixture and stir over a moderate heat until all the liquid has been absorbed. Stir in the stock, salt, whole chillies and peas, if using. Continue to cook, stirring occasionally, until all the liquid has been absorbed and the rice is just tender.

5 Remove the pan from the heat, cover it with a tight-fitting lid and leave it to stand in a warm place for 5–10 minutes. Remove the chillies, fluff up the rice lightly and serve, sprinkled with black pepper. The chillies may be used as a garnish, if liked.

Cook's Tip
Do not stir the rice too often after adding the stock or the grains will break down and the mixture will become starchy.

Spiced Vietnamese Chilli Rice Energy 252kcal/1066kJ; Protein 5g; Carbohydrate 51g, of which sugars 1g; Fat 5g, of which saturates 1g; Cholesterol 0mg; Calcium 24mg; Fibre 0.3g; Sodium 500mg.
Mexican Rice Energy 162kcal/676kj; Protein 2.8g; Carbohydrate 28.4g; of which sugars 1.6g; Fat 4g; of which saturates 0.5g; Cholesterol 0mg; Calcium 11mg; Fibre 0.5g; Sodium 167mg.

Spicy Bulgur and Pine Nut Pilaff

Although not rice, bulgur makes a delicious pilaff, and is a popular staple throughout the Middle East and Africa. This version comes from North Africa.

Serves 4

30ml/2 tbsp olive oil
1 onion, chopped
1 garlic clove, crushed
5ml/1 tsp ground saffron or turmeric
2.5ml/½ tsp ground cinnamon
1 fresh green chilli, seeded and chopped
600ml/1 pint/2½ cups chicken or vegetable stock
150ml/¼ pint/⅔ cups white wine
225g/8oz/1⅓ cups bulgur wheat
15g/½oz/1 tbsp butter or margarine
30–45ml/2–3 tbsp pine nuts
30ml/2 tbsp chopped fresh parsley

1 Heat the oil in a large pan and fry the onion until soft. Add the garlic, saffron or turmeric, ground cinnamon and chopped chilli, and fry for a few seconds more.

2 Add the stock and wine to the pan and mix well. Bring to the boil, then reduce the heat and simmer for 8 minutes.

3 Rinse the bulgur wheat under cold water, drain and add to the pan. Cover and simmer gently for about 15 minutes until the stock has been absorbed.

4 Melt the butter in a small pan, add the pine nuts and fry for a few minutes until golden. Add to the pan containing the other ingredients. Add the chopped parsley to the pan and stir with a fork to mix.

5 Spoon into a warmed serving dish and serve immediately. This pilaff would make a tasty accompaniment to grilled and roasted meats or a vegetable stew.

Cook's Tip
You can leave out the wine, if you prefer, and replace with water or stock. It is not essential, but it adds extra flavour.

Rice with Chilli Chicken and Potatoes

This tasty Indian dish is generally only made on special occasions.

Serves 4 to 6

1.3kg/3lb skinless chicken breast fillet, cut into large pieces
60ml/4 tbsp biryani masala paste
2 green chillies, chopped
15ml/1 tbsp crushed fresh root ginger
15ml/1 tbsp crushed garlic
50g/2oz coriander (cilantro) leaves, chopped
6–8 mint leaves, chopped
150ml/½ pint/⅔ cup natural (plain) yogurt, beaten
30ml/2 tbsp tomato purée (paste)
4 onions, finely sliced, deep-fried and crushed
450g/1lb basmati rice, washed and drained
5ml/1 tsp black cumin seeds
5cm/2in cinnamon stick
4 green cardamoms
2 black cardamoms
vegetable oil, for shallow-frying
4 large potatoes, peeled and quartered
175ml/6fl oz/¾ cup milk, mixed with 75ml/2½fl oz/⅓ cup water
1 sachet saffron powder, mixed with 90ml/6 tbsp milk
30ml/2 tbsp ghee or unsalted butter
salt, to taste

For the garnish
ghee or unsalted (sweet) butter, for shallow-frying
50g/2oz cashew nuts
50g/2oz sultanas (golden raisins)
deep-fried onion slices

1 Mix the chicken with the next ten ingredients and marinate for 2 hours. Place in a pan and cook for 10 minutes. Set aside. Boil a pan of salted water and soak the rice with the cumin seeds, cinnamon and cardamoms for 5 minutes. Drain well. Heat the oil for frying. Cook the potatoes until browned. Set aside.

2 Place half the rice on top of the chicken, then an even layer of potatoes. Add the remaining rice on the potatoes. Sprinkle the milky water all over the rice. Make a few holes through the rice and pour in a little saffron milk. Dot the surface with ghee or butter, cover and cook over a low heat for 35–45 minutes.

3 Make the garnish. Heat the ghee or butter and fry the nuts and sultanas until they swell. Set aside. When the rice is ready, gently toss the layers together. Garnish with the nut mixture and onion slices and serve immediately.

Spicy Bulgur Pilaff Energy 295kcal/1225kJ; Protein 4.8g; Carbohydrate 32.4g, of which sugars 2.7g; Fat 14.4g, of which saturates 3.1g; Cholesterol 8mg; Calcium 25mg; Fibre 0.7g; Sodium 26mg.
Chilli Chicken Energy 940kcal/3944kJ; Protein 66g; Carbohydrate 107.1g, of which sugars 15.5g; Fat 28.4g, of which saturates 5.9g; Cholesterol 153mg; Calcium 166mg; Fibre 4.9g; Sodium 195mg.

Spiced Chicken Biryani

Biryanis originated in Persia and are traditionally made with meat and rice.

Serves 4

275g/10oz/1½ cups basmati rice
30ml/2 tbsp vegetable oil
1 onion, thinly sliced
2 garlic cloves, crushed
1 green chilli, finely chopped
2.5cm/1in fresh root ginger, finely chopped
675g/1½lb skinless chicken breast fillets, cut into 2.5cm/1in cubes
45ml/3 tbsp curry paste
1.5ml/¼ tsp salt
1.5ml/¼ tsp garam masala
3 tomatoes, cut into thin wedges
1.5ml/¼ tsp ground turmeric
2 bay leaves
4 green cardamom pods
4 cloves
1.5ml/¼ tsp saffron strands
fresh coriander (cilantro), to garnish

1 Wash the rice in several changes of cold water. Put into a large bowl, cover with plenty of water and leave to soak for 30 minutes.

2 Meanwhile, heat the oil in a large frying pan and fry the onion for about 5–7 minutes until lightly browned, then add the garlic, chilli and ginger and fry for about 2 minutes.

3 Add the chicken to the pan and fry for about 5 minutes, stirring occasionally.

4 Add the curry paste, salt and garam masala and cook for 5 minutes. Add the tomatoes and continue to cook for a further 3–4 minutes. Remove from the heat and set aside.

5 Preheat the oven to 190°C/375°F/Gas 5. Bring a large pan of water to the boil. Drain the rice and add it to the pan with the turmeric. Cook for about 10 minutes, or until the rice is almost tender. Drain the rice and toss together with the bay leaves, cardamoms, cloves and saffron.

6 Layer the rice and chicken in a shallow, ovenproof dish until all the mixture has been used, finishing off with a layer of rice. Cover and bake in the oven for 15–20 minutes, or until the chicken is tender. Serve immediately, garnished with a fresh coriander sprig.

Fiery Lamb Pilau

In this Indian rice dish, lamb is first marinated in spices then pan-fried and cooked with the rice to create a tasty dish that can be served on its own or accompanied with Indian breads or a moist dhal.

Serves 4

450g/1lb stewing lamb
15ml/1 tbsp curry powder
1 onion, chopped
2 garlic cloves, crushed
2.5ml/½ tsp dried thyme
2.5ml/½ tsp dried oregano
1 fresh or dried chilli
25g/1oz/2 tbsp butter or margarine, plus more for serving
600ml/1 pint/2½ cups beef stock or chicken stock or coconut milk
5ml/1 tsp ground black pepper
2 tomatoes, chopped
10ml/2 tsp sugar
30ml/2 tbsp chopped spring onions (scallions)
450g/1lb basmati rice
spring onion (scallion) strips, to garnish

1 Cut the lamb into bitesize cubes and place in a shallow glass or china dish. Sprinkle with the curry powder, onion, garlic, herbs and chilli and stir until the spices are well combined and the lamb pieces are thoroughly coated. Cover the dish loosely with clear film (plastic wrap) and leave to marinate in a cool place for 1 hour.

2 Melt the butter or margarine in a large, heavy pan and fry the lamb for 5–10 minutes, until evenly browned on all sides.

3 Add the stock or coconut milk to the pan and stir well. Bring the mixture to the boil, then lower the heat and simmer for about 35 minutes or until the meat is tender.

4 Add the black pepper, tomatoes, sugar, spring onions and rice, stir well and reduce the heat. Make sure that the rice is covered by about 2.5cm/1in of liquid and add a little more water if necessary.

5 Simmer the pilau gently for about 25 minutes, or until the rice is tender and the liquid has been absorbed. Stir a little extra butter or margarine into the rice before serving. Garnish with the spring onion strips.

Chicken Biryani Energy 377kcal/1579kJ; Protein 30.3g; Carbohydrate 47.2g, of which sugars 8.3g; Fat 7.5g, of which saturates 1.2g; Cholesterol 71mg; Calcium 86mg; Fibre 1.8g; Sodium 255mg.
Fiery Lamb Pilau Energy 652kcal/2726kJ; Protein 32.1g; Carbohydrate 96.3g, of which sugars 5.7g; Fat 15g, of which saturates 7.3g; Cholesterol 97mg; Calcium 51mg; Fibre 1g; Sodium 231mg.

Savoury Fried Rice with Chilli and Cashew Nuts

This is typical Thai street food, eaten at all times of the day. The recipe can be adapted to use whatever vegetables you have available and you could also add meat or shellfish.

Serves 2

30ml/2 tbsp vegetable oil
2 garlic cloves, finely chopped
1 small fresh red chilli, seeded and finely chopped
50g/2oz/½ cup cashew nuts, toasted
50g/2oz/⅔ cup desiccated (dry unsweetened shredded) coconut, toasted
2.5ml/½ tsp palm sugar (jaggery) or light muscovado (brown) sugar
30ml/2 tbsp light soy sauce
15ml/1 tbsp rice vinegar
1 egg
115g/4oz/1 cup green beans, sliced
½ spring cabbage or 115g/4oz spring greens (collards) or pak choi (bok choy), shredded
90g/3½oz jasmine rice, cooked
lime wedges, to serve

1 Heat the oil in a wok or large, heavy frying pan. Add the garlic and cook over a medium to high heat until golden. Do not let it burn or it will taste bitter.

2 Add the red chilli, cashew nuts and toasted coconut to the wok or pan and stir-fry briefly, taking care to prevent the coconut from scorching.

3 Stir the sugar, soy sauce and rice vinegar into the pan. Cook, stirring, over the heat for 1–2 minutes.

4 Push the stir-fry to one side of the wok or pan and break the egg into the empty space. When the egg is almost set stir it into the garlic and chilli mixture.

5 Add the green beans, greens and cooked rice to the pan. Stir over the heat until the greens have just wilted.

6 Spoon the rice mixture into a warmed serving dish. Offer the lime wedges separately, for squeezing over the rice, and serve immediately in individual bowls.

Red Chilli Rice

This pretty Thai dish is traditionally shaped into a cone and surrounded by a variety of accompaniments before being served.

Serves 8

450g/1lb/2⅔ cups jasmine rice
60ml/4 tbsp vegetable oil
2 garlic cloves, crushed
2 onions, thinly sliced
2.5ml/½ tsp ground turmeric
750ml/1¼ pints/3 cups water
400ml/14fl oz can coconut milk
1–2 lemon grass stalks, bruised

For the accompaniments
omelette strips
2 fresh red chillies, seeded and shredded
cucumber chunks
tomato wedges
fried onions
prawn (shrimp) crackers

1 Put the jasmine rice in a large strainer and rinse it thoroughly under cold water. Drain well.

2 Heat the oil in a frying pan with a lid. Gently cook the garlic, onions and turmeric for 2–3 minutes, until the onions have softened. Add the rice and stir well to coat in the oil.

3 Pour in the water and coconut milk and add the lemon grass. Bring to the boil, stirring. Cover the pan and cook gently for about 12 minutes, or until all the liquid has been absorbed by the rice.

4 Remove the pan from the heat and lift the lid. Cover with a clean dish towel, replace the lid and leave to stand in a warm place for 15 minutes.

5 Remove the lemon grass, mound the rice mixture in a cone on a serving platter and garnish with the accompaniments, then serve immediately.

Cook's Tip

Jasmine rice is an aromatic rice from Thailand. It is widely available in most supermarkets and Asian stores. It is also known as Thai fragrant rice.

Fried Rice Energy 548kcal/2271kJ; Protein 14.6g; Carbohydrate 25.1g, of which sugars 7g; Fat 43.9g, of which saturates 18.2g; Cholesterol 110mg; Calcium 183mg; Fibre 7.5g; Sodium 1200mg.
Red Chilli Rice Energy 285kcal/1204kJ Protein 4.6g; Carbohydrate 52.6g, of which sugars 3.8g; Fat 7.7g, of which saturates 0.7g; Cholesterol 0mg; Calcium 49mg; Fibre 0.6g; Sodium 58mg.

Pumpkin Rice with Fried Fish and Ginger and Chilli

This is a tasty dish combining pumpkin, spicy fish, and a spicy aromatic mixture added at the end.

Serves 4

30ml/2 tbsp plain (all-purpose) flour
5ml/1 tsp ground coriander
2.5ml/½ tsp ground turmeric
450g/1lb sea bass or other firm fish, skinned, boned and cubed
30–45ml/2–3 tbsp olive oil
6 spring onions (scallions), sliced 1 garlic clove, finely chopped
500g/1¼lb pumpkin, cubed
275g/10oz/1½ cups basmati rice, soaked
550ml/18fl oz/2½ cups fish stock
salt and ground black pepper
lime wedges and fresh coriander (cilantro) sprigs, to garnish

For the flavouring mixture

45ml/3 tbsp finely chopped fresh coriander (cilantro)
10ml/2 tsp finely chopped fresh root ginger
½–1 fresh chilli, seeded and chopped
45ml/3 tbsp lime or lemon juice

1 Mix the flour, coriander, turmeric and salt and pepper in a plastic bag, add the fish and shake so that the fish is coated. Set aside. Mix all the flavouring mixture ingredients in a small bowl.

2 Heat 15ml/1 tbsp oil in a flameproof casserole and stir-fry the spring onions and garlic for a few minutes. Add the pumpkin and cook gently for 4–5 minutes or until it begins to soften.

3 Drain the rice, add it to the mixture and toss over a brisk heat for 2–3 minutes. Stir in the stock, with a little salt. Bring to simmering point, then lower the heat, cover and cook for 12–15 minutes, until both the rice and the pumpkin are tender.

4 About 4 minutes before the rice is ready, heat the remaining oil in a frying pan and fry the spiced fish over a moderately high heat for about 3 minutes until the outside is lightly browned and crisp and the flesh is cooked through but still moist.

5 Stir the flavouring mixture into the rice and transfer to a warm serving dish. Lay the fish pieces on top. Serve, garnished with coriander and lime wedges for squeezing over the fish.

Spicy Moroccan Paella Rice

This dish has crossed the sea from Spain to Morocco, and acquired some spicy touches.

Serves 6

150g/5oz prepared squid, cut into rings
275g/10oz cod or haddock fillets, skinned, cut into bitesize chunks
8–10 raw king prawns (jumbo shrimp), peeled and deveined
8 scallops, trimmed and halved
2 skinless chicken breast fillets
350g/12oz fresh mussels
250g/9oz/1⅓ cups long grain rice
30ml/2 tbsp sunflower oil
1 bunch spring onions (scallions), cut into strips
2 courgettes (zucchini), cut in strips
1 red (bell) pepper, cored, seeded and cut into strips
400ml/14fl oz/1⅔ cups chicken stock
250ml/8fl oz/1 cup passata (bottled strained tomatoes)
salt and ground black pepper
fresh coriander (cilantro) sprigs and lemon wedges, to garnish

For the marinade

2 red chillies, seeded and chopped
handful of fresh coriander (cilantro)
10–15ml/2–3 tsp ground cumin
15ml/1 tbsp paprika
2 garlic cloves
45ml/3 tbsp olive oil
60ml/4 tbsp sunflower oil
juice of 1 lemon

1 Place all the marinade ingredients in a food processor with 5ml/1 tsp salt and blend. Place the fish and shellfish (except the mussels) in one bowl, and the chicken in another. Split the marinade between the two. Cover and marinate for 2 hours.

2 Scrub the mussels, discarding any that do not close when tapped, and chill. Place the rice in a bowl, cover with boiling water and leave for 30 minutes. Drain the chicken and fish, and reserve the marinade. Heat the oil in a wok. Fry the chicken until browned.

3 Fry the spring onions for 1 minute, add the courgettes and pepper and fry for 3–4 minutes. Transfer the chicken and the vegetables to separate plates. Cook the marinade for 1 minute. Add the drained rice, stock, passata and chicken. Bring to the boil, cover and simmer for 15 minutes.

4 Add the vegetables to the pan and top with the seafood. Cook for 12 minutes until the fish is tender and the mussels are open. Discard any not open. Garnish with coriander and lemon wedges.

Pumpkin Rice Energy 436kcal/1825kJ; Protein 27.9g; Carbohydrate 64.2g, of which sugars 3g; Fat 7.2g, of which saturates 1.1g; Cholesterol 52mg; Calcium 101mg; Fibre 2.3g; Sodium 73mg.
Spicy Moroccan Rice Energy 490kcal/2056kJ; Protein 46.9g; Carbohydrate 44.1g, of which sugars 8.7g; Fat 14g, of which saturates 2g; Cholesterol 202mg; Calcium 94mg; Fibre 2.2g; Sodium 367mg.

Squid Risotto with Coriander

Squid is marinated in lime and kiwi fruit before being cooked in this spicy risotto.

Serves 3 to 4

450g/1lb squid, cleaned and gutted
about 45ml/3 tbsp olive oil
15g/½oz/1 tbsp butter
1 onion, finely chopped
2 garlic cloves, crushed
1 fresh red chilli, seeded and finely sliced
275g/10oz/1½ cups risotto rice
175ml/6fl oz/¾ cup white wine
1 litre/1¾ pints/4 cups fish stock
30ml/2 tbsp chopped fresh coriander (cilantro)
salt and ground black pepper

For the marinade

2 kiwi fruit, chopped
1 fresh red chilli, seeded and finely sliced
30ml/2 tbsp fresh lime juice

1 Cut the squid body into thin strips and the tentacles into short pieces. Mash the kiwi fruit for the marinade in a bowl, then stir in the chilli and lime juice. Add the squid, stirring to coat. Season with salt and ground black pepper, cover with clear film (plastic wrap) and chill for 4 hours or overnight.

2 Drain the squid. Heat 15ml/1 tbsp of the olive oil in a frying pan and cook, in batches if necessary, for 30–60 seconds over a high heat. It is important that the squid cooks very quickly. Transfer to a plate and set aside. If too much juice accumulates in the pan, pour this into a jug (pitcher) and add more olive oil when cooking the next batch. Reserve the accumulated juices.

3 Heat the remaining oil with the butter in a large pan and gently fry the onion and garlic for 5–6 minutes until soft. Add the sliced chilli to the pan and fry for 1 minute more. Add the rice. Cook for a few minutes, stirring, until the rice is coated with oil, then stir in the wine until it has been absorbed.

4 Heat the stock, and gradually add it and the reserved liquid from the squid, a ladleful at a time, to the pan. Stir constantly and wait until each addition is absorbed before adding the next.

5 When the rice is about three-quarters cooked, add the squid and cook until the stock has gone and the rice is tender. Stir in the coriander, cover, and leave for a few minutes before serving.

Chilli Rice with Chinese Sausage

Traditional Vietnamese stir-fried rice includes cured Chinese pork sausage, or thin strips of pork combined with prawns or crab meat. Prepared this way, the dish can be eaten as a snack, or as part of the meal with grilled and roasted meats accompanied by a vegetable dish or salad.

Serves 4

25g/1oz dried cloud ear (wood ear) mushrooms, soaked for 20 minutes
15ml/1 tbsp vegetable or sesame oil
1 onion, sliced
2 green or red Thai chillies, seeded and finely chopped
2 Chinese sausages (15cm/6in long), each sliced into 10 pieces
175g/6oz prawns (shrimp), shelled and deveined
30ml/2 tbsp Thai fish sauce, plus extra for drizzling
10ml/2 tsp five-spice powder
1 bunch of fresh coriander (cilantro), stalks removed, leaves finely chopped
450g/1lb/4 cups cold steamed rice
ground black pepper

1 Drain the soaked cloud ear mushrooms then cut into thin strips. Heat a wok or large, heavy pan and add the oil. Add the onion and chillies and fry until they begin to colour, then stir in the cloud ear mushrooms.

2 Add the Chinese sausage slices, moving them around the wok or pan until they begin to brown.

3 Add the prawns and move them around until they turn opaque. Stir in the fish sauce, the five-spice powder and 30ml/2 tbsp of the coriander.

4 Season well with ground black pepper. Add the rice, and cook, stirring constantly to make sure it doesn't stick to the pan.

5 As soon as the rice is heated through, sprinkle with the remainder of the chopped fresh coriander and serve with Thai fish sauce to drizzle over it.

Squid Risotto Energy 645kcal/2722kJ; Protein 31g; Carbohydrate 86g, of which sugars 5g; Fat 22g, of which saturates 6g; Cholesterol 348mg; Calcium 84mg; Fibre 1.2g; Sodium 1000mg.
Chilli Rice Energy 398kcal/1673kJ; Protein 19g; Carbohydrate 44g, of which sugars 4g; Fat 18g, of which saturates 5g; Cholesterol 116mg; Calcium 158mg; Fibre 2g; Sodium 800mg.

Spicy Beef and Vegetable Rice

This dish looks a little daunting but is well worth the effort. It is the perfect dish to serve on a special occasion for guests who like spicy food.

Serves 4

400g/14oz/2 cups short grain rice or pudding rice, rinsed
a drop of sunflower oil
1 sheet dried seaweed
4 quail's eggs
vegetable oil, for shallow-frying
sesame seeds, to garnish

For the marinated beef

30ml/2 tbsp dark soy sauce
15ml/1 tbsp garlic, crushed
15ml/1 tbsp sliced spring onions (scallions)
5ml/1 tsp sesame oil
5ml/1 tsp rice wine
200g/7oz beef, shredded
10ml/2 tsp vegetable oil
salt and ground black pepper

For the namul vegetables

150g/5oz mooli (daikon), peeled
1 courgette (zucchini)
150g/5oz/generous ½ cup soya beansprouts, trimmed
150g/5oz fern fronds (optional)
6 dried shiitake mushrooms, soaked in warm water for about 30 minutes until softened
½ cucumber

For the namul seasoning

5ml/1 tsp sugar
12.5ml/2½ tsp salt
30ml/2 tbsp sesame oil
5ml/1 tsp crushed garlic
a splash of dark soy sauce
1.5ml/¼ tsp chilli powder
5ml/1 tsp sesame seeds
vegetable oil, for stir-frying

For the gochujang sauce

15ml/3 tbsp gochujang
7.5ml/1½ tsp sugar or honey
10ml/2 tsp sesame oil

1 Place the rice in a pan and add water to 5mm/¼in above the rice. Add the sunflower oil, cover and bring to the boil. Simmer for 12–15 minutes. Remove from the heat and leave for 5 minutes.

2 For the marinade, blend the soy sauce, garlic, spring onions, sesame oil, rice wine, and salt and pepper. Add the beef, mix well and marinate for 1 hour. Roll up the seaweed and slice into strips. Mix the gochujang sauce ingredients and place in a serving bowl.

3 Cut the mooli and courgette into strips. Blend 5ml/1 tsp sugar, 5ml/1 tsp salt and 5ml/1 tsp sesame oil, with 2.5ml/½ tsp garlic, and fry. Use to coat the mooli. Transfer to a plate.

4 Blend 5ml/1 tsp salt and 5ml/1 tsp sesame oil with 2.5ml/½ tsp garlic and a little water. Use to coat the courgette. Heat 5ml/1 tsp vegetable oil and fry the courgette until soft. Transfer to the plate.

5 Briefly boil the beansprouts. Mix 15ml/1 tbsp sesame oil with 2.5ml/½ tsp salt, 1.5ml/¼ tsp chilli powder and 2.5ml/½ tsp sesame seeds and sugar. Use to coat the beansprouts. Transfer to the plate.

6 Parboil the fern fronds, if using, and drain. Stir-fry in 5ml/1 tsp sesame oil, with a little soy sauce and 2.5ml/½ tsp sesame seeds. Drain and slice the mushrooms, discarding the stems. Quickly fry in 5ml/1 tsp vegetable oil and season. Transfer to the plate. Seed the cucumber, cut into thin strips and add to the mushrooms.

7 Heat 10ml/2 tsp vegetable oil and fry the beef until tender. Serve the rice in four bowls and top with the vegetables and beef. Fry the eggs, and place one in each bowl. Garnish with sesame seeds and dried seaweed. Serve with gochujang sauce.

Fried Rice with Pork and Chillies

This classic rice dish looks particularly pretty garnished with strips of omelette.

Serves 4 to 6

45ml/3 tbsp vegetable oil
1 onion, chopped
15ml/1 tbsp chopped garlic
115g/4oz pork, cut into small cubes
2 eggs, beaten
1kg/2¼lb/4 cups cooked rice
30ml/2 tbsp Thai fish sauce
15ml/1 tbsp dark soy sauce
2.5ml/½ tsp caster (superfine) sugar

For the garnish

4 spring onions (scallions), finely sliced
2 fresh red chillies, seeded and finely sliced
1 lime, cut into wedges

1 Heat the oil in a wok or large frying pan. Add the onion and garlic and cook for about 2–3 minutes until the onion is beginning to turn soft and translucent.

2 Add the pork to the softened onion and garlic. Fry, stirring constantly, until the pork changes colour and is cooked through.

3 Add the beaten eggs to the pan and cook, stirring, until they are scrambled into small lumps.

4 Add the cooked rice to the pan and continue to stir and toss, to coat it with the oil and prevent it from sticking to the base of the pan.

5 Add the fish sauce, soy sauce and sugar and mix well. Continue to fry until the rice is thoroughly heated.

6 Spoon the rice into warmed individual bowls and serve immediately, garnished with sliced spring onions, sliced chillies and lime wedges.

Cook's Tip

To make 1kg/2¼lb/4 cups cooked rice, you will need approximately 400g/14oz/2 cups uncooked rice.

Spicy Beef Energy 645kcal/2688kJ; Protein 23.7g; Carbohydrate 88.5g, of which sugars 7.7g; Fat 21.4g, of which saturates 4.4g; Cholesterol 86mg; Calcium 73mg; Fibre 2.3g; Sodium 1781mg.
Rice with Pork Energy 513kcal/2165kJ; Protein 17.1g; Carbohydrate 80g, of which sugars 2.1g; Fat 16.1g, of which saturates 2.3g; Cholesterol 132mg; Calcium 75mg; Fibre 0.7g; Sodium 511mg.

Morning Glory with Fried Garlic Shallots and Chilli

Morning glory is a green leafy vegetable with long jointed stems and arrow-shaped leaves. The stems remain crunchy while the leaves wilt like spinach when cooked. It is perfect as a stir-fried side dish and combines well with the flavours of garlic and chilli.

Serves 4

2 bunches morning glory, total weight about 250g/9oz, trimmed and coarsely chopped into 2.5cm/1in lengths
30ml/2 tbsp vegetable oil
4 shallots, thinly sliced
6 large garlic cloves, thinly sliced
sea salt
1.5ml/¼ tsp dried chilli flakes

1 Place the morning glory in a steamer and steam over a pan of boiling water for 30 seconds, until just wilted. If necessary, cook it in batches. Place the leaves in a bowl or spread them out on a large serving plate.

2 Heat the oil in a wok and stir-fry the shallots and garlic over a medium to high heat until golden.

3 Spoon the mixture over the morning glory on the plate, sprinkle with a little sea salt and the dried chilli flakes and serve immediately.

Cook's Tip

Morning glory goes by various names, including water spinach, water convolvulus and swamp cabbage – owing to the fact it is cultivated both on water-logged and dry land. Although not related to spinach, its flavour and fragrance are similar. Look for it in Asian markets and refrigerate for up to 4 days.

Variation

Use spinach instead of morning glory, or substitute young spring greens (collards), sprouting broccoli or Swiss chard.

Pak Choi in a Spicy Lime and Coconut Dressing

The coconut dressing for this Thai speciality is traditionally made using fish sauce, but vegetarians could use mushroom sauce instead. Beware, this is a fiery dish.

Serves 4

30ml/2 tbsp vegetable oil
3 fresh red chillies, cut into strips
4 garlic cloves, thinly sliced
6 spring onions (scallions), sliced diagonally
2 pak choi (bok choy), shredded
15ml/1 tbsp crushed peanuts
salt

For the dressing

30ml/2 tbsp fresh lime juice
15–30ml/1–2 tbsp Thai fish sauce
250ml/8fl oz/1 cup coconut milk

1 Make the dressing. Put the lime juice and fish sauce in a bowl and mix well together, then gradually whisk in the coconut milk.

2 Heat the oil in a wok and stir-fry the chillies for 2–3 minutes, until crisp. Transfer to a plate using a slotted spoon. Add the garlic to the wok and stir-fry for 30–60 seconds, until golden brown. Transfer to the plate.

3 Stir-fry the white parts of the spring onions for about 2–3 minutes, then add the green parts and stir-fry for 1 minute more. Transfer to the plate.

4 Bring a large pan of lightly salted water to the boil and add the pak choi. Stir twice, then drain immediately.

5 Place the pak choi in a bowl, add the dressing and toss to mix. Spoon into a large serving bowl and sprinkle with the peanuts and the stir-fried chilli mixture. Serve warm or cold.

Variation

This recipe can be adapted for diners who don't particularly like spicy food. Simply substitute red (bell) pepper strips for some or all of the chillies.

Morning Glory Energy 64kcal/263kJ; Protein 1.3g; Carbohydrate 1.4g, of which sugars 1.2g; Fat 5.9g, of which saturates 0.7g; Cholesterol 0mg; Calcium 92mg; Fibre 1.5g; Sodium 9mg.
Pak Choi Energy 79kcal/329kJ; Protein 1.8g; Carbohydrate 4.5g, of which sugars 4.4g; Fat 6.1g, of which saturates 0.8g; Cholesterol 0mg; Calcium 99mg; Fibre 1.2g; Sodium 398mg.

Thai Asparagus with Ginger and Chilli

This is an excitingly different way of cooking asparagus. The crunchy texture is retained and the flavour is complemented by the addition of galangal and chilli.

Serves 4

350g/12oz asparagus stalks
30ml/2 tbsp vegetable oil
1 garlic clove, crushed
15ml/1 tbsp sesame seeds, toasted
2.5cm/1in piece fresh galangal, finely shredded
1 fresh red chilli, seeded and finely chopped
15ml/1 tbsp Thai fish sauce
15ml/1 tbsp light soy sauce
45ml/3 tbsp water
5ml/1 tsp palm sugar (jaggery) or light muscovado (brown) sugar

1 Snap the asparagus stalks. They will break naturally at the junction between the woody base and the more tender upper portion of the stalk. Discard the woody parts of the stems.

2 Heat the oil in a wok and stir-fry the garlic, sesame seeds and galangal for 3–4 seconds. Do not allow to brown but cook until the garlic is just beginning to turn golden.

3 Add the asparagus stalks and chilli to the pan. Cook for 1 minute, stirring constantly, then add the fish sauce, soy sauce, water and sugar.

4 Using two spoons, toss over the heat for a further 2 minutes, or until the asparagus just begins to soften and the liquid is reduced by about half.

5 Carefully transfer the asparagus to a warmed serving dish and serve immediately.

Variation
This is a very versatile recipe. Try using broccoli or pak choi (bok choy) in place of the asparagus. The sauce will also work very well with green beans.

Stir-fried Asparagus with Chilli, Galangal and Lemon Grass

One of the culinary legacies of French colonization in Vietnam and Cambodia is asparagus. Today it is grown in Vietnam and finds its way into stir-fries in both countries. Cambodian in style, this is a lovely spicy way to eat asparagus.

Serves 2 to 4

30ml/2 tbsp groundnut (peanut) oil
2 garlic cloves, finely chopped
2 Thai chillies, seeded and finely chopped
25g/1oz galangal, finely shredded
1 lemon grass stalk, trimmed and finely sliced
350g/12oz fresh asparagus stalks, trimmed
30ml/2 tbsp tuk trey
30ml/2 tbsp soy sauce
5ml/1 tsp sugar
30ml/2 tbsp unsalted roasted peanuts, finely chopped
1 small bunch fresh coriander (cilantro), finely chopped

1 Heat a large wok and add the oil. Stir in the garlic, chillies, galangal and lemon grass and stir-fry until they become fragrant and begin to turn golden.

2 Add the asparagus and stir-fry for a further 1–2 minutes, until it is just tender but not too soft.

3 Stir in the tuk trey, soy sauce and sugar. Stir in the peanuts and coriander and serve immediately.

Cook's Tip
Tuk trey is a popular condiment in Cambodian cuisine. It is a nutty and pungent fish sauce made from fermented fish with the addition of ground, roasted peanuts.

Variation
This recipe also works well with broccoli, green beans and courgettes (zucchini), cut into strips.

Thai Asparagus Energy 120kcal/492kJ; Protein 4.1g; Carbohydrate 2.4g, of which sugars 2.3g; Fat 10.4g, of which saturates 1.4g; Cholesterol 0mg; Calcium 75mg; Fibre 2.1g; Sodium 537mg.
Stir-fried Aaparagus Energy 117kcal/482kJ; Protein 5g; Carbohydrate 3.3g, of which sugars 2.7g; Fat 9g, of which saturates 1g; Cholesterol 0mg; Calcium 30mg; Fibre 2g; Sodium 535mg.

Spicy Spinach with Mushrooms and Red Pepper

A tasty and nutritious vegetable, spinach cooked in this way is wonderful served with chapatis.

Serves 4

450g/1lb fresh or frozen spinach
30ml/2 tbsp corn oil
2 medium onions, diced
6–8 curry leaves
1.5ml/¼ tsp onion seeds
5ml/1 tsp crushed garlic
5ml/1 tsp crushed ginger
5ml/1 tsp chilli powder
5ml/1 tsp salt
7.5ml/1½ tsp ground coriander
1 large red (bell) pepper, seeded and sliced
115g/4oz mushrooms, roughly chopped
225g/8oz/1 cup fromage frais or low-fat cream cheese
30ml/2 tbsp fresh coriander (cilantro) leaves

1 If using fresh spinach, blanch it briefly in boiling water and drain thoroughly. If using frozen spinach, thaw first, then drain. Set aside.

2 Heat the oil in a wok or frying pan and fry the onions with the curry leaves and the onion seeds for 1–2 minutes.

3 Add the garlic, ginger, chilli powder, salt and ground coriander to the pan. Stir-fry for 2–3 minutes.

4 Add half the red pepper slices and all the mushrooms and continue to stir-fry for 2–3 minutes. Add the spinach and stir-fry for 4–6 minutes.

5 Finally, add the fromage frais or cream cheese and half the fresh coriander, followed by the remaining red pepper slices. Stir-fry for a further 2–3 minutes before serving, garnished with the remaining coriander.

Cook's Tip
Different types of mushrooms will work well in this dish, use whatever variety you have available.

Spring Greens with Green Chillies

This spicy side dish is simple and delicious. Spring greens are taken from cabbages early in the season and have a lovely fresh, tender taste.

Serves 4

450g/1lb spring greens (collards)
60ml/4 tbsp olive oil
2 small red onions, finely chopped
1 garlic clove, crushed
2.5ml/½ tsp grated fresh root ginger
2 fresh green chillies, seeded and sliced
150ml/¼ pint/⅔ cup vegetable stock or water
1 red (bell) pepper, seeded and sliced
salt and ground black pepper

1 Wash the spring greens, then strip the leaves from the stalks and steam the leaves over a pan of boiling water for about 5 minutes until slightly wilted. Set aside on a plate to cool, then place in a sieve (strainer) or colander and press to squeeze out the excess water.

2 Using a large sharp knife, slice the drained spring greens into very thin strips.

3 Heat the oil in a pan and fry the onions for 3–4 minutes until browned. Add the garlic and ginger and stir-fry with the onions for a few minutes.

4 Add the chillies and a little of the stock or water to the pan and cook for about 2 minutes.

5 Add the greens, red pepper and the remaining stock or water. Season with salt and pepper, mix well, then cover and cook over a low heat for about 15 minutes. Serve immediately.

Cook's Tip
Traditionally this dish is cooked with more liquid and for longer. The cooking time has been reduced from 45 minutes to 15 minutes. However, if you fancy a more authentic taste, cook for longer and increase the amount of liquid. Green cabbage is a good substitute for spring greens.

Spicy Spinach Energy 220kcal/913kJ; Protein 14.4g; Carbohydrate 16.3g, of which sugars 12g; Fat 12.1g, of which saturates 3.9g; Cholesterol 14mg; Calcium 296mg; Fibre 4.8g; Sodium 412mg.
Spinach with Chillies Energy 149kcal/615kJ; Protein 4.1g; Carbohydrate 6g, of which sugars 4.8g; Fat 12.3g, of which saturates 1.7g; Cholesterol 0mg; Calcium 248mg; Fibre 4.3g; Sodium 24mg.

Cauliflower and Potatoes Chilli-style

Cauliflower and potatoes are encrusted with Indian spices in this delicious recipe. It is a popular side dish or can be served as a main course with other dishes such as a salad, dhal or simply with Indian breads.

Serves 4

450g/1lb potatoes, cut into 2.5 cm/1 in chunks
30ml/2 tbsp vegetable oil
5ml/1 tsp cumin seeds
1 green chilli, finely chopped
450g/1lb cauliflower, broken into florets
5ml/1 tsp ground coriander
5ml/1 tsp ground cumin
1.5ml/¼ tsp chilli powder
2.5ml/½ tsp ground turmeric
2.5ml/½ tsp salt
chopped fresh coriander (cilantro), to garnish
tomato and onion salad and pickle, to serve

1 Par-boil the potatoes in a large pan of boiling water for 10 minutes. Drain well and set aside.

2 Heat the oil in a wok or large frying pan and fry the cumin seeds for about 2 minutes, until they begin to splutter and release their fragrance. Add the chilli to the pan and fry, stirring constantly, for a further 1 minute.

3 Add the cauliflower florets to the pan and fry, stirring constantly, for 5 minutes.

4 Add the potatoes, the ground spices and salt and cook for 7–10 minutes, or until both the vegetables are tender.

5 Garnish with fresh coriander and serve with a tomato and onion salad and pickle.

Variation
Try using sweet potatoes instead of ordinary potatoes for an alternative curry with a sweeter flavour. The cauliflower could also be replaced with the same amount of broccoli.

Spiced Eggs and Spinach

This is a superbly balanced dish for those who don't eat meat. Egusi, or ground melon seed, is widely used in West African cooking, adding a creamy texture and a nutty flavour to many recipes. It is especially good with fresh spinach.

Serves 4

900g/2lb fresh spinach
115g/4oz ground egusi
90ml/6 tbsp groundnut (peanut) or vegetable oil
4 tomatoes, peeled and chopped
1 onion, chopped
2 garlic cloves, crushed
1 slice fresh root ginger, finely chopped
150ml/¼ pint/⅔ cup vegetable stock
1 fresh red chilli, seeded and finely chopped
6 eggs
salt

1 Roll up the spinach into bundles and slice into strips. Place the strips in a bowl. Cover with boiling water, then drain through a sieve (strainer). Press with your fingers to remove excess water.

2 Place the egusi in a bowl and gradually add enough water to form a paste, stirring all the time.

3 Heat the oil in a pan, add the tomatoes, onion, garlic and ginger and fry for about 10 minutes, stirring frequently.

4 Add the egusi paste, stock, chilli and salt, and cook for about 10 minutes, then add the spinach and stir into the sauce. Cook for 15 minutes, uncovered, stirring frequently.

5 Meanwhile hard-boil the eggs, stand them in cold water for a few minutes to cool and then shell and cut in half. Arrange in a serving dish and pour the egusi spinach over the top. Serve hot.

Cook's Tip
Instead of using boiled eggs, you could make an omelette flavoured with herbs and garlic. Serve it either whole, or sliced, with the egusi sauce. If you can't find egusi, use ground almonds as a substitute.

Cauliflower Chilli-style Energy 181kcal/759kJ; Protein 6.7g; Carbohydrate 23.2g, of which sugars 4.3g; Fat 7.5g, of which saturates 1.1g; Cholesterol 0mg; Calcium 40mg; Fibre 3.2g; Sodium 24mg.
Spiced Eggs Energy 436kcal/1803kJ; Protein 21.5g; Carbohydrate 12.6g, of which sugars 7.5g; Fat 33.3g, of which saturates 5.1g; Cholesterol 285mg; Calcium 464mg; Fibre 7.3g; Sodium 428mg.

Chilli Cucumber Stuffed with Onions and Spices

A classic summer variety of kimchi, the refreshing natural succulence of cucumber is perfect on a hot, humid day. The spiciness of the chilli is cooled by the cucumber, with flavours that invigorate the palate.

Serves 4

15 small pickling cucumbers
30ml/2 tbsp sea salt
1 bunch Chinese chives

For the seasoning

1 onion, finely chopped
4 spring onions (scallions), thinly sliced
75ml/5 tbsp Korean chilli powder
15ml/1 tbsp Thai fish sauce
10ml/2 tsp salt
1 garlic clove, crushed
7.5ml/1½ tsp grated fresh root ginger
5ml/1 tsp sugar
5ml/1 tsp sesame seeds

1 If the cucumbers are long, cut them in half widthways. Make two slits in a cross down the length of each cucumber or cucumber half, making sure not to cut all the way to the end. Coat with the sea salt, and leave for 1 hour. Cut the Chinese chives into 2.5cm/1in lengths, cutting off and discarding the bulb.

2 Combine the onion and spring onions with the Chinese chives in a bowl. Add 45ml/3 tbsp of the chilli powder and add the Thai fish sauce, salt, garlic, ginger, sugar and sesame seeds. Mix the ingredients thoroughly by hand, using plastic gloves to prevent the chilli powder from staining your skin.

3 Lightly rinse the cucumbers to remove the salt crystals. Coat with the remaining chilli powder, and press the seasoning into the slits. Put the cucumber into an airtight container and leave at room temperature for 12 hours before serving.

Cook's Tip
Cucumber kimchi can be stored in the refrigerator, although it is best eaten within two days.

Mooli with Chilli and Ginger

Mooli kimchi from Korea is traditionally eaten as the autumn evenings start to draw in, with a spiciness that fortifies against the cold. The pungent aromas and tangy flavours make this one of the most popular and tasty kimchi varieties.

Serves 4

1.5kg/3½lb mooli (daikon), peeled
225g/8oz/2 cups coarse sea salt
5ml/1 tsp sugar

For the seasoning

75ml/5 tbsp Korean chilli powder
1 garlic clove, crushed
¼ onion, finely chopped
3 spring onions (scallions), finely sliced
15ml/1 tbsp sea salt
5ml/1 tsp Thai fish sauce
5ml/1 tsp fresh root ginger, peeled and finely chopped
22.5ml/4½ tsp light muscovado (brown) sugar

1 Cut the mooli into 2cm/¾in cubes. Place in a bowl and coat with the sea salt and sugar. Leave for 2 hours, draining off any water that collects at the bottom of the bowl.

2 Combine all the ingredients for the seasoning and mix well with the salted mooli. Place the mooli in an airtight container and seal. Leave at room temperature for 24 hours and chill before serving.

Cook's Tip
Kimchi is a pungent condiment served at almost every Korean meal. Various vegetables – such as cabbage or turnips – are pickled then traditionally stored in sealed pots to ferment.

Variations
- *Blend half an onion in a food processor and add it to the seasoning for a tangier taste and subtle sweetness.*
- *For extra kick you could add a finely chopped red chilli to the seasoning, but be warned, this will make the dish extremely hot.*

Stuffed Chilli Cucumber Energy 32kcal/131kJ; Protein 2.5g; Carbohydrate 3.9g, of which sugars 3.4g; Fat 2.1g, of which saturates 0.2g; Cholesterol 0mg; Calcium 88mg; Fibre 1.4g; Sodium 2067mg.
Mooli with Ginger Energy 73kcal/302kJ; Protein 3.1g; Carbohydrate 14g, of which sugars 13.6g; Fat 0.8g, of which saturates 0.4g; Cholesterol 0mg; Calcium 81mg; Fibre 3.7g; Sodium 1203mg.

Korean Spicy Cabbage

There are many varieties of kimchi, which is fermented vegetables. This version takes two days to prepare.

Serves 10

1 head Chinese leaves (Chinese cabbage), about 2kg/4½lb
30ml/2 tbsp table salt
50g/2oz/½ cup coarse sea salt

For the seasoning

2 oysters (optional)
½ mooli (daikon), about 500g/1¼lb, peeled and sliced
25g/1oz Korean chives
25g/1oz minari or watercress
5 garlic cloves
15g/½oz fresh root ginger, peeled
½ onion
½ Asian pear, or ½ kiwi fruit
1 chestnut, sliced
3 spring onions (scallions), sliced
50g/2oz Korean chilli powder
120ml/4fl oz/½ cup Thai fish sauce
5ml/1 tsp sugar
1 red chilli, sliced
salt

1 Make a deep cut across the base of the head of Chinese leaves and split it into two. Split the two halves into quarters. Place the quartered head in a bowl and cover with water, adding the table salt. Leave to soak for 2 hours.

2 Drain the cabbage and sprinkle with the sea salt, making sure to coat between the leaves. Leave for 4 hours.

3 Hold an oyster with the rounded shell up. Push the tip of a short-bladed knife into the hinge of the oyster and twist to prise open. Cut the two muscles. Run the blade between the shells to open. Remove the oyster from the shell. Season with salt.

4 Cut the mooli slices into fine strips. Cut the chives and minari or watercress into 5cm/2in lengths. Finely chop or blend the garlic, ginger, onion and Asian pear or kiwi fruit. Mix all the seasoning ingredients together with 120ml/4fl oz/½ cup water.

5 Rinse the quarters of Chinese leaves in cold running water. Place in a bowl and coat with the seasoning mixture. Place the Chinese leaves in an airtight container. Leave at room temperature for 5 hours, then chill for 24 hours.

Stir-fried Pineapple with Ginger and Chilli

Throughout South-east Asia, fruit is often treated like a vegetable and tossed in a salad, or stir-fried, to accompany spicy dishes. In this Cambodian dish, the pineapple is combined with the tangy flavours of ginger and chilli and served as a side dish.

Serves 4

30ml/2 tbsp groundnut (peanut) oil
2 garlic cloves, finely shredded
40g/1½oz fresh root ginger, peeled and finely shredded
2 red Thai chillies, seeded and finely shredded
1 pineapple, trimmed, peeled, cored and cut into bitesize chunks
15ml/1 tbsp fish sauce
30ml/2 tbsp soy sauce
15ml–30ml/1–2 tbsp sugar
30ml/2 tbsp roasted unsalted peanuts, finely chopped
1 lime, cut into quarters, to serve

1 Heat a large wok or large, heavy frying pan and add the groundnut oil. Stir in the garlic, ginger and chillies. Stir-fry for 2 minutes until the ingredients begin to colour. Ensure that the garlic does not burn, otherwise it will impart a bitter taste to the rest of the dish.

2 Add the pineapple to the pan and stir-fry for a further 1–2 minutes, until the edges turn golden.

3 Add the fish sauce and soy sauce to the pan and mix well. Add sugar to taste and continue to stir-fry until the pineapple begins to caramelize.

4 Transfer to a serving dish, sprinkle with the roasted peanuts and serve with lime wedges.

Cook's Tip

This dish is an excellent accompaniment to grilled (broiled) meats, and will be perfect on a summer's day to be eaten alongside spicy chicken or satays cooked on the barbecue.

Korean Spicy Cabbage Energy 73kcal/303kJ; Protein 3.6g; Carbohydrate 13.5g, of which sugars 12.9g; Fat 0.6g, of which saturates 0.1g; Cholesterol 0mg; Calcium 121mg; Fibre 5.1g; Sodium 383mg.
Stir-fried Pineapple Energy 185kcal/780kJ; Protein 3g; Carbohydrate 24.1g, of which sugars 23.6g; Fat 9g, of which saturates 1g; Cholesterol 0mg; Calcium 43mg; Fibre 2.9g; Sodium 271mg.

Spicy Bitter Gourds

Bitter gourds are widely used in Indian cooking, both on their own as a side dish and combined with other vegetables in a curry.

Serves 4

675g/1½lb bitter gourds
60ml/4 tbsp vegetable oil
2.5ml/½ tsp cumin seeds
6 spring onions (scallions), chopped
5 tomatoes, finely chopped
2.5cm/1in piece root ginger, finely chopped
2 garlic cloves, crushed
2 fresh green chillies, seeded and finely chopped
2.5ml/½ tsp salt, plus extra to taste
2.5ml/½ tsp chilli powder
5ml/1 tsp ground coriander
5ml/1 tsp ground cumin
45ml/3 tbsp peanuts, crushed
45ml/3 tbsp soft dark brown sugar
15ml/1 tbsp gram flour
fresh coriander (cilantro) sprigs, to garnish

1 Bring a large pan of lightly salted water to the boil. Peel the bitter gourds using a small sharp knife and halve them. Discard the seeds. Cut into 2cm/¾in pieces, then cook in the water for about 10–15 minutes, or until they are tender. Drain well and set aside.

2 Heat the oil in a large pan and fry the cumin seeds for about 2 minutes until they begin to splutter. Add the spring onions and fry for 3–4 minutes. Add the tomatoes, ginger, garlic and chillies and cook for 5 minutes.

3 Add the salt, remaining spices, the peanuts and sugar and cook for about 2–3 minutes, stirring constantly.

4 Add the bitter gourds and mix well. Sprinkle over the gram flour. Cover and simmer over a low heat for 5–8 minutes, or until all of the gram flour has been absorbed into the sauce. Serve garnished with fresh coriander sprigs.

Cook's Tip
For a quick and easy way to crush peanuts, put into a food processor or blender and process for about 20–30 seconds.

Masala Okra with Chilli and Coriander

Okra, or 'ladies' fingers', are a popular Indian vegetable. In this recipe they are stir-fried with a dry masala spice mixture to make a delicious side dish.

Serves 4

450g/1lb okra
2.5ml/½ tsp ground turmeric
5ml/1 tsp chilli powder
15ml/1 tbsp ground cumin
15ml/1 tbsp ground coriander
1.5ml/¼ tsp salt
1.5ml/¼ tsp sugar
15ml/1 tbsp lemon juice
15ml/1 tbsp desiccated (dry unsweetened shredded) coconut
30ml/2 tbsp chopped fresh coriander (cilantro)
45ml/3 tbsp vegetable oil
2.5ml/½ tsp cumin seeds
2.5ml/½ tsp black mustard seeds
chopped tomatoes, to garnish
poppadums, to serve

1 Wash, dry and trim the okra. In a bowl, mix together the turmeric, chilli powder, cumin, ground coriander, salt, sugar, lemon juice, desiccated coconut and the fresh coriander.

2 Heat the oil in a wok or large, heavy frying pan that has a tight-fitting lid. Add the cumin seeds and mustard seeds and fry for about 2 minutes, or until they begin to splutter and release their fragrances.

3 Add the spice mixture to the pan and continue to fry, stirring constantly, for 2 minutes.

4 Add the okra to the pan, cover, and cook over a low heat for about 10 minutes, or until the okra is tender.

5 Transfer to a serving dish and garnish with the chopped fresh tomatoes. Serve immediately with poppadums.

Cook's Tip
Poppadums are wafer-thin crisp breads from India. Buy them in Asian stores and look out for the versions with added spices.

Spicy Bitter Gourds Energy 304kcal/1268kJ; Protein 8.9g; Carbohydrate 27g, of which sugars 19.6g; Fat 18.6g, of which saturates 2.8g; Cholesterol 0mg; Calcium 89mg; Fibre 3.8g; Sodium 19mg.
Masala Okra Energy 211kcal/873kJ; Protein 5g; Carbohydrate 6.3g, of which sugars 5.2g; Fat 18.7g, of which saturates 7.1g; Cholesterol 0mg; Calcium 246mg; Fibre 7.6g; Sodium 15mg.

Aubergines with Garlic, Chilli and Hot Pepper

This is a delicious way of serving aubergines. They are first fried with garlic and tomatoes then cooked in a rich stock with chilli and bell peppers and finished with fresh coriander.

Serves 4

45ml/3 tbsp vegetable oil
2 garlic cloves, crushed
3 tomatoes, peeled and chopped
900g/2lb aubergines (eggplants), cut into chunks
150ml/¼ pint/⅔ cup vegetable stock or water
30ml/2 tbsp soy sauce
60ml/4 tbsp chopped spring onions (scallions)
½ red (bell) pepper, chopped
1 hot chilli pepper, seeded and chopped
30ml/2 tbsp chopped fresh coriander (cilantro)
salt and ground black pepper

1 Heat the oil in a wok or large frying pan and fry the garlic and tomatoes for a few minutes, stirring constantly, until slightly softened. Add the aubergines and toss together with the garlic and tomatoes.

2 Pour in the stock or water and cover the pan. Simmer gently until the aubergines are very soft. Stir in the soy sauce and half of the spring onions.

3 Add the red pepper, hot chilli pepper and seasoning to the pan and stir well.

4 Stir in the coriander and transfer to a warmed serving dish. Garnish with the remaining spring onion and serve immediately.

Variation
You can make this dish more substantial and even tastier by adding little strips of smoked salmon to the pan at the last minute. All it needs is stirring in and then warming through for a minute or two.

Okra with Spicy Filling

A delicious accompaniment to any dish, this can also be served on a bed of creamy yogurt, which gives an excellent contrast in flavour.

Serves 4 to 6

225g/8oz okra (see Cook's Tip)
15ml/1 tbsp amchur (dry mango powder)
2.5ml/½ tsp ground ginger
2.5ml/½ tsp ground cumin
2.5ml/½ tsp chilli powder
2.5ml/½ tsp ground turmeric
a few drops of vegetable oil
30ml/2 tbsp cornflour (cornstarch), placed in a plastic bag
vegetable oil, for frying
salt, to taste

1 Wash the okra and pat dry using kitchen paper. Carefully trim off the tops without making a hole. Using a sharp knife, make a slit lengthways in the centre of each okra but do not cut all the way through.

2 In a bowl, mix together the amchur, ginger, cumin, chilli powder, turmeric and salt with a few drops of oil. Leave the mixture to rest for 1 or 2 hours.

3 Using your fingers, part the slit of each okra carefully without opening it all the way. Fill each okra pod with as much of the spicy filling as possible.

4 Put all the okra into the plastic bag with the cornflour. Seal the opening of the bag and shake carefully for a minute or two until the okra is evenly covered with the cornflour.

5 Fill the frying pan with enough oil to sit 2.5cm/1in deep, heat it and fry the okra in small batches for about 5–8 minutes, turning, until they are browned and slightly crisp. Serve the okra immediately.

Cook's Tip
Okra has a ridged skin and a tapered, oblong shape. Buy okra pods that are firm and brightly coloured and are less than 10cm/4in long.

Aubergines with Garlic Energy 132kcal/551kJ; Protein 3.2g; Carbohydrate 9.3g, of which sugars 8.7g; Fat 9.5g, of which saturates 1.3g; Cholesterol 0mg; Calcium 36mg; Fibre 5.7g; Sodium 550mg.
Okra with Spices Energy 176kcal/734kJ; Protein 1.7g; Carbohydrate 15.5g, of which sugars 1.4g; Fat 12.4g, of which saturates 1.6g; Cholesterol 0mg; Calcium 92mg; Fibre 2.3g; Sodium 12mg.

Smoked Aubergine with a Spring Onion and Chilli Dressing

Aubergines can be placed in the flames of a fire, or over hot charcoal, or directly over the gas flame of a stove, and still taste great. This way of smoking or roasting them has its roots in North Africa, the Middle East, India and across South-east Asia, producing many delicious dips, purées and salads. This spicy Vietnamese version is served as a side salad to accompany meat and poultry dishes.

Serves 4

2 aubergines (eggplants)
30ml/2 tbsp groundnut (peanut) or vegetable oil
2 spring onions (scallions), finely sliced
1–2 red serrano chillies, seeded and finely sliced
15ml/1 tbsp fish sauce
25g/1oz/½ cup fresh basil leaves
salt
15ml/1 tbsp roasted peanuts, crushed, to garnish
chilli sauce, to serve

1 Place the aubergines over a barbecue or under a hot grill (broiler), or hold them on a fork or skewer directly over a gas flame on the stove and cook, turning them from time to time, until they are soft when pressed.

2 Carefully lift the aubergines by the stalk and put them into a plastic bag to sweat for 1 minute.

3 Holding the aubergines by the stalk once again, carefully peel off the skin under cold running water. Gently squeeze the excess water from the peeled flesh, remove the stalk and pull the flesh apart in long strips. Place these strips in a serving dish.

4 Heat the oil in a small pan and quickly stir in the spring onions. Remove the pan from the heat and stir in the chillies, fish sauce, basil leaves and a little salt to taste. Pour this dressing over the aubergines, toss gently and sprinkle the peanuts over the top.

5 Serve at room temperature and, for those who like a little extra fire, splash on some chilli sauce.

Red-hot Chilli Cauliflower

Vegetables are seldom served plain in Mexico. The cauliflower here is flavoured with a simple tomato salsa and fetacheese. The salsa could be any table salsa; tomatillo is particularly good. The contrast of the hot spicy salsa with the texture and mild flavour of the cauliflower makes for a tasty dish.

Serves 6

1 small onion
1 lime
1 medium cauliflower
400g/14oz can chopped tomatoes
4 fresh serrano chillies, seeded and finely chopped
1.5ml/¼ tsp caster (superfine) sugar
75g/3oz feta cheese, crumbled
salt
chopped fresh flat leaf parsley, to garnish

1 Chop the onion very finely and place in a bowl. With a cannelle knife (zester), peel away the rind of the lime in thin strips. Add to the chopped onion.

2 Cut the lime in half and add the juice from both halves to the bowl containing the onions and lime rind mixture. Set aside so that the lime juice can soften the onion. Cut the cauliflower into florets.

3 Place the tomatoes in a pan and add the chillies and sugar. Heat the mixture gently. Meanwhile, place the cauliflower in a pan of boiling water, reduce the heat and cook gently for about 5–8 minutes, until tender.

4 Add the onions to the tomato salsa in the pan, with salt to taste, stir in and heat through, then spoon about a third of the salsa into a serving dish.

5 Arrange the drained cauliflower florets on top of the salsa in the serving dish and then spoon the remaining salsa on top of the florets.

6 Sprinkle the feta cheese over the top – it should soften a little on contact. Serve immediately, sprinkled with chopped fresh flat leaf parsley.

Smoked Aubergine Energy 215kcal/890kJ; Protein 10g; Carbohydrate 6g, of which sugars 4g; Fat 17g, of which saturates 3g; Cholesterol 0mg; Calcium 425mg; Fibre 0.8g; Sodium 700mg
Red-hot Chilli Cauliflower Energy 63kcal/262kJ; Protein 4.2g; Carbohydrate 4.5g, of which sugars 4g; Fat 3.2g, of which saturates 1.9g; Cholesterol 9mg; Calcium 74mg; Fibre 1.9g; Sodium 192mg.

Steamed Vegetables with Spicy Dip

In Thailand, steamed vegetables are often partnered with raw ones to create the contrasting textures and flavours that are such a feature of the national cuisine. By happy coincidence, it is also an extremely healthy way to serve them.

Serves 4

1 head broccoli, divided into florets
130g/4½oz/1 cup green beans, trimmed
130g/4½oz asparagus, trimmed
½ head cauliflower, divided into florets
8 baby corn cobs
130g/4½oz mangetouts (snow peas) or sugar snap peas
salt

For the dip

1 fresh green chilli, seeded
4 garlic cloves, peeled
4 shallots, peeled
2 tomatoes, halved
5 pea aubergines (eggplants)
30ml/2 tbsp lemon juice
30ml/2 tbsp soy sauce
2.5ml/½ tsp salt
5ml/1 tsp sugar

1 Place the broccoli, green beans, asparagus and cauliflower in a steamer and steam them over a pan of boiling water for about 4–6 minutes, until they are just tender but still retain a slight crunch.

2 Transfer the steamed vegetables to a large bowl and add the corn cobs and mangetouts or sugar snap peas. Season to taste with a little salt. Toss to mix, then set aside.

3 Meanwhile, make the dip. Preheat the grill (broiler). Wrap the chilli, garlic cloves, shallots, tomatoes and aubergines in a foil package. Grill (broil) for 10 minutes, until the vegetables have softened, turning the package over once or twice.

4 Unwrap the foil and transfer its contents into a mortar or food processor. Add the lemon juice, soy sauce, salt and sugar. Pound with a pestle or process to a fairly liquid paste, adding a little water if necessary.

5 Scrape the dip into a serving bowl or four individual bowls. Serve, surrounded by the steamed and raw vegetables.

Deep-fried Aubergine with Spicy Garlic Sauce

This dish is often served at the many rice stalls throughout Singapore as an accompaniment to a main rice dish. Many of the cooks at the stalls, and in the home, make up batches of different sambals to be stored and used for making quick and simple dishes like this one. Generally, the aubergines will be cooked by deep-frying at the hawker stalls, but you could bake them in the oven at home. Serve this dish as a spicy snack to go with a chunk of fresh bread or as a side dish to accompany a more substantial rice dish or grilled meats.

Serves 2 to 4

6 shallots, chopped
4 garlic cloves, chopped
2 red chillies, seeded and chopped
1 lemon grass stalk, trimmed and chopped
5ml/1 tsp shrimp paste
15ml/1 tbsp sesame oil
15–30ml/1–2 tbsp soy sauce
7.5ml/1½ tsp sugar
vegetable oil, for deep-frying
2 slender, purple aubergines (eggplants), partially peeled in strips and halved lengthways

To garnish

1 green chilli, seeded and finely chopped
a small bunch each of fresh mint and coriander (cilantro), stalks removed, finely chopped

1 Using a mortar and pestle or food processor, grind the shallots, garlic, chillies and lemon grass to a paste. Beat in the shrimp paste and mix well.

2 Heat the sesame oil in a small wok or heavy pan. Stir in the spice paste and cook until fragrant and brown. Stir in the soy sauce and sugar and cook until smooth. Remove from the heat.

3 Heat enough oil for deep-frying in a wok or heavy pan. Drop in the aubergine halves and fry until tender. Drain on kitchen paper, then press the centres to make a dip or shallow pouch.

4 Arrange the aubergine halves on a plate and smear with the spicy sauce. Garnish with the chopped green chilli, mint and coriander and serve at room temperature.

Steamed Vegetables Energy 70kcal/295kJ; Protein 6.8g; Carbohydrate 8.1g, of which sugars 7.2g; Fat 1.4g, of which saturates 0.3g; Cholesterol 0mg; Calcium 37mg; Fibre 4.7g; Sodium 1005mg.
Deep-fried Aubergine Energy 158kcal/654kJ; Protein 1.6g; Carbohydrate 6.5g, of which sugars 5.1g; Fat 14.2g, of which saturates 1.8g; Cholesterol 0mg; Calcium 24mg; Fibre 2.7g; Sodium 271mg.

Banana Curry with Chilli Spices

An unusual partnership, but the sweetness of bananas combines well with the spices used, producing a mild, sweet curry. Choose bananas that are slightly under-ripe so that they retain their shape and do not become mushy.

Serves 4

4 under-ripe bananas
30ml/2 tbsp ground coriander
15ml/1 tbsp ground cumin
5ml/1 tsp chilli powder
2.5ml/½ tsp salt
1.5ml/¼ tsp ground turmeric
5ml/1 tsp sugar
15ml/1 tbsp gram flour
45ml/3 tbsp chopped fresh coriander (cilantro)
90ml/6 tbsp vegetable oil
1.5ml/¼ tsp cumin seeds
1.5ml/¼ tsp black mustard seeds
fresh coriander (cilantro) sprigs, to garnish
chapatis, to serve

1 Trim the bananas and cut each into three equal pieces leaving the skin on. Make a lengthways slit in each piece of banana, without cutting through.

2 Mix together on a plate, the coriander, cumin, chilli powder, salt, turmeric, sugar, gram flour, fresh coriander and 15ml/1 tbsp of the oil.

3 Carefully stuff each piece of banana with the spice mixture, taking care not to break them in half.

4 Heat the remaining oil in a large heavy pan and fry the cumin and mustard seeds for 2 minutes, or until they begin to splutter and release their fragrances.

5 Add the stuffed banana pieces to the pan and toss very gently in the oil until coated in the seeds. Cover the pan and simmer over a low heat for 15 minutes, stirring from time to time until the bananas are soft, but be careful to avoid letting them go too mushy.

6 When the bananas are ready, transfer them to a warmed serving dish. Garnish with the fresh coriander and serve with warm chapatis.

Curried Spiced Cauliflower

In this tasty and popular Indian side dish, the creamy, aromatic and spicy coconut sauce complements the texture and mild flavour of the cauliflower. Serve with a fiery meat curry, together with Indian breads.

Serves 4 to 6

15ml/1 tbsp gram flour
100ml/3½fl oz/scant ½ cup water
5ml/1 tsp chilli powder
15ml/1 tbsp ground coriander
5ml/1 tsp ground cumin
5ml/1 tsp mustard powder
5ml/1 tsp ground turmeric
60ml/4 tbsp vegetable oil
6–8 curry leaves
5ml/1 tsp cumin seeds
1 cauliflower, broken into florets
175ml/6fl oz/¾ cup thick coconut milk
juice of 2 lemons
salt, to taste

1 In a bowl, mix together the gram flour with a little of the water to make a smooth paste.

2 Add the chilli, coriander, cumin, mustard and turmeric, and season with a little salt. Slowly add the remaining water to the bowl and keep mixing to ensure all the ingredients are thoroughly blended together.

3 Heat the oil in a frying pan and fry the curry leaves and cumin seeds for 1–2 minutes, until the seeds begin to splutter and release their fragrance.

4 Add the spice paste to the pan and cook, stirring constantly, for about 5 minutes. If the sauce has become too thick, add a little hot water to thin it down.

5 Add the cauliflower florets to the pan and pour in the coconut milk, stirring until it is well combined with the other ingredients in the pan.

6 Bring the mixture to the boil, reduce the heat, cover the pan and cook until the cauliflower is tender but still slightly crunchy. Cook longer, if you prefer.

7 Add the lemon juice, and mix well. Serve immediately.

Banana Curry Energy 321kcal/1340kJ; Protein 4g; Carbohydrate 36.7g, of which sugars 26.4g; Fat 18.7g, of which saturates 2.3g; Cholesterol 0mg; Calcium 56mg; Fibre 2.1g; Sodium 10mg.
Spiced Cauliflower Energy 122kcal/504kJ; Protein 3.7g; Carbohydrate 7.4g, of which sugars 3.3g; Fat 8.8g, of which saturates 1.2g; Cholesterol 0mg; Calcium 34mg; Fibre 1.4g; Sodium 41mg.

Chilli Yam Fries

These tasty spicy fries will make a welcome change from using potatoes. If you can't find yams then you can use sweet potatoes for a similar taste.

Serves 4
450g/1lb white yam
good pinch of chilli powder or cayenne pepper
salt and ground black pepper
vegetable oil, for deep-frying

1 Peel the yam and cut into slices, then into chips (French fries). Place the yam chips in a pan and cover with salted water.

2 Bring the water to the boil, cook for 5 minutes, then drain the chips in a colander or on kitchen paper for 5 minutes. Sprinkle with chilli powder or cayenne pepper.

3 Heat the oil in a heavy pan or deep-fat fryer until hot, then fry the yam chips for about 6–8 minutes, until cooked through, golden brown and crisp.

4 Drain well, then transfer into a dish lined with kitchen paper. Sprinkle with salt and serve immediately.

Thai Salad with a Yam Dressing

Here 'yam' does not refer to the vegetable but to a style of Thai cooking where raw or cooked vegetables are dressed with a special spicy sauce.

Serves 4
50g/2oz watercress or baby spinach, chopped
½ cucumber, finely diced
2 celery sticks, finely diced
2 carrots, finely diced
1 red (bell) pepper, seeded and finely diced
2 tomatoes, seeded and diced
small bunch fresh mint, chopped
90g/3½oz cellophane noodles

For the yam dressing
2 small fresh red chillies, seeded and finely chopped
60ml/4 tbsp light soy sauce
45ml/3 tbsp lemon juice
5ml/1 tsp palm sugar (jaggery) or light muscovado (brown) sugar
60ml/4 tbsp water
1 head pickled garlic, finely chopped, plus 15ml/1 tbsp vinegar from the jar
50g/2oz/scant ½ cup peanuts, roasted and chopped
90g/3½oz fried tofu, finely chopped
15ml/1 tbsp sesame seeds, toasted

1 Mix together the watercress or spinach, cucumber, celery, carrots, pepper and tomatoes in a bowl with the chopped mint.

2 Soak the noodles in boiling water for 3 minutes, then drain and cut into shorter lengths. Add them to the vegetables.

3 Make the yam dressing. Put the chillies in a pan with the soy sauce, lemon juice, sugar and water. Stir over a medium heat until the sugar has completely dissolved. Add the garlic, with the pickling vinegar from the jar, then mix in the nuts, tofu and sesame seeds.

4 Pour the yam over the vegetables and noodles, toss together until well mixed, and serve immediately.

Hot Plantain and Yam

The plantain, a very large, firm variety of banana, is also known as 'cooking banana'. It is extremely popular in Latin American countries as well as parts of Africa, Asia and India. It has a mild flavour similar to that of squash and is used very much as a potato would be in vegetable dishes.

Serves 4
2 green plantains
450g/1lb white yam
2 tomatoes, peeled and chopped
1 red chilli, seeded and chopped
1 onion, chopped
½ vegetable stock (bouillon) cube
15ml/1 tbsp palm oil
15ml/1 tbsp tomato purée (paste)
salt

1 Peel the plantains and cut them into six rounds, then peel and dice the yam.

2 Place the plantains and yam in a large heavy pan with 600ml/1 pint/2½ cups water, bring to the boil, reduce the heat and cook for 5 minutes.

3 Add the tomatoes, chilli and onion to the pan and simmer for a further 10 minutes.

4 Crumble the vegetable stock cube into the pan and stir well until completely dissolved. Cover the pan and simmer for a further 5 minutes.

5 Stir in the oil and tomato purée and continue cooking for about 5 minutes until the plantains are tender.

6 Season the vegetables with a little salt. Transfer to a warmed serving dish. Serve immediately.

Cook's Tips
- *To peel the plantains, cut them in half, slit the plantains along the natural ridges, then lift off the skin in sections.*
- *Serve this mild-tasting side dish with an aromatic and fiery curry or dhal to fully enjoy the contrasting flavours and textures.*

Chilli Yam Fries Energy 277kcal/1159kJ; Protein 1.7g; Carbohydrate 31.7g, of which sugars 0.8g; Fat 16.8g, of which saturates 2.1g; Cholesterol 0mg; Calcium 17mg; Fibre 1.5g; Sodium 2mg.
Thai Salad Energy 225kcal/939kJ; Protein 8.3g; Carbohydrate 31.4g, of which sugars 11.6g; Fat 7.4g, of which saturates 1.4g; Cholesterol 0mg; Calcium 176mg; Fibre 3.6g; Sodium 1101mg.
Hot Plantain and Yam Energy 258kcal/1097kJ; Protein 3.2g; Carbohydrate 57.1g, of which sugars 8g; Fat 3.5g, of which saturates 1.6g; Cholesterol 0mg; Calcium 32mg; Fibre 3.3g; Sodium 19mg.

Fragrant Chilli Mushrooms in Lettuce Leaves

This quick and easy vegetable dish is served on lettuce leaf 'saucers' so can be eaten with the fingers – a great treat for children.

Serves 2

30ml/2 tbsp vegetable oil
2 garlic cloves, finely chopped
2 baby cos or romaine lettuces, or 2 Little Gem (Bibb) lettuces
1 lemon grass stalk, finely chopped
2 kaffir lime leaves, rolled in cylinders and thinly sliced
200g/7oz/3 cups oyster or chestnut mushrooms, sliced
1 small fresh red chilli, seeded and finely chopped
juice of ½ lemon
30ml/2 tbsp light soy sauce
5ml/1 tsp palm sugar (jaggery) or light muscovado (brown) sugar
small bunch fresh mint, leaves removed from the stalks

1 Heat the oil in a wok or frying pan. Add the garlic and cook over a medium heat, stirring occasionally, until golden. Do not let it burn or it will taste bitter.

2 Meanwhile, separate the individual lettuce leaves into a stack and set aside until needed.

3 Increase the heat under the wok or pan and add the lemon grass, lime leaves and sliced mushrooms. Stir-fry for about 2 minutes.

4 Add the chilli, lemon juice, soy sauce and sugar to the wok or pan. Toss the mixture over the heat to combine the ingredients together, then stir-fry for a further 2 minutes.

5 Arrange the lettuce leaves on a large plate. Spoon a small amount of the mushroom mixture on to each leaf, top with a mint leaf and serve.

Cook's Tip
If serving this dish to children, ensure that the amount of chilli used won't make it too spicy for them to enjoy.

Mushrooms with Chipotle Chillies

Chipotle chillies are jalapeños that have been smoke-dried and are extremely popular in Mexican and Tex-Mex cuisine. Their smoky flavour and significant spicy kick is the perfect foil for the earthy taste of the mushrooms in this simple and delicious salad.

Serves 6

2 chipotle chillies
450g/1lb/6 cups button (white) mushrooms
60ml/4 tbsp vegetable oil
1 onion, finely chopped
2 garlic cloves, crushed or chopped
salt
small bunch of fresh coriander (cilantro), to garnish

1 Soak the dried chillies in a bowl of hot water for about 10 minutes until they are softened. Drain them, cut off the stalks, then slit the chillies and scrape out the seeds. Chop the flesh finely.

2 Trim the mushrooms, then clean them with a damp cloth or kitchen paper. If they are large, cut them in half.

3 Heat the oil in a large, heavy frying pan. Add the onion and cook, stirring, for 2–3 minutes until just beginning to soften and turn translucent.

4 Add the garlic, chillies and mushrooms to the pan and stir until evenly coated in the oil. Fry for 6–8 minutes, stirring occasionally, until the onion and mushrooms are cooked.

5 Season to taste and spoon into a serving dish. Chop some of the coriander, leaving some whole leaves, and use to garnish. Serve immediately.

Variation
Baby button mushrooms are perfect for this dish, if you can get them. You can, of course, use other varieties of mushrooms, such as brown cap (cremini) or chestnut, but larger ones will work better if halved or quartered.

Fragrant Mushrooms Energy 136kcal/561kJ; Protein 3.1g; Carbohydrate 4.7g, of which sugars 4.4g; Fat 11.7g, of which saturates 1.4g; Cholesterol 0mg; Calcium 22mg; Fibre 1.3g; Sodium 1076mg.
Mushrooms with Chillies Energy 84kcal/346kJ; Protein 1.7g; Carbohydrate 1.9g, of which sugars 1.4g; Fat 7.8g, of which saturates 1.2g; Cholesterol 0mg; Calcium 9mg; Fibre 1.4g; Sodium 5mg..

Hot Mushroom Curry

This is a deliciously spicy way of cooking mushrooms, and they will go perfectly well with any meat dish.

Serves 4

30ml/2 tbsp vegetable oil
2.5ml/½ tsp cumin seeds
1.5ml/¼ tsp black peppercorns
4 green cardamom pods
1.5ml/¼ tsp ground turmeric
1 onion, finely chopped
5ml/1 tsp ground cumin
5ml/1 tsp ground coriander
2.5ml/½ tsp garam masala
1 fresh green chilli, seeded and finely chopped
2 garlic cloves, crushed
2.5cm/1in piece fresh root ginger, grated
400g/14oz can chopped tomatoes
1.5ml/¼ tsp salt
450g/1lb button (white) mushrooms, halved
chopped fresh coriander (cilantro), to garnish

1 Heat the oil in a large pan and fry the cumin seeds, peppercorns, cardamom pods and turmeric for about 2–3 minutes, until the seeds start to splutter and the spices release their fragrances.

2 Add the onion to the pan and fry, stirring occasionally, for about 5–7 minutes, until soft and beginning to turn golden.

3 Stir in the cumin, coriander and garam masala and fry for a further 2 minutes, stirring constantly.

4 Add the chilli, garlic and ginger and fry for 2–3 minutes, stirring all the time to prevent the spices from sticking to the bottom of the pan.

5 Add the tomatoes and salt. Bring to the boil and simmer for 5 minutes.

6 Add the mushrooms to the pan and mix well to coat with the spices and sauce. Cover the pan and simmer over a low heat for 10 minutes until the mushrooms are tender.

7 Transfer to a warmed serving dish. Garnish with chopped fresh coriander and serve immediately.

Chilli Mushrooms in a Creamy Garlic Sauce

This is a simple and delicious dish which makes a great accompaniment to a spicy rice dish, or a fiery curry.

Serves 4

350g/12oz/4½ cups button (white) mushrooms
45ml/3 tbsp olive oil
1 bay leaf
3 garlic cloves, roughly chopped
2 fresh green chillies, seeded and chopped
225g/8oz/1 cup fromage frais or low-fat cream cheese
15ml/1 tbsp chopped fresh mint
15ml/1 tbsp chopped fresh coriander (cilantro)
5ml/1 tsp salt
fresh mint and coriander (cilantro) leaves, to garnish

1 Trim the mushrooms, then clean them with a damp cloth or kitchen paper. Cut them in half, or quarters if particularly large, and set them aside.

2 Heat the oil in a non-stick wok or large frying pan, then add the bay leaf, garlic and chillies and cook for about 1–2 minutes, until just beginng to soften and colour. Ensure that the garlic does not burn, otherwise it will taste bitter.

3 Add the mushrooms. Continue to stir-fry for about 2 minutes, until the juices are released from the mushrooms.

4 Remove the pan from the heat and stir in the fromage frais or low-fat cream cheese, followed by the mint, coriander and salt. Cook for about 2 minutes, until the sauce is bubbling and all the ingredients are heated through and combined.

5 Transfer to a warmed serving dish and garnish with mint and coriander leaves. Serve immediately.

Cook's Tip

Cook the mushrooms for longer if you prefer them well cooked and browned.

Hot Mushroom Curry Energy 110kcal/459kJ; Protein 4.2g; Carbohydrate 7.1g, of which sugars 3.3g; Fat 7.7g, of which saturates 1.1g; Cholesterol 0mg; Calcium 32mg; Fibre 2.2g; Sodium 18mg.
Chilli Mushrooms Energy 75kcal/314kJ; Protein 6.5g; Carbohydrate 4.9g, of which sugars 2.8g; Fat 3.4g, of which saturates 0.5g; Cholesterol 5mg; Calcium 90mg; Fibre 1.1g; Sodium 520mg.

Green Butter Beans in a Chilli Sauce

Make the most of butter beans or broad beans by teaming them with tomatoes and fresh chillies in this simple accompaniment.

Serves 4

450g/1lb fresh butter (wax) beans or broad (fava) beans
30ml/2 tbsp olive oil
1 onion, finely chopped
2 garlic cloves, crushed
400g/14oz can plum tomatoes, drained and chopped
25g/1oz/about 3 tbsp drained pickled jalapeño chilli slices, chopped
salt
fresh coriander (cilantro) and lemon slices, to garnish

1 Bring a pan of lightly salted water to the boil. Add the butter beans or broad beans and cook for 15 minutes, or until the beans are just tender.

2 Meanwhile, heat the olive oil in a frying pan, add the onion and garlic and fry, stirring occasionally, for 5–6 minutes until the onion is soft and translucent.

3 Add in the tomatoes and continue to cook, stirring, until the mixture thickens. Add the chilli slices and cook for 1–2 minutes. Season with salt to taste.

4 Drain the beans and return them to the pan. Pour over the tomato mixture and stir over the heat for a few minutes until the beans are heated through. If the sauce thickens too quickly add a little water.

5 Spoon the spicy beans into a warmed serving dish, garnish with the coriander and lemon slices and serve immediately.

Cook's Tip
Pickled chillies can often be hotter than roasted chillies – taste one before adding to the dish and adjust the quantity to suit your personal taste.

Pumpkin with Spices

Roasted pumpkin has a wonderful, rich flavour. Eat it straight from the skin, eat the skin too, or scoop out the cooked flesh, add a spoonful of salsa and wrap it in a warm tortilla. It also makes flavoursome soups and sauces.

Serves 6

1kg/2¼lb pumpkin
50g/2oz/¼ cup butter
10ml/2 tsp hot chilli sauce
2.5ml/½ tsp salt
2.5ml/½ tsp ground allspice
5ml/1 tsp ground cinnamon
chopped fresh herbs, to garnish
Classic Spiced Tomato Salsa (see p248) and crème fraîche, to serve

1 Preheat the oven to 220°C/425°F/Gas 7. Cut the pumpkin into large pieces. Scoop out and discard the fibre and seeds, then put the pumpkin pieces in a roasting pan.

2 Melt the butter in a pan over a low heat, or in a heatproof bowl in the microwave. Mix together the melted butter and chilli sauce and drizzle the mixture evenly over the pumpkin pieces in the roasting pan.

3 Put the salt in a small bowl and add the ground allspice and cinnamon. Mix together well and sprinkle the mixture over the pumpkin pieces.

4 Place the roasting pan in the oven and roast for 25 minutes, turning halfway through the cooking. The pumpkin flesh should yield when pressed gently when it is ready.

5 Transfer the spiced pumpkin pieces to a warmed serving dish and serve. Offer the salsa and crème fraîche separately.

Cook's Tip
Green, grey or orange-skinned pumpkins all roast well and would work in this recipe. The orange-fleshed varieties are, however, the most vibrantly coloured and will look wonderful when used in this dish.

Green Butter Beans Energy 170kcal/714kJ; Protein 10.1g; Carbohydrate 18.7g, of which sugars 6.3g; Fat 6.6g, of which saturates 1g; Cholesterol 0mg; Calcium 80mg; Fibre 8.7g; Sodium 19mg.
Pumpkin with Spices Energy 84kcal/347kJ; Protein 1.2g; Carbohydrate 3.7g, of which sugars 2.9g; Fat 7.2g, of which saturates 4.5g; Cholesterol 18mg; Calcium 50mg; Fibre 1.7g; Sodium 214mg.

Refried Chilli Beans

If the only refried beans you've tried have been the canned ones, you may have found them rather bland. These, however, are superb.

Serves 4

25g/1oz/2 tbsp lard or white cooking fat
2 onions, finely chopped
5ml/1 tsp ground cumin
5ml/1 tsp ground coriander
250g/9oz/1¼ cups dried pinto beans, soaked overnight and cooked
3 garlic cloves, crushed
small bunch of fresh coriander (cilantro) or 4–5 dried avocado leaves
50g/2oz feta cheese
salt

1 Melt the lard in a large frying pan. Add the onions, cumin and ground coriander. Cook gently over a low heat for about 30 minutes, or until the onions caramelize and become soft.

2 Add a ladleful of the soft, cooked beans. Fry them for only a few minutes simply to heat. Mash the beans into the onions as they cook, using a fork or a potato masher. Continue until all the beans have been added, a little at a time, then stir in the crushed garlic.

3 Lower the heat and cook the beans to form a thick paste. Season with salt and spoon into a warmed serving dish. Chop the coriander or crumble the avocado leaves, and sprinkle most of them over the beans. Crumble the feta cheese over the top, then garnish with the reserved sprigs or leaves.

Mung Bean Stew with Chillies

This is a simple and tasty stew from Kenya.

Serves 4

225g/8oz/1¼ cups mung beans, soaked overnight in water
25g/1oz/2 tbsp ghee or butter
2 garlic cloves, crushed
1 red onion, chopped
30ml/2 tbsp tomato purée (paste)
½ green (bell) pepper, seeded and cut into small cubes
½ red (bell) pepper, seeded and cut into small cubes
1 green chilli, seeded and finely chopped
300ml/½ pint/1¼ cups water

1 Drain the mung beans, put them in a large pan, cover with fresh water and boil until the beans are soft and the water has evaporated. Remove from the heat and mash roughly with a fork or potato masher until smooth.

2 Heat the ghee or butter in a separate pan, add the garlic and onion and fry for 4–5 minutes until golden brown, then add the tomato purée and cook for a further 2–3 minutes, stirring all the time.

3 Stir in the mashed beans, then the green and red peppers and the chopped chilli. Add the water, stirring well to mix all the ingredients together.

4 Pour the mixture back into a clean pan and simmer for about 10 minutes, then spoon into a serving dish and serve immediately.

Spiced Mexican Beans

Traditionally, clay pots are used in Mexico for this spicy dish, which give the beans a wonderful, slightly earthy flavour.

Serves 4

250g/9oz/1¼ cups dried pinto beans, soaked overnight in water to cover
1.75 litres/3 pints/7½ cups water
2 onions
10 whole garlic cloves, peeled
small bunch of fresh coriander (cilantro)
salt

For the toppings

2 fresh red fresno chillies
1 tomato, peeled and chopped
2 spring onions (scallions), finely chopped
60ml/4 tbsp sour cream
50g/2oz feta cheese

1 Drain the beans, rinse them under cold water and drain again. Put the water in a large pan, bring to the boil and add the beans. Cut the onions in half and add them to the pan, with the whole garlic cloves. Boil again, then simmer for 1½ hours, until the beans are tender and there is only a little liquid remaining.

2 While the beans are cooking, prepare the toppings. Spear the chillies on a long-handled metal skewer and roast them over the flame of a gas burner until the skins blister and darken. Alternatively, dry fry them in a griddle pan until the skins are scorched. Put the roasted chillies in a plastic bag and tie the top immediately to keep the steam in. Set aside for 20 minutes.

3 Remove the chillies from the bag and peel. Discard the stalks, then slit the chillies and discard the seeds. Slice into thin strips and put in a bowl. Put the other toppings into separate bowls.

4 Ladle about 250ml/8fl oz/1 cup of the beans and liquid into a food processor or blender. Process to a smooth purée. Return the purée to the pan, and stir it in. Chop the coriander and stir it in, reserving some for the garnish. Season with salt.

5 Serve the beans in individual bowls along with the toppings and add coriander to garnish. Each guest spoons a little of the chillies, tomatoes and spring onions over the beans, then adds a spoonful of sour cream, and finally a crumbling of feta cheese.

Refried Beans Energy 279kcal/1174kJ; Protein 16.9g; Carbohydrate 32.8g, of which sugars 5.4g; Fat 9.9g, of which saturates 4.4g; Cholesterol 15mg; Calcium 148mg; Fibre 11.3g; Sodium 197mg.
Mung Bean Stew Energy 229kcal/965kJ; Protein 14.5g; Carbohydrate 31.1g, of which sugars 5.5g; Fat 6g, of which saturates 3.5g; Cholesterol 13mg; Calcium 61mg; Fibre 6.8g; Sodium 65mg.
Spiced Beans Energy 259kcal/1094kJ; Protein 17.6g; Carbohydrate 34.1g, of which sugars 6.9g; Fat 6.8g, of which saturates 3.8g; Cholesterol 18mg; Calcium 166mg; Fibre 11.7g; Sodium 2,700mg.

Chilli Chickpea and Okra Fry

This is a delicious dish combining the nutty taste and firm texture of chickpeas with the fresh, subtle flavour of okra. It makes an excellent side dish for a larger meal or is perfect as a light lunch.

Serves 4

450g/1lb okra
15ml/1 tbsp vegetable oil
15ml/1 tbsp mustard oil
15g/½oz/1 tbsp butter or margarine
1 onion, finely chopped
1 garlic clove, crushed
2 tomatoes, finely chopped
1 green chilli, seeded and finely chopped
2 slices fresh root ginger
5ml/1 tsp ground cumin
15ml/1 tbsp chopped fresh coriander (cilantro)
425g/15oz can chickpeas, drained
salt and ground black pepper

1 Wash and dry the okra, remove the tops and tails and chop the pods roughly.

2 Heat the vegetable and mustard oils and the butter or margarine in a large frying pan.

3 Fry the onion and garlic for 5 minutes until the onion is slightly softened and turning translucent.

4 Add the chopped tomatoes, chilli and ginger and stir well, then add the okra, cumin and coriander. Simmer for 5 minutes, stirring frequently.

5 Stir in the drained chickpeas and mix well. Season with a little salt and black pepper.

6 Cook gently for a few minutes for the chickpeas to heat through, then spoon into a serving bowl and serve immediately.

Variations

Other vegetables can be added to this stir-fry to make a pleasing side dish. Mushrooms, cooked potatoes, courgettes (zucchini) or green beans would all be suitable additions.

Black Gram in a Spiced Cream Sauce

Dhabas are highway cafés throughout India and are very lively eating places serving a variety of dishes. This bean recipe is commonly served, and is one of the most popular.

Serves 4 to 6

175g/6oz black gram, (lentils) soaked overnight
50g/2oz red gram (lentils)
120ml/4fl oz/½ cup double (heavy) cream
120ml/4fl oz/½ cup natural (plain) yogurt
5ml/1 tsp cornflour (cornstarch)
45ml/3 tbsp ghee
1 onion, finely chopped
5cm/2in piece fresh root ginger, crushed
4 green chillies, chopped
1 tomato, chopped
2.5ml/½ tsp chilli powder
2.5ml/½ tsp ground turmeric
2.5ml/½ tsp ground cumin
2 garlic cloves, sliced
salt

1 Drain the black gram and place in a heavy pan with the red gram. Cover with water and bring to the boil. Reduce the heat, cover the pan and simmer until the gram are tender. The black gram will remain whole but the red gram will be mushy. Gently mash with a spoon. Allow to cool.

2 In a bowl, mix together the cream, yogurt and cornflour. Mix into the gram without breaking the black gram grains.

3 Heat 15ml/1 tbsp of the ghee in a frying pan and fry the onion, ginger, two of the green chillies and the tomato until the onion is soft and translucent. Add the spices and salt and fry for a further 2 minutes. Add it all to the gram mixture and mix well. Reheat, transfer to a heatproof serving dish and keep warm.

4 Heat the remaining ghee in a frying pan and fry the garlic slices and the remaining chillies until the garlic is golden.

5 Pour over the gram and serve, folding the garlic and chilli into the gram just before serving. Place extra cream on the table for the diners to add more, if they wish.

Chilli Chick-pea Fry Energy 241kcal/1010kJ; Protein 10.9g; Carbohydrate 22.2g, of which sugars 5.6g; Fat 12.8g, of which saturates 3.3g; Cholesterol 8mg; Calcium 231mg; Fibre 9.3g; Sodium 257mg.
Spicy Gram Energy 283kcal/1181kJ; Protein 10.1g; Carbohydrate 23g, of which sugars 5.6g; Fat 17.4g, of which saturates 9.3g; Cholesterol 23mg; Calcium 86mg; Fibre 6.8g; Sodium 32mg.

Lentils with Chilli, Ginger and Coconut Milk

For the largely vegetarian South Indian population spicy dhal dishes such as this one are an important source of protein.

Serves 4

30ml/2 tbsp ghee, or 15ml/1 tbsp vegetable oil and 15g/½oz/1 tbsp butter
1 onion, chopped
4 garlic cloves, chopped
2 fresh red chillies, seeded and chopped
50g/2oz fresh root ginger, peeled and chopped
10ml/2 tsp sugar
7.5ml/1½ tsp cumin seeds
5ml/1 tsp ground turmeric
15ml/1 tbsp garam masala
225g/8oz/generous 1 cup brown lentils, washed thoroughly and drained
600ml/1 pint/2½ cups coconut milk
salt
natural (plain) yogurt or curry, rice and chutney, to serve

For the garnish

10ml/2 tsp mustard seeds
a small handful dried curry leaves
1–2 dried red chillies
15ml/1 tbsp ghee

1 Heat the ghee, or oil and butter, in a heavy pan. Stir in the onion, garlic, chillies and ginger and fry until fragrant and beginning to colour.

2 Add the sugar, cumin seeds, turmeric and garam masala, taking care not to burn the spices. Stir in the lentils and coat in the spices and ghee. Pour in 600ml/1 pint/2½ cups water, mix thoroughly, and bring to the boil. Reduce the heat and allow to simmer gently for 35–40 minutes until the mixture is thick.

3 Stir in the coconut milk and simmer for a further 30 minutes until thick and mushy – if at any time the dhal seems too dry, add more water or coconut milk. Season to taste with salt.

4 In a small pan, heat the mustard seeds. As soon as they begin to pop, add the curry leaves and chillies. When the chillies start to darken, stir in the ghee until it melts. Spoon the mixture over the dhal, or fold it in until well mixed. Serve the dhal with yogurt or with a curry, rice and chutney.

Dhal Seasoned with Fried Spices

Dhals, made with lentils, are cooked in every house in India in one form or another. This recipe is for a quick and easy version of this spicy classic.

Serves 4 to 6

115g/4oz red gram, washed and picked over
50g/2oz Bengal gram, washed and picked over
350ml/12floz/1½ cups water
4 whole green chillies
5ml/1 tsp ground turmeric
1 large onion, sliced
400g/14oz canned plum tomatoes, crushed
60ml/4 tbsp vegetable oil
2.5ml/½ tsp mustard seeds
2.5ml/½ tsp cumin seeds
1 clove garlic, crushed
6 curry leaves
2 whole dried red chillies
1.5ml/¼ tsp asafoetida
salt
fresh coriander (cilantro) leaves, to garnish

1 Put both kinds of lentils, the water, chillies, turmeric and onion in a heavy pan and bring to the boil. Cover the pan and simmer until the pulses are soft and the water has been absorbed.

2 Mash the lentils with the back of a spoon. When nearly smooth, add the salt and tomatoes and mix well. If necessary, thin the mixture with hot water.

3 Heat the vegetable oil in a large frying pan and cook the mustard and cumin seeds for 1–2 minutes until they start to splutter and release their fragrances.

4 Add the garlic, curry leaves, dried chillies and asafoetida to the pan. Fry until the garlic begins to turn brown. Ensure that it does not burn, otherwise it will taste bitter.

5 Pour the spice mixture over the lentils and cover the pan. Return to the heat. After 5 minutes, mix well, garnish and serve.

Cook's Tip

If you prefer a little more heat in your spicy dishes, then increase the number of dried chillies used in this dish.

Lentils with Chilli Energy 322kcal/1358kJ; Protein 14g; Carbohydrate 41.3g, of which sugars 10.6g; Fat 12.4g, of which saturates 5.7g; Cholesterol 0mg; Calcium 77mg; Fibre 3g; Sodium 186mg.
Dhal with Fried Spices Energy 213kcal/893kJ; Protein 9.1g; Carbohydrate 25.7g, of which sugars 6.5g; Fat 9.1g, of which saturates 1.1g; Cholesterol 0mg; Calcium 50mg; Fibre 3g; Sodium 21mg.

Piquant Potato Salad

Colourful vegetables in a creamy smooth dressing make this piquant potato salad an excellent dish. It is ideal to serve as one of a selection of salads or with grilled or cold meats for a more substantial meal.

Serves 6

900g/2lb small waxy or salad potatoes
2 red (bell) peppers, seeded and diced
2 celery sticks, finely chopped
1 shallot, finely chopped
2 or 3 spring onions (scallions), finely chopped
1 mild fresh green chilli, seeded and finely chopped
1 garlic clove, crushed
10ml/2 tsp finely chopped fresh chives
10ml/2 tsp finely chopped fresh basil
15ml/1 tbsp finely chopped fresh parsley
15ml/1 tbsp single (light) cream
30ml/2 tbsp salad cream
15ml/1 tbsp mayonnaise
5ml/1 tsp Dijon mustard
7.5ml/1½ tsp sugar
chopped chives, to garnish
chopped red chilli, to garnish

1 Cook the potatoes in a large pan of boiling water until tender but still firm. Drain and leave to one side.

2 When the potatoes are cool enough to handle, cut into 2.5cm/1in cubes and place in a large salad bowl.

3 Add all the vegetables to the potatoes in the salad bowl, together with the chilli, garlic and all the chopped herbs, mixing thoroughly until well combined.

4 Mix together the cream, salad cream, mayonnaise, mustard and sugar in a small bowl. Stir well until the mixture is thoroughly combined and forms a smooth dressing.

5 Pour the dressing over the potato mixture and stir gently until all the ingredients are evenly coated.

6 Serve the salad garnished with the chopped chives and chopped red chilli.

Potatoes with Crushed Red Chillies and Spices

If you like chillies, you'll love these spicy potatoes. If you're not a fan of fiery flavours, leave out the chilli seeds and just use the flesh.

Serves 4

12–14 small new or salad potatoes, halved
30ml/2 tbsp vegetable oil
2.5ml/½ tsp crushed dried red chillies
2.5ml/½ tsp white cumin seeds
2.5ml/½ tsp fennel seeds
2.5ml/½ tsp crushed coriander seeds
5ml/1 tsp salt
1 onion, sliced
1–4 fresh red chillies, chopped
15ml/1 tbsp chopped fresh coriander (cilantro)
chopped fresh coriander (cilantro), to garnish

1 Cook the potatoes in boiling salted water until just tender. Remove from the heat and drain. Set aside until needed.

2 In a deep frying pan, heat the oil over a medium-high heat, then reduce the heat to medium. Add the crushed chillies, cumin, fennel and coriander seeds and salt and fry, stirring, for 30–40 seconds, until the spices start to release their fragrances.

3 Add the sliced onion to the pan and fry for 4–5 minutes until golden brown. Then add the potatoes, red chillies and coriander and stir well.

4 Reduce the heat to very low, then cover the pan and cook for about 5–7 minutes.

5 Serve the potatoes hot, garnished with fresh coriander.

Cook's Tip

To prepare fresh chillies, slit down one side and scrape out the seeds, unless you want a really hot dish. Finely slice or chop the flesh. Wear rubber gloves if you have very sensitive skin that is irritated by the oils in chillies.

Piquant Potato Salad Energy 167kcal/705kJ; Protein 3.7g; Carbohydrate 30.2g, of which sugars 7.1g; Fat 4.3g, of which saturates 0.7g; Cholesterol 4mg; Calcium 24mg; Fibre 3.5g; Sodium 90mg.
Potatoes with Chillies Energy 101kcal/421kJ; Protein 1.4g; Carbohydrate 11.4g, of which sugars 1.8g; Fat 5.8g, of which saturates 0.7g; Cholesterol 0mg; Calcium 20mg; Fibre 1.2g; Sodium 501mg.

Potato Curry with Yogurt and Green Chillies

Variations of this simple Indian curry are popular in Singapore at market stalls, where it is served with flatbread. Generally, it is served with a meat curry and rice, but it is also delicious on its own, served with yogurt and a spicy pickle or chutney.

Serves 4

6 garlic cloves, chopped
25g/1oz fresh root ginger, peeled and chopped
30ml/2 tbsp ghee, or 15ml/1 tbsp oil and 15g/½oz/1 tbsp butter
6 shallots, halved lengthways and sliced along the grain
2 green chillies, seeded and finely sliced
10ml/2 tsp sugar
a handful of fresh or dried curry leaves
2 cinnamon sticks
5–10ml/1–2 tsp ground turmeric
15ml/1 tbsp garam masala
500g/1¼lb waxy potatoes, cut into bitesize pieces
2 tomatoes, peeled, seeded and quartered
250ml/8fl oz/1 cup Greek (US strained plain) yogurt
salt and ground black pepper
5ml/1 tsp red chilli powder, and fresh coriander (cilantro) and mint leaves, chopped, to garnish
1 lemon, quartered, to serve

1 Using a mortar and pestle or a food processor, grind the garlic and ginger to a coarse paste. Heat the ghee in a heavy pan and stir in the shallots and chillies, until fragrant. Add the garlic and ginger paste with the sugar, and stir until the mixture begins to colour. Stir in the curry leaves, cinnamon sticks, turmeric and garam masala, and toss in the potatoes, making sure they are coated in the spice mixture.

2 Pour in just enough cold water to cover the potatoes. Bring to the boil, then reduce the heat and simmer until the potatoes are just cooked – they should still have a bite to them.

3 Season with salt and pepper to taste. Gently toss in the tomatoes to heat them through. Fold in the yogurt so that it is streaky rather than completely mixed in. Sprinkle with the chilli powder, coriander and mint. Serve immediately from the pan, with lemon to squeeze over it and flatbread for scooping it up.

Chilli Bombay Potatoes

A classic Indian vegetarian dish of potatoes slowly cooked in a richly flavoured curry sauce with fresh chillies for an added kick.

Serves 4 to 6

450g/1lb new or small salad potatoes
5ml/1 tsp ground turmeric
60ml/4 tbsp vegetable oil
2 dried red chillies
6–8 curry leaves
2 onions, finely chopped
2 fresh green chillies, finely chopped
50g/2oz coriander (cilantro) leaves, coarsely chopped
1.5ml/¼ tsp asafoetida
2.5ml/½ tsp each cumin, mustard, onion, fennel and nigella seeds
lemon juice
salt
fresh fried curry leaves, to garnish (optional)

1 Chop the potatoes into small chunks and cook in boiling lightly salted water with 2.5ml/½ tsp of the turmeric until tender. Drain, then coarsely mash. Set aside.

2 Heat the oil in a large, heavy frying pan and fry the red chillies and curry leaves, stirring constantly, until the chillies are nearly burnt.

3 Add the onions, green chillies, coriander, the remaining turmeric, asafoetida and spice seeds to the pan. Cook for about 4–5 minutes, stirring occasionally, until the onions are soft and turning translucent, the seeds are spluttering and the spices are releasing their fragrances.

4 Fold in the potatoes and add a few drops of water. Cook on a low heat for about 10 minutes, mixing well to ensure the even distribution of the spices.

5 When the potatoes are heated through, remove the dried chillies and curry leaves from the pan.

6 Transfer the spicy potatoes to a warmed serving dish and serve immediately, with lemon juice squeezed or poured over, to taste. Garnish the potatoes with the fresh fried curry leaves, if you wish.

Potato Curry Energy 231kcal/967kJ; Protein 6.7g; Carbohydrate 26.2g, of which sugars 7.4g; Fat 12.4g, of which saturates 4.1g; Cholesterol 0mg; Calcium 110mg; Fibre 2g; Sodium 63mg.
Chilli Bombay Potatoes Energy 208kcal/869kJ; Protein 4g; Carbohydrate 24g, of which sugars 6g; Fat 12g, of which saturates 1g; Cholesterol 0mg; Calcium 59mg; Fibre 2.2g; Sodium 100mg.

Spicy Potato Chips with Sesame Seeds

This recipe is a variation of the well-known Bombay potatoes, in which the potatoes are fried to give them a crispy texture, and then tossed with the spices and sesame seeds.

Serves 4

900g/2lb potatoes
vegetable oil, for deep-frying
1.5ml/¼ tsp ground turmeric
1.5ml/¼ tsp chilli powder
1.5ml/¼ tsp salt
30ml/2 tbsp vegetable oil
1.5ml/¼ tsp black mustard seeds
1 green chilli, finely chopped
1 garlic clove, crushed
30ml/2 tbsp sesame seeds

1 Cut the potatoes into thick even chips (French fries). Heat the oil for deep-frying to 160°C/325°F. Fry the chips in batches for about 5 minutes, until golden brown. Drain the chips well on plenty of kitchen paper.

2 Put the chips in a bowl and sprinkle over the turmeric, chilli powder and salt. Cool, then toss the chips in the spices until they are evenly coated.

3 Heat the 30ml/2 tbsp oil in a large pan and fry the mustard seeds for 2 minutes until they splutter. Add the chilli and garlic and fry for 2 minutes.

4 Add the sesame seeds and fry for 3–4 minutes until the seeds begin to brown. Remove from the heat then add to the potatoes. Toss together until all the ingredients are thoroughly combined.

5 Serve the potatoes cold, or reheat for about 5 minutes in an oven preheated to 200°C/400°F/Gas 6.

Cook's Tip

Make sure the chips are as uniform in size as possible to ensure that they cook evenly.

Potatoes with Chorizo and Chillies

Mexicans make their own chorizo sausage, sometimes using it fresh, but also putting it into casings to dry, when it resembles the Spanish version which is now popular the world over. This recipe makes a delicious brunch dish. Typical of peasant food, it is based on the combination of plenty of potato mixed with strongly flavoured meat to help it go further.

Serves 4 to 6

900g/2lb potatoes, peeled and diced
30ml/2 tbsp vegetable oil
2 garlic cloves, crushed
4 spring onions (scallions), chopped
2 jalapeño chillies, diced
300g/11oz chorizo sausage, skinned
150g/5oz/1¼ cups grated Monterey Jack or Cheddar cheese
salt (optional)

1 Bring a large pan of water to the boil and add the potatoes. Simmer the potatoes for 5 minutes. Transfer to a colander and drain thoroughly.

2 Heat the oil in a large frying pan, add the garlic, spring onions and chillies and cook for 3–4 minutes. Add the diced potato and cook until the cubes begin to brown a little.

3 Cut the chorizo into cubes and add these to the pan. Cook for 5 minutes more, until the sausage has heated through.

4 Season with salt if necessary, then add the cheese. Mix quickly and carefully, trying not to break up the cubes of potato. Serve immediately, while the cheese is still melting.

Potatoes in a Fiery Red Sauce

This dish should be hot and sour but, if you wish, reduce the chillies and add extra tomato purée instead.

Serves 4 to 6

450g/1lb small new potatoes, washed and dried
25g/1oz whole dried red chillies, preferably Kashmiri
5ml/1½ tsp cumin seeds
4 garlic cloves
90ml/6 tbsp vegetable oil
60ml/4 tbsp thick tamarind juice
30ml/2 tbsp tomato purée (paste)
4 curry leaves
5ml/1 tsp sugar
1.5ml/¼ tsp asafoetida
salt
coriander (cilantro) leaves and lemon wedges, to garnish

1 Boil the potatoes until they are fully cooked, ensuring they do not break. To test, insert a thin sharp knife into the potatoes. The potatoes should feel tender when they are fully cooked. Drain well.

2 Soak the chillies for 5 minutes in warm water. Drain and grind with the cumin seeds and garlic to a coarse paste using a mortar and pestle or food processor.

3 Fry the paste, tamarind juice, tomato purée, curry leaves, salt, sugar and asafoetida until the oil separates. Add the potatoes. Reduce the heat, cover and simmer for 5 minutes. Garnish with coriander and lemon wedges and serve immediately.

Spicy Potato Chips Energy 377kcal/1574kJ; Protein 4.9g; Carbohydrate 38.9g, of which sugars 2.9g; Fat 23.6g, of which saturates 2.9g; Cholesterol 0mg; Calcium 27mg; Fibre 2.3g; Sodium 27mg.
Potatoes and Chorizo Energy 443kcal/1847kJ; Protein 16g; Carbohydrate 32.4g, of which sugars 3.6g; Fat 28.1g, of which saturates 12.3g; Cholesterol 49mg; Calcium 226mg; Fibre 1.9g; Sodium 728mg.
Potatoes in a Fiery Red Sauce Energy 208kcal/869kJ; Protein 4g; Carbohydrate 24g, of which sugars 6g; Fat 12g, of which saturates 1g; Cholesterol 0mg; Calcium 59mg; Fibre 2.2g; Sodium 100mg.

Hot Tomato Potatoes

This curry makes an excellent accompaniment to almost any other savoury dish. It's perfect with fish or meat curries and rice.

Serves 4

10ml/2 tsp corn oil
1.5ml/¼ tsp onion seeds
4 curry leaves
2 medium onions, diced
400g/14oz can tomatoes
5ml/1 tsp ground cumin
7.5ml/1½ tsp ground coriander
5ml/1 tsp chilli powder
5ml/1 tsp crushed fresh root ginger
5ml/1 tsp crushed garlic
1.5ml/¼ tsp ground turmeric
5ml/1 tsp salt
15ml/1 tbsp lemon juice
15ml/1 tbsp chopped fresh coriander (cilantro)
2 medium potatoes, diced

1 Heat the oil in a wok or large frying pan and fry the onion seeds, curry leaves and onions over a medium heat for 3–4 minutes, until the seeds start to splutter and the onions are becoming soft and translucent.

2 Meanwhile, place the canned tomatoes in a bowl and add the cumin, ground coriander, chilli powder, ginger, garlic, turmeric, salt, lemon juice and fresh coriander. Mix well so all the ingredients are thoroughly combined.

3 Pour this mixture into the wok and stir for about 1 minute to mix thoroughly with the onions.

4 Add the potatoes to the pan and stir to mix well with the sauce. Cover the pan and simmer for 10–12 minutes over a low heat, stirring occasionally.

5 When the potatoes are tender, transfer the contents of the pan to a warmed serving dish. Serve immediately to accompany a curry and boiled rice.

Variation
This curry is also delicious if you add a few cauliflower florets to the pan with the potatoes.

Indonesian Potatoes with Onions and Chilli Sauce

This adds another dimension to potato chips, with the addition of crisply fried onions and a hot soy sauce and chilli dressing. Eat this dish hot, warm or cold, as a tasty side dish.

Serves 6

3 large potatoes, about 225g/8oz each, peeled
sunflower or groundnut (peanut) oil, for deep-frying
2 onions, finely sliced
salt

For the dressing
1–2 fresh red chillies, seeded and ground, or 2.5ml/½ tsp chilli sauce
45ml/3 tbsp dark soy sauce

1 Cut the potatoes into chips (French fries) and then pat dry thoroughly with kitchen paper.

2 Heat the oil in a large pan. Deep-fry the chips, until they are golden brown in colour and evenly crisp.

3 Drain the chips on kitchen paper and then transfer to a dish, sprinkle with salt and keep warm.

4 Fry the onion slices in the hot oil until they are similarly crisp and golden brown. Drain well on kitchen paper and then add to the potato chips.

5 Mix the ground chillies or chilli sauce with the soy sauce and heat gently.

6 Pour over the potato and onion mixture and serve immediately if you want them hot or leave to cool before serving.

Variation
Alternatively, you could boil the potatoes in their skins. Drain, cool and slice them and then shallow-fry until golden. Cook the onions and pour over the dressing, as above.

Hot Tomato Potatoes Energy 158kcal/667kJ; Protein 4.7g; Carbohydrate 29.7g, of which sugars 10g; Fat 3.3g, of which saturates 0.5g; Cholesterol 0mg; Calcium 52mg; Fibre 3.4g; Sodium 26mg.
Indonesian Potatoes Energy 194kcal/815kJ; Protein 2.9g; Carbohydrate 25.6g, of which sugars 3.1g; Fat 9.6g, of which saturates 1.3g; Cholesterol 0mg; Calcium 13mg; Fibre 1.6g; Sodium 551mg.

Spicy Mooli Salad

The sweet, slightly vinegary taste of mooli provides a refreshing foundation to this healthy dish. The red chilli and sesame oil dressing adds an understated spiciness and nutty aftertaste. The mooli, also known as Chinese white radish or daikon, is a commonly used ingredient in Asian cooking and is highly valued for its medicinal properties.

Serves 2

225g/8oz mooli (daikon), peeled
¼ red chilli, shredded, and 1.5ml/¼ tsp sesame seeds, to garnish

For the marinade

5ml/1 tsp cider vinegar
2.5ml/½ tsp sugar
1.5ml/¼ tsp salt
7.5ml/1½ tsp lemon juice
2.5ml/½ tsp Korean chilli powder

1 Using a sharp knife, slice the mooli into thin strips approximately 5cm/2in long.

2 To make the marinade, mix the cider vinegar, sugar, salt, lemon juice and chilli powder together in a small bowl, ensuring the ingredients are thoroughly blended.

3 Place the mooli strips in a bowl, and pour over the marinade, mixing well to ensure all the ingredients are well combined. Leave in a cool place to marinate for 20 minutes, then place the bowl in the refrigerator until the salad has chilled thoroughly.

4 Garnish the salad with the shredded chilli and sesame seeds before serving.

Variation

The mooli in this salad will take on some of the red colouring of the chilli powder. For an interesting alternative you could try replacing the chilli powder with about 2.5ml/½ tsp of wasabi, the Japanese pungent paste made from a root with a similar taste to horseradish. Wasabi will give the salad an unusual green colour from the as well as giving it a sharper taste.

Hot Korean Cucumber Salad

The refreshing, succulent taste of this simple salad makes a perfect accompaniment for a main meal on a hot summer's night. Small pickling cucumbers are the best for this dish; they are not as watery as the larger specimens and they do not require peeling.

Serves 2

400g/14oz pickling or salad cucumber
30ml/2 tbsp salt

For the dressing

2 spring onions (scallions), finely chopped
2 garlic cloves, crushed
5ml/1 tsp cider vinegar
5ml/1 tsp salt
3ml/½ tsp Korean chilli powder
10ml/2 tsp toasted sesame seeds
10ml/2 tsp sesame oil
5ml/1 tsp hot chilli paste
10ml/2 tsp sugar

1 Cut the cucumber lengthways into thin slices and put into a colander. Sprinkle with the salt, mix well and set aside for about 30 minutes so the salt can draw moisture from the cucumber.

2 Place the cucumber slices in a damp dish towel and gently squeeze out as much of the water as possible.

3 Place the spring onions in a large bowl. Add the crushed garlic, vinegar, salt and chilli powder, and stir to combine. Sprinkle in the sesame seeds and mix in the sesame oil, chilli paste and sugar.

4 Blend the cucumber with the dressing and chill before serving.

Cucumber, Sesame and Chilli Salad

This sautéed dish retains the natural succulence of the cucumber, while also infusing the recipe with a pleasantly refreshing hint of garlic and a kick of chilli.

Serves 2

200g/7oz cucumber
15ml/1 tbsp vegetable oil
5ml/1 tsp spring onion (scallion), finely chopped
1 garlic clove, crushed
5ml/1 tsp sesame oil
salt
sesame seeds, and seeded and shredded red chilli, to garnish

1 Thinly slice the cucumber and place in a colander. Sprinkle with salt, then leave to stand for 10 minutes. Drain off any excess liquid and transfer to a clean bowl.

2 Coat a frying pan or wok with the vegetable oil, and heat it over a medium heat. Add the spring onion, garlic and cucumber, and quickly stir-fry together.

3 Remove the pan from the heat, add the sesame oil and toss lightly to blend the ingredients. Place in a shallow serving dish and garnish with the sesame seeds and the shredded chilli before serving.

Spicy Mooli Salad Energy 22kcal/91kJ; Protein 1g; Carbohydrate 3.2g, of which sugars 3.2g; Fat 0.7g, of which saturates 0.2g; Cholesterol 0mg; Calcium 27mg; Fibre 1.1g; Sodium 209mg.
Hot Cucumber Salad Energy 105kcal/432kJ; Protein 3.3g; Carbohydrate 9.2g, of which sugars 7.4g; Fat 6.2g, of which saturates 0.9g; Cholesterol 0mg; Calcium 78mg; Fibre 2.2g; Sodium 1973mg.
Cucumber and Sesame Salad Energy 74kcal/304kJ; Protein 0.8g; Carbohydrate 1.7g, of which sugars 1.6g; Fat 7.1g, of which saturates 0.9g; Cholesterol 0mg; Calcium 20mg; Fibre 0.7g; Sodium 4mg.

Cucumber, Leek and Chilli Salad

This subtle dish combines the sweetness of white radish with leek and nutty sesame oil. Blanching the sticks of white radish softens it, leaving it with a silky texture.

Serves 2

400g/14oz mooli (daikon), peeled
50g/2oz leek, finely sliced
20ml/4 tsp sesame oil, plus extra for drizzling
5ml/1 tsp salt
60ml/4 tbsp vegetable oil
½ red chilli, seeded and finely shredded, to garnish

1 Slice the mooli into 5cm/2in matchstick lengths. Blanch in a pan of boiling water for 30 seconds. Drain, and gently squeeze to remove any excess water.

2 Place the leek together with the sesame oil and salt in a large bowl, and mix until well combined.

3 Place a pan over a medium heat, and add the vegetable oil. Add the mooli and fry gently for 1–2 minutes. Add the leek mixture to the pan, then fry for a further 2 minutes. Remove from the heat.

4 Garnish with the shredded chilli and a drizzle of the sesame oil before serving.

Soya Beansprout and Chilli Salad

The delicate spiciness of the red chilli and nutty flavour of the sesame oil create a tantalizing and crunchy dish. Crispy soya beansprouts can be replaced with mung beansprouts.

Serves 2

300g/10oz/2 cups soya beansprouts
60ml/4 tbsp vegetable oil
⅔ red chilli, seeded and sliced
1 baby leek, finely sliced
10ml/2 tsp sesame oil
salt

1 Wash the soya beansprouts and trim the tail ends. Cover them with a light sprinkling of salt and leave to stand for 10 minutes.

2 Bring a large pan of water to the boil and add the beansprouts. Cover the pan and bring back to the boil for 3 minutes, then drain the beansprouts thoroughly.

3 Place a frying pan or wok over a medium heat and add the vegetable oil. Add the soya beansprouts and fry gently for about 30 seconds.

4 Add the chilli and leek to the pan, and fry together for 2–3 minutes, stirring all the time so that the ingredients are thoroughly blended.

5 Transfer to a shallow dish and drizzle with a little sesame oil before serving.

Korean Green Chilli and Chive Salad

This dish is the perfect accompaniment for any grilled meat, and is a tasty alternative to the classic shredded spring onion salad.

Serves 2

180g/7oz fresh Korean or Chinese chives
1 fresh green chilli, seeded and finely sliced
10ml/2 tsp sesame seeds, to garnish

For the seasoning

30ml/2 tbsp dark soy sauce
2 garlic cloves, crushed
10ml/2 tsp Korean chilli powder
10ml/2 tsp sesame oil
10ml/2 tsp sugar

1 Clean the chives, then trim off the bulbs and discard. Slice the chives roughly into 4cm/1½in lengths. Combine with the chilli in a bowl.

2 To make the seasoning, mix the soy sauce, garlic, chilli powder, sesame oil and sugar together, and then add it to the bowl with the chives and chilli. Mix until well coated, then chill.

3 Garnish with sesame seeds and serve.

Cook's Tip

The Korean chive has a garlic nuance in both taste and aroma, and the leaves have a soft, grasslike texture. Look for it in Asian supermarkets and food stores. If unavailable you can substitute Chinese chives.

Variation

For a traditional alternative to this chive salad, use about 150g/5oz shredded spring onion (scallion) in place of the Korean chives, and add 15ml/1 tbsp cider vinegar and 15ml/1 tbsp soy sauce to the seasoning.

Cucumber Salad Energy 137kcal/565kJ; Protein 1.8g; Carbohydrate 4.5g, of which sugars 4.3g; Fat 12.5g, of which saturates 1.8g; Cholesterol 0mg; Calcium 45mg; Fibre 2.4g; Sodium 1005mg.
Soya Beansprout Salad Energy 282kcal/1167kJ; Protein 5.2g; Carbohydrate 7.5g, of which sugars 4.4g; Fat 26g, of which saturates 3.2g; Cholesterol 0mg; Calcium 42mg; Fibre 3.4g; Sodium 9mg.
Korean Green Chilli Salad Energy 105kcal/434kJ; Protein 4.3g; Carbohydrate 7g, of which sugars 6.7g; Fat 6.7g, of which saturates 0.9g; Cholesterol 0mg; Calcium 196mg; Fibre 2.3g; Sodium 1196mg.

Vinegared Chilli Cabbage

Anybody who thinks that cabbage cannot be an exciting and tasty vegetable should try this delectable dish. This tangy salad is the perfect way to cook and spice up cabbage, and it will prove to be the ideal accompaniment to grilled chicken or a plate of various cold meats.

Serves 4 to 6

1 fresh red chilli, halved, seeded and shredded
25g/1oz/2 tbsp lard, white cooking fat or butter
2 garlic cloves, crushed (optional)
1 medium white cabbage, cored and shredded
10ml/2 tsp cider vinegar
5ml/1 tsp cayenne pepper
salt

1 Put the chilli with the lard, white cooking fat or butter into a large pan and cook over a medium heat, stirring constantly, until the chilli sizzles, releases its fragrance and just begins to curl at the edges.

2 Add the garlic and cabbage to the pan and stir, over the heat, until the cabbage is thoroughly coated in the other ingredients and warmed through.

3 Add salt to taste and 75ml/5 tbsp water. Bring to the boil, cover and lower the heat.

4 Cook for a further 3–4 minutes, shaking the pan regularly to mix up the ingredients, until the cabbage wilts. Remove the pan lid, raise the heat and cook until the excess liquid in the pan has all evaporated.

5 Check the seasoning and add more salt if necessary. Sprinkle with the vinegar and cayenne.

Cook's Tip
A wok with a domed lid is an almost essential piece of kitchen equipment for people who like cooking and eating spicy Asian food. It is ideal for this salad dish and the part-frying, part-steaming method of cooking the cabbage.

Coleslaw in Triple-hot Dressing

This is a real treat for lovers of spicy food. The triple hotness is supplied by mustard, horseradish and Tabasco sauce.

Serves 6

½ white cabbage, cored and shredded
2 celery sticks, finely sliced
1 green (bell) pepper, seeded and finely sliced
4 spring onions (scallions), finely shredded
30ml/2 tbsp chopped fresh dill
cayenne pepper

For the dressing

15ml/1 tbsp Dijon mustard
10ml/2 tsp creamed horseradish
5ml/1 tsp Tabasco sauce
30ml/2 tbsp red wine vinegar
75ml/5 tbsp olive oil
salt and ground black pepper

1 Mix together the cabbage, celery, green pepper and spring onions in a large salad bowl. Toss the ingredients together until they are well combined.

2 Make the dressing. In a small bowl, mix the mustard, horseradish and Tabasco sauce, then gradually stir in the vinegar with a fork and finally beat in the olive oil and seasoning.

3 Pour the dressing over the bowl of vegetables, mix until well combined and evenly coated, and leave to stand, if possible, for at least an hour. During this time turn the salad once or twice in its dressing.

4 Immediately before serving, season the salad if necessary, toss again and sprinkle with the dill and cayenne.

Cook's Tip
This is a good salad for a buffet table or picnic as it improves with some standing in its dressing (could be overnight in the refrigerator) and travels well in a covered plastic bowl or box. However, if there are any children at the buffet or picnic, you may want to tone down some of the heat in the salad by reducing the amount of the hot items in it: the mustard, Tabasco sauce or the creamed horseradish.

Vinegared Chilli Cabbage Energy 80kcal/333kJ; Protein 2g; Carbohydrate 6g, of which sugars 6g; Fat 5g, of which saturates 3g; Cholesterol 13mg; Calcium 58mg; Fibre 2.4g; Sodium 100mg.
Coleslaw in Dressing Energy 113kcal/466kJ; Protein 1g; Carbohydrate 4g, of which sugars 4g; Fat 10g, of which saturates 1g; Cholesterol 0mg; Calcium 36mg; Fibre 1.6g; Sodium 200mg.

Hot Pepper, Mango and Tomato Salad

This salad makes an excellent appetizer. The under-ripe mango has a subtle sweetness and the flavour blends well with the tomato. There is a pleasant kick from the hot pepper sauce.

Serves 4

1 firm under-ripe mango
2 large tomatoes or 1 beefsteak tomato, sliced
½ red onion, sliced into rings
½ cucumber, peeled and thinly sliced
30ml/2 tbsp sunflower or vegetable oil
15ml/1 tbsp lemon juice
1 garlic clove, crushed
2.5ml/½ tsp hot pepper sauce
salt and ground black pepper
sugar, to taste
chopped chives, to garnish

1 Prepare the mango. Cut away two thick slices from either side of the mango stone (pit) and cut them into slices. Peel the skin from the slices.

2 Arrange the mango, tomato, onion and cucumber slices on a large serving plate.

3 Blend the oil, lemon juice, garlic, hot pepper sauce, salt and black pepper in a blender or food processor, or place in a small jar and shake vigorously. Add a pinch of sugar and mix again.

4 Pour the dressing over the salad and garnish with chopped chives before serving.

Cook's Tip
There are many varieties of hot pepper sauces from around the world available to buy and there will be a version to suit all palates. They range from the surprisingly mild sauces to extremely hot varieties that should be approached with a high degree of caution. As a rule, unless you are familiar with the sauce, start by using a small amount – you can always add more afterwards.

Hot Cajun Potato Salad

In Cajun country in Louisiana, where Tabasco sauce originates, hot means really hot, so you can go to town with this salad if you think you can take it.

Serves 6 to 8

8 waxy potatoes
1 green (bell) pepper, diced
1 large gherkin, chopped
4 spring onions (scallions), shredded
3 hard-boiled eggs, shelled and chopped
250ml/8fl oz/1 cup mayonnaise
15ml/1 tbsp Dijon mustard
salt and ground black pepper
Tabasco sauce, to taste
pinch or two of cayenne
sliced gherkin, to garnish
mayonnaise, to serve

1 Cook the potatoes in their skins in boiling salted water until tender. Drain and leave to cool.

2 When the potatoes are cool enough to handle, but while they are still warm, peel them and cut into coarse chunks. Place them in a large bowl.

3 Add the green pepper, gherkin, spring onions and hard-boiled eggs to the potatoes and toss gently to combine.

4 In a separate bowl, mix the mayonnaise with the mustard and season with salt, black pepper and Tabasco sauce to taste.

5 Pour the dressing over the potato mixture and toss gently so that the potatoes are well coated. Sprinkle with a pinch or two of cayenne and garnish with a few slices of gherkin. Serve with extra mayonnaise.

Cook's Tips
- *The salad is good to eat immediately, when the potatoes are just cool. If you make it in advance and chill it, let it come back to room temperature before serving.*
- *Tabasco is one of thousands of commercial hot pepper sauces on the market, of varying intensity: use your favourite brand to make this salad.*

Hot Pepper Salad Energy 93kcal/390kJ; Protein 1g; Carbohydrate 10.1g; of which sugars 9.5g; Fat 5.8g; of which saturates 0.7g; Cholesterol 0mg; Calcium 17mg; Fibre 2.1g; Sodium 600mg.
Cajun Salad Energy 289kcal/1197kJ; Protein 4g; Carbohydrate 10.3g, of which sugars 2.7g; Fat 26.1g, of which saturates 4.2g; Cholesterol 95mg; Calcium 21mg; Fibre 0.9g; Sodium 229mg.

Red Hot Seaweed Salad with Green Mango

In the Philippines various types of seaweed are enjoyed in salads and the occasional stir-fry. Serve this spicy salad as an appetizer or as an accompaniment to grilled meats and fish.

Serves 4

50g/2oz fine thread seaweed, reconstituted in water, or 225g/8oz fresh seaweed, cut into strips
1 green mango, grated
2–3 ripe tomatoes, skinned, seeded and chopped
4–6 spring onions (scallions), white parts only, sliced
25g/1oz fresh root ginger, grated
45ml/3 tbsp coconut or cane vinegar
10ml/2 tsp chilli oil
15ml/1 tbsp sugar
salt and ground black pepper

1 Bring a large pan of water to the boil, drop in the seaweed, remove from the heat and leave to soak for 15 minutes. Drain and refresh under cold running water. Using your hands, squeeze the seaweed dry.

2 Put the seaweed, mango, tomatoes, spring onions and ginger into a large bowl and mix to combine.

3 In a separate bowl, mix together the coconut vinegar, chilli oil and sugar until the sugar has dissolved.

4 Pour the dressing over the salad, toss well together and season with salt and pepper to taste. Serve as an appetizer or with grilled (broiled) meat or fish.

Cook's Tip
Fresh and dried seaweeds are widely available from Chinese and South-east Asian supermarkets and food stores. Some dried varieties are also available from health food stores. For this recipe, you need the fine thread seaweed available in Chinese stores.

Thai Seafood Salad with Pomelo and Peanuts

A Thai meal will include a selection of dishes, one of which is often a refreshing and palate-cleansing salad that features tropical fruit, as with the pomelo here.

Serves 4 to 6

30ml/2 tbsp vegetable oil
4 shallots, finely sliced
2 garlic cloves, finely sliced
1 large pomelo, peeled
15ml/1 tbsp roasted peanuts
115g/4oz cooked peeled prawns (shrimp)
115g/4oz cooked crab meat
10–12 small fresh mint leaves

For the dressing
30ml/2 tbsp Thai fish sauce
15ml/1 tbsp palm sugar (jaggery) or light muscovado (brown) sugar
30ml/2 tbsp fresh lime juice

For the garnish
2 spring onions (scallions), thinly sliced
2 fresh red chillies, seeded and thinly sliced
fresh coriander (cilantro) leaves
grated fresh coconut (optional)

1 Make the dressing. Mix the fish sauce, sugar and lime juice in a bowl. Whisk well, then cover and set aside.

2 Heat the oil in a frying pan, add the shallots and garlic and cook until they are golden. Remove from the pan and set aside.

3 Break the pomelo flesh into small pieces, taking care to remove any membranes. Grind the peanuts and mix with the pomelo, prawns, crab, mint and shallots. Toss in the dressing and sprinkle with spring onions, chillies and coriander. Add the coconut, if using. Serve immediately.

Cook's Tip
The pomelo is a large citrus fruit that looks like a grapefruit, although it is not, as is often thought, a hybrid. It is slightly pear-shaped with thick, yellow, dimpled skin and pinkish-yellow flesh that is drier than a grapefruit's. It also has a sharper taste.

Red Hot Seaweed Salad Energy 75kcal/315kJ; Protein 2.4g; Carbohydrate 12g, of which sugars 11.8g; Fat 2.2g, of which saturates 0.3g; Cholesterol 0mg; Calcium 110mg; Fibre 2.8g; Sodium 85mg.
Thai Seafood Salad Energy 159kcal/665kJ; Protein 13.4g; Carbohydrate 8.4g, of which sugars 8.1g; Fat 4.9g, of which saturates 0.9g; Cholesterol 44mg; Calcium 107mg; Fibre 1.1g; Sodium 612mg.

Green Papaya Salad with Red Chillies

Throughout South-east Asia, unripe green mangoes and papayas are used for salads. Their tart, crunchy flesh complements spicy grilled or stir-fried dishes beautifully. This Filipino version is sweet and sour, achieving the desired balance to go perfectly with grilled or deep-fried pork and chicken.

Serves 4

2 green papayas, seeded and grated
4 shallots, finely sliced
1–2 red chillies, seeded, halved lengthways and finely sliced
150g/5oz/1 cup plump sultanas (golden raisins) or raisins
2 garlic cloves, crushed
25g/1oz fresh root ginger, grated
45–60ml/3–4 tbsp coconut or cane vinegar
50g/2oz palm sugar (jaggery) or light muscovado (brown) sugar
1 small bunch of fresh coriander (cilantro), chopped, to garnish

1 Put the papayas, shallots, chillies, sultanas or raisins, garlic and ginger into a bowl. Mix thoroughly until the ingredients are all well combined.

2 In a separate small bowl, mix together the coconut vinegar and sugar until the sugar has dissolved.

3 Pour the sweet vinegar dressing over the salad and toss well together. Leave the salad to marinate for at least 1 hour or, for the best flavour, in the refrigerator overnight to allow the flavours to fully mingle.

4 Serve the salad garnished with the coriander leaves.

Variation

Use green mango or grated carrots in this salad, if you wish, or you could combine the papayas with carrots for the vibrant colours they will bring to the dish.

Refreshing Fruit Salad in a Tangy Dressing

Entrenched in the Indonesian culinary culture, this salad appears in many guises – as a snack, as a salad to accompany fried and grilled dishes, or as a festive dish. Designed to be flexible, this refreshing salad, tossed in a pungent and tangy dressing, can include any choice of fruit and vegetables that you have available.

Serves 4 to 6

1 green mango, finely sliced
1 ripe, firm papaya, finely sliced
1–2 star fruit (carambola), finely sliced
½ pineapple, finely sliced and cut into bitesize pieces
½ pomelo, segmented
1 small cucumber, roughly peeled, seeded, and finely sliced
1 yam bean, finely sliced
a handful of beansprouts

For the sauce

10ml/2 tsp shrimp paste
225g/8oz roasted peanuts
4 garlic cloves, chopped
2–4 red chillies, seeded and chopped
15ml/1 tbsp tamarind paste
30ml/2 tbsp palm sugar (jaggery)
salt

1 To make the sauce, dry-roast the shrimp paste in a small, heavy frying pan, stirring, until browned and emitting a toasted, pungent aroma.

2 Using a mortar and pestle or an electric blender, grind the peanuts, garlic and chillies to form a coarse paste. Beat in the dry-fried shrimp paste, tamarind paste and the sugar. Add enough water to the mixture to make a thick, pouring sauce, then stir until the sugar has completely dissolved. Season the sauce with salt to taste.

3 Put all the fruit and vegetables, except the beansprouts, into a large bowl. Pour in some of the sauce and toss gently together. Leave the salad to stand for 30 minutes.

4 Transfer the salad into a serving dish. Sprinkle the beansprouts over the top and serve with the remaining sauce drizzled over the top.

Green Papaya Salad Energy 232kcal/988kJ; Protein 2.5g; Carbohydrate 58.3g, of which sugars 57.6g; Fat 0.4g, of which saturates 0g; Cholesterol 0mg; Calcium 81mg; Fibre 5.5g; Sodium 19mg.
Refreshing Fruit Salad Energy 321kcal/1344kJ; Protein 12.3g; Carbohydrate 30g, of which sugars 27.2g; Fat 17.7g, of which saturates 3.3g; Cholesterol 8mg; Calcium 91mg; Fibre 6.2g; Sodium 81mg.

Fruit and Vegetable Salad with a Hint of Chilli

This fruit salad is traditionally presented with the main course and serves as a cooler to counteract the heat of the chillies that will inevitably be present in the other dishes. It is a typically harmonious balance of flavours.

Serves 4 to 6

1 small pineapple
1 small mango, peeled and sliced
1 green apple, cored and sliced
6 rambutans or lychees, peeled and stoned (pitted)
115g/4oz/1 cup green beans, trimmed and halved
1 red onion, sliced
1 small cucumber, cut into short sticks
115g/4oz/½ cup beansprouts
2 spring onions (scallions), sliced
1 ripe tomato, quartered
225g/8oz cos, romaine or iceberg lettuce leaves
salt

For the coconut dipping sauce

30ml/2 tbsp coconut cream
30ml/2 tbsp sugar
75ml/5 tbsp boiling water
1.5ml/¼ tsp chilli sauce
15ml/1 tbsp Thai fish sauce
juice of 1 lime

1 Make the coconut dipping sauce. Spoon the coconut cream, sugar and boiling water into a screw-top jar. Add the chilli and fish sauces and lime juice, close tightly and shake to mix.

2 Trim both ends of the pineapple with a serrated knife, then cut away the outer skin. Remove the central core with an apple corer. Alternatively, quarter the pineapple lengthways and remove the portion of core from each wedge with a knife. Chop the pineapple and set aside with the other fruits.

3 Bring a small pan of lightly salted water to the boil over a medium heat. Add the green beans and cook for 3–4 minutes, until just tender but still retaining some 'bite'. Drain, refresh under cold running water, drain well again and set aside.

4 To serve, arrange all the fruits and vegetables in small heaps on a platter or in a shallow bowl. Pour the coconut sauce into a small serving bowl and serve separately as a dip.

Thai Spiced Cabbage Salad

This is a simple and delicious way of serving a somewhat mundane vegetable, with classic Thai flavours.

Serves 4 to 6

30ml/2 tbsp vegetable oil
2 large fresh red chillies, seeded and cut into thin strips
6 garlic cloves, thinly sliced
6 shallots, thinly sliced
1 small cabbage, shredded
salt
30ml/2 tbsp coarsely chopped roasted peanuts, to garnish

For the dressing

30ml/2 tbsp Thai fish sauce
grated rind of 1 lime
30ml/2 tbsp fresh lime juice
120ml/4fl oz/½ cup coconut milk

1 Make the dressing by mixing the fish sauce, lime rind and juice and coconut milk together in a bowl. Whisk until thoroughly combined, then set aside.

2 Heat the oil in a wok or large frying pan. Fry the chillies, garlic and shallots over a medium heat, stirring constantly, for 3–4 minutes, until the shallots have turned brown and crisp. Remove the ingredients from the pan with a slotted spoon and set aside until needed.

3 Bring a large pan of lightly salted water to the boil. Add the cabbage and blanch for 2–3 minutes. Transfer it into a colander, drain well and put into a bowl.

4 Whisk the dressing again. Pour it over the warm cabbage and toss to mix until the cabbage is evenly coated in the dressing.

5 Transfer the salad to a serving dish. Sprinkle the fried shallot mixture and the chopped peanuts over the salad. Serve the salad immediately.

Variation
Other vegetables will also work in this versatile dish. Cauliflower, broccoli and Chinese leaves (Chinese cabbage) can be cooked in this way.

Fruit and Vegetable Salad Energy 159kcal/673kJ; Protein 3.5g; Carbohydrate 32.2g, of which sugars 31g; Fat 2.7g, of which saturates 1.7g; Cholesterol 0mg; Calcium 69mg; Fibre 4.7g; Sodium 188mg.
Thai Spiced Cabbage Salad Energy 124kcal/513kJ; Protein 3.4g; Carbohydrate 7.1g, of which sugars 6.5g; Fat 9.2g, of which saturates 1.4g; Cholesterol 0mg; Calcium 57mg; Fibre 2.3g; Sodium 306mg.

Serrano Chilli and Spinach Salad

Young spinach leaves make a welcome change from lettuce and are excellent in salads. The roasted garlic is an inspired addition to the spicy dressing.

Serves 6

500g/1¼lb baby spinach leaves
50g/2oz/⅓ cup sesame seeds
50g/2oz/¼ cup butter
30ml/2 tbsp olive oil
6 shallots, sliced
8 fresh serrano chillies, seeded and cut into strips
4 tomatoes, sliced

For the dressing
6 roasted garlic cloves
120ml/4fl oz/½ cup white wine vinegar
2.5ml/½ tsp ground white pepper
1 bay leaf
2.5ml/½ tsp ground allspice
30ml/2 tbsp chopped fresh thyme, plus extra sprigs, to garnish

1 Make the dressing. Remove the skins from the garlic when cool, then chop and combine with the vinegar, pepper, bay leaf, allspice and chopped thyme in a jar with a screw-top lid. Close the lid tightly, shake well, then put the dressing in the refrigerator until needed.

2 Wash the spinach leaves and dry them in a salad spinner or clean dish towel. Put them in a plastic bag in the refrigerator.

3 Toast the sesame seeds in a dry frying pan, shaking frequently over a moderate heat until golden. Set aside.

4 Heat the butter and oil in a frying pan. Fry the shallots for 4–5 minutes, until softened, then stir in the chilli strips and fry for 2–3 minutes more.

5 In a large bowl, layer the spinach with the shallot and chilli mixture, and the tomato slices. Pour over the dressing. Sprinkle with sesame seeds and serve, garnished with thyme sprigs.

Cook's Tip
To roast garlic, place in a roasting pan in the oven at 180°C/350°F/Gas 4 for about 15 minutes until soft.

Raw Vegetable and Coconut Salad in a Chilli Lime Dressing

This Indonesian salad is typical of the type of dish that is served as a snack on a banana leaf with rice, or with grilled or fried fish and meat. Street stalls often prepare a simple salad of this kind to accompany the main dish. Crunchy and easy to eat with the fingers, the salad varies according to what is in season. Serve it as a spicy accompaniment to meat, poultry or fish along with bowls of rice.

Serves 4 to 6

225g/8oz yard-long beans, cut into bitesize pieces
3–4 tomatoes, skinned, seeded and cut into bitesize chunks
4–6 spring onions (scallions), finely sliced
225g/8oz/1 cup beansprouts
½ fresh coconut, grated

For the dressing
1–2 red or green chillies, seeded and chopped
2 garlic cloves, chopped
25g/1oz galangal or fresh root ginger, grated
5–10ml/1–2 tsp shrimp paste
juice of 2–3 limes
salt and ground black pepper

1 Make the dressing. Using a mortar and pestle or a food processor, grind the chillies, garlic and galangal or ginger to a paste.

2 Add the shrimp paste and juice of 2 limes. If the limes are not juicy, then squeeze the juice from the extra lime and add to the dressing. Alternatively, add a little water, so that it is of pouring consistency. Season the dressing with a little salt and pepper to taste.

3 Put the yard-long beans, tomatoes, spring onions, beansprouts and grated coconut into a large bowl. Using your fingers or two spoons, mix the ingredients together.

4 Pour the dressing over the vegetables in the bowl and mix thoroughly until everything is evenly coated. Serve as an accompaniment to meat, poultry or fish and bowls of fragrant boiled rice.

Serrano and Spinach Salad Energy 181kcal/748kJ; Protein 4.7g; Carbohydrate 4.2g, of which sugars 4.1g; Fat 16.3g, of which saturates 5.7g; Cholesterol 18mg; Calcium 209mg; Fibre 3.4g; Sodium 177mg.
Raw Vegetable Salad Energy 141kcal/584kJ; Protein 4.5g; Carbohydrate 6.4g, of which sugars 5.1g; Fat 11g, of which saturates 9.1g; Cholesterol 8mg; Calcium 54mg; Fibre 4.6g; Sodium 86mg.

Persimmon and Bamboo Shoot Salad with Chilli

This is a refreshing salad, lightly seasoned with a sweet and sour soy dressing.

Serves 1 to 2

200g/7oz can bamboo shoots, drained and rinsed in water
2 dried shiitake mushrooms, soaked in warm water for about 30 minutes until softened
50g/2oz beef flank, thinly sliced
25ml/1½ tbsp vegetable oil
115g/4oz/½ cup beansprouts
1 egg
90g/3½oz watercress or rocket (arugula)
salt
½ red chilli, seeded and thinly sliced, to garnish

For the seasoning
7.5ml/1½ tsp dark soy sauce
10g/¼oz red persimmon, finely chopped
½ spring onion (scallion), finely chopped
1 garlic clove, crushed
5ml/1 tsp sesame seeds
2.5ml/½ tsp sesame oil
ground white pepper

For the dressing
60ml/4 tbsp dark soy sauce
60ml/4 tbsp water
30ml/2 tbsp rice vinegar
40g/1½oz red persimmon, finely chopped
5ml/1 tsp sesame seeds

1 Thinly slice the bamboo shoots and cut into bitesize pieces. Drain the mushrooms and thinly slice them, discarding the stems. Put the beef slices in a bowl. Add the seasoning ingredients and the shiitake mushrooms, and mix together well.

2 Heat 15ml/1 tbsp of the oil in a frying pan. Stir-fry the beef and mushrooms until cooked. Cool, then put in the refrigerator. Trim the beansprouts and blanch for 3 minutes. Drain.

3 In a bowl, combine all the dressing ingredients and mix well. Set aside. Beat the egg and season with a pinch of salt. Heat the remaining oil, add the egg and make an omelette, browning gently on each side. Remove from the pan and cut into strips.

4 Arrange the beef on a serving plate with the bamboo shoots, watercress or rocket, and beansprouts. Garnish with the sliced chilli and egg strips before serving.

Spicy Bamboo Shoot Salad

This hot, sharp-flavoured salad originated in north-eastern Thailand. Use canned whole bamboo shoots, if you can find them – they have more flavour than the sliced ones.

Serves 4

400g/14oz canned bamboo shoots, in large pieces
25g/1oz glutinous rice
30ml/2 tbsp chopped shallots
15ml/1 tbsp chopped garlic
45ml/3 tbsp chopped spring onions (scallions)
30ml/2 tbsp Thai fish sauce
30ml/2 tbsp fresh lime juice
5ml/1 tsp sugar
2.5ml/½ tsp dried chilli flakes
20–25 small fresh mint leaves
15ml/1 tbsp toasted sesame seeds

1 Rinse the bamboo shoots under cold running water, then drain them, pat thoroughly dry with kitchen paper and set aside.

2 Dry-roast the glutinous rice in a wok or frying pan until it is golden brown. Leave it to cool slightly, then transfer into a mortar and grind to fine crumbs with a pestle, or use a food processor or blender.

3 Transfer the rice to a bowl and add the shallots, garlic, spring onions, fish sauce, lime juice, sugar, chilli flakes and half the mint leaves. Mix well, ensuring that the rice is evenly coated in the other ingredients.

4 Add the bamboo shoots to the bowl and toss to mix. Serve sprinkled with the toasted sesame seeds and the remaining mint leaves.

Cook's Tip
Glutinous rice does not, in fact, contain any gluten – it is just particularly sticky when boiled due to a higher starch content. This type of rice is generally preferred in much Asian cuisine precisely because it is sticky and therefore easier to handle with chopsticks. It is used in many Chinese and Japanese dishes, especially when it is boiled.

Persimmon Salad Energy 268kcal/1115kJ; Protein 17g; Carbohydrate 9.1g, of which sugars 6.1g; Fat 18.6g, of which saturates 3.6g; Cholesterol 119mg; Calcium 164mg; Fibre 3.5g; Sodium 2489mg.
Spicy Bamboo Shoot Salad Energy 80kcal/336kJ; Protein 4.5g; Carbohydrate 9.4g, of which sugars 2.9g; Fat 2.8g, of which saturates 0.4g; Cholesterol 0mg; Calcium 51mg; Fibre 2g; Sodium 185mg.

Rice Salad with a Touch of Chilli

The sky's the limit with this recipe. Use whatever fruit, vegetables and even leftover meat that you might have, mix with cooked rice and pour over the fragrant dressing.

Serves 4 to 6

350g/12oz/3 cups cooked rice
1 Asian pear, cored and diced
50g/2oz dried shrimp, chopped
1 avocado, peeled, stoned (pitted) and diced
½ medium cucumber, finely diced
2 lemon grass stalks, finely chopped
30ml/2 tbsp sweet chilli sauce
1 fresh green or red chilli, seeded and finely sliced
115g/4oz/1 cup flaked (sliced) almonds, toasted
small bunch fresh coriander (cilantro), chopped
fresh Thai sweet basil leaves, to garnish

For the dressing

300ml/½ pint/1¼ cups water
10ml/2 tsp shrimp paste
15ml/1 tbsp palm sugar (jaggery) or light muscovado (brown) sugar
2 kaffir lime leaves, torn into small pieces
½ lemon grass stalk, sliced

1 Make the dressing. Put the measured water in a small pan with the shrimp paste, sugar, kaffir lime leaves and lemon grass. Heat gently, stirring, until the sugar dissolves, then bring to boiling point and simmer for 5 minutes. Strain into a bowl and set aside until cold.

2 Put the cooked rice in a large salad bowl and fluff up the grains with a fork.

3 Add the Asian pear, dried shrimp, avocado, cucumber, lemon grass and sweet chilli sauce to the rice. Mix well, ensuring that the rice is evenly coated.

4 Add the sliced chilli, flaked almonds and chopped coriander to the bowl and toss well.

5 Garnish the salad with the Thai basil leaves and serve immediately. Pass around the bowl of dressing so diners can help themselves and spoon it over the top of their individual portions of salad.

Hot and Sour Noodle Salad with Baby Corn

Noodles make the perfect basis for a salad, absorbing the spicy flavours and giving a contrast in texture to the crisp vegetables.

Serves 2

200g/7oz thin rice noodles
small bunch fresh coriander (cilantro)
2 tomatoes, seeded and sliced
130g/4½oz baby corn cobs, sliced
4 spring onions (scallions), thinly sliced
1 red (bell) pepper, seeded and finely chopped
juice of 2 limes
2 small fresh green chillies, seeded and finely chopped
10ml/2 tsp sugar
115g/4oz/1 cup peanuts, toasted and chopped
30ml/2 tbsp soy sauce
salt

1 Bring a large pan of salted water to the boil. Snap the noodles into short lengths, add to the pan and cook for about 4 minutes. Drain, rinse under cold water and drain again.

2 Set aside a few coriander leaves for the garnish. Chop the remaining leaves and place them in a large serving bowl.

3 Add the noodles to the bowl, with the tomato slices, corn cobs, spring onions, red pepper, lime juice, chillies, sugar and toasted peanuts.

4 Season the noodles with the soy sauce, then taste and add a little salt if you think the mixture needs it.

5 Toss the salad if you added salt, to mix it in thoroughly. Garnish the salad with the reserved coriander leaves and serve immediately.

Cook's Tip

Rice noodles come in a wide range of thicknesses, from the very thin variety often called vermicelli, to the wider ones, which are also known as rice sticks. Use whichever you have available.

Rice Salad Energy 404kcal/1689kj; Protein 16.1g; Carbohydrate 36.7g, of which sugars 8.5g; Fat 22.4g, of which saturates 2.6g; Cholesterol 63mg; Calcium 247mg; Fibre 4g; Sodium 550mg.
Noodle Salad Energy 761kcal/3173kj; Protein 24.1g; Carbohydrate 101.6g, of which sugars 15.6g; Fat 27.7g, of which saturates 5.2g; Cholesterol 0mg; Calcium 117mg; Fibre 7.9g; Sodium 1840mg.

Gypsy Salad with Feta, Chillies and Parsley

There are two common salads eaten as meze in Turkey, or served as accompaniments to meat and fish dishes. One, known as *çoban salatası* or 'shepherd's salad', is made of chopped cucumber, tomatoes, peppers, onion and flat leaf parsley; the other is this gypsy salad, *çingene pilavı*, meaning 'gypsy rice'. The mix is similar to shepherd's salad, only a chilli is included to give the desired kick, and crumbled feta is added to represent the rice.

Serves 3 to 4

2 red onions, cut in half lengthways and finely sliced along the grain
1 green (bell) pepper, seeded and finely sliced
1 fresh green chilli, seeded and chopped
2–3 garlic cloves, chopped
1 bunch of fresh flat leaf parsley, roughly chopped
225g/8oz firm feta cheese, rinsed and grated
2 large tomatoes, skinned, seeded and finely chopped
30–45ml/2–3 tbsp olive oil
salt and ground black pepper

To serve
scant 5ml/1 tsp Turkish red pepper flakes or paprika
scant 5ml/1 tsp ground sumac

1 Sprinkle the onions with a little salt to draw out the moisture. Leave for about 10 minutes, then rinse and pat dry with kitchen paper.

2 Put the red onions and green pepper in a large bowl. Add the chopped chilli, garlic, flat leaf parsley, feta cheese and tomatoes. Gently mix together.

3 Add the oil and seasoning and toss gently, ensuring that all the ingredients are mixed together and coated in oil.

4 Transfer the salad into a large serving dish and sprinkle with the red pepper or paprika and sumac.

Peppery Egg, Watercress and Chilli Salad

Chillies and eggs may seem unlikely partners, but actually work very well together. The peppery flavour of the watercress makes it the perfect foundation for this tasty salad.

Serves 2

15ml/1 tbsp groundnut (peanut) oil
1 garlic clove, thinly sliced
4 eggs
2 shallots, thinly sliced
2 small fresh red chillies, seeded and thinly sliced
½ small cucumber, finely diced
1cm/½in piece fresh root ginger, peeled and grated
juice of 2 limes
30ml/2 tbsp soy sauce
5ml/1 tsp caster (superfine) sugar
small bunch coriander (cilantro)
bunch watercress or rocket (arugula), coarsely chopped

1 Heat the oil in a frying pan. Add the garlic and cook over a low heat until it starts to turn golden.

2 Crack the eggs into the pan. Break the yolks with a wooden spatula, then fry until the eggs are almost firm. Remove from the pan and set aside.

3 In a bowl, mix together the shallots, chillies, cucumber and ginger until well blended.

4 In a separate bowl, whisk the lime juice with the soy sauce and sugar. Pour this dressing over the vegetables and toss lightly.

5 Set aside a few coriander sprigs for the garnish. Chop the rest and add it to the salad. Toss it again.

6 Reserve a few watercress or rocket sprigs and arrange the remainder on two serving plates. Cut the fried eggs into slices and divide them between the watercress or rocket mounds.

7 Spoon the shallot mixture over the eggs and serve immediately, garnished with the reserved coriander and watercress or rocket.

Gypsy Salad Energy 253kcal/1049kJ; Protein 11.1g; Carbohydrate 13.4g, of which sugars 11g; Fat 17.6g, of which saturates 8.6g; Cholesterol 39mg; Calcium 260mg; Fibre 3.2g; Sodium 824mg.
Egg and Chilli Salad Energy 215kcal/894kJ; Protein 14.2g; Carbohydrate 2.4g, of which sugars 2.2g; Fat 16.9g, of which saturates 4.2g; Cholesterol 381mg; Calcium 112mg; Fibre 0.8g; Sodium 1223mg.

Aubergine Salad with Shrimp, Egg and Chilli

An appetizing and unusual salad that you will find yourself making over and over again. Roasting the aubergines really brings out their flavour.

Serves 4 to 6

2 aubergines (eggplants)
15ml/1 tbsp vegetable oil
30ml/2 tbsp dried shrimp, soaked in warm water for 10 minutes
15ml/1 tbsp coarsely chopped garlic
1 hard-boiled egg, chopped
4 shallots, thinly sliced into rings
fresh coriander (cilantro) leaves and 2 fresh red chillies, seeded and sliced, to garnish

For the dressing
30ml/2 tbsp fresh lime juice
5ml/1 tsp palm sugar (jaggery) or light muscovado (brown) sugar
30ml/2 tbsp Thai fish sauce

1 Preheat the grill (broiler) to medium or preheat the oven to 180°C/350°F/Gas 4. Prick the aubergines several times with a skewer, then arrange on a baking sheet. Cook them under the grill for 30–40 minutes, or until they are charred and tender. Alternatively, roast them by placing them directly on the shelf of the oven for 1 hour, turning them at least twice. Remove the aubergines and set aside until cool enough to handle.

2 Meanwhile, make the dressing. Put the lime juice, palm or muscovado sugar and fish sauce into a small bowl. Mix well. Cover with clear film (plastic wrap) and set aside until required.

3 When the aubergines are cool enough to handle, peel off the skin and cut the flesh into medium slices.

4 Heat the oil in a small frying pan. Drain the dried shrimp thoroughly and add to the pan with the garlic. Cook over a medium heat for about 3 minutes, until golden. Set aside.

5 Arrange the aubergine slices on a serving dish. Top with the hard-boiled egg, shallots and dried shrimp mixture. Drizzle over the dressing and garnish with the coriander and red chillies.

Squid and Seaweed with Chilli Dressing

This chilled seafood salad makes a great appetizer, and really stimulates the appetite. The flavours of chilli and rice vinegar are balanced by sweet maple syrup, with the kelp providing a tantalizing aroma and taste.

Serves 2

400g/14oz squid, cleaned and gutted
180g/7oz dried kelp, roughly chopped
2 cucumbers, thinly sliced
10ml/2 tsp sesame seeds
6 spring onions (scallions), finely chopped
2 dried red chillies, finely chopped
salt

For the dressing
30ml/2 tbsp rice vinegar
2 garlic cloves, crushed
60ml/4 tbsp gochujang chilli paste
60ml/4 tbsp maple syrup
15ml/1 tbsp grated fresh root ginger

1 Use a sharp knife to score the squid with a criss-cross pattern, and slice into generous pieces about 4cm/1½in long.

2 Soak the kelp in cold water for 20 minutes and blanch in boiling water for 1 minute, draining it almost immediately to retain its texture and colour. Squeeze any excess water from the leaves by hand. Roughly chop the kelp into bitesize pieces.

3 Place the thinly sliced cucumber in a colander and sprinkle with salt. Leave for 10 minutes for the salt to draw out some of the cucumber's moisture, and then pour away any excess liquid.

4 Combine all the dressing ingredients in a large bowl, mixing well to ensure they are thoroughly combined.

5 Bring a pan of water to the boil over high heat. Blanch the squid for 3 minutes, stirring constantly, then drain under cold running water. Place the squid, cucumber and kelp on a serving platter and pour the dressing over the dish. Chill in the refrigerator, and sprinkle with the sesame seeds, spring onions and chillies before serving.

Aubergine Salad Energy 90kcal/376kJ; Protein 7.2g; Carbohydrate 4.7g, of which sugars 4.3g; Fat 4.9g, of which saturates 0.9g; Cholesterol 86mg; Calcium 113mg; Fibre 3g; Sodium 612mg.
Squid and Seaweed Energy 321kcal/1354kJ; Protein 35.6g; Carbohydrate 30g, of which sugars 27.3g; Fat 7.3g, of which saturates 1.3g; Cholesterol 450mg; Calcium 247mg; Fibre 3.3g; Sodium 433mg.

Seafood Salad in Chilli Oil and Mustard Dressing

Though not traditional in this Korean dish, English mustard adds a pleasant heat, and perfectly complements the seafood with a unique and slightly mysterious taste. Or, for a more authentic flavour, use Korean mustard. Simple to prepare, this dish is a perfect quick snack or appetizer.

Serves 2

50g/2oz squid, cleaned, gutted and prepared
50g/2oz king prawns (jumbo shrimp), shelled and deveined
50g/2oz jellyfish (optional)
50g/2oz cooked whelks
90g/3½oz Asian pear
⅓ carrot
½ medium cucumber
25g/1oz Chinese leaves (Chinese cabbage), shredded
25g/1oz canned chestnuts, drained and sliced
25g/1oz crab meat or seafood stick

For the dressing

15ml/1 tbsp ready-made English (hot) mustard
30ml/2 tbsp sugar
15ml/1 tbsp milk
45ml/3 tbsp cider vinegar
5ml/1 tsp chilli oil
2.5ml/½ tsp dark soy sauce
5ml/1 tsp salt

1 Score the squid with a criss-cross pattern, and slice into strips about 2cm/¾in wide. Slice the prawns and jellyfish, if using, into similar-sized pieces.

2 Bring a pan of lightly salted water to the boil and blanch the squid, prawns and jellyfish for about 3 minutes, then drain. Thinly slice the whelks.

3 Peel the Asian pear. Cut the pear and carrot into thin julienne strips. Seed the cucumber and cut into thin julienne strips.

4 Mix all the dressing ingredients in a bowl. Take a large serving platter and arrange the julienne vegetables, Chinese leaves and chestnuts in rows, or fan them around the centre of the plate. Add the seafood, including the crab meat or seafood stick. Pour over the dressing and chill in the refrigerator before serving.

Scented Fish Salad with Chilli and Mango

For a tropical taste of the Far East, try this delicious fish salad scented with coconut, fruit and warm Thai spices.

Serves 4

350g/12oz fillet of red mullet, sea bream or snapper
1 cos or romaine lettuce
1 papaya or mango, peeled and sliced
1 pitaya, peeled and sliced
1 large ripe tomato, cut into wedges
½ cucumber, peeled and cut into batons
3 spring onions (scallions), sliced
salt

For the marinade

5ml/1 tsp coriander seeds
5ml/1 tsp fennel seeds
2.5ml/½ tsp cumin seeds
5ml/1 tsp caster (superfine) sugar
2.5ml/½ tsp hot chilli sauce
30ml/2 tbsp garlic oil

For the dressing

15ml/1 tbsp coconut cream
45ml/3 tbsp boiling water
60ml/4 tbsp groundnut (peanut) oil
grated rind and juice of 1 lime
1 fresh red chilli, seeded and finely chopped
5ml/1 tsp sugar
45ml/3 tbsp chopped fresh coriander (cilantro)

1 Cut the fish into even strips, removing any stray bones. Place it on a plate and set aside. Meanwhile, make the marinade. Put the coriander, fennel and cumin seeds in a mortar. Add the sugar and crush with a pestle. Stir in the chilli sauce, garlic oil, and salt to taste and mix to a paste.

2 Spread the paste over the fish, cover and leave to marinate in a cool place for at least 20 minutes. Make the salad dressing. Place the coconut cream and salt in a screw-top jar. Stir in the boiling water. Add the oil, lime rind and juice, chilli, sugar and coriander. Shake well.

3 Wash and dry the lettuce leaves. Place in a bowl and add the papaya or mango, pitaya, tomato, cucumber and spring onions. Pour in the dressing and toss well to coat.

4 Heat a large non-stick frying-pan, add the fish and cook for 5 minutes, turning once. Add to the salad, toss lightly and serve.

Seafood Salad Energy 206kcal/872kJ; Protein 18g; Carbohydrate 29.8g, of which sugars 23.9g; Fat 2.4g, of which saturates 0.6g; Cholesterol 230mg; Calcium 62mg; Fibre 2.4g; Sodium 1282mg.
Fish Salad Energy 304kcal/1269kJ; Protein 17.6g; Carbohydrate 11.7g, of which sugars 11.6g; Fat 21.1g, of which saturates 3.6g; Cholesterol 0mg; Calcium 89mg; Fibre 2.6g; Sodium 88mg.

Spicy Seafood Salad with Fragrant Herbs

This is a spectacular salad. The luscious combination of prawns, scallops and squid makes it the ideal choice for a special celebration. Any chilli-lovers will appreciate the presence of plenty of red chillies, which give this fragrant salad a deliciously spicy kick. Should you want it to be any hotter, use the seeds from the chillies in the salad as well.

Serves 4 to 6

250ml/8fl oz/1 cup fish stock or water
350g/12oz squid, cleaned and cut into rings
12 raw king prawns (jumbo shrimp), peeled and deveined, with tails intact
12 scallops
50g/2oz cellophane noodles, soaked in warm water for 30 minutes
½ cucumber, cut into thin batons
1 lemon grass stalk, finely chopped
2 kaffir lime leaves, finely shredded
2 shallots, thinly sliced
30ml/2 tbsp chopped spring onions (scallions)
30ml/2 tbsp fresh coriander (cilantro) leaves
12–15 fresh mint leaves, coarsely torn
4 fresh red chillies, seeded and cut into slivers
juice of 1–2 limes
30ml/2 tbsp Thai fish sauce
fresh coriander (cilantro) sprigs, to garnish

1 Pour the fish stock or water into a medium pan set over a high heat and bring to the boil. Cook each type of seafood separately in the stock for 3–4 minutes. Remove with a slotted spoon and set aside to cool.

2 Drain the noodles. Cut them into short lengths, about 5cm/2in long. Place them in a serving bowl and add the cucumber, lemon grass, lime leaves, shallots, spring onions, coriander, mint and chillies.

3 Pour over the lime juice and fish sauce. Mix well, then add the seafood. Toss lightly.

4 Garnish the salad with the fresh coriander sprigs and then serve immediately.

Thai Prawn Salad with Chilli and Garlic Dressing and Frizzled Shallots

In this salad, sweet prawns and mango are covered in a garlic dressing with the hot taste of chilli.

Serves 4 to 6

675g/1½lb prawns (shrimp), peeled and deveined, with tails intact
finely shredded rind of 1 lime
½ fresh red chilli, seeded and finely chopped
30ml/2 tbsp olive oil, plus extra for brushing
1 ripe firm mango, stoned (pitted)
2 carrots, cut into long thin shreds
10cm/4in piece cucumber, sliced
1 red onion, halved and thinly sliced
a few fresh mint sprigs
a few coriander (cilantro) sprigs
45ml/3 tbsp roasted peanuts, coarsely chopped
4 large shallots, thinly sliced and fried until crisp in 30ml/2 tbsp groundnut (peanut) oil
salt and ground black pepper

For the dressing

1 large garlic clove, chopped
10–15ml/2–3 tsp caster (superfine) sugar
juice of 2 limes
15–30ml/1–2 tbsp Thai fish sauce
1 red chilli, seeded and chopped
5–10ml/1–2 tsp light rice vinegar

1 In a glass dish, toss the prawns with the lime rind, half the chilli, oil and seasoning. Leave for 30–40 minutes.

2 Make the dressing. Place the garlic in a mortar with 10ml/2 tsp of the sugar. Pound until smooth, then add three-quarters of the lime juice and 15ml/1 tbsp of the Thai fish sauce. Transfer to a bowl. Stir in half the chilli and the vinegar. Taste and add more seasoning if necessary.

3 Cut the mango flesh into strips and remove any flesh from around the stone. Place the strips of mango in a bowl with the carrots, cucumber slices and red onion. Pour over about half the dressing and mix. Arrange the salad on four to six individual serving plates or in bowls.

4 Heat a griddle until hot. Brush with oil, then sear the prawns for 2–3 minutes on each side. Arrange on the salads. Pour the remaining dressing over and garnish with the mint and coriander, the remaining chilli, the peanuts and crisp-fried shallots.

Spicy Seafood Salad Energy 137kcal/578kJ; Protein 20g; Carbohydrate 10.2g, of which sugars 1.2g; Fat 1.8g, of which saturates 0.4g; Cholesterol 171mg; Calcium 61mg; Fibre 0.9g; Sodium 154mg.
Prawn Salad Energy 292kcal/1222kJ; Protein 33.5g; Carbohydrate 13.4g, of which sugars 11.8g; Fat 11.9g, of which saturates 2g; Cholesterol 329mg; Calcium 160mg; Fibre 2.7g; Sodium 596mg.

Piquant Prawn Salad

The fish sauce dressing adds a superb flavour to the noodles and prawns. This delicious salad can be enjoyed warm or cold, and will serve six as an appetizer.

Serves 4
200g/7oz rice vermicelli
8 baby corn cobs, halved
150g/5oz mangetouts (snow peas)
15ml/1 tbsp vegetable oil
2 garlic cloves, finely chopped
2.5cm/1in piece fresh root ginger, peeled and finely chopped
1 fresh red or green chilli, seeded and finely chopped
450g/1lb raw peeled tiger prawns (jumbo shrimp)
4 spring onions (scallions), very thinly sliced
15ml/1 tbsp sesame seeds, toasted
1 lemon grass stalk, thinly shredded

For the dressing
15ml/1 tbsp chopped fresh chives
15ml/1 tbsp Thai fish sauce
5ml/1 tsp soy sauce
45ml/3 tbsp groundnut (peanut) oil
5ml/1 tsp sesame oil
30ml/2 tbsp rice vinegar

1 Put the rice vermicelli in a wide, heatproof bowl, pour over boiling water to just cover and set aside to soak for 10 minutes. Drain the noodles and refresh them under cold running water, then drain them again thoroughly. Transfer to a large serving bowl and set aside until required.

2 Boil or steam the corn cobs and mangetouts for about 3 minutes, until tender but still crunchy. Refresh under cold running water and drain. Make the dressing by mixing all the ingredients in a screw-top jar. Close tightly and shake vigorously to combine.

3 Heat the oil in a large frying pan or wok. Add the garlic, ginger and red or green chilli and cook for 1 minute. Add the tiger prawns and toss over the heat for about 3 minutes, until they have just turned pink. Stir in the spring onions, corn cobs, mangetouts and sesame seeds, and toss lightly to mix.

4 Add the contents of the pan or wok to the rice vermicelli. Pour the dressing on top and toss well. Sprinkle with lemon grass and serve, or chill for 1 hour before serving.

Chilli Chicken and Prawn Salad

This delicious Indonesian salad is spicy and refreshing.

Serves 4
500g/1¼lb chicken breast fillets or thighs
225g/8oz prawns (shrimp), shelled and deveined
30ml/2 tbsp groundnut (peanut) oil
5ml/1 tsp blachan (shrimp paste)
10ml/2 tsp palm sugar (jaggery)
2 tomatoes, skinned, seeded and chopped
1 bunch fresh coriander (cilantro) leaves, chopped
1 bunch fresh mint leaves, chopped
juice of 1 lime
salt and ground black pepper

For the spice paste
2 shallots, chopped
2 garlic cloves, chopped
2–3 fresh red chillies, seeded and chopped
25g/1oz galangal, chopped
15g/½oz fresh turmeric, chopped, or 2.5ml/½ tsp ground turmeric
1 lemon grass stalk, chopped
2 candlenuts, chopped

To serve
1 lime, quartered
2 fresh green or red chillies, seeded and cut into quarters lengthways

1 Cook the chicken pieces according to your preference by steaming, roasting or boiling. When cooked, if using chicken breast fillets, cut the meat into thin strips and, if using thighs, shred the meat with your fingers. Set aside.

2 Boil or steam the prawns for 2–3 minutes, drain and refresh under cold running water, then drain again. Put aside.

3 To make the spice paste, using a mortar and pestle, grind the shallots, garlic, chillies, galangal, turmeric, lemon grass and candlenuts together to form a paste.

4 Heat the oil in a pan, stir in the spice paste and fry for a minute. Add the shrimp paste and sugar and stir for 3–4 minutes, until the paste browns. Add the tomatoes, coriander, mint and lime juice and cook for 5–10 minutes, until the sauce is reduced and thick. Season and put in a large bowl. Leave to cool.

5 Add the chicken and prawns to the bowl and toss well. Serve with the lime wedges, and the chillies to chew on.

Prawn Salad Energy 412kcal/1717kJ; Protein 25g; Carbohydrate 43.1g, of which sugars 1.8g; Fat 14.8g, of which saturates 2.4g; Cholesterol 219mg; Calcium 139mg; Fibre 1.5g; Sodium 702mg.
Chilli Chicken Salad Energy 274kcal/1154kJ; Protein 41.6g; Carbohydrate 10.4g, of which sugars 8.7g; Fat 7.7g, of which saturates 1.1g; Cholesterol 197mg; Calcium 99mg; Fibre 2.2g; Sodium 193mg.

Tangy Chicken Salad

This fresh and lively dish typifies the character of Thai cuisine. It is ideal for a spicy light lunch on a hot and lazy summer's day.

Serves 4 to 6

4 skinless chicken breast fillets
2 garlic cloves, crushed
30ml/2 tbsp soy sauce
30ml/2 tbsp vegetable oil
120ml/4fl oz/½ cup coconut cream
30ml/2 tbsp Thai fish sauce
juice of 1 lime
30ml/2 tbsp palm sugar (jaggery) or light muscovado (brown) sugar
115g/4oz/½ cup canned water chestnuts, sliced
50g/2oz/½ cup cashew nuts, roasted and coarsely chopped
4 shallots, thinly sliced
4 kaffir lime leaves, thinly sliced
1 lemon grass stalk, bruised and thinly sliced
5ml/1 tsp chopped fresh galangal
1 large fresh red chilli, seeded and finely chopped
10–12 fresh mint leaves, torn
2 spring onions (scallions), thinly sliced
2 fresh red chillies, seeded and sliced, to garnish
1 lettuce, separated into leaves, to serve

1 Place the chicken in a large dish. Rub with the garlic, soy sauce and 15ml/1 tbsp of the oil. Cover and leave to marinate for 1–2 hours.

2 Heat the remaining oil in a wok or frying pan and stir-fry the chicken for 3–4 minutes on each side, or until cooked. Remove and set aside to cool.

3 In a pan, heat the coconut cream, fish sauce, lime juice and sugar. Stir until the sugar has dissolved; set aside.

4 Tear the cooked chicken into strips and put it in a bowl. Add the water chestnuts, cashew nuts, shallots, kaffir lime leaves, lemon grass, galangal, red chilli, mint leaves and spring onions. Mix the ingredients together until well combined.

5 Pour the coconut dressing over the mixture and toss well again so that everything is evenly coated in the dressing. Serve the chicken on a bed of lettuce leaves and garnish with sliced red chillies.

Thai Chicken Salad

Chiang Mai is a city in the north-east of Thailand. The city is culturally very close to Laos. It is famous for its chicken salad, which was originally called 'laap' or 'larp'. Duck, beef or pork can be used instead of chicken.

Serves 4 to 6

450g/1lb minced (ground) chicken
lower 5cm/2in of 1 lemon grass stalk, root trimmed
3 kaffir lime leaves
4 fresh red chillies, seeded and chopped
60ml/4 tbsp fresh lime juice
30ml/2 tbsp Thai fish sauce
15ml/1 tbsp roasted ground rice (see Cook's Tip)
2 spring onions (scallions), finely chopped
30ml/2 tbsp fresh coriander (cilantro) leaves
thinly sliced kaffir lime leaves, mixed salad leaves and fresh mint sprigs, to garnish

1 Heat a wok or large, heavy frying pan. Add the minced chicken and moisten with a little water. Stir constantly over a medium heat for 7–10 minutes, until it is cooked through. Remove the pan from the heat and drain off any excess fat. Finely chop the trimmed lemon grass stalk and the kaffir lime leaves.

2 Transfer the cooked chicken to a large bowl and add the chopped lemon grass, lime leaves, chillies, lime juice, fish sauce, roasted ground rice, spring onions and coriander. Mix all the ingredients thoroughly.

3 Spoon the chicken mixture into a salad bowl. Sprinkle sliced lime leaves over the top and garnish with salad leaves and sprigs of mint.

Cook's Tip

Use glutinous rice for the roasted ground rice. Put the rice in a frying pan and dry-roast it until golden brown. Remove and grind to a powder, using a mortar and pestle or a food processor. When the rice is cold, store it in a glass jar in a cool and dry place.

Chicken Salad Energy 404kcal/1691kJ; Protein 40.4g; Carbohydrate 11.3g, of which sugars 9g; Fat 22.3g, of which saturates 9.8g; Cholesterol 105mg; Calcium 25mg; Fibre 0.8g; Sodium 666mg.
Thai Chicken Salad Energy 135kcal/572kJ; Protein 27.4g; Carbohydrate 3.4g, of which sugars 0.4g; Fat 1.3g, of which saturates 0.4g; Cholesterol 79mg; Calcium 8mg; Fibre 0.1g; Sodium 424mg.

Spicy Warm Pork Salad

Tender pork fillet is cut into strips before being grilled. Shredded and then tossed with a delicious sweet and sour sauce, it makes a marvellous warm salad, especially with the extra heat from the chilli.

Serves 4

30ml/2 tbsp dark soy sauce
15ml/1 tbsp clear honey
400g/14oz pork fillet (tenderloin)
6 shallots, very thinly sliced lengthways
1 lemon grass stalk, thinly sliced
5 kaffir lime leaves, thinly sliced
5cm/2in piece fresh root ginger, peeled and sliced into fine shreds
½ fresh long red chilli, seeded and sliced into fine shreds
small bunch fresh coriander (cilantro), chopped

For the dressing

30ml/2 tbsp palm sugar (jaggery) or light muscovado (brown) sugar
30ml/2 tbsp Thai fish sauce
juice of 2 limes
20ml/4 tsp thick tamarind juice, made by mixing tamarind paste with warm water

1 Preheat the grill (broiler) to medium. Mix the soy sauce with the honey in a small bowl or jug (pitcher) and stir until they are well blended.

2 Using a sharp knife, cut the pork fillet lengthways into quarters to make four long, thick strips. Place the pork strips in a grill pan. Brush generously with the soy sauce and honey mixture, then grill (broil) for about 10–15 minutes, until cooked through and tender. Turn the strips over frequently and baste with the soy sauce and honey mixture.

3 Transfer the cooked pork strips to a board. Slice the meat across the grain, then shred it with a fork. Place in a large bowl and add the shallot slices, lemon grass, kaffir lime leaves, ginger, chilli and chopped coriander.

4 Make the dressing. Place the sugar, fish sauce, lime juice and tamarind juice in a bowl. Mix until the sugar has dissolved.

5 Pour the dressing over the pork mixture and toss well to mix, then serve immediately.

Chilli Beef Salad

A hearty main meal salad from Thailand. It combines tender strips of sirloin steak with thinly shredded cucumber and a piquant chilli and lime dressing.

Serves 4

2 sirloin steaks, each weighing about 225g/8oz
1 lemon grass stalk, root trimmed
1 red onion or 4 Thai shallots, thinly sliced
½ cucumber, cut into strips
30ml/2 tbsp chopped spring onion (scallion)
juice of 2 limes
15–30ml/1–2 tbsp Thai fish sauce
2–4 fresh red chillies, seeded and finely chopped
Chinese mustard cress, salad cress or fresh coriander (cilantro), to garnish

1 Pan-fry the steaks in a large, heavy frying pan over a medium heat. Cook them for 4–6 minutes for rare, 6–8 minutes for medium and about 10 minutes for well done, depending on their thickness. (In Thailand the beef is traditionally served quite rare.) Alternatively, cook them under a preheated grill (broiler). Remove the steaks from the pan and leave to rest for 10–15 minutes. Meanwhile, cut off the lower 5cm/2in from the lemon grass stalk and chop it finely. Discard the remainder.

2 When the meat is cool, slice it thinly and put the slices in a large bowl. Add the sliced onion or shallots, cucumber, lemon grass and chopped spring onion to the meat slices.

3 Toss the salad and add lime juice and fish sauce to taste. Add the red chillies and toss again. Transfer to a serving bowl or plate. Serve the salad at room temperature or chilled, garnished with the Chinese mustard cress, salad cress or coriander leaves.

Cook's Tip

Look for gui chai leaves in Thai and Chinese groceries. These look like very thin spring onions (scallions) and are often used as a substitute for the more familiar vegetable.

Spicy Warm Pork Salad Energy 170kcal/718kJ; Protein 22g; Carbohydrate 12.2g, of which sugars 12.1g; Fat 4g, of which saturates 1.4g; Cholesterol 63mg; Calcium 16mg; Fibre 0.2g; Sodium 352mg.
Chilli Beef Salad Energy 161kcal/674kJ; Protein 26.9g; Carbohydrate 1.8g, of which sugars 1.4g; Fat 5.1g, of which saturates 2.3g; Cholesterol 57mg; Calcium 14mg; Fibre 0.3g; Sodium 873mg.

Chilli Beef and Mushroom Salad

All the ingredients for this traditional, tasty Thai salad, known as *yam nua yang*, are widely available in most large supermarkets as well as in Asian food stores.

Serves 4

675g/1½lb beef fillet or rump (round) steak
30ml/2 tbsp olive oil
2 small mild red chillies, seeded and sliced
225g/8oz/3¼ cups fresh shiitake mushrooms, stems removed and caps sliced

For the dressing

3 spring onions (scallions), finely chopped
2 garlic cloves, finely chopped
juice of 1 lime
15–30ml/1–2 tbsp Thai fish sauce
5ml/1 tsp soft light brown sugar
30ml/2 tbsp chopped fresh coriander (cilantro)

To serve

1 cos or romaine lettuce, in strips
175g/6oz cherry tomatoes, halved
5cm/2in piece cucumber, peeled, halved and thinly sliced
45ml/3 tbsp toasted sesame seeds

1 Preheat the grill (broiler) to medium, then cook the steak for 2–4 minutes on each side, depending on how well done you like it. (In Thailand, the beef is traditionally served quite rare.) Leave the steak to cool for at least 15 minutes.

2 Slice the beef fillet or rump steak as thinly as possible (freezing it for 30 minutes before slicing will help make this easier). Place the slices in a bowl.

3 Heat the olive oil in a small, heavy frying pan. Add the seeded and sliced red chillies and the sliced shiitake mushroom caps. Cook for 5 minutes, stirring occasionally. Remove from the heat and add the steak slices to the pan. Stir well to coat the beef slices in the chilli and mushroom mixture.

4 Make the dressing by mixing all the ingredients in a bowl, then pour it over the meat mixture and toss gently.

5 Arrange the lettuce, tomatoes and cucumber on a serving plate. Spoon the steak mixture in the centre and sprinkle the sesame seeds over. Serve immediately.

Lime-marinated Beef Salad

This is a great Chinese favourite and versions of it are enjoyed in Vietnam, Thailand, Cambodia and Laos. It is also one of the traditional dishes that appear in the *bo bay mon* – beef seven ways feast – in which there are seven different beef dishes. For the most delicious result, it is worth buying an excellent-quality piece of tender fillet steak because the meat is only just seared before being dressed in the spicy, fragrant lime dressing and tossed in a crunchy salad of beansprouts and fresh, aromatic herbs.

Serves 4

about 7.5ml/1½ tsp vegetable oil
450g/1lb beef fillet, cut into steaks 2.5cm/1in thick
115g/4oz/½ cup beansprouts
1 bunch each fresh basil and mint, stalks removed, leaves shredded
1 lime, cut into quarters, to serve

For the dressing

juice (about 80ml/3fl oz/⅓ cup) and rind of 2 limes
30ml/2 tbsp Thai fish sauce
30ml/2 tbsp raw cane sugar
2 garlic cloves, crushed
2 lemon grass stalks, very finely sliced
2 green serrano chillies, seeded and finely sliced

1 To make the marinade, beat the lime juice, rind and Thai fish sauce in a bowl with the sugar, until the sugar dissolves. Stir in the garlic, lemon grass and chillies and set aside.

2 Pour the oil into a heavy pan and rub it over the base with a piece of kitchen paper. Heat the pan and sear the steaks for 1–2 minutes each side. Transfer them to a board and leave to cool a little.

3 Using a sharp knife, cut the meat into thin slices. Toss the slices in the marinade, cover the bowl and leave to marinate for about 1–2 hours.

4 Drain the meat of any excess juice from the marinade and transfer it to a wide serving bowl. Add the beansprouts and herbs and toss it all together. Serve immediately with lime quarters to squeeze over.

Chilli Beef Salad Energy 381kcal/1588kJ; Protein 39.7g; Carbohydrate 4g, of which sugars 3.8g; Fat 23g, of which saturates 6.6g; Cholesterol 103mg; Calcium 105mg; Fibre 2.4g; Sodium 352mg.
Beef Salad Energy 233kcal/979kJ; Protein 26g; Carbohydrate 12g, of which sugars 9g; Fat 9g, of which saturates 3g; Cholesterol 69mg; Calcium 74mg; Fibre 0.5g; Sodium 400mg.

Lemon, Chilli and Garlic Relish

This powerful relish is flavoured with North African spices and punchy preserved lemons, which are widely available in Middle Eastern stores. It is great served with Moroccan tagines.

Makes 1 small jar

45ml/3 tbsp olive oil
3 large red onions, sliced
2 heads of garlic, separated into cloves and peeled
10ml/2 tsp coriander seeds, crushed
10ml/2 tsp light muscovado (brown) sugar, plus a little extra
pinch of saffron threads
5cm/2in piece cinnamon stick
2–3 small whole dried red chillies (optional)
2 fresh bay leaves
30–45ml/2–3 tbsp sherry vinegar
juice of ½ small orange
30ml/2 tbsp chopped preserved lemon
salt and ground black pepper

1 Gently heat the oil in a large heavy pan. Add the onions and stir, then cover and cook on the lowest setting for 10–15 minutes, stirring occasionally, until soft.

2 Add the garlic cloves and the coriander seeds. Cover and cook for 5–8 minutes, until soft.

3 Add a pinch of salt, lots of ground black pepper and the sugar to the onions and cook, uncovered, for a further 5 minutes.

4 Soak the saffron in about 45ml/3 tbsp warm water for 5 minutes, then add to the onions, together with the soaking water. Add the cinnamon, dried chillies, if using, and bay leaves. Stir in 30ml/2 tbsp of the sherry vinegar and the orange juice.

5 Cook very gently, uncovered, until the onions are very soft and most of the liquid has evaporated. Stir in the preserved lemon and cook gently for 5 minutes.

6 Taste the relish and adjust the seasoning, adding more salt, sugar and/or vinegar to taste.

7 Serve warm or cold (not hot or chilled). The relish tastes best if left to stand for 24 hours.

Tangy Nectarine Relish

This sweet and tangy fruit relish is a tasty partner for hot roast meats such as pork and game birds such as guinea fowl and pheasant. Once it is made, keep it tightly covered in the refrigerator and it will last for a few months.

Makes about 450g/1lb

45ml/3 tbsp olive oil
2 onions, thinly sliced
1 fresh green chilli, seeded and finely chopped
5ml/1 tsp finely chopped fresh rosemary
2 bay leaves
450g/1lb nectarines, stoned (pitted) and cut into chunks
150g/5oz/1 cup raisins
10ml/2 tsp crushed coriander seeds
350g/12oz/1½ cups demerara (raw) sugar
200ml/7fl oz/scant 1 cup red wine vinegar

1 Heat the oil in a large pan. Add the onions, chilli, rosemary and bay leaves. Cook, stirring frequently, for about 15 minutes, or until the onions are soft.

2 Add the nectarines, raisins, coriander seeds, demerara sugar and vinegar to the pan, then slowly bring to the boil, stirring frequently.

3 Reduce the heat and simmer gently for 1 hour, or until the relish is thick and sticky. Stir occasionally during cooking, and more frequently towards the end of the cooking time to prevent the relish sticking to the pan.

4 Spoon the relish into warmed, sterilized jars and seal. Leave the jars to cool completely, then store in the refrigerator. The relish will keep well in the refrigerator for up to 5 months.

Cook's Tip
Pots of this relish make a lovely gift. Store it in pretty jars and add a colourful label identifying the relish, and reminding the recipient that it should be stored in the refrigerator, and when it should be used by.

Lemon and Chilli Relish Energy 102kcal/422kJ; Protein 1.9g; Carbohydrate 11.4g, of which sugars 7.8g; Fat 5.7g, of which saturates 0.8g; Cholesterol 0mg; Calcium 28mg; Fibre 1.7g; Sodium 4mg.
Nectarine Relish Energy 2408kcal/10211kJ; Protein 16g; Carbohydrate 541.8g, of which sugars 532.6g; Fat 34.8g, of which saturates 4.7g; Cholesterol 0mg; Calcium 320mg; Fibre 23.5g; Sodium 121mg.

Chilli Strips with Lime

This fresh relish is ideal for serving with stews, rice dishes or bean dishes. The oregano adds a sweet note and the absence of sugar or oil makes this a very healthy choice.

Makes about 60ml/4 tbsp

10 fresh green chillies
½ white onion
4 limes
2.5ml/½ tsp dried oregano
salt

1 Roast the chillies in a griddle pan over a moderate heat until the skins are charred and blistered. The flesh should not be allowed to blacken as this might make the salsa bitter. Place the roasted chillies in a strong plastic bag and tie the top to keep the steam in. Set aside for 20 minutes.

2 Meanwhile, slice the onion very thinly and put it in a large bowl. Squeeze the limes and strain the juice into the bowl, adding any pulp that gathers in the strainer. The lime juice will soften the onion. Stir in the oregano.

3 Remove the chillies from the bag and peel off the skins. Slit them, scrape out the seeds with a small sharp knife, then cut the chillies into long strips.

4 Add the chilli strips to the onion mixture, mixing well, and season with salt.

5 Cover the bowl and chill in the refrigerator for at least 1 day before serving. This will allow the flavours to blend together. The salsa will keep for up to 2 weeks in a well-covered bowl in the refrigerator.

Cook's Tip

This method of roasting chillies is ideal if you need more than one or two, or if you do not have a gas burner. To roast over a burner, spear the chillies, four or five at a time, on a long-handled metal skewer and hold them over the flame until the skins blister.

Onion and Red Chilli Relish

This popular relish, known as *cebollas en escabeche*, is typical of the Yucatan region of Mexico and is often served alongside chicken, fish or turkey dishes. It is also delicious served with savoury crackers and cheese – it will add a lovely spicy, tangy taste and won't contribute any additional fat or sugar.

Makes 1 small jar

2 fresh red fresno chillies
5ml/1 tsp allspice berries
2.5ml/½ tsp black peppercorns
5ml/1 tsp dried oregano
2 white onions
2 garlic cloves, peeled
100ml/3½fl oz/⅓ cup white wine vinegar
200ml/7fl oz/scant 1 cup cider vinegar
salt

1 Spear the fresno chillies on a long-handled metal skewer and roast them over the flame of a gas burner until the skins blister. Do not let the flesh burn. Alternatively, dry-fry them in a griddle pan until the skins are scorched. Place the roasted chillies in a strong plastic bag and tie the top to keep the steam in. Set aside for 20 minutes.

2 Meanwhile, place the allspice, black peppercorns and oregano in a mortar or food processor. Grind the herbs and spices slowly by hand with a pestle or blend in the processor until coarsely ground.

3 Cut the onions in half and slice them thinly. Put them in a bowl. Dry-roast the garlic in a heavy frying pan until golden. Do not let it burn, otherwise it will taste bitter. Crush the roasted garlic and add to the onions in the bowl.

4 Remove the chillies from the bag and peel off the skins. Slit the chillies, scrape out the seeds with a small sharp knife and discard. Chop the chillies roughly.

5 Add the ground spices to the onion mixture, followed by the chopped chillies. Add both vinegars and stir well. Add salt to taste and mix thoroughly.

6 Cover the bowl and chill for at least 1 day before serving.

Chilli Strips with Lime Energy 45kcal/189kJ; Protein 3.8g; Carbohydrate 6.2g, of which sugars 4.9g; Fat 0.7g, of which saturates 0g; Cholesterol 49mg; Calcium 49mg; Fibre 0.9g; Sodium 9mg.
Onion and Red Chilli Relish Energy 151kcal/629kJ; Protein 5.8g; Carbohydrate 31.8g, of which sugars 22.6g; Fat 1g, of which saturates 0g; Cholesterol 0mg; Calcium 111mg; Fibre 5.6g; Sodium 14mg.

Dark Soy Sauce and Chilli Relish

This can be served as a dip for satays instead of the usual peanut sauce and is particularly good with beef and chicken satays and deep-fried chicken.

Makes about 150ml/¼ pint/⅔ cup

1 fresh red chilli, seeded and finely chopped
2 garlic cloves, crushed
60ml/4 tbsp dark soy sauce
20ml/4 tsp lemon juice, or 15–25ml/1–1½ tbsp prepared tamarind juice
30ml/2 tbsp hot water
30ml/2 tbsp fried onions (optional)

1 Mix together the red chilli, garlic, dark soy sauce, lemon juice or tamarind juice and the measured hot water in a bowl, ensuring they are well combined.

2 Stir in the fried onions, if using, and leave the relish to stand for about 30 minutes before serving.

Hot Tomato Sambal

In Indonesia, sambals are placed on the table as a condiment, mainly for dipping meat and fish. They are strong and pungent, so should be used sparingly.

Makes 120ml/4fl oz/½ cup

3 ripe tomatoes
2.5ml/½ tsp salt
5ml/1 tsp chilli sauce
60ml/4 tbsp fish sauce, or soy sauce
15ml/1 tbsp chopped coriander (cilantro) leaves

1 Cover the tomatoes with boiling water for 3–4 minutes to loosen the skins. Remove the skins, halve, discard the seeds and chop the flesh finely.

2 Place the chopped tomatoes in a bowl and add the salt, chilli sauce, fish sauce or soy sauce, and coriander. Mix well.

Hot Chilli and Garlic Dipping Sauce

This dipping sauce is particularly strong and pungent, so warn any guests who are unaccustomed to spicy foods. This sauce is especially good for serving with satays and as a side dish to a simple bowl of rice.

Makes 120ml/4fl oz/½ cup

1 clove garlic, crushed
2 small red chillies, seeded and finely chopped
10ml/2 tsp sugar
5ml/1 tsp tamarind sauce
60ml/4 tbsp soy sauce
juice of ½ lime

1 Pound the garlic, chillies and sugar until smooth using a pestle and mortar, or grind in a food processor.

2 Mix in the tamarind sauce, soy sauce and lime juice.

Chilli Sambal

This ubiquitous Indonesian sauce, known as *sambal ulek*, will keep for several weeks in a well-sealed jar in the refrigerator, so it is worth making up a reasonable quantity at a time. Use a stainless-steel or plastic spoon to measure it out. This sauce is fiercely hot and so only small amounts are needed as an accompaniment. It is also useful as a source of ready-prepared chillies for adding some heat to other dishes.

Makes 450g/1lb

450g/1lb fresh red chillies, seeded
10ml/2 tsp salt

1 Plunge the chillies into a pan of boiling water and cook for 5–8 minutes. Drain them well and then grind in a food processor, without making the paste too smooth.

2 Turn into a screw-topped glass jar, stir in the salt and cover with a piece of baking parchment or clear film (plastic wrap). Then screw on the lid and store in the refrigerator.

3 Spoon into small dishes, to serve as an accompaniment, or use in recipes as suggested.

Dark Soy Sauce Relish Energy 67kcal/282kJ; Protein 5.9g; Carbohydrate 10.2g, of which sugars 5.3g; Fat 0.5g, of which saturates 0g; Cholesterol 0mg; Calcium 34mg; Fibre 1.2g; Sodium 4277mg.
Hot Tomato Sambal Energy 83kcal/353kJ; Protein 4g; Carbohydrate 15.6g, of which sugars 15.1g; Fat 0.9g, of which saturates 0.3g; Cholesterol 0mg; Calcium 32mg; Fibre 3g; Sodium 4381mg.
Chilli Dipping Sauce Energy 89kcal/378kJ; Protein 4.2g; Carbohydrate 18.4g, of which sugars 14.3g; Fat 0.3g, of which saturates 0g; Cholesterol 0mg; Calcium 27mg; Fibre 1g; Sodium 3208mg.
Chilli Sambal Energy 90kcal/374kJ; Protein 13.1g; Carbohydrate 3.1g, of which sugars 3.1g; Fat 2.7g, of which saturates 0g; Cholesterol 0mg; Calcium 136mg; Fibre 0g; Sodium 3962mg.

Spicy Mixed Vegetable Pickle

If you can obtain fresh turmeric, it makes such a difference to the colour and appearance of this Malaysian pickle, called *acar campur*. You can use almost any vegetable, bearing in mind that you need a balance of textures, flavours and colours.

Makes 2 to 3 x 300g/11oz jars

1 fresh red chilli, seeded and sliced
1 onion, quartered
2 garlic cloves, crushed
1cm/½ in cube shrimp paste
4 macadamia nuts or 8 almonds
2.5cm/1in fresh turmeric, peeled and sliced, or 5ml/1 tsp ground turmeric
50ml/2fl oz/¼ cup sunflower oil
475ml/16fl oz/2 cups white vinegar
250ml/8fl oz/1 cup water
25–50g/1–2oz sugar
3 carrots
225g/8oz green beans
1 small cauliflower
1 cucumber
225g/8oz white cabbage
115g/4oz dry-roasted peanuts, roughly crushed
salt

1 Place the chilli, onion, garlic, shrimp paste, nuts and turmeric in a food processor and blend to a paste, or pound in a mortar with a pestle.

2 Heat the oil and stir-fry the paste briefly. Add the vinegar, water, sugar and salt. Bring to the boil, then simmer for 10 minutes.

3 Cut the carrots into flower shapes. Cut the green beans into short, neat lengths. Separate the cauliflower into neat, bitesize florets. Peel and seed the cucumber and cut the flesh in neat, bitesize pieces. Cut the cabbage in neat, bitesize pieces.

4 Blanch each vegetable separately, in a large pan of boiling water, for 1 minute. Transfer to a colander and rinse with cold water, to halt the cooking. Drain well.

5 Add the vegetables to the sauce. Slowly bring to the boil and allow to cook for 5–10 minutes. Do not overcook – the vegetables should still be crunchy.

6 Add the peanuts and mix well. Leave to cool. Spoon the pickle into clean jars with lids and store in the refrigerator.

Creamy Chilli and Tamarind Relish

Traditional flavourings for this dish, known as *sambal goreng*, are strips of calf's liver, chicken livers, green beans or hard-boiled eggs.

Makes 900ml/1½ pints/3¾ cups

2.5cm/1in cube shrimp paste
2 onions, quartered
2 garlic cloves, crushed
2.5cm/1in fresh galangal, peeled and sliced
10ml/2 tsp chilli sauce or 2 fresh red chillies, seeded and sliced
1.5ml/¼ tsp salt
30ml/2 tbsp vegetable oil
45ml/3 tbsp tomato purée (paste)
600ml/1 pint/2½ cups stock or water
60ml/4 tbsp tamarind juice
pinch sugar
45ml/3 tbsp coconut milk or cream

1 Grind the shrimp paste, with the onions and garlic, to a paste in a food processor or with a mortar and pestle. Add the galangal, Chilli Sambal or chillies and salt. Process or pound to a fine paste.

2 Fry the paste in hot oil for 1–2 minutes, without browning, until the mixture gives off a rich aroma.

3 Add the tomato purée and the stock or water and cook for about 10 minutes. Add one of the flavouring variations below to half the quantity of the sauce. Cook in the sauce for 3–4 minutes, then stir in the tamarind juice, sugar and coconut milk or cream at the last minute, before tasting and serving.

Variations

- *Chicken Sambal Goreng – Add 350g/12oz cooked chicken pieces and 50g/2oz cooked and sliced French beans.*
- *Tomato Sambal Goreng – Add 450g/1lb of skinned, seeded and coarsely chopped tomatoes, before the stock.*
- *Prawn Sambal Goreng – Add 350g/12oz cooked, peeled prawns (shrimp) and 1 green (bell) pepper, chopped.*
- *Egg Sambal Goreng – Add 3 or 4 hard-boiled eggs, shelled and chopped, and 2 tomatoes, skinned, seeded and chopped.*

Spicy Vegetable Pickle Energy 248kcal/1026kJ; Protein 6.1g; Carbohydrate 13.6g, of which sugars 12.2g; Fat 19g, of which saturates 2.8g; Cholesterol 0mg; Calcium 97mg; Fibre 5.7g; Sodium 35mg.
Chilli Relish Energy 432kcal/1793kJ; Protein 9.8g; Carbohydrate 48.4g, of which sugars 36.9g; Fat 23.5g, of which saturates 2.7g; Cholesterol 0mg; Calcium 169mg; Fibre 8.3g; Sodium 176mg.

Sesame Seed and Chilli Chutney

This is an extremely versatile Indian chutney, which doubles as a delicious dip for poppadums, pakora or bhajis. It also makes a tasty sandwich filling with cucumber.

Serves 4

175g/6oz sesame seeds
5ml/1 tsp salt
120–150ml/4–5fl oz/½–⅔ cup water
2 green chillies, seeded and diced
60ml/4 tbsp chopped fresh coriander (cilantro)
15ml/1 tbsp chopped fresh mint
15ml/1 tbsp tamarind paste
30ml/2 tbsp sugar
5ml/1 tsp corn oil
1.5ml/¼ tsp onion seeds
4 curry leaves
6 onion rings, 1 green chilli, seeded and sliced, 1 red chilli, seeded and sliced, and 15ml/1 tbsp fresh coriander (cilantro) leaves, to garnish

1 Dry-roast the sesame seeds and leave to cool. Place them in a spice grinder and grind to a grainy powder, or grind the seeds using a mortar and pestle.

2 Transfer the sesame powder to a bowl. Add the salt, water, diced chillies, coriander, mint, tamarind paste and sugar and, using a fork, mix everything together.

3 Taste and adjust the seasoning if necessary: the mixture should have a sweet-and-sour flavour.

4 Heat the oil in a heavy pan and fry the onion seeds and curry leaves, stirring constantly, for 2–3 minutes until the seeds begin to splutter and release their fragrances.

5 Add the sesame seed paste to the pan and fry the mixture for about 45 seconds, stirring constantly to avoid it sticking to the base of the pan. Transfer the mixture to a serving dish.

6 Garnish the chutney with onion rings, sliced green and red chillies and the fresh coriander leaves. If it is not to be eaten immediately, cover the chutney and store it in the refrigerator until it is required.

Bombay Duck and Chilli Pickle

The bummalo fish is found off the west coast of India during the monsoon season. It is salted and dried in the sun and is characterized by a strong smell and distinctive piquancy. How this fish acquired the name Bombay duck in the Western world is far from certain.

Serves 4 to 6

6–8 pieces bummalo (Bombay duck), soaked in water for 5 minutes
60ml/4 tbsp vegetable oil
2 fresh red chillies, crushed
15ml/1 tbsp sugar
450g/1lb cherry tomatoes, halved
115g/4oz fried onions

1 Pat the soaked fish dry with kitchen paper. Heat the oil in a frying pan and fry the fish pieces for about 30–45 seconds on both sides until crisp. Be careful not to burn them as they will taste bitter. Drain well on kitchen paper. When cool, break the fish into small pieces.

2 To the same oil, add the chillies and fry, stirring constantly, for about 2–3 minutes, until the chillies release their aromas.

3 Add the sugar, cherry tomatoes and fried onions to the pan and mix well. Continue to cook, stirring frequently, until the tomatoes become pulpy and the mixture is blended into a fairly thick sauce.

4 Fold the fish pieces into the tomato sauce and cook for a minute until all the ingredients are heated through. Serve immediately if eating hot, or it will be equally delicious if left to cool and eaten cold.

Cook's Tip

The origin of the term 'Bombay duck' is uncertain. Some believe that, during the British Raj, the dried fish was often transported on the railway and that the mail carriages of the train (dak means 'mail' in Hindi) would smell of the fish, consequently leading the British to refer to the pungent smell of the fish as the 'Bombay dak', which became 'duck'.

Sesame Chutney Energy 303kcal/1256kJ; Protein 8.5g; Carbohydrate 8.6g, of which sugars 8.4g; Fat 26.3g, of which saturates 3.7g; Cholesterol 0mg; Calcium 327mg; Fibre 4.2g; Sodium 506mg.
Bombay Duck Pickle Energy 156kcal/652kJ; Protein 11.8g; Carbohydrate 5g, of which sugars 4.2g; Fat 10g, of which saturates 1.9g; Cholesterol 22mg; Calcium 22mg; Fibre 1.4g; Sodium 141mg.

Red-hot Lime Pickle

A good lime pickle is not only delicious served with any meal, but it increases the appetite and aids digestion. The tangy pickle is the perfect accompaniment to a curry, such as a biryani, and is delicious as a dip with poppadums and snacks such as pakora and samosas or spicy chicken wings.

Makes 450g/1lb/2 cups
25 limes
225g/8oz salt
50g/2oz ground fenugreek
50g/2oz mustard powder
150g/5oz chilli powder
15g/½oz ground turmeric
600ml/1 pint/2½ cups mustard oil
5ml/1 tsp asafoetida
25g/1oz yellow mustard seeds, crushed

1 Cut each lime into eight pieces and remove the pips (seeds), if you wish. Place the limes in a large sterilized jar or glass bowl.

2 Add the salt to the limes and toss together until well combined. Cover the jar or bowl and leave in a warm place until the limes become soft and dull brown in colour. This will take about 1 to 2 weeks.

3 Mix together the fenugreek, mustard powder, chilli powder and turmeric and add to the limes, mixing well to ensure the limes are evenly covered in the spices. Cover again and leave to rest in a warm place for a further 2 or 3 days.

4 Heat the mustard oil in a frying pan and fry the asafoetida and mustard seeds until the seeds begin to splutter. When the oil reaches smoking point, pour it over the limes.

5 Mix well, cover with a clean cloth and leave in a warm place for about 1 week before serving.

Cook's Tip
Asafoetida is a pungent spice obtained from the resin of a fennel-like plant. It has a very strong odour of garlic and onion and should only be used sparingly.

Green Chilli Pickle

Southern India is the source of some of the hottest curries and pickles, which are said to help cool the body in the hot climate. This fiery pickle should be used sparingly as an accompaniment to spicy food.

Makes 450–550g/1–1¼lb/2–2½ cups
50g/2oz yellow mustard seeds, crushed
50g/2oz freshly ground cumin seeds
25g/1oz ground turmeric
50g/2oz garlic cloves, crushed
150ml/¼ pint/⅔ cup white vinegar
75g/3oz sugar
10ml/2 tsp salt
150ml/¼ pint/⅔ cup mustard oil
20 small garlic cloves, peeled and left whole
450g/1lb small green chillies, washed, dried and halved

1 Mix the mustard seeds, cumin, turmeric, crushed garlic, vinegar, sugar and salt together in a sterilized glass bowl. Cover with a cloth and allow to rest for 24 hours. This enables the flavours of the spices to mingle together and allows time for the sugar and salt to dissolve.

2 Heat the mustard oil in a wok or frying pan and gently fry the spice mixture for about 5 minutes until it releases its fragrances. (Keep a window open while cooking with mustard oil as it is pungent and the smoke may irritate the eyes.)

3 Add the whole garlic cloves to the pan and fry, stirring constantly, for a further 5 minutes until they turn a light brown colour. Ensure that the garlic does not burn, otherwise it will impart a bitter taste to the pickle.

4 Add the chillies to the pan and cook them gently until they are tender but still green in colour. This will take about 30 minutes over a low heat.

5 Cool the mixture thoroughly and then pour into sterilized bottles. Ensure that the oil is evenly distributed if you are using more than one bottle. Leave the pickle to rest for about a week before serving to allow the flavours to merge and mingle. Serve as an accompaniment to Indian curries and other spicy food.

Lime Pickle Energy 4699kcal/19387kJ; Protein 57g; Carbohydrate 151.3g, of which sugars 64g; Fat 438.1g, of which saturates 53.4g; Cholesterol 0mg; Calcium 2173mg; Fibre 0g; Sodium 88610mg.
Chilli Pickle Energy 1953kcal/8134kJ; Protein 51.5g; Carbohydrate 176.9g, of which sugars 95.2g; Fat 123.3g, of which saturates 14.7g; Cholesterol 0mg; Calcium 488mg; Fibre 8.2g; Sodium 96mg.

Fiery Bengal Chutney

Not for timid tastebuds, this fiery chutney is the perfect choice for lovers of hot and spicy food. Although it can be eaten a month after making, it is better matured for longer.

Makes about 2kg/4½lb

115g/4oz fresh root ginger
1kg/2¼lb cooking apples
675g/1½lb onions
6 garlic cloves, finely chopped
225g/8oz/1½ cups raisins
450ml/¾ pint/scant 2 cups malt vinegar
400g/14oz/1¾ cups demerara (raw) sugar
2 fresh red chillies
2 fresh green chillies

1 Peel and finely shred the fresh root ginger. Peel, core and roughly chop the apples. Peel and quarter the onions, then slice as thinly as possible. Place in a preserving pan with the garlic, raisins and vinegar.

2 Bring to the boil, then simmer steadily for 15–20 minutes, stirring occasionally, until the apples and onions are thoroughly softened. Add the sugar and stir over a low heat until the sugar has dissolved. Simmer the mixture for about 40 minutes, or until thick and pulpy, stirring frequently towards the end of the cooking time.

3 Halve the chillies and remove the seeds, then slice them finely. (Always wash your hands with soapy water immediately after handling chillies.)

4 Add the chillies to the pan and cook for a further 5–10 minutes, or until no excess liquid remains. Stir in the salt and turmeric.

5 Spoon the chutney into warmed sterilized jars, cover and seal them immediately, then label when cool.

6 Store the chutney in a cool, dark place and leave to mature for at least 2 months before eating. Use within 2 years of making. Once opened, store in the refrigerator and use within 1 month.

Hot Yellow Plum Chutney

It is well worth seeking out yellow plums to make this hot, fragrant chutney. They give it a slightly tart flavour and make it the perfect accompaniment to deep-fried Asian-style snacks such as spring rolls and wontons, or battered vegetablesand shellfish.

Makes 1.3kg/3lb

900g/2lb yellow plums, halved and stoned (pitted)
1 onion, finely chopped
7.5cm/3in piece fresh root ginger, peeled and grated
3 whole star anise
350ml/12fl oz/1½ cups white wine vinegar
225g/8oz/1 cup soft light brown sugar
5 celery sticks, thinly sliced
3 green chillies, seeded and finely sliced
2 garlic cloves, crushed

1 Put the halved plums, onion, ginger and star anise in a large pan and pour over half the white wine vinegar. Bring to the boil and simmer gently over a low heat for about 30 minutes, or until the plums have softened.

2 Stir the remaining vinegar, sugar, sliced celery, chillies and crushed garlic into the plum mixture. Cook very gently over a low heat, stirring frequently, until the sugar has dissolved.

3 Bring the mixture to the boil, then simmer for 45–50 minutes, or until thick, with no excess liquid. Stir frequently during the final stages of cooking to prevent the chutney sticking to the pan.

4 Spoon the plum chutney into warmed sterilized jars, then cover and seal immediately. Store the chutney in a cool, dark place then allow to mature for at least 1 month before using. Use within 2 years.

Cook's Tips

- *Once opened, store the chutney in the refrigerator and use within 3 months.*
- *Be sure to use jars with non-metallic lids to store the chutney.*

Fiery Chutney Energy 2789kcal/11889kJ; Protein 18.4g; Carbohydrate 717.3g, of which sugars 701.8g; Fat 3.5g, of which saturates 0g; Cholesterol 0mg; Calcium 573mg; Fibre 31.2g; Sodium 6163mg.
Hot Plum Chutney Energy 1243kcal/5312kJ; Protein 8g; Carbohydrate 320.4g, of which sugars 319g; Fat 1.3g, of which saturates 0g; Cholesterol 0mg; Calcium 313mg; Fibre 16.9g; Sodium 123mg.

Pickled Peach and Chilli Chutney

This is a spicy, rich chutney with a succulent texture. It is great served traditional-style, with cold roast meats such as ham, pork or turkey; it is also good with pan-fried chicken served in warm wraps. Try it with ricotta cheese as a filling for pitta bread.

Makes about 450g/1lb

475ml/16fl oz/2 cups cider vinegar
275g/10oz/1¼ cups light muscovado (brown) sugar
225g/8oz/1⅓ cups dried dates, stoned (pitted) and finely chopped
5ml/1 tsp ground allspice
5ml/1 tsp ground mace
450g/1lb ripe peaches, stoned (pitted) and cut into small chunks
3 onions, thinly sliced
4 fresh red chillies, seeded and finely chopped
4 garlic cloves, crushed
5cm/2in piece fresh root ginger, peeled and finely grated
5ml/1 tsp salt

1 Place the vinegar, sugar, dates, allspice and mace in a large pan and heat gently, stirring, until the sugar has dissolved. Bring to the boil, stirring occasionally.

2 Add the peaches, sliced onions, chopped chillies, crushed garlic, grated ginger and salt, and bring the mixture back to the boil, stirring occasionally.

3 Reduce the heat and simmer for 40–50 minutes, or until the chutney has thickened. Stir frequently to prevent the mixture sticking to the bottom of the pan.

4 Spoon the hot cooked chutney into warmed sterilized jars and seal immediately. When cold, store the jars in a cool, dark place and leave the chutney to mature for at least 2 weeks before eating. Use within 6 months.

Cook's Tip
To test the consistency of the chutney before bottling, spoon a little of the mixture on to a plate: if the chutney retains its shape then it is the right consistency.

Red Hot Relish

Make this relish during the summer months when tomatoes and peppers are plentiful. It enhances simple, plain dishes such as a cheese or mushroom omelette.

Makes about 1.3kg/3lb

800g/1¾lb ripe tomatoes, skinned and quartered
450g/1lb red onions, chopped
3 red (bell) peppers, seeded and chopped
3 fresh red chillies, seeded and finely sliced
200g/7oz/1 cup sugar
200ml/7fl oz/scant 1 cup red wine vinegar
30ml/2 tbsp mustard seeds
10ml/2 tsp celery seeds
15ml/1 tbsp paprika
5ml/1 tsp salt

1 Put the chopped tomatoes, onions, peppers and chillies in a preserving pan, cover with a lid and cook over a very low heat for about 10 minutes, stirring once or twice, until the tomato juices start to run.

2 Add the sugar and vinegar to the tomato mixture and slowly bring to the boil, stirring occasionally, until the sugar has dissolved completely.

3 Add the mustard seeds, celery seeds, paprika and salt to the pan and stir well to combine.

4 Increase the heat under the pan slightly and cook the relish, uncovered, for about 30 minutes, or until most of the liquid has evaporated and the mixture has a thick but moist consistency. Stir frequently towards the end of cooking time to prevent the mixture sticking to the pan.

5 Spoon the relish into warmed sterilized jars, cover and seal. Store in a cool, dark place and leave for at least 2 weeks before eating. Use the relish within 1 year of making.

Cook's Tip
Once opened, store the jar of relish in the refrigerator and use within 2 months.

Peach Chutney Energy 2039kcal/8684kJ; Protein 20.9g; Carbohydrate 517.3g, of which sugars 502.9g; Fat 2g, of which saturates 0.2g; Cholesterol 0mg; Calcium 407mg; Fibre 23.6g; Sodium 59mg.
Hot Relish Energy 1270kcal/5392kJ; Protein 17.8g; Carbohydrate 306.2g, of which sugars 294.1g; Fat 5.6g, of which saturates 1.4g; Cholesterol 0mg; Calcium 320mg; Fibre 23.5g; Sodium 121mg.

Thai Pickled Shallots with Chillies

Pickling Thai shallots in this way demands some patience while the vinegar and spices work their magic, but the results are definitely worth the wait. Thinly sliced, the shallots are often used as a condiment with South-east Asian meals.

Makes 2 to 3 jars

5–6 small red or green bird's eye chillies
500g/1¼lb Thai pink shallots, peeled
2 large garlic cloves, peeled, halved and green shoots removed

For the vinegar

40g/1½oz/3 tbsp sugar
10ml/2 tsp salt
5cm/2in piece fresh root ginger, peeled and sliced
15ml/1 tbsp coriander seeds
2 lemon grass stalks, cut in half lengthways
4 kaffir lime leaves or pared strips of lime rind
600ml/1 pint/2½ cups cider vinegar
15ml/1 tbsp chopped fresh coriander (cilantro)

1 The chillies can be left whole or halved and seeded, if you prefer. The pickle will be hotter if you leave the seeds in. If leaving the chillies whole, prick them several times with a cocktail stick (toothpick). Bring a large pan of water to the boil. Add the chillies, shallots and garlic. Blanch for 1–2 minutes, then drain. Rinse all the vegetables under cold water, then drain again.

2 Prepare the vinegar. Put the sugar, salt, ginger, coriander seeds, lemon grass and lime leaves or lime rind in a pan, pour in the vinegar and bring to the boil. Reduce the heat to low and simmer for 3–4 minutes. Leave to cool.

3 Remove and discard the ginger, then bring the vinegar back to the boil. Add the fresh coriander, garlic and chillies and cook for 1 minute.

4 Pack the shallots into sterilized jars, distributing the lemon grass, lime leaves, chillies and garlic among them. Pour over the hot vinegar. Cool, then seal and store in a cool, dark place for 2 months before eating.

Hot Pickled Mushrooms

This method of preserving mushrooms is popular throughout Europe. The pickle is good made with cultivated mushrooms, but it is worth including a couple of sliced ceps for their delicious flavour.

Makes about 900g/2lb

500g/1¼lb/8 cups mixed mushrooms, such as small ceps, chestnut mushrooms, shiitake and girolles
300ml/½ pint/1¼ cups white wine vinegar or cider vinegar
15ml/1 tbsp sea salt
5ml/1 tsp caster (superfine) sugar
300ml/½ pint/1¼ cups water
4–5 fresh bay leaves
8 large fresh thyme sprigs
15 garlic cloves, peeled, halved, with any green shoots removed
1 small red onion, halved and thinly sliced
2–3 small dried red chillies
5ml/1 tsp coriander seeds, lightly crushed
5ml/1 tsp black peppercorns
a few strips of lemon rind
250–350ml/8–12fl oz/1–1½ cups extra virgin olive oil

1 Trim the mushrooms and wipe clean. Cut any large mushrooms in half.

2 Put the vinegar, salt, sugar and water in a pan and bring to the boil. Add the bay leaves, thyme, garlic, onion, chillies, coriander seeds, peppercorns and lemon rind and simmer for 2 minutes.

3 Add the mushrooms to the pan and simmer for 3–4 minutes. Drain the mushrooms through a seive (strainer), retaining the herbs and spices, then set aside for a few minutes more until the mushrooms are thoroughly drained.

4 Fill one large or two small cool sterilized jars with the mushrooms. Distribute the garlic, onion, herbs and spices evenly among the layers of mushrooms, then add enough olive oil to cover by at least 1cm/½in. You may need to use extra oil if you are making two jars.

5 Leave the pickle to settle, then tap the jars on the work surface to dispel any air bubbles. Seal the tops, then store in the refrigerator. Use within 2 weeks.

Pickled Shallots Energy 129kcal/551kJ; Protein 3.9g; Carbohydrate 29.2g, of which sugars 29.2g; Fat 0.5g, of which saturates 0g; Cholesterol 0mg; Calcium 71mg; Fibre 305g; Sodium 1991mg.
Pickled Mushrooms Energy 579kcal/2392kJ; Protein 9g; Carbohydrate 7.2g, of which sugars 6.2g; Fat 57.4g, of which saturates 8.4g; Cholesterol 0mg; Calcium 33mg; Fibre 10.7g; Sodium 35mg..

Dill Pickles with Chillies

Redolent of garlic and piquant with fresh chilli, salty dill pickles can be supple and succulent or crisp and crunchy. Every pickle aficionado has a favourite type.

Makes about 900g/2lb

20 small, ridged or knobbly pickling (small) cucumbers
2 litres/3½ pints/8 cups water
175g/6oz/¾ cup coarse sea salt
15–20 garlic cloves, unpeeled
2 bunches fresh dill
15ml/1 tbsp dill seeds
30ml/2 tbsp mixed pickling spice
1 or 2 hot fresh chillies

1 Scrub the cucumbers and rinse well in cold running water. Leave to dry.

2 Put the measured water and salt in a large pan and bring to the boil. Turn off the heat and leave the salted water to cool to room temperature.

3 Using the flat side of a knife blade or a wooden mallet, lightly crush each garlic clove, breaking the papery skin.

4 Pack the cucumbers tightly into one or two wide-necked, sterilized jars, layering them with the garlic, fresh dill, dill seeds and pickling spice. Add one chilli to each jar.

5 Pour over the cooled brine, making sure that the cucumbers are completely covered. Tap the jars on the work surface to dispel any trapped air bubbles.

6 Cover the jars with lids and then leave to stand at room temperature for about 4–7 days before serving. Store the pickles in the refrigerator.

Cook's Tip
If you cannot find ridged or knobbly pickling cucumbers, use any kind of small cucumbers instead.

Spicy Pickled Limes

This hot, pungent pickle comes from Punjab in India. Salting softens the rind and intensifies the flavour of the limes, while they mature in the first month or two of storage. Pickled limes are extremely salty, so are best served with slightly under-seasoned dishes.

Makes about 1kg/2¼lb

1kg/2¼lb unwaxed limes
75g/3oz/⅓ cup salt
seeds from 6–8 green cardamom pods
6 whole cloves
5ml/1 tsp cumin seeds
4 fresh red chillies, seeded and sliced
5cm/2in piece fresh root ginger, peeled and finely shredded
450g/1lb/2¼ cups preserving or granulated (white) sugar

1 Put the limes in a large bowl and pour over cold water to cover. Set aside and leave the limes to soak for 8 hours, or overnight, if preferred.

2 The next day, remove the limes from the soaking water. Using a sharp knife, cut each lime in half from end to end, then cut each of the halves into slices that are approximately 5mm/¼in thick.

3 Place the lime slices in the bowl, sprinkling the salt between the layers, ensuring the slices are evenly covered. Cover the bowl and leave to stand for a further 8 hours.

4 Drain the limes, catching the juices from them in a large pan or a preserving pan.

5 Crush the cardamom seeds together with the cumin seeds. Add to the pan with the chillies, ginger and sugar. Bring to the boil, stirring constantly until the sugar completely dissolves. Simmer the mixture gently for about 2 minutes, stirring occasionally, and then set aside to cool.

6 Mix the limes in the syrup. Pack into sterilized jars, cover and seal. Store in a cool, dark place for at least 1 month before eating. Use within 1 year.

Dill Pickles Energy 76kcal/305kJ; Protein 5.3g; Carbohydrate 11.4g, of which sugars 10.7g; Fat 0.8g, of which saturates 0g; Cholesterol 0mg; Calcium 140mg; Fibre 4.6g; Sodium 1001 3mg.
Pickled Limes Energy 1963kcal/8354kJ; Protein 12.3g; Carbohydrate 502.3g, of which sugars 502.3g; Fat 3g; of which saturates 1g; Cholesterol 0mg; Calcium 1089mg; Fibre 0g; Sodium 2042mg.

Classic Spiced Tomato Salsa

This is the traditional tomato-based salsa that most people associate with Mexican food. There are innumerable recipes for it, but the basics of onion, tomato, chilli and coriander are common to all. Serve as a condiment with a wide variety of dishes.

Serves 6 as an accompaniment

3–6 fresh serrano chillies
1 large white onion
grated rind and juice of 2 limes, plus strips of rind, to garnish
8 ripe, firm tomatoes
bunch of fresh coriander (cilantro)
1.5ml/¼ tsp sugar
salt

1 Use three chillies for a salsa of medium heat; up to six if you like it hot. Spear the chillies on a metal skewer and roast them over a gas flame until the skins blister. Do not let the flesh burn. Alternatively, dry-fry them in a griddle. Place them in a strong plastic bag and tie the top. Set aside for 20 minutes.

2 Meanwhile, chop the onion finely and put it in a bowl with the lime rind and juice. The lime juice will soften the onion.

3 Remove the chillies from the bag and peel off the skins. Cut off the stalks, then slit the chillies and scrape out the seeds with a sharp knife. Chop the flesh roughly and set aside.

4 Cut a small cross in the base of each tomato. Place them in a heatproof bowl and pour over boiling water to cover.

5 Leave the tomatoes in the water for 3 minutes, then lift out and plunge into a bowl of cold water. Drain. The skins will be peeling back from the crosses. Remove the skins completely.

6 Dice the peeled tomatoes and put them in a bowl. Add the chopped onion and lime mixture; the onion should have softened. Chop the fresh coriander finely.

7 Add the coriander, with the chillies and the sugar. Mix gently until the sugar has dissolved and all the ingredients are coated in lime juice. Cover and chill for 2–3 hours. The salsa will keep for 3–4 days in the refrigerator. Garnish with lime rind before serving.

Roasted Tomato and Chilli Salsa

Slow roasting these tomatoes to a semi-dried state results in a very rich, full-flavoured sweet sauce. The costeno amarillo chilli is mild and has a fresh light flavour, making it the perfect partner for the rich tomato taste. This salsa is great to go with tuna or sea bass and makes a marvellous sandwich filling when teamed with creamy cheese.

Serves 6 as an accompaniment

500g/1¼ lb tomatoes
8 small shallots
5 garlic cloves
1 fresh rosemary sprig
2 costeno amarillo chillies
grated rind and juice of ½ small lemon
30ml/2 tbsp extra virgin olive oil
1.5ml/¼ tsp soft dark brown sugar
sea salt

1 Preheat the oven to 160°C/325°F/Gas 3. Cut the tomatoes into quarters and place them in a roasting pan.

2 Peel the shallots and garlic and add them to the roasting pan. Sprinkle with sea salt. Roast in the oven for 1¼ hours, or until the tomatoes are beginning to dry.

3 Leave the tomatoes to cool, then peel off the skins and chop the flesh finely. Place in a bowl. Remove the outer layer of skin from any shallots that have toughened.

4 Using a large, sharp knife, chop the shallots and garlic roughly, place them with the tomatoes in a bowl and mix.

5 Strip the rosemary leaves from the woody stem and chop finely. Add half to the tomato and shallot mixture and mix lightly.

6 Soak the chillies in hot water for 10 minutes until soft. Drain, remove the stalks, slit them and scrape out the seeds with a sharp knife. Chop the flesh finely and add to the tomato mixture.

7 Stir in the lemon rind and juice, the olive oil and the sugar. Mix well. Cover and chill for at least an hour before serving, sprinkled with the remaining rosemary. The salsa will keep for up to a week in the refrigerator.

Classic Spiced Tomato Salsa Energy 42kcal/176kJ; Protein 2g; Carbohydrate 8g, of which sugars 7g; Fat 1g, of which saturates 0g; Cholesterol 0mg; Calcium 31mg; Fibre 1.7g; Sodium 100mg.
Roasted Tomato Salsa Energy 54kcal/226kJ; Protein 0.8g; Carbohydrate 4.2g, of which sugars 3.7g; Fat 4g, of which saturates 0.6g; Cholesterol 0mg; Calcium 11mg; Fibre 1.1g; Sodium 8mg.

Sweet Potato and Jalapeño Salsa

Very colourful and delightfully sweet, with a satisfying heat from the jalapeño chillies, this salsa makes the perfect accompaniment to hot, spicy Mexican dishes. Add more dried chilli if you like your food a little more fiery.

Serves 4 as an accompaniment

675g/1½lb sweet potatoes
juice of 1 small orange
5ml/1 tsp crushed dried jalapeño chillies
4 small spring onions (scallions)
juice of 1 small lime (optional)
salt

1 Peel the sweet potatoes and dice the flesh finely. Bring a pan of water to the boil. Add the sweet potatoes and cook for about 8–10 minutes, until just soft.

2 Drain off the water, cover the pan and leave over a very low heat for about 5 minutes to dry out, then transfer to a bowl and set aside.

3 Mix the orange juice and crushed dried chillies in a bowl. Chop the spring onions finely and add them to the juice and chillies in the bowl.

4 When the sweet potatoes are cool, add the orange juice mixture and toss carefully until all the pieces of potato are evenly coated.

5 Cover the bowl and chill in the refrigerator for at least 1 hour, then taste and season with salt. Add lime juice for a fresher taste.

6 Serve the salsa as an accompaniment to spicy dishes. The salsa will keep for 2–3 days in a covered bowl in the refrigerator.

Cook's Tip

This fresh and tasty salsa is also very good served with a simple grilled (broiled) salmon fillet or other fish dishes, and makes a delicious accompaniment to veal escalopes (scallops) or grilled chicken breast fillets.

Mango and Chilli Salsa

This delicious salsa has a fresh, fruity taste and is perfect with fish or as a contrast to rich, creamy dishes. The bright colours make it an attractive addition to any table.

Serves 4 as an accompaniment

2 fresh red fresno chillies
2 ripe mangoes
½ white onion
bunch of fresh coriander (cilantro)
grated rind and juice of 1 lime

1 To loosen the skin of the chillies, spear them on a long-handled metal skewer and roast them over the flame of a gas burner until the skins blister and darken. Do not allow the flesh of the chillies to burn. Alternatively, dry-fry them in a griddle pan until the skins are scorched.

2 Place the roasted chillies in a strong plastic bag and tie the top to keep the steam in. Set aside for 20 minutes.

3 Meanwhile, put one of the mangoes on a board and cut off a thick slice close to the flat side of the stone (pit). Turn the mango round and repeat on the other side. Score the flesh on each thick slice with criss-cross lines at 1cm/½in intervals, taking care not to cut through the skin. Repeat this process with the second mango.

4 Fold the mango halves inside out so that the mango flesh stands proud of the skin, in neat dice. Carefully slice these off the skin and into a bowl. Cut off the flesh adhering to each stone, dice it and add it to the bowl.

5 Remove the roasted chillies from the bag and carefully peel off the skins. Cut off the stalks, then slit the chillies and scrape out the seeds.

6 Chop the white onion and the coriander finely and add them to the diced mango. Chop the chilli flesh finely and add it to the mixture in the bowl, together with the lime rind and juice.

7 Stir well to mix, cover and chill for at least 1 hour before serving. The salsa will keep for 2–3 days in the refrigerator.

Sweet Potato Salsa Energy 154kcal/657kJ; Protein 2.3g; Carbohydrate 37.4g, of which sugars 11g; Fat 0.6g, of which saturates 0g; Cholesterol 0mg; Calcium 46mg; Fibre 4.2g; Sodium 70mg.
Mango and Chilli Salsa Energy 56kcal/239kJ; Protein 1.2g; Carbohydrate 12.9g, of which sugars 12g; Fat 0.4g, of which saturates 0.1g; Cholesterol 0mg; Calcium 40mg; Fibre 2.9g; Sodium 7mg.

Fiery Habañero Chilli Salsa

This is a very fiery salsa with an intense heat level. A dab on the plate alongside meat or fish dishes adds a fresh, clean taste, but this is not for the faint-hearted. Habañero chillies, also called Scotch bonnets, are very hot. Lantern-shaped, they range in colour from yellow to a deep orange red. Costeno amarillo chillies are yellow when fresh and have a milder level of heat and a sharp citrus flavour.

Serve sparingly

5 dried roasted habañero chillies
4 dried costeno amarillo chillies
3 spring onions (scallions), finely chopped
juice of ½ large grapefruit or 1 Seville orange
grated rind and juice of 1 lime
bunch of fresh coriander (cilantro)
salt

1 Soak the habañero and costeno amarillo chillies in hot water for about 10 minutes until softened. Drain, reserving the soaking water.

2 Wear rubber gloves to handle the habañeros to avoid them irritating your skin. Remove the stalks from all chillies, then slit them and scrape out the seeds with a small sharp knife. Chop the chillies roughly.

3 Put the chillies in a food processor or blender and add a little of the soaking liquid. Blend to a fine paste. Do not lean over the processor – the fumes from the chillies may irritate your eyes and face. Remove the lid and scrape the chilli mixture into a bowl.

4 Put the chopped spring onions in another bowl and add the fruit juice, with the lime rind and juice, and mix well together. Roughly chop the coriander.

5 Carefully add the coriander to the bowl and stir thoroughly. Then add the spring onion mixture to the chillies, mixing well. Taste a tiny amount of the salsa and add salt.

6 Cover the salsa and chillin the refrigerator for at least 1 day before use. Serve the salsa very sparingly.

Red Chilli Salsa

Use this as a condiment with fish or meat dishes, or as a dipping sauce for baked potato wedges. It is often added to rice dishes.

Makes about 250ml/8fl oz/1 cup

3 large tomatoes
15ml/1 tbsp olive oil
3 ancho chillies
2 pasilla chillies
2 garlic cloves, peeled and left whole
2 spring onions (scallions)
10ml/2 tsp soft dark brown sugar
2.5ml/½ tsp paprika
juice of 1 lime
2.5ml/½ tsp dried oregano
salt

1 Preheat the oven to 200°C/400°F/Gas 6. Quarter the tomatoes and place in a roasting pan. Drizzle over the olive oil. Roast for about 40 minutes until slightly charred. Leave to cool slightly, then remove the skin.

2 Soak the chillies in hot water for about 10 minutes. Drain, remove the stalks, slit the flesh and then scrape out the seeds. Chop the flesh finely.

3 In a heavy frying pan, dry-roast the garlic until just golden. Ensure that it does not burn, otherwise it will impart a bitter taste to the salsa.

4 Finely chop most of the spring onions, retaining the top part of one for garnishing. Place the chopped onion in a bowl with the sugar, paprika, lime juice and oregano. Slice the remaining spring onion diagonally and set aside for the garnish.

5 Put the skinned tomatoes and chopped chillies in a food processor or blender and add the garlic. Process until smooth.

6 Add the sugar, paprika, lime juice, spring onions and oregano to the blender. Process for a few seconds, then taste and add salt.

7 Spoon into a pan and warm through before serving, or place in a bowl, cover and chill until required. Garnish with the sliced spring onion. The salsa will keep, covered, for up to 1 week in the refrigerator.

Fiery Habañero Chilli Salsa Energy 62kcal/259kJ; Protein 5.3g; Carbohydrate 7.4g, of which sugars 7.1g; Fat 1.5g, of which saturates 0g; Cholesterol 0mg; Calcium 147mg; Fibre 3g; Sodium 31mg.
Red Chilli Salsa Energy 195kcal/818kJ; Protein 2.6g; Carbohydrate 20.6g, of which sugars 20.6g; Fat 12g, of which saturates 1.9g; Cholesterol 0mg; Calcium 35mg; Fibre 3.3g; Sodium 29mg.

Chipotle Chilli Sauce

The delicious smoky flavour of this sauce makes it the ideal choice to go with barbecued food, either as a marinade or as an accompaniment. It is also wonderful stirred into cream cheese as a sandwich filling with chicken. Chipotle chillies are smoked dried jalapeño chillies.

Serves 6 as an accompaniment
500g/1¼ lb tomatoes
5 chipotle chillies
3 garlic cloves, roughly chopped
150ml/¼ pint/⅔ cup red wine
5ml/1 tsp dried oregano
60ml/4 tbsp clear honey
5ml/1 tsp American mustard
2.5ml/½ tsp ground black pepper
salt

1 Preheat the oven to 200°C/400°F/Gas 6. Cut the tomatoes into quarters and place them in a roasting pan. Roast for 45 minutes to 1 hour, until the skins of the tomatoes are charred and softened.

2 Meanwhile, soak the chillies in a bowl of cold water to cover for about 20 minutes, or until soft. Remove the stalks, slit the chillies and scrape out the seeds with a small sharp knife. Chop the flesh roughly.

3 Remove the tomatoes from the oven, let them cool slightly, then remove the skins. If you prefer a smooth sauce, remove the seeds. Chop the tomatoes and put them in a blender or food processor.

4 Add the chopped chillies and garlic with the red wine to the blender or food processor. Blend the mixture until smooth, then add the oregano, honey, mustard and black pepper. Process briefly to mix, then taste and season with salt.

5 Scrape the mixture into a small pan. Place over a moderate heat and stir until the mixture boils. Lower the heat and simmer the sauce for about 10 minutes, stirring occasionally, until it has reduced and thickened.

6 Spoon the salsa into a serving bowl and serve immediately if using hot, or set aside to cool before serving cold.

Guajillo Chilli Sauce

This sauce can be served over enchiladas or steamed vegetables. It is also good with meats, and makes a fine seasoning for soups or stews. The dried chillies give it a well rounded, fruity flavour and it is not too hot.

Serves 4 as an accompaniment
2 tomatoes, total weight about 200g/7oz
2 red (bell) peppers, cored, seeded and quartered
3 garlic cloves, in their skins
2 ancho chillies
2 guajillo chillies
30ml/2 tbsp tomato purée (paste)
5ml/1 tsp dried oregano
5ml/1 tsp soft dark brown sugar
300ml/½ pint/1¼ cups chicken stock

1 Preheat the oven to 200°C/400°F/Gas 6. Cut the tomatoes into quarters and place them in a roasting pan with the peppers and garlic cloves. Roast for 45 minutes to 1 hour, until the tomatoes and peppers are slightly charred and the garlic is soft.

2 Put the peppers in a strong plastic bag and tie the top. Set aside for 20 minutes. Remove the skin from the tomatoes. Meanwhile, soak the chillies in boiling water for 15 minutes.

3 Remove the peppers from the bag and rub off the skins. Cut them in half, remove the cores and seeds, then chop the flesh roughly and put it in a food processor or blender. Drain the chillies, remove the stalks, then slit them and scrape out the seeds and discard. Chop the chillies and add to the peppers.

4 Add the roasted tomatoes to the food processor or blender. Squeeze the roasted garlic out of the skins and add to the tomato mixture, with the tomato purée, oregano, brown sugar and stock. Process until smooth.

5 Pour the mixture into a pan, place over a moderate heat and bring to the boil. Lower the heat and simmer for 10–15 minutes until the sauce has reduced to about half. Transfer to a bowl and serve immediately or, if serving cold, cover, leave to cool, then chill until required. Keep in the refrigerator for up to a week.

Chipotle Chilli Sauce Energy 63kcal/265kJ; Protein 1g; Carbohydrate 10.4g, of which sugars 10.4g; Fat 0.3g, of which saturates 0.1g; Cholesterol 0mg; Calcium 12mg; Fibre 0.8g; Sodium 11mg.
Guajillo Chilli Sauce Energy 43kcal/181kJ; Protein 1.6g; Carbohydrate 8.3g, of which sugars 8g; Fat 0.6g, of which saturates 0.2g; Cholesterol 0mg; Calcium 15mg; Fibre 1.9g; Sodium 9mg.

Fiery Guacamole

One of the best loved Mexican salsas, this blend of creamy avocado, tomatoes, chillies, coriander and lime now appears on tables the world over. Bought guacamole usually contains mayonnaise, which helps to preserve the avocado, but this is not an ingredient in traditional recipes.

Serves 6 to 8

4 medium tomatoes
4 ripe avocados, preferably fuerte
juice of 1 lime
½ small onion
2 garlic cloves
small bunch of fresh coriander (cilantro), chopped
3 fresh red fresno chillies
salt
tortilla chips, to serve

1 Cut a cross in the base of each tomato. Place the tomatoes in a heatproof bowl and pour over boiling water to cover.

2 Leave the tomatoes in the water for 3 minutes, then lift them out using a slotted spoon and plunge them into a bowl of cold water. Drain. The skins will have begun to peel back from the crosses. Remove the skins completely. Cut the tomatoes in half, remove the seeds with a teaspoon, then chop the flesh roughly and set it aside.

3 Cut the avocados in half then remove the stones (pits). Scoop the flesh out of the shells and place it in a food processor or blender. Process until almost smooth, then scrape into a bowl and stir in the lime juice.

4 Chop the onion finely, then crush the garlic. Add both to the avocado and mix well. Stir in the coriander.

5 Remove the stalks from the chillies, slit them and scrape out the seeds with a small sharp knife. Chop the chillies finely and add them to the avocado mixture, with the chopped tomatoes. Mix well.

6 Check the seasoning and add salt to taste. Cover closely with clear film (plastic wrap) or a tight-fitting lid and chill for 1 hour before serving as a dip with tortilla chips. If it is well covered, guacamole will keep in the refrigerator for 2–3 days.

Black Bean and Chilli Salsa

This salsa has a very striking appearance. The pasado chillies add a subtle citrus flavour. Leave the salsa for a day or two after making to allow the flavours to develop fully.

Serves 4 as an accompaniment

130g/4½ oz/generous ½ cup black beans, soaked overnight in water to cover
1 pasado chilli
2 fresh red fresno chillies
1 red onion
grated rind and juice of 1 lime
30ml/2 tbsp Mexican beer (optional)
15ml/1 tbsp olive oil
small bunch of fresh coriander (cilantro), chopped
salt

1 Drain the beans and put them in a large pan. Pour in water to cover and place the lid on the pan. Bring to the boil, lower the heat slightly and simmer the beans for 40 minutes, or until tender. They should still have a little bite and should not have begun to disintegrate. Drain, rinse under cold water, then drain again and leave the beans until cold.

2 Soak the pasado chilli in hot water for about 10 minutes until softened. Drain, remove the stalk, then slit the chilli and scrape out the seeds with a small sharp knife. Chop the flesh finely.

3 Spear the fresno chillies on a long-handled metal skewer and roast them over the flame of a gas burner until the skins blister and darken. Do not let the flesh burn. Alternatively, dry fry them in a griddle pan until the skins are scorched. Then place the roasted chillies in a strong plastic bag and tie the top to keep the steam in. Set aside for 20 minutes.

4 Meanwhile, chop the red onion finely. Remove the chillies from the bag and peel off the skins. Slit them, remove the seeds and chop them finely.

5 Transfer the beans to a bowl and add the onion and both types of chilli. Stir in the lime rind and juice, beer, oil and coriander. Season with salt and mix well. Chill before serving.

Fiery Guacamole Energy 262kcal/1083kJ; Protein 3.2g; Carbohydrate 5g, of which sugars 3g; Fat 25.4g, of which saturates 5.4g; Cholesterol 0mg; Calcium 37mg; Fibre 5.5g; Sodium 15mg.
Bean and Chilli Salsa Energy 129kcal/544kJ; Protein 8g; Carbohydrate 17.6g, of which sugars 3.2g; Fat 3.5g, of which saturates 0.5g; Cholesterol 0mg; Calcium 67mg; Fibre 6.3g; Sodium 11mg.

Roasted Red Pepper and Chilli Jelly

The hint of chilli in this glowing red jelly makes it ideal for spicing up hot or cold roast meat, sausages or hamburgers. The jelly is also good stirred into sauces or used as a glaze for poultry.

Makes about 900g/2lb

8 red (bell) peppers, quartered and seeded
4 fresh red chillies, halved and seeded
1 onion, roughly chopped
2 garlic cloves, roughly chopped
250ml/8fl oz/1 cup water
250ml/8fl oz/1 cup white wine vinegar
7.5ml/1 ½ tsp salt
450g/1lb/2 ¼ cups preserving or granulated (white) sugar
25ml/1 ½ tbsp powdered pectin

1 Arrange the peppers, skin side up, on a rack in a grill (broiling) pan and grill (broil) until the skins blister and blacken.

2 Put the peppers in a polythene bag until they are cool enough to handle, then remove the skins.

3 Put the skinned peppers, chillies, onion, garlic and water in a food processor or blender and process to a purée.

4 Press the purée through a nylon sieve (strainer) set over a bowl, pressing it hard with a wooden spoon, to extract as much of the juice as possible. There should be roughly 750ml/1 ¼ pints/3 cups of purée.

5 Scrape the purée into a large stainless steel pan, then stir in the white wine vinegar and salt.

6 In a bowl, combine the sugar and pectin, then stir it into the pepper mixture. Heat gently, stirring constantly, until the sugar and pectin have dissolved completely, then bring the mixture to a rolling boil.

7 Cook the jelly, stirring frequently, for exactly 4 minutes, then remove the pan from the heat.

8 Pour the jelly into warmed, sterilized jars. Leave to cool and set, then cover, label and store.

Yogurt Cheese in a Herb Chilli Oil

Sheep's milk is widely used in cheese-making in the Eastern Mediterranean, particularly in Greece where sheep's yogurt is hung in muslin to drain off the whey before patting into balls of soft cheese. Here it's preserved in extra virgin olive oil with chilli and herbs. It is good as part of a Greek meze platter.

Makes two 450g/1lb jars

750g/10oz/1 ¼ cups Greek sheep's yogurt
2.5ml/½ tsp salt
10ml/2 tsp crushed dried chillies or chilli powder
15ml/1 tbsp chopped fresh rosemary
15ml/1 tbsp chopped fresh thyme or oregano
about 300ml/½ pint/1 ¼ cups olive oil, preferably garlic-flavoured

1 Sterilize a 30cm/12in square of muslin (cheesecloth) by steeping it in boiling water. Drain and lay over a large plate. Mix the yogurt with the salt and place in the centre of the muslin.

2 Bring up the sides of the muslin and tie firmly with string. You should now have a secured bag that can be hung. Use extra string and bag fixtures and fastenings if necessary.

3 Hang the bag in a suitable position where it can be suspended with a bowl underneath to catch the whey as it drips. Leave for 2–3 days, or until the whey stops dripping.

4 Wash thoroughly and dry two 450g/1lb glass preserving jars or jam jars. Sterilize them by heating them in an oven preheated to 150°C/300°F/Gas 2 for 15 minutes.

5 Mix together the chilli and herbs. Take teaspoonfuls of the cheese and roll into balls with your hands. Lower into the jars, sprinkling each layer with the herb mixture.

6 Pour the olive oil over the soft cheese balls until covered. Mix with the handle end of a wooden spoon in order to blend the flavourings. Store in the refrigerator for up to 3 weeks.

7 To serve the cheese, spoon out of the jars with a little of the flavoured olive oil and spread on to lightly toasted bread.

Pepper and Chilli Jelly Energy 2275kcal/9665kJ; Protein 18g; Carbohydrate 571g, of which sugars 565.1g; Fat 6.1g, of which saturates 1.5g; Cholesterol 0mg; Calcium 373mg; Fibre 24.8g; Sodium 89mg.
Yogurt Cheese in Oil Energy 1,331kcal/5,485kJ; Protein 24g; Carbohydrate 7.5g, of which sugars 7.5g; Fat 138.2g, of which saturates 33.8g; Cholesterol 0mg; Calcium 563mg; Fibre 0g; Sodium 758mg.

Index